SOLARO

STUDY GUIDE

High School Precalculus

SOLARO Study Guide is designed to help students achieve success in school. The content in each study guide is 100% curriculum aligned and serves as an excellent source of material for review and practice. To create this book, teachers, curriculum specialists, and assessment experts have worked closely to develop the instructional pieces that explain each of the key concepts for the course. The practice questions and sample tests have detailed solutions that show problem-solving methods, highlight concepts that are likely to be tested, and point out potential sources of errors. ***SOLARO Study Guide*** is a complete guide to be used by students throughout the school year for reviewing and understanding course content, and to prepare for assessments.

Rao, Gautam, 1961 –
SOLARO STUDY GUIDE – High School Precalculus (2015 Edition) Texas

1. Mathematics – Juvenile Literature. I. Title

Castle Rock Research Corporation
2410 Manulife Place
10180 – 101 Street
Edmonton, AB T5J 3S4

1 2 3 MP 16 15 14

Printed in the United States of America

Publisher
Gautam Rao

Dedicated to the memory of Dr. V. S. Rao

THE *SOLARO STUDY GUIDE*

The ***SOLARO Study Guide*** is designed to help students achieve success in school and to provide teachers with a road map to understanding the concepts of the regional State Standards.

The content in each study guide is 100% curriculum aligned and serves as an excellent source of material for review and practice. The ***SOLARO Study Guide*** introduces students to a process that incorporates the building blocks upon which strong academic performance is based. To create this resource, teachers, curriculum specialists, and assessment experts have worked closely to develop instructional pieces that explain key concepts. Every exercise question comes with a detailed solution that offers problem-solving methods, highlights concepts that are likely to be tested, and points out potential sources of errors.

The ***SOLARO Study Guide*** is intended to be used for reviewing and understanding course content, to prepare for assessments, and to assist each student in achieving their best performance in school.

The ***SOLARO Study Guide*** consists of the following sections:

TABLE OF CORRELATIONS

The Table of Correlations is a critical component of the ***SOLARO Study Guide***.

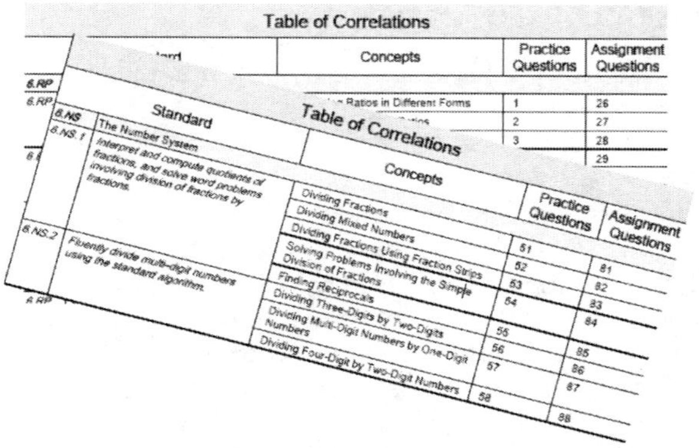

Castle Rock Research has designed the ***SOLARO Study Guide*** by correlating each question and its solution to regional State Standards. Each unit begins with a Table of Correlations, which lists the standards and questions that correspond to those standards.

For students, the Table of Correlations provides information about how each question fits into a particular course and the standards to which each question is tied. Students can quickly access all relevant content associated with a particular standard.

For teachers, the Table of Correlations provides a road map for each standard, outlining the most granular and measurable concepts that are included in each standard. It assists teachers in understanding all the components involved in each standard and where students are excelling or require improvement. The Table of Correlations indicates the instructional focus for each content strand, serves as a standards checklist, and focuses on the standards and concepts that are most important in the unit and the particular course of study.

Some concepts may have a complete lesson aligned to them but cannot be assessed using a paper-and-pencil format. These concepts typically require ongoing classroom assessment through various other methods.

LESSONS

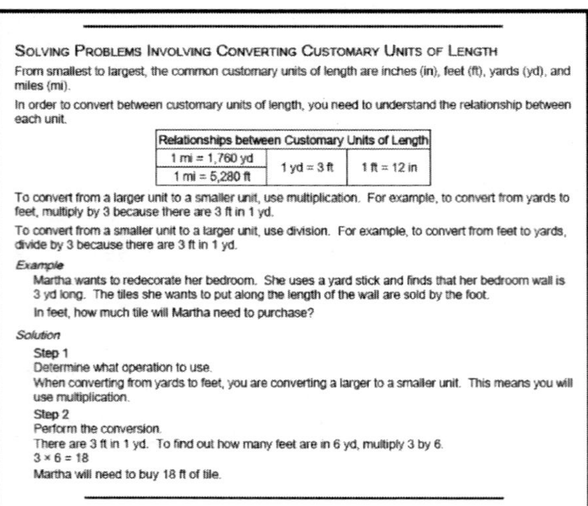

SOLVING PROBLEMS INVOLVING CONVERTING CUSTOMARY UNITS OF LENGTH

From smallest to largest, the common customary units of length are inches (in), feet (ft), yards (yd), and miles (mi).

In order to convert between customary units of length, you need to understand the relationship between each unit.

Relationships between Customary Units of Length		
1 mi = 1,760 yd	1 yd = 3 ft	1 ft = 12 in
1 mi = 5,280 ft		

To convert from a larger unit to a smaller unit, use multiplication. For example, to convert from yards to feet, multiply by 3 because there are 3 ft in 1 yd.

To convert from a smaller unit to a larger unit, use division. For example, to convert from feet to yards, divide by 3 because there are 3 ft in 1 yd.

Example

Martha wants to redecorate her bedroom. She uses a yard stick and finds that her bedroom wall is 3 yd long. The tiles she wants to put along the length of the wall are sold by the foot.

In feet, how much tile will Martha need to purchase?

Solution

Step 1
Determine what operation to use.
When converting from yards to feet, you are converting a larger to a smaller unit. This means you will use multiplication.

Step 2
Perform the conversion.
There are 3 ft in 1 yd. To find out how many feet are in 6 yd, multiply 3 by 6.
$3 \times 6 = 18$
Martha will need to buy 18 ft of tile.

Following the Table of Correlations for each unit are lessons aligned to each concept within a standard. The lessons explain key concepts that students are expected to learn according to regional State Standards.

As each lesson is tied to state standards, students and teachers are assured that the information will be relevant to what is being covered in class.

EXERCISE QUESTIONS

Each set of lessons is followed by two sets of exercise questions that assess students on their understanding of the content. These exercise questions can be used by students to give them an idea of the type of questions they are likely to face in the future in terms of format, difficulty, and content coverage.

DETAILED SOLUTIONS

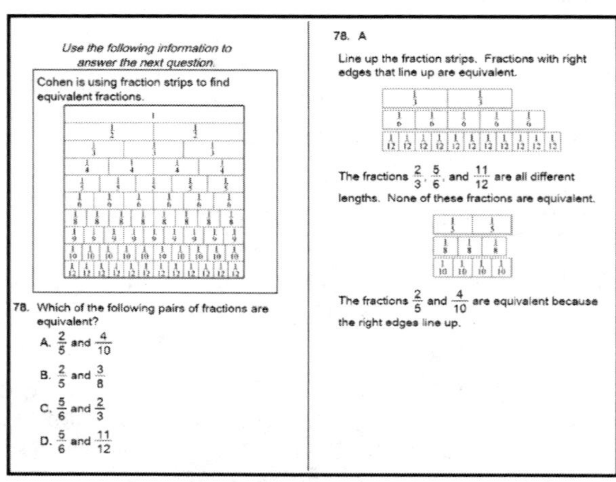

Use the following information to answer the next question.

Cohen is using fraction strips to find equivalent fractions.

78. Which of the following pairs of fractions are equivalent?

A. $\frac{2}{5}$ and $\frac{4}{10}$

B. $\frac{2}{5}$ and $\frac{3}{8}$

C. $\frac{5}{6}$ and $\frac{2}{3}$

D. $\frac{5}{6}$ and $\frac{11}{12}$

78. A

Line up the fraction strips. Fractions with right edges that line up are equivalent.

The fractions $\frac{2}{3}$, $\frac{5}{6}$, and $\frac{11}{12}$ are all different lengths. None of these fractions are equivalent.

The fractions $\frac{2}{5}$ and $\frac{4}{10}$ are equivalent because the right edges line up.

Some study guides only provide an answer key, which will identify the correct response but may not be helpful in determining what led to the incorrect answer. Every exercise question in the ***SOLARO Study Guide*** is accompanied by a detailed solution. Access to complete solutions greatly enhances a student's ability to work independently, and these solutions also serve as useful instructional tools for teachers. The level of information in each detailed solution is intended to help students better prepare for the future by learning from their mistakes and to help teachers discern individual areas of strengths and weaknesses.

For the complete curriculum document, visit http://www.tea.state.tx.us/index2.aspx?id=6148.

SOLARO Study Guides are available for many courses. Check www.solaro.com/orders for a complete listing of books available for your area.

For more enhanced online resources, please visit www.SOLARO.com.

Student-Oriented Learning, Assessment, and Reporting Online

SOLARO is an online resource that provides students with regionally and age-appropriate lessons and practice questions. Students can be confident that SOLARO has the right materials to help them when they are having difficulties in class. SOLARO is 100% compliant with each region's core standards. Teachers can use SOLARO in the classroom as a supplemental resource to provide remediation and enrichment. Student performance is reported to the teacher through various reports, which provide insight into strengths and weaknesses.

TABLE OF CONTENTS

CREDITS

Key Tips for Being Successful at School

KEY TIPS FOR BEING SUCCESSFUL AT SCHOOL

KEY FACTORS CONTRIBUTING TO SCHOOL SUCCESS

In addition to learning the content of your courses, there are some other things that you can do to help you do your best at school. You can try some of the following strategies:

- **Keep a positive attitude:** Always reflect on what you can already do and what you already know.
- **Be prepared to learn:** Have the necessary pencils, pens, notebooks, and other required materials for participating in class ready.
- **Complete all of your assignments:** Do your best to finish all of your assignments. Even if you know the material well, practice will reinforce your knowledge. If an assignment or question is difficult for you, work through it as far as you can so that your teacher can see exactly where you are having difficulty.
- **Set small goals for yourself when you are learning new material:** For example, when learning the parts of speech, do not try to learn everything in one night. Work on only one part or section each study session. When you have memorized one particular part of speech and understand it, move on to another one. Continue this process until you have memorized and learned all the parts of speech.
- **Review your classroom work regularly at home:** Review to make sure you understand the material you learned in class.

- **Ask your teacher for help:** Your teacher will help you if you do not understand something or if you are having a difficult time completing your assignments.
- **Get plenty of rest and exercise:** Concentrating in class is hard work. It is important to be well-rested and have time to relax and socialize with your friends. This helps you keep a positive attitude about your schoolwork.
- **Eat healthy meals:** A balanced diet keeps you healthy and gives you the energy you need for studying at school and at home.

HOW TO FIND YOUR LEARNING STYLE

Every student learns differently. The manner in which you learn best is called your learning style. By knowing your learning style, you can increase your success at school. Most students use a combination of learning styles. Do you know what type of learner you are? Read the following descriptions. Which of these common learning styles do you use most often?

- **Linguistic Learner:** You may learn best by saying, hearing, and seeing words. You are probably really good at memorizing things such as dates, places, names, and facts. You may need to write down the steps in a process, a formula, or the actions that lead up to a significant event, and then say them out loud.
- **Spatial Learner:** You may learn best by looking at and working with pictures. You are probably really good at puzzles, imagining things, and reading maps and charts. You may need to use strategies like mind mapping and webbing to organize your information and study notes.
- **Kinesthetic Learner:** You may learn best by touching, moving, and figuring things out using manipulatives. You are probably really good at physical activities and learning through movement. You may need to draw your finger over a diagram to remember it, tap out the steps needed to solve a problem, or feel yourself writing or typing a formula.

SCHEDULING STUDY TIME

You should review your class notes regularly to ensure that you have a clear understanding of all the new material you learned. Reviewing your lessons on a regular basis helps you to learn and remember ideas and concepts. It also reduces the quantity of material that you need to study prior to a test. Establishing a study schedule will help you to make the best use of your time.

Regardless of the type of study schedule you use, you may want to consider the following suggestions to maximize your study time and effort:

- Organize your work so that you begin with the most challenging material first.
- Divide the subject's content into small, manageable chunks.
- Alternate regularly between your different subjects and types of study activities in order to maintain your interest and motivation.
- Make a daily list with headings like "Must Do," "Should Do," and "Could Do."
- Begin each study session by quickly reviewing what you studied the day before.
- Maintain your usual routine of eating, sleeping, and exercising to help you concentrate better for extended periods of time.

Creating Study Notes

Mind-Mapping or Webbing

Use the key words, ideas, or concepts from your reading or class notes to create a mind map or web (a diagram or visual representation of the given information). A mind map or web is sometimes referred to as a knowledge map. Use the following steps to create a mind map or web:

1. Write the key word, concept, theory, or formula in the centre of your page.
2. Write down related facts, ideas, events, and information, and link them to the central concept with lines.
3. Use coloured markers, underlining, or symbols to emphasize things such as relationships, timelines, and important information.

The following examples of a Frayer Model illustrate how this technique can be used to study vocabulary.

Perimeter

Definition	**Notes**
• Perimeter is the distance around the outside of a polygon.	• Perimeter is measured in linear units (e.g., metres, centimetres, and so on).
Examples	**Non-Examples**
• The length of a fence around a yard • The distance around a circle (circumference)	• The area of grass covering a lawn • The size of a rug lying on a floor

Cube

Definition	**Notes**
• A cube is a solid 3-D object with six faces.	• A cube is different from other shapes because it has six equally-sized square faces, eight vertices, and twelve equal edges.
Examples	**Non-Examples**
	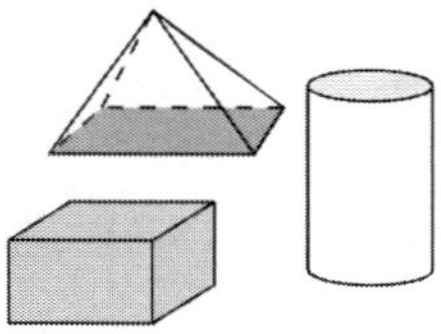

INDEX CARDS

To use index cards while studying, follow these steps:

1. Write a key word or question on one side of an index card.
2. On the reverse side, write the definition of the word, answer to the question, or any other important information that you want to remember.

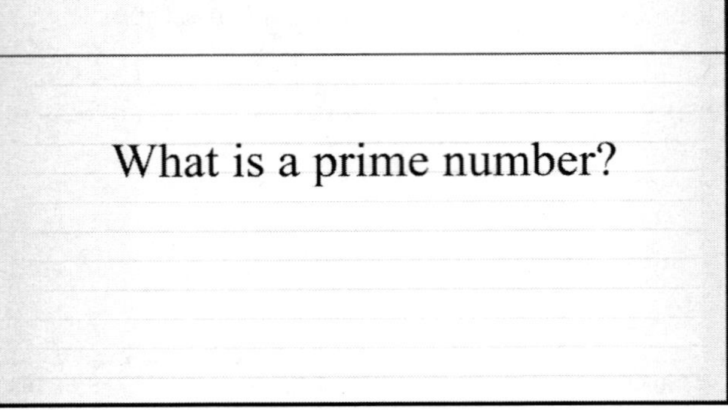

What is a prime number?

A prime number is any number that has exactly 2 factors.
A prime number can be divided evenly only by itself and one.
For example, 2, 3, 5, 7, 19.
The number 1 is not a prime number.

SYMBOLS AND STICKY NOTES—IDENTIFYING IMPORTANT INFORMATION

Use symbols to mark your class notes. The following are some examples:

- An exclamation mark (!) might be used to point out something that must be learned well because it is a very important idea.
- A question mark (?) may highlight something you are not certain about
- A diamond (◊) or asterisk (*) could highlight interesting information that you want to remember.

Sticky notes are useful in the following situations:

- Use sticky notes when you are not allowed to put marks in books.
- Use sticky notes to mark a page in a book that contains an important diagram, formula, explanation, or other information.
- Use sticky notes to mark important facts in research books.

MEMORIZATION TECHNIQUES

- **Association** relates new learning to something you already know. For example, to remember the spelling difference between dessert and desert, recall that the word *sand* has only one *s*. So, because there is sand in a desert, the word *desert* has only one *s*.
- **Mnemonic** devices are sentences that you create to remember a list or group of items. For example, the first letter of each word in the phrase "Every Good Boy Deserves Fudge" helps you to remember the names of the lines on the treble-clef staff (E, G, B, D, and F) in music.

- **Acronyms** are words that are formed from the first letters or parts of the words in a group. For example, RADAR is actually an acronym for Radio Detecting and Ranging, and MASH is an acronym for Mobile Army Surgical Hospital. HOMES helps you to remember the names of the five Great Lakes (Huron, Ontario, Michigan, Erie, and Superior).
- **Visualizing** requires you to use your mind's eye to "see" a chart, list, map, diagram, or sentence as it is in your textbook or notes, on the chalkboard or computer screen, or in a display.

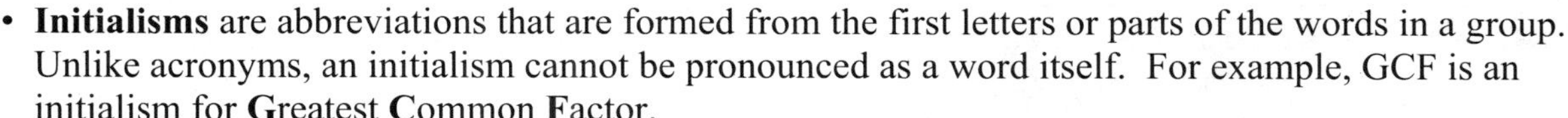

- **Initialisms** are abbreviations that are formed from the first letters or parts of the words in a group. Unlike acronyms, an initialism cannot be pronounced as a word itself. For example, GCF is an initialism for **G**reatest **C**ommon **F**actor.

KEY STRATEGIES FOR REVIEWING

Reviewing textbook material, class notes, and handouts should be an ongoing activity. Spending time reviewing becomes more critical when you are preparing for a test. You may find some of the following review strategies useful when studying during your scheduled study time:

- Before reading a selection, preview it by noting the headings, charts, graphs, and chapter questions.
- Before reviewing a unit, note the headings, charts, graphs, and chapter questions.
- Highlight key concepts, vocabulary, definitions, and formulas.
- Skim the paragraph, and note the key words, phrases, and information.
- Carefully read over each step in a procedure.
- Draw a picture or diagram to help make the concept clearer.

KEY STRATEGIES FOR SUCCESS: A CHECKLIST

Reviewing is a huge part of doing well at school and preparing for tests. Here is a checklist for you to keep track of how many suggested strategies for success you are using. Read each question, and put a check mark (✓) in the correct column. Look at the questions where you have checked the "No" column. Think about how you might try using some of these strategies to help you do your best at school.

Key Strategies for Success	Yes	No
Do you attend school regularly?		
Do you know your personal learning style—how you learn best?		
Do you spend 15 to 30 minutes a day reviewing your notes?		
Do you study in a quiet place at home?		
Do you clearly mark the most important ideas in your study notes?		
Do you use sticky notes to mark texts and research books?		
Do you practise answering multiple-choice and written-response questions?		
Do you ask your teacher for help when you need it?		
Are you maintaining a healthy diet and sleep routine?		
Are you participating in regular physical activity?		

Graphing Functions

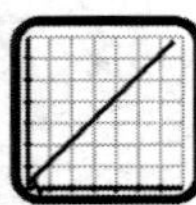

GRAPHING FUNCTIONS

Table of Correlations

Standard		Concepts	Exercise #1	Exercise #2
PC.1	The student defines functions, describes characteristics of functions, and translates among verbal, numerical, graphical, and symbolic representations of functions, including polynomial, rational, power (including radical), exponential, logarithmic, trigonometric, and piecewise-defined functions.			
PC. 1.A	*Describe parent functions symbolically and graphically, including f(x)=xn, f(x)=1n(x), f(x)=log$_a$(x), f(x)=1/x, f(x)=ex, f(x)=|x|, f(x)=ax, f(x)=sin(x), f(x)=arcsin(x), etc.*	Graphs of Logarithmic Functions	1, 2	22, 23
		Graphing the Natural Logarithm Function		
		Graphing the Inverse of the Sine Function: $y = \arcsin x$		
		Graphing the Inverse of the Cosine Function $y = \arccos x$		
		Graphing the Inverse of the Tangent Function $y = \arctan x$		
		Sketching the Graph of the Sine Function Using Degrees		
		Sketching the Graph of the Sine Function Using Radians		
		Sketching the Graph of the Cosine Function Using Degrees		
		Sketching the Graph of the Cosine Function Using Radians		
		Sketching the Graph of the Tangent Function Using Degrees		
		Sketching the Graph of the Tangent Function Using Radians		
		Defining the Domain and Range of a Function	3, 4	24, 25
		Determining the Domain and Range for Continuous Data	5, 6	26, 27
		Graphing log$_b$, Where b Is Not Equal to Zero	7, 8	28, 29
		Graphing the Function $y = e^x$		
		The Graph of $y = x^n$, where $0 < n < 5$	9, 10	30, 31
		Understanding Absolute Values		
PC. 1.B	*Determine the domain and range of functions using graphs, tables, and symbols.*	Graphing the Natural Logarithm Function		
		Graphing the Inverse of the Sine Function: $y = \arcsin x$		
		Graphing the Inverse of the Cosine Function $y = \arccos x$		
		Graphing the Inverse of the Tangent Function $y = \arctan x$		
		Sketching the Graph of the Sine Function Using Degrees		
		Sketching the Graph of the Sine Function Using Radians		

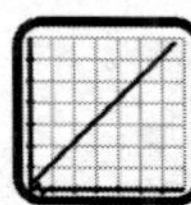

		Sketching the Graph of the Cosine Function Using Degrees		
		Sketching the Graph of the Cosine Function Using Radians		
		Sketching the Graph of the Tangent Function Using Degrees		
		Sketching the Graph of the Tangent Function Using Radians		
		Defining the Domain and Range of a Function	3, 4	24, 25
		Determining the Domain and Range for Continuous Data	5, 6	26, 27
		Graphing $\log_b$, Where b Is Not Equal to Zero	7, 8	28, 29
		Graphing the Function $y = e^x$		
		The Graph of $y = x^n$, where $0 < n < 5$	9, 10	30, 31
		Graphing $y = \| x \|$		
PC. 1.C	*Describe symmetry of graphs of even and odd functions.*	Determining the Properties of Even and Odd Polynomial Functions	11, 12	32
PC. 1.D	*Recognize and use connections among significant values of a function (zeros, maximum values, minimum values, etc.), points on the graph of a function, and the symbolic representation of a function.*	Identifying the Properties of a Trigonometric Function from an Equation or a Graph	13, 14	33
PC. 1.E	*Investigate the concepts of continuity, end behavior, asymptotes, and limits and connect these characteristics to functions represented graphically and numerically.*	The Graph of $y = x^n$, where $0 < n < 5$	9, 10	30, 31
		Determining the Properties of Even and Odd Polynomial Functions	11, 12	32
		Sketching the Graph of a Polynomial Function	15	
		Determining Horizontal Asymptotes of Rational Functions	16, 17	34
		Determining the Vertical Asymptotes of Rational Functions	18, 19	35, 36
		Determining the Oblique Asymptotes of a Rational Function	20, 21	37, 38

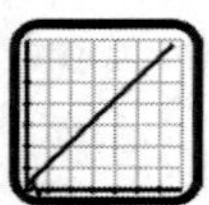

PC.1.A Describe parent functions symbolically and graphically, including f(x)=xn, f(x)=1n(x), f(x)=log$_a$(x), f(x)=1/x, f(x)=ex, f(x)=|x|, f(x)=ax, f(x)=sin(x), f(x)=arcsin(x), etc.

Graphs of Logarithmic Functions

To investigate the graphs of logarithmic functions that are not base 10 or base *e* logarithms, apply the change-of-base formula. This will express the desired function in terms of $y = \log x$ or $y = \ln x$.

Usually, base 10 logarithms are used, and the required application is $\log_b x = \frac{\log x}{\log b}$.

Using a TI-83 calculator, compare the graphs of the functions $f(x) = \log_2 x$, $g(x) = \log_3 x$, and $h(x) = \log_{10} x$. These functions are all of the type $y = \log_b x$, in which $b > 1$.

Applying the change-of-base formula, input the following three functions into the Y = editor:
Y_1 = log (X)/log (2)
Y_2 = log (X)/log (3)
Y_3 = log (X)

The graphs shown here appear in the display when the viewing window is set at the following values: $X_{min} = -5$, $X_{max} = 5$, $X_{scl} = 1$, $Y_{min} = -5$, $Y_{max} = 5$, and $Y_{scl} = 1$.

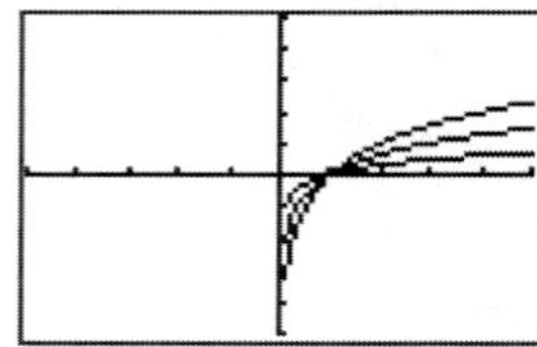

Notice that the graphs do not extend into quadrants 2 and 3. This implies that the domain must be $x > 0$ or $x \geq 0$. All three graphs appear to intersect the *y*-axis but, in fact, do not. A graphing calculator does not always show graphs the way they really should appear.

The graphs shown here appear when the viewing window is changed to the following values: $X_{min} = 0$, $X_{max} = 2$, $X_{scl} = 1$, $Y_{min} = -3$, $Y_{max} = 2$, and $Y_{scl} = 1$.

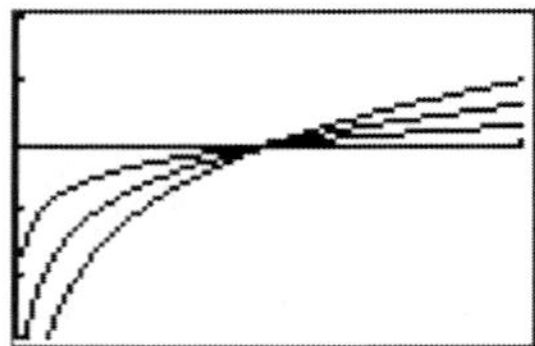

The graph of $h(x) = \log_{10} x$ still appears to intersect the *y*-axis.

The graphs sketched here are not drawn to scale to emphasize the fact that they do not intersect the *y*-axis.

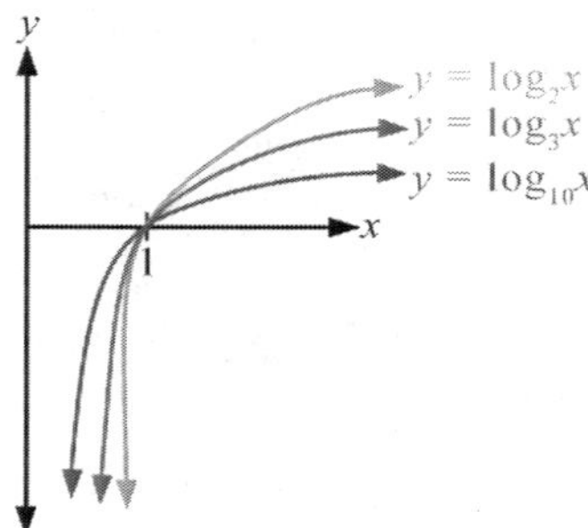

Through this investigation, you can observe the following key features of logarithmic functions and their graphs:

- The *y*-axis is a vertical asymptote, so the domain is $x > 0$, $x \in R$.
- The range is $y \in R$, since the graph extends infinitely upward and downward.
- The *x*-intercept is 1 for all graphs. This is because $b^0 = 1$ for all permissible values of *b*, which is equivalent to $\log_b(1) = 0$.
- There is no *y*-intercept or horizontal asymptote.
- The functions are increasing over the entire domain, since, as *x* increases, the corresponding value of *y* increases and the graph rises. Observe that increasing the value of the base, *b*, compresses the graph vertically toward the *x*-axis.

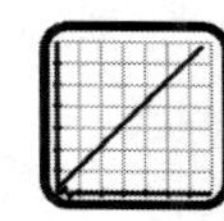

Graphing $f(x) = \log_{\frac{1}{2}} x$, $g(x) = \log_{\frac{1}{3}} x$, and $h(x) = \log_{\frac{1}{10}} x$, in which $0 < b < 1$, on the same axes produces the following three graphs. Note that these graphs are not drawn to scale.

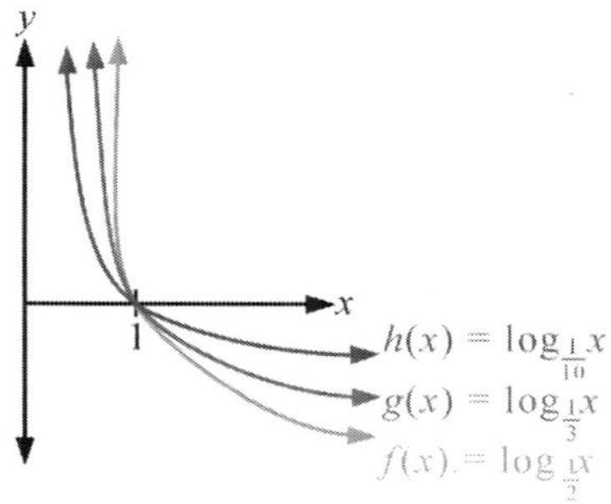

Many of the features of the previous graphs (when $b > 1$) apply to these graphs as well. Notice, however, that the function values now decrease as the x-values increase, and that decreasing the value of b compresses the graph toward the x-axis.

Key features of the graph of $f(x) = \log_b x$, $b > 0$, $b \neq 1$ are as follows:

Domain	$x > 0$
Range	$y \in R$
Vertical asymptote	$x = 0$
x-intercept	1
y-intercept	None
Increasing/decreasing behavior	Decreasing if $0 < b < 1$; increasing if $b > 1$

Example

A student draws the graph of the function $f(x) = \log_5 x$. Then, on the same axes, the student draws the graphs of $g(x) = \log_2 x$ and $h(x) = \log_{\frac{1}{3}} x$.

Describe the similarities and differences of the key features that the student will notice in the three graphs.

Solution

All three graphs have the same domain, $x > 0$; the same x-intercept, 1; the same range, $y \in R$; and the same vertical asymptote, the y-axis. If the base is greater than 1($b > 1$), the function increases over the entire domain, so both $f(x) = \log_5 x$ and $g(x) = \log_2 x$ are increasing. However, the graph of $f(x) = \log_5 x$ is more compressed toward the x-axis than is the graph of $g(x) = \log_2 x$, since it does not increase as rapidly.
The function $h(x) = \log_{\frac{1}{3}} x$ decreases as x increases because its base is between 0 and 1 ($0 < b < 1$).

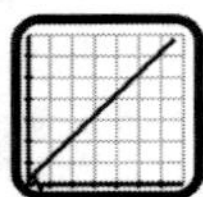

Graphing the Natural Logarithm Function

A **natural logarithm** is any logarithm that has a base of e, where e is a unique numerical value approximately equal to 2.71828. The notation ln (pronounced *lawn*) is used to represent the natural logarithm $\log_e$. The function $f(x) = \log_e x$ is written as $f(x) = \ln(x)$. The inverse of the natural logarithmic function $f(x) = \log_e x = \ln(x)$ is $f(x) = e^x$. The graphs of $y = e^x$ and $y = \ln(x)$ will appear as reflections across the line $y = x$.

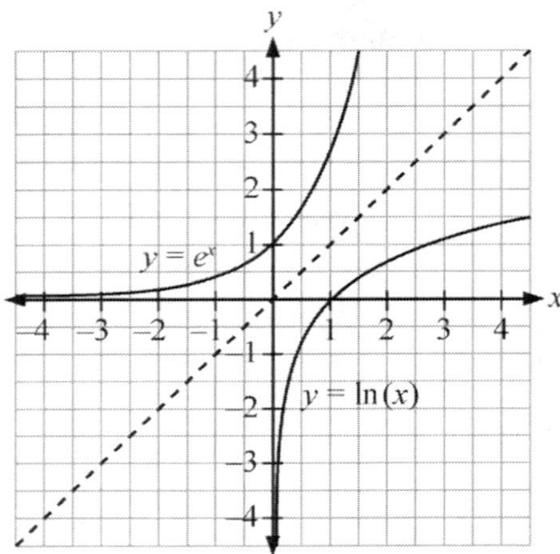

Graph of the functions $y = e^x$ and $y = \ln(x)$

The graph of the natural logarithmic function $y = \ln(x)$ has two important characteristics:

- The domain of $y = \ln(x)$ can be any positive real number: $x > 0$, where $x \in \mathbb{R}$.
- The range of $y = \ln(x)$ can be any real number: $y \in \mathbb{R}$.

Example

Graph the natural logarithmic function $y = \ln(x)$.

Solution

Step 1

Determine if there is an x-intercept.

To determine if there are any x-intercepts, let $y = 0$ and solve the given function for x.

$y = \ln(x)$
$0 = \ln(x)$

Take the exponential form of both sides of the equation (remember that the natural logarithm uses base e), and solve for x.

$e^0 = e^{\ln(x)}$
$1 = x$

The given function, $y = \ln(x)$, crosses the x-axis at $x = 1$.

Step 2

Determine if there is a y-intercept.

To determine if there is a y-intercept, let $x = 0$ and solve the given function for y.

$y = \ln(x)$
$y = \ln(0)$

Take the exponential form of both sides of the equation (remember that the natural logarithm uses base e), and solve for x.

$e^y = e^{\ln(0)}$
$e^y = 0$

There is no solution to the equation above, so there is no y-intercept.

Step 3

Calculate any asymptotes.

An asymptote occurs on the graph of $y = \ln(x)$ at the line $x = 0$. Transforming the given natural logarithmic equation, $0 = \ln(x)$, into its exponential form $0 = e^y$ (as shown in step 2) makes it more obvious that there is no real number (no matter how infinitely small) that will satisfy the equation $y = \ln(0)$. The smaller the value of y becomes, the closer the x-value gets to 0, but there is no real number small enough to satisfy the equation $0 = e^y$.

Since there is no real number small enough to satisfy the equation $y = \ln(0)$, the function will only ever approach the line $x = 0$.

Step 4
Graph the function by using the identified key features.

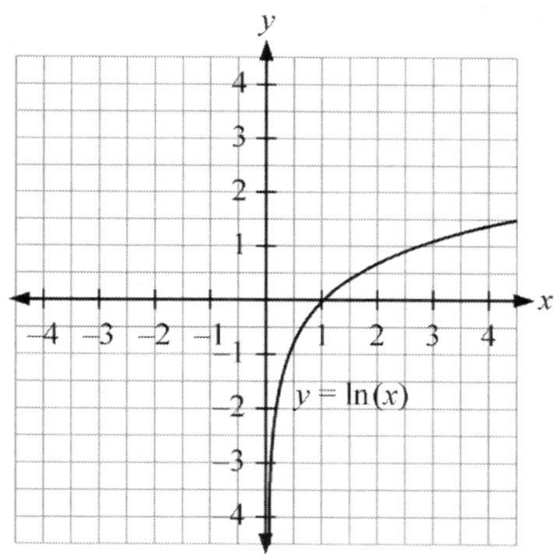

Graphing the Inverse of the Sine Function: $y = \arcsin x$

Recall that only **one-to-one functions** have **inverse functions**. Since the function $y = \sin x$ is not one-to-one, in order to define its inverse function, the domain must be restricted.

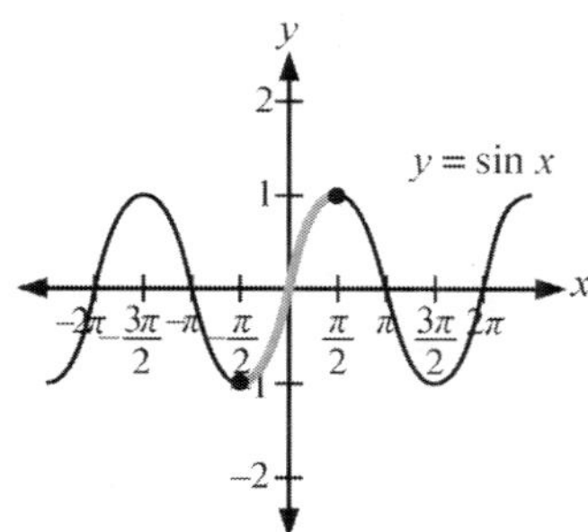

Observe that the portion of the graph of $y = \sin x$ in the domain $-\frac{\pi}{2} \leq x \leq \frac{\pi}{2}$, highlighted in the image, is one-to-one and will have an inverse function.

To graph the inverse function $y = \sin^{-1} x$, or $y = \arcsin x$, reflect the graph of $y = \sin x$ on the restricted domain about the line $y = x$, as shown.

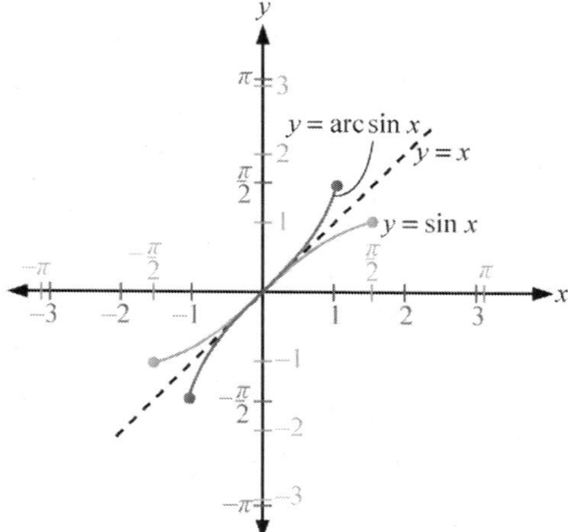

As the range of $y = \sin x$ is $-1 \leq y \leq 1$, the function $y = \arcsin x$ is defined on the domain of $-1 \leq x \leq 1$ and has a range of $-\frac{\pi}{2} \leq y \leq \frac{\pi}{2}$.

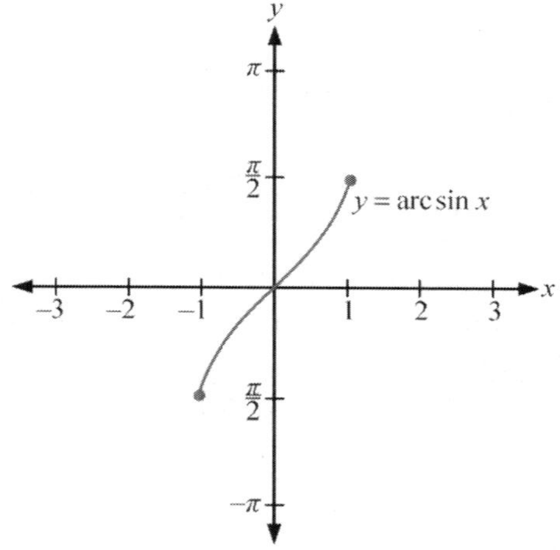

The graph of $y = \arcsin x$ begins at the point $\left(-1, -\frac{\pi}{2}\right)$, increases, passes through the origin, and continues increasing to the point $\left(1, \frac{\pi}{2}\right)$, where the graph stops.

Note that if the required angle measures were in degrees instead of radians, the range of $y = \arcsin x$ would be $-90° \leq y \leq 90°$. The graph of $y = \arcsin x$ would have the same shape, beginning at the point $(-1, -90°)$ and terminating at the point $(1, 90°)$.

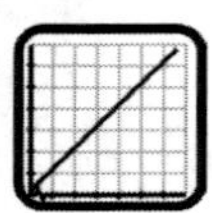

Graphing the Inverse of the Cosine Function $y = \arccos x$

Only one-to-one functions have **inverse functions**. Since the function $y = \cos x$ is not one-to-one, you must restrict the domain to define its inverse function. The portion of the graph of $y = \cos x$ in the domain $0 \le x \le \pi$ is one-to-one and will have an inverse function.

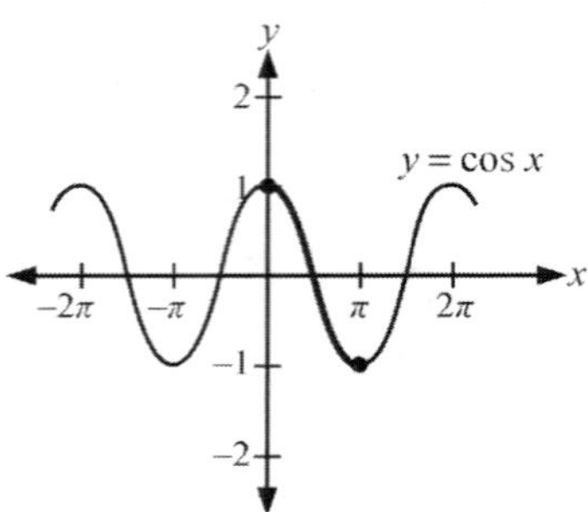

To graph the inverse function, $y = \cos^{-1} x$ or $y = \arccos x$, reflect the graph of $y = \cos x$ on the restricted domain about the line $y = x$.

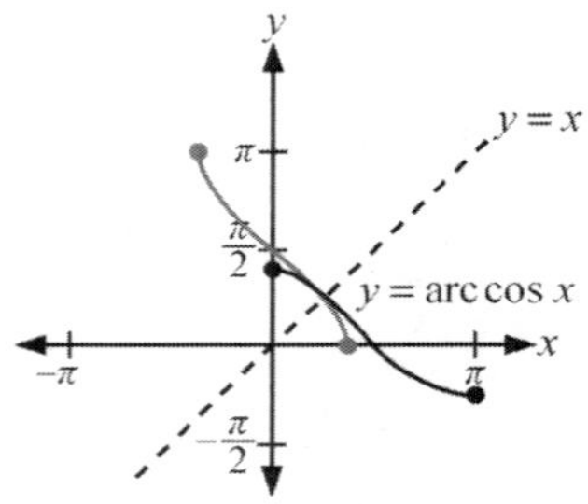

Since the range of $y = \cos x$ is $-1 \le y \le 1$, the function $y = \arccos x$ is defined on the domain of $-1 \le x \le 1$ and has a range of $0 \le x \le \pi$.

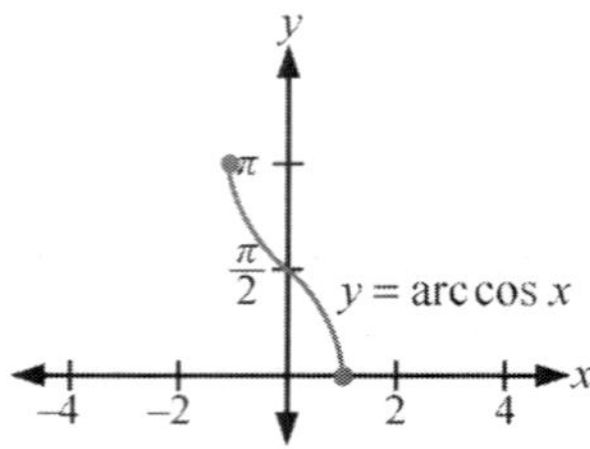

The graph of $y = \arccos x$ begins at the point $(-1, \pi)$, decreases, passes through the y-axis at $\left(0, \frac{\pi}{2}\right)$, and continues decreasing until the point $(1, 0)$, where the graph stops.

If the required angle measures were in degrees instead of radians, the range of $y = \arccos x$ would be $0 \le y \le 180°$. The graph of $y = \arccos x$ would have the same shape, beginning at the point $(-1, 180°)$, decreasing to pass through the y-axis at $(0, 90°)$, and terminating at the point $(1, 0)$.

Graphing the Inverse of the Tangent Function $y = \arctan x$

Only **one-to-one functions** have **inverse functions**. Since the function $y = \tan x$ is not one-to-one, to define its inverse function, you must restrict the domain. The portion of the graph of $y = \tan x$ that is in the domain $-\frac{\pi}{2} < x < \frac{\pi}{2}$ is one-to-one and will have an inverse function.

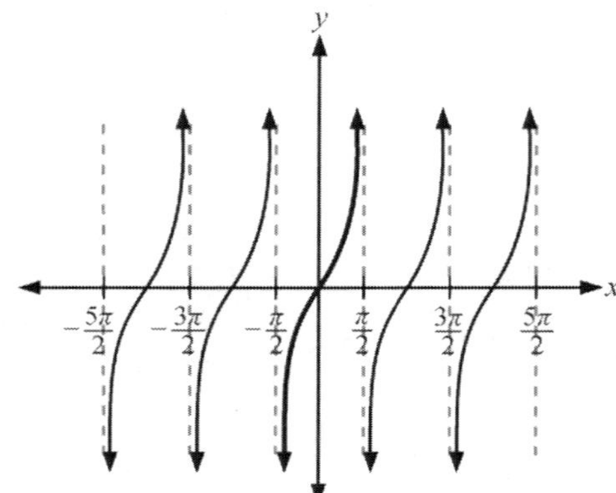

To graph the inverse function, $y = \tan^{-1} x$ or $y = \arctan x$, reflect the graph of $y = \tan x$ on the restricted domain about the line $y = x$.

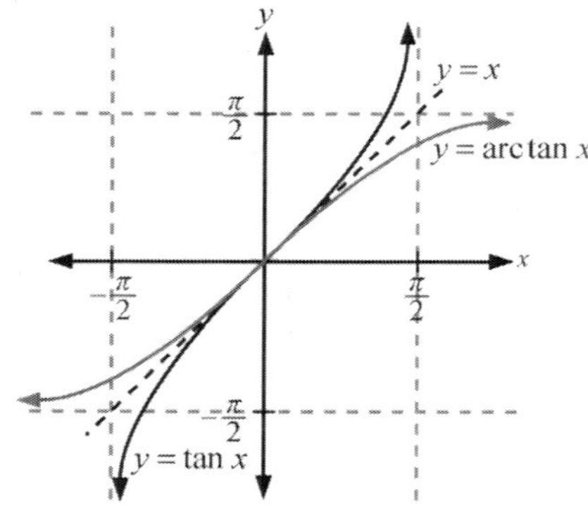

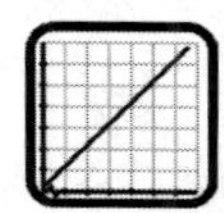

Since the range of $y = \tan x$ is $y \in \mathbb{R}$, the function $y = \arctan x$ is defined on the domain of $x \in \mathbb{R}$ and has a range of $-\frac{\pi}{2} < y < \frac{\pi}{2}$.

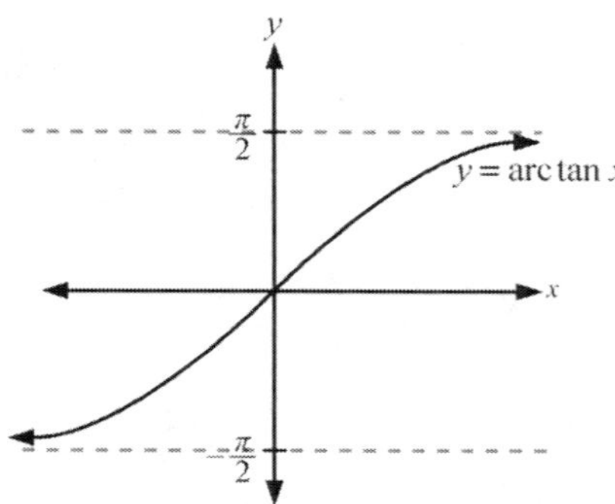

Since the domain of $y = \arctan x$ is the set of real numbers, the graph extends from $-\infty$ to $+\infty$ on the x-axis and has horizontal asymptotes of $y = -\frac{\pi}{2}$ and $y = \frac{\pi}{2}$.

If the required angle measures were in degrees instead of radians, the range of $y = \arctan x$ would be $-90° < y < 90°$. The graph of $y = \arctan x$ would have the same shape, extending from $-\infty$ to $+\infty$ on the x-axis with horizontal asymptotes of $y = -90°$ and $y = 90°$.

Sketching the Graph of the Sine Function Using Degrees

The notations $f(x) = \sin x$ and $f(\theta) = \sin \theta$ are used interchangeably to refer to the sine function. When the sine function is graphed, the first notation uses the x-axis, while the second notation uses the θ-axis to represent the domain of the function (the values of all possible angles).

The function value, $f(x)$, for any angle, x, can be determined with a calculator. The resulting function values of x-values between 0° and 360° that are multiples of 30° are shown in the following table.

x	$f(x) = \sin x$	x	$f(x) = \sin x$
0°	0	210°	−0.5
30°	0.5	240°	−0.866
60°	0.866	270°	−1
90°	1	300°	−0.866
120°	0.866	330°	−0.5
150°	0.5	360°	0
180°	0		

If the values from the table are placed on the Cartesian plane and connected with a smooth curve, the graph of $f(x) = \sin x$ is formed for all angles between 0° and 360°.

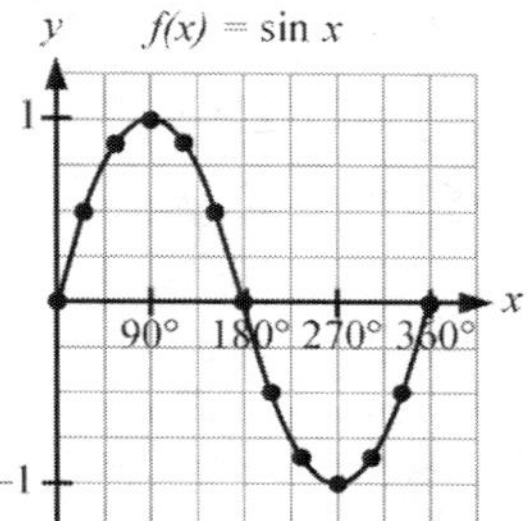

Sketching the Graph of the Sine Function Using Radians

The notations $f(x) = \sin x$ and $f(\theta) = \sin \theta$ are used interchangeably to refer to the sine function. When the sine function is graphed, the first notation uses the x-axis, while the second notation uses the θ-axis to represent the domain of the function (the values of all possible angles).

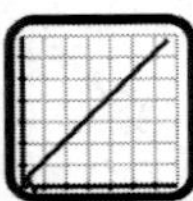

The function value, $f(x)$, for any angle, x, can be determined using a calculator. The resulting function values of x-values between 0 and 2π radians that are multiples of $\frac{\pi}{6}$ are shown in the following table.

x	$f(x) = \sin x$	x	$f(x) = \sin x$
0	0	$\frac{7\pi}{6}$	−0.5
$\frac{\pi}{6}$	0.5	$\frac{4\pi}{3}$	−0.866
$\frac{\pi}{3}$	0.866	$\frac{3\pi}{2}$	−1
$\frac{\pi}{2}$	1	$\frac{5\pi}{3}$	−0.866
$\frac{2\pi}{3}$	0.866	$\frac{11\pi}{6}$	−0.5
$\frac{5\pi}{6}$	0.5	2π	0
π	0		

If the values from the table are placed on the Cartesian plane and connected with a smooth curve, the graph of $f(x) = \sin x$ is formed for all angles between 0 and 2π radians.

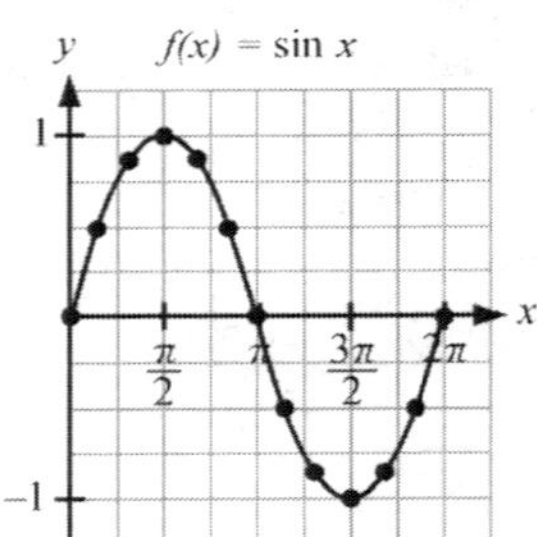

Sketching the Graph of the Cosine Function Using Degrees

The notations $f(x) = \cos x$ and $f(\theta) = \cos \theta$ are used interchangeably to refer to the cosine function. When the cosine function is graphed, the first notation uses the x-axis, while the second notation uses the θ-axis to represent the domain of the function (the values of all possible angles).

The function value, $f(x)$, for any angle, x, can be determined using a calculator. The resulting function values of x-values between 0° and 360° that are multiples of 30° are shown in the following table.

x	$f(x) = \cos x$	x	$f(x) = \cos x$
0°	1	210°	−0.866
30°	0.866	240°	−0.5
60°	0.5	270°	0
90°	0	300°	0.5
120°	−0.5	330°	0.866
150°	−0.866	360°	1
180°	−1		

If the values from the table are placed on the Cartesian plane and connected with a smooth curve, the graph of $f(x) = \cos x$ is formed for all angles between 0° and 360°.

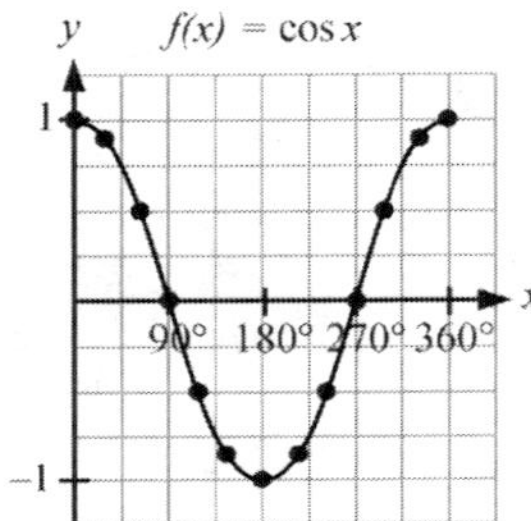

Sketching the Graph of the Cosine Function Using Radians

The notations $f(x) = \cos x$ and $f(\theta) = \cos \theta$ are used interchangeably to refer to the cosine function. When the cosine function is graphed, the first notation uses the x-axis, while the second notation uses the θ-axis to represent the domain of the function (the values of all possible angles).

The function value, $f(x)$, for any angle, x, can be determined using a calculator. The resulting function values of x-values between 0 and 2π radians that are multiples of $\frac{\pi}{6}$ are shown in the following table.

x	$f(x) = \cos x$	x	$f(x) = \cos x$
0	1	$\frac{7\pi}{6}$	−0.866
$\frac{\pi}{6}$	0.866	$\frac{4\pi}{3}$	−0.5
$\frac{\pi}{3}$	0.5	$\frac{3\pi}{2}$	0
$\frac{\pi}{2}$	0	$\frac{5\pi}{3}$	0.5
$\frac{2\pi}{3}$	−0.5	$\frac{11\pi}{6}$	0.866
$\frac{5\pi}{6}$	−0.866	2π	1
π	−1		

If the values from the table are placed on the Cartesian plane and connected with a smooth curve, the graph of $f(x) = \cos x$ is formed for all angles between 0 and 2π radians.

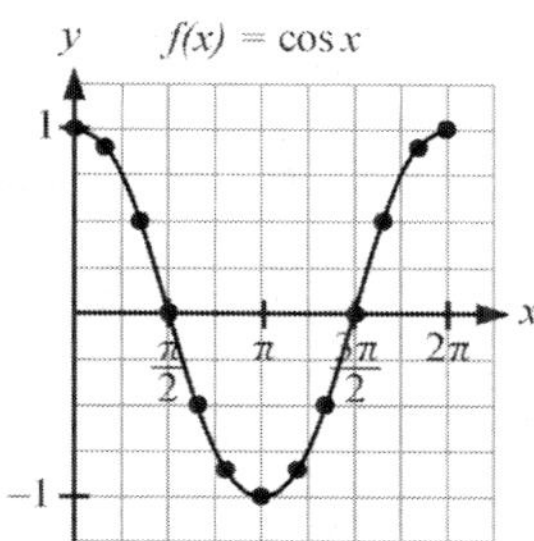

Sketching the Graph of the Tangent Function Using Degrees

The notations $f(x) = \tan x$ and $f(\theta) = \tan \theta$ are used interchangeably to refer to the tangent function. When the tangent function is graphed, the first notation uses the x-axis, while the second notation uses the θ-axis to represent the domain of the function. The domain of the function includes the values of all possible angles.

The function value, $f(\theta)$, for any angle, θ, can be determined using a calculator. The resulting function values of θ-values between 0° and 360° that are multiples of 30° and 45°are shown in the following table:

Angle Measure (θ)	Tangent Ratio ($f(\theta)$)
0°	0
30°	0.577
45°	1.0
60°	1.732
90°	Undefined
120°	−1.732
135°	−1.0
150°	−0.577
180°	0
210°	0.577
225°	1.0
240°	1.732
270°	Undefined
300°	−1.732
315°	−1.0
330°	−0.577
360°	0

There are two angles in the table for which the tangent ratio is undefined. This means a vertical asymptote occurs at $\theta = 90°$ and at any multiple of 180° to the left or right of 90°.

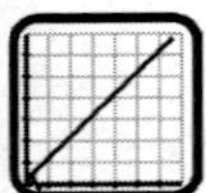

The asymptotes are placed on the Cartesian plane using a dotted line to help graph the tangent function. If the values from the table are placed on the Cartesian plane and connected with a smooth curve between the asymptotes, the graph of $f(\theta) = \tan\theta$ is formed for angles that are defined between 0° and 360°.

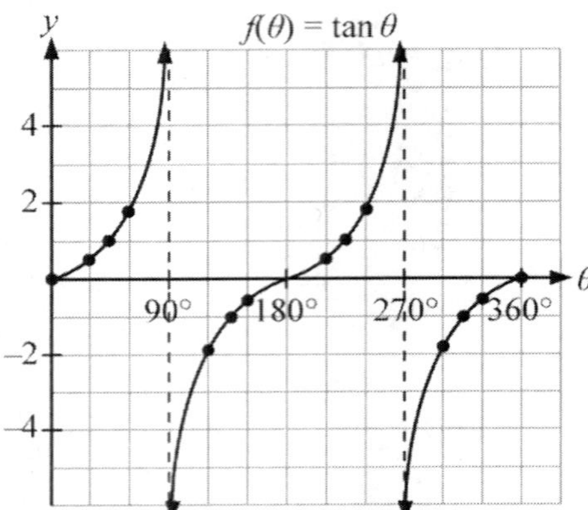

Sketching the Graph of the Tangent Function Using Radians

The notations $f(x) = \tan x$ and $f(\theta) = \tan\theta$ are used interchangeably to refer to the tangent function. When the tangent function is graphed, the first notation uses the x-axis, while the second notation uses the θ-axis to represent the domain of the function. The domain of the function includes the values of all possible angles.

The function value, $f(\theta)$, for any angle, θ, can be determined using a calculator. The resulting function values of θ-values between 0 and 2π radians that are multiples of $\frac{\pi}{6}$ and $\frac{\pi}{4}$ are shown in the following table:

Angle Measure (θ)	Tangent Ratio ($f(\theta)$)
0	0
$\frac{\pi}{6}$	0.577
$\frac{\pi}{4}$	1.0
$\frac{\pi}{3}$	1.732
$\frac{\pi}{2}$	Undefined
$\frac{2\pi}{3}$	−1.732
$\frac{3\pi}{4}$	−1.0
$\frac{5\pi}{6}$	−0.577
π	0
$\frac{7\pi}{6}$	0.577
$\frac{5\pi}{4}$	1.0
$\frac{4\pi}{3}$	1.732
$\frac{3\pi}{2}$	Undefined
$\frac{5\pi}{3}$	−1.732
$\frac{7\pi}{4}$	−1.0
$\frac{11\pi}{6}$	−0.577
2π	0

There are two angles in the table for which the tangent ratio is undefined. This means a vertical asymptote occurs at $\frac{\pi}{2}$ and at any multiple of π to the left or right of $\frac{\pi}{2}$.

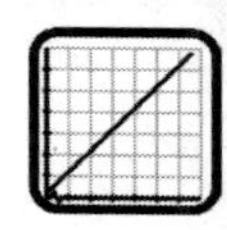

The asymptotes are placed on the Cartesian plane using a dotted line to help graph the tangent function. If the values from the table are placed on the Cartesian plane and connected with a smooth curve between the asymptotes, the graph of $f(\theta) = \tan \theta$ is formed for the angles that are defined between 0 and 2π.

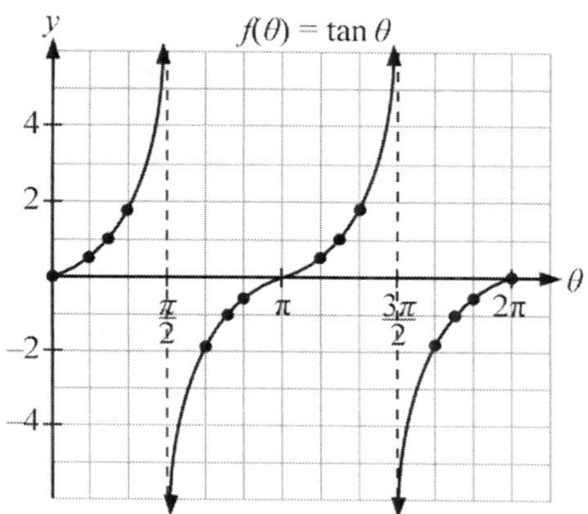

Defining the Domain and Range of a Function

The **domain** of a function is the set of all possible x-values (valid input values) represented by the graph or the equation of the function. The **range** of a function is the set of all possible y-values (valid output values) represented by the graph or the equation of the function. On a graph, the domain is found by referring to the x-axis, and the range is found by referring to the y-axis.

Sometimes, the values contained in the domain and range can be stated in the form of a list. At other times, it is impossible to list all the values, and it is better to state the domain and range as intervals. The following inequality symbols are used when stating an interval:

- $>$ —greater than
- $\geq$ —greater than or equal to
- $<$ —less than
- $\leq$ —less than or equal to

Example

Find the domain and range of the function $y = x - 2$.

Solution

Graph or provide a table of values to visualize the domain and range of the given function.

$y = x - 2$

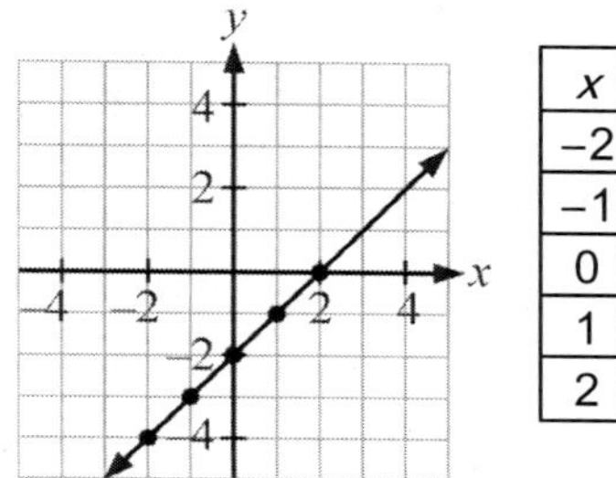

x	y
−2	−4
−1	−3
0	−2
1	−1
2	0

The graph continues infinitely to the right and left for all positive and negative real input elements, or x-values. Therefore, the domain is the set of real numbers. It is written as $x \in \mathbb{R}$, which reads as "x is defined by or belongs to the real numbers." The input values (x) of the table imply this reasoning as well.

The graph of the function $y = x - 2$ and sample output values (y) in the table show that the graph continues infinitely upward and downward for all positive and negative real numbers. Therefore, the range of this function is the set of all real numbers, $y \in \mathbb{R}$.

Example

Find the domain and range of the function $y = x^2 - 3$.

Solution

Graph or provide a table of values to visualize the domain and range of the given function.

$y = x^2 - 3$

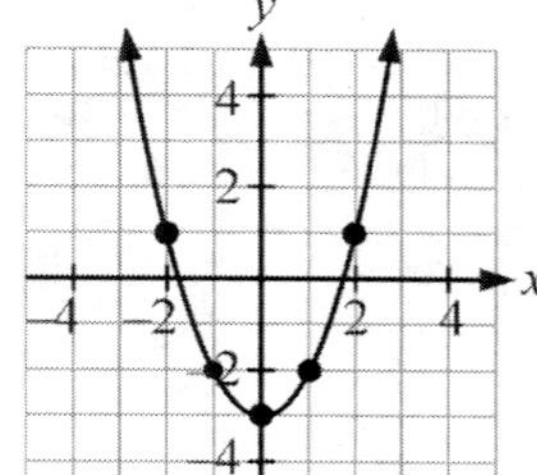

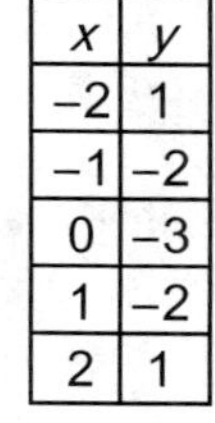

x	y
−2	1
−1	−2
0	−3
1	−2
2	1

The graph continues infinitely to the right and left for all positive and negative real input elements, or *x*-values. Therefore, the domain is the set of real numbers. It is written as $x \in \mathbb{R}$, which reads as "*x* is defined by or belongs to the real numbers." The input values (*x*) of the table imply this reasoning as well.

The graph of the function and sample output values $f(x)$ in the table show that the function's *y*-values do not go lower than –3, but increase infinitely for all real numbers above and including –3. This description of the range is written as $y \geq -3$.

Determining the Domain and Range for Continuous Data

A **continuous** relation includes all values between points.

Example

Since a linear graph continues indefinitely in both directions, both the domain and range contain the set of all real numbers.

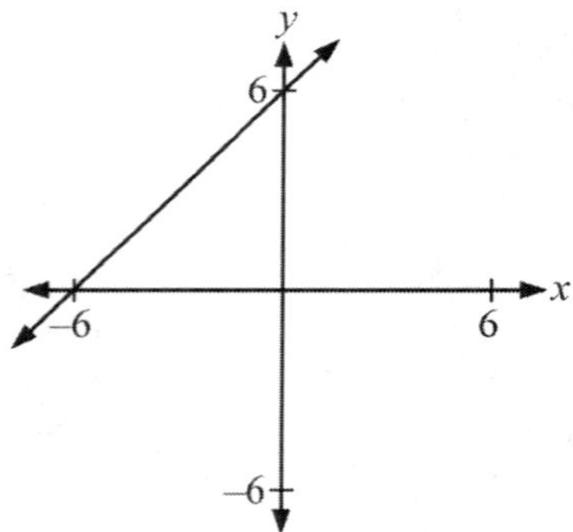

In this case, the domain can be written as $x \in \mathbb{R}$, and the range can be written as $y \in \mathbb{R}$.

The following inequality symbols are used when stating an interval:

- >—greater than
- ≥—greater than or equal to
- <—less than
- ≤—less than or equal to

Example

The given graph is the graph of a particular linear function.

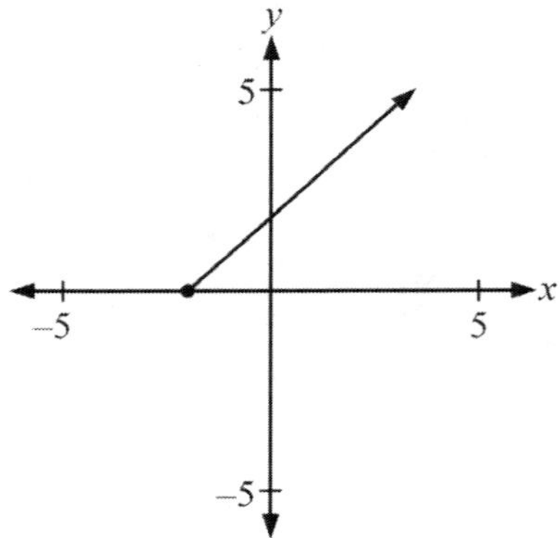

State the domain and range of this function.

Solution

For the domain, the *x*-values start at –2 and increase infinitely. This statement can be written as $x \geq -2$. The given inequality means that *x* is greater than or equal to –2.

For the range, the *y*-values start at 0 and increase infinitely. This statement can be written as $y \geq 0$. The given inequality means that *y* is greater than or equal to 0.

Example

Consider the relation shown in the graph of $y = -x^2 + 4x + 2$.

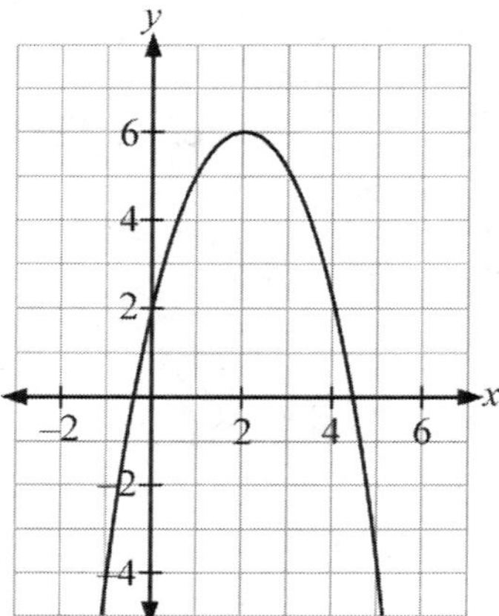

State the domain and range of the given relation.

Solution

The graph is continuous to the right and left for all positive and negative real input or *x*-values. The domain is the set of real numbers, which is written as $x \in \mathbb{R}$.

The graph also shows that the output or *y*-values decrease infinitely for all numbers less than or equal to 6. The range can be expressed as the inequality $y \leq 6$.

Graphing $\log_b$, Where *b* Is Not Equal to Zero

The graph of the logarithmic function $y = \log_b(x)$, where $b \neq 0$, has the two following important characteristics:

- The *domain* can be any positive real number, written as $x > 0$, where $x \in \mathbb{R}$.
- The *range* can be any real number, written as $y \in \mathbb{R}$.

Use the following steps to sketch the graph of the logarithmic function $y = \log_b(x)$, where $b \neq 0$:

1. Determine if there is an *x*-intercept.
2. Determine if there is a *y*-intercept.
3. Calculate any asymptotes.
4. Graph the function using the identified key features.

Example

Graph the logarithmic function $y = \log_2(x)$.

Solution

Step 1

Determine if there is an *x*-intercept.

To determine if there are any *x*-intercepts, let $y = 0$ and solve the resulting equation for *x*.

$y = \log_2(x)$

$0 = \log_2(x)$

Take the exponential form of both sides of the equation (the logarithm uses base 2) and solve for *x*.

$2^0 = 2^{\log_2(x)}$

$1 = x$

The given function, $y = \log_2(x)$, crosses the *x*-axis at $x = 1$.

Step 2

Determine if there is a *y*-intercept.

To determine if there is a *y*-intercept, let $x = 0$ and solve for *y*.

$y = \log_2(x)$

$y = \log_2(0)$

Take the exponential form of both sides of the equation (the logarithm uses base 2) and solve for *y*.

$2^y = 2^{\log_2(0)}$

$2^y = 0$

There is no solution to the equation above; therefore, there is no *y*-intercept.

Step 3

Calculate any asymptotes.

Asymptotes occur wherever $y = \log_2(0)$ occurs. Transforming the logarithmic equation $y = \log_2(0)$ into its exponential form, $0 = 2^y$, makes it more obvious that there is no real number for *y* (no matter how infinitely small) that will satisfy the equation. Therefore, a vertical asymptote occurs at $x = 0$.

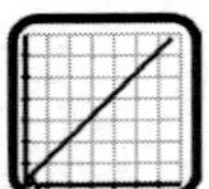

Step 4
Graph the function using the identified key features. It might be useful to determine another point or two on the graph to help graph the function more accurately.

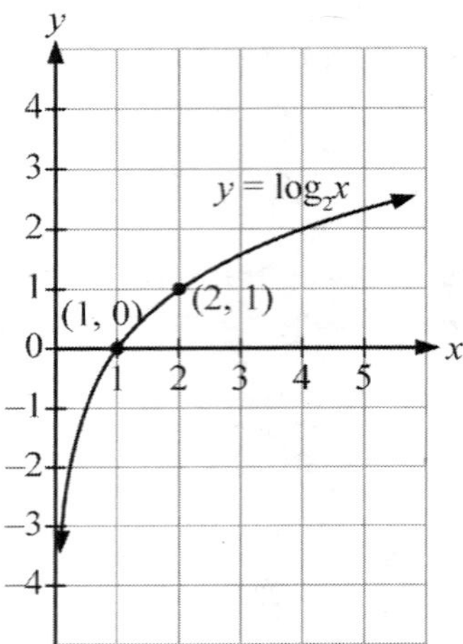

The function $f(x) = \log_b(x)$ is increasing when $b > 1$ and decreasing when $0 < b < 1$.

Example

Graph the logarithmic function $y = \log_{\frac{1}{2}}(x)$.

Solution

Step 1
Determine if there is an x-intercept.
To determine if there are any x-intercepts, let $y = 0$ and solve for x.

$$y = \log_{\frac{1}{2}}(x)$$
$$0 = \log_{\frac{1}{2}}(x)$$

Take the exponential form of both sides of the equation (the logarithm uses base $\frac{1}{2}$) and solve for x.

$$\left(\frac{1}{2}\right)^0 = \left(\frac{1}{2}\right)^{\log_{\frac{1}{2}}(x)}$$
$$1 = x$$

The given function, $y = \log_{\frac{1}{2}}(x)$, crosses the x-axis at $x = 1$.

Step 2
Determine if there is a y-intercept.
To determine if there is a y-intercept, let $x = 0$ and solve for y.

$$y = \log_{\frac{1}{2}}(x)$$
$$y = \log_{\frac{1}{2}}(0)$$

Take the exponential form of both sides of the equation (the logarithm uses base $\frac{1}{2}$) and solve for y.

$$\left(\frac{1}{2}\right)^y = \left(\frac{1}{2}\right)^{\log_{\frac{1}{2}}(0)}$$
$$\left(\frac{1}{2}\right)^y = 0$$

There is no solution to the equation above; therefore, there is no y-intercept.

Step 3
Calculate any asymptotes.
Asymptotes occur wherever $y = \log_{\frac{1}{2}}(0)$ occurs. Transforming the logarithmic equation $y = \log_{\frac{1}{2}}(0)$ into its exponential form, $0 = \left(\frac{1}{2}\right)^y$, makes it more obvious that there is no real number for y (no matter how infinitely small) that will satisfy the equation. Therefore, an asymptote occurs at $x = 0$.

Step 4
Graph the function using the identified key features. It might be useful to determine another point or two on the graph to help sketch the function more accurately.

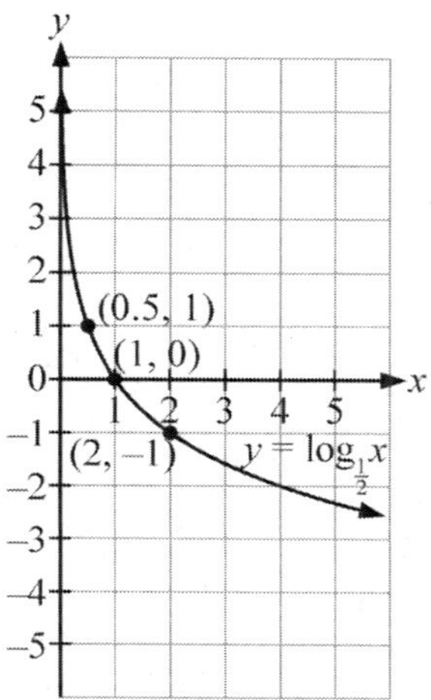

GRAPHING THE FUNCTION $y = e^x$

The unique numeric value e, where $e \approx 2.71828$, has many applications in the field of mathematics. The function $y = e^x$ is called an exponential function because it is the exponent that is the independent variable. The inverse of the exponential function $y = e^x$ is the natural logarithmic function $f(x) = \log_e x = \ln(x)$.

The graphs of $y = e^x$ and $y = \ln(x)$ will appear as reflections across the line $y = x$.

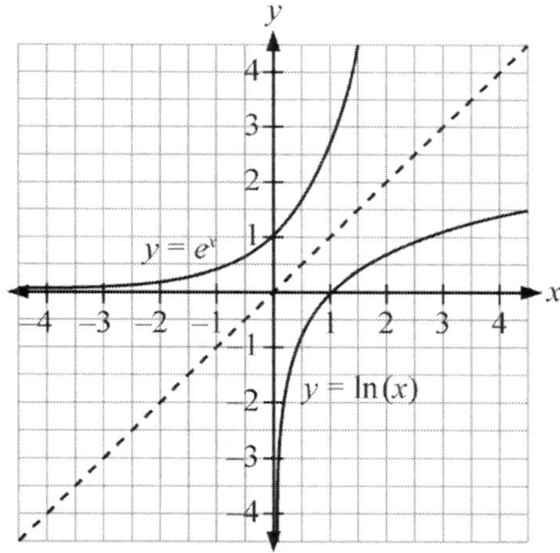

The graph of the exponential function $y = e^x$ has the following two important characteristics:

- The **domain** of $y = e^x$ can be any real number written as $x \in \mathbb{R}$.
- The **range** of $y = e^x$ can be any real positive number written as $y > 0$, where $y \in \mathbb{R}$.

Example

Draw a graph of the exponential function $y = e^x$.

Solution

Step 1
Determine if there is a y-intercept.
Substitute $x = 0$ into the given exponential equation, and solve for y.

$y = e^x$
$y = e^0$
$y = 1$

The given exponential function, $y = e^x$, crosses the y-axis at $y = 1$.

Step 2
Determine if there is an x-intercept.
Substitute $y = 0$ into the given exponential equation, and solve for x.

$y = e^x$
$0 = e^x$

A solution does not exist to the given equation, meaning there is no x-intercept for the exponential function $y = e^x$.

Step 3
Calculate any asymptotes.

An asymptote occurs on the graph of $y = e^x$ at the line $y = 0$. There is no real number (no matter how infinitely small) that will satisfy the equation $0 = e^x$. The smaller the value of x becomes, the closer the given function gets to 0. Since there is no real number small enough to satisfy the equation $0 = e^x$, the function will only ever approach 0.

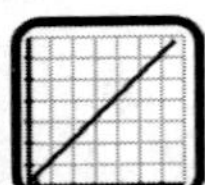

Step 4
Graph the function using the identified key features.

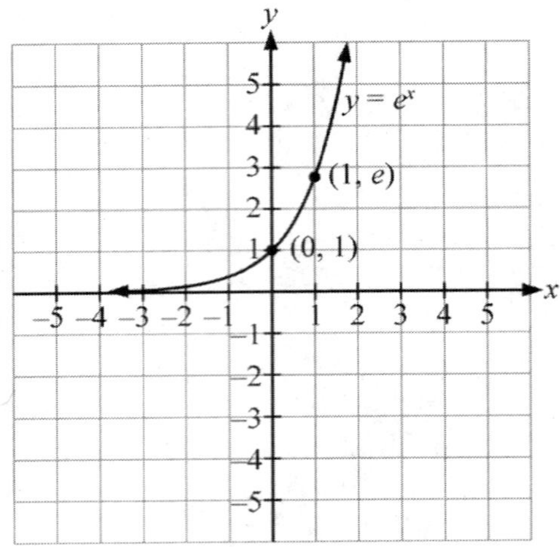

THE GRAPH OF $y = x^n$, WHERE $0 < n < 5$

The graph of $y = x^n$ becomes a different function depending on the value of n.

LINEAR FUNCTION

When $n = 1$, the equation $y = x^n$ becomes a linear function $y = x$.

The graph of $y = x$ is a line passing through the origin (0, 0), bisecting quadrants 3 and 1 as shown.

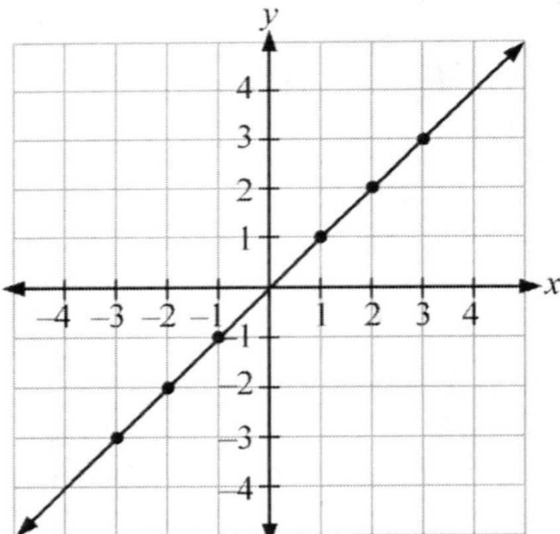

The domain and range are $x \in \mathbb{R}$ and $y \in \mathbb{R}$.

QUADRATIC FUNCTION

When $n = 2$, the equation $y = x^n$ becomes a quadratic function $y = x^2$.

The graph of $y = x^2$ is a parabola with its vertex at the origin (0, 0) as shown.

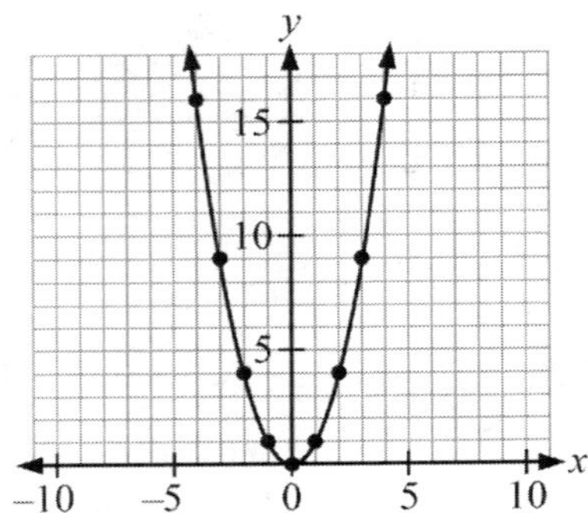

The domain and range are $x \in \mathbb{R}$ and $y \geq 0$.

CUBIC FUNCTION

When $n = 3$, the equation $y = x^n$ becomes a cubic function $y = x^3$.

The graph of $y = x^3$ is a curve passing through the origin (0, 0) as shown.

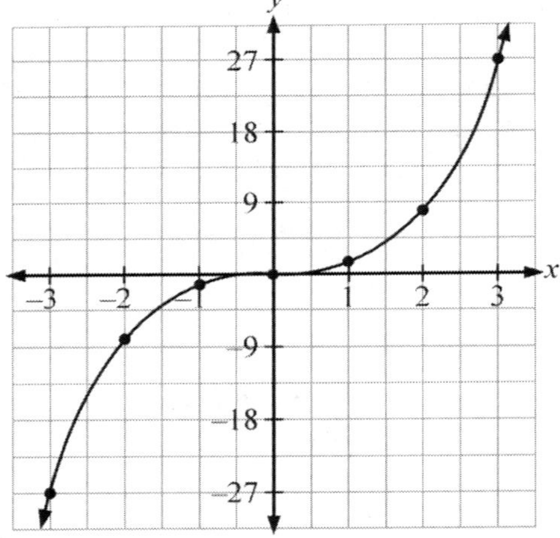

The domain and range are $x \in \mathbb{R}$ and $y \in \mathbb{R}$.

Quartic Function

When $n = 4$, the equation $y = x^n$ becomes a quartic function $y = x^4$.

The graph of $y = x^4$ is a curve passing through the origin (0, 0) as shown.

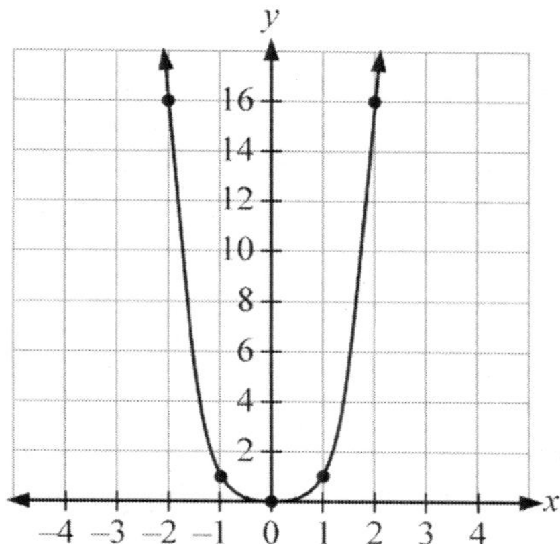

The domain and range are $x \in \mathbb{R}$ and $y \geq 0$.

The Graph of $y = x^n$

In general, for values of $n \geq 5$, the graph of $y = x^n$ will resemble the graph of $y = x^3$ when n is odd and $y = x^4$ when n is even. This is because for odd values of n, the value of x^n is negative when x is negative and positive when x is positive. But when n is even, the value of x^n is positive for both negative and positive values of x.

All graphs of functions of the form $y = x^n$ must pass through the origin (0, 0) since $0^n = 0$. The graph will also pass through the point (1, 1) since $1^n = 1$.

When n is odd, the graph will pass through $(-1, -1)$ since $(-1)^n = -1$ for odd values of n.

When n is even, the graph will pass through $(-1, 1)$ since $(-1)^n = 1$ for even values of n.

As the value of n increases, the graph of all functions of the form $y = x^n$ will get closer to the x-axis in the domain of $-1 < x < 1$ and will move away from the x-axis faster in the domains $x < 1$ and $x > 1$.

Understanding Absolute Values

Every real number has an absolute value. The absolute value of a number is shown by the symbol | | surrounding the number. It is equal to the number of units that the number is from zero on a number line. However, it only indicates the distance from zero, not the direction from zero.

The number $|-3|$ is read "the absolute value of negative three." Since –3 is three units away from zero on a number line, $|-3| = 3$.

The number $|+3|$ is read "the absolute value of positive three" or "the absolute value of three." Since it is three units from zero on a number line, $|+3| = 3$.

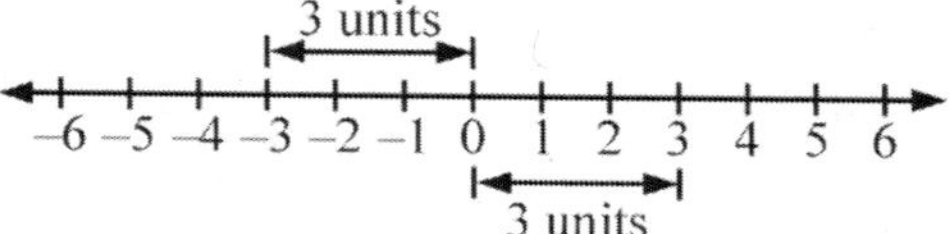

You can use the following guidelines to find the absolute value of real numbers:

1. If the number is positive or zero, then the absolute value of that number is equal to the number.
2. If the number is negative, then the absolute value of that number is equal to the additive inverse of that number.

Example

Simplify $|-7.2| + |16.3|$.

Solution

Step 1

Determine $|-7.2|$.

Since the number is negative, its absolute value is equal to the additive inverse of the number. The additive inverse of –7.2 is 7.2, since $-7.2 + 7.2 = 0$. Therefore, $|-7.2| = 7.2$.

This is equivalent to taking the negative of the number.

$$\begin{aligned}|-7.2| &= -(-7.2)\\ &= 7.2\end{aligned}$$

Step 2

Determine $|16.3|$.

Since the number is positive, its absolute value equals the number.

$|16.3| = 16.3$

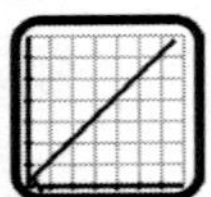

Step 3
Determine $|-7.2| + |16.3|$.

$$|-7.2| + |16.3| = 7.2 + 16.3$$
$$= 23.5$$

The operations within the absolute value symbol must be completed first. The absolute value of the number can then be found.

Example

Simplify $|9 - 3|$.

Solution

Step 1
Determine $|9 - 3|$.
Subtract the terms within the absolute value symbol.
$|9 - 3| = |6|$

Step 2
Determine $|6|$.
Since the number is a positive number, its absolute value equals the number.
$|6| = 6$

When given a variable instead of a number such as $|x|$, where $x \in \mathbb{R}$, it is read as "the absolute value of x."

- When $x \geq 0$, the absolute value of x will be $|x| = x$, since the value of x is a positive number.
- When $x < 0$, the absolute value of x will be $|x| = -x$, since the value of x is a negative number.

The negative sign (–) indicates that the number will be multiplied by –1 to obtain a positive number. If $x = -2$, then $|-2| = -(-2) = 2$.

PC.1.B Determine the domain and range of functions using graphs, tables, and symbols.

GRAPHING $y = |x|$

The definition of the absolute value of the variable x is given as follows:
$|x| = x$ when $x \geq 0$
$|x| = -x$ when $x < 0$

The graph of $y = |x|$ can be obtained by using the definition of absolute value to write $y = |x|$ as two distinct functions.

Example

Use tables of values and the definition of absolute value to sketch the graph of $y = |x|$.

Solution

Step 1
Create a table of values.
The function $y = |x|$ can be written as two functions: $y = x$ when $x \geq 0$ and $y = -x$ when $x < 0$.
Construct a table of values using these two functions.

$y = x, x \geq 0$		$y = -x, x < 0$		
x	y	x	y	
0	0			
1	1	–1	1	
		–2	2	2
		–3	3	3
		–4	4	4

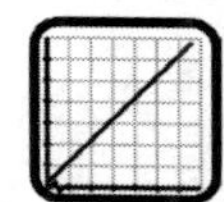

Step 2
Sketch the graph.
Plotting the ordered pairs from the table of values on the Cartesian plane and drawing lines through the points gives a graph of the function. Since the values for x and y can be any real numbers, ordered pairs, such as (7.4, 7.4) and $(-\sqrt{5}, \sqrt{5})$, are part of the graph. Therefore, the lines are continuous and without end for extreme values.

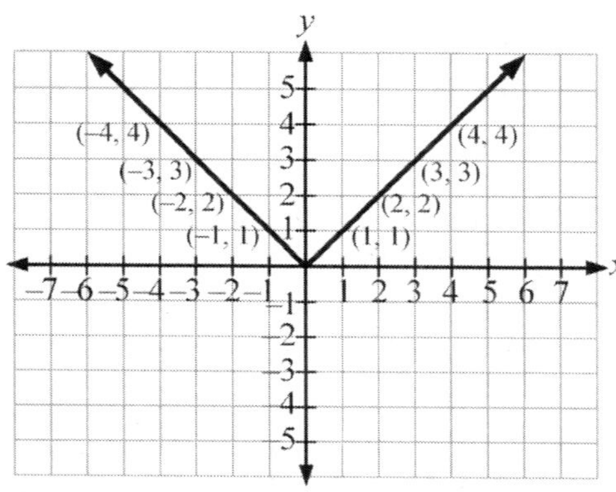

The graph of $y = |x|$ has the following key features:

- The graph consists of the graphs of two functions, $y = x$ when $x \geq 0$, and $y = -x$ when $x < 0$, that result in a V-shape with a corner at (0, 0).
- The domain (the set of possible x-values) is $\{x| \ x \in \mathbb{R}\}$.
- The range (the set of possible y-values) is $\{y| \ y \geq 0\}$.
- The minimum value of the function is 0.

PC.1.C Describe symmetry of graphs of even and odd functions.

Determining the Properties of Even and Odd Polynomial Functions

A function $f(x)$ is considered to be even if it satisfies the condition that $f(-x) = f(x)$ for all values of x in its domain. This means that the y-coordinate for any value of x must equal the y-coordinate at $-x$. For every point on the right side of the y-axis, a mirror image exists on the left side of the y-axis. Therefore, the graph of an even function is symmetrical about the y-axis.

Example
Since all the features of the graph $f(x) = x^4 - 18x^2 - 19$ on the left of the y-axis are duplicated in the reflection on the right, it is an even function.

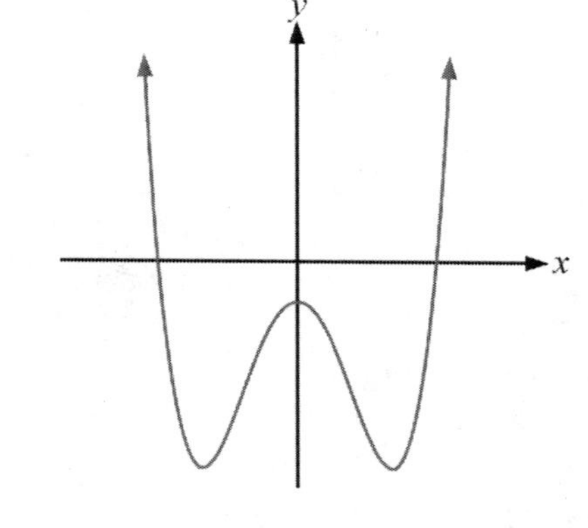

A function $f(x)$ is considered to be odd if it satisfies the condition that $f(-x) = -f(x)$ for all values of x in its domain. This means that the y-coordinate for any value of x must equal the negative of the y-coordinate at $-x$. For every point on the graph, there must be another point located directly through the origin, the same distance from the origin as the point itself. Therefore, the graph of an odd function is symmetrical about the origin.

Example

Since the graph $y = x^3 - 20x$ is symmetrical about the origin, it is an odd function.

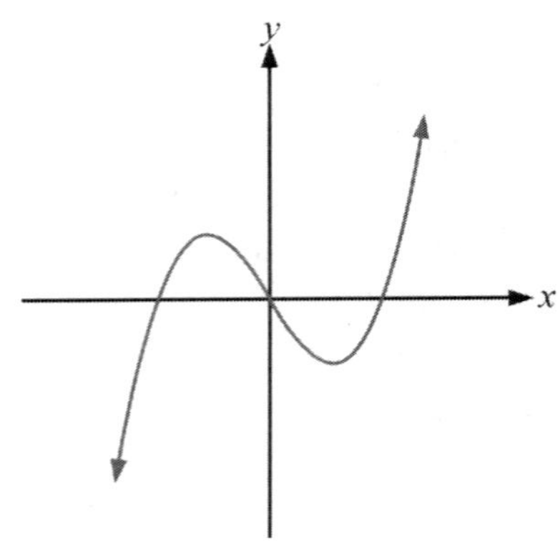

To determine whether or not a function $y = f(x)$ is even, find $y = f(-x)$. If $f(x) = f(-x)$, then the function is even. To determine if a function is odd, find both $f(-x)$ and $-f(x)$. If $f(-x) = -f(x)$, then the function is odd.

Example

Determine if the polynomial function $f(x) = 2x^3 - 5x$ is odd, even, or neither.

Solution

Substitute $-x$ for x into the equation $f(x) = 2x^3 - 5x$.

$$\begin{aligned} f(-x) &= 2(-x)^3 - 5(-x) \\ &= -2x^3 + 5x \\ &= -(2x^3 - 5x) \\ &= -f(x) \end{aligned}$$

Since $f(-x) = -f(x)$, $f(x)$ is an odd function and its corresponding graph is symmetrical about the origin.

It can be shown that any polynomial function whose terms consist of only odd degree monomials is an odd function and any polynomial function consisting of only even degree monomials is an even function. If the polynomial function has any combination of odd degree and even degree terms, then the function is neither odd nor even. For example, the function $f(x) = 2x^6 - 3x^4 + 5x^2 - 9$ is an even function since it consists of only even degree monomials. The function $g(x) = 2x^5 - 3x^4 + 5x^3 \quad 9$ consists of a combination of odd degree and even degree terms, so is neither even nor odd.

PC.1.D Recognize and use connections among significant values of a function (zeros, maximum values, minimum values, etc.), points on the graph of a function, and the symbolic representation of a function.

Identifying the Properties of a Trigonometric Function from an Equation or a Graph

When identifying the properties of a trigonometric function from an equation, identify the value of each parameter in order from left to right.

The parameters a, b, c, and d for sine functions, $y = a\sin[b(\theta - c)] + d$, and cosine functions, $y = a\cos[b(\theta - c)] + d$, indicate the following properties:

- The value $|a|$ indicates a stretch of the amplitude.
- The value $\frac{2\pi}{|b|}$ or $\frac{360^\circ}{|b|}$ indicates the range of the period.
- The value of c indicates the horizontal phase shift.
  - Shift right if $c > 0$.
  - Shift left if $c < 0$.
- The value of d indicates the vertical displacement.
  - Move up if $d > 0$.
  - Move down if $d < 0$.

The effects of changing each parameter are consistent with the effects of transformations of general functions described by $y = af[b(x - c)] + d$.

It is essential that the equations of the functions be written in the general form because factoring out the value of b is often required.

When identifying the properties of a transformed trigonometric function given a graph, it is best to compare the transformed graph with the original one. This makes it easier to determine the values of the parameters a, b, c, and d.

The properties of the sine function can be identified from this original graph of $y = \sin \theta$.

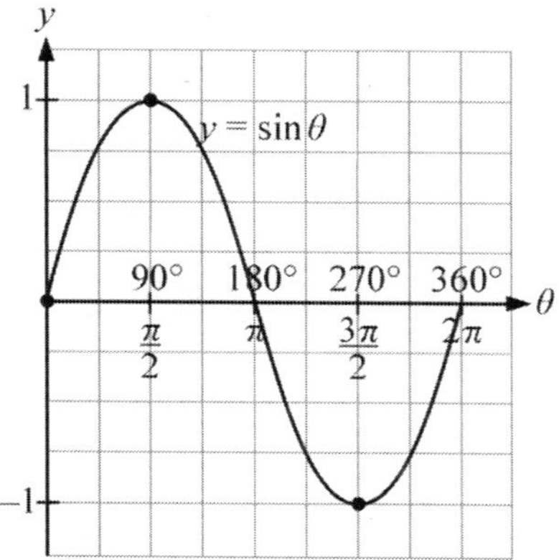

The properties of the cosine function can be identified from this original graph of $y = \cos \theta$.

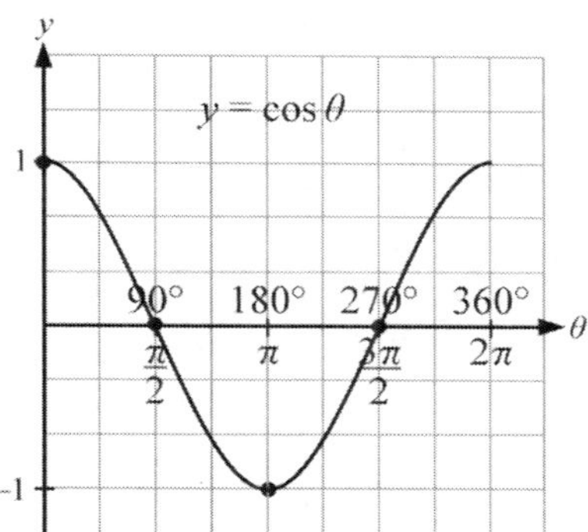

The amplitude is the vertical distance from the horizontal midline axis to the maximum or minimum value of the graph and can be calculated using the formula $a = \dfrac{\text{maximum} - \text{minimum}}{2}$.

The value of b can be determined using the formula period $= \dfrac{360°}{|b|}$ or period $= \dfrac{2\pi}{|b|}$.

The values of c and d can be determined by referring to the original graph of the trigonometric function and applying the horizontal midline axis, $y = d$.

Example

Determine the amplitude, period, phase shift, and vertical displacement for the trigonometric function $y = -2\cos(3\theta + \pi) + 6$.

Solution

Step 1

Rewrite the trigonometric function in the form of $y = a\cos[b(\theta - c)] + d$.

The value of b needs to be factored out of the equation, and the horizontal translation needs to be written as $(\theta - c)$.

$$y = -2\cos(3\theta + \pi) + 6$$

$$y = -2\cos 3\left(\theta + \frac{\pi}{3}\right) + 6$$

$$y = -2\cos 3\left(\theta - \left(-\frac{\pi}{3}\right)\right) + 6$$

Step 2

Determine the amplitude.

Amplitude $= |a| = |-2| = 2$

Step 2

Determine the period of the transformed function.

The period is calculated by substituting the value of b into the expression $\dfrac{2\pi}{|b|}$.

The value of b is 3.

$$\frac{2\pi}{|b|} = \frac{2\pi}{|3|} = \frac{2}{3}\pi$$

The period of the transformed trigonometric function is $\dfrac{2}{3}\pi$.

Step 3

Determine the phase shift.

$$c = -\frac{\pi}{3}$$

Since the value of c is negative, the graph shifts $\dfrac{\pi}{3}$ to the left.

Step 4

Determine the vertical displacement.

$d = 6$

Since the value of d is positive, the graph moves 6 units up.

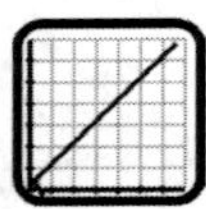

PC.1.E Investigate the concepts of continuity, end behavior, asymptotes, and limits and connect these characteristics to functions represented graphically and numerically.

Sketching the Graph of a Polynomial Function

When a polynomial function is expressed in its factored form, it is easy to identify the zeros of the function from the factors.

The zeros are x-coordinates whose corresponding y-coordinate is zero. These values are also the x-intercepts of the graph of the function.

If a factor occurs only once in the factored form of a polynomial function, then the graph of the function will cross the x-axis at the corresponding zero.

Example
In the function $f(x) = 3(x+2)(x-3)(x-5)$, the zeros are $x = -2$, 3, and 5.

For $f(x) = 3(x+2)(x-3)(x-5)$, the graph will cross the x-axis at $x = -2$, 3, and 5, as shown.

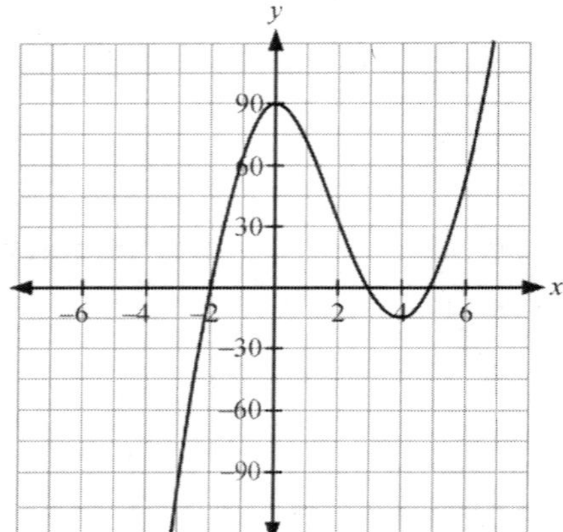

If a factor occurs exactly twice in the factored form of a polynomial function, then the graph of the function will be tangent to the x-axis at the corresponding zero.

Example
For the function

$$\begin{aligned} f(x) &= -3(x+2)(x+2)(x-5) \\ &= -3(x+2)^2(x-5) \end{aligned}$$

the factor $(x+2)$ occurs twice. There are two zeros: $x = -2$ and 5. At $x = -2$, the graph will approach the x-axis, touch, and turn away, as shown below.

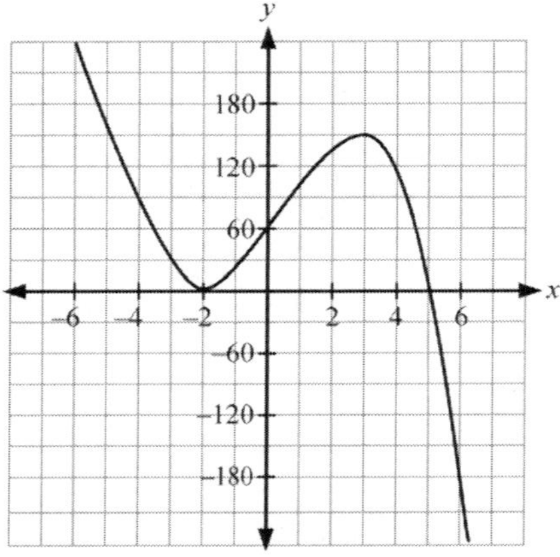

If a factor occurs three times in the factored form of a polynomial function, then the graph will pass through the x-axis with a point of inflection at the corresponding zero.

Example

When a factor occurs three times, as in
$f(x) = 2(x-3)(x-3)(x-3)(x+2)$
$= 2(x-3)^3(x+2)$
the graph will pass through the x-axis with a point of inflection at the corresponding zero, as shown at $x = 3$ in the graph below.

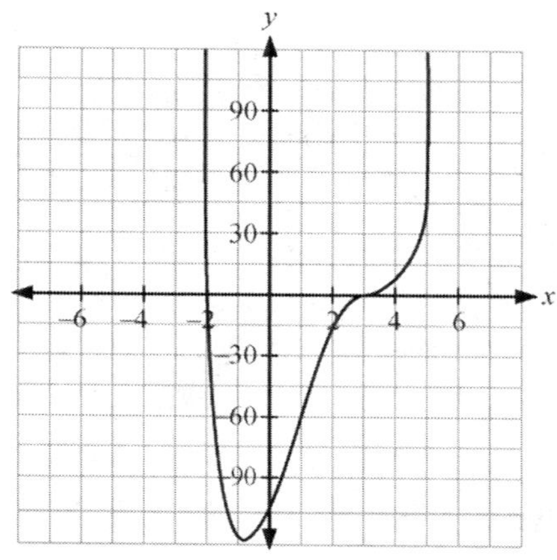

Example

Give the x-intercepts, end behavior and shape of the graph of $f(x) = -2x(x+3)^2(x-4)$, and provide a sketch of the graph.

Solution

The function is a fourth-degree polynomial function with a leading term of $-2x^4$ when expressed in standard form.

Substituting either an extreme negative number or positive number into this term produces a negative result. So, the end behavior is away from the x-axis toward $-\infty$ in both quadrants III and IV.

There are three zeros: $x = -3$, 0, and 4.

Since the factor $x + 3$ occurs twice, the graph will be tangent to the x-axis at $x = -3$.
The graph will cross the x-axis at $x = 0$ and 4.

From left to right, the graph will rise to the x-axis in quadrant III, touch the x-axis at −3, and turn back into quadrant III.

The graph will then turn again and pass through the origin, reach a maximum in quadrant I, turn once more, pass through $x = 4$, and finally head toward $-\infty$ in quadrant IV.

The graph is given.

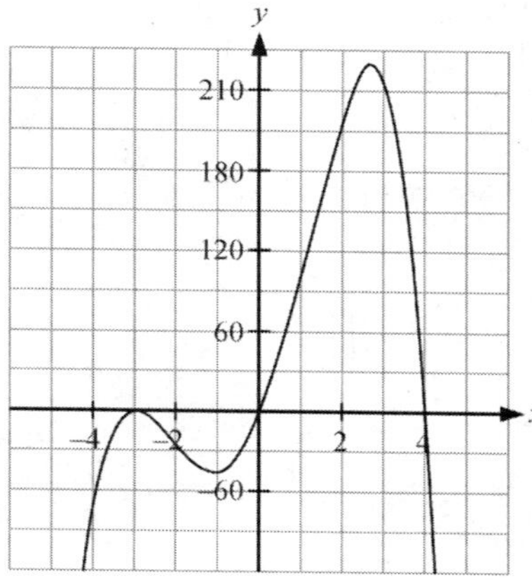

Determining Horizontal Asymptotes of Rational Functions

A rational function is a function in the form $R(x) = \dfrac{P(x)}{Q(x)}$, where $P(x)$ and $Q(x)$ are polynomial functions and $Q(x) \neq 0$. Rational functions have the following properties when it comes to horizontal asymptotes:

- When the degree of the numerator is less than the degree of the denominator, the horizontal asymptote occurs at $y = 0$.
- When the degree of the numerator is equal to the degree of the denominator, the horizontal asymptote occurs at $y = \dfrac{a}{b}$, where a and b are the leading coefficients of the numerator and denominator, respectively.
- When the degree of the numerator is greater than the degree of the denominator, there is no horizontal asymptote.

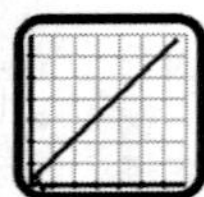

If a rational function has a horizontal asymptote, its graph can intersect or cross the horizontal asymptote.

Example

Consider the graph of $f(x) = \dfrac{x+1}{x^2+3}$.

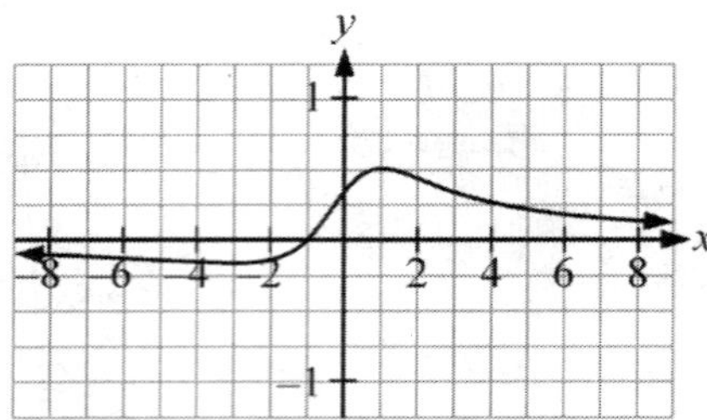

As the *x*-values increase, the *y*-values become smaller and closer to zero. As the *x*-values decrease below zero, the *y*-values again approach zero. The graph of $f(x) = \dfrac{x+1}{x^2+3}$ has a horizontal asymptote at $y = 0$. Notice that the curve crosses over the *x*-axis, the horizontal asymptote, when $x = -1$.

Example

Determine the equation of the horizontal asymptote of the rational function

$$f(x) = \frac{x^2-2}{3x^3+2x-5}.$$

Solution

Step 1

Determine the degree of the numerator and the degree of the denominator.

The degree of the numerator, $x^2 - 2$, is 2.

The degree of the denominator, $3x^3 + 2x - 5$, is 3.

Step 2

Determine the equation of the asymptote.

Since the degree of the numerator is less than the degree of the denominator, the horizontal asymptote occurs at $y = 0$

Example

Determine the equation of the horizontal asymptote of the rational function

$$f(x) = \frac{5x^3-2x^2+4x-7}{-2x^3+6x^2-4x+8}.$$

Solution

Step 1

Determine the degree of the numerator and the degree of the denominator.

The degree of the numerator, $5x^3 - 2x^2 + 4x - 7$, is 3. The degree of the denominator, $-2x^3 + 6x^2 - 4x + 8$, is 3.

Step 2

Determine the equation of the asymptote.

Since the degrees of the numerator and the denominator are equal, the horizontal asymptote occurs at $y = \dfrac{a}{b}$, where *a* and *b* are the leading coefficients of the numerator and denominator, respectively.

$$y = \frac{a}{b}$$

$$y = \frac{5}{-2}$$

The equation of the horizontal asymptote is $y = -\dfrac{5}{2}$.

Determining the Vertical Asymptotes of Rational Functions

A rational function is one of the form $R(x) = \dfrac{P(x)}{Q(x)}$, where $P(x)$ and $Q(x)$ are polynomial functions and $Q(x) \neq 0$.

Notice that a polynomial function qualifies as a rational function because it can be written as $R(x) = \dfrac{P(x)}{1}$ and $Q(x) = 1$ is a polynomial function.

An asymptote is a straight line that a curve approaches more and more closely.

A vertical asymptote is a vertical line that a function approaches but never reaches.

Since a rational function contains a denominator, its non-permissible values must be determined. When you graph rational functions, note that either the non-permissible values will become asymptotes or the graph will be discontinuous at those values.

Example

Sketch the graph of the rational function $\frac{12}{x}$.

The resulting graph will look like the one shown here.

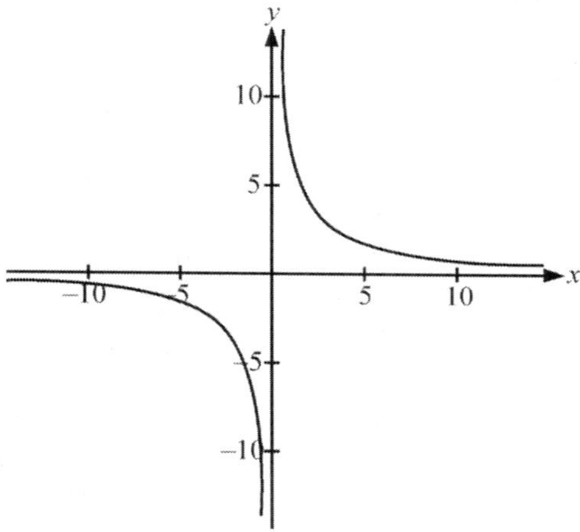

Notice from the graph that as the x-values approach 0 from the right side, the y-values become larger (5, 10, 100, etc.), and when the x-values approach 0 from the left side, the y-values become smaller (–5, –10, –100, etc.). There is no y-value when $x = 0$ and, correspondingly, no x-value when $y = 0$. The graph approaches the y-axis vertically, so there is a vertical asymptote at $x = 0$.

The equation of the vertical asymptote is in the form $x = a$. To determine the vertical asymptote, set the denominator equal to 0 and solve for x.

Example

Determine the vertical asymptotes for the graph of $R(x) = \frac{x^2}{x^2 + 2x - 3}$.

Solution

Determine the equations of the vertical asymptotes.

Set the denominator $x^2 + 2x - 3$ equal to 0, and solve for x.

$$\begin{aligned} x^2 + 2x - 3 &= 0 \\ x^2 + 3x - x - 3 &= 0 \\ x(x + 3) - 1(x + 3) &= 0 \\ (x + 3)(x - 1) &= 0 \end{aligned}$$

Solve for each x.

$x = 1$

$x = -3$

Therefore, the vertical asymptotes for the graph of $R(x) = \frac{x^2}{x^2 + 2x - 3}$ are at $x = 1$ and $x = -3$.

Determining the Oblique Asymptotes of a Rational Function

A rational function is a function of the form $R(x) = \frac{P(x)}{Q(x)}$, where $P(x)$ and $Q(x)$ are polynomial functions, and $Q(x) \neq 0$.

When the degree of the numerator, $P(x)$, is exactly one more than the degree of the denominator, $Q(x)$, the graph of the rational function has an oblique or slant asymptote. An oblique asymptote is a slanted line that is neither horizontal nor vertical.

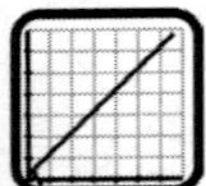

Example

Consider the rational function $f(x) = \dfrac{x^2 + 3x + 7}{x - 2}$.

The degree of the numerator is one more than the degree of the denominator. Therefore, the graph of the rational function has an oblique asymptote.

A graph of $f(x) = \dfrac{x^2 + 3x + 7}{x - 2}$ is given.

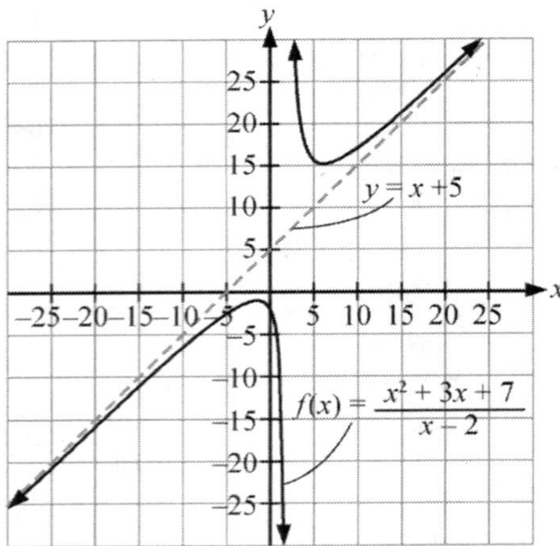

In the graph there is an oblique asymptote at the line $y = x + 5$.

The oblique asymptote can be found by dividing the numerator by the denominator. The quotient is equal to the equation of the oblique asymptote, which is a linear function in the form $y = mx + b$.

When dividing the numerator by the denominator to determine the equation of an oblique asymptote, only the quotient is important, not the remainder.

To determine the oblique asymptote of a rational function, take the following steps:

1. Determine the degree of the numerator and the denominator.
2. Determine the equation of the oblique asymptote. Use synthetic or long division to obtain the quotient.

Example

Determine the equation of the oblique asymptotes of the rational function

$f(x) = \dfrac{2x^2 + 9x - 12}{x + 3}$.

Solution

Step 1

Determine the degree of the numerator, $P(x)$, and denominator, $Q(x)$.

- The degree of the numerator, $2x^2 + 9x - 12$, is 2.
- The degree of the denominator, $x + 3$, is 1.

Since the degree of $P(x)$ is one larger than the degree of $Q(x)$, the graph of $f(x)$ has an oblique asymptote.

Step 2

Determine the equation of the asymptote. Use synthetic division to determine the quotient.

$$\begin{array}{r|rrr} 3 & 2 & 9 & -12 \\ & \downarrow & 6 & 9 \\ \hline & 2 & 3 & \boxed{-21} \end{array}$$

The quotient is $2x + 3$, and the remainder is −21. Therefore, the line $y = 2x + 3$ is an oblique asymptote for the graph of $f(x)$.

Example

Determine the equation of the oblique asymptote of the rational function

$f(x) = \dfrac{4x^3 - 2x^2 - x - 1}{2x^2 + 1}$.

Solution

Step 1

Determine the degree of the numerator and the denominator.

- The degree of the numerator, $4x^3 - 2x^2 - x - 1$, is 3.
- The degree of the denominator, $2x^2 + 1$, is 2.

The degree of the numerator is one more than the degree of the denominator. Therefore, the graph of the rational function has an oblique asymptote.

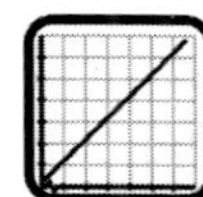

Step 2
Determine the equation of the oblique asymptote. Use long division to obtain the quotient.

$$
\begin{array}{r}
2x - 1 \\
2x^2 + 1 \overline{)\, 4x^3 - 2x^2 - x - 1} \\
\underline{-(4x^3 + 0x^2 + 2x)} \\
-2x^2 - 3x - 1 \\
\underline{-(-2x^2 + 0x - 1)} \\
-3x
\end{array}
$$

The quotient is $2x-1$ and the remainder is $-3x$. Therefore, the equation of the oblique asymptote is $y = 2x - 1$.

GRAPHING FUNCTIONS EXERCISE #1

1. Dale is asked to graph $y = 2\log x$ and $y = \log_2 x$ by using a graphing calculator. If Dale graphs the two equations properly, which of the following statements about the graphs of $y = 2\log x$ and $y = \log_2 x$ will he find to be **true**?
   A. Both graphs are exactly the same.
   B. The domains of the graphs are different.
   C. One of the graphs intersects the *y*-axis.
   D. The graphs have the same vertical asymptote.

2. Using only common logarithms, the graph of $y = \log_5 x$ can be obtained by graphing
   A. $y = \dfrac{\log 5}{\log x}$
   B. $y = \dfrac{\log x}{\log 5}$
   C. $y = \log x - \log 5$
   D. $y = \log 5 - \log x$

Use the following information to answer the next question.

The graph of the function $f(x) = 0x + 3$ is shown.

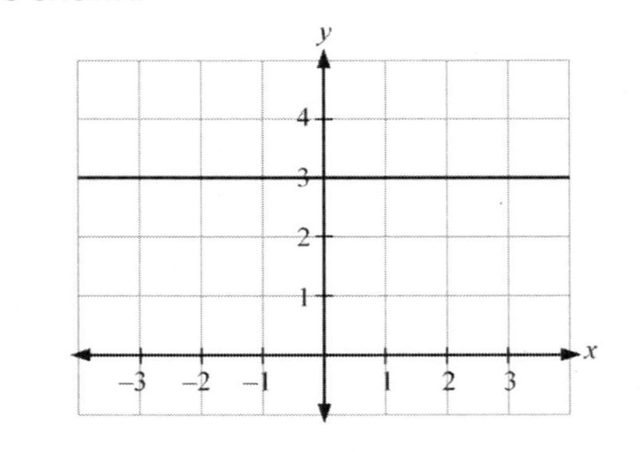

3. The domain (D) and range (R) of this linear function, respectively, are
   A. D: $x \in \mathbb{R}$ R: $y \in \mathbb{R}$
   B. D: $x = 3$ R: $y \in \mathbb{R}$
   C. D: $x \in \mathbb{R}$ R: $y = 3$
   D. D: $x \geq -4$ R: $y = 3$

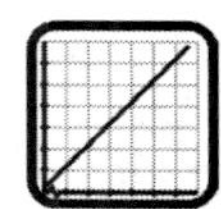

Use the following information to answer the next question.

The equations for four different functions are shown:

1. $y = 3$
2. $y = 3x$
3. $y = x^2 - 3$
4. $y = 3 - x^2$

4. Which of the following statements about the given functions is **false**?

A. All the functions have domains of $x \in \mathrm{R}$.

B. The linear functions have a range of $y \in \mathrm{R}$.

C. The quadratic functions do not have a range of $y \in \mathrm{R}$.

D. Only one function has a domain of $x \in \mathrm{R}$ and a range of $y \in \mathrm{R}$.

Use the following information to answer the next question.

Sandy likes to take walks. One day, she decided to make a graph of the distance she walked in relation to the time it took. She plotted these three points for reference.

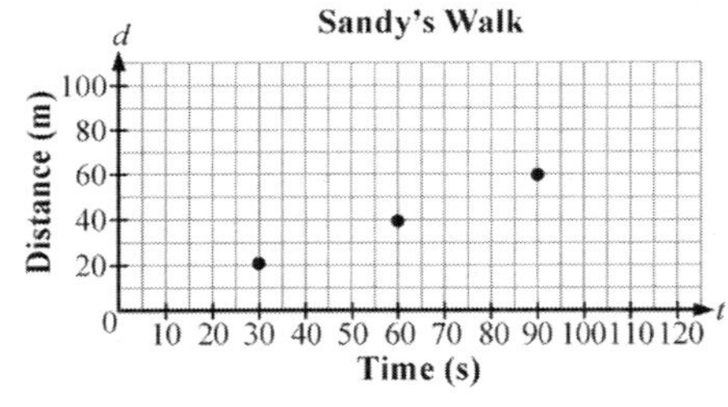

5. What are the domain and range of the relation if she walks for 2 min?

A. D:$\{0 \le t \le 90\}$ and R:$\{0 \le d \le 60\}$

B. D:$\{30, 60, 90\}$ and R:$\{20, 40, 60\}$

C. D:$\{0 \le t \le 120\}$ and R:$\{0 \le d \le 80\}$

D. D:$\{30, 60, 90, 120\}$ and R:$\{20, 40, 60, 80\}$

Use the following information to answer the next question.

The air pressure in a car tire changes during a trip, as shown in the graph. The graph consists of five line segments.

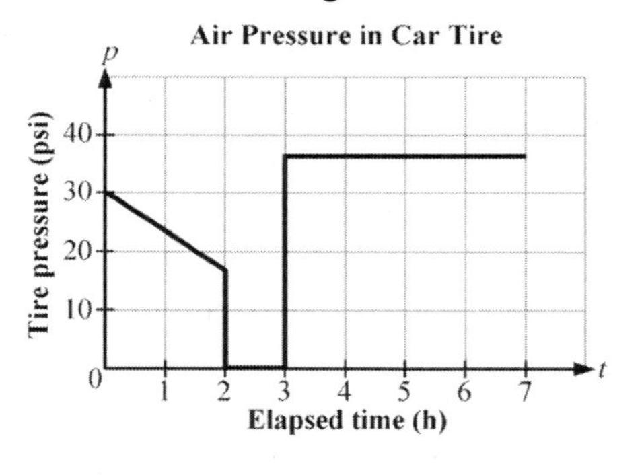

6. If the maximum tire pressure is 37 psi, what are the domain and range of the relation?

A. D:$\{0 \le t \le 2\}$ and R:$\{0 \le p \le 30\}$

B. D:$\{0 \le t \le 7\}$ and R:$\{0 \le p \le 37\}$

C. D:$\{0 \le p \le 30\}$ and R:$\{0 \le t \le 2\}$

D. D:$\{0 \le p \le 37\}$ and R:$\{0 \le t \le 7\}$

Use the following information to answer the next question.

The partial graphs of four different logarithmic functions of the form $y = \log_b x$ are drawn on the same grid, as shown.

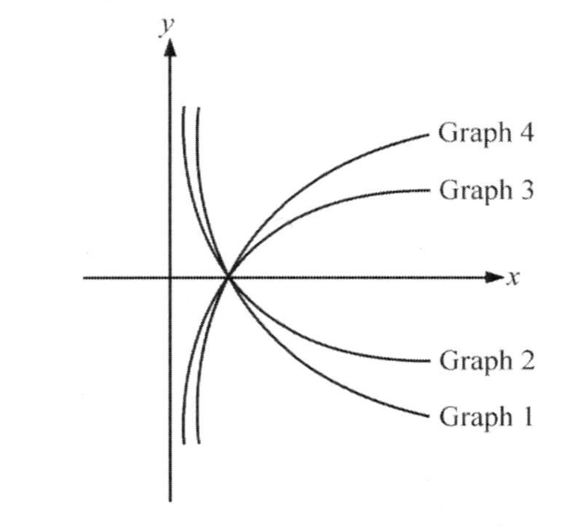

7. Which graph represents the function with the greatest b value?

A. Graph 1 **B.** Graph 2

C. Graph 3 **D.** Graph 4

8. Which of the following changes in the value of b in the function $f(x) = \log_b x$ will cause the function to change from decreasing to increasing as x increases?

A. $b = 2$ to $b = 3$

B. $b = 2$ to $b = \frac{1}{3}$

C. $b = \frac{1}{2}$ to $b = 3$

D. $b = \frac{1}{2}$ to $b = \frac{1}{3}$

9. Which of the following grids illustrates the graphs of the functions $y = x^5$ and $y = x^7$?

A.

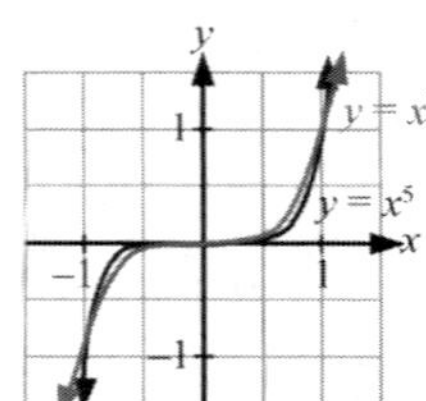

B.

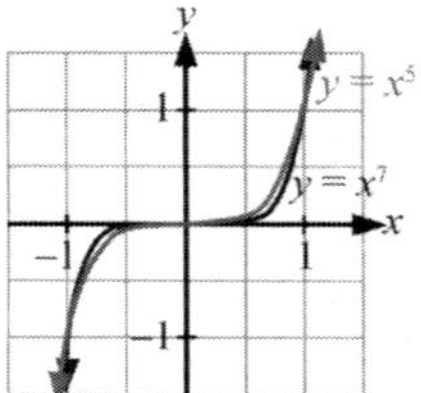

C.

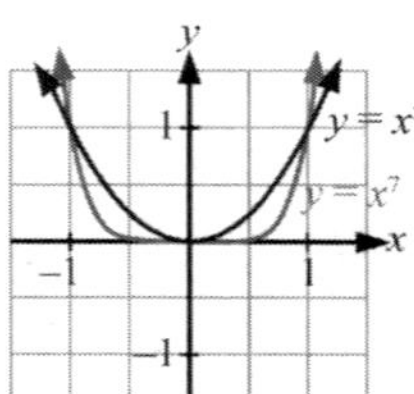

D.

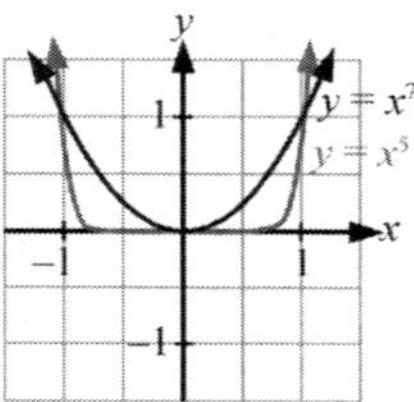

10. Which of the following grids illustrates the graphs of the functions $y = x^5$ and $y = x^6$?

A.

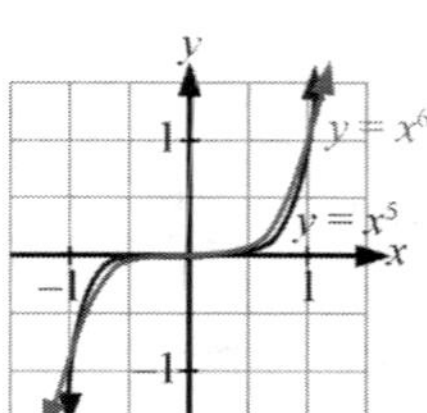

B.

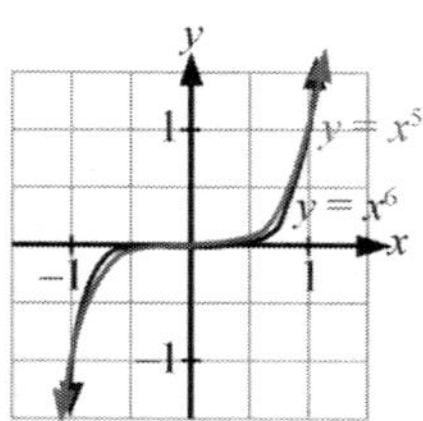

C.

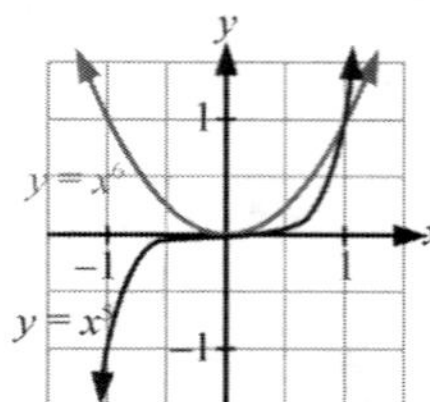

D.

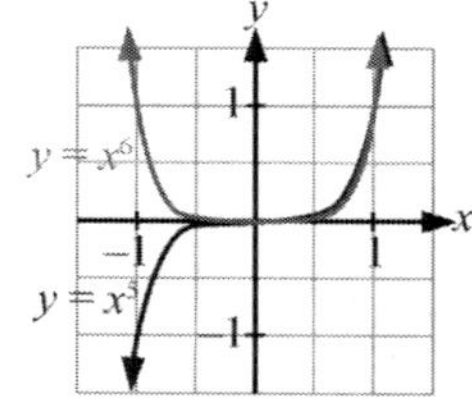

11. Which of the following functions is odd?

A. $f(x) = x^2 - 3x + 2$

B. $f(x) = -x^4 - x^3 - x^2$

C. $f(x) = 5x^5 + 2x^3 - 3x$

D. $f(x) = 3x^3 + 4x^2 - 5x - 1$

12. Which of the following equations is an even function?

A. $y = x^2 + 3 + \frac{3x}{4x^4}$

B. $y = \frac{1}{3} + \frac{1}{3x} + \frac{1}{3x^4}$

C. $y = x^2 + \frac{5x^5}{x} + \frac{1}{x^2}$

D. $y = 2x + 4x + 6x^2$

Use the following information to answer the next question.

The given graph is a transformation of the graph $y = \cos\theta$. The graph is restricted to the domain $0 \le \theta \le 8\pi$.

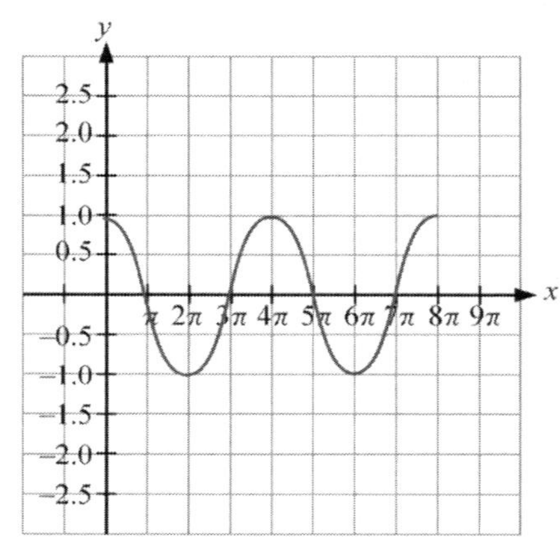

13. Expressed in radians, what is the period of the given graph?

A. 4

B. 8

C. 4π

D. 8π

Use the following information to answer the next question.

The graph shown is a transformed function of the graph of $y = \tan\theta$.

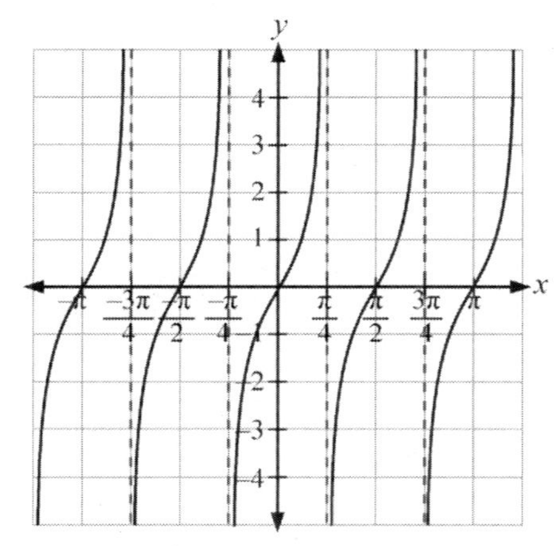

14. What is the range of the given graph?

A. $\left\{\theta \middle| \; \theta \in \mathrm{R},\ \theta \neq \frac{\pi}{4} + \frac{\pi}{2}n,\ n \in I\right\}$

B. $\left\{y \middle| \; y \in \mathrm{R},\ \theta \neq \frac{\pi}{4} + \frac{\pi}{2}n,\ n \in I\right\}$

C. $\{\theta \mid \theta \in \mathrm{R}\}$

D. $\{y \mid y \in \mathrm{R}\}$

Use the following information to answer the next question.

Sarah wants to graph the polynomial function $p(x) = -4(x-2)(x+2)(x-1)$ without the help of technology. She decides to locate positive and negative regions of the graph using test values.

15. Which of the following regions represents the set of test regions that Sarah will need to use?

A. $-2 < x < 1$ and $1 < x < 2$

B. $-2 < x < -1$ and $-1 < x < 2$

C. $x < -2$, $-2 < x < 1$, $1 < x < 2$, and $x > 2$

D. $x < -2$, $-2 < x < 1$, $-1 < x < 2$, and $x > 2$

16. The equation of the horizontal asymptote for the graph of $y = \dfrac{6x^2}{4 - 2x^2}$ is

A. $y = 3$ **B.** $y = \dfrac{3}{2}$

C. $y = -\dfrac{3}{2}$ **D.** $y = -3$

17. The equation of the horizontal asymptote for the graph of $\dfrac{\sqrt{x^2 - 2x + 1}}{x^2 - 1} = 1$ is written in the form $y = k$. Rounded to the nearest whole number, the value of k is __________.

18. For the graph of the function $y = \dfrac{-6x^2}{2x^2 + x - 6}$, the equation of one of the vertical asymptotes is

A. $x = -3$ **B.** $x = -2$

C. $x = 0$ **D.** $x = 2$

19. The equation of one of the vertical asymptotes for the graph of $y = \dfrac{2x^2}{x^2 + 3x - 4}$ is

A. $x = -4$ **B.** $x = -1$

C. $x = 0$ **D.** $x = 2$

20. Which of the following rational functions has an oblique asymptote?

A. $f(x) = \dfrac{5x^2 - 10x + 13}{6x^2 + 5x - 11}$

B. $f(x) = \dfrac{x^3 - 4x - 10}{x^2 + 8}$

C. $f(x) = \dfrac{x^3 - 2x + 4}{x - 9}$

D. $f(x) = \dfrac{x - 5}{x^2 - 6x + 3}$

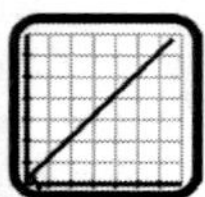

21. What is the equation of the oblique asymptote for the graph of $f(x) = \dfrac{2x^3 + 4x + 3}{x^2 - 2}$?

A. $y = 2x$

B. $y = 4x$

C. $y = x - 2$

D. $y = 3x + 2$

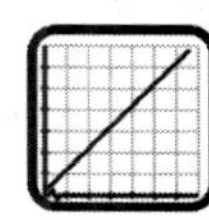

GRAPHING FUNCTIONS EXERCISE #1 ANSWERS AND SOLUTIONS

1. D	7. C	13. C	19. A
2. B	8. C	14. D	20. B
3. C	9. B	15. C	21. A
4. B	10. D	16. D	
5. C	11. C	17. 0	
6. B	12. C	18. B	

1. D

Step 1

Enter the equations into a TI-83 or similar calculator. Press the [Y =] button. Enter $Y_1 = 2\log x$, and then enter $Y_2 = \frac{\log(x)}{\log(2)}$ for the second function, $y = \log_2 x$.

Step 2

Press the [ZOOM] button, and select 0:ZoomFit. The graph shown here should appear.

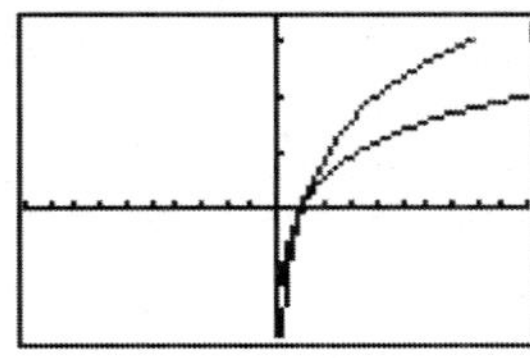

Step 3

Analyze the graph.

The graphs are not the same. Both graphs have a domain of $x > 0$. Neither of the graphs intersects the y-axis. Both graphs have the y-axis as a vertical asymptote.

2. B

Apply the base conversion formula $\log_b c = \frac{\log_a c}{\log_a b}$.

The function $y = \log_5 x$ can be written as

$y = \frac{\log_{10} x}{\log_{10} 5}$ or simply $y = \frac{\log x}{\log 5}$.

Therefore, the graph of $y = \log_5 x$ can be obtained by graphing $y = \frac{\log x}{\log 5}$.

3. C

Any linear function, except for $x = a$, has a domain that is $x \in \mathbb{R}$. Thus, the function $f(x) = 0x + 3$ has a domain of $x \in \mathbb{R}$. This is shown in the graph that extends left and right infinitely due to the fact that all real numbers can be substituted for x to give a corresponding y-value. For all values of x, the corresponding y-values are always 3 (e.g., $f(1) = 0(1) + 3 = 3$, $f(-3) = 0(-3) + 3 = 3$). Therefore, the range of this function is $y = 3$.

4. B

Step 1

Draw the graph of function 1, and determine the type of function, the domain, and the range of the graph.

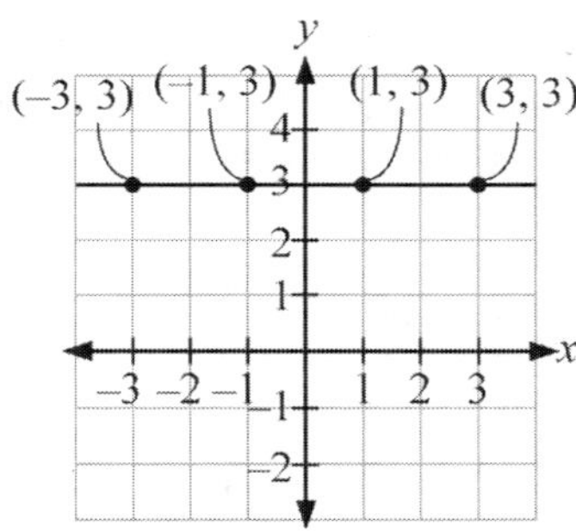

This is a linear function, where the domain is $x \in \mathrm{R}$ and the range is $y = 3$.

Step 2
Draw the graph of function 2, and determine the type of function, the domain, and the range of the graph.

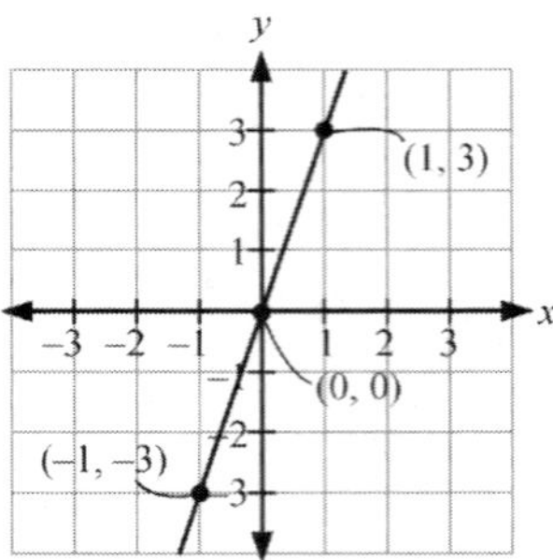

This is a linear function, where the domain is $x \in \mathrm{R}$ and the range is $y \in \mathrm{R}$.

Step 3
Draw the graph of function 3, and determine the type of function, the domain, and the range of the graph.

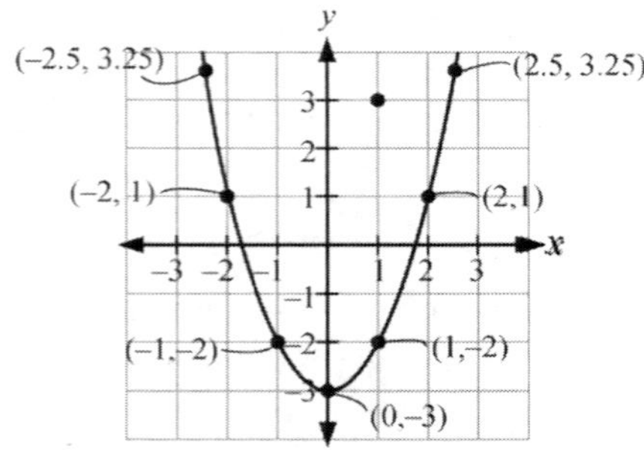

This is a quadratic function, where the domain is $x \in \mathrm{R}$ and the range is $y \geq -3$.

Step 4
Draw the graph of function 4, and determine the type of function, the domain, and the range of the graph.

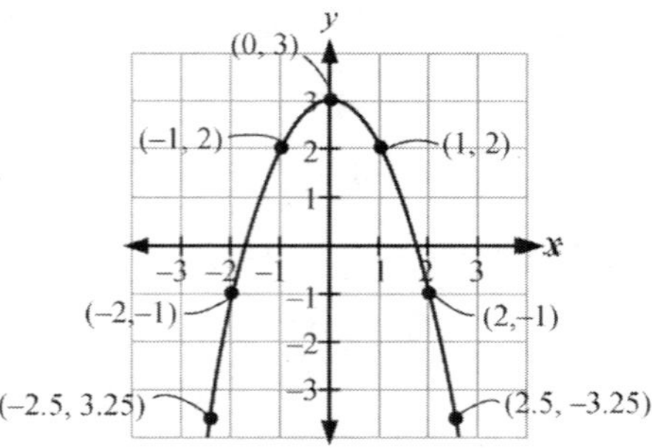

This is a quadratic function, where the domain is $x \in \mathrm{R}$ and the range is $y \leq 3$.

Step 5
Examine all graphs, and determine which statement is false.

All the functions have domains of $x \in \mathrm{R}$, so that statement is true.

Quadratic functions 3 and 4 do not have a range of $y \in \mathrm{R}$, so that statement is true.

Only function 2 has a domain of $x \in \mathrm{R}$ and a range of $y \in \mathrm{R}$, so that statement is true.

The linear functions (functions 1 and 2) do not have a range of $y \in \mathrm{R}$ since the range of function 1 is $y = 3$.

Therefore, the statement that the linear functions have a range of $y \in \mathrm{R}$ is false.

5. C

Step 1
Connect the points by a line segment.

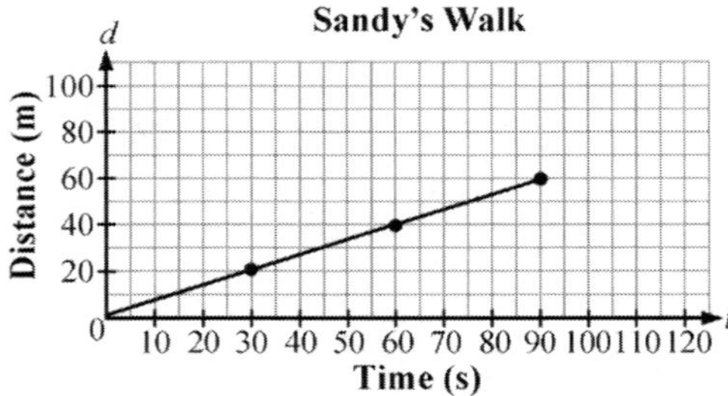

Step 2
Extend the line segment.

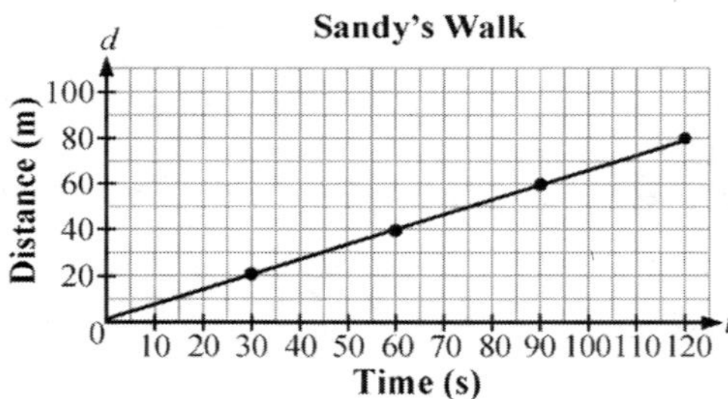

Identify the point on the line segment that corresponds to the x-coordinate of 120 (2 min). This point is (120, 80).

Step 3
Determine the domain and range of the relation.

The domain is 0 to 120 s inclusive. If t represents the time, the domain is $D{:}\{0 \leq t \leq 120\}$.

The range is 0 to 80 m inclusive. If d represents the distance, the range is $R{:}\{0 \leq d \leq 80\}$.

6. B

Step 1
Determine the domain of the relation.
Looking at the graph, the horizontal axis starts at 0 h and continues to 7 h before it stops. Therefore, the domain is 0 h to 7 h inclusive. If t represents the time, the domain is $D:\{0 \le t \le 7\}$.

Step 2
Determine the range of the relation.
Looking at the vertical axis, the lowest value is 0 psi, and the highest value is 37 psi. Therefore, the range is 0 psi to 37 psi inclusive. If p represents the tire pressure, the range is $R:\{0 \le p \le 37\}$.
Thus, the domain and range of the relation are $D:\{0 \le t \le 7\}$ and $R:\{0 \le p \le 37\}$.

7. C

Step 1
Analyze graphs 1 and 2 with respect to their corresponding functions' b values.
The orientation of the two graphs indicates that the values of b for both functions are between 0 and 1 $(0 < b < 1)$.

Step 2
Analyze graphs 3 and 4 with respect to their corresponding functions' b values.
The orientation of the two graphs indicates that the values of b for both functions are greater than 1 $(b > 1)$.

Step 3
Since steps 1 and 2 reveal that functions 3 and 4 will have greater b values than functions 1 and 2, determine which one of functions 3 and 4 has the larger b value.
Functions of the form $y = \log_b(x)$ can also be written as $y = \frac{\log x}{\log b}$. The larger the b value, the larger the value of $\log b$, and thus the smaller the value of the function $y = \log_b(x)$.

As x increases in value, the corresponding y values for graph 3 are smaller than the corresponding y values for graph 4. Therefore, function 3 has a larger b value than function 4.
Note: To verify this statement, graph (using technology) two functions of the form $y = \log_b x$, where $b > 1$, such as $y = \log_2 x$ and $y = \log_8 x$. Then, compare the two graphs with respect to their corresponding functions' b values.

8. C

The function $f(x) = \log_b x$ is increasing when $b > 1$ and decreasing when $0 < b < 1$, so the change from decreasing to increasing would occur when b changes from $\frac{1}{2}$ to 3.

9. B

Step 1
Identify the quadrants in which the graphs will reside.
If the value of n is even for a function of the form $y = x^n$, the graph of the function exists in quadrants 2 and 1. If the value of n is odd, the graph is in quadrants 3 and 1.
Since the value of n is odd for both functions, they will exist in quadrants 3 and 1.

Step 2
Determine the relative location for each graph.
As the value of n increases for functions of the form $y = x^n$, the graph will get closer to the x-axis in the domain $-1 < x < 1$. It will move away from the x-axis faster in the domains $x < 1$ and $x > 1$.

Therefore, the graph of $y = x^7$ must be closer to the x-axis than the graph of $y = x^5$ in the domain $-1 < x < 1$.

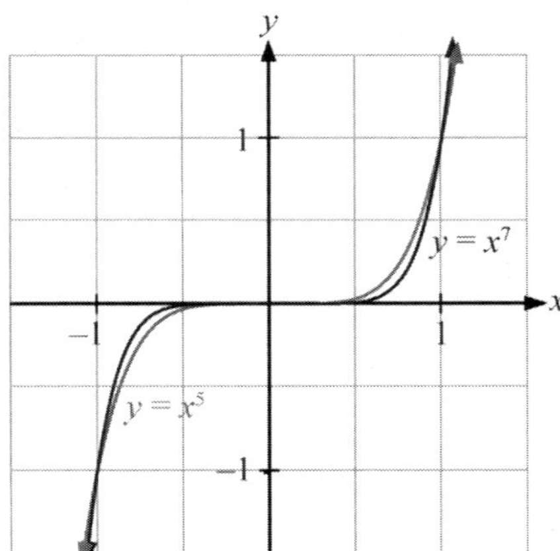

10. D

Step 1
Identify the quadrants in which the graphs will reside.
If the value of n is even for a function of the form $y = x^n$, the graph of the function exists in quadrants 2 and 1. If the value of n is odd, the graph is in quadrants 3 and 1.
Since the value of n is odd for one function, it will exist in quadrants 3 and 1. Since the value of n is even for the other function, it will exist in quadrants 2 and 1.

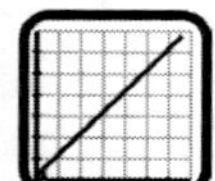

Step 2

Determine the relative location for each graph.

As the value of n increases for functions of the form $y = x^n$, the graph will get closer to the x-axis in the domain $-1 < x < 1$. It will move away from the x-axis faster in the domains $x < 1$ and $x > 1$.

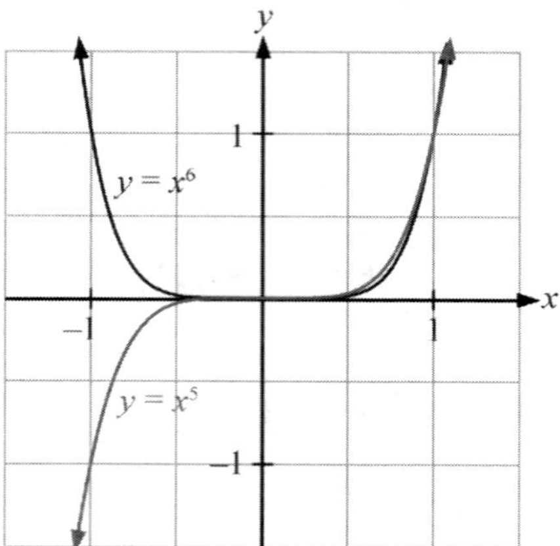

11. C

A function $f(x)$ is odd if and only if $f(-x) = -f(x)$. Evaluate each of the given functions to determine which is odd.

Step 1

Evaluate the function $f(x) = x^2 - 3x + 2$, when $f(-x)$.

$$f(x) = x^2 - 3x + 2$$
$$f(-x) = (-x)^2 - 3(-x) + 2$$
$$f(-x) = x^2 + 3x + 2$$

Since $f(-x) \neq -f(x)$, $f(x) = x^2 - 3x + 2$ is not an odd function.

Step 2

Evaluate the function $f(x) = -x^4 - x^3 - x^2$, when $f(-x)$.

$$f(x) = -x^4 - x^3 - x^2$$
$$f(-x) = -(-x)^4 - (-x)^3 - (-x)^2$$
$$f(-x) = -x^4 + x^3 - x^2$$

Since $f(-x) \neq -f(x)$, $f(x) = -x^4 - x^3 - x^2$ is not an odd function.

Step 3

Evaluate the function $f(x) = 5x^5 + 2x^3 - 3x$, when $f(-x)$.

$$f(x) = 5x^5 + 2x^3 - 3x$$
$$f(-x) = 5(-x)^5 + 2(-x)^3 - 3(-x)$$
$$f(-x) = -5x^5 - 2x^3 + 3$$

Since $f(-x) = -f(x)$, $f(x) = 5x^5 + 2x^3 - 3x$ is an odd function.

Step 4

Evaluate the function $f(x) = 3x^3 + 4x^2 - 5x - 1$, when $f(-x)$.

$$f(x) = 3x^3 + 4x^2 - 5x - 1$$
$$f(-x) = 3(-x)^3 + 4(-x)^2 - 5(-x) - 1$$
$$f(-x) = -3x^3 + 4x^2 + 5x - 1$$

Since $f(-x) \neq -f(x)$, $f(x) = 3x^3 + 4x^2 - 5x - 1$ is not an odd function.

12. C

Any polynomial function consisting of only even-degree monomials is an even function, and any polynomial function whose terms consist of only odd-degree monomials is an odd function. If the polynomial function has any combination of odd-degree and even-degree terms, it is neither odd nor even.

The equation $y = x^2 + \frac{5x^5}{x} + \frac{1}{x^2}$ is an even function. Since $\frac{5x^5}{x}$ simplifies to $5x^4$, the equation contains only even-degree monomials.

The other equations are neither odd nor even functions. The equation $y = \frac{1}{3} + \frac{1}{3x} + \frac{1}{3x^4}$ contains the odd-degree monomial $\frac{1}{3x}$.

The equation $y = x^2 + 3 + \frac{3x}{4x^4}$ contains $\frac{3x}{4x^4}$, which simplifies to the odd-degree monomial $\frac{3}{4x^3}$.

The equation $y = 2x + 4x + 6x^2$ contains the odd-degree monomials $2x$ and $4x$, which simplify to $6x$.

13. C

To determine the period, look for repetitive behavior in the graph.

It can be seen from the graph that the maximum value occurs every 4π rad.

Since a maximum value occurs only once in one period, the period is 4π rad.

14. D

Since the graph extends up and down indefinitely, the range includes all real numbers.

15. C

The zeros of the polynomial function $p(x) = -4(x-2)(x+2)(x-1)$ are $x = 2, -2$, and 1. Arranged in ascending order, the zeros are $x = -2$, 1, and 2. The test regions Sarah will need to use are $x < -2$, $-2 < x < 1$, $1 < x < 2$, and $x > 2$.

16. D

Step 1
Determine the degree of the numerator and the denominator:

The degree of the numerator, $6x^2$, is 2. The degree of the denominator, $4 - 2x^2$, is 2.

Step 2
Determine the equation for the horizontal asymptote. Since the degrees of the numerator and the denominator are equal, the horizontal asymptote occurs at $y = \frac{a}{b}$, where a and b are the leading coefficients of the numerator and denominator, respectively.

$$y = \frac{a}{b}$$
$$y = \frac{6}{-2}$$
$$y = -3$$

17. 0

Step 1
Determine the degree of the numerator and the degree of the denominator.
Rewrite the numerator to remove the radical.

$$\begin{aligned}\sqrt{x^2 - 2x + 1} &= \sqrt{x^2 - x - x + 1}\\ &= \sqrt{x(x-1) - (x-1)}\\ &= \sqrt{(x-1)^2}\\ &= x - 1\end{aligned}$$

The degree of the numerator, $x - 1$, is 1.

The degree of the denominator, $x^2 - 1$, is 2.

Step 2
Determine the equation of the horizontal asymptote. Since the degree of the numerator is less than the degree of the denominator, the horizontal asymptote occurs at $y = 0$. Therefore, the value of k is 0.

18. B

Step 1
Determine the equations of the vertical asymptotes. To determine the vertical asymptotes, set the denominator equal to zero, and solve for x.

$$\begin{aligned}2x^2 + x - 6 &= 0\\ 2x^2 + 4x - 3x - 6 &= 0\\ 2x(x+2) - 3(x+2) &= 0\\ (2x-3)(x+2) &= 0\end{aligned}$$

Solve for each x.

$x = \frac{3}{2}$ or $x = -2$

The vertical asymptotes are at $x = -2$ and $x = \frac{3}{2}$.

19. A

To determine the vertical asymptotes, set the denominator equal to zero and solve for x.

$$\begin{aligned}x^2 + 3x - 4 &= 0\\ x^2 + 4x - x - 4 &= 0\\ x(x+4) - 1(x+4) &= 0\\ (x-1)(x+4) &= 0\end{aligned}$$

Solve for each x.
$x = 1$ or $x = -4$

Therefore, the vertical asymptotes are at $x = 1$ and $x = -4$.

20. B

When the degree of the numerator is exactly one degree more than the degree of the denominator, the graph of the rational function has an oblique asymptote.

Step 1
Determine the degree of the numerator and denominator for $f(x) = \frac{5x^2 - 10x + 13}{6x^2 + 5x - 11}$.

- The degree of the numerator, $5x^2 - 10x + 13$, is 2.
- The degree of the denominator, $6x^2 + 5x - 11$, is 2.

The numerator and the denominator have the same degree. Therefore, the graph of the rational function does not have an oblique asymptote.

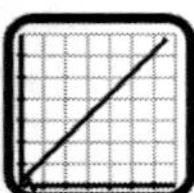

Step 2
Determine the degree of the numerator and denominator for $f(x) = \dfrac{x^3 - 4x - 10}{x^2 + 8}$.

- The degree of the numerator, $x^3 - 4x - 10$, is 3.
- The degree of the denominator, $x^2 + 8$, is 2.

The degree of the numerator is one degree more than the degree of the denominator. Therefore, the graph of the rational function has an oblique asymptote.

Step 3
Determine the degree of the numerator and denominator for $f(x) = \dfrac{x^3 - 2x + 4}{x - 9}$.

- The degree of the numerator, $x^3 - 2x + 4$, is 3.
- The degree of the denominator, $x - 9$, is 1.

The degree of the numerator is more than one degree larger than the degree of the denominator. Therefore, the graph of the rational function does not have an oblique asymptote.

Step 4
Determine the degree of the numerator and denominator for $f(x) = \dfrac{x - 5}{x^2 - 6x + 3}$.

- The degree of the numerator, $x - 5$, is 1.
- The degree of the denominator, $x^2 - 6x + 3$, is 2.

The degree of the numerator is less than the degree of the denominator. Therefore, the graph of the rational function does not have an oblique asymptote.

21. A

Step 1
Determine the degree of the numerator and denominator.

The degree of the numerator, $2x^3 + 4x + 3$, is 3.

The degree of the denominator, $x^2 - 2$, is 2.
Since the degree of the numerator is one more than the degree of the denominator, the graph of the rational function has an oblique asymptote.

Step 2
Determine the equation of the oblique asymptote. Use long division to obtain the quotient.

$$\begin{array}{r} 2x \\ x^2 - 2\overline{\smash{)}2x^3 + 0x^2 + 4x + 3} \\ \underline{-(2x^3 + 0x^2 - 4x)} \\ 8x + 3 \end{array}$$

The quotient is $2x$. Therefore, the equation of the oblique asymptote is $y = 2x$.

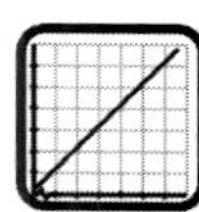

GRAPHING FUNCTIONS EXERCISE #2

22. Which of the following functions could a student enter into a graphing calculator to obtain the graph of $y = 2\log_4 x$?

A. $y = \dfrac{2\log 4}{\log x}$

B. $y = \dfrac{\log 4}{2\log x}$

C. $y = \dfrac{\log x}{2\log 4}$

D. $y = \dfrac{2\log x}{\log 4}$

Use the following information to answer the next question.

> In order to illustrate that $\log(x-3)^2 = 2\log(x-3)$, Paula used a graphing calculator to graph $y = \log(x-3)^2$ and $y = 2\log(x-3)$.

23. If Paula correctly graphs the two functions, she will discover that the

A. functions have the same graph
B. ranges of the two functions are different
C. domains of the two functions are different
D. vertical asymptotes of the graphs of the functions are different

Use the following information to answer the next question.

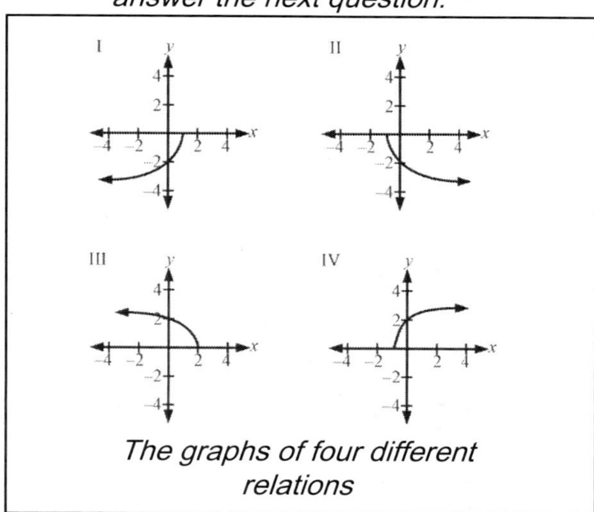

The graphs of four different relations

24. Which two of the illustrated relations could have the same domain?

A. I and II **B.** I and III
C. II and IV **D.** III and IV

25. Which of the following quadratic functions has a range of $y \geq 4$?

A. $y = 4x^2$

B. $y = -x^2 + 4$

C. $y = x^2 + 4$

D. $y = x^2 + 2x + 1$

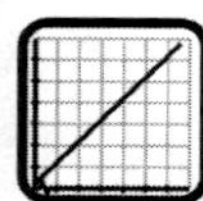

Use the following information to answer the next question.

A graph of a function is given.

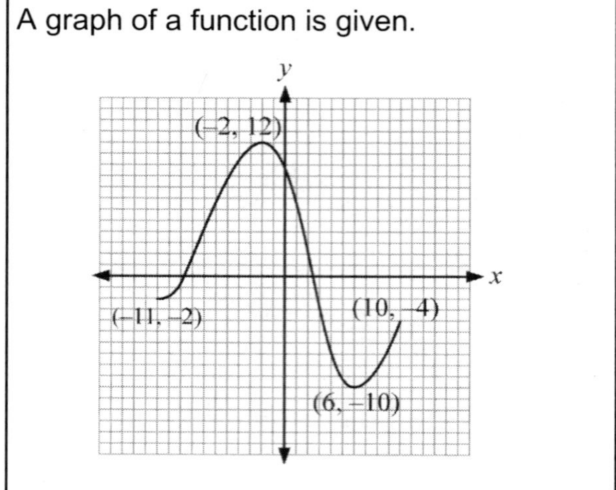

26. What are the domain and the range of the graph?

A. The domain is $\{-11 \le x \le 10\}$, and the range is $\{-10 \le y \le 12\}$.

B. The domain is $\{-10 \le x \le 12\}$, and the range is $\{-11 \le y \le 10\}$.

C. The domain is $\{-11 \le x \le 10\}$, and the range is $\{-4 \le y \le -2\}$.

D. The domain is $\{-2 \le x \le 6\}$, and the range is $\{-10 \le y \le 12\}$.

Use the following information to answer the next question.

Ryan measured the height of a tree over a seven month growing period. Ryan showed his measurements on a graph.

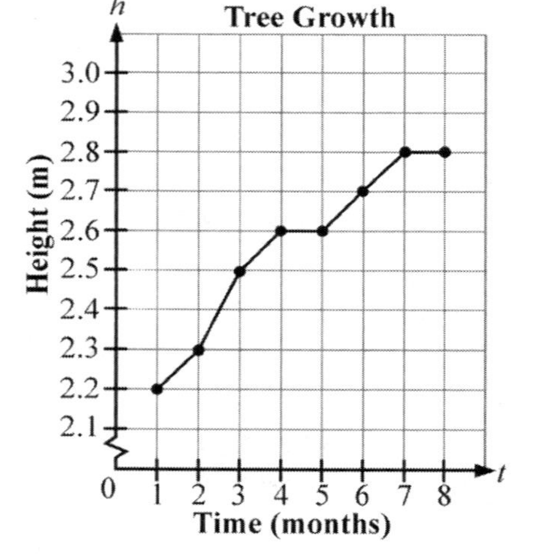

27. What are the domain and range of the relation on Ryan's graph?

A. D:$\{1 \le t \le 8\}$ and R:$\{2.2 \le h \le 2.8\}$

B. D:$\{2.2 \le t \le 2.8\}$ and R:$\{1 \le h \le 8\}$

C. D:$\{1 \le t \le 8\}$ and R:$\{2.1 \le h \le 3.0\}$

D. D:$\{0 \le t \le 7\}$ and R:$\{2.1 \le h \le 3.0\}$

28. The graphs of the logarithmic functions $y = \log_b x$, $b > 1$ and $y = \log_a x$, $0 < a < 1$ will intersect at the ordered pair

A. (0, 0) **B.** (0, 1)

C. (1, 0) **D.** (1, 1)

29. Which of the following statements regarding the graph of $y = \log_8 x$ is **true**?

A. The range of the graph is $y > 0$.

B. The y-intercept of the graph is (0, 1).

C. The graph passes through the point $\left(\frac{1}{8}, -1\right)$.

D. The equation of the horizontal asymptote of the graph is $y = 0$.

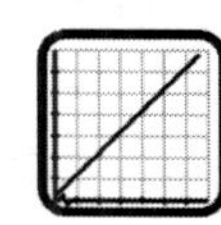

Use the following information to answer the next question.

The graphs of two functions of the form $y = x^n$ are shown.

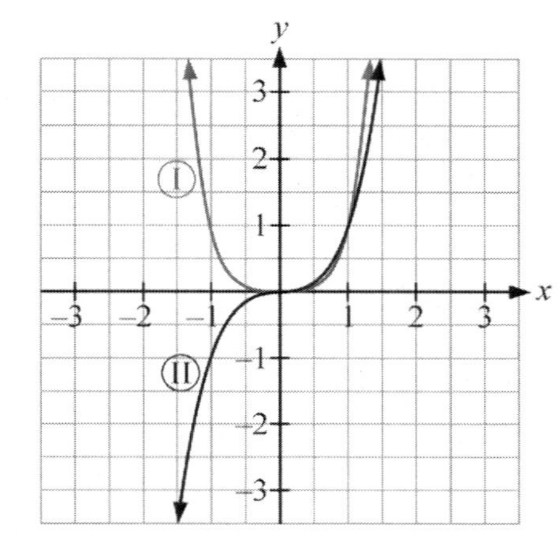

30. The equations of graphs I and II respectively could be

A. $y = x^3$ and $y = x^4$

B. $y = x^5$ and $y = x^4$

C. $y = x^4$ and $y = x^3$

D. $y = x^4$ and $y = x^5$

Use the following information to answer the next question.

The graphs of two functions of the form $y = x^n$ are shown.

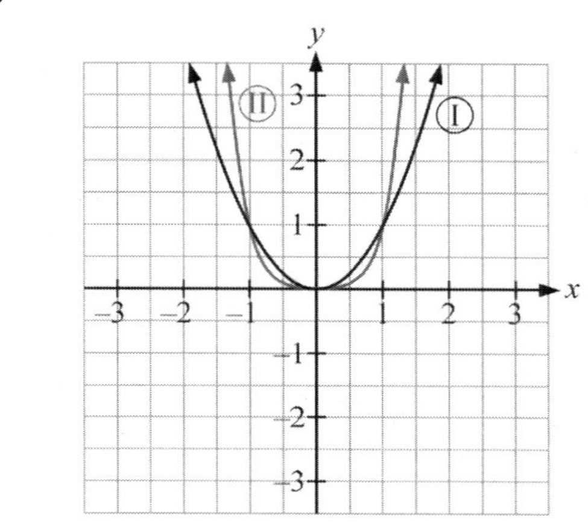

31. What are the equations of graphs I and II, respectively?

A. $y = x^2$ and $y = x^4$

B. $y = x^2$ and $y = x^3$

C. $y = x^4$ and $y = x^2$

D. $y = x^4$ and $y = x^3$

32. Which of the following graphs of four different functions of the form $y = f(x)$ illustrates that $f(-x) = -f(x)$?

A.

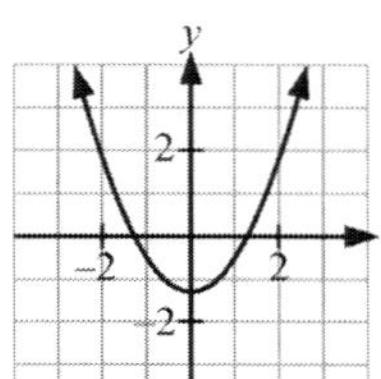

B.

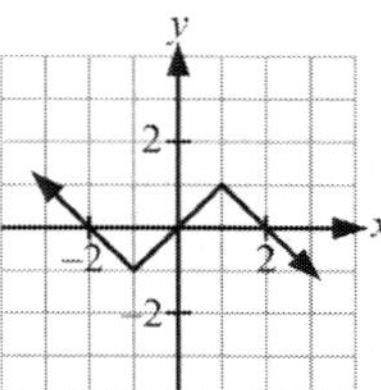

C.

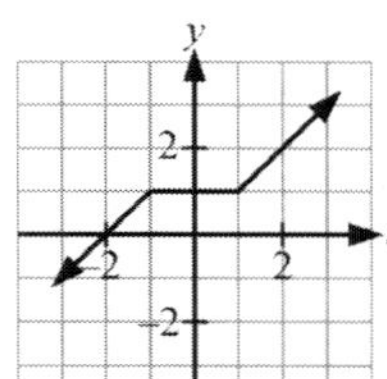

D.

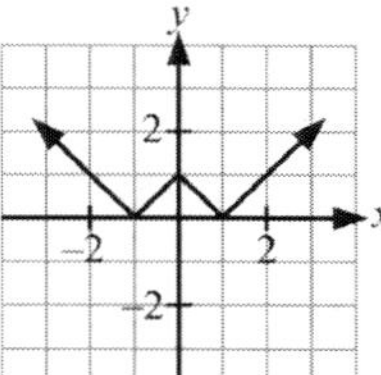

33. For the trigonometric function $y = -2\cos\left(\frac{2}{3}(x + 90°)\right) - 2$, determine the amplitude, period, phase shift, and vertical displacement.

34. What is the equation of the horizontal asymptote for the graph of $f(x) = \frac{5x-2}{3x-2}$?

A. $y = \frac{5}{3}$ **B.** $y = 1$

C. $y = \frac{2}{3}$ **D.** $y = 0$

35. The equation of the vertical asymptote of the function $f(x) = \frac{x^2-9}{2x-3}$ is

A. $x = -3$ **B.** $x = \frac{3}{2}$

C. $x = \frac{2}{3}$ **D.** $x = 3$

36. What is the equation of the vertical asymptote of the function $y = \frac{3x^2}{x^2-2x+1}$?

A. $x = -3$ **B.** $x = -1$

C. $x = 0$ **D.** $x = 1$

37. What is the equation of the oblique asymptote for the graph of $R(x) = \frac{-2x^2+11x+7}{x-2}$?

A. $y = -x - 21$ **B.** $y = -2x + 7$

C. $y = 2x - 7$ **D.** $y = x + 21$

Use the following information to answer the next question.

The equation of the oblique asymptote for the graph of $f(x) = \frac{6x^2+15x-2}{x+5}$ is in the form $y = mx + b$.

38. The value of b is

A. 73 **B.** 6

C. –15 **D.** –45

Operations of Functions

OPERATIONS OF FUNCTIONS

Table of Correlations

Standard		Concepts	Exercise #1	Exercise #2
PC.2	The student interprets the meaning of the symbolic representations of functions and operations on functions to solve meaningful problems.			
PC. 2.A	*Apply basic transformations, including a•f(x), f(x)+d, f(x-c), f(b•x), and compositions with absolute value functions, including |f(x)|, and f(|x|), to the parent functions.*	Understanding Absolute Values		
		Graphing $y = \| x \|$		
		Absolute Value Function	39, 40	81
		Vertical and Horizontal Translations of $y = \| x \|$	41, 42	82
		Reflections of $y = \| x \|$ in the x-axis	43, 44	83
		Vertical Stretches of $y = \| x \|$ about the x-axis	45, 46	84
		Combined Transformations of $y = \| x \|$	47, 48	85, 86
		Horizontal Stretches	49, 50	87
		Vertical Stretches	51, 52	88
		Horizontal Translations	53, 54	89
		Vertical Translations	55, 56	90
		The Graph of $y = f(\| x \|)$	57, 58	91, 92
		Stretches about Lines Parallel to the x- and y-Axes	59, 60	93
PC. 2.B	*Perform operations including composition on functions, find inverses, and describe these procedures and results verbally, numerically, symbolically, and graphically.*	Sketching the Inverse Graph of a Function		
		Determining the Equation of the Inverse of a Function Algebraically	61, 62	94
		Combining Functions Using Arithmetic Operations	63, 64	95, 96
		Compositions of Two Functions	65, 66	97
		Defining the Inverse of a Function Given Numeric Representations	67, 68	98
PC. 2.C	*Investigate identities graphically and verify them symbolically, including logarithmic properties, trigonometric identities, and exponential properties.*	Verifying Reciprocal, Quotient, and Pythagorean Identities	69, 80	99
		Properties of Exponential Functions	70, 71	100, 101
		Logarithm Identities	72, 73	102
		Verifying Sum, Difference, and Double-Angle Identities	74, 75	103
		Developing the Pythagorean Identities		
		Proving Simple Trigonometric Identities Using Reciprocal, Quotient, and Pythagorean Identities	76, 77	104, 105
		Developing Reciprocal and Quotient Identities		
		Understanding the Laws of Rational Exponents	78, 79	106

PC.2.A Apply basic transformations, including a•f(x), f(x)+d, f(x-c), f(b•x), and compositions with absolute value functions, including |f(x)|, and f(|x|), to the parent functions.

Absolute Value Function

If a function $f(x)$ is given, the absolute value function is defined by the equation $y = |f(x)|$. When the graph of $y = f(x)$ is transformed to the graph of the absolute value function $y = |f(x)|$, the part of the graph that is below the x-axis on the graph of $y = f(x)$ is reflected above the x-axis on the graph of $y = |f(x)|$, and the part of the graph that is above the x-axis on the graph of $y = f(x)$ remains the same.

To sketch the graph of $y = |f(x)|$ given the graph of $y = f(x)$, follow these steps:

1. Sketch the graph of $y = f(x)$.
2. Identify points where the graph of $y = f(x)$ is zero or positive (above the x-axis) and where the graph of $y = f(x)$ is negative (below the x-axis).
3. Reflect the negative parts of $y = f(x)$ about the x-axis.

The graph of $y = |f(x)|$ will consist of the parts of the graph of $y = f(x)$ that are above the x-axis and the parts that were reflected about the x-axis, as illustrated in the following example.

Example

Given the function $f(x) = x + 2$, sketch the graph of $y = |f(x)|$.

Solution

Step 1

Sketch the graph of $f(x) = x + 2$.

The graph of $f(x) = x + 2$ is a line with a slope of 1 and a y-intercept at 2.

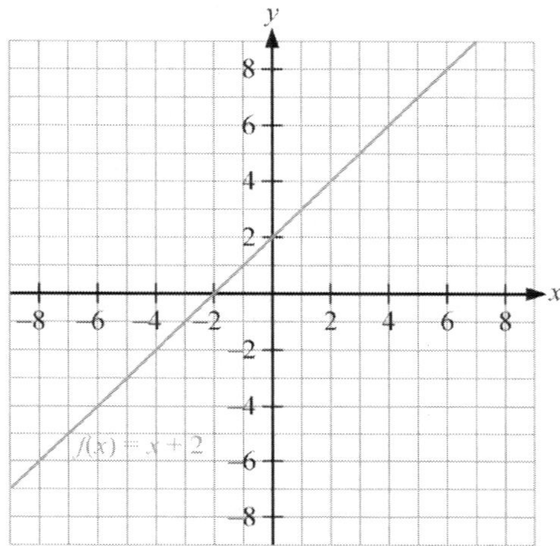

Step 2

Identify points where the function $f(x)$ is zero or positive (above the x-axis) and where the function $f(x)$ is negative (below the x-axis).

The function $f(x)$ is zero or positive for x-values greater than or equal to −2 or $x \geq -2$.

The function $f(x)$ is negative for x-values less than −2 or $x < -2$.

Step 3
Reflect the negative part of the graph of $y = f(x)$ about the x-axis.

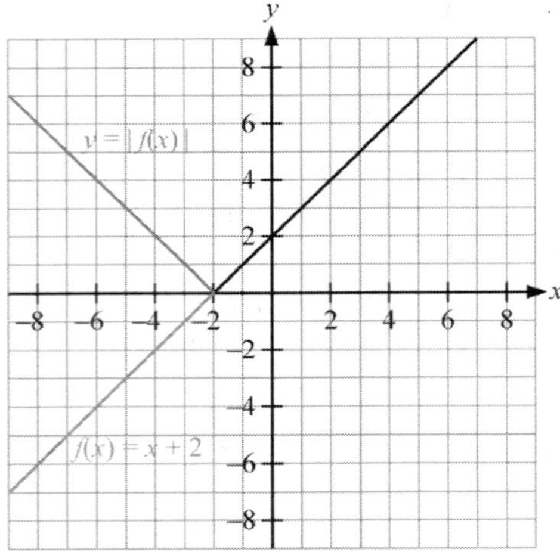

Step 4
Show the sketch of $y = | f(x) |$.

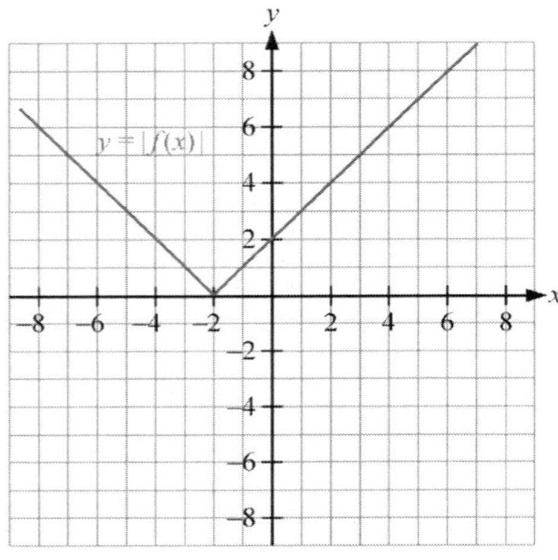

Vertical and Horizontal Translations of $y = | x |$

Vertical and horizontal translations cause a shift in a graph's position, either left, right, up, or down.

Vertical Translations

Adding a positive number, k, to the right side of the equation $y = | x |$ translates the graph k units up, and subtracting a positive number (or adding a negative number), k, from the right side of the equation $y = | x |$ translates the graph k units down.

Example

Sketch the graph of $y = | x | + 4$ using a table of values.

Solution

Step 1
Create a table of values.

$y = \| x \| + 4$	
x	**y**
−3	$\| -3 \| + 4 = 3 + 4$ $= 7$
−2	$\| -2 \| + 4 = 2 + 4$ $= 6$
−1	$\| -1 \| + 4 = 1 + 4$ $= 5$
0	$\| 0 \| + 4 = 0 + 4$ $= 4$
1	$\| 1 \| + 4 = 1 + 4$ $= 5$
2	$\| 2 \| + 4 = 2 + 4$ $= 6$
3	$\| 3 \| + 4 = 3 + 4$ $= 7$

Step 2
Plot the ordered pairs from the table of values on the Cartesian plane, and draw lines through the points to find the graph of the function $y = | x | + 4$.

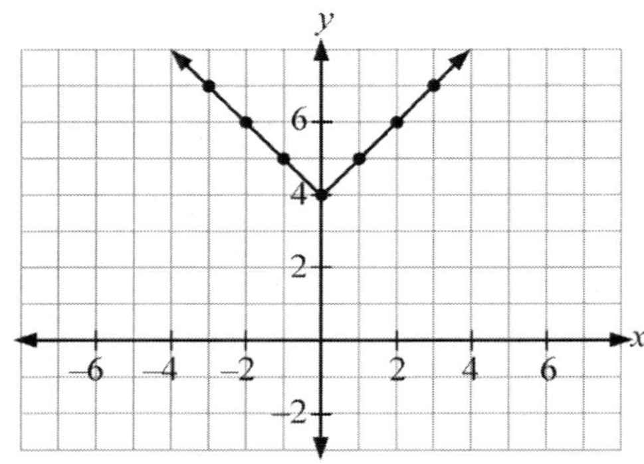

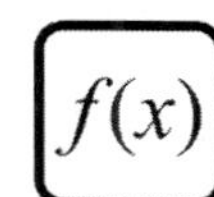

Example

Sketch the graph of $y = |x| - 1$ using a table of values.

Solution

Step 1

Create a table of values.

$y = \vert x \vert - 1$	
−3	$\vert -3 \vert - 1 = 3 - 1$ $= 2$
−2	$\vert -2 \vert - 1 = 2 - 1$ $= 1$
−1	$\vert -1 \vert - 1 = 1 - 1$ $= 0$
0	$\vert 0 \vert - 1 = 0 - 1$ $= -1$
1	$\vert 1 \vert - 1 = 1 - 1$ $= 0$
2	$\vert 2 \vert - 1 = 2 - 1$ $= 1$
3	$\vert 3 \vert - 1 = 3 - 1$ $= 2$

Step 2

Plot the ordered pairs from the table of values on the Cartesian plane, and draw lines through the points to find the graph of the function $y = |x| - 1$.

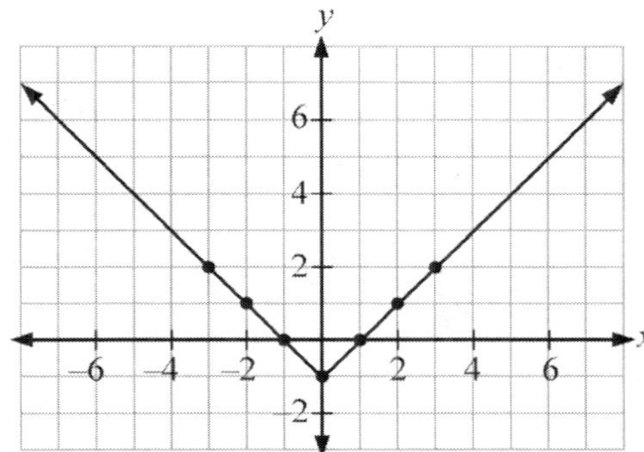

To summarize, the graph of $y = |x| + k$ is the graph of $y = |x|$ translated k units up when $k > 0$ and k units down when $k < 0$.

HORIZONTAL TRANSLATIONS

Subtracting a positive number, h, from the x-variable translates the graph h units to the right, and adding a positive number (or subtracting a negative number), h, to the x-variable translates the graph h units to the left.

Example

Sketch the graph of $y = |x - 2|$ using a table of values.

Solution

Step 1

Create a table of values.

$y = \vert x - 2 \vert$	
x	**y**
−2	$\vert -2 - 2 \vert = \vert -4 \vert$ $= 4$
−1	$\vert -1 - 2 \vert = \vert -3 \vert$ $= 3$
0	$\vert 0 - 2 \vert = \vert -2 \vert$ $= 2$
1	$\vert 1 - 2 \vert = \vert -1 \vert$ $= 1$
2	$\vert 2 - 2 \vert = \vert 0 \vert$ $= 0$
3	$\vert 3 - 2 \vert = \vert 1 \vert$ $= 1$
4	$\vert 4 - 2 \vert = \vert 2 \vert$ $= 2$
5	$\vert 5 - 2 \vert = \vert 3 \vert$ $= 3$

Step 2
Plot the ordered pairs from the table of values on the Cartesian plane, and draw lines through the points to find the graph of the function $y = |x - 2|$.

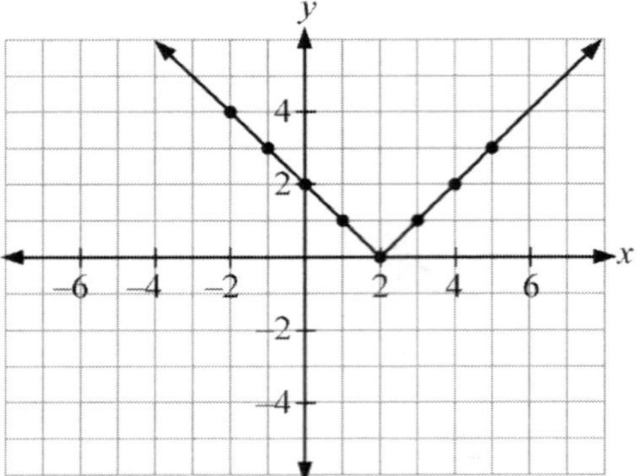

Example

Sketch the graph of $y = |x + 3|$ using a table of values.

Solution

Step 1
Create a table of values.

$y = \|x + 3\|$	
x	**y**
−5	$\|-5+3\| = \|-2\|$ $= 2$
−4	$\|-4+3\| = \|-1\|$ $= 1$
−3	$\|-3+3\| = \|0\|$ $= 0$
−2	$\|-2+3\| = \|1\|$ $= 1$
−1	$\|-1+3\| = \|2\|$ $= 2$
0	$\|0+3\| = \|3\|$ $= 3$
1	$\|1+3\| = \|4\|$ $= 4$

Step 2
Plot the ordered pairs from the table of values on the Cartesian plane, and draw lines through the points to find the graph of the function $y = |x + 3|$.

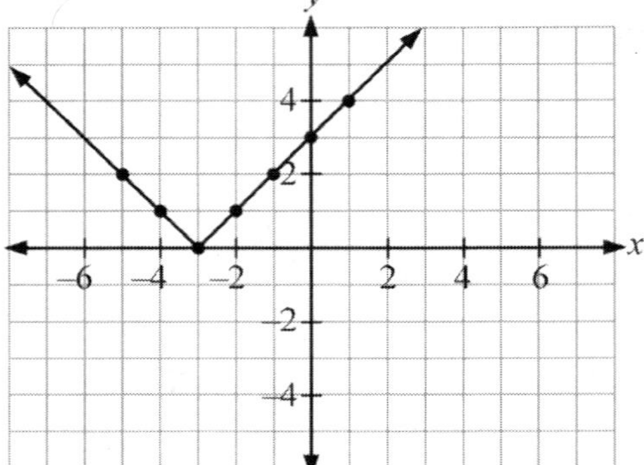

To summarize, the graph of $y = |x - h|$ is the graph of $y = |x|$ translated h units right when $h > 0$ and h units left when $h < 0$.

Notice that when h is negative, such as −3, $y = |x - h|$ gives $y = |x - (-3)|$, which is $y = |x + 3|$.

Example

Determine the equation of the graph of $y = |x|$ after it has been translated 11 units to the left.

Solution

The graph of $y = |x - h|$ is the graph of $y = |x|$ translated h units right when $h > 0$ and $|h|$ units left when $h < 0$.

Since the required translation is to the left, $h < 0$ and therefore h must be −11.

Thus, the equation is $y = |x - (-11)|$, which simplifies to $y = |x + 11|$.

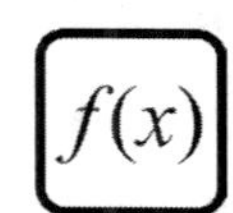

Reflections of $y = |x|$ in the x-axis

Reflections in the x-axis cause a graph to flip upside down.

Example

Sketch the graphs of both $y = |x|$ and $y = -|x|$ on the same grid, using tables of values.

Solution

Step 1

Create a table of values for each of the given functions.

x	$y = \|x\|$	$y = -\|x\|$
−3	3	−3
−2	2	−2
−1	1	−1
0	0	0
1	1	−1
2	2	−2
3	3	−3

Step 2

Sketch the graphs of the two functions.

From the given tables of values, it can be seen that for each x-value, the y-value for $y = -|x|$ is the negative of the y-value for $y = |x|$.

Graphically, this means that for each x-value, the corresponding y-values of the two functions are equally displaced on either side of the x-axis.

The graph of $y = |x|$ is in the shape of a right-side up V, and the graph of $y = -|x|$ is in the shape of an upside-down V.

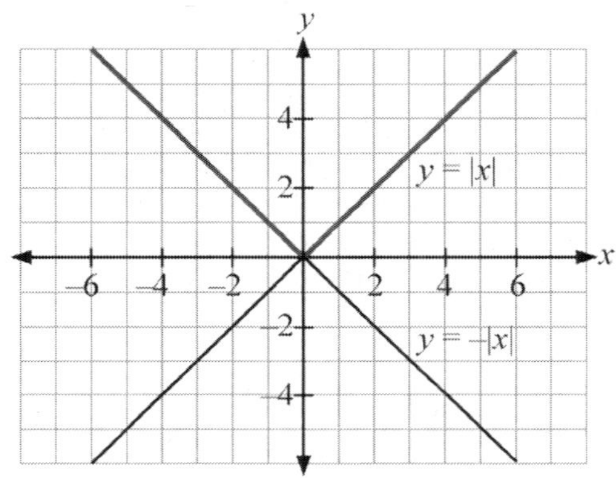

The graph of $y = -|x|$ is the graph of $y = |x|$ reflected in the x-axis.

Vertical Stretches of $y = |x|$ about the x-axis

For the graph of the function $y = a|x|$, parameter a causes a vertical expansion by a factor of $|a|$ about the x-axis when $|a| > 1$ and a vertical compression by a factor of $|a|$ about the x-axis when $0 < |a| < 1$. Sometimes, the word stretch is used in place of the words expansion and compression. In these situations, find the value of the factor to determine whether the stretch is in fact an expansion or a compression. The graph is also reflected in the x-axis when $a < 0$.

Example

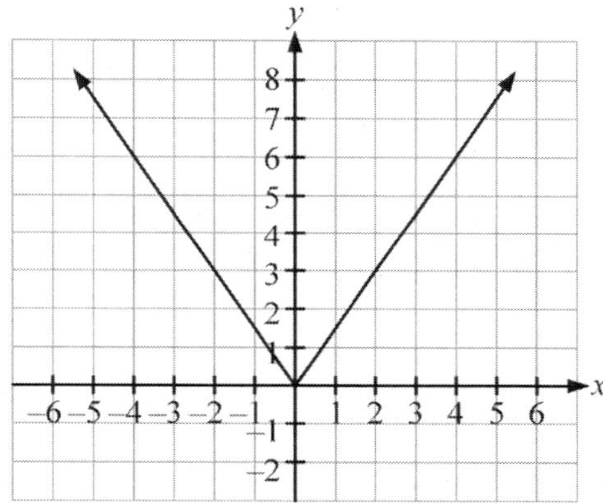

This graph is a stretched form of the graph $y = |x|$.

Determine the equation of the stretched graph.

Solution

The point (2, 2) would be on the graph of $y = |x|$ because $2 = |2|$. Since the point with coordinates (2, 3) is on the graph that is shown, it appears the graph of $y = |x|$ has been stretched vertically about the x-axis by a factor of $\frac{3}{2}$. This is confirmed by other points on the graph such as (−2, 3) and (4, 6).

The equation of the graph that is given is $y = \frac{3}{2}|x|$, or $y = 1.5|x|$.

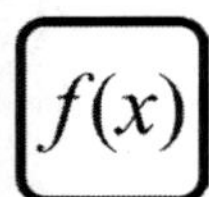

Example

Sketch the graphs of $y = |x|$, $y = 2|x|$, and $y = \frac{1}{2}|x|$ on the same grid with the help of a table of values.

Solution

Step 1

Create a table of values.

x	$y = \lvert x \rvert$	$y = 2\lvert x \rvert$	$y = \frac{1}{2}\lvert x \rvert$
−3	3	6	$\frac{3}{2}$
−2	2	4	1
−1	1	2	$\frac{1}{2}$
0	0	0	0
1	1	2	$\frac{1}{2}$
2	2	4	1
3	3	6	$\frac{3}{2}$

The table of values shows that for any particular x-value, the y-value is double for $y = 2|x|$ and half for $y = \frac{1}{2}|x|$ when compared to the y-value for $y = |x|$. This is expected from observing the two equations $y = 2|x|$ and $y = \frac{1}{2}|x|$ while comparing them with $y = |x|$.

Step 2

Sketch the graphs of the three functions. Graphically, the effects are that the graph of $y = 2|x|$ is a vertical stretch (expansion) of the graph of $y = |x|$ by a factor of 2 about the x-axis, and the graph of $y = \frac{1}{2}|x|$ is a vertical stretch (compression) of the graph of $y = |x|$ by a factor of $\frac{1}{2}$ about the x-axis.

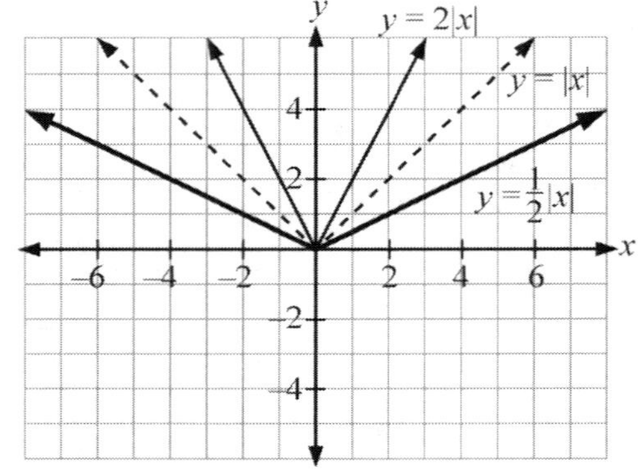

Combined Transformations of $y = |x|$

The graph of $y = a|x - h| + k$ can be obtained from the graph of $y = |x|$ by the following combination of transformations:

1. A vertical stretch by a factor of $|a|$ about the x-axis
2. A reflection in the x-axis when $a < 0$
3. A horizontal translation of h units right when $h > 0$ and $|h|$ units left when $h < 0$
4. A vertical translation of k units up when $k > 0$ and $|k|$ units down when $k < 0$

In general, the order of the transformations makes a difference in the following situations:

- When there is a stretch and a translation in the same direction (both horizontal or both vertical)
- When reflections and translations in the same direction are combined

In most cases, because of the effect of the order of transformations, the following order is applied when transforming graphs or describing the transformations that have been applied:

1. Stretches with respect to one or both axes
2. Reflections in one or both axes
3. Vertical and horizontal translations

Example

The partial graphs of the functions $y = |x|$ and $y = 2|x-3|-4$ are shown.

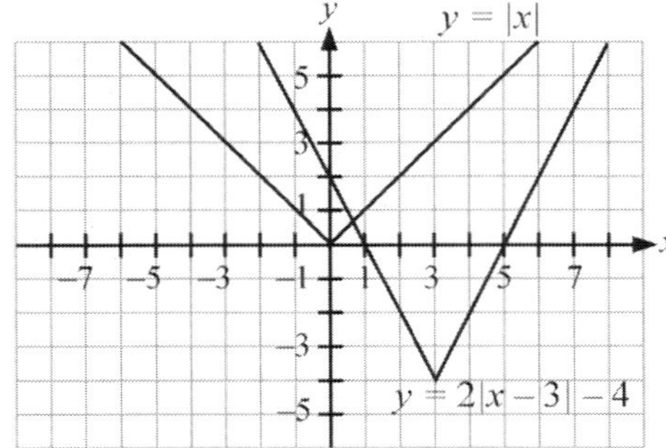

Compare the graphs of the functions $y = |x|$ and $y = 2|x-3|-4$.

Solution

By comparing the two graphs, it can be seen that the following transformations of the graph of $y = |x|$ will create the graph of $y = 2|x-3|-4$:

1. A vertical stretch by a factor of 2 about the *x*-axis
2. A translation of 3 units right
3. A translation of 4 units down

Example

The partial graphs of the functions $y = |x|$ and $y = -\frac{1}{3}|x+1|+5$ are shown.

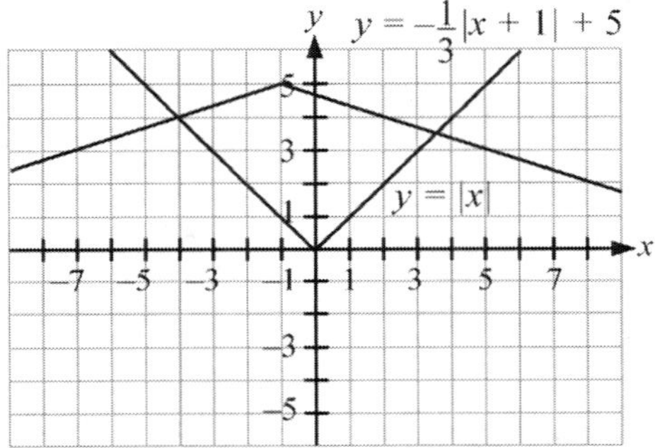

Compare the graphs of the functions $y = |x|$ and $y = -\frac{1}{3}|x+1|+5$.

Solution

When you compare the two graphs, you can see that the following transformations of the graph of $y = |x|$ will create the graph of $y = -\frac{1}{3}|x+1|+5$:

1. A vertical stretch by a factor of $\frac{1}{3}$ about the *x*-axis
2. A reflection in the *x*-axis
3. A horizontal translation of 1 unit left
4. A vertical translation of 5 units up

Example

Use the concepts of transformations of $y = |x|$ to sketch the graph of $y = -\frac{1}{4}|x+2|-1$ on the Cartesian plane.

Solution

The transformations of the graph of $y = |x|$ that will create the graph of $y = -\frac{1}{4}|x+2|-1$ are listed in order as follows:

1. A vertical stretch by a factor of $\frac{1}{4}$ about the *x*-axis (equation: $y = \frac{1}{4}|x|$)
2. A reflection in the *x*-axis (equation: $y = -\frac{1}{4}|x|$)
3. A horizontal translation of 2 units left (equation: $y = -\frac{1}{4}|x+2|$)
4. A vertical translation of 1 unit down (equation: $y = -\frac{1}{4}|x+2|-1$)

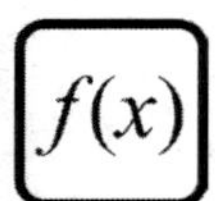

Using the transformations of $y = |x|$, the graph of $y = -\frac{1}{4}|x+2| - 1$ can be sketched as shown.

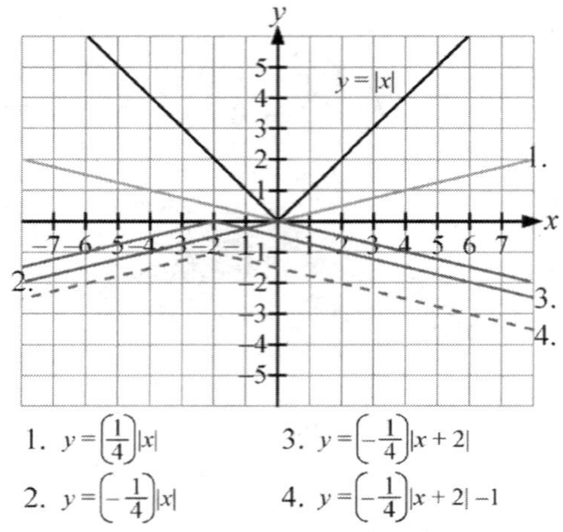

Horizontal Stretches

A horizontal stretch occurs when a graph is stretched horizontally about a vertical line by a specific factor. The graph is usually stretched about the y-axis. When the graph of $y = f(x)$ is transformed to the graph of $y = f(bx)$, the value of b causes a horizontal stretch about the y-axis by a factor of $\frac{1}{|b|}$, where $b \neq 0$. If $b < 0$, there is a reflection in the y-axis.

The x-coordinate of a transformed point is equal to $\frac{1}{b}$ times the value of the x-coordinate of the original corresponding point. The y-coordinates of the original and the corresponding transformed point are equal.

Example

When the graph of $y = \sqrt{x} + 3$ is stretched horizontally about the y-axis by a factor of $\frac{1}{2}$, the resulting graph is $y = \sqrt{2x} + 3$.

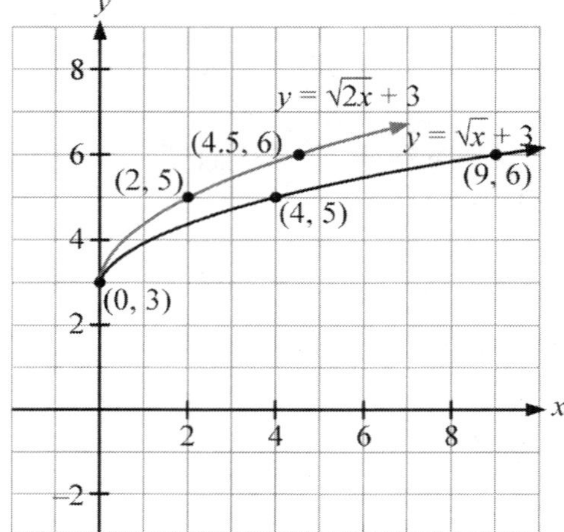

To produce the equation $y = \sqrt{2x} + 3$ from $y = \sqrt{x} + 3$, it is necessary to replace x with $2x$. Observe that the y-coordinate of any ordered pair on the original graph is equal to the y-coordinate of the corresponding ordered pair on the transformed graph. However, the x-coordinates of the ordered pairs on the transformed graph of $y = \sqrt{2x} + 3$ are $\frac{1}{2}$ the value of the x-coordinates of the corresponding ordered pairs on the graph of $y = \sqrt{x} + 3$. The y-intercept of each graph, (0, 3), does not change, so it is an invariant point.

When a graph is stretched horizontally about the y-axis by a factor of b, the horizontal distance from the y-axis to each transformed point is b times the original horizontal distance.

Example

If the graph of $y = f(x)$ contains the point (2, 5), then the corresponding point on the graph of $y = f\left(\frac{1}{2}x\right)$ is (4, 5). The horizontal distance from (4, 5) to the y-axis is 4 units, which is twice the horizontal distance from (2, 5) to the y-axis.

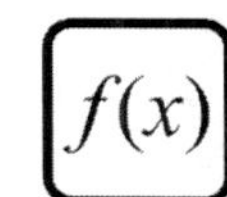

Example

How does the graph of $y = f(3x)$ compare with the graph of $y = f(x)$?

Solution

In order to transform the equation $y = f(x)$ to the equation $y = f(3x)$, x is replaced with $3x$ in the equation $y = f(x)$. When x is replaced with $3x$ in the equation $y = f(x)$, the graph of $y = f(x)$ will be horizontally stretched about the y-axis by a factor of $\frac{1}{3}$. Thus, $y = f(3x)$ is the graph of $y = f(x)$ stretched horizontally about the y-axis by a factor of $\frac{1}{3}$.

When a graph is stretched horizontally, the y-coordinates remain constant. It follows that the y-intercepts are not affected by a horizontal stretch about the y-axis. Since the y-coordinates are constant, the range of the graph is also constant.

When a graph is stretched horizontally by a factor of b, the x-coordinates are replaced by bx. It follows that the x-intercepts change from $(x, 0)$ to $(bx, 0)$. Since the x-coordinates change, the domain of the graph will be changed from $m \le x \le n$ to $bm \le x \le bn$.

Example

The graph of $y = f(x)$ is given.

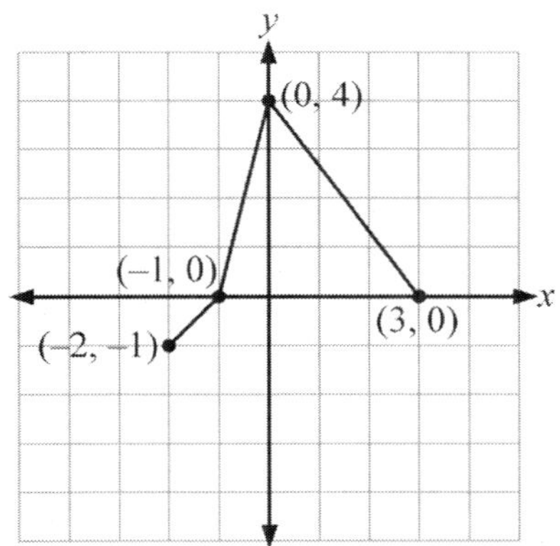

Determine the domain and range of the function after a horizontal stretch about the y-axis by a factor of 3.

Solution

Step 1
Determine the domain and range of $y = f(x)$.

- The domain of $y = f(x)$ is $-2 \le x \le 3$.
- The range of $y = f(x)$ is $-1 \le y \le 4$.

Step 2
Determine the domain and range of $y = f(x)$ after a horizontal stretch about the y-axis by a factor of 3.

When a graph is stretched about the y-axis by a factor of b, the domain of the graph will be changed from $m \le x \le n$ to $bm \le x \le bn$. It follows that the domain of the transformed function is $3(-2) \le x \le 3(3)$, or $-6 \le x \le 9$.

The range of a function does not change after a horizontal stretch about the y-axis; therefore, the range of the stretched function is $-1 \le y \le 4$.

Determine the x- and y-intercepts of the given function after a horizontal stretch about the y-axis by a factor of 3.

Solution

Step 1
Determine the x and y-intercepts of $y = f(x)$.

- The x-intercepts of $y = f(x)$ are $(-1, 0)$ and $(3, 0)$.
- The y-intercept of $y = f(x)$ is $(0, 4)$.

Step 2
Determine the x- and y-intercepts of the stretched function.

When a graph is stretched horizontally by a factor of b, the x-intercepts change from $(x, 0)$ to $(bx, 0)$. The x-intercepts of the stretched function are $(3(-1), 0)$ and $(3(3), 0)$, or $(-3, 0)$ and $(9, 0)$.

Since y-intercepts are not affected by a stretch about the y-axis, the y-intercept of the stretched function is $(0, 4)$.

To sketch the graph of $y = f(bx)$ by transforming the graph of $y = f(x)$, take the following steps:

1. Select appropriate ordered pairs located on the graph of $y = f(x)$.
2. Apply the stretch factor to the x-coordinate of each selected ordered pair on the graph of $y = f(x)$. Since the graph is stretched horizontally about the y-axis by a factor of $\frac{1}{|b|}$, a point, (x, y), on the graph of $y = f(x)$ will be transformed to the corresponding point $\left(\frac{1}{b}x, y\right)$ on the graph of $y = f(bx)$. The reciprocal of b is $\frac{1}{b}$.
3. Plot the corresponding ordered pairs on a grid, and join the points to form the transformed graph.

Example

The graph of $y = x + 4$ is shown.

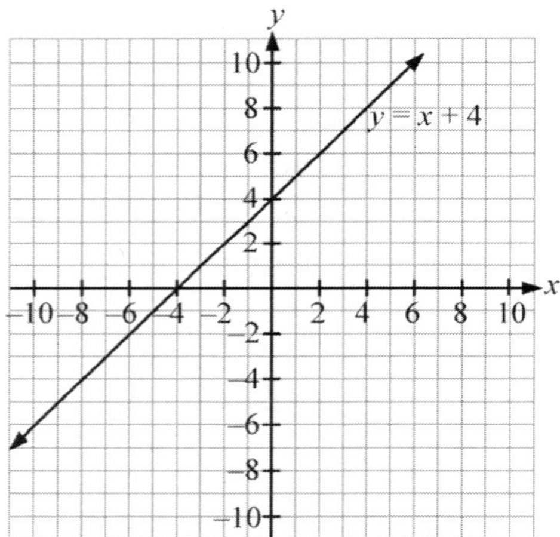

On the same axis, sketch the graph of the transformed function $y = \frac{1}{2}x + 4$.

Solution

Step 1
Determine the transformations applied to the graph of $y = x + 4$ in order to transform it to the graph of $y = \frac{1}{2}x + 4$.

Since the graph of $y = x + 4$ is transformed to the graph of $y = \frac{1}{2}x + 4$, x has been replaced by $\frac{1}{2}x$ in the equation $y = x + 4$. Thus, the graph of $y = x + 4$ will be horizontally stretched about the y-axis by a factor of 2. (The reciprocal of $\frac{1}{2}$ is 2.)

Step 2
Select appropriate ordered pairs located on the graph of $y = x + 4$.
One option is to choose the ordered pairs (2, 6), (0, 4), (−4, 0), and (−5, −1).

Step 3
Apply the stretch factor to the x-coordinate of each ordered pair on the graph of $y = x + 4$. Since the graph is stretched horizontally about the y-axis by a factor of 2, a point (x, y) on the graph of $y = x + 4$ will be transformed to the corresponding point $(2x, y)$ on the graph of $y = \frac{1}{2}x + 4$. (The reciprocal of 2 is $\frac{1}{2}$.)

- Point (2, 6) becomes $(2 \times 2, 6) = (4, 6)$.
- Point (0, 4) becomes $(2 \times 0, 4) = (0, 4)$.
- Point (−4, 0) becomes $(2 \times -4, 0) = (-8, 0)$.
- Point (−5, −1) becomes $(2 \times -5, -1) = (-10, -1)$.

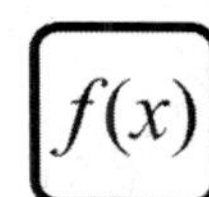

Step 4
Plot the corresponding ordered pairs on a grid, and join the points to form the basis for creating the graph of the transformed graph.

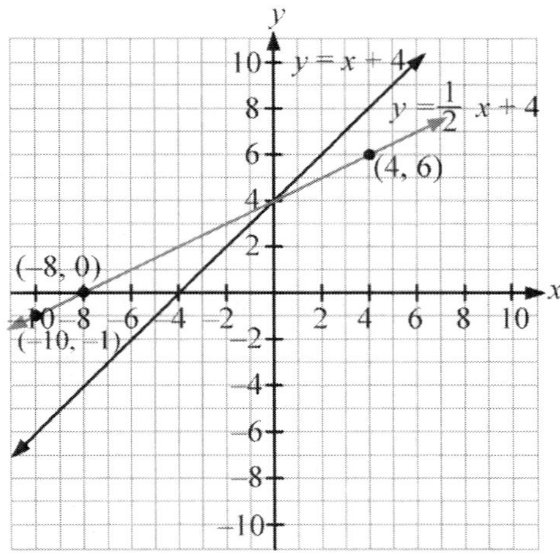

Vertical Stretches

A vertical stretch occurs when a given graph is stretched vertically about a horizontal line (usually the x-axis) by a certain factor. When the graph of $y = f(x)$ is transformed to the graph of $\frac{1}{a}y = f(x)$, or $y = af(x)$, the value of a causes a vertical stretch about the x-axis by a factor of $|a|$, $a \neq 0$. If $a < 0$, there is a reflection in the x-axis.

Example

When the graph of $y = \sqrt{x}$ is stretched vertically about the x-axis by a factor of 2, the resulting graph is $\frac{1}{2}y = \sqrt{x}$.

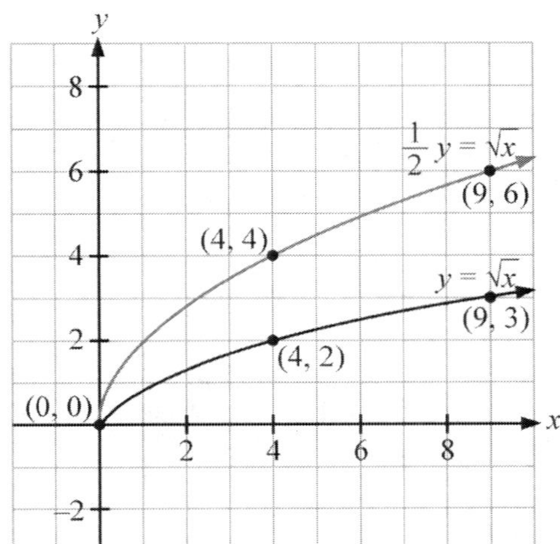

To produce the equation $\frac{1}{2}y = \sqrt{x}$ from $y = \sqrt{x}$, y is replaced with $\frac{1}{2}y$. The x-coordinate of an ordered pair on the original graph and the x-coordinate of the corresponding ordered pair on the transformed graph are equal. However, the y-coordinate of an ordered pair on the transformed graph, $\frac{1}{2}y = \sqrt{x}$, is twice the value of the y-coordinate of the corresponding ordered pair on the graph of $y = \sqrt{x}$.

When y is replaced with $\frac{1}{a}y$ in the equation $y = f(x)$, the graph of $y = f(x)$ is stretched vertically about the x-axis by a factor of $|a|$, resulting in the graph of $\frac{1}{a}y = f(x)$, or $y = af(x)$. As a result, a point (x, y) on the graph of $y = f(x)$ will be transformed to the point (x, ay) on the graph of $\frac{1}{a}y = f(x)$ because the reciprocal of $\frac{1}{a}$ is a. Thus, the y-coordinate of a transformed point is equal to a times the value of the y-coordinate of the original point, and the x-coordinates of the original and transformed points are equal.

When a graph is stretched vertically about the x-axis, the x-intercept is an invariant point.

Example

How can the graph of $\frac{1}{3}y = f(x)$ be obtained from the graph of $y = f(x)$?

Solution

In order to transform the equation $y = f(x)$ to the equation $\frac{1}{3}y = f(x)$, y is replaced with $\frac{1}{3}y$ in the equation $y = f(x)$.

Since $\frac{1}{a} = \frac{1}{3}$, the vertical stretch factor is 3.

Thus, the graph of $y = f(x)$ is stretched vertically about the x-axis by a factor of 3 to give the graph of $\frac{1}{3}y = f(x)$.

Since $\frac{1}{3}y = f(x)$ is usually changed to $y = 3f(x)$, the coefficient 3 is the vertical stretch factor.

In order to transform the graph of $y = f(x)$ into the graph of $\frac{1}{a}y = f(x)$, follow these steps:

1. Determine the vertical stretch factor.
2. Select appropriate ordered pairs located on the graph of $y = f(x)$.
3. Apply the stretch factor to the y-coordinate of each selected ordered pair on the graph of $y = f(x)$. Since the graph is stretched vertically about the x-axis by a factor of a, a point (x, y) on the graph of $y = f(x)$ will be transformed to the corresponding point (x, ay) on the graph of $\frac{1}{a}y = f(x)$, or $y = af(x)$, because the reciprocal of a is $\frac{1}{a}$.
4. Plot the corresponding ordered pairs on a grid, and use these ordered pairs to create the necessary graph.

Example

The graph of $y = x^2 - 4$ is shown.

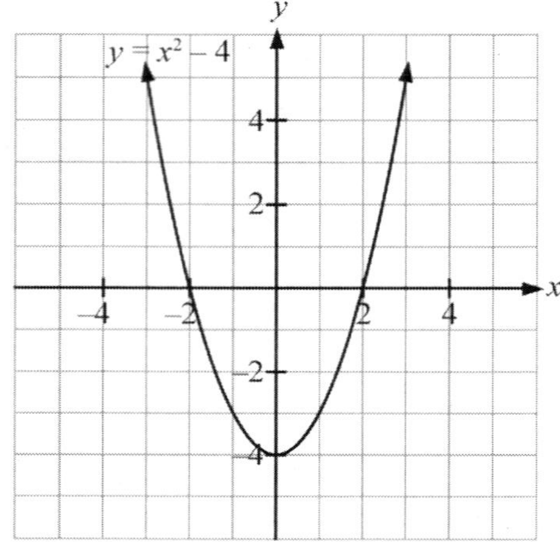

On the same axis, sketch the graph of the transformed function $y = \frac{1}{2}x^2 - 2$.

Solution

Step 1

Determine the stretch factor by rewriting the transformed equation of the function in the form $\frac{1}{a}y = f(x)$.

The equation $y = \frac{1}{2}x^2 - 2$ can be written as $y = \frac{1}{2}(x^2 - 4)$ by factoring out $\frac{1}{2}$ from the expression $\frac{1}{2}x^2 - 2$. The equation $y = \frac{1}{2}(x^2 - 4)$ is equivalent to $2y = x^2 - 4$.

Since the graph of $y = x^2 - 4$ is transformed to the graph of $2y = x^2 - 4$, y has been replaced by $2y$ in the equation $y = x^2 - 4$.

Thus, the graph of $y = x^2 - 4$ will be vertically stretched about the x-axis by a factor of $\frac{1}{2}$.

(The reciprocal of 2 is $\frac{1}{2}$.)

Step 2

Select appropriate ordered pairs located on the graph of $y = x^2 - 4$.

One option is to choose the ordered pairs $(-3, 5)$, $(-2, 0)$, $(0, -4)$, $(2, 0)$, and $(3, 5)$.

Step 3
Apply the stretch factor to the y-coordinate of each selected ordered pair on the graph of $y = x^2 - 4$.
Since the graph is stretched vertically about the x-axis by a factor of $\frac{1}{2}$, a point (x, y) on the graph of $y = x^2 - 4$ will be transformed to the corresponding point $\left(x, \frac{1}{2}y\right)$ on the graph of $2y = x^2 - 4$. (The reciprocal of 2 is $\frac{1}{2}$).

- Point $(-3, 5)$ becomes $\left(-3, \frac{1}{2} \times 5\right) = (-3, 2.5)$.
- Point $(-2, 0)$ becomes $\left(-2, \frac{1}{2} \times 0\right) = (-2, 0)$.
- Point $(0, -4)$ becomes $\left(0, \frac{1}{2} \times -4\right) = (0, -2)$.
- Point $(2, 0)$ becomes $\left(2, \frac{1}{2} \times 0\right) = (2, 0)$.
- Point $(3, 5)$ becomes $\left(3, \frac{1}{2} \times 5\right) = (3, 2.5)$.

Step 4
Plot the corresponding ordered pairs on the grid, and use these points to create the necessary graph.

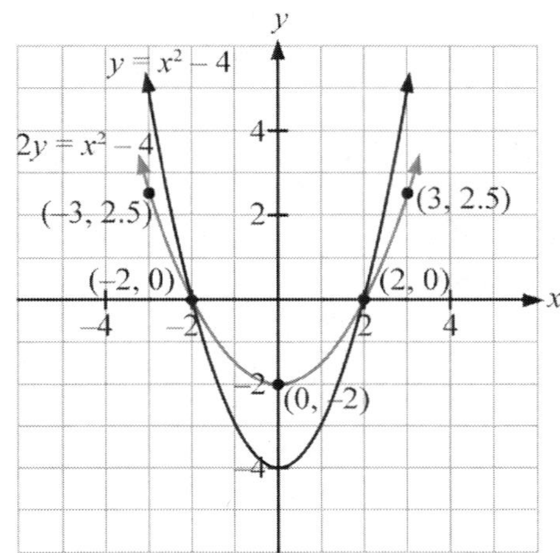

When a graph is stretched vertically about the x-axis by a factor of 2, the vertical distance from the x-axis to each transformed point is twice the original vertical distance.

Example
If the graph of $y = f(x)$ contains the point $(2, 5)$, the corresponding point on the graph of $y = 2f(x)$ is $(2, 10)$. The vertical distance from $(2, 10)$ to the x-axis is 10 units, which is twice the vertical distance from $(2, 5)$ to the x-axis.

When a graph is stretched vertically, the x-coordinate remains constant.

Horizontal Translations

A horizontal translation occurs when a graph is shifted left or right a certain number of units. When the graph of $y = f(x)$ is transformed into the graph of $y = f(x - h)$, the value of h causes a horizontal translation. When $h < 0$, the graph of $y = f(x)$ is translated to the left $|h|$ units, and when $h > 0$, the graph is translated to the right h units.

In general, to produce the equation $y = f(x - h)$ from $y = f(x)$, x is replaced with $x - h$.

Example

The graphs of $f(x) = x^2$ and $f(x) = (x - 2)^2$ are given.

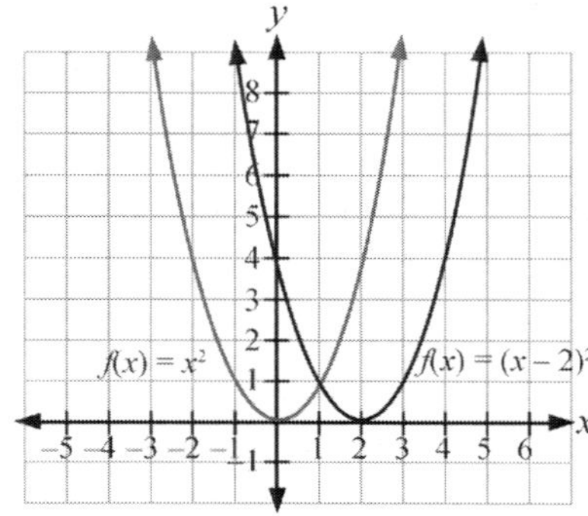

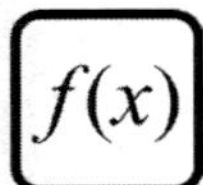

How can the graph of $f(x) = (x - 2)^2$ be obtained by translating the graph of $f(x) = x^2$?

Solution

The graph of $f(x) = (x - 2)^2$ is translated 2 units to the right of $f(x) = x^2$. This is because the equation $f(x) = (x - 2)^2$ is produced from $f(x) = x^2$ by replacing x with $(x - 2)$.

Example

The graphs of $f(x) = x^2$ and $f(x) = (x + 2)^2$ are given.

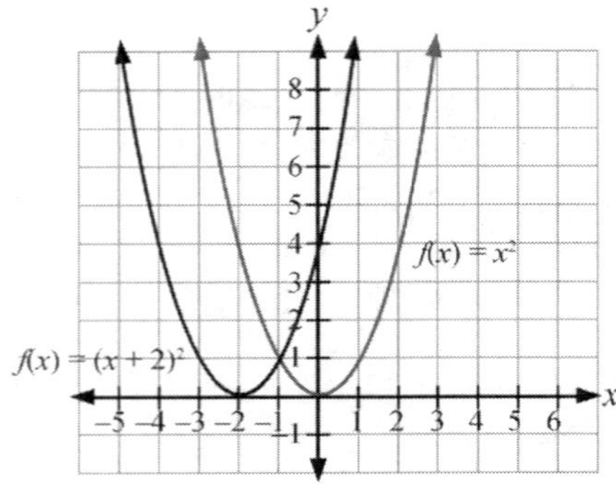

Describe how the graph of $f(x) = (x + 2)^2$ can be obtained by translating the graph of $f(x) = x^2$.

Solution

The graph of $f(x) = (x + 2)^2$ is translated 2 units to the left of $f(x) = x^2$. This is because the equation $f(x) = (x + 2)^2$ is produced from $f(x) = x^2$ by replacing x with $(x - (-2))$, or simply $(x + 2)$.

Example

Use a graphing calculator to graph $y = \sqrt{x}$ and $y = \sqrt{x + 6}$. Describe how the second graph can be obtained by translating the first graph.

Solution

The graphs of $y = \sqrt{x}$ and $y = \sqrt{x + 6}$ are shown using a window setting of x:[−10, 10, 1] and y:[−5, 5, 1].

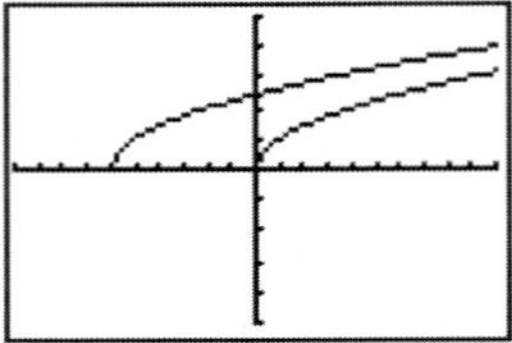

$y = \sqrt{x + 6}$ can be rewritten in the general form $y = f(x - h)$ as $y = \sqrt{x - (-6)}$. Since $h = -6$, the horizontal translation is 6 units to the left.

Thus, the graph of $y = \sqrt{x + 6}$ can be obtained from the graph of $y = \sqrt{x}$ by translating the graph of $y = \sqrt{x}$ 6 horizontal units to the left.

When a graph is translated horizontally, the y-coordinate of a given point will remain constant. Only the x-coordinate of that point changes. A coordinate point (x, y) on the graph of $y = f(x)$ will be transformed to the point $(x + h, y)$ on the graph of $y = f(x - h)$.
For example, if the coordinate point (−4, 1) is on the graph of $y = f(x)$, the corresponding point on the graph of $y = f(x + 2)$ is $(-4 - 2, 1) = (-6, 2)$. Remember that $y = f(x + 2)$ is equivalent to $y = f(x - (-2))$.

It follows that the x-intercepts are transformed from $(x, 0)$ to $(x + h, 0)$. There are no special rules for determining y-intercepts after a horizontal translation.

Example

Point (3, 9) is on the graph of $y = x^2$.
If $y = x^2$ is changed to $y = (x - 2)^2$, how will the point (3, 9) change?

Solution

When the graph of $y = x^2$ is transformed to the graph of $y = (x - 2)^2$, the graph of $y = x^2$ will be horizontally translated 2 units to the right. Thus, every point (x, y) on the graph of $y = x^2$ will be transformed to the point $(x + 2, y)$ on the graph of $y = (x - 2)^2$. Since the point (3, 9) is on the graph of $y = x^2$, the graph of $y = (x - 2)^2$ will contain the point $(3 + 2, 9) = (5, 9)$.

The point (3, 9) will be translated 2 units to the right.

Since the y-coordinates of $y = f(x - h)$ are the same as $y = f(x)$, the range of the translated graph does not change. The domain of the graph will be transformed h units to the right, from $m \le x \le n$ to $m + h \le x \le n + h$.

Example

The graph of $y = f(x)$ has a domain of $6 \le x \le 11$ and a range of $4 \le y \le 8$.

Determine the domain and range of $y = f(x + 6)$.

Solution

The domain of the graph of $y = f(x - h)$ will be $m + h \le x \le n + h$, where $m \le x \le n$ is the domain of $y = f(x)$. The value of h is –6 because $y = f(x + 6)$ is equivalent to $y = f(x - (-6))$. The domain of $y = f(x + 6)$ is $(6 - 6) \le x \le (11 - 6)$, or $0 \le x \le 5$.

Since the y-coordinates have not changed, the range of the translated graph will not change. The range is $4 \le y \le 8$.

VERTICAL TRANSLATIONS

A vertical translation occurs when a given graph is shifted down or up a certain number of units. When the graph of $y = f(x)$ is transformed to the graph of $y - k = f(x)$, the value of k causes a vertical translation. The equation $y - k = f(x)$ can also be written as $y = f(x) + k$. When $k < 0$, the graph of $y = f(x)$ is translated down $|k|$ units, and when $k > 0$, the graph is translated up k units.

For example, compare the graph of $f(x) = x^2$ with the graph of $f(x) = x^2 - 2$.

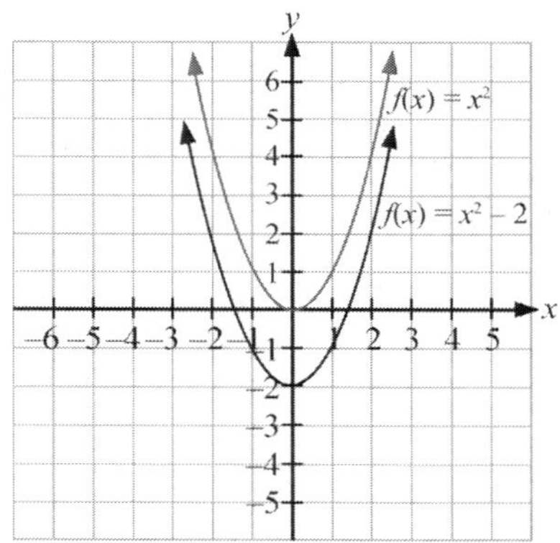

The graph of $f(x) = x^2 - 2$ is the graph of $f(x) = x^2$ translated 2 units down.

Next, compare the graph of $f(x) = x^2$ with the graph of $f(x) = x^2 + 2$.

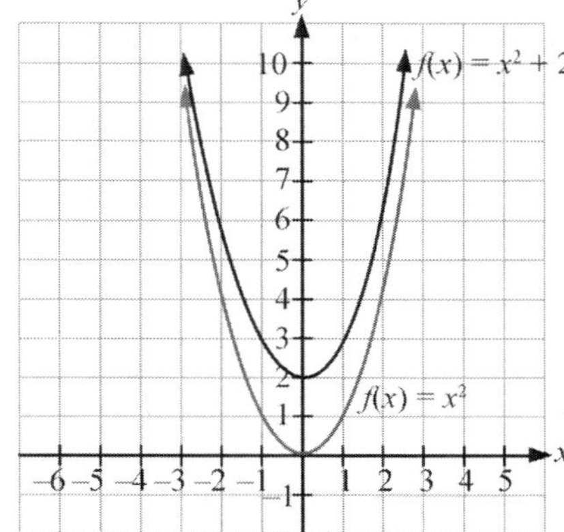

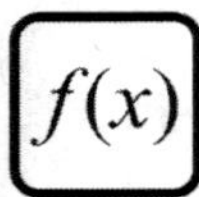

The graph of $f(x) = x^2 + 2$ is the graph of $f(x) = x^2$ translated 2 units up.

To produce the equation $f(x) = x^2 - 2$ from $f(x) = x^2$, follow these steps:

1. Write $f(x) = x^2$ as $y = x^2$.
2. Since the graph of $y = x^2$ is translated 2 units down, replace y with $y + 2$. Remember that $y + 2$ is equivalent to $y - (-2)$. $y + 2 = x^2$
3. Solve for y. $y = x^2 - 2$
4. Write $y = x^2 - 2$ in function notation. $f(x) = x^2 - 2$

Similarly, to produce the equation $f(x) = x^2 + 2$ from $f(x) = x^2$, follow these steps:

1. Write $f(x) = x^2$ as $y = x^2$.
2. Since the graph of $y = x^2$ is translated 2 units up, replace y with $y - 2$. Remember that $y - 2$ is equivalent to $y - (+2)$. $y - 2 = x^2$
3. Solve for y. $y = x^2 + 2$
4. Write $y = x^2 + 2$ in function notation. $f(x) = x^2 + 2$

In general, to produce the equation $y - k = f(x)$ from $y = f(x)$, replace y with $y - k$.

Example

Use a graphing calculator to graph $y = \sqrt{x}$ and $y = \sqrt{x} + 5$. Describe how the second graph can be obtained by translating the first graph.

Solution

The graphs of $y = \sqrt{x}$ and $y = \sqrt{x} + 5$ are shown using a window setting of x:[−5, 5, 1] and y:[−2, 10, 1].

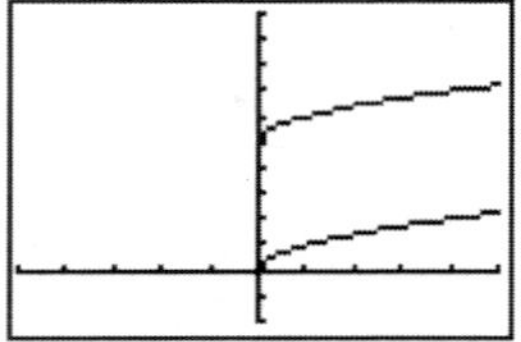

Recall that the function $y = \sqrt{x} + 5$ can be written in the general form, $y - k = f(x)$, as $y - 5 = \sqrt{x}$. Notice that $k = 5$ so the vertical translation is 5 units up. In the form $y = \sqrt{x} + 5$, the constant 5 is used to describe the vertical translation. Thus, the graph of $y = \sqrt{x} + 5$ can be obtained from the graph of $y = \sqrt{x}$ by translating the graph of $y = \sqrt{x}$ 5 vertical units up.

When a graph is translated vertically, the x-coordinate of a given point remains constant, but the y-coordinate of that point will change. A coordinate point (x, y) on the graph of $y = f(x)$ will be transformed to the point $(x, y + k)$ on the graph of $y - k = f(x)$. For example, if the coordinate point $(3, -1)$ is on the graph of $y = f(x)$, then the corresponding point on the graph of $y + 4 = f(x)$ is $(3, -1 - 4) = (3, -5)$. Since $y + 4 = f(x)$ is equivalent to $y - (-4) = f(x)$, $k = -4$.

It follows that the y-intercepts are transformed from $(0, y)$ to $(0, y + k)$. There are no special rules for determining x-intercepts after a vertical translation.

Example

The point (3, 9) is on the graph of $y = x^2$. If $y = x^2$ is changed to $y - 2 = x^2$, how will the point (3, 9) change?

Solution

When the graph of $y = x^2$ is transformed to the graph of $y - 2 = x^2$ (or $y = x^2 + 2$), the graph of $y = x^2$ will be translated 2 units up. Thus, every point (x, y) on the graph of $y = x^2$ will be transformed to the point $(x, y + 2)$ on the graph of $y - 2 = x^2$. Since (3, 9) is on the graph of $y = x^2$, the graph of $y - 2 = x^2$ will contain the point $(3, 9 + 2) = (3, 11)$.

The point (3, 9) will be translated vertically 2 units up.

Since the x-coordinates of $y - k = f(x)$ are the same as $y = f(x)$, the domain of the translated graph will not change. The range of the graph will be transformed from $s \le y \le t$ to $s + k \le y \le t + k$.

Example

The graph of $y = f(x)$ has a domain of $6 \le x \le 11$ and a range of $4 \le y \le 8$.

Determine the domain and range of $y - 3 = f(x)$.

Solution

Since the x-coordinates have not changed, the domain of the translated graph will not have changed. The domain is $6 \le x \le 11$.

The range of the graph $y - k = f(x)$ will be $s + k \le y \le t + k$, where $s \le y \le t$ is the range of $y = f(x)$. The range of $y - 3 = f(x)$ is $(4 + 3) \le y \le (8 + 3)$, or $7 \le y \le 11$.

The Graph of $y = f(|x|)$

When the function $y = f(x)$ is transformed into the function $y = f(|x|)$, the main consequence of the transformation occurs initially to the x-coordinates. All x-coordinates are made positive or zero before the function values are determined, since the absolute value operator is applied to x.

Example

A partial table is given.

x	$f(x)$	$\|x\|$	$f(\|x\|)$
–3	10		
–2	5		
–1	3		
0	0		
1	–3		
2	–5		
3	–10		

Given the function values for $y = f(x)$, complete the table of values for the transformation $y = f(|x|)$, describe the relation between the points whose x-coordinates are additive inverses after the transformation has been applied, and identify the coordinates of all invariant points.

Solution

Step 1

Complete the table of values for the transformation $y = f(|x|)$.

Since $|-3| = 3$, then $f(|-3|) = f(3)$. The corresponding value of $f(3)$ is -10. Similarly, $|-2| = 2$, so $f(|-2|) = f(2)$. The value of $f(2)$ is -5.

Complete the table by doing the same for all the other values of x.

x	$f(x)$	$\|x\|$	$f(\|x\|)$
–3	10	3	–10
–2	5	2	–5
–1	3	1	–3
0	0	0	0
1	–3	1	–3
2	–5	2	–5
3	–10	3	–10

Step 2

Describe the relation between the points whose x-coordinates are additive inverses after the transformation.

The points whose x-coordinates are additive inverses, such as the points with x-coordinates of –3 and 3 or –2 and 2, will have the same y-coordinate. Graphically, this means that for any point (a, b) on the graph of $y = f(x)$, where $a > 0$, the point $(-a, b)$ will be on the graph of $y = f(|x|)$. The point $(-a, b)$ is a reflection of the point (a, b) in the y-axis.

Step 3

Identify the coordinates of all invariant points.

The points (0, 0), (1, –3), (2, –5), and (3, –10) are invariant because they are unchanged after the transformation.

When $y = f(x)$ is transformed, the following effects of the transformation $y = f(|x|)$ are noted:

- For all $x \geq 0$, the graph of $y = f(|x|)$ will be the graph of $f(x)$.
- For all $x < 0$, the graph of $y = f(|x|)$ will be a mirror image of the part of the graph to the right of the y-axis.
- Since the invariant points remain in the same location after the transformation, they are all points with x-coordinates such that $x \geq 0$.

To draw or sketch the graph of $y = f(|x|)$, first sketch the graph of $y = f(x)$ for all $x \geq 0$. Then, draw or sketch in the reflection of the first part about the y-axis.

Example

Sketch the graph of $y = f(|x|)$ for the function $f(x) = (x - 3)^2$, and verify the result with a graphing calculator.

Solution

Step 1

Sketch the graph of $f(x) = (x - 3)^2$.

The graph of $f(x) = (x - 3)^2$ is a parabola that opens upward with its vertex at (3, 0) and y-intercept of 9.

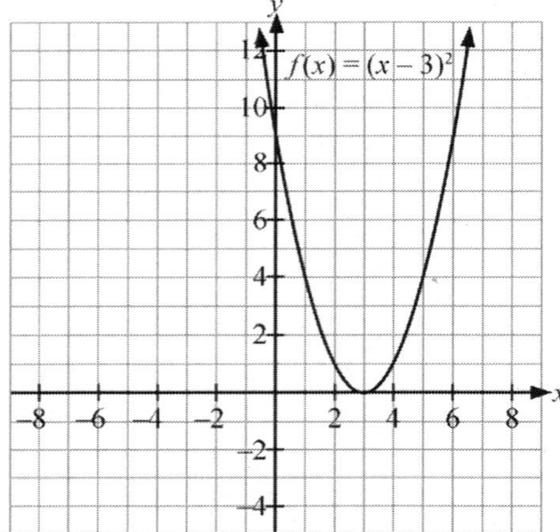

Step 2

Sketch the graph of $y = f(|x|)$.

Sketch the y-intercept and the part of the parabola to the right of the y-axis.

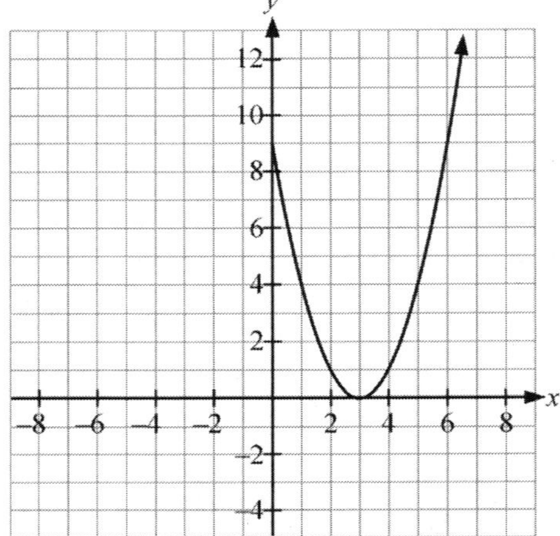

Reflect the part of the graph drawn about the y-axis to complete the graph of $y = f(|x|)$.

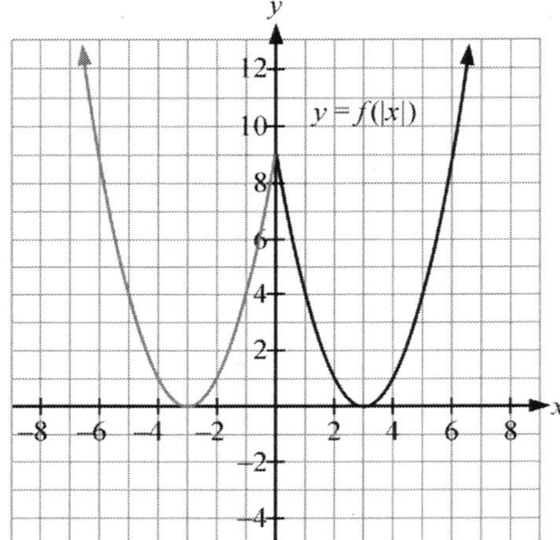

Step 3

Verify with a graphing calculator.

For $f(x) = (x - 3)^2$, the transformation $f(|x|) = (|x| - 3)^2$.

Using a TI-83 calculator, input $Y_1 = (\text{abs}(X) - 3)^2$ on an appropriate viewing window such as x:−8, 8, 1 and y:−2, 30, 5.

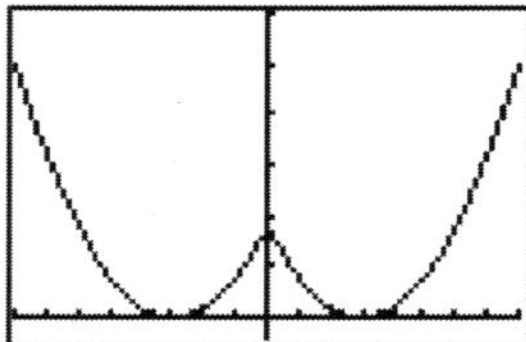

The domain and range of $y = f(|x|)$ can be different from the domain of $y = f(x)$.

Example

Sketch the graph of $y = f(|x|)$, and identify the domain for both $f(x)$ and $f(|x|)$ for the function $f(x) = \log x$.

Solution

Step 1

Sketch the graph of $f(x) = \log x$.

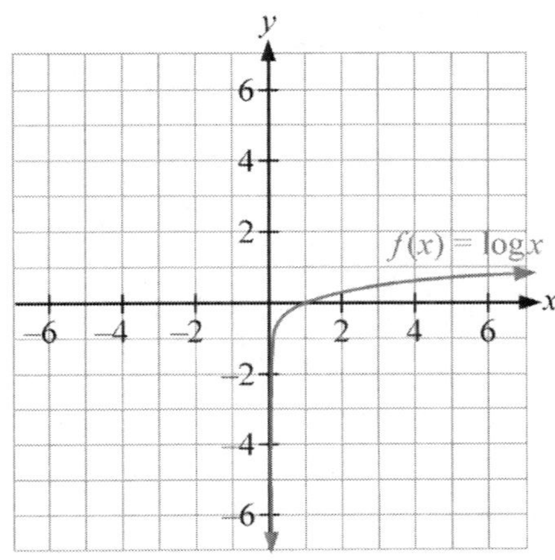

Step 2

Sketch the graph of $f(|x|) = \log |x|$ by adding the reflection of the graph of $f(x) = \log x$ about the y-axis.

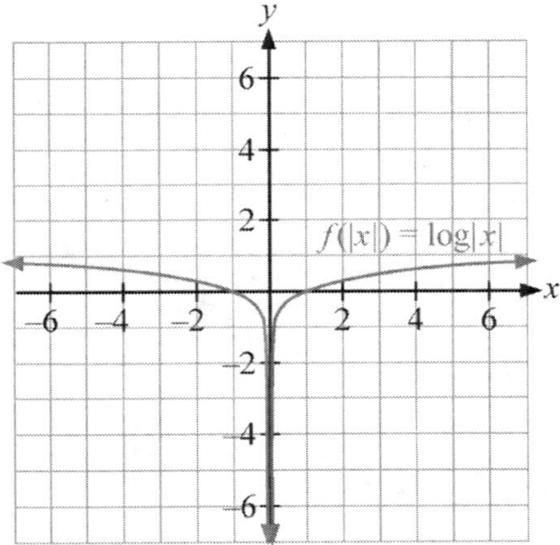

Step 3

Identify the domains.

The domain of $f(x) = \log x$ is $x > 0$.

The domain of $f(|x|) = \log |x|$ is $x > 0$ or $x < 0$, which is more simply written as $x \neq 0$.

Example

Sketch the graph of $y = f(|x|)$, and identify the domain for both $f(x)$ and $f(|x|)$ for the function $f(x) = \dfrac{1}{x-3}$.

Solution

Step 1

Sketch the graph of $f(x) = \dfrac{1}{x-3}$, for $x \geq 0$.

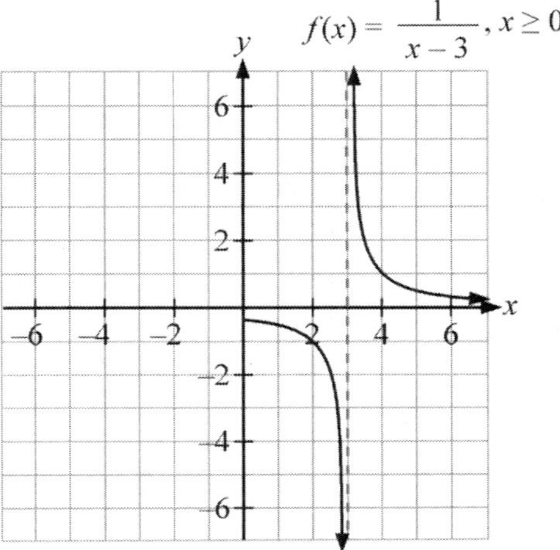

Step 2

Sketch the graph of $f(|x|) = \dfrac{1}{|x| - 3}$ by adding the reflection of the graph in step 1 about the y-axis.

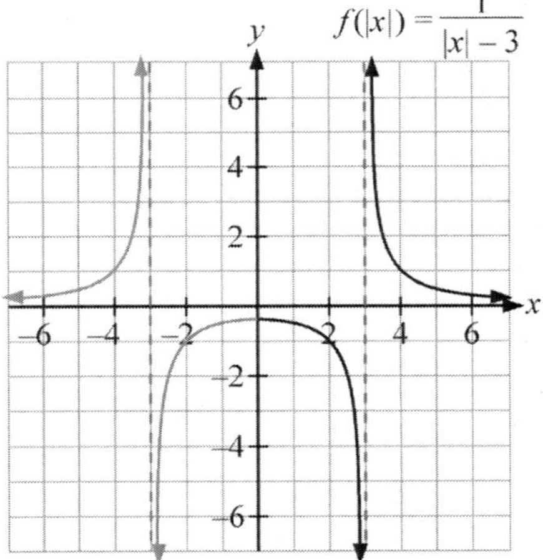

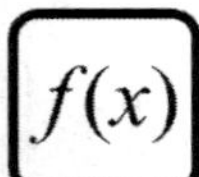

Step 3
Identify the domains.

The domain of $f(x) = \dfrac{1}{x-3}$ is $x \neq 3$, and the domain of $f(|x|) = \dfrac{1}{|x| - 3}$ is $x \neq \pm 3$.

Example

The graph of function $y = g(x)$ is given.

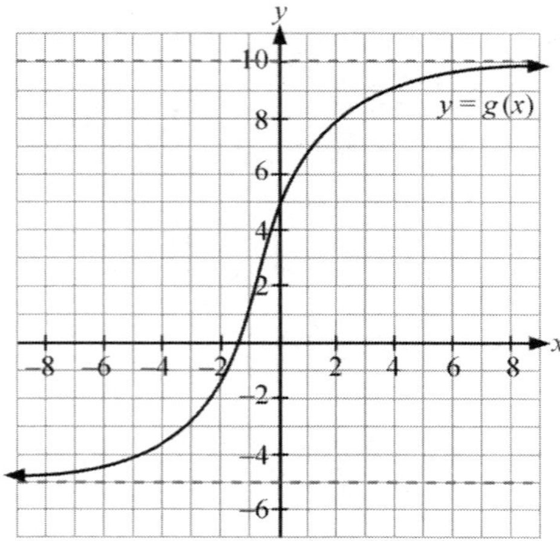

Sketch the graph of the transformation $y = g(|x|)$, and identify the range for both $y = g(x)$ and $y = g(|x|)$.

Solution

Step 1
Sketch the graph of $g(x)$ for $x \geq 0$.

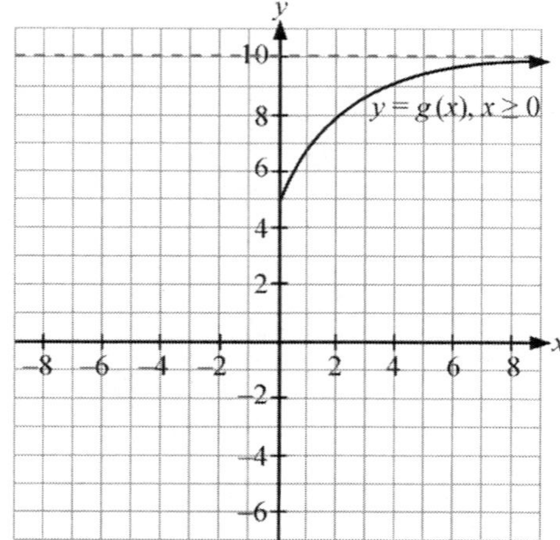

Step 2
Sketch the graph of $g(|x|)$ by adding the reflection of the graph in step 1 about the y-axis.

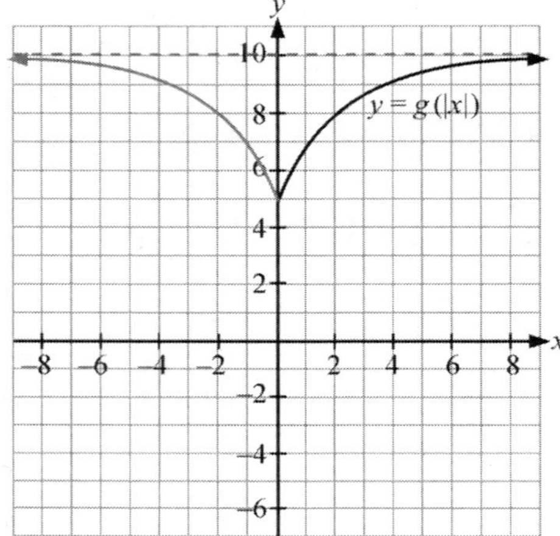

Step 3
Identify the ranges.
The range of $g(x)$ is $-5 < y < 10$, as $g(x)$ has horizontal asymptotes of $y = -5$ and $y = 10$.
The range of $g(|x|)$ is $5 \leq y < 10$.

The following conclusions can be drawn from the transformation of $y = f(|x|)$:

- The domain of $y = f(|x|)$ can be different from the domain of $y = f(x)$.
- If $f(x)$ has a vertical asymptote at $x = a$, $a > 0$, then $y = f(|x|)$ will have vertical asymptotes at both $x = a$ and $x = -a$.
- The range of $y = f(|x|)$ will be equal to the range of $y = f(x)$ on the domain of $x \geq 0$.

Stretches about Lines Parallel to the x- and y-Axes

A graph can be stretched vertically about any line that is parallel to the x-axis—this includes any horizontal line other than the x-axis. Likewise, a graph can be stretched horizontally about any line that is parallel to the y-axis—this includes any vertical line other than the y-axis.

$f(x)$

Vertical Stretches about Any Horizontal Line

If the vertical stretch factor is c, where $c \in \mathrm{N}$, then the vertical distance from the horizontal line to a translated point is c times the original vertical distance from the original point to the horizontal line.

Example

The graph of $y = f(x)$ contains the point (2, 5).

If the graph of $y = f(x)$ is stretched vertically by a factor of 2 about the line $y = 3$, determine the new point that is transformed from the original point (2, 5).

Solution

The vertical distance from the line $y = 3$ to the point (2, 5) is 2 units. Since the stretch factor is 2, the vertical distance from the transformed point to the line $y = 3$ is now 4 units ($2 \times 2 = 4$). The new point (2, 7) is 4 vertical units from the line $y = 3$.

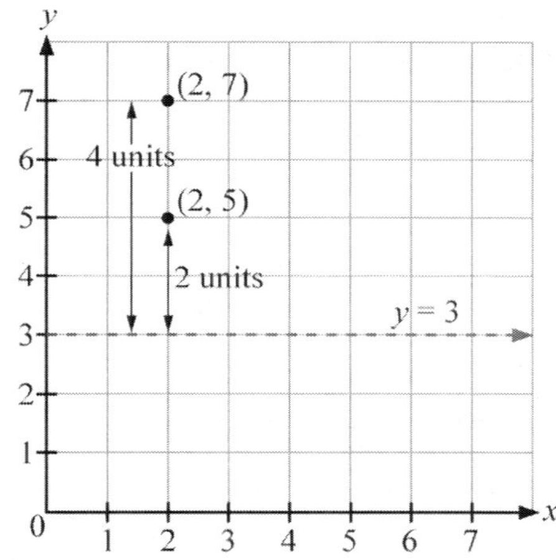

Therefore, the original point (2, 5) is transformed to become the new point (2, 7).

Example

The graph of $y = x^2$ is shown.

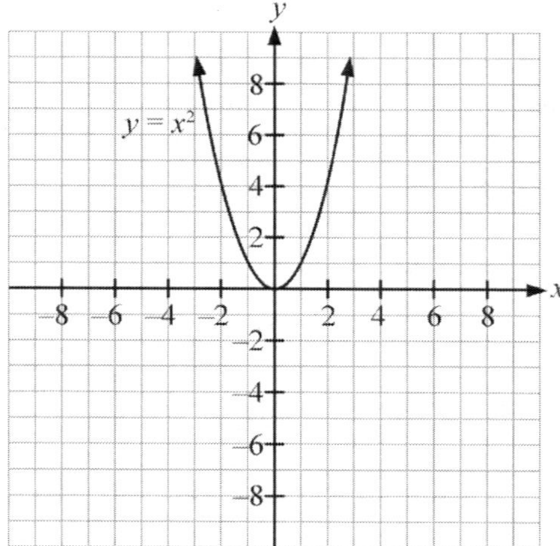

Sketch the transformed function if the graph of $y = x^2$ is stretched vertically by a factor of 3 about the line $y = 2$.

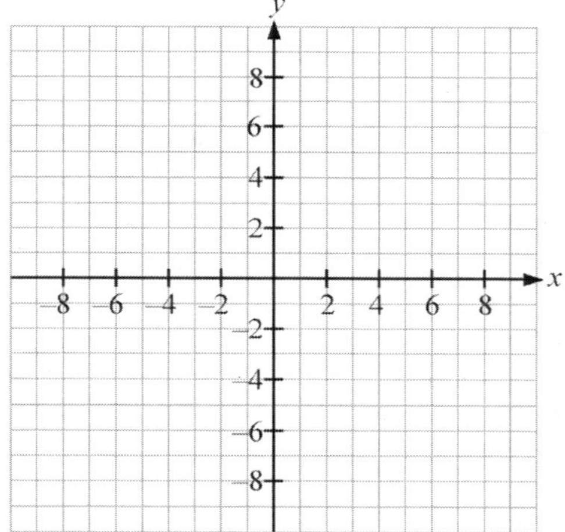

Solution

Step 1

Select particular ordered pairs on the graph of $y = x^2$, and determine the number of vertical units that each ordered pair is from the line $y = 2$.

- (−2, 4) is 2 vertical units above the line $y = 2$.
- (−1, 1) is 1 vertical unit below the line $y = 2$.
- (0, 0) is 2 vertical units below the line $y = 2$.
- (1, 1) is 1 vertical unit below the line $y = 2$.
- (2, 4) is 2 vertical units above the line $y = 2$.

Step 2
Determine the number of vertical units that each transformed ordered pair is from the line $y = 2$.
Since the given graph is stretched vertically by a factor of 3 about the line $y = 2$, each of the derived vertical units outlined in step1 must be multiplied by 3.

- (−2, 4) must be 2 × 3 = 6 vertical units above the line $y = 2$.
- (−1, 1) must be 1 × 3 = 3 vertical units below the line $y = 2$.
- (0, 0) must be 2 × 3 = 6 vertical units below the line $y = 2$.
- (1, 1) must be 1 × 3 = 3 vertical units below the line $y = 2$.
- (2, 4) must be 2 × 3 = 6 vertical units above the line $y = 2$.

Notice that every point on the transformed function is 3 times as far as the original point from the line $y = 2$. If the point is below the line $y = 2$, the transformed point is 3 times as far away as the original point in the negative direction.

Step 3
Determine the corresponding transformed ordered pair for each selected ordered pair on the graph of $y = x^2$.

- (−2, 4) is transformed to (−2, 2 + 6) = (−2, 8).
- (−1, 1) is transformed to (−1, 2 − 3) = (−1, −1).
- (0, 0) is transformed to (0, 2 − 6) = (0, −4).
- (1, 1) is transformed to (1, 2 − 3) = (1, −1).
- (2, 4) is transformed to (2, 2 + 6) = (2, 8).

Step 4
Plot the transformed ordered pairs, and use these ordered pairs as a basis for creating the graph of the transformed function.

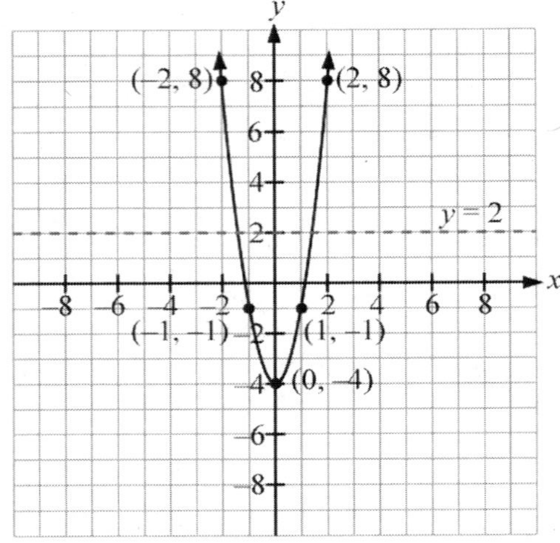

Horizontal Stretches about Any Vertical Line

If the horizontal stretch factor is c, where $c \in \mathrm{N}$, then the horizontal distance from the vertical line to a translated point is c times the original horizontal distance from the original point to the vertical line.

Example

The graph of $y = f(x)$ contains the point (3, 1).

If the graph of $y = f(x)$ is stretched horizontally by a factor of 3 about the line $x = 1$, determine the new point that is transformed from the original point (3, 1).

Solution

The horizontal distance from the line $x = 1$ to the point (3, 1) is 2 units. Since the stretch factor is 3, the horizontal distance from a transformed point to the line $x = 1$ is now 6 units ($2 \times 3 = 6$). The transformed point (7, 1) is 6 horizontal units from the line $x = 1$.

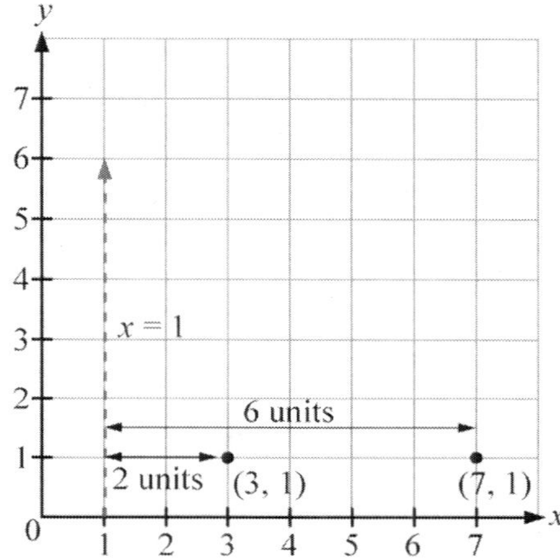

Therefore, the original point (3, 1) is transformed to become the new point (7, 1).

Example

The graph of $y = x^2$ is shown.

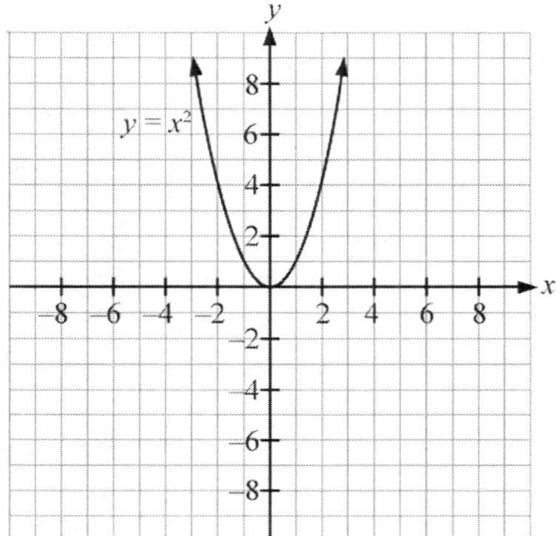

Sketch the transformed function if the graph of $y = x^2$ is stretched horizontally by a factor of 3 about the line $x = 2$.

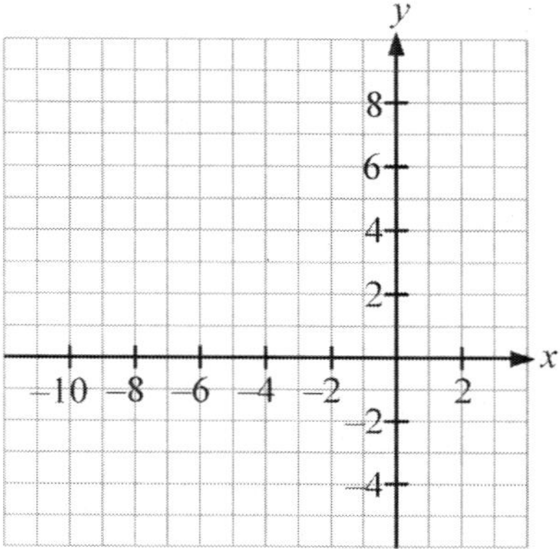

Solution

Step 1

Select particular ordered pairs on the graph of $y = x^2$, and determine the number of horizontal units that each ordered pair is from the line $x = 2$.

- (−2, 4) is 4 horizontal units left of the line $x = 2$.
- (−1, 1) is 3 horizontal units left of the line $x = 2$.
- (0, 0) is 2 horizontal units left of the line $x = 2$.
- (1, 1) is 1 horizontal unit left of the line $x = 2$.
- (2, 4) is 0 horizontal units from the line $x = 2$.

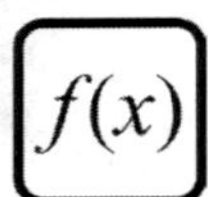

Step 2
Determine the number of horizontal units that each transformed ordered pair is from the line $x = 2$.
Since the given graph is stretched horizontally by a factor of 3 about the line $x = 2$, each of the derived horizontal units must be multiplied by 3.

- (−2, 4) must be 4 × 3 = 12 horizontal units left of the line $x = 2$.
- (−1, 1) must be 3 × 3 = 9 horizontal units left of the line $x = 2$.
- (0, 0) must be 2 × 3 = 6 horizontal units left of the line $x = 2$.
- (1, 1) must be 1 × 3 = 3 horizontal units left of the line $x = 2$.
- (2, 4) must be 0 × 3 = 0 horizontal units from the line $x = 2$.

Notice that every point on the transformed function is 3 times as far as the original point from the line $x = 2$. If the point is to the left of the line $x = 2$, the transformed point is 3 times as far away as the original point in the negative direction.

Step 3
Determine the corresponding transformed ordered pair for each selected ordered pair on the graph of $y = x^2$.

- (−2, 4) is transformed to (2 − 12, 4) = (−10, 4).
- (−1, 1) is transformed to (2 − 9, 1) = (−7, 1).
- (0, 0) is transformed to (2 − 6, 0) = (−4, 0).
- (1, 1) is transformed to (2 − 3, 1) = (−1, 1).
- (2, 4) is transformed to (2 − 0, 4) = (2, 4).

Note that (2, 4) is an invariant point.

Step 4
Plot the transformed ordered pairs, and then use these ordered pairs as a basis for creating the graph of the transformed function.

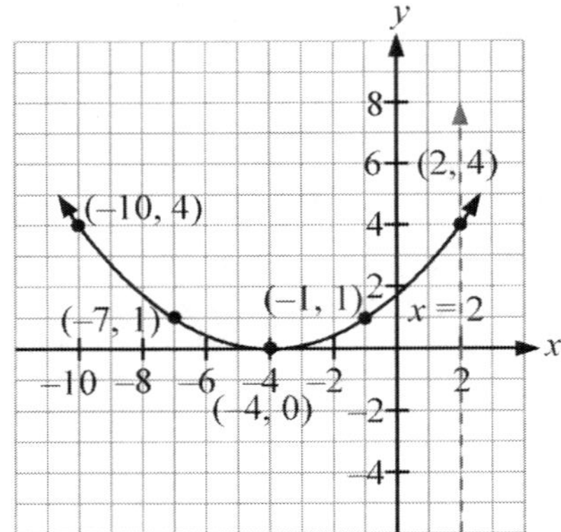

PC.2.B Perform operations including composition on functions, find inverses, and describe these procedures and results verbally, numerically, symbolically, and graphically.

Sketching the Inverse Graph of a Function

A function is a set of ordered pairs in which every element of the domain is paired with exactly one element of the range.

The inverse of a function is the relation that exists from interchanging the values in the ordered pairs of the function. The inverse of a function must generate every original domain value for every original range value as an input. The domain of the inverse relation is the range of the original function. The range of the inverse relation is the domain of the original function.

When sketching the inverse graph of a function, switch the coordinates of the points found on the graph of the original function around.
The x-coordinates now become the y-coordinates and the y-coordinates become the x-coordinates. Plot the new set of points, and draw a line through them.

It can be shown that for any relation, the graph of the relation and the graph of its inverse are reflections in the line $y = x$.

Example

The graph of a function is given.

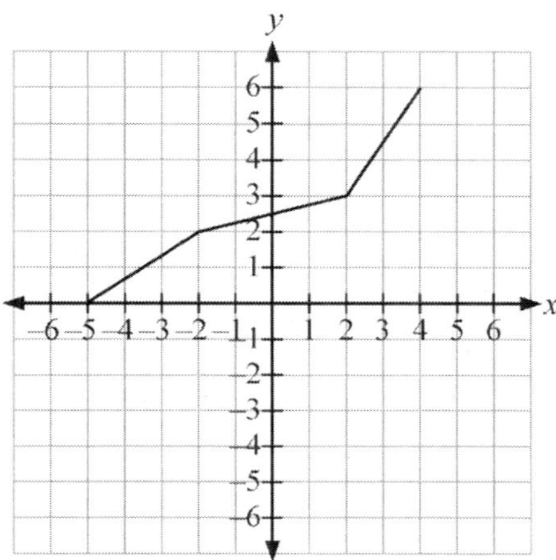

Sketch the graph of the inverse.

Solution

Step 1

Determine the ordered pairs of the inverse.

Some ordered pairs of points that are on the graph of the given function are (−5, 0), (−2, 2), (2, 3), and (4, 6).

Since the inverse of this function has the domain and range values interchanged, some ordered pairs of points on the inverse are (0, −5), (2, −2), (3, 2), and (6, 4).

Step 2

Plot and connect these points to get the graph of the inverse.

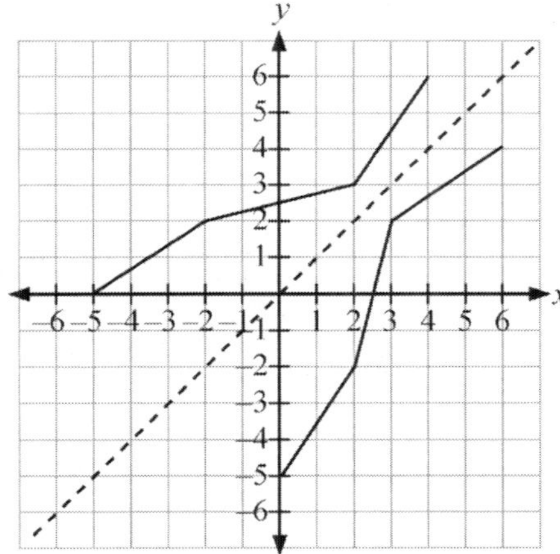

Notice that the inverse is a reflection of the original function in the line $y = x$ (drawn with the dotted line).

Apply the vertical line test to determine if the inverse of the original function is itself a function. If a vertical line can be drawn so that it touches the graph in more than one place, then the relation is not a function.

Example

Determine if the inverse of $y = x^2$ is a function.

Solution

Step 1

Determine the coordinates of the points on the inverse graph.

Some points on the graph of $y = x^2$ are (−2, 4), (−1, 1), (0, 0), (1, 1), and (2, 4).

The points on the inverse graph will be (4, −2), (1, −1), (0, 0), (1, 1), and (4, 2).

Step 2

Sketch the original graph and the inverse graph.

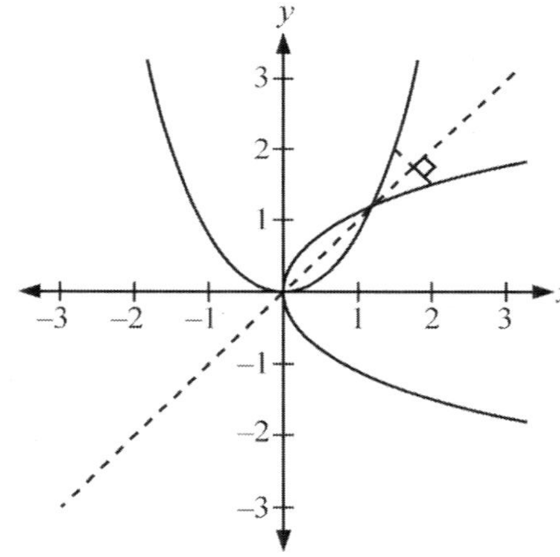

The graphs are reflections in the line $y = x$ so that any point on the original graph (P) has an image point on the graph of the inverse (P′).

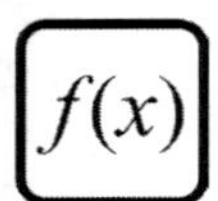

Step 3

Determine if the inverse of $y = x^2$ is a function.
Apply the vertical line test to its graph.
The graph of the inverse does not pass the vertical line test.

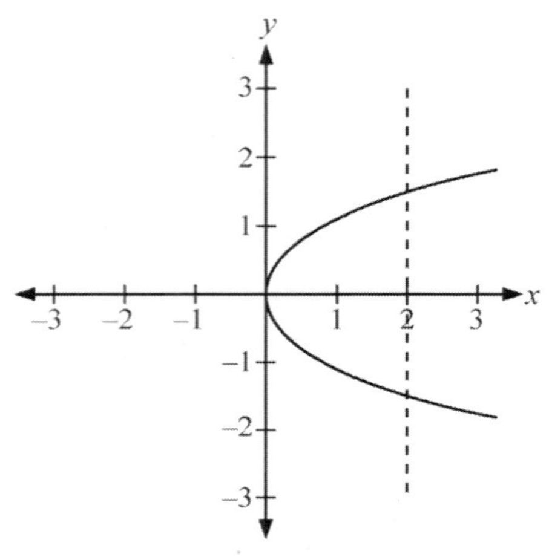

Using a Graphing Calculator to Graph the Inverse of a Function

A TI-83 graphing calculator can be used to graph a function and its inverse. For example, you can graph the function $2x^2 - 4x + 1$ and its inverse by following these steps:

1. Press Y = , enter the equation $2x^2 - 4x + 1$, and press GRAPH . This image will appear on the calculator screen.

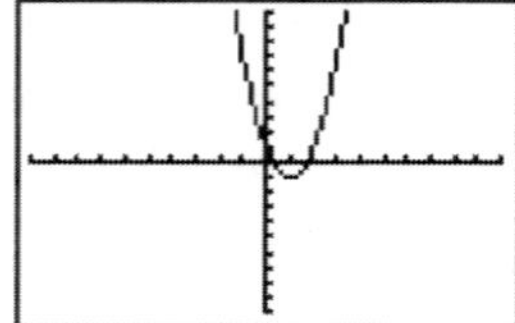

2. Press 2nd PRGM and select 8:DrawInv from the menu.

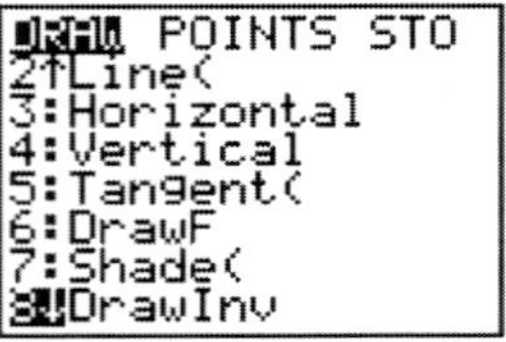

3. Press VARS ▷ (Y-VARS is highlighted) ENTER , select 1:Y_1 from the menu, and press ENTER . These graphs will result.

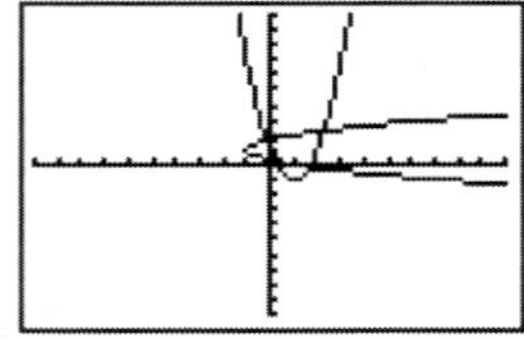

If only the graph of the inverse is required, remove the highlighting from the equal sign of the function in the Y = menu. To do this, place the cursor on the = sign, and press ENTER .

To clear all the graphs from the calculator screen, press 2nd PRGM select 1:ClrDraw from the menu and ENTER ENTER .

Determining the Equation of the Inverse of a Function Algebraically

A **function** is a set of ordered pairs in which every element of the domain is paired with exactly one element of the range. The **inverse** of a function is the relation that exists from interchanging the values in the ordered pairs of the function.
The function notation for the inverse of a function is $f^{-1}(x)$, and it is read "*f* inverse."

Note that −1 is not an exponent—it is just part of the symbol. The $f^{-1}(x)$ form can only be used when the inverse is a function.

Follow these steps when determining the equation of the inverse of a function:

1. Replace $f(x)$ with y.
2. Interchange x and y.
3. Resolve for y.
4. Replace y with $f^{-1}(x)$ if the inverse of the original function is also a function.

Example

Write the inverse of $f(x) = \frac{1}{3}x + 4$.

Solution

Step 1
Replace $f(x)$ with y.

$y = \frac{1}{3}x + 4$

Step 2
Interchange x and y.

$x = \frac{1}{3}y + 4$

Step 3
Solve for y.

$$\begin{aligned} x &= \frac{1}{3}y + 4 \\ 3x &= y + 12 \\ 3x - 12 &= y \\ y &= 3x - 12 \end{aligned}$$

Step 4
Replace y with $f^{-1}(x)$.
Since $y = 3x - 12$ is a linear function, it can be written using function notation.

$f^{-1}(x) = 3x - 12$

Example

Write the inverse of $f(x) = -(x+2)^2$.

Solution

Step 1
Replace $f(x)$ with y.

$$\begin{aligned} f(x) &= -(x+2)^2 \\ y &= -(x+2)^2 \end{aligned}$$

Step 2
Interchange x and y.

$x = -(y+2)^2$

Step 3
Resolve for y.

$$\begin{aligned} x &= -(y+2)^2 \\ -x &= (y+2)^2 \\ \pm\sqrt{-x} &= y + 2 \\ -2 \pm \sqrt{-x} &= y \\ y &= -2 \pm \sqrt{-x} \end{aligned}$$

Since the inverse of $f(x)$ is not a function, the equation of the inverse remains as $y = -2 \pm \sqrt{-x}$.

The inverses of other functions are determined using the same procedures as for linear and quadratic functions. The important thing is that the domain and range are exactly interchanged between any function or relation and its inverse.

Example

Determine the inverse of $f(x) = \frac{3}{x-4}$, writing the inverse in function notation if appropriate.

Solution

Step 1
Replace $f(x)$ with y.

$$\begin{aligned} f(x) &= \frac{3}{x-4} \\ y &= \frac{3}{x-4} \end{aligned}$$

Step 2
Interchange x and y.

$x = \frac{3}{y-4}$

Step 3
Resolve for y.

$$\begin{aligned} (y-4)x &= 3 \\ y - 4 &= \frac{3}{x} \\ y &= \frac{3}{x} + 4 \end{aligned}$$

$y = \frac{3}{x} + 4$ or $y = \frac{3+4x}{x}$

Since the inverse is a function, it can be written as $f^{-1}(x) = \frac{3}{x} + 4$ or $f^{-1}(x) = \frac{3+4x}{x}$.

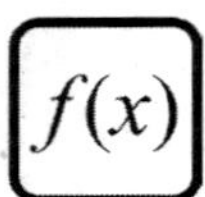

Example

Write the inverse of $f(x) = \sqrt{x-2}$, writing the inverse in function notation if appropriate.

Solution

Step 1

Replace $f(x)$ with y.

$$f(x) = \sqrt{x-2}$$
$$y = \sqrt{x-2}$$

Step 2

Interchange x and y.

$$x = \sqrt{y-2}$$

Step 3

Resolve for y.

$$x = \sqrt{y-2}$$
$$x^2 = y-2$$
$$x^2 + 2 = y$$
$$y = x^2 + 2$$

In the original function $f(x) = \sqrt{x-2}$, the range is $y \geq 0$.

Thus, the domain of the inverse, $y = x^2 + 2$, must be $x \geq 0$.

Since the inverse is a function, it can be written as $f^{-1}(x) = x^2 + 2,\ x \geq 0$.

Combining Functions Using Arithmetic Operations

Functions are often created by applying the four basic operations to combine other simpler functions. Operations with functions are performed according to the rules and operations for polynomial, rational, and other representations of real numbers. Non-permissible values must be considered when working with rational functions and should be determined for the original function before any simplification occurs.

The non-permissible values are retained for the function after the common factors have been removed.

Example

It is given that $g(x) = x^2 - x - 12$ and $h(x) = x + 3$.

Determine $f(x)$ if $f(x) = g(x) + h(x)$.

Solution

Step 1

Substitute $x^2 - x - 12$ for $g(x)$ and $x + 3$ for $h(x)$ into the equation $f(x) = g(x) + h(x)$.

$$f(x) = (x^2 - x - 12) + (x + 3)$$

Step 2

Combine like terms and simplify.

$$\begin{aligned} f(x) &= (x^2 - x - 12) + (x + 3) \\ &= x^2 - x - 12 + x + 3 \\ &= x^2 - 9 \end{aligned}$$

Determine $f(x)$ if $f(x) = g(x) - h(x)$.

Solution

Step 1

Substitute $x^2 - x - 12$ for $g(x)$ and $x + 3$ for $h(x)$ into the equation $f(x) = g(x) - h(x)$.

$$f(x) = (x^2 - x - 12) - (x + 3)$$

Step 2

Combine like terms and simplify.

$$\begin{aligned} f(x) &= (x^2 - x - 12) - (x + 3) \\ &= x^2 - x - 12 - x - 3 \\ &= x^2 - 2x - 15 \end{aligned}$$

Determine $f(x)$ if $f(x) = g(x) \cdot h(x)$.

Solution

Step 1
Substitute $x^2 - x - 12$ for $g(x)$ and $x + 3$ for $h(x)$ into the equation $f(x) = g(x) \cdot h(x)$.

$f(x) = (x^2 - x - 12)(x + 3)$

Step 2
Expand using the distributive property and then simplify by combining like terms.

$$\begin{aligned} f(x) &= (x^2 - x - 12)(x + 3) \\ &= x^3 + 3x^2 - x^2 - 3x - 12x - 36 \\ &= x^3 + 2x^2 - 15x - 36 \end{aligned}$$

Determine $f(x)$ if $f(x) = \dfrac{g(x)}{h(x)}$.

Solution

Step 1
Substitute $x^2 - x - 12$ for $g(x)$ and $x + 3$ for $h(x)$ in the equation $f(x) = \dfrac{g(x)}{h(x)}$.

$$f(x) = \frac{x^2 - x - 12}{x + 3}$$

Step 2
Factor the numerator and denominator, and reduce.

$$\begin{aligned} f(x) &= \frac{x^2 - x - 12}{x + 3} \\ &= \frac{(x - 4)(x + 3)}{x + 3} \\ &= x - 4 \end{aligned}$$

State the non-permissible values.

$$\begin{aligned} x + 3 &\neq 0 \\ x &\neq -3 \end{aligned}$$

The non-permissible value of x is -3.

Compositions of Two Functions

The composition of two functions involves using the result of one function as the input of another. Instead of calculating each function separately, the composition of two functions is written as a single function. A composite function is represented with the notation $g(f(x))$, or $g \circ f$. The notation $g(f(x))$ (or $g \circ f$) means that every x-variable in $g(x)$ is replaced with the function $f(x)$.

The notation $g(f(x))$ (or $g \circ f$) is read as "g of f of x."

Example

$f(x) = 2x + 1$ and $g(x) = x^2 - 3$

Determine $g(f(x))$.

Solution

Step 1
Replace each variable x in $g(x)$ with the function $f(x)$.

$$\begin{aligned} g(x) &= x^2 - 3 \\ g(f(x)) &= (2x + 1)^2 - 3 \end{aligned}$$

Step 2
Simplify the expression.

$$\begin{aligned} g(f(x)) &= (2x + 1)^2 - 3 \\ &= 4x^2 + 4x + 1 - 3 \\ &= 4x^2 + 4x - 2 \end{aligned}$$

Example

It is given that $f(x) = x + 2$ and $g(x) = x^2 + x$.

Determine $f(g(x))$.

Solution

Substitute $x^2 + x$ into the function $f(x)$ wherever the variable x appears; then, simplify the expression.

$$\begin{aligned} f(x) &= x + 2 \\ f(g(x)) &= (x^2 + x) + 2 \\ &= x^2 + x + 2 \end{aligned}$$

Determine $g \circ f$.

Solution

Substitute $x + 2$ into the function $g(x)$ wherever the variable x appears; then, simplify the expression.

$$\begin{aligned} g(x) &= x^2 + x \\ g \circ f &= (x + 2)^2 + (x + 2) \\ &= x^2 + 4x + 4 + x + 2 \\ &= x^2 + 5x + 6 \end{aligned}$$

If $g(x) = x^2 + x$, then determine $g(g(x))$.

Solution

Substitute $x^2 + x$ into the function $g(x)$ wherever the variable x appears; then, simplify the expression.

$$\begin{aligned} g(x) &= x^2 + x \\ g(g(x)) &= (x^2 + x)^2 + (x^2 + x) \\ &= x^4 + 2x^3 + x^2 + x^2 + x \\ &= x^4 + 2x^3 + 2x^2 + x \end{aligned}$$

When asked to evaluate a composition of functions $g(f(x))$ for a specific value $x = n$, one method is to calculate the value of the inner function $f(n)$ and use that result as input for the outer function $g(f(n))$. For example, to determine the value of $g(g(-2))$, first calculate the value of $g(-2)$, and then use the resulting value to calculate $g(g(-2))$. The following example outlines this process.

Example

If $g(x) = x^2 + x$, determine the value of the function $g(g(-2))$.

Solution

Step 1

Calculate the value of $g(-2)$.

Substitute -2 into the function $g(x)$ wherever the variable x appears; then, simplify the expression.

$$\begin{aligned} g(x) &= x^2 + x \\ g(-2) &= (-2)^2 + (-2) \\ &= 4 - 2 \\ &= 2 \end{aligned}$$

So, $g(-2) = 2$.

Step 2

Calculate the value of $g(g(-2))$.

Since $g(-2) = 2$, then $g(g(-2)) = g(2)$.

Substitute 2 into the function $g(x)$ wherever the variable x appears; then, simplify the expression.

$$\begin{aligned} g(x) &= x^2 + x \\ g(2) &= (2)^2 + (2) \\ &= 6 \end{aligned}$$

Another method of evaluating a composition of functions for a specific value is to determine the composite function first and then substitute the specific value into that composite function.

Example

If $g(x) = x^2 - 3$, determine the value of $g(g(-2))$.

Solution

Step 1

Determine $g(g(x))$.

Substitute $x^2 - 3$ wherever the variable x appears; then, simplify the expression.

$$g(x) = x^2 - 3$$
$$g(g(x)) = (x^2 - 3)^2 - 3$$
$$g(g(x)) = x^2 - 6x + 9 - 3$$
$$g(g(x)) = x^2 - 6x + 6$$

Step 2

Calculate the value of $g(g(-2))$.

Substitute -2 for x in the composite function.

$$g(g(-2)) = (-2)^2 + 6(-2) + 6$$
$$= 4 - 12 + 6$$
$$= -2$$

Defining the Inverse of a Function Given Numeric Representations

The inverse of a function is the relation that is obtained by interchanging the x- and y-values in the ordered pairs of the function. The inverse of a function is a relation that may or may not be a function. The function is often written as F, and the inverse of a function is written as F'. However, there are many different notations used for functions and their inverses, such as function $f(x)$ and inverse $f^{-1}(x)$, where $f^{-1}(x) \neq \frac{1}{f(x)}$.

Because the notations vary, it is important to be aware of the notation being used in a particular problem.

Example

G:{(1, 2), (2, 3), (3, 4), (4, 4)}

Write the inverse of function G, defined by the given set of ordered pairs, and determine if the inverse is a function.

Solution

The inverse of function G, labeled G′, is obtained by interchanging the x and y-values in the ordered pairs as follows:

G′:{(2, 1), (3, 2), (4, 3), (4, 4)}

Notice how the domain and range are interchanged.

This relation is not a function because it has two ordered pairs with the same input (4) paired with two different outputs (3 and 4). A mapping diagram can be used to illustrate a function and its inverse.

The mapping diagrams for the function G and its inverse, G′, are as follows.

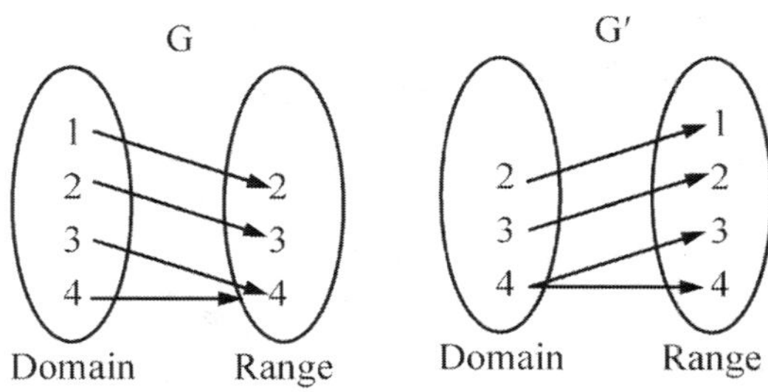

For the inverse relation G′, notice how the element 4 from the domain is mapped to 3 and 4 from the range.

PC.2.C Investigate identities graphically and verify them symbolically, including logarithmic properties, trigonometric identities, and exponential properties.

Verifying Reciprocal, Quotient, and Pythagorean Identities

An identity is an equality that is true for all permissible value replacements of variables. For example, the product rule for exponents, $x^m \cdot x^n = x^{m+n}$, is true for all permissible values of x, m, and n. Similarly, a trigonometric identity is an equality involving trigonometric expressions that is true for all permissible angle-measure replacements of variables.

There are three basic types of trigonometric identities that become the building blocks for creating and examining more complex identities:

- Reciprocal identities
  $\csc\theta = \frac{1}{\sin\theta}$, $\sec\theta = \frac{1}{\cos\theta}$, $\cot\theta = \frac{1}{\tan\theta}$
- Quotient identitiestan $\theta = \frac{\sin\theta}{\cos\theta}$, $\cot\theta = \frac{\cos\theta}{\sin\theta}$
- Pythagorean identities
  $\sin^2\theta + \cos^2\theta = 1$, $1 + \tan^2\theta = \sec^2\theta$,
  $1 + \cot^2\theta = \csc^2\theta$

To verify that an identity is true for one or more values, use either or both of the following methods:

1. Test the identity for a particular angle value.
2. Graph each side of the identity as separate functions and see if the graphs appear identical. In other words determine whether one graph lies on top of the other.

Verifying Identities for a Particular Angle Value

Verifying an identity requires that the two sides of the identity be evaluated separately, as shown in the following examples.

Example

Verify the identity $\sec x = \tan x \csc x$ for $x = 30°$.

Solution

Substitute 30° for x on both sides of the equation and then evaluate each side separately to show that they result in the same numerical value.

	LHS	RHS
Substitute 30° for x.	$\sec 30°$	$\tan 30° \times \csc 30°$
Write in terms of primary trigonometric ratios.	$\frac{1}{\cos 30°}$	$\tan 30° \times \frac{1}{\sin 30°}$
Evaluate each side separately.	$\frac{1}{\frac{\sqrt{3}}{2}}$	$\frac{1}{\sqrt{3}} \times \frac{1}{\frac{1}{2}}$
	$\frac{2}{\sqrt{3}}$	$\frac{2}{\sqrt{3}}$
	LHS =	RHS

Since LHS = RHS, the identity $\sec x = \tan x \csc x$ is true for $x = 30°$.

Because 30° is one of the special angles, exact values were used in the verification shown in the previous example.

If verification is required for an angle that is not special, a calculator can be used to evaluate each side of the equation (approximately) to determine if the identity is true for the given angle.

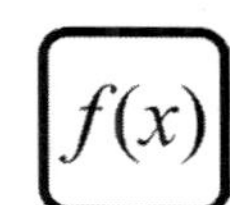

Example

Verify the identity $1 + \tan^2 \theta = \sec^2 \theta$ for $\theta = 2$ rad.

Solution

	LHS	RHS
Substitute 2 for θ.	$1 + \tan^2 (2)$	$\sec^2 (2)$
Write in terms of primary trigonometric ratios.	$1 + \tan^2 (2)$	$\frac{1}{\cos^2 (2)}$
Evaluate each side separately.	$1 + 4.774\ldots$	$5.774\ldots$
	$= 5.774\ldots$	$5.774\ldots$

LHS = RHS

Since LHS = RHS, the identity is true for $\theta = 2$ rad.

VERIFYING IDENTITIES GRAPHICALLY

A graphing calculator can also be used to verify identities. This involves graphing the left-hand side and the right-hand side of the identity as two separate functions, and checking whether or not the graphs overlap.

If both functions share the same graph, then the given equation is an identity.

Example

Use a graphing method to verify the identity $\tan \theta = \frac{\sin \theta}{\cos \theta}$.

Solution

Using a graphing calculator, graph the functions $Y_1 = \tan \theta$ and $Y_2 = \frac{\sin \theta}{\cos \theta}$ in the same window.

Press [Y =] to bring up the Y = editor.

Press [TAN] [X, T, *θ*, *n*] [)] [ENTER] to enter the first function.

To enter the second function, press [SIN] [X, T, *θ*, *n*] [)] [÷] [COS] [X, T, *θ*, *n*] [)] [ENTER]. The resulting window should be

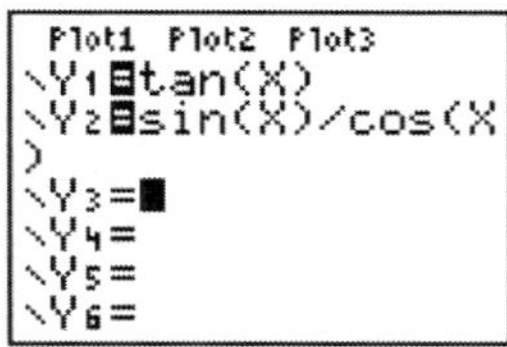

Since this is a comparison of the graphs of two functions, it would be useful to make one of the graphs appear different than the other. Display the first graph as a thick line in order to differentiate it from the second graph.

Use the directional arrows, [△] and [◁], to position the cursor on the far left of the Y_1 row.

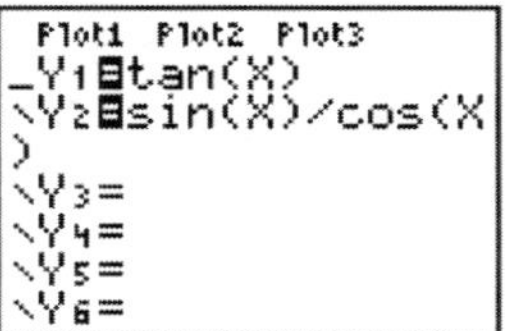

Press ENTER once to select a thick line style for the function Y_1.

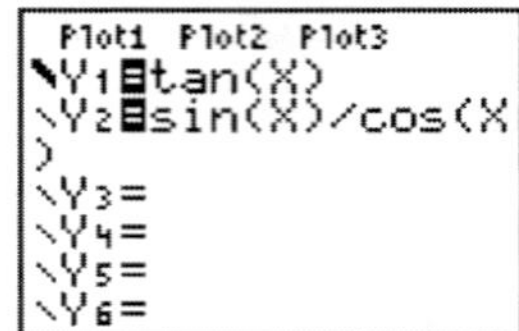

This setting will display the first graph with a thick line and the second graph with a regular line.

Set the calculator to radian mode and the viewing window to ZTrig.

Press GRAPH to display both graphs.

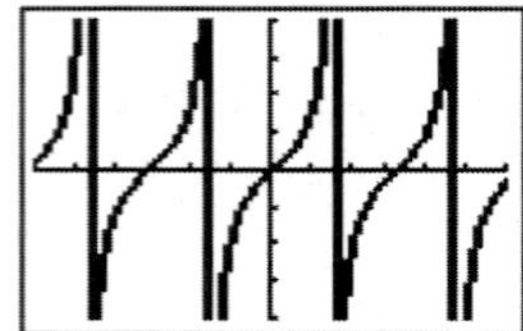

It appears that the identity $\tan\theta = \dfrac{\sin\theta}{\cos\theta}$ holds true because the graphs of $y = \tan\theta$ and $y = \dfrac{\sin\theta}{\cos\theta}$ overlap and appear to be the same.

Although graphing using technology is a useful method to test the validity of potential identities, it should be noted that it is not a proof. Although two functions may appear to have identical graphs, it is possible, although unlikely, that they are not equivalent. The graphs may be so close together that their differences cannot be seen in the limited space of the calculator's viewing window.

Properties of Exponential Functions

The graphs of exponential functions of the form $y = b^x$, where the variable, x, is the exponent will be analyzed. The graph of $y = b^x$ changes depending on the value of the base, b. There are two sets of positive values for b:

- $b > 1$
- $0 < b < 1$

Negative values of b are not included because exponential expressions with negative bases do not always give real number values when the exponents are rational numbers. Consider the following examples.

1. Evaluate $(-125)^{\frac{1}{3}}$. Write $(-125)^{\frac{1}{3}}$ as $\sqrt[3]{-125}$, which is -5 because $(-5)^3 = -125$. There is no difficulty here.
2. Evaluate $(-4)^{\frac{3}{2}}$. Write $(-4)^{\frac{3}{2}}$ as $\sqrt{(-4)^3} = \sqrt{-64}$. $\sqrt{-64}$ cannot be evaluated because -64 is a negative number and there is no real number that when multiplied by itself gives a negative result. Thus, there is no real number value here.
3. Evaluate $(-8)^{\frac{2}{3}}$. Write $(-8)^{\frac{2}{3}}$ as $\sqrt[3]{(-8)^2}$. Now, $\sqrt[3]{(-8)^2} = \sqrt[3]{64} = 4$. Because this has a real number value, there is no difficulty here.

When the base is negative, some expressions can be evaluated and some cannot. In summary, the problem arises when the expression results in an even root of a negative number. To avoid problems associated with exponential functions of the form $y = b^x$, negative bases are avoided.

The graph of $y = 1^x$, where the base (b) is 1, is just a horizontal line.

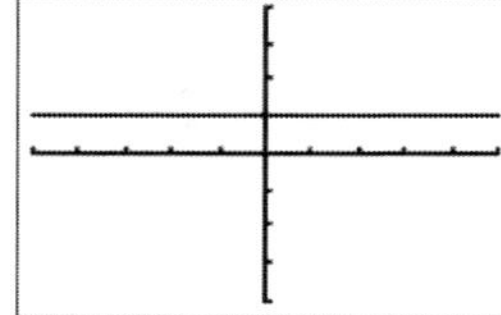

This graph is described by the constant function $y = 1$. Thus, exponential functions where the base is 1 are also not considered.

$f(x)$

In general, the graphs of $y = b^x$ ($b > 0$, where $b \neq 1$) have the following characteristics:

- **Domain:** $x \in \mathrm{R}$, since all x-values are permissible.
- **Range:** $y > 0$, since each graph has y-values that get closer and closer to the y-axis, but never become 0.
- **Horizontal asymptote:** $y = 0$Note that an asymptote is the line a curve approaches but never touches, which in this case, is the x-axis defined by the equation $y = 0$.
- **y-intercept:** (0, 1) or 1, since for all exponential functions, $y = b^x$, $b^0 = 1$.
- **x-intercept:** None, since the graph never touches the x-axis.

The following are graphs of functions where the base, b, is greater than 1.

- $y = 2^x$: 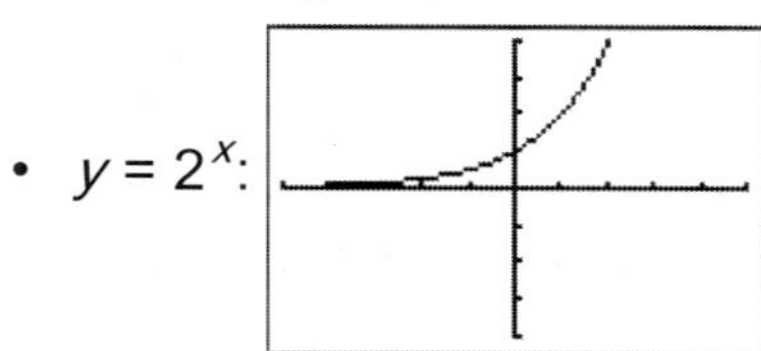
- $y = 3^x$: 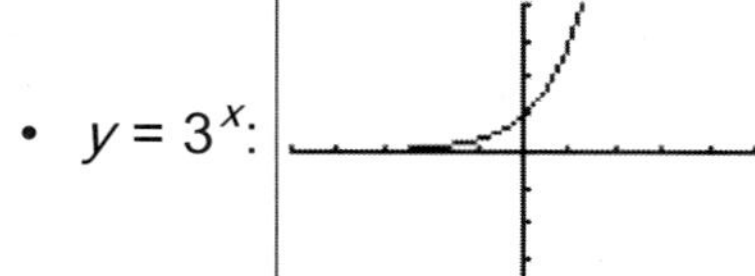
- $y = 9^x$: 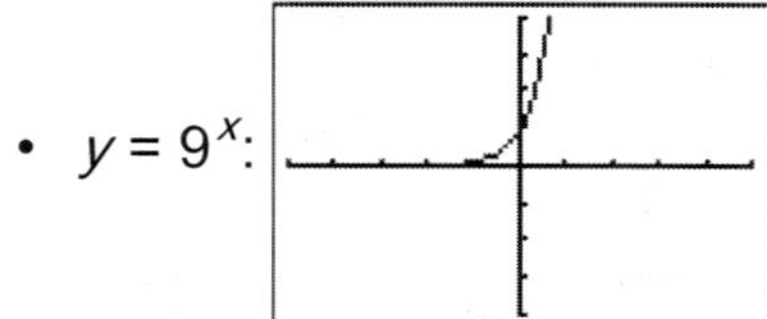

Notice that as the value of b increases, the graph of $y = b^x$ climbs more quickly from left to right.

When $b > 1$, the graph has these characteristics:

- It has this shape:

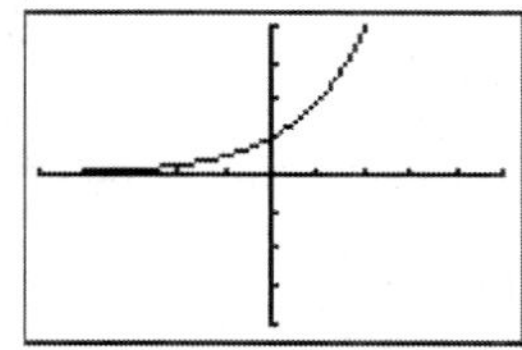

- It is an increasing function as you move from left to right through the domain.
- It is also flatter on the left side of the y-axis and steeper or increases more rapidly on the right side of the y-axis as the value of b increases.

Now, examine the following exponential graphs where the base, b, is between 0 and 1.

- $y = \left(\frac{1}{2}\right)^x$: 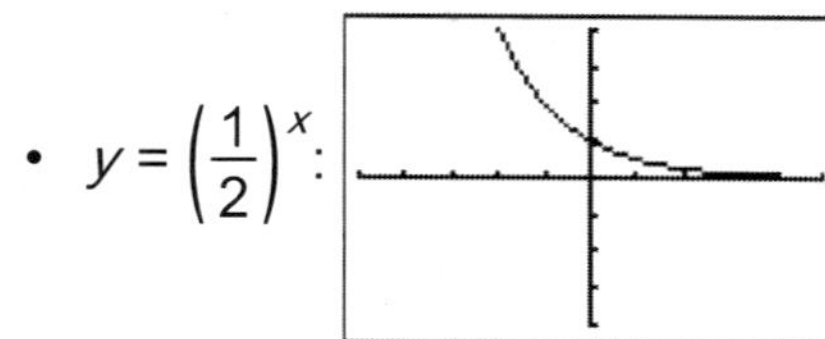
- $y = \left(\frac{1}{3}\right)^x$: 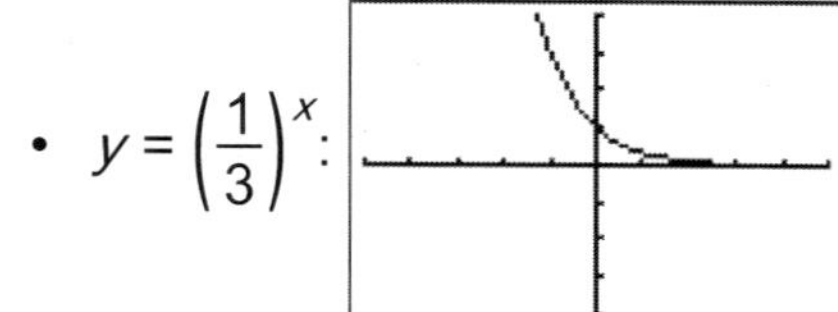
- $y = \left(\frac{1}{9}\right)^x$: 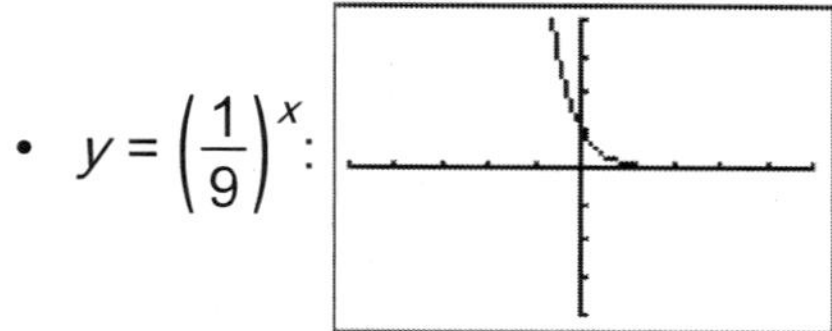

Notice that as the value of b decreases, the graph of $y = b^x$ falls more quickly from left to right.

When $0 < b < 1$, the graph has these characteristics:

- It has this shape:

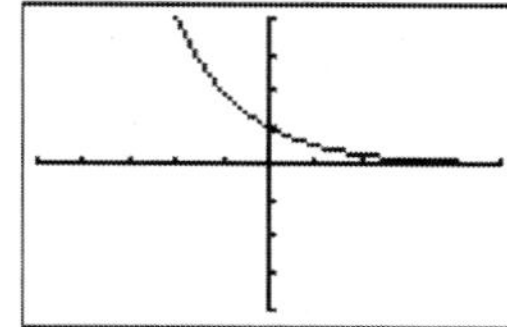

- It is a decreasing function as you move from left to right through the domain.
- It is also flatter on the right side of the y-axis and steeper or decreases more rapidly on the left side of the y-axis as the value of b decreases or gets closer to 0.

Notice that the graphs of the functions $y = b^x$ and $y = \left(\frac{1}{b}\right)^x$ are mirror reflections of each other in the y-axis. Observe that $y = \left(\frac{1}{b}\right)^x$ can be written as $y = \left(b^{-1}\right)^x = b^{-x}$.

Recall that when x is replaced with $-x$ in a function, the result is that the graph is a reflection of the original graph in the y-axis. Thus, the graph of $y = \left(\frac{1}{b}\right)^x = b^{-x}$ is a reflection of the graph of $y = b^x$ in the y-axis.

LOGARITHM IDENTITIES

There are some special logarithm identities that can be used to simplify or change logarithms into a different form. These special identities can be used to simplify more complex logarithm expressions.

1. $\log_b 1 = 0$, where $b > 0$ and $b \neq 1$.
2. $\log_b b = 1$
3. $\log_b (b^x) = x$
4. $b^{\log_b x} = x$
5. $\log_b c = \dfrac{\log_a c}{\log_a b}$

IDENTITY 1

To evaluate $\log_b 1$, set the logarithmic expression equal to x, and then change the logarithmic equation into exponential form.

$\log_b 1 = x$
$b^x = 1$

Since $b^0 = 1$ as long as $b > 0$ and $b \neq 1$, the value of the exponent x is 0. Therefore, $\log_b 1 = 0$.

Example

Evaluate $\log_{\frac{1}{3}} 1$.

Solution

The expression $\log_{\frac{1}{3}} 1$ is of the form $\log_b 1$, so it can be evaluated by using the identity $\log_b 1 = 0$, where $b > 0$ and $b \neq 1$.

Thus, $\log_{\frac{1}{3}} 1 = 0$.

IDENTITY 2

To evaluate $\log_b b$, set the logarithmic expression equal to x, and then change the logarithmic equation into the exponential form.

$\log_b b = x$
$b^x = b$

Whenever a base is raised to the power of 1, the result will be that base. Therefore, $x = 1$ in the expression $b^x = b$, so $\log_b b = 1$.

Example

Evaluate $\log_{3.7} 3.7$.

Solution

The expression $\log_{3.7} 3.7$ is of the form $\log_b b$, so it can be evaluated by using the identity $\log_b b = 1$.

Thus, $\log_{3.7} 3.7 = 1$.

IDENTITY 3

To evaluate $\log_b (b^x)$, set the logarithmic expression equal to y, and then change the logarithmic equation to exponential form.

$\log_b (b^x) = y$
$b^x = b^y$

Since the bases on both sides of the equation are equal, then the exponents are also equal. Therefore, $x = y$, and $\log_b (b^x) = x$.

Example

Evaluate $\log_{2.1} (2.1^5)$.

Solution

The expression $\log_{2.1} (2.1^5)$ is of the form $\log_b (b^x)$, so it can be evaluated by using the identity $\log_b (b^x) = x$.

Thus, $\log_{2.1} (2.1^5) = 5$.

IDENTITY 4

To evaluate $b^{\log_b x}$, set the expression equal to y, and then solve for y. Notice that the base of the power in the expression $b^{\log_b x}$ is equal to the base in the logarithm.

$b^{\log_b x} = y$

Change this exponential equation to logarithmic form.
$\log_b y = \log_b x$

Since the two logarithmic expressions are equal, then $y = x$. Thus, $b^{\log_b x} = x$.

The identity $b^{\log_b x} = x$ is useful for evaluating logarithmic exponents where x is not a power of the base b.

Example

Evaluate $\left(\frac{1}{10}\right)^{\log_{\frac{1}{10}} 10{,}000}$.

Solution

The expression $\left(\frac{1}{10}\right)^{\log_{\frac{1}{10}} 10{,}000}$ is of the form $b^{\log_b x}$, so it can be evaluated by using the identity $b^{\log_b x} = x$.

Thus, $\left(\frac{1}{10}\right)^{\log_{\frac{1}{10}} 10{,}000} = 10{,}000$.

Identity 5: The Base Conversion Formula

Some logarithmic expressions have bases that are not convenient for calculations. The **base conversion formula** can be used to rewrite this logarithm using another base. When changing the base, any base could be chosen for the logarithms in the resulting ratio, but it would be most useful to use a base that would make the expression easier to evaluate.

To evaluate the logarithmic expression $\log_b c$, set the expression equal to y.
$\log_b c = y$

Change the logarithmic equation to exponential form.
$b^y = c$

Take the common logarithm of both sides of the equation with a base of a.
$\log_a b^y = \log_a c$

Apply the power law of logarithms to the right side of the equation.
$y\log_a b = \log_a c$

Divide both sides of the equation by $\log_a b$.

$$y = \frac{\log_a c}{\log_a b}$$

Therefore, the expression $\log_b c$ can be rewritten using the base conversion formula

$$\log_b c = \frac{\log_a c}{\log_a b}.$$

Example
Evaluate $\log_9 27$.

Apply the base conversion formula.
To change the base for the expression $\log_9 27$, a good choice for the new base would be 3 because both 9 and 27 can easily be written as powers of 3. Thus, the expression can be rewritten as follows:

$$\log_9 27 = \frac{\log_3 27}{\log_3 9}$$

Evaluate the numerator and denominator, and simplify.

$$\frac{\log_3 27}{\log_3 9} = \frac{3}{2}$$

Example

Evaluate $\log_{32} \frac{1}{8}$.

Solution

Step 1
Apply the base conversion formula.

Choose a new base such that 32 and $\frac{1}{8}$ are both powers of that new base. Base 2 is appropriate because 32 and $\frac{1}{8}$ are both powers of 2.

$$\log_{32} \frac{1}{8} = \frac{\log_2 \frac{1}{8}}{\log_2 32}$$

Step 2
Evaluate the numerator and denominator, and then simplify.

$$\frac{\log_2 \frac{1}{8}}{\log_2 32} = \frac{-3}{5} = -\frac{3}{5}$$

The base conversion formula can also be used in the opposite direction in order to write a rational expression as a single logarithm.

$$\frac{\log_a c}{\log_a b} = \log_b c$$

Example

In the rational expression $\frac{\log_6 1{,}000}{\log_6 10}$, the logarithms in the numerator and the denominator have the same base (base 6). Therefore, the base conversion formula can be used to write the expression as a single logarithm in order to evaluate the expression more easily.

$$\frac{\log_6 1{,}000}{\log_6 10} = \log_{10} 1{,}000 = 3$$

The base conversion formula can also be used to evaluate logarithmic expressions with a calculator.

Consider the expressions $\log_7 23$ and $\log_3 \frac{1}{4}$.

These expressions cannot be easily evaluated without a calculator, but most calculators do not have a logarithm function that accepts the entry of logarithms of any base. Most calculators are only programmed to directly evaluate **common logarithms** (logarithms with a base of 10). When a logarithm is written without a base indicated, the base is assumed to be 10.

Example
The expression log 300 is assumed to be $\log_{10} 300$.

To evaluate common logarithms with a calculator, use the log button, which usually looks like this: [LOG]

Example
Evaluate the common logarithm expression log 78 to the nearest thousandth.

There are two possible methods for evaluating log 78, depending on the calculator being used.

1. On most scientific calculators, enter [7] [8] and then press [LOG].
2. On most graphing calculators, press [LOG] [7] [8] and [ENTER].

Using either method, $\log 78 \approx 1.892$.
If $\log 78 \approx 1.892$, then it must follow that $10^{1.892} \approx 78$. Use the calculator to verify that this evaluation is correct.

$f(x)$

Example

Evaluate $\dfrac{\log_3 55}{\log_3 10}$ to the nearest thousandth.

Solution

Step 1

The logarithm in the numerator has the same base as the logarithm in the denominator. Use the reverse of the base conversion formula to write the expression as a single logarithm.

$$\frac{\log_3 55}{\log_3 10} = \log_{10} 55$$

Step 2

The simplified logarithm is a common logarithm of base 10. Use a calculator to evaluate $\log_{10} 55$ (or $\log 55$).

$\log 55 \approx 1.740$

Thus, $\dfrac{\log_3 55}{\log_3 10} \approx 1.740$.

Using the base conversion formula, a logarithmic expression can be written in any base as long as it is a positive number not equal to 1. However, as most calculators will evaluate only common logarithms (base 10), it is useful to choose base 10 when writing the expression.

Example

To evaluate the expression $\log_7 23$, apply the base conversion formula using a base of 10.

$$\log_7 23 = \frac{\log 23}{\log 7}$$

For the sake of accuracy, evaluate this expression with a calculator by entering $\dfrac{\log(23)}{\log(7)}$ in one step, as shown.

```
log(23)/log(7)
        1.61132528
█
```

Although the value of this expression can be determined using a calculator by evaluating the numerator and denominator separately and then dividing the results, it is recommened to enter the expression in a calculator in one step.

$$\begin{aligned}&\log_7 23\\ &= \frac{\log 23}{\log 7}\\ &\approx \frac{1.362}{0.845}\\ &\approx 1.611\end{aligned}$$

A calculator can also be used to verify that 1.611 is correct. Since $\log_7 23 \approx 1.611$, the result of $7^{1.611}$ should be very close to 23.

Example

Evaluate $\log_3 \dfrac{1}{4}$ to the nearest thousandth.

Solution

Step 1

Write the expression using the base conversion formula. Choose base 10 in order to evaluate the new expression on a calculator.

$$\log_3 \frac{1}{4} = \frac{\log \frac{1}{4}}{\log 3}$$

Step 2

Evaluate the entire expression with a graphing calculator by entering $\log(1 \div 4) \div \log 3$ and then pressing ENTER.

$\log(1 \div 4) \div \log 3 \approx -1.262$

Thus, $\log_3 \dfrac{1}{4} \approx -1.262$

Example

Evaluate $\log_5 12 + \log_5 4 - \log_5 8$ to the nearest thousandth.

Solution

Step 1

All three terms have the same base 5. Combine the terms into a single logarithm by applying the product and quotient laws of logarithms.

$\log_5 12 + \log_5 4 - \log_5 8$

$= \log_5\left(\frac{12 \times 4}{8}\right)$

$= \log_5 6$

Step 2

Rewrite the expression $\log_5 6$ by applying the base conversion formula. Choose a new base of 10 so that the expression can be evaluated using a calculator.

$\log_5 6 = \frac{\log 6}{\log 5}$

Step 3

Using a graphing calculator, enter log (6) ÷ log (5), and then press ENTER.

$\log_5 6 = \frac{\log 6}{\log 5} \approx 1.113$

Thus, $\log_5 12 + \log_5 4 - \log_5 8 \approx 1.113$.

Verifying Sum, Difference, and Double-Angle Identities

Another category for trigonometric identities includes those that deal with more than one angle. The angles can appear as a sum, a difference, or a double-angle identity.

Sum and Difference Identities

$\sin(A + B) = \sin A\cos B + \cos A\sin B$

$\sin(A - B) = \sin A\cos B - \cos A\sin B$

$\cos(A + B) = \cos A\cos B - \sin A\sin B$

$\cos(A - B) = \cos A\cos B + \sin A\sin B$

Double-Angle Identities

$\sin(2A) = 2\sin A\cos A$

$\cos(2A) = \cos^2 A - \sin^2 A$

The sum, difference, and double-angle identities can be verified for particular angle measures of A and B. They can also be verified graphically.

Verifying Identities for a Particular Value of the Angle

When given the particular angle measures, substitute those values into both the left and right sides of the equation to verify the identity.

Example

Verify $\cos(A + B) = \cos A\cos B - \sin A\sin B$ for $A = 60°$ and $B = 45°$.

Solution

	LHS	RHS
Substitute $A = 60°$ and $B = 45°$.	$\cos(60° + 45°)$	$\cos 60°\cos 45° - \sin 60°\sin 45°$
Simplify.	$\cos 105°$	
Evaluate.	$-0.2588...$	$-0.2588...$

LHS = RHS

Since LHS = RHS, the equation is verified for $A = 60°$ and $B = 45°$.

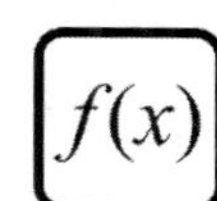

Example

Verify the identity $\frac{1 + \cos(2x)}{\sin(2x)} = \cot x$ for $x = 30°$.

Solution

Substitute 30° into the identity.

	LHS	RHS
Substitute 30° for *x*.	$\frac{1 + \cos(2(30°))}{\sin(2(30°))}$	$\cot(30°)$
Simplify.	$\frac{1 + \cos 60°}{\sin 60°}$	
Evaluate each term.	$\frac{1 + \frac{1}{2}}{\frac{\sqrt{3}}{2}}$	$\sqrt{3}$
Simplify.	$\frac{\frac{3}{2}}{\frac{\sqrt{3}}{2}}$	$\sqrt{3}$
On LHS, multiply by the reciprocal.	$\frac{3}{2} \times \frac{2}{\sqrt{3}}$	$\sqrt{3}$
	$\sqrt{3}$	$\sqrt{3}$

LHS = RHS

Since LHS = RHS, the identity holds true for $x = 30°$.

VERIFYING IDENTITIES GRAPHICALLY

To verify that an identity is true for one value or a few values using a graphical method, graph each side of the identity as a separate function, and observe whether the graphs appear identical.

Example

Verify the identity

$\frac{(\sin x + \cos x)^2}{\sin 2x} = 1 + \csc(2x)$ graphically.

Solution

Step 1

Graph the functions $y = \frac{(\sin x + \cos x)^2}{\sin 2x}$ and $y = 1 + \csc(2x)$.

To graph the function $y = 1 + \csc(2x)$, rewrite it as $y = 1 + \frac{1}{\sin(2x)}$.

Using a TI-83 graphing calculator, press Y = to bring up the Y = editor.

Enter the functions as shown.

Optional: Move the cursor to the left of Y_2 and press ENTER once to change the style of the line to bold.

Set the calculator to radian mode, and the viewing window to ZTrig.

Press GRAPH to display both graphs.

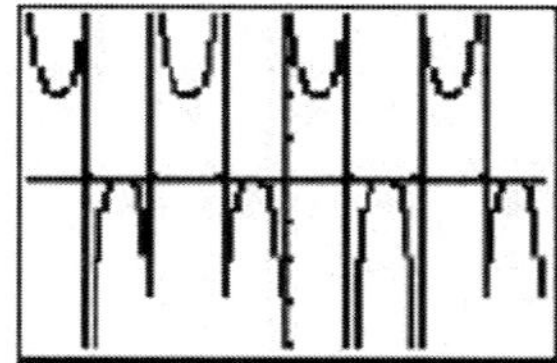

Step 2

Interpret the graph.

Since the graphs of $Y_1 = \frac{(\sin x + \cos x)^2}{\sin(2x)}$ and $Y_2 = 1 + \csc(2x)$ overlap, the identity appears to hold true.

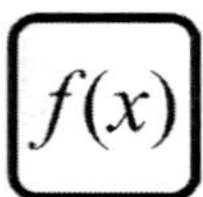

Developing the Pythagorean Identities

To derive the Pythagorean identities, consider an angle, θ, drawn in standard position on the Cartesian plane with $P(x, y)$ on the terminal arm of angle θ.

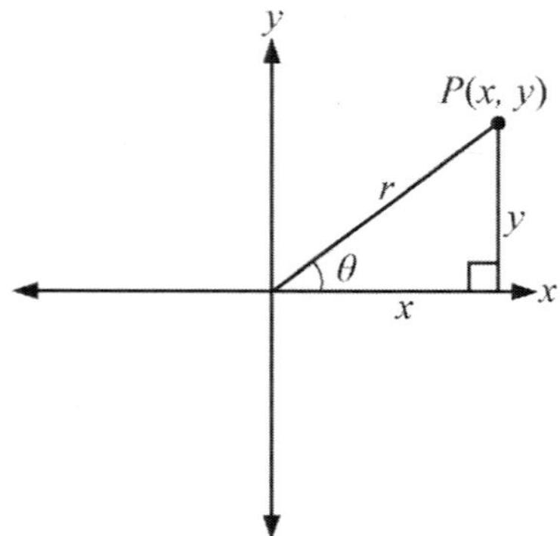

The equation $x^2 + y^2 = r^2$ can be derived by applying the Pythagorean theorem to the right triangle in the given diagram. This equation is true for all x- and y-values on the Cartesian plane.

Also, in the given triangle, $\sin\theta = \frac{y}{r}$ and $\cos\theta = \frac{x}{r}$.

The Pythagorean identity can be derived using the equation $x^2 + y^2 = r^2$ and the definitions of sine and cosine.

First, divide each term in the equation $x^2 + y^2 = r^2$ by r^2, $r \neq 0$.

$$\frac{x^2}{r^2} + \frac{y^2}{r^2} = \frac{r^2}{r^2}$$

The equation $\frac{x^2}{r^2} + \frac{y^2}{r^2} = \frac{r^2}{r^2}$ can be written as $\left(\frac{x}{r}\right)^2 + \left(\frac{y}{r}\right)^2 = 1$.

Next, substitute $\cos\theta$ for $\frac{x}{r}$ and $\sin\theta$ for $\frac{y}{r}$.

$$(\cos\theta)^2 + (\sin\theta)^2 = 1$$

The resulting equation can be written as $\cos^2\theta + \sin^2\theta = 1$ or rearranged as $\sin^2\theta + \cos^2\theta = 1$. These two equations are the first versions of the Pythagorean identity.

Two more versions of the Pythagorean identity can also be derived algebraically using the identity $\cos^2\theta + \sin^2\theta = 1$, the reciprocal identities, and the quotient identities.

First, divide each side of the identity $\cos^2\theta + \sin^2\theta = 1$ by $\cos^2\theta$, and simplify.

$$\cos^2\theta + \sin^2\theta = 1$$
$$\frac{\cos^2\theta + \sin^2\theta}{\cos^2\theta} = \frac{1}{\cos^2\theta}$$
$$\frac{\cos^2\theta}{\cos^2\theta} + \frac{\sin^2\theta}{\cos^2\theta} = \frac{1}{\cos^2\theta}$$
$$1 + \frac{\sin^2\theta}{\cos^2\theta} = \frac{1}{\cos^2\theta}$$

Apply the quotient and reciprocal identities.

$$1 + \frac{\sin^2\theta}{\cos^2\theta} = \frac{1}{\cos^2\theta}$$
$$1 + \tan^2\theta = \sec^2\theta$$

The second form of the Pythagorean identity is $1 + \tan^2\theta = \sec^2\theta$.

To derive a third form of the Pythagorean identity, divide each side of the identity $\cos^2\theta + \sin^2\theta = 1$ by $\sin^2\theta$, and simplify.

$$\cos^2\theta + \sin^2\theta = 1$$
$$\frac{\cos^2\theta + \sin^2\theta}{\sin^2\theta} = \frac{1}{\sin^2\theta}$$
$$\frac{\cos^2\theta}{\sin^2\theta} + \frac{\sin^2\theta}{\sin^2\theta} = \frac{1}{\sin^2\theta}$$
$$\frac{\cos^2\theta}{\sin^2\theta} + 1 = \frac{1}{\sin^2\theta}$$

Apply the quotient and reciprocal identities.

$$\frac{\cos^2\theta}{\sin^2\theta} + 1 = \frac{1}{\sin^2\theta}$$
$$\cot^2\theta + 1 = \csc^2\theta$$

This form of the Pythagorean identity is often written as $1 + \cot^2\theta = \csc^2\theta$.

The three forms of the Pythagorean identities are listed as follows:

1. $\sin^2\theta + \cos^2\theta = 1$
2. $1 + \tan^2\theta = \sec^2\theta$
3. $1 + \cot^2\theta = \csc^2\theta$

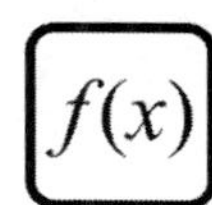

PROVING SIMPLE TRIGONOMETRIC IDENTITIES USING RECIPROCAL, QUOTIENT, AND PYTHAGOREAN IDENTITIES

Reciprocal, quotient, and Pythagorean identities are often used to prove other more complex identities. These three basic identities are given by the following formulas:

- Reciprocal identities—
  $\csc\theta = \dfrac{1}{\sin\theta}$, $\sec\theta = \dfrac{1}{\cos\theta}$, $\cot\theta = \dfrac{1}{\tan\theta}$
- Quotient identities—
  $\tan\theta = \dfrac{\sin\theta}{\cos\theta}$, $\cot\theta = \dfrac{\cos\theta}{\sin\theta}$
- Pythagorean identities—
  $\sin^2\theta + \cos^2\theta = 1$, $1 + \tan^2\theta = \sec^2\theta$,
  $1 + \cot^2\theta = \csc^2\theta$

During the process of proving an identity, each side of the equation is handled separately. The goal is to make legitimate substitutions and simplifications on each side of the equation to show that the two sides are equal.

Prove identities using the following general strategies:

1. Split the equation into two parts, left-hand side (LHS) and right-hand side (RHS), without the equal sign between them.
2. Look for obvious substitutions using the basic identities—consider using the Pythagorean identities if squares of trigonometric expressions are involved.
3. Simplify the most complicated side to make it equal to the other side.
4. If necessary, write in terms of sines and cosines by applying the quotient and reciprocal identities.
5. Write expressions containing fractions as a single fraction.
6. Divide out common factors.
7. Multiply numerators and denominators by the same expression (possibly a conjugate) if necessary.

Example

Prove the identity $\dfrac{\sec\theta \cdot \sin\theta \cdot \cot\theta}{\tan\theta \cdot \csc\theta} = \cos\theta$.

Solution

Use a chart to help you work through the required steps of the proof.

	LHS	RHS
	$\dfrac{\sec\theta \cdot \sin\theta \cdot \cot\theta}{\tan\theta \cdot \csc\theta}$	$\cos\theta$
Apply the reciprocal and quotient identities.	$\dfrac{\left(\dfrac{1}{\cos\theta}\right)\sin\theta\left(\dfrac{\cos\theta}{\sin\theta}\right)}{\left(\dfrac{\sin\theta}{\cos\theta}\right)\left(\dfrac{1}{\sin\theta}\right)}$	
Multiply and reduce.	$\dfrac{1}{\left(\dfrac{1}{\cos\theta}\right)}$	
Divide.	$\cos\theta$	
	LHS =	RHS

In certain proofs, it may be helpful to recognize that the Pythagorean identities can be rearranged. For example, $\sin^2\theta + \cos^2\theta = 1$ can also be written as $\sin^2\theta = 1 - \cos^2\theta$ or as $\cos^2\theta = 1 - \sin^2\theta$.

Example

Prove the identity $\dfrac{\sin^2 x}{1 + \cos x} = 1 - \cos x$.

Solution

	LHS	RHS
	$\dfrac{\sin^2 x}{1 + \cos x}$	$1 - \cos x$
Apply the Pythagorean identity.	$\dfrac{1 - \cos^2 x}{1 + \cos x}$	
Factor.	$\dfrac{(1 - \cos x)(1 + \cos x)}{1 + \cos x}$	
Reduce.	$1 - \cos x$	
	LHS =	RHS

Example

Prove the identity $\frac{\sec x}{\sin x} - \frac{\sin x}{\cos x} = \cot x$.

Solution

	LHS	RHS
	$\frac{\sec x}{\sin x} - \frac{\sin x}{\cos x}$	$\cot x$
Apply the reciprocal identity.	$\frac{\frac{1}{\cos x}}{\sin x} - \frac{\sin x}{\cos x}$	
Simplify.	$\frac{1}{\sin x \cdot \cos x} - \frac{\sin x}{\cos x}$	
Find the common denominator and combine.	$\frac{1 - \sin^2 x}{\sin x \cdot \cos x}$	
Apply the Pythagorean identity.	$\frac{\cos^2 x}{\sin x \cdot \cos x}$	
Reduce $(\cos x)$.	$\frac{\cos x}{\sin x}$	
Apply the quotient identity.	$\cot x$	

LHS = RHS

Developing Reciprocal and Quotient Identities

A trigonometric identity is an equality involving trigonometric expressions that is true for all permissible angle-measure replacements of the given variables.

The trigonometric and reciprocal ratios of an acute angle (e.g., angle A) for right-triangle trigonometry are defined as follows:

$\sin A = \frac{\text{opposite}}{\text{hypotenuse}}$	$\csc A = \frac{\text{hypotenuse}}{\text{opposite}}$
$\cos A = \frac{\text{adjacent}}{\text{hypotenuse}}$	$\sec A = \frac{\text{hypotenuse}}{\text{adjacent}}$
$\tan A = \frac{\text{opposite}}{\text{adjacent}}$	$\cot A = \frac{\text{adjacent}}{\text{opposite}}$

To extend the trigonometric ratios to angles of any measure (θ), consider angles in **standard position** on the Cartesian plane.

An angle, θ, drawn in standard position on the Cartesian plane with $P(x, y)$ on the terminal arm of angle θ, is shown here.

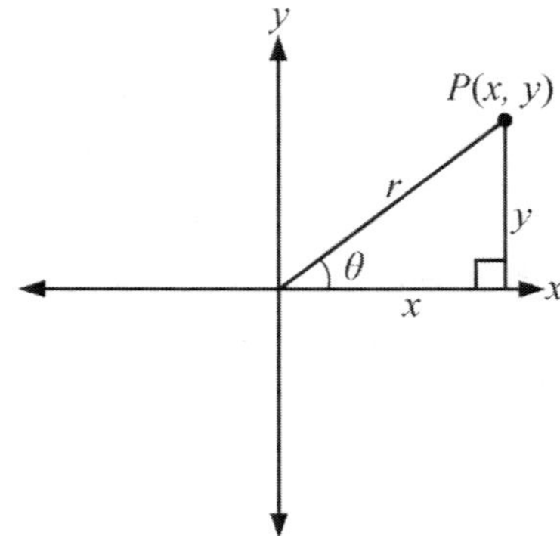

The following relationships are observed:

$\sin \theta = \frac{y}{r}$

$\cos \theta = \frac{x}{r}$

$\tan \theta = \frac{y}{x}$

$\csc \theta = \frac{r}{y}$

$\sec \theta = \frac{r}{x}$

$\cot \theta = \frac{x}{y}$

The reciprocal identities can be derived using the definitions of the primary trigonometric ratios.

Since $\frac{y}{r}$ is the reciprocal of $\frac{r}{y}$, it follows that $\sin \theta$ is the reciprocal of $\csc \theta$.

Thus, $\sin \theta = \frac{1}{\csc \theta}$ or $\csc \theta = \frac{1}{\sin \theta}$. Similarly, since $\frac{x}{r}$ is the reciprocal of $\frac{r}{x}$, it follows that $\cos \theta$ is the reciprocal of $\sec \theta$. Thus, $\cos \theta = \frac{1}{\sec \theta}$ or $\sec \theta = \frac{1}{\cos \theta}$. As well, since $\frac{y}{x}$ is the reciprocal of $\frac{x}{y}$, it follows that $\tan \theta$ is the reciprocal of $\cot \theta$. Thus, $\tan \theta = \frac{1}{\cot \theta}$ or $\cot \theta = \frac{1}{\tan \theta}$.

The quotient identities can also be derived using the definitions of the primary trigonometric ratios. An equivalent form of $\frac{\sin\theta}{\cos\theta}$ can be determined as follows:

$$\begin{aligned}\frac{\sin\theta}{\cos\theta} &= \frac{\frac{y}{r}}{\frac{x}{r}}\\ &= \frac{y}{r}\times\frac{r}{x}\\ &= \frac{y}{x}\\ &= \tan\theta\end{aligned}$$

Thus, the quotient identity for tangent is defined as $\tan\theta = \frac{\sin\theta}{\cos\theta}$.

Since $\cot\theta$ is the reciprocal of $\tan\theta$, it follows that the quotient identity for cotangent is $\cot\theta = \frac{\cos\theta}{\sin\theta}$.

Understanding the Laws of Rational Exponents

A rational exponent is an exponent that can be written in the form of a rational number, $\frac{a}{b}$, where a and b are integers and $b \neq 0$.

Example

Evaluate the expression $4^{\frac{1}{2}}$.

Solution

Step 1

Create an equation in which multiples of $4^{\frac{1}{2}}$ equal 4^m, where m is a whole number exponent.

$4^{\frac{1}{2}} \times 4^{\frac{1}{2}} = 4^{\frac{1}{2}+\frac{1}{2}} = 4^1$

Step 2

Substitute x for $4^{\frac{1}{2}}$.

$(x)(x) = 4^1$

$x^2 = 4$

Step 3

Solve for x.

$x = \pm\sqrt{(4)}$

Note: Dismiss $-\sqrt{4}$, since the base is greater than 0.

Since $x = 4^{\frac{1}{2}}$, $4^{\frac{1}{2}} = \sqrt{(4)^1} = 2$.

Example

Evaluate the expression $64^{-\frac{1}{3}}$.

Solution

Step 1

Create an equation in which multiples of $64^{-\frac{1}{3}}$ equal 64^m, where m is a whole number.

$64^{-\frac{1}{3}} \times 64^{-\frac{1}{3}} \times 64^{-\frac{1}{3}} = 64^{-\frac{3}{3}} = 64^{-1}$

Step 2

Substitute x for $64^{-\frac{1}{3}}$.

$(x)(x)(x) = 64^{-1}$

$x^3 = \frac{1}{(64)^1}$

Step 3

Solve for x by taking the cube root of both sides.

$x = \frac{1}{\sqrt[3]{64}}$

$64^{-\frac{1}{3}} = \frac{1}{\sqrt[3]{(64)^1}} = \frac{1}{4}$

Radicals can be written as powers with rational exponents, and powers with rational exponents can be written as radicals.

In general, the rational exponent property is $x^{\frac{m}{n}} = \sqrt[n]{x^m} = \left(\sqrt[n]{x}\right)^m$.

Once a radical is expressed as a power with a rational exponent, the regular laws of exponents can be applied. These laws are stated as follows:

- When multiplying powers with the same bases, add the exponents together.
  $b^x \times b^y = b^{x+y}$
- When dividing powers with the same bases, subtract the exponents.
  $\frac{b^x}{b^y} = b^{x-y}$, in which $b \neq 0$
- When a power is raised to a power, multiply the exponents.
  $(b^x)^y = b^{xy}$
- When the product of powers inside brackets is raised to a power, each power in the brackets is raised to the power outside the brackets.
  $(ab)^x = a^x b^x$
- When the quotient of powers inside brackets is raised to a power, each power in the numerator and denominator in the brackets is raised to the power outside the brackets.
  $\left(\frac{a}{b}\right)^x = \frac{a^x}{b^x}$, in which $b \neq 0$
- When a base is raised to a negative exponent, it can be represented as 1 over the base raised to a positive exponent.
  $b^{-x} = \frac{1}{b^x}$, in which $b \neq 0$
- Any base other than 0 raised to the exponent 0 is equal to 1.
  $b^0 = 1[b \neq 0]$
- Zero raised to any exponent (except 0) is equal to 0.
  $0^x = 0[x \neq 0]$
- The expression 0^0 is undefined.

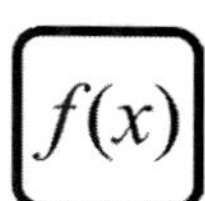

OPERATIONS OF FUNCTIONS EXERCISE #1

Use the following information to answer the next question.

The point with coordinates $(2, -6)$ lies on the graph of the function $y = f(x)$.

39. What are the coordinates of the corresponding point on the graph of $y = |f(x)| + 2$?

A. $(2, 4)$ **B.** $(2, 8)$

C. $(-2, 4)$ **D.** $(-2, -8)$

40. If the range of the function $y = f(x)$ is $-3 \leq y \leq 5$, then the range of the function $y = |f(x)|$ is

A. $-3 \leq y \leq 5$ **B.** $0 \leq y \leq 3$

C. $0 \leq y \leq 5$ **D.** $3 \leq y \leq 5$

Use the following information to answer the next question.

The graph of $y = |x|$ is transformed into the graph of $y - 7 = |x + 5|$.

41. As a result of this transformation, what does point $(-3, 3)$ become on the transformed graph?

A. $(-8, -4)$ **B.** $(-8, 10)$

C. $(2, -4)$ **D.** $(2, 10)$

Use the following information to answer the next question.

The graph of $y = |x|$ was transformed to the graph of $y = |x - 5| + 7$.

42. Which of the following statements describes the transformation?

A. The graph of $y = |x|$ has been translated 7 units to the right and 5 units upward.

B. The graph of $y = |x|$ has been translated 5 units to the left and 7 units downward.

C. The point (x, y) on the graph of $y = |x|$ has been translated to point $(x + 5, y + 7)$.

D. The point (x, y) on the graph of $y = |x|$ has been translated to point $(x - 5, y - 7)$.

43. If $f(x) = |x|$, then the graph of $g(x) = -f(x)$ will have

A. a different domain and a different range from f

B. the same domain but a different range from f

C. the same domain and the same range as f

D. a different domain but the same range as f

Use the following information to answer the next question.

The partial graph of $f(x) = |x|$ is given.

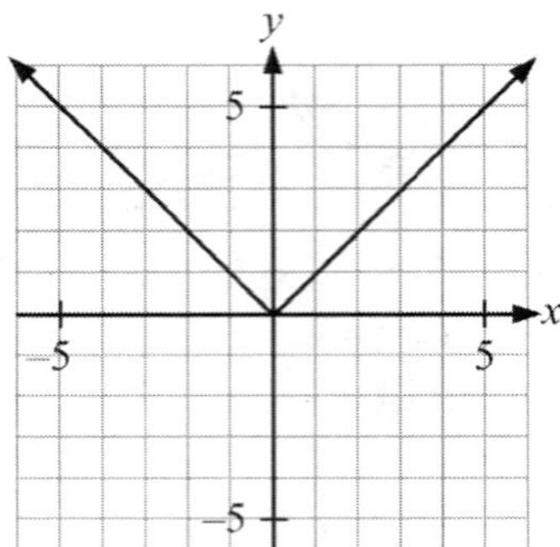

The following descriptions identify transformations that are separately applied to the graph of the function, $f(x) = |x|$:

I. A vertical translation 6 units down, followed by a reflection in the x-axis
II. A horizontal translation 6 units left, then a vertical translation 6 units up, followed by a reflection in the x-axis
III. A reflection in the x-axis, followed by a vertical translation 6 units up
IV. A reflection in the x-axis, followed by a vertical translation 6 units down, and a horizontal translation 6 units right

44. Which two descriptions of the transformations of $f(x) = |x|$ will produce two new and identical graphs?

A. I and II **B.** I and III
C. II and III **D.** II and IV

Use the following information to answer the next question.

The partial graph of $y = f(x)$ and a transformation of the graph of $y = f(x)$ are shown.

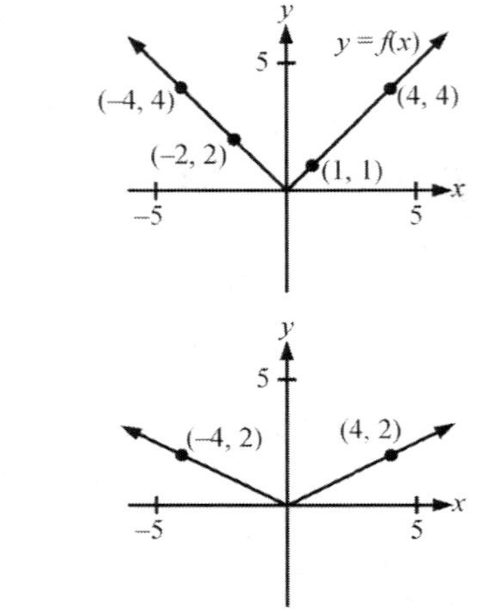

45. An equation which could define the graph of the transformed function is

A. $y = f(x) - 2$
B. $y = f(x) + 2$
C. $y = \frac{1}{2} f(x)$
D. $y = 2 f(x)$

Use the following information to answer the next question.

The partial graph of $y = f(x)$, where $f(x) = |x|$, is shown.

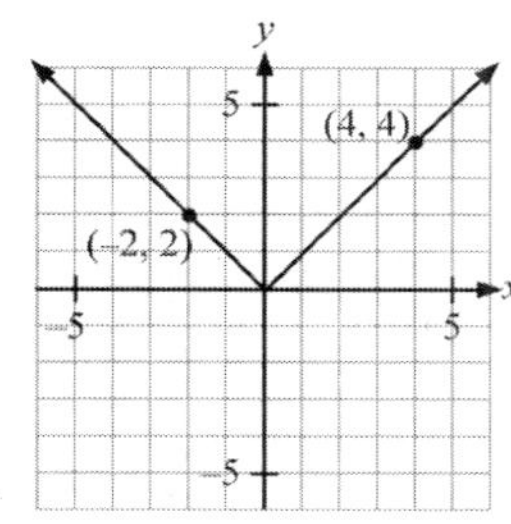

46. If the function $f(x)$ is transformed to $y = \frac{3}{2}|x|$, which of the following graphs shows the transformed function?

A.

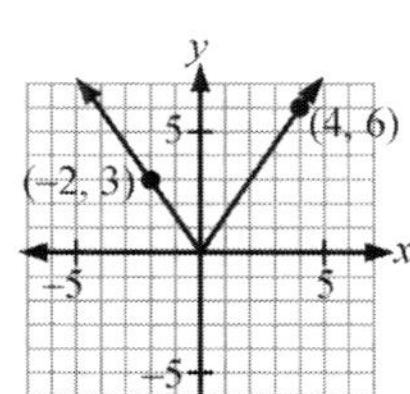

B.

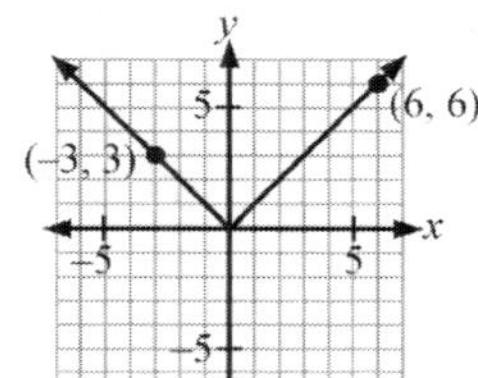

C.

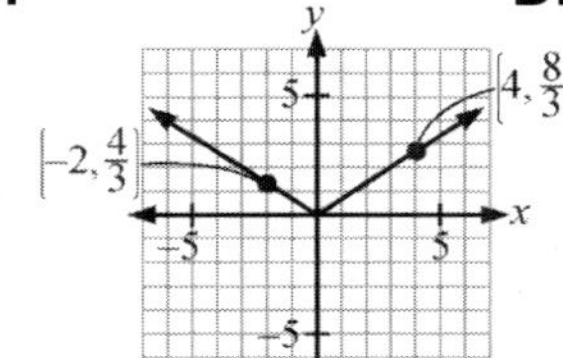

D.

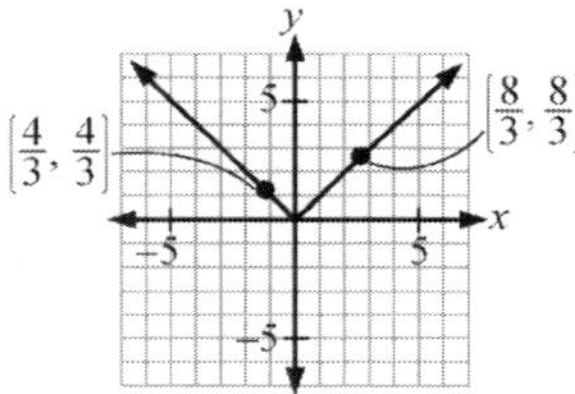

Use the following information to answer the next question.

The graph of the function $f(x) = |x|$ is vertically stretched about the x-axis by a factor of 2 and then translated 5 units down.

47. A function, g, that will have the same domain and range as the transformed function of f is

A. $g(x) = -|x + 3| + 5$

B. $g(x) = -2|x| + 5$

C. $g(x) = 2|x - 5|$

D. $g(x) = |x - 3| - 5$

Use the following information to answer the next question.

The graph of $y = |x|$ and the transformed image of the graph of $y = |x|$ are shown.

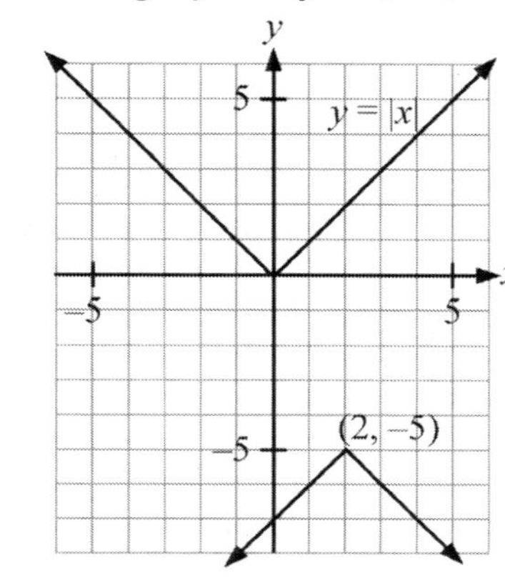

48. If the two graphs are congruent, then the equation of the graph of the transformed image is

A. $y = -|x - 2| - 5$

B. $y = -|x + 2| - 5$

C. $y = |x - 2| - 5$

D. $y = |x + 2| - 5$

Use the following information to answer the next question.

Two graphs are as shown. Graph 2 is a transformation of Graph 1.

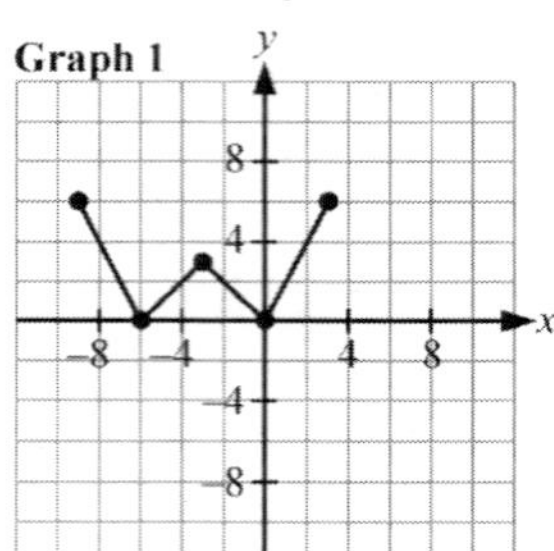

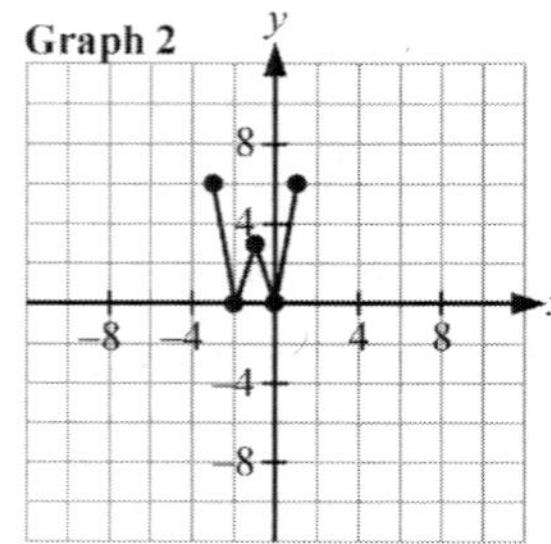

49. If the equation of Graph 1 is $y = f(x)$, then the equation of Graph 2 could be

A. $y = f(3x)$

B. $y = f\left(\frac{1}{3}x\right)$

C. $y = 3f(x)$

D. $y = \frac{1}{3}f(x)$

Use the following information to answer the next question.

The graph of $y = 9x^2 - 1$ is stretched horizontally about the y-axis by a factor of 6.

50. The equation of the transformed graph is

A. $y = \frac{1}{4}x^2 - 1$

B. $y = 54x^2 - 1$

C. $y = 54x^2 - 6$

D. $y = 324x^2 - 1$

Use the following information to answer the next question.

The graph of $y = f(x)$ is shown.

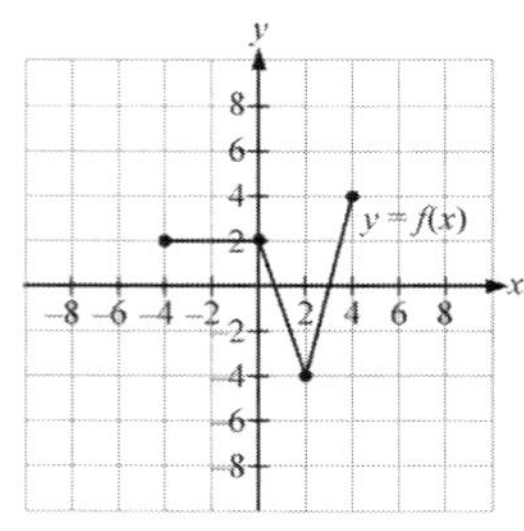

51. Which of the following graphs could be the graph of $y = 2f(x)$?

A.

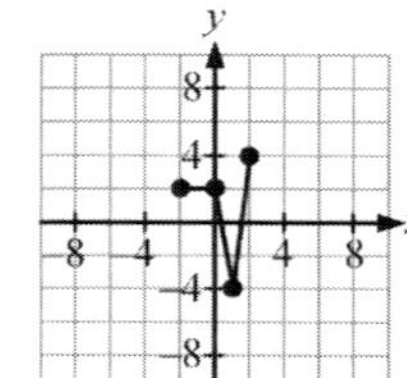

B.

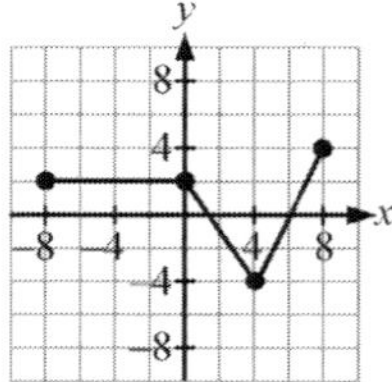

C.

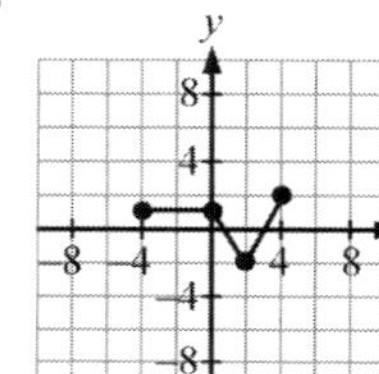

D.

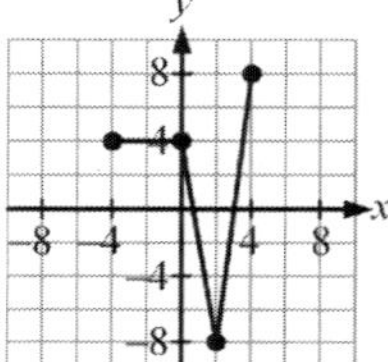

Use the following information to answer the next question.

The partial graph of $y = f(x)$ is as shown.

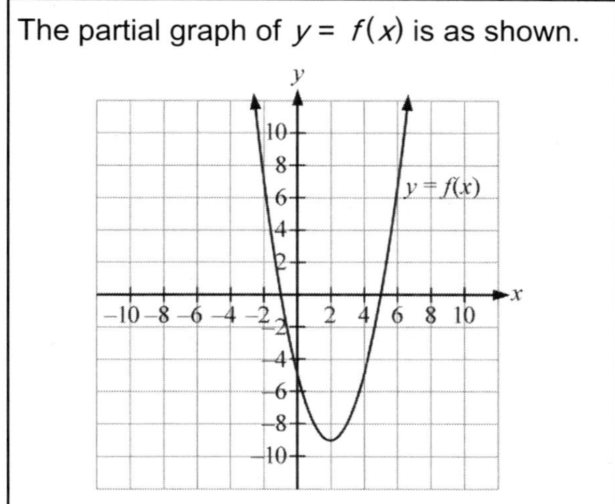

52. If the graph of $y = f(x)$ is vertically stretched about the x-axis by a factor of $\frac{1}{5}$, the x-intercepts of the transformed graph will be located at the ordered pairs

A. $\left(-\frac{1}{5}, 0\right)$ and $(25, 0)$

B. $\left(-\frac{1}{5}, 0\right)$ and $(1, 0)$

C. $(-5, 0)$ and $(25, 0)$

D. $(-1, 0)$ and $(5, 0)$

Use the following information to answer the next question.

The graph of $y = f(x)$ is translated to the graph of $y = f(x - 8)$. If the ordered pair $(12, 7)$ is on the graph of $y = f(x - 8)$, then the corresponding ordered pair $(k, 7)$ is on the graph of $y = f(x)$.

53. The value of k is _________.

Use the following information to answer the next question.

The graph of $y = f(x)$ is given.

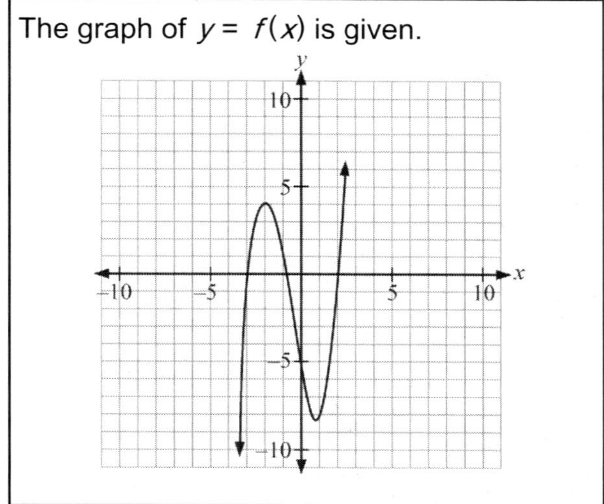

54. One x-intercept of the graph of $y = f(x - 7)$ is located at the ordered pair

A. $(-8, 0)$ **B.** $(-7, 0)$

C. $(6, 0)$ **D.** $(7, 0)$

55. Given the graph of $y = f(x)$, the graph of $y + 1 = f(x) - 4$ can be drawn by translating the graph of $y = f(x)$ vertically

A. down by 4 units

B. down by 5 units

C. up by 4 units

D. up by 5 units

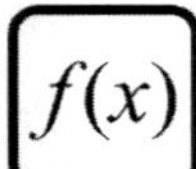

Use the following information to answer the next question.

The graph of $y = f(x)$ is given.

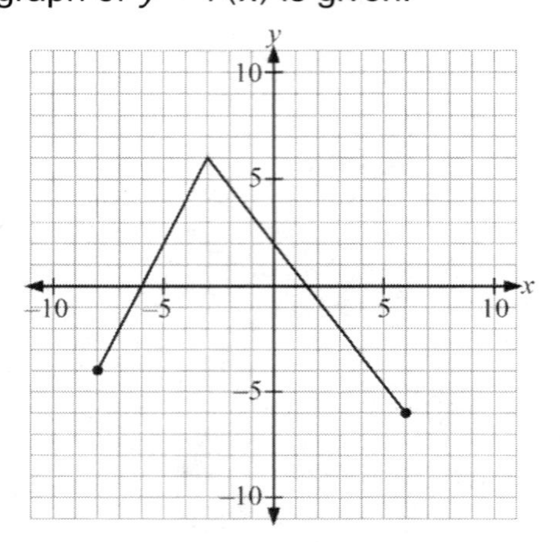

56. On the grid provided, sketch the graph of $y = f(x) + 2$.

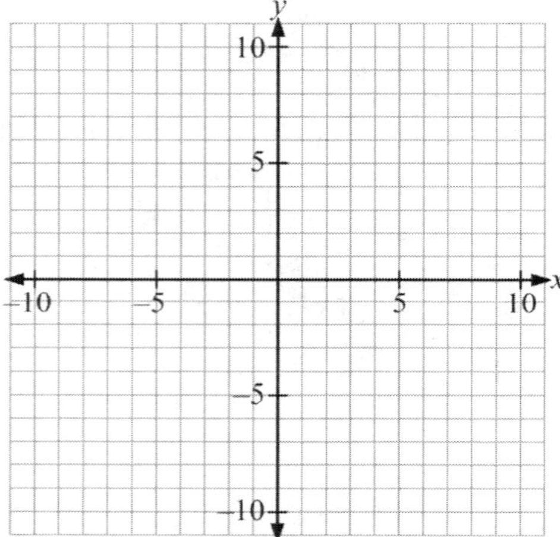

57. The function $g(x)$ is defined by the equation $g(x) = \frac{5}{(3x-2)(x+3)(x-5)}$. What are the vertical asymptotes of the graph of the transformation $y = g(|x|)$?

A. $x = \pm\frac{3}{2}$, $x = \pm 5$, $x = \pm 3$

B. $x = \pm\frac{2}{3}$, $x = \pm 5$, $x = \pm 3$

C. $x = \pm\frac{3}{2}$, $x = \pm 5$

D. $x = \pm\frac{2}{3}$, $x = \pm 5$

Use the following information to answer the next question.

The graph of the function $y = g(x)$ is shown.

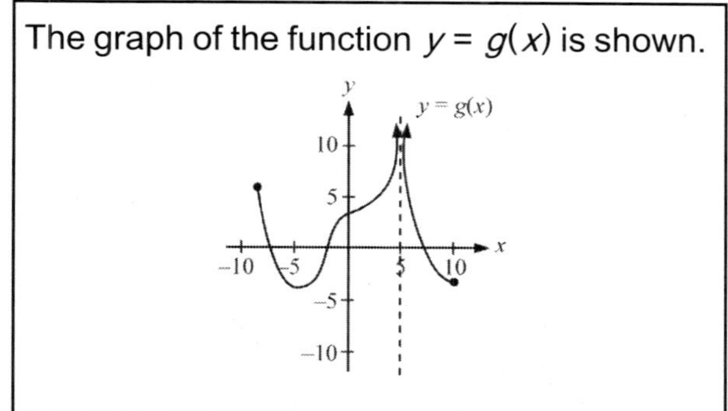

58. What is the graph and the domain of the transformed function $y = g(|x|)$?

A.

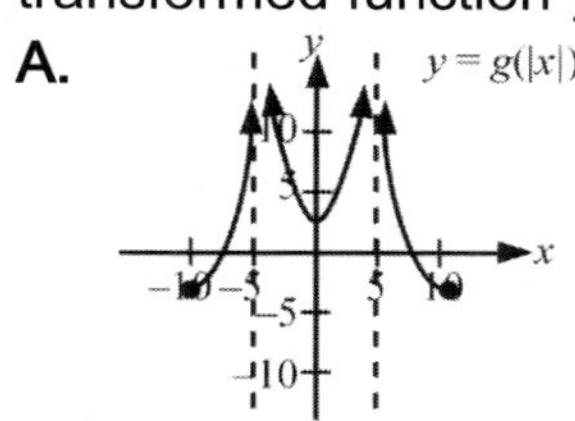

$-10 \leq x \leq 10,\ x \neq \pm 5$

B.

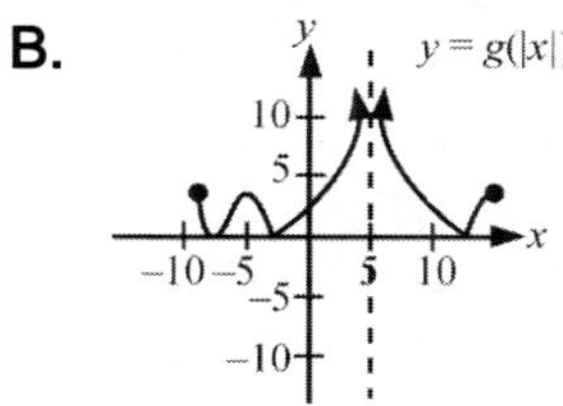

$-8 \leq x \leq 10,\ x \neq 5$

C.

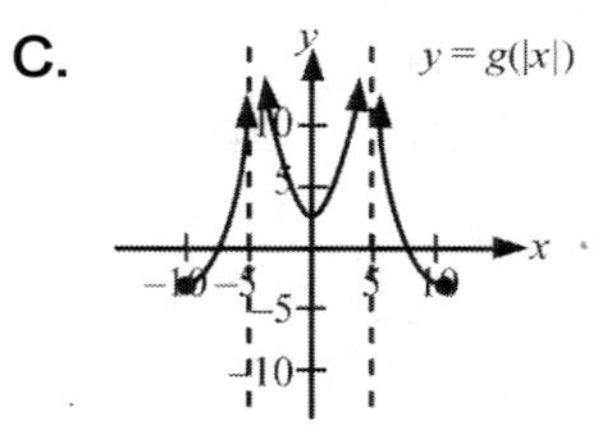

$x \neq \pm 5$

D.

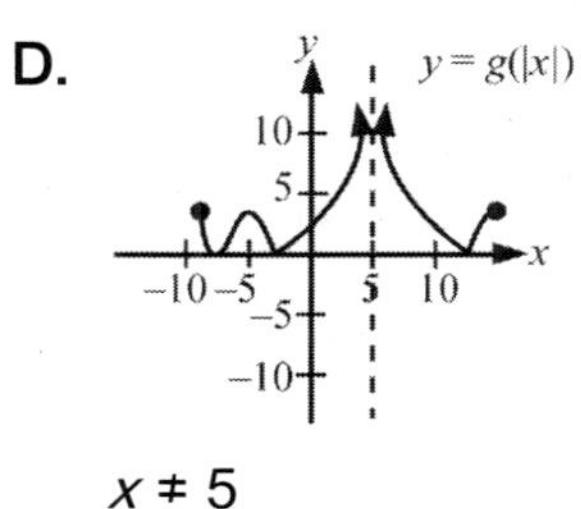

$x \neq 5$

Use the following information to answer the next question.

Point $Q(-2, 5)$ lies on the graph of $y = f(x)$. If the graph of $y = f(x)$ is stretched horizontally by a factor of $\frac{1}{4}$ about the line $x = 6$, point Q is transformed to point (m, n), where m and n represent integers.

59. What is the numerical value of $m + n$?

A. –26 **B.** –21

C. 2 **D.** 9

Use the following information to answer the next question.

Point $A(1, 2)$ lies on the graph of $y = f(x)$. If the graph of $y = f(x)$ is stretched vertically by a factor of 3 about the line $y = -4$, point A is transformed to point (m, n), where m and n represent integers.

60. What is the numerical value of $m + n$?

A. 3 **B.** 9

C. 15 **D.** 21

Use the following information to answer the next question.

A function is defined as follows: y is determined by adding 4 to x and then multiplying by 6.

61. Which of the following statements describes the operations required to determine the inverse of the given function?

A. Divide by 6, and then add 4.

B. Divide by 6, and then subtract 4.

C. Subtract 4, and then divide by 6.

D. Subtract 4, and then multiply by 6.

62. The inverse of the quadratic function $f(x) = \frac{1}{2}(x + 6)^2 - 5$ is

A. $y = \pm\sqrt{2x + 5} - 6$

B. $y = \pm\sqrt{2x + 10} - 6$

C. $y = \pm 2\sqrt{x + 5} - 6$

D. $y = \pm 2\sqrt{x - 6} + 5$

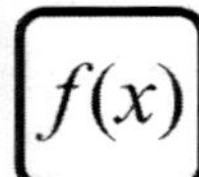

Use the following information to answer the next question.

A function is given by $f(x) = \frac{g(x)}{h(x)}$, where $g(x) = x^2 - 25$, $h(x) = x + 5$, and $h(x) \neq 0$.

63. The simplified form of $f(x)$ is

A. $x + 5,\ x \neq 5$

B. $x - 5,\ x \neq 5$

C. $x - 5,\ x \neq -5$

D. $x + 5,\ x \neq -5$

64. If $f(x) = x^2 + 2x - 4$, $g(x) = x^2 + 25$, and $h(x) = f(x)g(x)$, what is $h(x)$ in simplified form?

A. $x^4 + 2x^3 - 21x^2 + 50x - 100$

B. $x^4 - 2x^3 - 29x^2 - 50x + 100$

C. $x^4 + 2x^3 + 29x^2 + 50x + 100$

D. $x^4 + 2x^3 + 21x^2 + 50x - 100$

65. If $f(x) = 6 - 4x$ and $g(x) = \frac{1}{2}x - 3$, the value of $g\left(f\left(-\frac{1}{2}\right)\right)$ is

A. −5 **B.** −1

C. 1 **D.** 19

66. If $f(x) = 3x^2 - 12$, then determine the value of the function $f(f(-1))$. __________

Use the following information to answer the next question.

A relation, N, is defined by the following set of ordered pairs.

N:{(4, y), (7, 8), (x, 6)}

67. If both N and the inverse of N can be classified as functions, which of the following statements stating the value of an unknown variable is **false**?

A. The x variable cannot equal 4 or 7.

B. The y variable cannot equal 6 or 8.

C. The x variable can never equal the value of y.

D. The y variable can equal 4, and x can equal 6.

68. If $f(x) = x^2 - 4$, where x is a member of the integers and $0 \leq x \leq 3$, then which of the following sets of ordered pairs could define $f^{-1}(x)$?

A. $\left\{\left(-\frac{1}{4}, 0\right), \left(-\frac{1}{3}, 0\right), (0, 2), \left(\frac{1}{5}, 3\right)\right\}$

B. {(−4, 0), (−3, 1), (0, 2), (5, 3)}

C. $\left\{\left(\frac{1}{4}, 0\right), \left(\frac{1}{3}, 0\right), (0, 2), \left(-\frac{1}{5}, 2\right)\right\}$

D. {(4, 0), (3, 1), (0, 2), (−5, 3)}

69. When verifying that the identity $\frac{\cos x}{1 - \sin x} = \frac{1 + \sin x}{\cos x}$ is true for $x = 60°$, the exact value of the equation is

A. $1 - \sqrt{3}$ **B.** $2 - \sqrt{2}$

C. $2 + \sqrt{3}$ **D.** $3 + \sqrt{2}$

70. Which of the following functions has a base of 3, a y-intercept of 4, and a range of $y > 1$?

A. $f(x) = 4(3)^{x+1}$

B. $f(x) = (3)^x + 3$

C. $f(x) = 4(3)^x + 1$

D. $f(x) = (3)^{x+1} + 1$

$f(x)$

71. Sketch the graph of $y = 5^{x-4} + 1$, and state the domain, range, and equation of the asymptote.

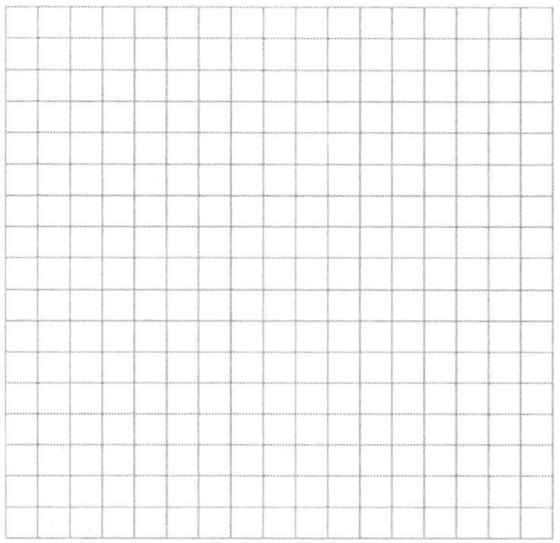

72. The expression $\log_7 1 - 7$ is equal to

A. −7 **B.** −6

C. 0 **D.** 7

73. The expression $z + \log_{2z} 1$ where $z > 0$ and $z \neq \frac{1}{2}$, is equivalent to

A. $z + 2$ **B.** $z + 1$

C. $2z$ **D.** z

74. To verify the identity $\frac{\cos(2x) + 1}{\sin(2x)} = \cot x$ for $x = \frac{\pi}{6}$, the left and right side of the equation, to the nearest hundredth, will equal _______.

Use the following information to answer the next question.

Three of the given functions have identical graphs in the domain $-\pi \leq x \leq \pi$.

1. $y = \sin(8x)$
2. $y = \cos(8x)\tan(8x)$
3. $y = 2\sin(4x)\cos(4x)$
4. $y = \left(\begin{matrix} 4\sin(2x)\cos(2x) \\ \times\ (\cos^2(2x) - \sin^2(2x)) \end{matrix}\right)$

75. Which of the given functions has a graph that differs from the others?

A. 1 **B.** 2

C. 3 **D.** 4

76. Prove the identity $\sec x = \frac{\csc x}{\cot x}$.

77. Prove the identity $\sin^2 x + \cos^2 x \tan^2 x = 2\sin^2 x$.

78. The expression $x^{-\frac{4}{3}}$ is equivalent to

A. $\sqrt[4]{x^3}$ **B.** $-\sqrt[3]{x^4}$

C. $-\frac{1}{\sqrt[4]{x^3}}$ **D.** $\frac{1}{\sqrt[3]{x^4}}$

79. Written using a single radical, what is the expression $\sqrt[5]{w^2} \times \sqrt{w^4}$?

A. $\sqrt[5]{w^{12}}$ **B.** $\sqrt[5]{w^4}$

C. $\sqrt[12]{w^5}$ **D.** $\sqrt[4]{w^5}$

Use the following information to answer the next question.

Charles wants to verify the identity $\csc x \tan x = \sec x$.

80. When verifying that the given identity is true for $x = \frac{\pi}{6}$ rad, the LHS of the equation, to the nearest hundredth, will equal _________.

OPERATIONS OF FUNCTIONS EXERCISE #1 ANSWERS AND SOLUTIONS

39. B	50. A	61. B	72. A
40. C	51. D	62. B	73. D
41. B	52. D	63. C	74. 1.73
42. C	53. See solution	64. D	75. B
43. B	54. C	65. C	76. See solution
44. B	55. B	66. 231	77. See solution
45. C	56. See solution	67. C	78. D
46. A	57. D	68. B	79. A
47. D	58. A	69. C	80. 1.15
48. A	59. D	70. D	
49. A	60. C	71. See solution	

39. B

To sketch the graph of the absolute value of $y = f(x)$, the part of the graph that lies below the x-axis on the graph of $y = f(x)$ is reflected in the x-axis; that is, it is reflected to lie above the line $y = 0$.
Thus, the point $(2, -6)$ becomes $(2, 6)$ on the graph of $y = |f(x)|$.
The graph of $y = |f(x)| + 2$ is then obtained by translating the graph of $y = |f(x)|$ up 2 units.

The point $(2, 6)$ becomes the point $(2, 8)$.
Therefore, the corresponding point on the graph of $y = |f(x)| + 2$ has the coordinates $(2, 8)$.

40. C

The graph of the absolute function $y = |f(x)|$ will reflect in the x-axis any portion of the graph of $y = f(x)$ that is below the x-axis. For example, let $y = f(x)$ be represented by the graph shown.

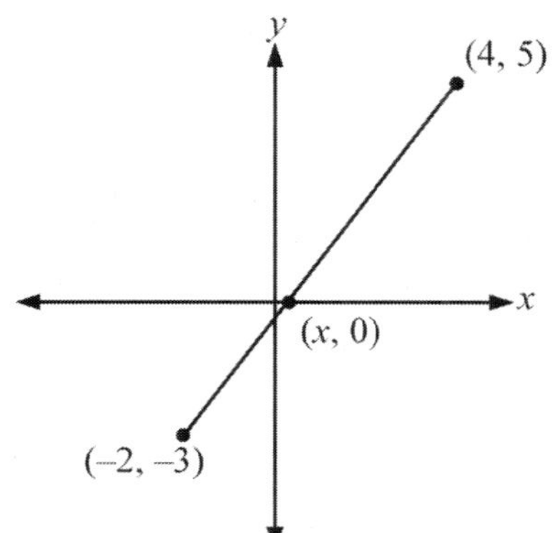

The graph of $y = |f(x)|$ will then appear as shown here.

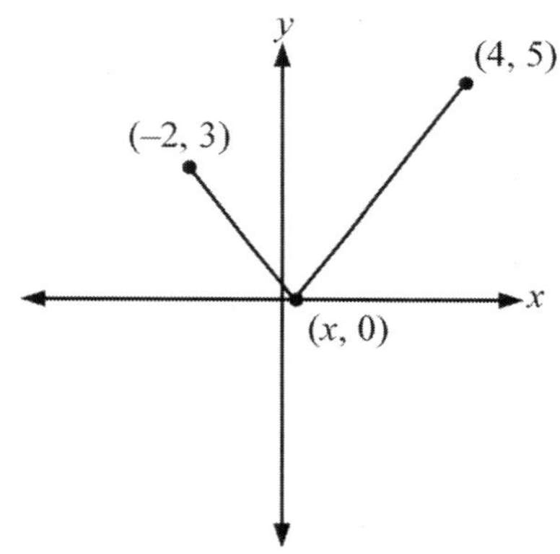

The range of $y = |f(x)|$ is therefore $0 \le y \le 5$.

41. B

To arrive at the equation $y - 7 = |x + 5|$ from $y = |x|$, substitute $x + 5$ for x and $y - 7$ for y in the equation $y = |x|$. When $x + 5$ is substituted for x and $y - 7$ is substituted for y, the graph of $y = |x|$ will be translated 5 units left and 7 units up. Thus, point $(-3, 3)$, which is on the graph of $y = |x|$, becomes point $(-3 - 5, 3 + 7) = (-8, 10)$ on the graph of $y - 7 = |x + 5|$.

42. C

To arrive at the equation $y = |x - 5| + 7$, or $y - 7 = |x - 5|$, from the equation $y = |x|$, substitute $x - 5$ for x and $y - 7$ for y in the equation $y = |x|$. When $x - 5$ is substituted for x and $y - 7$ is substituted for y, the point (x, y) on the graph of $y = |x|$ will be translated 5 units to the right and 7 units up. Therefore, the corresponding point to (x, y) on the graph of $y = |x|$ will be $(x + 5, y + 7)$ on the graph of $y = |x - 5| + 7$.

43. B

Since $g(x) = -f(x)$, the graph of function g is the graph of function f reflected in the x-axis. Therefore, any point (x, y) on the graph of function f will become the point $(x, -y)$ on the graph of function g. Notice that the x-coordinate of the points (x, y) and $(x, -y)$ are the same and that the y-coordinates have different signs. It then follows that since the domain of $f(x) = |x|$ is $x \in \mathbb{R}$, the domain of $g(x) = -f(x)$ is also $x \in \mathbb{R}$. However, the range of $f(x) = |x|$ is different from the range of $g(x) = -f(x)$. The range of $f(x) = |x|$ is $y \geq 0$, and the range of $g(x) = -f(x)$ is $y \leq 0$. Thus, the graph of function g will have the same domain but a different range than f.

44. B

Determine the equation of the graph of the transformed function for each description.

Step 1
Determine the equation of the graph of the transformed function for description I.

If the graph of $y = |x|$ is translated 6 units down, the equation of the resulting graph is $y = |x| - 6$.

If the graph of $y = |x| - 6$ is then reflected in the x-axis, the equation of the transformed graph can be determined by substituting $-y$ for y as follows:
$-y = |x| - 6$
Divide each term by -1.
$y = -|x| + 6$

The equation of the transformed graph will be $y = -|x| + 6$.

Step 2
Determine the equation of the graph of the transformed function for description II.

If the graph of $y = |x|$ is translated 6 units left and 6 units up, the equation of the resulting graph is $y - 6 = |x + 6|$ or $y = |x + 6| + 6$.

If this graph is then reflected in the x-axis, the equation of the transformed graph will be $-y = |x + 6| + 6$ or $y = -|x + 6| - 6$.

Step 3
Determine the equation of the graph of the transformed function for description III.

If the graph of $y = |x|$ is reflected in the x-axis, then the equation of the resulting graph is $-y = |x|$ or $y = -|x|$.

If this graph is then translated 6 units up, the equation of the transformed graph will be $y - 6 = -|x|$ or $y = -|x| + 6$.

Step 4
Determine the equation of the graph of the transformed function for description IV.
If the graph of $y = |x|$ is reflected in the x-axis, then the equation of the resulting graph is $y = -|x|$.
If this graph is then translated 6 units down and 6 units to the right, the equation of the transformed graph will be $y + 6 = -|x - 6|$ or $y = -|x - 6| - 6$.

Step 5
Identify the two new and identical graphs.
In order for the graphs to be identical, their respective defining equations must be identical.
The equations $y = -|x| + 6$ from step 1 and $y = -|x| + 6$ from step 3 are identical.
Therefore, descriptions I and III will produce two new and identical graphs.

45. C

Observe that the point $(-4, 4)$ on the graph of $y = f(x)$ becomes the point $(-4, 2)$ on the graph of the transformed function. As well, the point $(4, 4)$ on the graph of $y = f(x)$ becomes the point $(4, 2)$ on the graph of the transformed function.

The x-coordinates of the points $(-4, 4)$ and $(-4, 2)$ are the same, and the y-coordinate of the point $(-4, 2)$ is half the y-coordinate of the point $(-4, 4)$. The same relationship between the x- and y-coordinates exists for the points $(4, 4)$ and $(4, 2)$. Therefore, to arrive at the graph of the transformed function from the graph of $y = f(x)$, the graph of $y = f(x)$ must be vertically stretched by a factor of $\frac{1}{2}$ about the x-axis.

The equation of the transformed function can be obtained by substituting $2y$ (the reciprocal of $\frac{1}{2}$ is 2) for y in the equation $y = f(x)$. It then follows that the equation of the transformed function is $2y = f(x)$, or $y = \frac{1}{2} f(x)$.

46. A

To obtain the graph of $y = \frac{3}{2}|x|$ from the graph of $y = |x|$, vertically stretch the graph of $y = |x|$ by a factor of $\frac{3}{2}$ (the coefficient of $|x|$ in the equation $y = \frac{3}{2}|x|$) about the x-axis.

Any point (x, y) on the graph of $y = |x|$ becomes the point $\left(x, \frac{3}{2} \times y\right) = \left(x, \frac{3}{2}y\right)$ on the graph of $y = \frac{3}{2}|x|$.

Observe that the points (4, 4) and (−2, 2) are on the graph of $y = |x|$. Therefore, the corresponding points on the graph of $y = \frac{3}{2}|x|$ must be $\left(4, \frac{3}{2} \times 4\right) = (4, 6)$ and $\left(-2, \frac{3}{2} \times 2\right) = (-2, 3)$, respectively.

Only the graph shown here passes through points (4, 6) and (−2, 3).

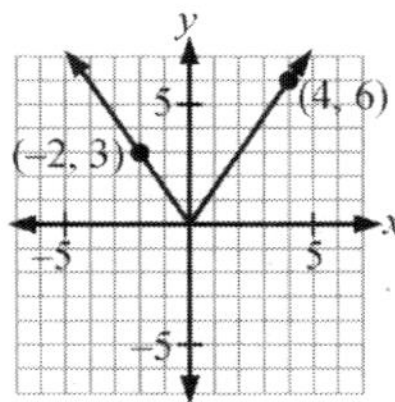

47. D

Step 1

Determine the equation of the function if the graph of $f(x) = |x|$ (or $y = |x|$) is vertically stretched about the x-axis by a factor of 2.

If the graph of $y = |x|$ is vertically stretched about the x-axis by a factor of 2, then the equation of the resulting transformed graph can be determined by substituting $\frac{1}{2}y$ (the reciprocal of 2 is $\frac{1}{2}$) for y in the equation $y = |x|$.

This results in the equation $\frac{1}{2}y = |x|$, or $y = 2|x|$.

Step 2

Determine the equation of the function if the graph of $y = 2|x|$ is translated 5 units down.

If the graph of $y = 2|x|$ is translated 5 units down, the equation of the resulting transformed function can be obtained by substituting $y + 5$ for y in the equation $y = 2|x|$.

This results in the equation $y + 5 = 2|x|$, or $y = 2|x| - 5$.

Step 3

Determine the domain and range of $y = 2|x| - 5$.

The domain of $y = 2|x| - 5$ is $x \in \mathbb{R}$, and the range is $y \geq -5$.

Step 4

Determine which of the given functions has the same domain and range as the transformed function $y = 2|x| - 5$.

The functions $g(x) = -2|x| + 5$ and $g(x) = -|x+3| + 5$ have each been reflected in the x-axis. Function f has not been reflected in the x-axis. Therefore, these functions will not have the same range as the transformed function $y = 2|x| - 5$.

Function $g(x) = 2|x-5|$ has the range $y \geq 0$. Therefore, this function does not have the same range as $y = 2|x| - 5$.

The domain of $g(x) = |x-3| - 5$ is $x \in \mathbb{R}$, and the range is $y \geq -5$. This function has the same domain and range as $y = 2|x| - 5$.

48. A

Since the graph of $y = |x|$ opens upward and the graph of the transformed image opens downward, the graph of $y = |x|$ has been reflected in the x-axis. If the graph of $y = |x|$ is reflected in the x-axis, the equation of the resulting transformed graph is $y = -|x|$.

Observe that the vertex of the graph of the transformed image is at the point (2, −5). The vertex of the graph of $y = -|x|$ is at the point (0, 0). Thus, the graph of $y = -|x|$ has been translated 2 units to the right and 5 units down in order to correspond to the graph of the transformed image. It then follows that the equation of the graph of the transformed image can be determined by substituting $x - 2$ for x and $y + 5$ for y in the equation $y = -|x|$.

$$\begin{aligned} y &= -|x| \\ y + 5 &= -|x-2| \\ y &= -|x-2| - 5 \end{aligned}$$

The equation of the graph of the transformed image is $y = -|x-2| - 5$.

49. A

Step 1

Identify appropriate points on Graph 1.

Possible points on Graph 1 include (−9, 6), (−6, 0), (−3, 3), (0, 0), and (3, 6).

Step 2

For each of the points (−9, 6), (−6, 0), (−3, 3), (0, 0), and (3, 6), identify the corresponding point on Graph 2.

Point (−9, 6) corresponds to point (−3, 6), point (−6, 0) corresponds to point (−2, 0), point (−3, 3) corresponds to point (−1, 3), point (0, 0) corresponds to point (0, 0), and point (3, 6) corresponds to point (1, 6).

Step 3
Determine how each transformed point can be obtained from the corresponding point on Graph 1. Notice that the y-coordinate of any point on Graph 2 is the same as the y-coordinate of the corresponding point on graph 1. Also, notice that the x-coordinate of any point on Graph 2 is $\frac{1}{3}$ the x-coordinate of the corresponding point. Point (x, y) on graph 1 is transformed to point $\left(\frac{1}{3}x, y\right)$ on Graph 2.

Step 4`
Determine a possible equation for Graph 2.
Since point (x, y) on Graph 1 is transformed to point $\left(\frac{1}{3}x, y\right)$ on Graph 2, Graph 2 is obtained by horizontally stretching Graph 1 about the y-axis by a factor of $\frac{1}{3}$. The equation of Graph 2 can be arrived at by substituting $3x$ for x (the reciprocal of $\frac{1}{3}$ is 3) in the equation $y = f(x)$. Thus, a possible equation of Graph 2 is $y = f(3x)$.

50. A

Since the graph of $y = 9x^2 - 1$ is stretched horizontally about the y-axis by a factor of 6, the equation of the transformed graph can be obtained by substituting $\frac{1}{6}x$ (the reciprocal of 6 is $\frac{1}{6}$) for x in the equation $y = 9x^2 - 1$.

$$\begin{aligned} y &= 9x^2 - 1 \\ &= 9\left(\frac{1}{6}x\right)^2 - 1 \\ &= 9\left(\frac{1}{36}x^2\right) - 1 \\ &= \frac{1}{4}x^2 - 1 \end{aligned}$$

The equation of the transformed graph is $y = \frac{1}{4}x^2 - 1$.

51. D

Step 1
Determine the transformation required to transform the graph of $y = f(x)$ to the graph of $y = 2f(x)$.
To arrive at the equation $y = 2f(x)$ (which is equivalent to $\frac{y}{2} = f(x)$) from the equation $y = f(x)$, substitute $\frac{y}{2}$ for y in the equation $y = f(x)$. When $\frac{y}{2}$ (or $\frac{1}{2}y$) is substituted for y in the equation $y = f(x)$, the graph of $y = f(x)$ will be vertically stretched about the x-axis by a factor of 2 (the reciprocal of $\frac{1}{2}$ is 2).

Step 2
Identify appropriate ordered pairs on the graph of $y = f(x)$.
Some ordered pairs on the graph of $y = f(x)$ are $(-4, 2)$, $(0, 2)$, $(2, -4)$, and $(4, 4)$.

Step 3
For each of the ordered pairs $(-4, 2)$, $(0, 2)$, $(2, -4)$, and $(4, 4)$, determine the corresponding point on the graph of $y = 2f(x)$.
Since the graph of $y = f(x)$ must be stretched vertically about the x-axis by a factor of 2 to obtain the graph of $y = 2f(x)$, a point (x, y) on the graph of $y = f(x)$ will be transformed to the corresponding point $(x, 2 \times y) = (x, 2y)$ on the graph of $y = 2f(x)$.
Thus, for the ordered pairs $(-4, 2)$, $(0, 2)$, $(2, -4)$, and $(4, 4)$, the corresponding points are as follows:

- Point $(-4, 2)$ corresponds to $(-4, 2 \times 2) = (-4, 4)$.
- Point $(0, 2)$ corresponds to $(0, 2 \times 2) = (0, 4)$.
- Point $(2, -4)$ corresponds to $(2, -4 \times 2) = (2, -8)$.
- Point $(4, 4)$ corresponds to $(4, 4 \times 2) = (4, 8)$.

Step 4
Determine which graph passes through points $(-4, 4)$, $(0, 4)$, $(2, -8)$, and $(4, 8)$.
Graph D passes through these four points; therefore, it is the graph of $y = 2f(x)$.

52. D

Step 1
Identify the ordered pairs that define the x-intercepts of the graph $y = f(x)$.
Since the graph of $y = f(x)$ crosses the x-axis where $x = -1$ and $x = 5$, the x-intercepts of the graph of $y = f(x)$ are located at the ordered pairs $(-1, 0)$ and $(5, 0)$.

Step 2
Determine the x-intercepts of the transformed graph. Since the graph of $y = f(x)$ is vertically stretched about the x-axis by a factor of $\frac{1}{5}$, a point (x, y) on the graph of $y = f(x)$ will be transformed to the corresponding point $\left(x, \frac{1}{5} \times y\right) = \left(x, \frac{1}{5}y\right)$ on the graph of the transformed function. Thus, the ordered pair $(-1, 0)$ corresponds to the point $\left(-1, 0 \times \frac{1}{5}\right) = (-1, 0)$, and the point $(5, 0)$ corresponds to the point $\left(5, 0 \times \frac{1}{5}\right) = (5, 0)$ on the graph of the transformed function. It then follows that the x-intercepts of the graph of the transformed function are also located at the ordered pairs $(-1, 0)$ and $(5, 0)$.

53.

The equation $y = f(x - 8)$ can be obtained from the equation $y = f(x)$ by substituting $x - 8$ for x in the equation $y = f(x)$.

When $x - 8$ is substituted for x in the equation $y = f(x)$, the graph of $y = f(x)$ will be translated 8 units to the right. Therefore, the ordered pair $(k, 7)$, which is on the graph of $y = f(x)$, will be transformed to the ordered pair$(k + 8, 7)$ on the graph of $y = f(x - 8)$.

Since it is given that $(k, 7)$ is transformed to the ordered pair $(12, 7)$, the value of k can be determined as follows:

$$k + 8 = 12$$
$$k = 4$$

54. C

Step 1
Determine the x-intercepts of the graph of $y = f(x)$. The x-intercepts of the graph are $(-3, 0)$, $(-1, 0)$, and $(2, 0)$.

Step 2
Determine how the graph of $y = f(x - 7)$ can be obtained from the graph of $y = f(x)$.
In order to generate the equation $y = f(x - 7)$ from the equation $y = f(x)$, it is necessary to substitute $x - 7$ for x in the equation $y = f(x)$. Therefore, the graph of $y = f(x)$ must be translated 7 units to the right in order to arrive at the graph of $y = f(x - 7)$.

Step 3
Determine the x-intercepts of the graph of $y = f(x - 7)$.
Since the graph of $y = f(x - 7)$ is 7 units to the right of the graph of $y = f(x)$, the x-intercepts of $y = f(x - 7)$are located at the ordered pairs $(-3 + 7, 0) = (4, 0)$, $(-1 + 7, 0) = (6, 0)$, and $(2 + 7, 0) = (9, 0)$. Only alternative C gives one of these x-intercepts.

55. B

The equation $y + 1 = f(x) - 4$ can be written as $y + 5 = f(x)$.

To obtain the equation $y + 5 = f(x)$ from the equation $y = f(x)$, it is necessary to substitute $y + 5$ for y in the equation $y = f(x)$.

When $y + 5$ is substituted for y, the graph of $y = f(x)$ will be translated vertically 5 units down.

56.

Step 1
Rewrite the equation $y = f(x) + 2$ as $y - 2 = f(x)$.

Step 2
Determine what transformation has been applied to the graph of $y = f(x)$.
To obtain the equation $y - 2 = f(x)$ from $y = f(x)$, $y - 2$ is substituted for y in $y = f(x)$. As a result, the graph of $y = f(x)$ will be translated 2 units up, and every ordered pair (x, y) on the graph of $y = f(x)$ will be translated to the ordered pair $(x, y + 2)$ on the graph of $y - 2 = f(x)$.

Step 3
Determine at least 3 points that best represent the graph of $y = f(x)$.
Select the endpoints $(-8, -4)$, $(-3, 6)$, and $(6, -6)$ on the graph of $y = f(x)$. These points will become $(-8, -4 + 2) = (-8, -2)$, $(-3, 6 + 2) = (-3, 8)$ and $(6, -6 + 2) = (6, -4)$ on the graph of $y = f(x) + 2$.

Step 4
Sketch the translated graph.
Plot the new endpoints, and sketch the graph of $y = f(x) + 2$.

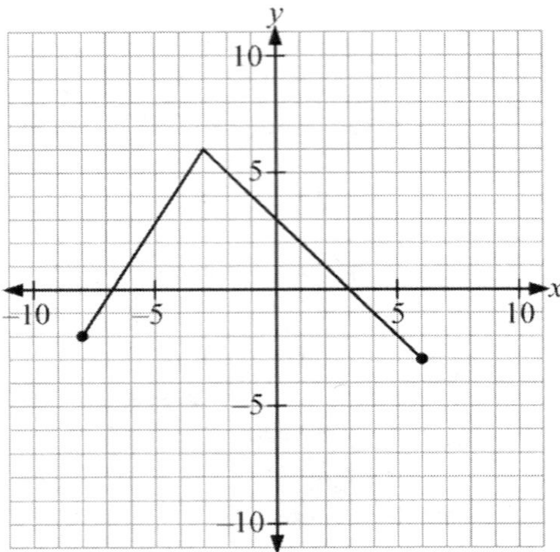

57. D

Step 1
Determine the vertical asymptotes of $g(x)$ for which $x \geq 0$.
Equate each factor in the denominator to 0, and solve.

$$3x - 2 = 0$$
$$3x = 2$$
$$x = \frac{2}{3}$$

$$x + 3 = 0$$
$$x = -3$$

$$x - 5 = 0$$
$$x = 5$$

The vertical asymptotes for which $x \geq 0$ are at $x = \frac{2}{3}$ and $x = 5$.

Step 2
Determine the vertical asymptotes of $g(|x|)$.
The graph of $y = g(|x|)$ is formed by the graph of $y = g(x)$, $x \geq 0$, and its reflection about the y-axis. For every vertical asymptote $x = a$, $a > 0$, on the graph of $y = g(x)$, there is also a vertical asymptote at $x = -a$ on the graph of $y = g(|x|)$.

Therefore, there are vertical asymptotes at $x = \pm\frac{2}{3}$ and $x = \pm 5$.

58. A

Step 1
Sketch the graph of $y = g(x)$ for $x \geq 0$.

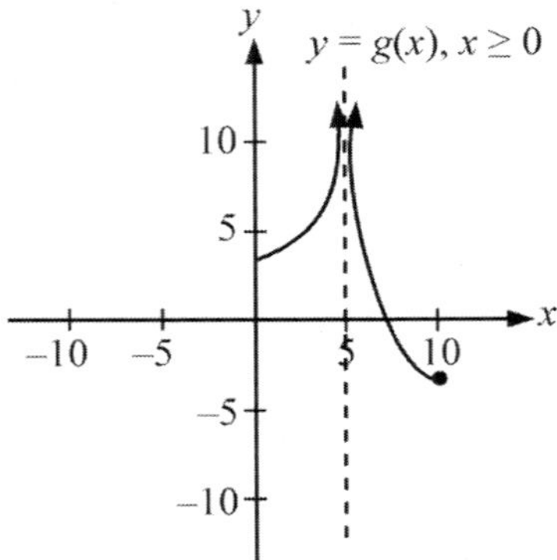

Step 2
Sketch the graph of the transformation $y = g(|x|)$ by adding the reflection of the graph in step 1 about the y-axis.

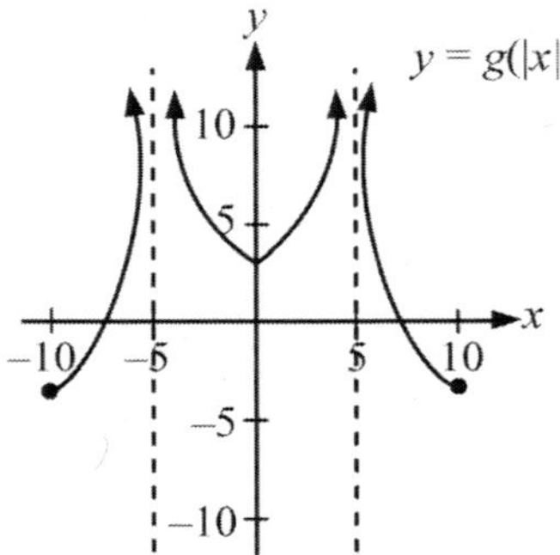

Step 3
Identify the domain of $y = g(|x|)$.
The transformed function $y = g(|x|)$ is defined for $-10 \leq x \leq 10$ but has vertical asymptotes at $x = \pm 5$, so the domain is $-10 \leq x \leq 10$, $x \neq \pm 5$.

59. D

Step 1
Sketch a graph that shows point $Q(-2, 5)$ and the line $x = 6$.

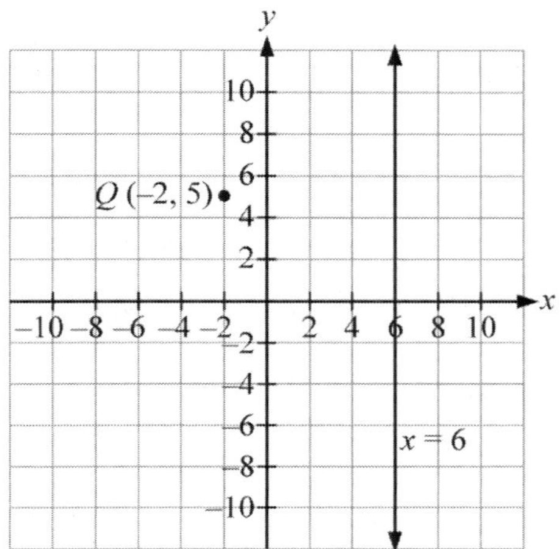

Step 2
Determine the distance from point $Q(-2, 5)$ to the line $x = 6$.
Point $Q(-2, 5)$ is $6 - (-2) = 8$ units from the line $x = 6$.

Step 3
Determine the distance from the transformed point (m, n) to the line $x = 6$.
Since the graph of $y = f(x)$ is stretched horizontally by a factor of $\frac{1}{4}$ about the line $x = 6$, the distance from point $Q(-2, 5)$ to $x = 6$ must be reduced to a quarter of what it was originally. Therefore, the transformed point must be $8 \times \frac{1}{4} = 2$ units from $x = 6$.

Step 4
Determine the coordinates of the transformed point.
The point that is 2 units to the left of the line $x = 6$ and has the same y-coordinate (since only a horizontal stretch has taken place) as point Q is the point $((6 - 2), 5) = (4, 5)$.

Step 5
Determine the value of m and n.
From the given information, point Q is transformed to point (m, n). Since point Q has been transformed to point $(4, 5)$, it follows that $(m, n) = (4, 5)$; therefore, $m = 4$ and $n = 5$.

Step 6
Determine the value of $m + n$.

$$\begin{aligned} m + n &= 4 + 5 \\ &= 9 \end{aligned}$$

60. C

Step 1
Sketch a graph that shows point $A(1, 2)$ and the line $y = -4$.

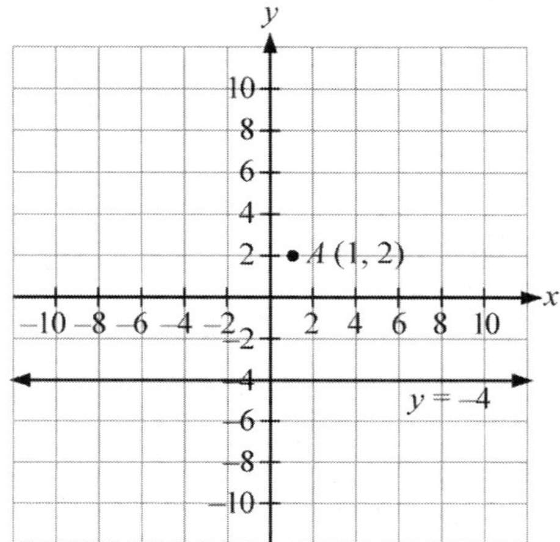

Step 2
Determine the distance from point $A(1, 2)$ to the line $y = -4$.
Point $A(1, 2)$ is $2 - (-4) = 6$ units from $y = -4$.

Step 3
Determine the distance from the transformed point (m, n) to the line $y = -4$.
Since the graph of $y = f(x)$ is stretched vertically by a factor of 3 about the line $y = -4$, the distance from point $A(1, 2)$ to $y = -4$ must be increased by a factor of 3. Point $A(1, 2)$ is 6 units from $y = -4$, so the transformed point must be $6 \times 3 = 18$ units from $y = -4$.

Step 4
Determine the coordinates of the transformed point.
The point that is 18 units above the line $y = -4$ and has the same x-coordinate (since only a vertical stretch has taken place) as point A is the point $(1, (-4 + 18)) = (1, 14)$.

Step 5
Determine the values of m and n.
From the given information, point A is transformed to point (m, n). Since point A has been transformed to point $(1, 14)$, it follows that $(m, n) = (1, 14)$. Thus, $m = 1$ and $n = 14$.

Step 6
Determine the value of $m + n$.

$$\begin{aligned} &m + n \\ &= 1 + 14 \\ &= 15 \end{aligned}$$

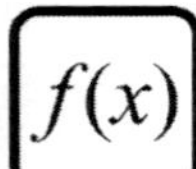

61. B

The given function can be expressed as $y = (x+4) \times 6$.

Determine the inverse of this function by first interchanging the variables and then solving for y.

$$x = (y+4) \times 6$$
$$\frac{x}{6} = \frac{(y+4) \times 6}{6}$$
$$\frac{x}{6} = y + 4$$
$$\frac{x}{6} - 4 = y + 4 - 4$$
$$\frac{x}{6} - 4 = y$$

To determine the inverse of a function following the interchanging of variables, the operations on the original function must be reversed (opposite operations performed) as must the order in which each operation was performed.

In this case, dividing by 6 must be done first since multiplying by 6 was the last operation performed on the original function. Then, the reverse of adding 4, which is subtracting 4, must be performed.

62. B

Step 1
Replace $f(x)$ with y.

$$f(x) = \frac{1}{2}(x+6)^2 - 5$$
$$y = \frac{1}{2}(x+6)^2 - 5$$

Step 2
Interchange x and y.

$$y = \frac{1}{2}(x+6)^2 - 5$$
$$x = \frac{1}{2}(y+6)^2 - 5$$

Step 3
Solve for y.

$$x = \frac{1}{2}(y+6)^2 - 5$$
$$x + 5 = \frac{1}{2}(y+6)^2$$
$$2x + 10 = (y+6)^2$$
$$\pm\sqrt{2x+10} = y + 6$$
$$\pm\sqrt{2x+10} - 6 = y$$
$$y = \pm\sqrt{2x+10} - 6$$

Note that y cannot be replaced by $f^{-1}(x)$ since the inverse is not a function.

63. C

Step 1

Substitute $x^2 - 25$ for $g(x)$ and $x + 5$ for $h(x)$ in the equation $f(x) = \frac{g(x)}{h(x)}$.

$$f(x) = \frac{x^2 - 25}{x + 5}$$

Step 2
State the non-permissible values.

$$x + 5 \neq 0$$
$$x \neq -5$$

The non-permissible value of x is -5.

Step 3
Factor the numerator, and reduce.

$$f(x) = \frac{x^2 - 25}{x + 5}$$
$$= \frac{(x-5)(x+5)}{x+5}$$
$$= x - 5$$

64. D

Step 1

Substitute $x^2 + 2x - 4$ for $f(x)$ and $x^2 + 25$ for $g(x)$ into the equation $h(x) = f(x)g(x)$.

$$h(x) = (x^2 + 2x - 4)(x^2 + 25)$$

Step 2
Expand by using the distributive property, and simplify by combining like terms.

$$h(x) = (x^2 + 2x - 4)(x^2 + 25)$$
$$= x^4 + 2x^3 - 4x^2 + 25x^2 + 50x - 100$$
$$= x^4 + 2x^3 + 21x^2 + 50x - 100$$

65. C

Step 1

Determine the value of $f\left(-\frac{1}{2}\right)$.

Substitute $-\frac{1}{2}$ for x in $f(x)$.

$$f\left(-\frac{1}{2}\right) = 6 - 4\left(-\frac{1}{2}\right)$$

Evaluate.

$$6 - 4\left(-\frac{1}{2}\right) = 6 + 2$$
$$= 8$$

Step 2

Determine the value of $g\left(f\left(-\frac{1}{2}\right)\right)$ or $g(8)$.

Substitute 8 for x in $g(x)$.

$g(8) = \frac{1}{2}(8) - 3$

Evaluate.

$$\begin{aligned}\frac{1}{2}(8) - 3 &= 4 - 3\\ &= 1\end{aligned}$$

$g\left(f\left(-\frac{1}{2}\right)\right) = 1$

66. 231

Step 1

Calculate the value of $f(-1)$.

Substitute -1 into the function $f(x)$, wherever the variable x appears. Then, simplify the expression.

$$\begin{aligned}f(x) &= 3x^2 - 12\\ f(-1) &= 3(-1)^2 - 12\\ &= 3 - 12\\ &= -9\end{aligned}$$

Step 2

Calculate the value of $f(f(-1))$.

Since $f(-1) = -9$, $f(f(-1)) = f(-9)$.

Substitute -9 into the function $f(x)$, wherever the variable x appears, and then simplify the expression.

$$\begin{aligned}f(x) &= 3x^2 - 12\\ f(-9) &= 3(-9)^2 - 12\\ &= 3(81) - 12\\ &= 243 - 12\\ &= 231\end{aligned}$$

67. C

Step 1

Write the inverse of function N.

The inverse of function N is obtained by interchanging the values in the ordered pairs of function N. Therefore, the inverse of function N, N', is N':{(y, 4), (8, 7), (6, x)}.

Step 2

Determine whether the statement "The x variable cannot equal 4 or 7" is true.

In order for N to be classified as a function, the first component of each ordered pair in function N must be different. Therefore, the value of x cannot be 4 or 7. The statement is true.

Step 3

Determine whether the statement "The y variable cannot equal 6 or 8" is true.

In order for the inverse of function N to be classified as a function, the first component of each of its ordered pairs must be different. Therefore, the value of y cannot be 6 or 8. The statement is true.

Step 4

The statement "The x variable can never equal the value of y" is false. There are a few values where the value of x cannot equal the value of y.

For example, when $x = y = 8$ or $x = y = 4$. However, there are an infinite number of values where the value of x can equal the value of y. For example, when $x = y = 2$ or $x = y = 5$.

Step 5

Determine whether the statement "The y variable can equal 4, and x can equal 6" is true.

The statement is true. If $x = 6$, and $y = 4$, then N and N' are as follows:

N:{(4, 4), (7, 8), (6, 6)}
N':{(4, 4), (8, 7), (6, 6)}

For the given values of x and y, both N and N' can be classified as functions.

68. B

Step 1

Write the set of ordered pairs that define function f.

Since $0 \le x \le 3$ and x is a member of the integers, begin by substituting each of the values 0, 1, 2, and 3 for x in the equation $f(x) = x^2 - 4$ as follows:

$f(0) = (0)^2 - 4 = -4$

$f(1) = (1)^2 - 4 = -3$

$f(2) = (2)^2 - 4 = 0$

$f(3) = (3)^2 - 4 = 5$

Next, write the set of ordered pairs that define function f. These are
{(0, −4), (1, −3), (2, 0), (3, 5)}.

Step 2

Write the set of ordered pairs that define $f^{-1}(x)$.

In order to write the ordered pairs that define $f^{-1}(x)$, it is necessary to interchange the values in the ordered pairs that define function f. Therefore, the set of ordered pairs that could define the inverse of function f, $f^{-1}(x)$, is
{(−4, 0), (−3, 1), (0, 2), (5, 3)}.

69. C

Verify for $x = 60°$.

	LHS	RHS
Substitute 60° for *x*.	$\dfrac{\cos 60°}{1 - \sin 60°}$	$\dfrac{1 + \sin 60°}{\cos 60°}$
Calculate the exact values.	$\dfrac{\frac{1}{2}}{1 - \frac{\sqrt{3}}{2}}$	$\dfrac{1 + \frac{\sqrt{3}}{2}}{\frac{1}{2}}$
Find a common denominator.	$\dfrac{\frac{1}{2}}{\frac{2 - \sqrt{3}}{2}}$	$\dfrac{\frac{2 + \sqrt{3}}{2}}{\frac{1}{2}}$
Multiply the numerator by the reciprocal of the denominator.	$\dfrac{1}{2} \times \dfrac{2}{(2 - \sqrt{3})}$	$\dfrac{(2 + \sqrt{3})}{2} \times \dfrac{2}{1}$
Simplify.	$\dfrac{1}{2 - \sqrt{3}}$	$2 + \sqrt{3}$
Rationalize the denominator.	$\dfrac{1}{(2 - \sqrt{3})} \times \dfrac{(2 + \sqrt{3})}{(2 + \sqrt{3})}$	$2 + \sqrt{3}$
Simplify.	$\dfrac{(2 + \sqrt{3})}{4 - 3}$	$2 + \sqrt{3}$
	$2 + \sqrt{3}$	$2 + \sqrt{3}$
	LHS =	RHS

The exact value of the equation is $2 + \sqrt{3}$.

70. D

Step 1

Interpret the required range in terms of transformations to the graph of an exponential function of the form $y = b^x$, $b > 1$.

Eliminate any functions that do not have a range of $y > 1$.

Since the desired exponential function has a range of $y > 1$, the function has been vertically translated up 1 unit ($y = b^x$ has a range of $y > 0$).

The function $f(x) = 4(3)^{x+1}$ has not been vertically translated, so its range is $y > 0$, not $y > 1$.

The function $f(x) = (3)^x + 3$ has been vertically translated up 3 units, so the range is $y > 3$, not $y > 1$.

The functions $f(x) = 4(3)^x + 1$ and $f(x) = (3)^{x+1} + 1$ have both been translated up 1 unit, and both functions will have a range of $y > 1$.

Step 2

Determine which of the remaining two functions have a *y*-intercept of 4.

If the desired function has a *y*-intercept of 4, $f(0) = 4$.

Using the function $f(x) = 4(3)^x + 1$, determine the value of $f(0)$.

$$\begin{aligned} f(x) &= 4(3)^x + 1 \\ f(0) &= 4(3)^0 + 1 \\ &= 4(1) + 1 \\ &= 4 + 1 \\ &= 5 \end{aligned}$$

Using the function $f(x) = (3)^{x+1} + 1$, determine the value of $f(0)$.

$$\begin{aligned} f(x) &= (3)^{x+1} + 1 \\ f(0) &= (3)^{0+1} + 1 \\ &= (3)^1 + 1 \\ &= 3 + 1 \\ &= 4 \end{aligned}$$

Therefore, $f(x) = (3)^{x+1} + 1$ is the correct function.

71.

Step 1

Sketch the graph of $y = 5^x$.

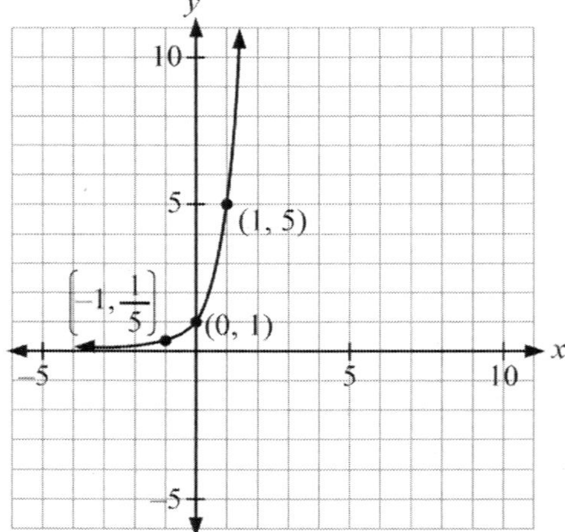

Step 2

Determine the transformations required to produce the graph of $y = 5^{x-4} + 1$.

The equation $y = 5^{x-4} + 1$ can be written as $y - 1 = 5^{x-4}$. To arrive at the equation $y - 1 = 5^{x-4}$, it is necessary to substitute $y - 1$ for *y* and $x - 4$ for *x* in the equation $y = 5^x$. The graph of $y = 5^{x-4} + 1$ is produced by translating the graph of $y = 5^x$1 unit up and 4 units to the right.

$f(x)$

Step 3

Sketch the graph of $y = 5^{x-4} + 1$.

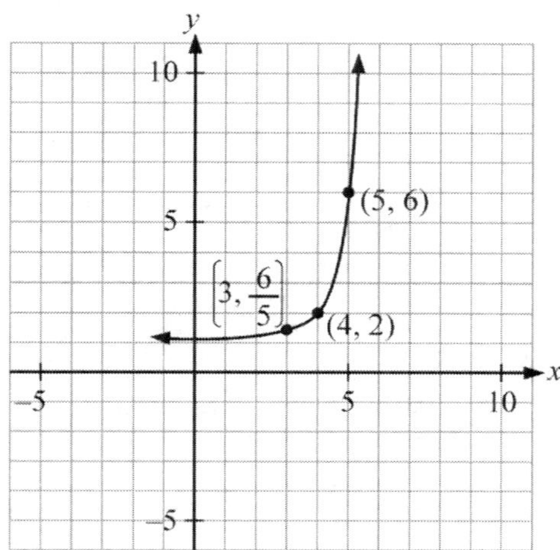

Step 4

From the graph of $y = 5^{x-4} + 1$, state the domain, range, and equation of the asymptote.

The domain is $x \in R$.

The range is $y > 1$. The range of the function $y = 5^x$ is $y > 0$. The graph of the function $y = 5^{x-4} + 1$ is $y > (0 + 1)$ or $y > 1$ since the graph of $y = 5^x$ is translated 1 unit up.

The equation of the horizontal asymptote is $y = 1$. The equation of the horizontal asymptote of the graph of the function $y = 5^x$ is $y = 0$. The equation of the horizontal asymptote of the graph of the function $y = 5^{x-4} + 1$ is $y = (0 + 1)$ or $y = 1$ since the graph of $y = 5^x$ is translated 1 unit up.

72. A

Evaluate the logarithmic expression. The expression $\log_7 1$ is of the form $\log_b 1$ and can be simplified by using the identity $\log_b 1 = 0$. Thus, $\log_7 1 = 0$.

It follows that,

$$\begin{aligned}\log_7 1 - 7 &= 0 - 7\\ &= -7\end{aligned}$$

73. D

Evaluate the logarithmic expression.

The expression $\log_{2z} 1$ is of the form $\log_b 1$ and can be evaluated by using the identity $\log_b 1 = 0$. It follows that $\log_{2z} 1 = 0$.

Therefore,

$$\begin{aligned}z + \log_{2z} 1 &= z + 0\\ &= z\end{aligned}$$

74. 1.73

Substitute $x = \frac{\pi}{6}$ into the left side and right side of the equation and evaluate each side.

LHS	RHS
$\dfrac{\cos\left(2\left(\frac{\pi}{6}\right)\right) + 1}{\sin\left(2\left(\frac{\pi}{6}\right)\right)}$	$\cot\left(\frac{\pi}{6}\right)$
$\dfrac{\cos\left(\frac{\pi}{3}\right) + 1}{\sin\left(\frac{\pi}{3}\right)}$	$\sqrt{3}$
$\dfrac{\frac{1}{2} + 1}{\frac{\sqrt{3}}{2}}$	≈ 1.73
$\dfrac{3}{\sqrt{3}}$	
$\sqrt{3}$	
≈ 1.73	

Since LHS = RHS, the identity is verified for $x = \frac{\pi}{6}$.

The left side and the right side of the given equation will equal 1.73.

75. B

In trigonometry, a number of identities can be used to represent the same function despite looking very different. The function $y = \sin(8x)$ includes a double angle that has no restriction on its domain in the given interval. Simplify the remaining functions, and compare the results, keeping in mind the function $y = \sin(8x)$ has a double angle with no restriction on the domain.

Step 1

Simplify the function $y = \cos(8x)\tan(8x)$.

$y = \cos(8x)\tan(8x)$

$y = \cos(8x)\left(\dfrac{\sin(8x)}{\cos(8x)}\right)$

$y = \sin(8x)$

Keep in mind that the $\cos(8x)$ in the denominator cannot equal zero, so the domain of the function must be restricted accordingly. Therefore, this function will have holes wherever $\cos(8x) = 0$, which is at $x = \frac{\pi}{16} \pm \frac{\pi n}{8}$.

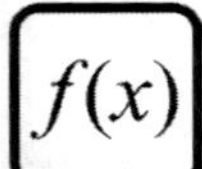

Step 2
Simplify the function $y = 2\sin(4x)\cos(4x)$.
Apply the double identity, $\sin(2A) = 2\sin(A)\cos(A)$.
$y = 2\sin(4x)\cos(4x)$
$y = \sin(2(4x))$
$y = \sin(8x)$
There are no restrictions on the domain.

Step 3
Simplify the function $y = 4\sin(2x)\cos(2x)\left(\cos^2(2x) - \sin^2(2x)\right)$. Apply the double-angle identities $\cos(2A) = \cos^2(A) - \sin^2(A)$ and $\sin(2A) = 2\sin(A)\cos(A)$.

$y = \begin{pmatrix} 4\sin(2x)\cos(2x) \\ \times\ (\cos^2(2x) - \sin^2(2x)) \end{pmatrix}$

$y = \begin{pmatrix} 2(2\sin(2x)\cos(2x)) \\ \times\ (\cos^2(2x) - \sin^2(2x)) \end{pmatrix}$

$y = 2(\sin(4x))(\cos(4x))$
$y = \sin(2 \times 4x)$
$y = \sin(8x)$
There are no restrictions on the domain.

Therefore, the only graph that would differ would be the graph of the function $y = \cos(8x)\tan(8x)$ because of the holes that would appear every time the function was undefined.

76.

Separately simplify the left- and right-hand sides of the equation, and show that the left-hand side of the equation equals the right-hand side of the equation. The given table shows the steps that can be used to prove the identity.

	LHS	RHS	
	$\sec x$	$\dfrac{\csc x}{\cot x}$	
Use the reciprocal identity.	$\dfrac{1}{\cos x}$	$\dfrac{\frac{1}{\sin x}}{\frac{\sin x}{\cos x}}$	Use the reciprocal and quotient identities.
		$\dfrac{1}{\sin x} \times \dfrac{\sin x}{\cos x}$	Multiply by the reciprocal.
		$\dfrac{1}{\cos x}$	Simplify.
	LHS =	RHS	

77.

Separately simplify the left- and right-hand sides of the equation. Show that the left-hand side of the equation equals the right-hand side of the equation. The given table shows the steps that can be used to prove the identity.

	LHS	RHS
	$\sin^2 x + \cos^2 x\tan^2 x$	$2\sin^2 x$
Use the quotient identity.	$\sin^2 x + \cos^2 x\left(\dfrac{\sin^2 x}{\cos^2 x}\right)$	
Simplify.	$\sin^2 x + \sin^2 x$	
Add.	$2\sin^2 x$	
	LHS =	RHS

78. D

Step 1
Apply the negative exponent property.
$x^{-\frac{4}{3}}$ can be written as $\dfrac{1}{x^{\frac{4}{3}}}$.

Step 2
Apply the rational exponent property.
$\dfrac{1}{x^{\frac{4}{3}}}$ is equivalent to $\dfrac{1}{\sqrt[3]{x^4}}$.

79. A

Step 1
Write the radicals as rational exponents.
$\sqrt[5]{w^2} \times \sqrt{w^4} = w^{\frac{2}{5}} \times w^{\frac{4}{2}}$

Step 2
Use the product law of exponents.

$$\begin{aligned} w^{\frac{2}{5}} \times w^{\frac{4}{2}} &= w^{\frac{2}{5}+\frac{4}{2}} \\ &= w^{\frac{2}{5}+\frac{2}{1}} \\ &= w^{\frac{2}{5}+\frac{10}{5}} \\ &= w^{\frac{12}{5}} \end{aligned}$$

Step 3
Write the rational expression as a radical.
$w^{\frac{12}{5}} = \sqrt[5]{w^{12}}$

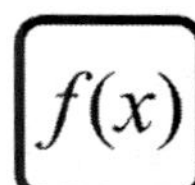

80. 1.15

Substitute $\frac{\pi}{6}$ for x, and evaluate each side of the equation.

LHS	RHS
$\csc\left(\frac{\pi}{6}\right)\tan\left(\frac{\pi}{6}\right)$	$\sec\left(\frac{\pi}{6}\right)$
$(2)\left(\frac{1}{\sqrt{3}}\right)$	$\frac{2}{\sqrt{3}}$
$\frac{2}{\sqrt{3}}$	≈ 1.15
≈ 1.15	

To the nearest hundredth, the LHS of the equation is 1.15.

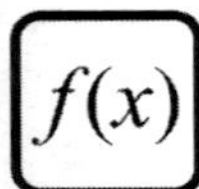

OPERATIONS OF FUNCTIONS EXERCISE #2

Use the following information to answer the next question.

The given figure shows the graph of the function $y = g(x)$.

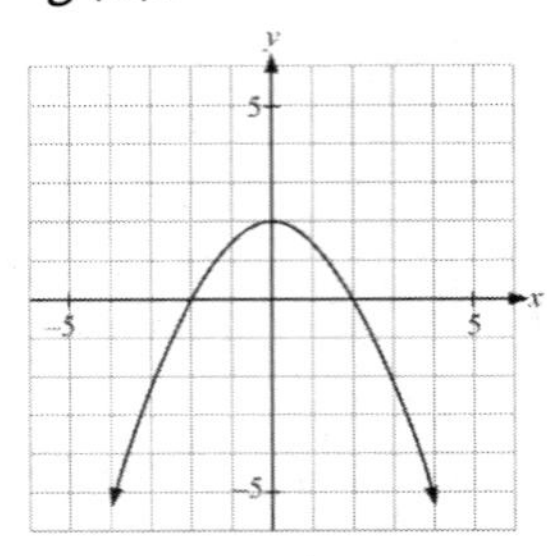

81. Which of the following graphs is the graph of the function $y = |g(x)|$?

A.

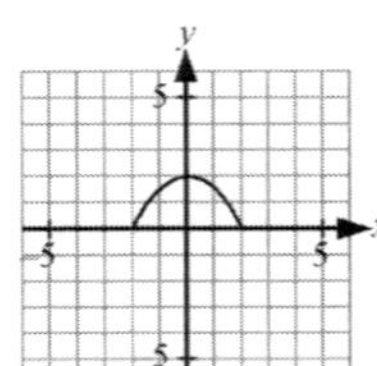

B.

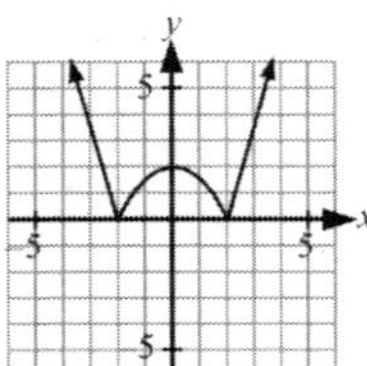

C.

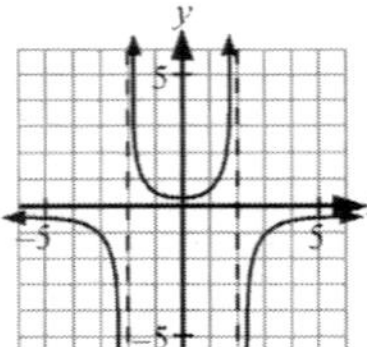

D.

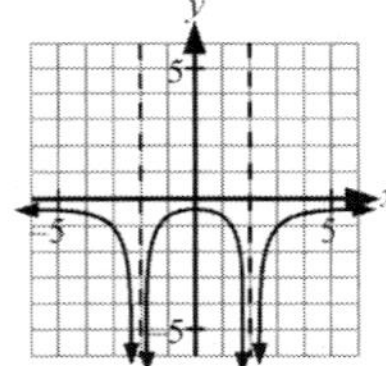

Use the following information to answer the next question.

The partial graph of $y = |x|$ is shown.

82. If the graph of $y = |x|$ is translated horizontally 2 units right and vertically 4 units up, the y-intercept of the transformed graph is __________.

Use the following information to answer the next question.

The partial graph of $y = f(x)$ is shown.

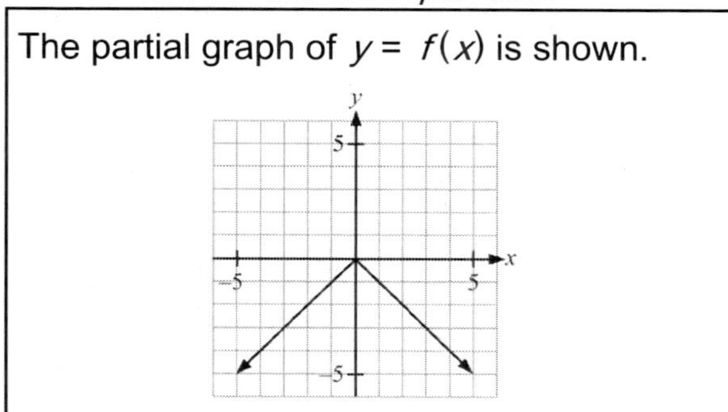

83. Which of the following graphs is the graph of $y = | f(x) |$?

A.

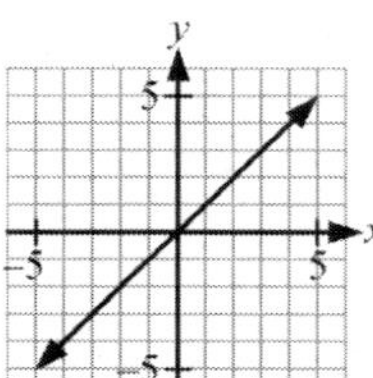

B.

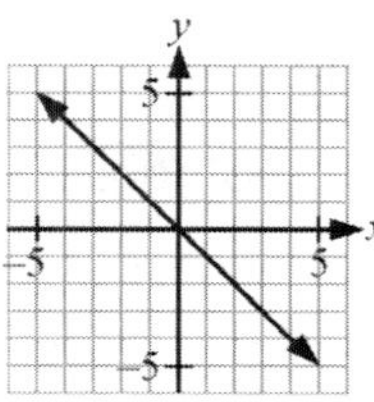

C.

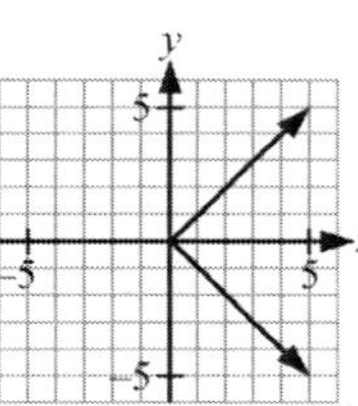

D.

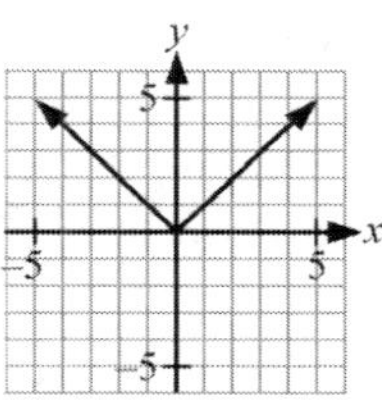

84. If y is replaced with $\frac{1}{3}y$ in the equation $y = | x |$, then the graph of $y = | x |$ will be stretched

A. horizontally about the y-axis by a factor of $\frac{1}{3}$

B. horizontally about the y-axis by a factor of 3

C. vertically about the x-axis by a factor of $\frac{1}{3}$

D. vertically about the x-axis by a factor of 3

Use the following information to answer the next question.

The graph of $y = | x |$ is vertically stretched about the x-axis by a factor of 2 and reflected in the x-axis. It is then horizontally translated 8 units left and vertically translated 12 units down.

85. The y-intercept of the graph of the resulting transformed function is

A. −4 **B.** −8

C. −16 **D.** −28

Use the following information to answer the next question.

The partial graph of $y = | f(x) |$ is shown.

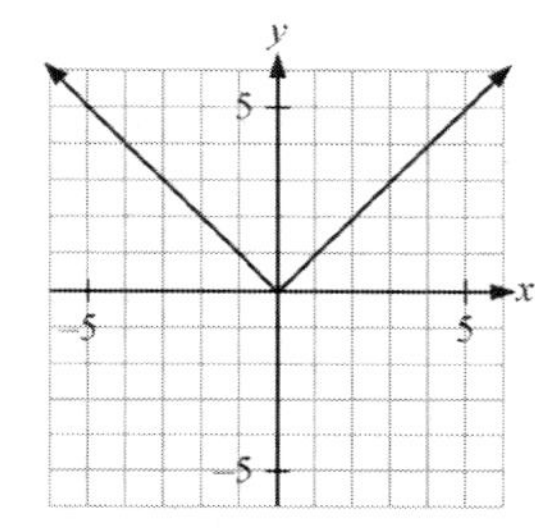

86. If the partial graph of $y = | f(x) |$ is reflected in the x-axis and then translated 4 units to the left and 3 units down, which of the following graphs shows the resulting transformed function?

A.

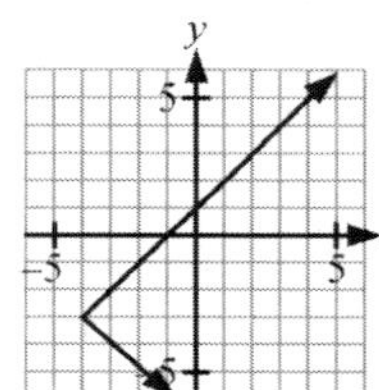

B.

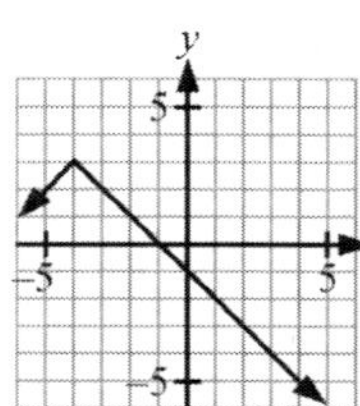

C.

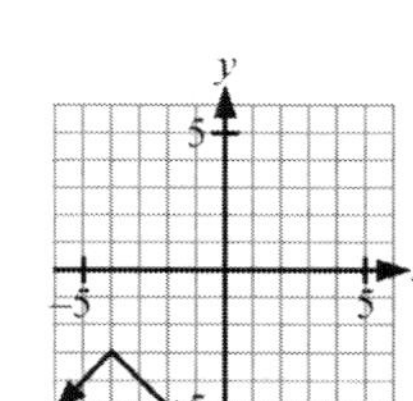

D.

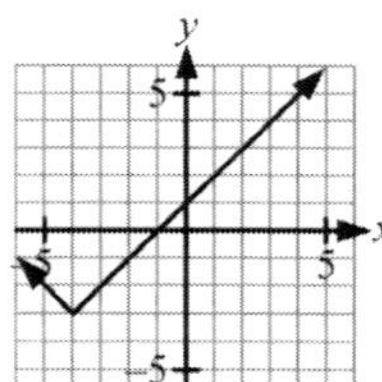

87. If the graph of the function $y = f(x)$ is transformed to the graph of $y = f(bx)$, where $b < 0$, then the graph of $y = f(x)$ will be

A. reflected in the y-axis.

B. reflected in the x-axis.

C. reflected about a point b.

D. translated along the y-axis.

Use the following information to answer the next question.

The partial graph of $y = g(x)$ is obtained by vertically stretching the graph of $y = |x|$ about the x-axis.

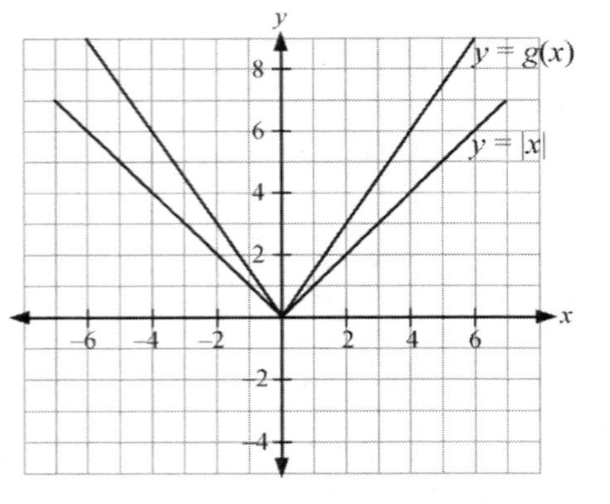

88. What is the equation of the graph of $y = g(x)$ in terms of $y = |x|$?

Use the following information to answer the next question.

The graph of $y = f(x)$ is shown.

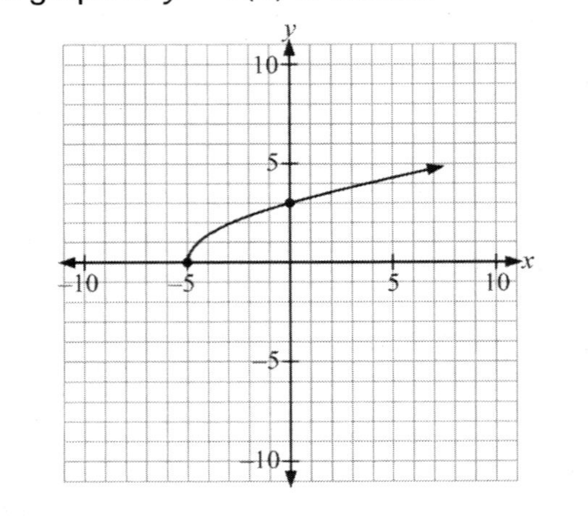

89. The domain of $y = f(x + 2)$ is

A. $x \in \mathrm{R}$

B. $x \geq -6$

C. $x \geq -2$

D. $-3 \leq x \leq 1$

90. If the graph of $y + 5 = f(x)$ is translated vertically 8 units up, then the equation of the graph of the transformed function is

A. $y = f(x) + 3$

B. $y = f(x) - 3$

C. $y = f(x) + 13$

D. $y = f(x) - 13$

91. The function $f(x) = \dfrac{x^2}{x - 2}$ has a domain of $-5 \leq x \leq 5,\ x \in I$. When the transformation $f(|x|)$ is applied to function $f(x)$, what are the invariant points?

A. $\left(-1, -\frac{1}{3}\right)$, (0, 0), (1, −1), (3, 9), (4, 8), $\left(5, \frac{25}{3}\right)$

B. (0, 0), (1, −1), (2, 0), (3, 9), (4, 8), $\left(5, \frac{25}{3}\right)$

C. (0, 0), (1, −1), (3, 9), (4, 8), $\left(5, \frac{25}{3}\right)$

D. (1, −1), (2, 0), (3, 9), (4, 8), $\left(5, \frac{25}{3}\right)$

Use the following information to answer the next question.

The graph of the function $y = g(x)$ is shown.

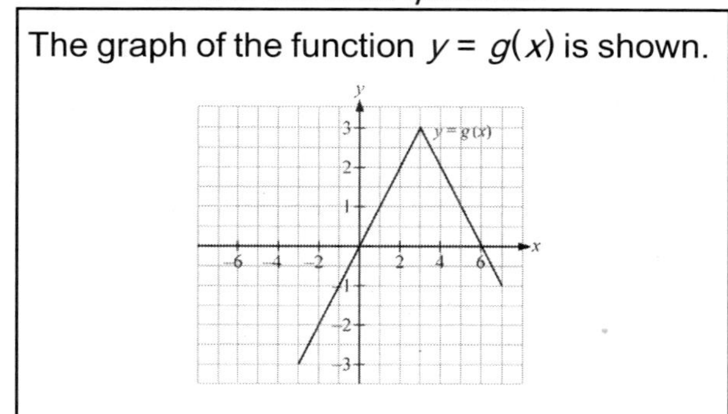

92. What is the graph and the range of the transformation $y = g(|x|)$?

A.

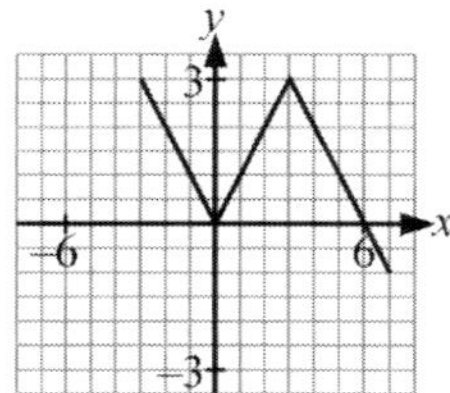

$-1 \leq y \leq 3$

B.

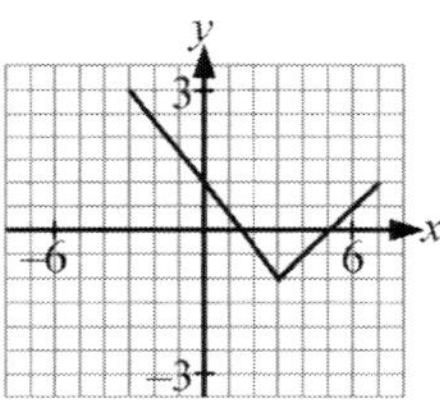

$-3 \leq y \leq 3$

C.

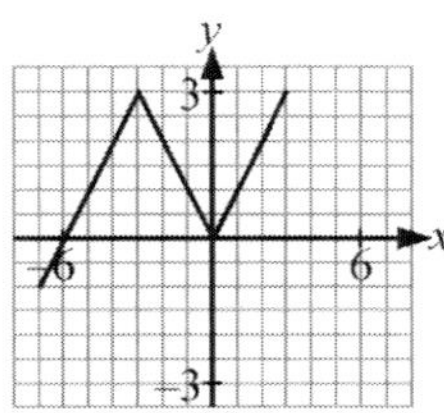

$-3 \leq y \leq 3$

D.

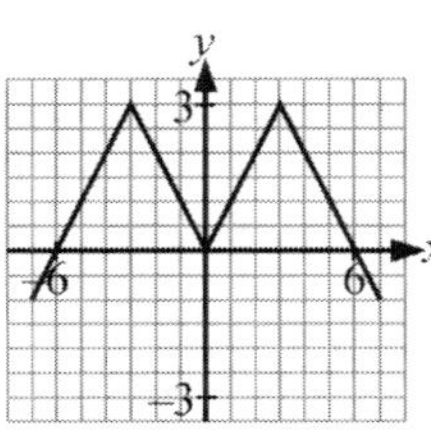

$-1 \leq y \leq 3$

Use the following information to answer the next question.

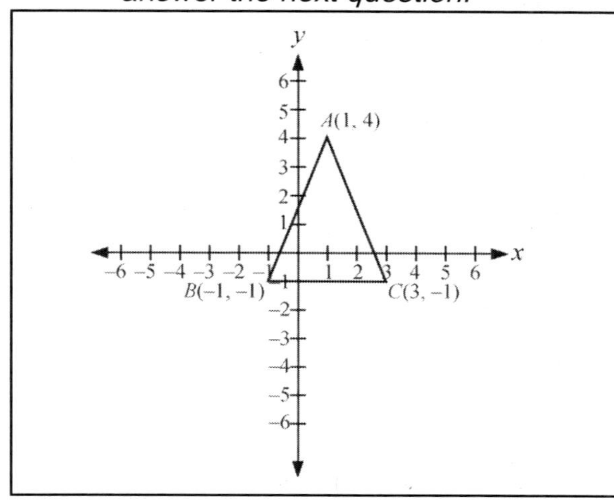

93. If the graph of the triangle shown is horizontally stretched about the line $x = 2$ by a factor of 3, the vertices A', B', and C' of the transformed triangle will be

A. $A'(3, 4)$, $B'(-3, -1)$, $C'(9, -1)$

B. $A'(2, 4)$, $B'(2, -1)$, $C'(9, -1)$

C. $A'(-1, 4)$, $B'(-7, -1)$, $C'(5, -1)$

D. $A'(3, 4)$, $B'(-2, -1)$, $C'(5, -1)$

94. The restriction on $f(x) = (x - 5)^2$ that will make $f^{-1}(x)$ a function is

A. $x \geq 5$ **B.** $x \geq -5$

C. $f(x) \geq 5$ **D.** $f(x) \geq -5$

95. If $f(x) = 2x - 15$ and $g(x) = 4x^2 + x - 2$, then $f(x) + g(x)$ is equal to

A. $4x - 30$

B. $-4x^2 - 13$

C. $4x^2 - x + 13$

D. $4x^2 + 3x - 17$

Use the following information to answer the next question.

For functions $g(x) = x^2 - 2x + 1$ and $h(x) = x^2 + 3x - 4$, a third function $f(x)$ is defined as $f(x) = g(x) - h(x)$.

96. The simplified form of $f(x)$ is

A. $x - 3$ **B.** $5x - 5$

C. $-5x + 5$ **D.** $-5x - 3$

97. If $g(f(x)) = 4$, where $f(x) = 3x - 7$ and $g(x) = 5 - 2x$, then x, correct to the nearest tenth, is equal to

A. -2.5 **B.** -0.7

C. 0.7 **D.** 2.5

Use the following information to answer the next question.

Each of the following sets of ordered pairs defines a unique function.

M:{(3, 5), (7, 1), (8, 0), (1, 7)}
N:{(5, 9), (0, 6), (7, 9), (6, 5)}
O:{(4, 4), (7, 7), (8, 8), (9, 9)}
P:{(6, 9), (9, 6), (7, 8), (8, 7)}

98. The inverse of which of the four given functions is **not** a function?

A. M **B.** N

C. O **D.** P

99. When verifying the identity $\frac{\sin^2 x}{1 + \cos x} = 1 - \cos x$ for $x = \frac{\pi}{2}$, the left and right sides of the equation, to the nearest tenth, are equal to

A. 0 **B.** 0.5

C. 1.0 **D.** 2.0

100. The range and y-intercept of the function $f(x) = 5^x$ are

A. $y \in R$ and $y = 1$

B. $y \in R$ and $y = 0$

C. $y > 0$ and $y = 0$

D. $y > 0$ and $y = 1$

Use the following information to answer the next question.

Four exponential functions are given.

1. $f(x) = 5^x$
2. $f(x) = \left(\frac{2}{3}\right)^x$
3. $f(x) = 3^x$
4. $f(x) = \left(\frac{1}{5}\right)^x$

101. When these functions are ordered from the function whose graph is closest to the positive x-axis to the function whose graph is farthest from the positive x-axis, the order is __________. (Record your answer as a four-digit number.)

102. The expression $\log_c c - 3c$ can be simplified to

A. $-3c$ **B.** $-2c$

C. $1 - 3c$ **D.** $c^c - 3c$

103. To show that $\frac{1 + \cos 2x}{\sin 2x} = \cot x$ is an identity, which of the following pairs of equations could be graphed?

A. $Y_1 = 1 + \cot(2x)$ and $Y_2 = \frac{1}{\tan(x)}$

B. $Y_1 = 1 + \cos(2x)$ and $Y_2 = \cos(2x)$

C. $Y_1 = \frac{1}{\sin(2x)} + \frac{1}{\tan(2x)}$ and $Y_2 = \frac{1}{\tan x}$

D. $Y_1 = \cos(2x)$ and $Y_2 = (\cos(x))^2 - (\sin(x))^2$

$f(x)$

104. Prove that $\dfrac{\sec\theta\cos\theta\tan\theta}{\cot\theta\csc\theta\sin\theta} = \tan^2\theta$.

105. Prove $\cos x \tan x = \sin x$ algebraically.

106. The expression $\sqrt[4]{\sqrt[3]{x^5}}$ is equivalent to which of the following expressions?

A. $x^{\frac{5}{12}}$ **B.** $x^{\frac{6}{7}}$

C. $x^{\frac{3}{20}}$ **D.** $x^{\frac{23}{12}}$

NOTES

Modeling and Solving Functions

MODELING AND SOLVING FUNCTIONS

Table of Correlations

Standard		Concepts	Exercise #1	Exercise #2
PC.3	The student uses functions and their properties, tools and technology, to model and solve meaningful problems.			
PC.3.A	*Investigate properties of trigonometric and polynomial functions.*	Determining the Properties of Even and Odd Polynomial Functions	11, 12	32
		Identifying the Properties of a Trigonometric Function from an Equation or a Graph	13, 14	33
		Describing Properties of Real-World Periodic Functions when Given a Graph	107, 143	144, 164
		Describing Properties of Real-World Periodic Functions when Given Numerical Representations	108, 109	145
PC.3.B	*Use functions such as logarithmic, exponential, trigonometric, polynomial, etc. to model real-life data.*	Describing Properties of Real-World Periodic Functions when Given Numerical Representations	108, 109	145
		Solving Real-World Problems Using Logarithms	110, 111	146
		Solving Real-World Problems Using Quadratic Regression	112, 113	147
		Modeling Exponential Functions of Growth	114, 115	148
		Modeling Exponential Functions of Decay	116, 117	149, 150, 153
		Solving Real-World Quadratic Problems Given a Graph	118, 119	151
		Representing Situations Using Quadratic Expressions in One Variable	120, 121	
		Solving Real-World Quadratic Problems Graphically when Given an Equation	122, 123	152
		Identify Exponential Functions in Real-World Problems	124	153
		Solving Problems Using Exponential Regression	125, 126	154, 155
PC.3.C	*Use regression to determine the appropriateness of a linear function to model real-life data (including using technology to determine the correlation coefficient).*	Identifying The Best Regression Equation for a Sequence of Data	127, 128	156
		Solve Problems Involving the Applications of Functions	129, 130	157
PC.3.D	*Use properties of functions to analyze and solve problems and make predictions.*	Solve Problems Involving the Applications of Functions	129, 130	157
PC.3.E	*Solve problems from physical situations using trigonometry, including the use of Law of Sines, Law of Cosines, and area formulas and incorporate radian measure where needed.*	Calculating the Area of a Triangle Given One Angle and Two Adjacent Sides	131, 132	158, 159
		Calculating Arc Lengths	133, 134	160
		Solving Problems Using the Sine Law for Acute Triangles	135, 136	

		Solving Problems Using the Cosine Law for Acute Triangles	137, 138	161
		Solving Problems Using Sine Laws for Obtuse Triangles	139, 140	162
		Solving Problems Using Cosine Laws for Obtuse Triangles	141, 142	163

PC.3.A Investigate properties of trigonometric and polynomial functions.

Describing Properties of Real-World Periodic Functions when Given a Graph

The properties of periodic functions, such as period, amplitude, horizontal midline axis, range, maxima, and minima can be described in the context of graphs representing real-world events.

Example

The given graph is a model of the average high temperatures of a town in northern Ontario over an entire year. The numbers on the horizontal axis are the 365 days of the year.

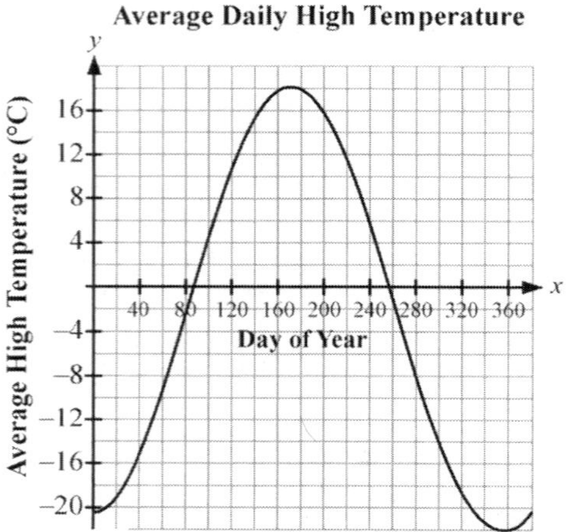

Determine the equation of the horizontal midline axis for the graph of the periodic function, and explain its meaning in the context of the given scenario.

Solution

The equation of the horizontal midline axis, $y = d$, is found by knowing the maximum and minimum y-values of the graph. The maximum value of about 18°C occurs at about day 170, and one of the minimum values of about −22°C occurs at about day 350.

Find the equation of the horizontal midline axis.

$$y = d$$

$$y = \frac{\text{maximum} + \text{minimum}}{2}$$

$$y = \frac{18 + (-22)}{2}$$

$$y = -2$$

The equation of the horizontal midline axis is $y = d = -2$. This value of −2°C reflects the average high temperature of all high temperatures throughout any year.

Describing Properties of Real-World Periodic Functions when Given Numerical Representations

The properties of periodic functions, such as period, amplitude, horizontal midline axis, range, maxima, and minima can be described in the context of data representing real-world events.

Example

The given table lists the maximum and minimum heights of the tide at St. Andrews, Station 40, in the Bay of Fundy on September 1, 2008.

2008-09-01 (Monday)

Time (ADT)	Height (m)
01:23	7.3
07:44	0.3
13:47	7.3
20:07	0.4

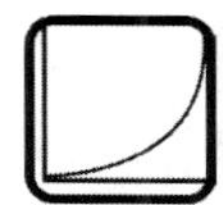

The height of the tide defines a periodic function with respect to time, starting at 00:00, on September 1, 2008.

What is the period, to the nearest minute, and amplitude, to the nearest tenth of a meter, of the function?

Solution

High tide occurs first at 01:23 and then again at 13:47. The period is the length of time lapsed between the two maxima.
Period = 13:47 – 1:23 = 12:24.
The period is 12 hours and 24 minutes.

The amplitude of the periodic function can be found as follows:

$$\begin{aligned}\text{Amplitude} &= \frac{\text{Maximum} - \text{Minimum}}{2}\\ &= \frac{7.3 - 0.3}{2}\\ &= 3.5\end{aligned}$$

The amplitude of the function is 3.5 m.

PC.3.B Use functions such as logarithmic, exponential, trigonometric, polynomial, etc. to model real-life data.

Solving Real-World Problems Using Logarithms

The use of logarithms to represent relative size allows for large differences to be represented by relatively small numbers. For example, 1,000 is one hundred times greater than 10, but their logarithms (using base 10) are 3 and 1, respectively (log 1,000 = 3 and log 10 = 1).

Three examples where logarithmic scales are used are the Richter scale for measuring intensity of earthquakes, the decibel scale for measuring the loudness of sounds, and the pH scale for measuring acidity or alkalinity.

Earthquake Intensity

The magnitude of an earthquake is measured using the Richter scale with the formula $m = \log\left(\frac{I}{I_r}\right)$, where I is the intensity of the earthquake, I_r is the reference intensity, and m is the magnitude on the Richter scale. Written in exponential form, this formula is $I = I_r(10)^m$.

The reference intensity, I_r, is the intensity of a very small and barely measurable earthquake.

The logarithmic or exponential form of the formula can be used to solve for the magnitude or the intensity. These formulas can also be used to compare the intensities of two different earthquakes.

In general, to solve earthquake intensity problems, follow these steps:

1. Let I_1 equal the earthquake with the greater intensity. Substitute I_1 for I and the magnitude for m, if given, in the exponential form of the formula, $I = I_r(10)^m$.
2. Let I_2 equal the earthquake with the weaker intensity. Substitute I_2 for I and the magnitude for m, if given, in the exponential form of the formula, $I = I_r(10)^m$.
3. Set up a ratio to compare the earthquake with the greater intensity to the weaker one, $\frac{I_1}{I_2}$.
4. Substitute for I_1 and I_2.
5. Cancel the I_r variable.
6. Simplify using the quotient law of exponents.
7. If necessary, convert the exponential equation into logarithmic form.
8. Evaluate.

Example

To the nearest tenth, how many times more intense is an earthquake with a magnitude of 4.5 compared to an earthquake with a magnitude of 2.9?

Solution

Step 1

Let I_1 represent the intensity of the stronger earthquake that has a magnitude of 4.5. Substitute I_1 for I and 4.5 for m in the exponential equation $I = I_r(10)^m$.

$I_1 = I_r(10)^{4.5}$

Step 2

Let I_2 represent the intensity of the weaker earthquake that has a magnitude of 2.9. Substitute I_2 for I and 2.9 for m in the exponential equation $I = I_r(10)^m$.

$I_2 = I_r(10)^{2.9}$

Step 3

Compare the intensities of the two earthquakes.

Set up a ratio that compares the stronger earthquake to the weaker one.

$$\frac{I_1}{I_2}$$

Step 4

Substitute $I_r(10)^{4.5}$ for I_1 and $I_r(10)^{2.9}$ for I_2.

$$\frac{I_1}{I_2} = \frac{I_r(10)^{4.5}}{I_r(10)^{2.9}}$$

Step 5

Cancel the I_r variable.

$$\frac{I_1}{I_2} = \frac{(10)^{4.5}}{(10)^{2.9}}$$

Step 6

Apply the quotient law of exponents.

$$\frac{I_1}{I_2} = (10)^{4.5-2.9}$$

Step 7

Simplify and evaluate.

$$\frac{I_1}{I_2} = 10^{1.6}$$

$$\approx 39.81$$

Therefore, an earthquake with a magnitude of 4.5 is approximately 39.8 times more intense than an earthquake with a magnitude of 2.9.

Example

A seismologist measures the intensities of an earthquake from different locations to determine the earthquake's epicentre.

The seismologist notices that the earthquake was 86 times more intense at location A than at location B.

If the earthquake in San Francisco was a magnitude 4.1 earthquake, what was the magnitude of the earthquake in Japan to the nearest tenth?

Solution

Step 1

Let I_1 represent the intensity of the earthquake in Japan.

Substitute I_1 for I in the exponential equation $I = I_r(10)^m$.

$I_1 = I_r(10)^m$

Step 2

Let I_2 represent the intensity of the earthquake in San Francisco.

Substitute I_2 for I and 4.1 for m in the exponential equation $I = I_r(10)^m$.

$I_2 = I_r(10)^{4.1}$

Step 3

It is given that the earthquake in Japan is 86 times more intense than the earthquake in San Francisco. Write a ratio that compares the intensity of the earthquakes.

$$\frac{I_1}{I_2} = 86$$

Step 4
Substitute $I_r(10)^m$ for I_1 and $I_r(10)^{4.1}$ for I_2 in the equation $\frac{I_1}{I_2} = 86$.

$$\frac{I_r(10)^m}{I_r(10)^{4.1}} = 86$$

Step 5
Cancel the I_r variables.

$$\frac{(10)^m}{(10)^{4.1}} = 86$$

Step 6
Apply the quotient law of exponents.
$(10)^{m-4.1} = 86$

Step 7
Rewrite the exponential equation in logarithmic form.
$\log_{10}86 = m - 4.1$

Step 8
Evaluate $\log_{10}86$, and solve for m.
$1.934 \approx m - 4.1$
$6.034 \approx m$
The earthquake in Japan was approximately a magnitude 6.0 earthquake.

Intensity of Sound

The loudness of sound is measured in decibels so that the decibel measurement (dB) is $\text{dB} = 10\log L$, where L is the relative loudness of the sound compared to the threshold of hearing, where $L = 1$.

For example, the loudness of ordinary traffic is 10,000,000 times louder than the threshold of hearing (TOH), so its decibel measure is as follows:

$$\begin{aligned} 10\log 10{,}000{,}000 &= 10(7) \\ &= 70 \end{aligned}$$

The decibel measures of some common sounds are given in the following chart.

Sound	Relative Loudness Compared to TOH	Decibel Measure (dB)
Jet plane (20 m away)	10^{14}	140
Rock concert music	10^{12}	120
Large orchestra	$10^{9.8}$	98
Heavy traffic	10^9	90
Vacuum cleaner	10^8	80
Ordinary traffic	10^7	70
Normal conversation	10^5	50
Whisper	10^2	20
Rustling leaves	10^1	10
Threshold of hearing (TOH)	1	0

In general, to solve sound intensity problems, follow these steps:

1. For a given dB value of a sound, substitute this value into the equation $\text{dB} = 10\log L$.
2. Simplify this equation and solve for L. It is not necessary to evaluate the power, however.
3. Compare the greatest sound intensity to the weaker intensity. Set up a ratio, $\frac{L_1}{L_2}$.
4. Substitute the values for L_1 and L_2 and evaluate.

Example

The measure of ordinary conversation is 50 dB. Amplified rock music is 10^{12} times louder than the threshold of hearing, which has a reading of 0 dB.

How many times louder is rock music than ordinary conversation?

Solution

Step 1
It is given that for ordinary conversation, dB = 50. Substitute 50 for dB in the equation dB = 10log L_c, where L_c is the loudness of ordinary conversation.
$50 = 10\log L_c$

Step 2
Simplify and solve for L_c.

$$\frac{50}{10} = \log L_c$$
$$5 = \log L_c$$
$$L_c = 10^5$$

Step 3
Compare the stronger sound intensity to the weaker intensity.
The ratio comparing relative loudness of rock music compared with ordinary conversation is $\frac{L_r}{L_c}$.

Step 4
It is given that the loudness of rock music L_r is 10^{12}. Substitute 10^{12} for L_r and 10^5 for L_c in the ratio $\frac{L_r}{L_c}$, and then evaluate.

$$\begin{aligned}\frac{L_r}{L_c} &= \frac{10^{12}}{10^5}\\ &= 10^7\\ &= 10{,}000{,}000\end{aligned}$$

Rock music is 10,000,000 times louder than ordinary conversation.

Acidity and Alkalinity

The acidity or alkalinity of a liquid is measured using the pH scale. The formula to determine pH is $\text{pH} = -\log\left[\text{H}^+\right]$, where $\left[\text{H}^+\right]$ represents the concentration of the hydrogen ion.

Written in exponential form, the equation is $\left[\text{H}^+\right] = 10^{-\text{pH}}$ or $\left[\text{H}^+\right] = \frac{1}{10^{\text{pH}}}$.

The logarithmic and exponential forms of the formula can be used to solve for the pH or the concentration of hydrogen ions. They can also be used to compare the acidity of two different liquids.

A liquid that is very acidic has a relatively small pH value, and one that is very alkaline has a relatively large pH value. The range of pH values is from 0 to 14. Pure water, which is neutral (neither acidic or alkaline), has a pH value of 7.

The approximate pH values for some common liquids are shown on this scale.

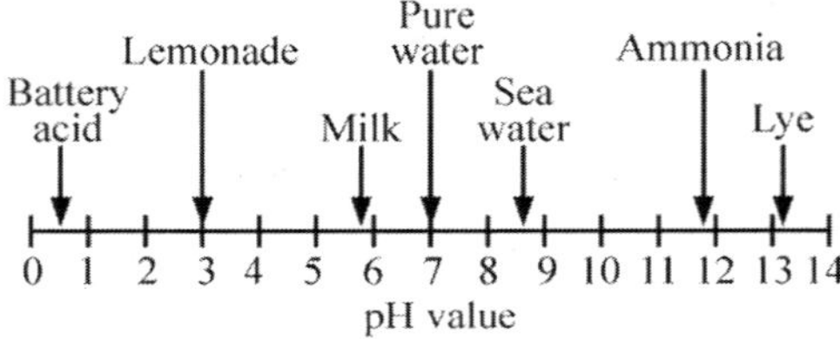

In general, to solve pH problems, follow these steps:

1. Given the pH of two solutions, make two equations by substituting the pH value into the formula $\text{pH} = -\log\left[\text{H}^+\right]$.
2. Convert each logarithmic equation into exponential form.
3. Compare the stronger concentration to the weaker one. Set up a ratio, $\frac{H_1^+}{H_2^+}$.
4. Evaluate the ratio.

Example

Vinegar has a pH of 2.8, while baking soda has a pH of 8.2.

How many times more acidic is vinegar than baking soda?

Solution

Determine the concentration of H^+ for the vinegar and baking soda, then set up a ratio to compare the acidities.

Step 1
For vinegar, substitute 2.8 for pH in the equation $pH = -\log[H^+]$.
$2.8 = -\log[H^+]$
For baking soda, substitute 8.2 for pH in the equation $pH = -\log[H^+]$.
$8.2 = -\log[H^+]$

Step 2
Convert each logarithmic equation to exponential form.

For vinegar, $[H^+] = 10^{-2.8} = \frac{1}{10^{2.8}}$.

For baking soda, $[H^+] = 10^{-8.2} = \frac{1}{10^{8.2}}$.

Step 3
Set up a ratio comparing the concentration of vinegar to the concentration of baking soda.

The ratio of the concentrations is $\dfrac{\frac{1}{10^{2.8}}}{\frac{1}{10^{8.2}}}$.

Step 4

Evaluate $\dfrac{\frac{1}{10^{2.8}}}{\frac{1}{10^{8.2}}}$.

$$\begin{aligned}\dfrac{\frac{1}{10^{2.8}}}{\frac{1}{10^{8.2}}} &= \frac{1}{10^{2.8}} \times \frac{10^{8.2}}{1} \\ &= \frac{10^{8.2}}{10^{2.8}} \\ &= 10^{5.4} \\ &\approx 251{,}189\end{aligned}$$

Therefore, vinegar is approximately 251,189 times more acidic than baking soda.

Solving Real-World Problems Using Quadratic Regression

When data from real-world problems has been collected and organized in a table of values, it sometimes models a quadratic function. Quadratic data has *y*-values (dependent variables) that increase then decrease, or decrease then increase.

If a quadratic function describes the data, then a graphing calculator, such as the TI-83, can be used to perform a quadratic regression. A quadratic regression is a method for determining the equation of the parabola, or the parabola of best fit, that models the data. The graph or the equation of the quadratic function can be used to answer questions related to the data.

Example

The given table shows the height of a ball, in meters, with respect to time, in seconds, after a football player kicked it.

Time (s)	Height (m)
0	0.25
1	15.85
2	21.15
3	16.65
4	2.35

Determine the height of the ball at 2.7 s, to the nearest hundredth of a meter.

Solution

Step 1

Determine the equation that defines the given data.

The y-values increase then decrease, so perform a quadratic regression.

```
QuadReg
 y=ax²+bx+c
 a=-4.971428571
 b=20.38571429
 c=.3071428571
```

To minimize rounding errors, round the values of the coefficients and the constant value to at least three decimal places.

A possible equation that defines the data is $h = -4.971t^2 + 20.386t + 0.307$, in which h is the height of the ball, in meters, and t is the time, in seconds.

Step 2

Use the derived equation of the function to solve the given problem. Substitute 2.7 for t.

$$\begin{aligned} h &= -4.971t^2 + 20.386t + 0.307 \\ &= -4.971(2.7)^2 + 20.386(2.7) + 0.307 \\ &\approx 19.12 \end{aligned}$$

At 2.7 s, the ball will be approximately 19.12 m above the ground.

Example

Teresa is preparing to open a hot-dog stand. To determine how much people are willing to pay for a hot dog, Teresa surveyed a number of potential customers. The results of the survey are shown in the given table.

Cost of Hot Dog ($)	Resulting Revenue ($)
1.00	160
2.00	216
3.00	177
4.00	12

Given the results of the survey, what should Teresa charge for a hot dog to acquire the maximum revenue?

Solution

Step 1

Determine the equation that defines the given data.

The dependent variables appear to increase then decrease, so perform a quadratic regression.

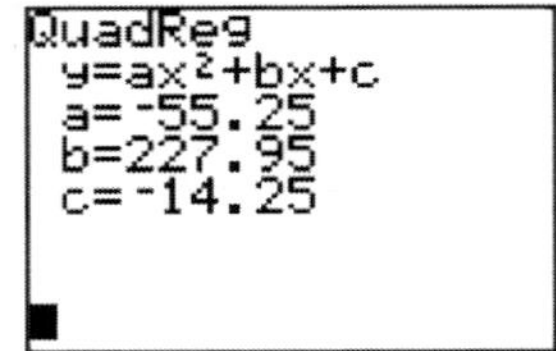

A possible equation that defines the data is $R = -55.25c^2 + 227.95c - 14.25$, where R is the total revenue, in dollars, and c is the cost of one hot dog, in dollars.

Step 2

Graph the function and determine the maximum point of the parabola in order to solve the given problem.

Enter the resulting equation in Y_1 and use the MAXIMUM feature to determine the maximum point on the graph.

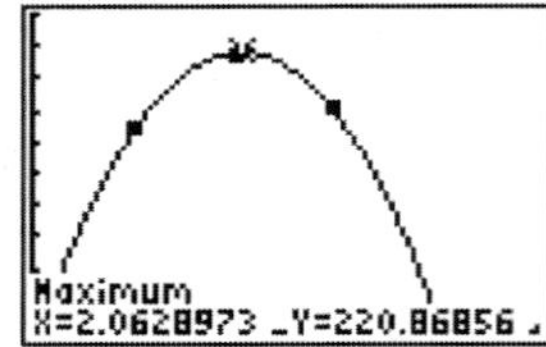

The maximum point is at approximately (2.06, 220.87).

Teresa should achieve a maximum revenue of $220.87 if the hot dogs are sold for $2.06 each.

Modeling Exponential Functions of Growth

Applications of exponential functions often involve exponential growth. Equations, graphs, and tables of values of exponential functions are often used to model real-life examples in which quantities increase or grow at an exponential rate.

A common example in which an exponential function is used to model exponential growth is population growth.

Example

The population in an ant colony doubles every 3 hours. At time $t = 0$, the population is 50.

Create a table of values showing the population growth of the ant colony.

Solution

Create a table of values.

Time, t (h)	Population, P	Calculation
0	50	Given
3	100	$50(2) = 50(2^1)$
6	200	$50(2)(2) = 50(2^2)$
9	400	$50(2)(2)(2) = 50(2^3)$
12	800	$50(2)(2)(2)(2) = 50(2^4)$
15	1,600	$50(2)(2)(2)(2)(2) = 50(2^5)$
18	3,200	$50(2)(2)(2)(2)(2)(2) = 50(2^6)$

The population behaves as an exponential function of time, t. The amount of time it takes for the population to double is called the **doubling period**.

Example

The population in an ant colony doubles every 3 h. At time $t = 0$, the population is 50.

Determine the equation of the exponential function representing the population growth of the ant colony in terms of time elapsed, t.

Solution

The equation of an exponential function can be expressed in the form $y = ab^x$, where a is the value of the function when $x = 0$ and $b > 0$, $b \neq 1$.

For the equation of an exponential growth function, $b > 1$.

At any given time, the ant colony's population, P, is given by $P = 50(2^n)$, where n is the number of doubling periods. Since the population doubles every 3 h, the number of doubling periods is equal to $\frac{t}{3}$, where t is the elapsed time.

The general population equation for the ant colony can be rewritten as $P = 50\left(2^{\frac{t}{3}}\right)$.

If the growth of the ant colony's population can be modeled by the equation $P = 50\left(2^{\frac{t}{3}}\right)$, where P is the population and t is the elapsed time in hours, use a graphing calculator to sketch the graph of the population function.

Solution

Using the Y = feature of a TI-83 Plus graphing calculator, enter the function Y = 50(2)^(x/3). Use a window setting of X:[0, 50, 10], Y:[0, 1,000,000, 100,000]. The graph is shown.

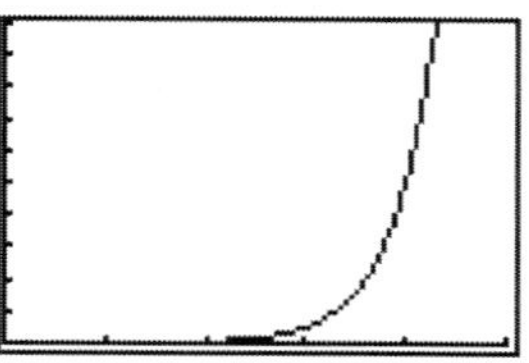

If the growth of the ant colony's population can be modeled by the equation $P = 50\left(2^{\frac{t}{3}}\right)$, where P is the population and t is the elapsed time in hours, what will the population of the colony be after 40 h?

Solution

Since the elapsed time is 40 h, substitute 40 for t in the formula, and solve for P.

$P = 50\left(2^{\frac{t}{3}}\right)$
$P = 50\left(2^{\frac{40}{3}}\right)$
$P \approx 50(10{,}321.27)$
$P \approx 516{,}063.7$

The population after 40 h will be approximately 516,064 ants.

If the growth of the ant colony's population can be modeled by the equation $P = 50\left(2^{\frac{t}{3}}\right)$, where P is the population and t is the elapsed time in hours, how long will it take, to the nearest hour, for the ant colony to reach a population of 10,000,000?

Solution

Step 1
Substitute 10,000,000 for P.

$10{,}000{,}000 = 50\left(2^{\frac{t}{3}}\right)$

Step 2
Divide both sides by 50.

$200{,}000 = 2^{\frac{t}{3}}$

Step 3
Take the common logarithm of both sides of the equation.

$\log 200{,}000 = \log\left(2^{\frac{t}{3}}\right)$

Step 4
Apply the power law of logarithms.

$\log 200{,}000 = \frac{t}{3}\log 2$

Step 5
Divide both sides of the equation by log 2.

$\frac{\log 200{,}000}{\log 2} = \frac{t}{3}$

Step 6
Multiply both sides by 3.

$\frac{3\log 200{,}000}{\log 2} = t$

Step 7
Evaluate using a calculator.

$52.83 \approx t$

It will take approximately 53 h for the colony to reach a population of 10,000,000.

A general formula that defines a quantity growing exponentially is given by $N_t = N_0 \times R^{\frac{t}{p}}$, where the following apply:

- N_t—The quantity at time t
- N_0—The initial size or value (when $t = 0$)
- R—The growth rate, $R > 1$. For example, when a quantity doubles in size, $R = 2$; when it triples, $R = 3$; when it increases by 25 %, $R = 1.25$, and so on.
- t—The elapsed time
- p—The period of time that it takes the quantity to grow by rate R. For example, if it takes 3 h for a population to double, $p = 3$.

The general formula $N_t = N_0 \times R^{\frac{t}{p}}$ can be used to determine the exponential equation that defines a particular problem.

To begin, the variables that have defined values need to be determined from the given problem.

Example

A certain island has 30 spiders.

If the population quadruples every 9 days, what is the island's spider population after 100 days?

Solution

Step 1

Determine the exponential equation that defines the problem.

Define the variables whose values are given in the problem with respect to the general formula $N_t = N_0 \times R^{\frac{t}{p}}$.

- At time zero, the population is 30: $N_0 = 30$.
- If the population quadruples, then the growth rate is 4: $R = 4$.
- The population after 100 days needs to be determined: $t = 100$.
- It takes 9 days for the population to quadruple, so the period is 9: $p = 9$.

Step 2

Substitute the values $N_0 = 30$, $R = 4$, $t = 100$, and $p = 9$ into the general formula $N_t = N_0 \times R^{\frac{t}{p}}$.

$$N_{100} = 30 \times 4^{\frac{100}{9}}$$

Step 3

Evaluate N_{100}.

$$\begin{aligned} N_{100} &= 30 \times 4^{\frac{100}{9}} \\ &\approx 146{,}783{,}323 \end{aligned}$$

After 100 days, the spider population is approximately 146,783,323.

Modeling Exponential Functions of Decay

Applications of exponential functions often involve exponential decay. Equations, graphs, and tables of values of exponential functions can also be used to model real-life examples in which quantities decrease or decay at an exponential rate. Common examples in which exponential functions are used to model exponential decay are depreciating assets or investments and radioactive half-lives.

The general formula for exponential growth $N_t = N_0 \times R^{\frac{t}{p}}$ also applies when a quantity or value is decreasing at an exponential rate. However, for exponential decay, the variable R refers to the rate of decay and will have a value of $0 < R < 1$. For example, when a quantity decreases to half its original value, $R = \frac{1}{2}$; when it depreciates by 25%, $R = 0.75$, and so on.

The general formula can be used to determine the exponential decay equation that defines a particular problem as a function of time. To begin, the variables that have defined values need to be determined from the given problem.

Example

A car that was originally worth $50,000 depreciates at a rate of 15% each year.

What is the exponential equation that defines the value of the car as a function of time?

Solution

The general formula for exponential decay is given by $N_t = N_0 \times R^{\frac{t}{p}}$.

Step 1

Define the variables that have values given in the problem.

- At time 0, the car's value is $50,000, so $N_0 = 50{,}000$.
- If the car depreciates at 15%, the growth rate is 0.85. In other words, each year the car is worth 85% of what its value was the previous year. Thus, $R = 0.85$.
- It takes 1 year for the car's value to reduce to 85% of the previous year's value, so $p = 1$.
- The number of years is defined by t.

Step 2

Substitute the values $N_0 = 50{,}000$, $R = 0.85$, and $P = 1$ into the general formula.

$N_t = 50{,}000 \times (0.85)^{\frac{t}{1}}$

Example

The value of a car after t years is given by the function $N_t = 50{,}000 \times (0.85)^{\frac{t}{1}}$.

What will the value of the car be after 14 years?

Solution

Substitute 14 for t in the equation $N_t = 50{,}000 \times (0.85)^{\frac{t}{1}}$, and evaluate.

$$\begin{aligned} N_{14} &= 50{,}000 \times (0.85)^{\frac{14}{1}} \\ &\approx 5{,}138.48 \end{aligned}$$

The car's value after 14 years is represented by N_{14}.

The car will be worth approximately $5,138.48 in 14 years.

The amount of time that it takes for a radioactive substance to decrease to half its original mass is called its half-life.

Radioactive decay questions are approached in a similar manner to a depreciating asset. When a radioactive substance decays, the substance's mass decreases.

Example

The mass of a certain radioactive substance is currently 300 g, and its half-life is 7 years.

To the nearest thousandth of a gram, what will its mass be in 100 years? __________

Solution

Step 1

Determine the exponential equation that defines the problem.

Define the variables whose values are given in the problem with respect to the general formula $N_t = N_0 \times R^{\frac{t}{p}}$.

- At time 0, the mass is 300 g.
  $N_0 = 300$
- The substance is reduced to $\frac{1}{2}$ its mass during each period.
  $R = \frac{1}{2}$
- The mass in 100 years needs to be determined, so $t = 100$.
- It takes 7 years for the substance to reduce to $\frac{1}{2}$ its mass, so the period is 7:
  $p = 7$

Step 2

Substitute the values $N_0 = 300$, $R = \frac{1}{2}$, $t = 100$, and $p = 7$ into the general formula $N_t = N_0 \times R^{\frac{t}{p}}$.

$$N_{100} = 300 \times \left(\frac{1}{2}\right)^{\frac{100}{7}}$$

Step 3
Evaluate N_{100}.

$$N_{100} = 300 \times \left(\frac{1}{2}\right)^{\frac{100}{7}}$$
$$\approx 0.0150208$$

The mass of the substance will be approximately 0.015 g in 100 years.

Solving Real-World Quadratic Problems Given a Graph

Quadratic functions can be used to model real-world situations and solve problems that require an analysis of the graph of the given quadratic function.

Most real-world problems involving quadratic functions can be solved by analyzing the graph of the corresponding parabola and identifying the y-intercept, the x-intercept, the coordinates of the vertex, or another particular point on the parabola.

Example

The trajectory of a baseball is represented by the given graph.

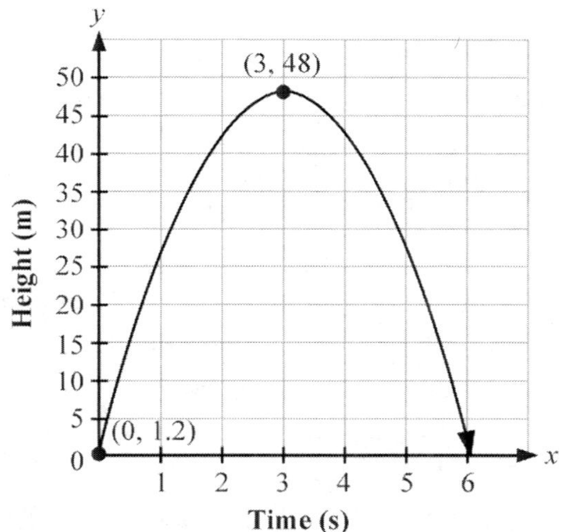

What is the maximum height of the baseball's trajectory?

Solution

The given parabola opens downward and has a vertex at (3, 48).

The maximum value (since the parabola opens downwards) of the quadratic function represented by the given parabola is equal to the y-coordinate of the vertex of the parabola.

Therefore, the maximum height of the baseball is 48 m.

What was the initial height of the baseball when it was hit?

Solution

At 0 s, the baseball was at its initial height. This corresponds to the ordered pair (0, 1.2) on the parabola.

Thus, the baseball was hit from an initial height of 1.2 m.

How long does the baseball remain in the air?

Solution

The ball remains in the air until it hits the ground. This occurs at the point where the parabola intersects the x-axis after reaching its maximum value.

Since the graph intersects the x-axis at 6, the ball remains in the air for 6 s.

Representing Situations Using Quadratic Expressions in One Variable

Some problems can be represented by quadratic expressions in one variable that can be expanded and simplified.

Example

A 2×3 picture is to be framed with a matte that has a width of x and a frame with a length of l and a width of w. All the measures are in inches.

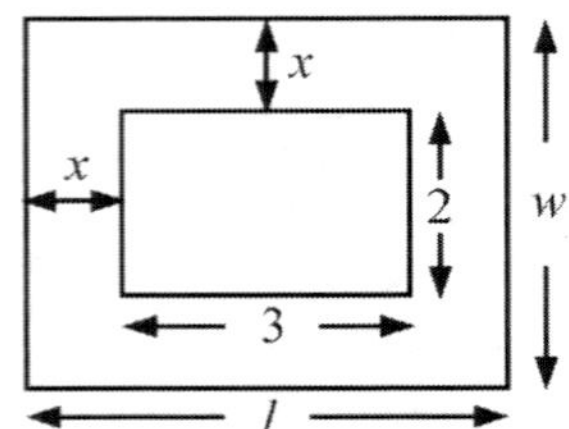

Determine the algebraic expression in terms of x that represents the total area of the picture frame, including the matte.

Solution

The length, l, can be expressed as $x + 3 + x = 2x + 3$, and the width, w, can be expressed as $x + 2 + x = 2x + 2$.

The area of the frame is $A = lw$.

$A = lw$
$A = (2x + 3)(2x + 2)$

Simplify the expression for the area of the picture frame.

Solution

The expression for the area of the picture frame is $(2x + 3)(2x + 2)$.

Expand the expression using the FOIL method, and then collect like terms.

$(2x + 3)(2x + 2)$
$= (2x)(2x) + (2)(2x) + (3)(2x) + (3)(2)$
$= 4x^2 + 4x + 6x + 6$
$= 4x^2 + 10x + 6$

The simplified expression representing the area of the picture frame is $4x^2 + 10x + 6$.

Solving Real-World Quadratic Problems Graphically when Given an Equation

Quadratic functions can be used to describe real-world situations.

The problems related to the equation can be solved graphically.

Example

A city's population can fluctuate. A small Ontario city that has a declining population is expecting the population to begin increasing in the near future because of the introduction of several industrial development initiatives.

The city planners predict that the city's population can be modeled by the quadratic function $P = 150t^2 - 1{,}200t + 14{,}900$, $t \geq 0$, in which t represents the time in years since January 1st, 2006, and P represents the population.

Using a graphing calculator, determine the year the city's population will be the lowest.

Solution

Press the [Y=] button on your calculator, and enter the equation $P = 150t^2 - 1{,}200t + 14{,}900$ into the $Y_1 =$ value as follows:
$Y_1 = 150X^2 - 1{,}200X + 14{,}900$.

Press [WINDOW], and use settings such as x: [−5, 12, 2] and y: [7,500, 20,000, 2,500].

Use the Minimum feature of your calculator. Press [2nd] [TRACE] to access the CALC menu.

Choose 3:minimum from the list. Follow the prompts given by the calculator. Provide a left bound, a right bound, and press [ENTER] when prompted for a guess.

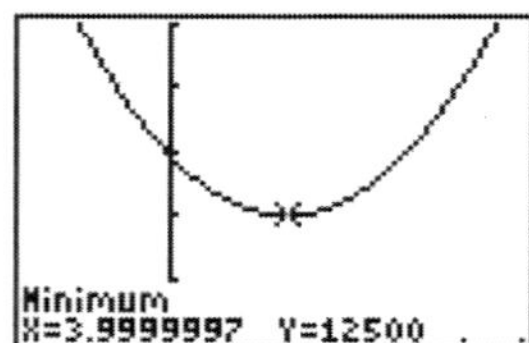

Since the graphing calculator's cursor is at $x \approx 4$, the minimum population will occur at the beginning of $t = 4$, or 2,006 + 4 = 2,010.

Using a graphing calculator, determine the first year that the city's population will be more than 24,000.

Solution

Press the [Y=] button on your calculator, and enter the equation $P = 150t^2 - 1{,}200t + 14{,}900$ into the Y_1 = value as follows:
$Y_1 = 150X^2 - 1{,}200X + 14{,}900$.

Use the Intersection feature of your calculator to find the first positive intersection point between this line and the line of the quadratic function, $Y_1 = 150X^2 - 1{,}200X + 14{,}900$.

Enter the line referring to the population of 24,000 into the Y_2 = value as follows:
$Y_2 = 24{,}000$.

Press [WINDOW], and use settings such as x: [−5, 20, 2] and y: [7,500, 35,000, 2,500].

Press [2nd] [TRACE] to access the CALC menu.

Choose 5:intersect from the list. Follow the prompts given by the calculator. Choose a point near the intersection on the first function (the quadratic function), and a point near the intersection on the second function (the line). Press [ENTER] when prompted for a guess.

The first positive intersection point occurs when $x = 12.76$, as shown in the given diagram.

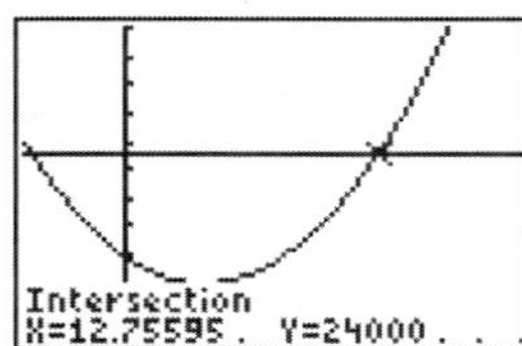

The first year that the population will be more than 24,000 is 2,006 + 12.76 = 2,018.76, or 2019.

Identify Exponential Functions in Real-World Problems

Exponential function equations are often broken down into two different forms:

1. **Exponential growth:** Equations, graphs, and tables of values of exponential functions are often used to model real-life examples in which quantities increase or grow at an exponential rate. A common example in which an exponential function is used to model exponential growth is population growth.
2. **Exponential decay:** Equations, graphs, and tables of values of exponential functions can also be used to model real-life examples in which quantities decrease or decay at an exponential rate. Common examples in which exponential functions are used to model exponential decay are depreciating assets or investments and radioactive half-lives.

A general formula that defines a quantity exponentially growing or decaying is given by $N_t = N_0 \times R^{\frac{t}{p}}$, in which the following apply:

- N_t: The quantity at time, t
- N_0: The initial size or value (when $t = 0$)
- R: The growth rate. When $R > 1$, it is an exponential growth. For example, when the quantity doubles in size, $R = 2$; when it triples, $R = 3$; when it increases by 25%, $R = 1.25$; and so on. When R has a value of $0 < R < 1$, it is an exponential decay. For example, when a quantity decreases to half its original value, $R = \frac{1}{2}$; when it depreciates by 25%, $R = 0.75$; and so on.
- t: The elapsed time
- p: The period of time it takes the quantity to grow by a rate, R. For example, if it takes 3 hours for a population to double, $p = 3$.

Example

A petri dish contains 25 bacteria. The number of bacteria, *N*, doubles every hour.

Construct a table of values, a graph, and an equation to represent the time, *t*, for the first 4 hours. Highlight the growth factor, *r*, and explain any restrictions on the domain and range.

Solution

Step 1

Construct a table of values.

t (h)	*N*	Ratio (*r*)
0	25	
1	50	$\frac{50}{25} = 2$
2	100	$\frac{100}{50} = 2$
3	200	$\frac{200}{100} = 2$
4	400	$\frac{400}{200} = 2$

Step 2

Sketch the graph.

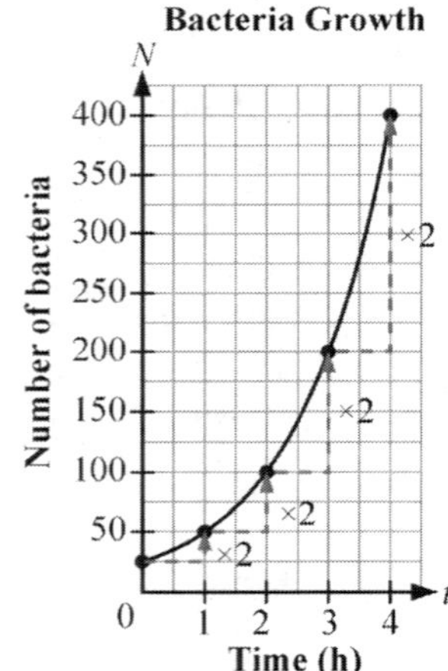

Step 3

Determine the exponential function.

Using the general formula of an exponential function, $N_t = N_0 \times R^{\frac{t}{p}}$, substitute 25 for N_0, 2 for *R*, and 1 for *p*.

$$N_t = N_0 \times R^{\frac{t}{p}}$$

$$N_t = 25 \times (2)^{\frac{t}{1}}$$

$$N_t = 25(2)^t$$

Step 4

State any restrictions on the domain and range.

The domain of the scenario is $t \geq 0$ up to a value of *t*, at which point the bacteria stops growing in the dish because of lack of food. The range is $N \geq 25$ up to a value of *N*, at which point the number of bacteria reaches its maximum.

Example

A lab technician had an 80 mg sample of a radioactive substance called iodine-131 with a half-life of 8 days. (Half-life means the time it takes for a radioactive substance to decay to $\frac{1}{2}$ its original mass.)

Construct a table of values, a graph, and an equation to represent the amount of mass, *m*, remaining over time, *t*, in the first 32 days. Highlight the decay factor, *r*, and explain any restrictions on the domain and range.

Solution

Step 1

Construct a table of values.

t (d)	*m*	Ratio (*r*)
0	80	-
8	40	$\frac{40}{80} = \frac{1}{2}$
16	20	$\frac{20}{40} = \frac{1}{2}$
24	10	$\frac{10}{20} = \frac{1}{2}$
32	5	$\frac{5}{10} = \frac{1}{2}$

Step 2
Sketch a graph from the table of values.

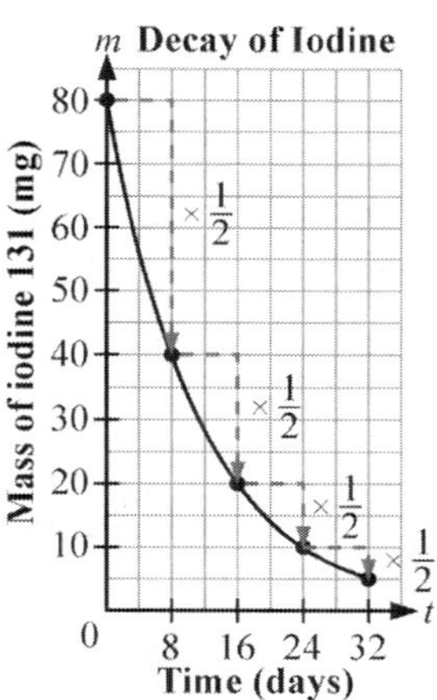

Step 3
Determine the equation of the exponential function.

Using the general formula of an exponential function, $N_t = N_0 \times R^{\frac{t}{p}}$, substitute 80 for N_0, $\frac{1}{2}$ for R, and 8 for p.

$$N_t = N_0 \times R^{\frac{t}{p}}$$

$$N_t = 80 \times \left(\frac{1}{2}\right)^{\frac{t}{8}}$$

$$N_t = 80\left(\frac{1}{2}\right)^{\frac{t}{8}}$$

Note: The exponent in the equation is $\frac{t}{8}$.

A value is placed in the denominator when the growth or decay time is not given as a unit value (e.g., 4 min → $\frac{t}{4}$, 16.5 years → $\frac{t}{16.5}$, 175 m → $\frac{d}{175}$).

Step 4
State the restrictions on the domain and range.

The domain of this scenario is $t \geq 0$ up to the time that only one molecule of iodine is left (t= infinity). Therefore, the domain is $t \geq 0$.

The range is $0 < m \leq 80$, since the mass would realistically never get to 0 mg and also would never become a negative amount.

Solving Problems Using Exponential Regression

When ordered pairs or tables of values are used to model real-life examples of exponential data, exponential regression is often performed. Exponential regression is a technique for finding the best-fitting exponential graph that passes through a set of ordered pairs.

An exponential regression takes data and produces an equation of the form $y = ab^x$. The a variable represents either the y-intercept or the initial value. The b variable is always positive, that is $b > 0$. The b variable determines the rate of growth or decay in the following way:

- If $b > 1$, the function is growing. The larger b is, the faster it is growing.
- If $0 < b < 1$, the function is decaying. The closer b is to 0, the faster it is decaying.

The following steps can be used to perform an exponential regression with a TI-83 or similar calculator:

1. Determine which variable is the independent variable and which is the dependent variable.
2. Press [STAT], and select 1:Edit... to access the list editor. Enter the values for the independent variable into list L_1 and the values for the dependent variable into list L_2.
3. Calculate the exponential regression. Press [STAT] and the right arrow once to access the CALC menu. Select 0:ExpReg, and specify lists L_1 and L_2 by pressing [2nd] [1] [,] [2nd] [2].
4. Run the regression by pressing [ENTER].

Example

Terrence did an experiment in which he studied the growth rate of bacteria. He examined a bacterial culture through a microscope every ten minutes. He counted the number of bacteria in a small area and used that number to estimate the total number of bacteria. He recorded his observations in a table.

Time (min)	Bacteria Count
10	538
20	590
30	626
40	691
50	732
60	808

What is the rate of growth of the bacteria each hour?

Solution

First, determine which variable is the independent variable and which is the dependent variable.

- Since Terrence decided when to observe the bacteria, time is the independent variable.
- Therefore, the bacteria count is the dependent variable.

Next, enter the values for the independent variable into list L_1 and the values for the dependent variable into list L_2.

1. Start by clearing any lists already present. Press [2nd] [+], select 4:ClrAllLists, and press [ENTER].
2. Press [STAT], and select 1:Edit....
   Enter the values for time into L_1. Since the question is asking for the rate in hours, convert the given time from minutes by dividing each value by 60. This can be done directly in the list editor by typing the value in minutes divided by 60. The calculator will compute the value.

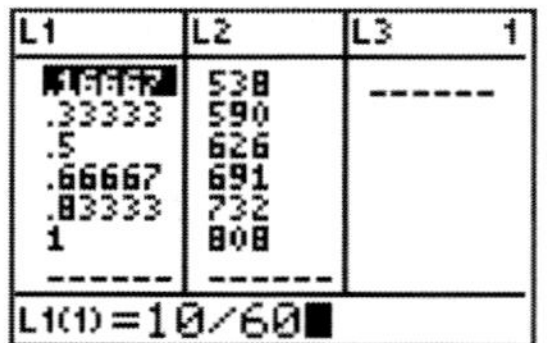

3. Enter the values for the bacteria count in L_2.

Next, calculate the exponential regression.

1. Press the [STAT] button, and then press the right arrow to access the CALC menu. Select 0:ExpReg.
2. Specify the lists L_1 and L_2 by pressing [2nd] [1] [,] [2nd] [2].

3. Press [ENTER] to run the exponential regression.

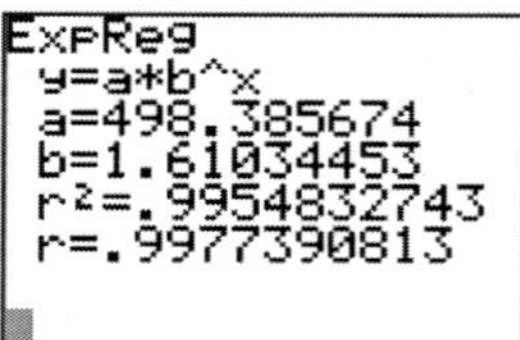

Finally, determine the growth rate.

- Since the value of b is about 1.61, the number of bacteria is increasing by 61% each hour.
- Therefore, the growth rate of the bacteria each hour is 61%.

After you find the values of a and b, you can use the regression function to make predictions.

Example

How many bacteria should Terrence expect to observe after 120 min?

Solution

First, substitute the values from the exponential regression into the exponential equation $y = ab^x$.

The results of the exponential regression are provided in this screen shot of a TI-83 graphing calculator.

```
ExpReg
 y=a*b^x
 a=498.385674
 b=1.61034453
 r²=.9954832743
 r=.9977390813
```

Substitute the values of a and b into $y = ab^x$.

$y = ab^x$
$y \approx (498)(1.61)^x$

Next, convert the given time from minutes to hours.

Divide the number of minutes by 60 to get the number of hours.

$x = \frac{120}{60}$
$x = 2$

Finally, substitute the time in hours for x in the exponential equation, and evaluate to find the value for y (the bacteria count).

Substitute $x = 2$ into $y \approx (498)(1.61)^x$, and evaluate.

$y \approx (498)(1.61)^x$
$y \approx (498)(1.61)^2$
$y \approx (498)(2.5921)$
$y \approx 1{,}290.8658$

Therefore, the number of bacteria Terrence should expect to observe after 120 min is approximately 1,291.

You can also use your graphing calculator to help make predictions from the exponential regression.

Example

What should the bacteria count be after 200 min?

Solution

First, enter the exponential equation that models the bacteria count into Y_1 on the calculator.

The calculator can do this automatically when calculating the exponential regression if a y-variable is specified to store the equation in.

1. Press the STAT button, and then press the right arrow to access the CALC menu. Select 0:ExpReg.Specify the lists L_1 and L_2 by pressing 2nd 1 , 2nd 2, but wait before actually running the command.

Run the exponential regression by pressing ENTER.

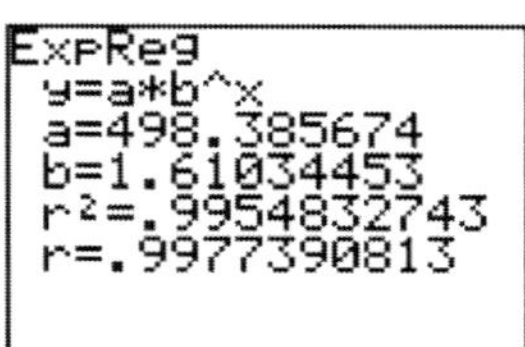

If the ExpReg command is given a third variable, it will store the expression ab^x with a and b automatically substituted in that third variable. In this example, Y_1 will be used as the third variable.

2. Press [,], and then specify the third variable.
3. Press [VARS], and then the right arrow to move to the Y-VARS menu. Select 1:Function…, and then select 1:Y_1.

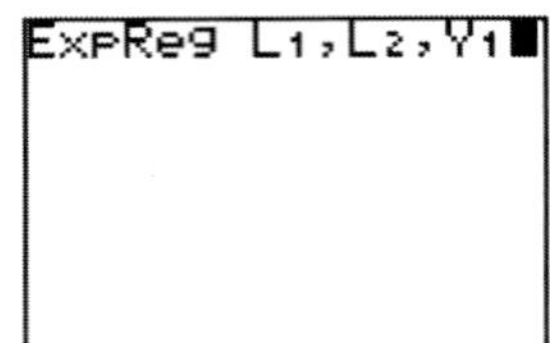

The exponential equation should now be stored in Y_1.

Next, set an appropriate window.

Before setting the window, turn on the stat plot.

1. Press [2nd] [Y=] to access the STAT PLOTS menu. Select 1:Plot1, and press [ENTER].
2. Highlight On, and press [ENTER]. Make sure that Xlist is set to L_1 and that Ylist is set to L_2.

Ensure that both the equation for Y_1 and Plot1 are turned on in the Y= screen.

3. Press [Y =], and verify that both Plot1 and the equals sign for Y_1 are highlighted in black. If either of them is not, move your cursor to the appropriate place and press [ENTER] to toggle that setting.

4. Set the window using ZoomStat. Press [ZOOM], and select 9:ZoomStat.

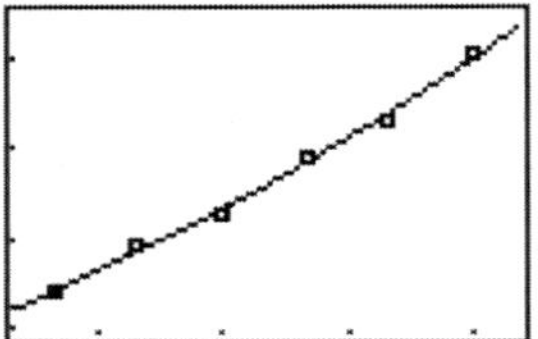

Adjust the window to include the desired value.

1. Calculate the time in hours by dividing the given time in minutes by 60. This will help determine what the window should be on the graphing calculator. Since time is the independent variable, the result will be an x-value.
   $x = \frac{200}{60}$
   $x \approx 3.33$
2. Change the Xmax of the window to be a value greater than 3.33.Press WINDOW, and set Xmin to 0 and Xmax to 4. Graph the function again.

3. The Ymax has to be much larger so that more of the function is visible in the domain.Press WINDOW, and set Ymin to 400, Ymax to 4,000, and Yscl to 100. Graph the function again.

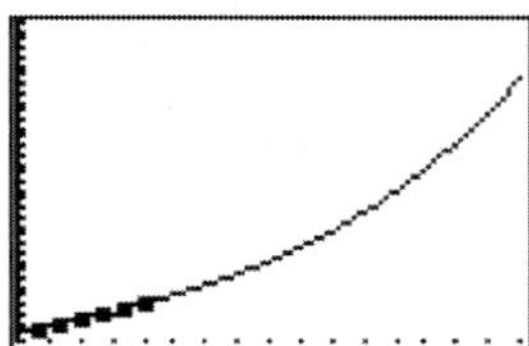

Finally use the trace function to determine the desired y-value.

1. Press TRACE, and use the up or down arrow to select the curve (instead of the points).
2. Type in 3.33, and press ENTER.

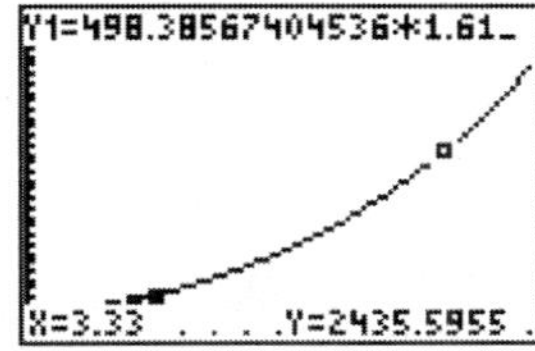

When $x = 3.33$, $y \approx 2{,}435.6$.

Therefore, after 200 min, Terrence should observe a bacterial count of approximately 2,436 bacteria.

PC.3.C Use regression to determine the appropriateness of a linear function to model real-life data (including using technology to determine the correlation coefficient).

Identifying The Best Regression Equation for a Sequence of Data

There are many instances in which it is helpful to be able to identify the most appropriate regression equation for a sequence of data. Being able to identify the equation of the best-fit line enables the user to more completely understand the nature of the relationship being analyzed and thus to be able to make accurate predictions.

The types of relationships that are commonly analyzed are linear, quadratic, exponential, and sinusoidal. Most graphing calculators have the ability to find regression equations from an entered sequence of data and also to calculate the correlation coefficient of the regression so that the user can decide which regression is the most appropriate.

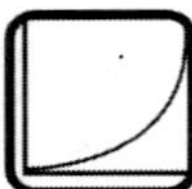

To perform a regression on a TI- 83 graphing calculator, follow these general steps:

1. Press 2nd + and select 4:ClrAllLists. Press ENTER.
2. Press 2nd 0, scroll down to select DiagnosticOn, and press ENTER.
3. Press STAT and select 1:Edit and enter the independent data into L1 and the dependent data into L2.
4. Press STAT, scroll right to highlight "CALC", then scroll down to the required regression.

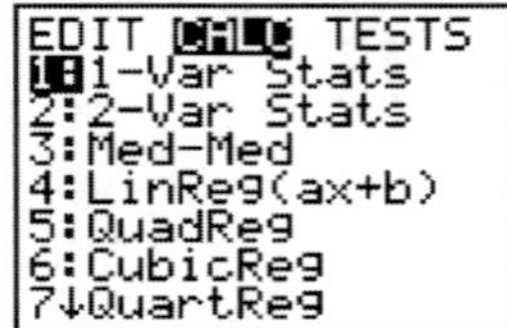

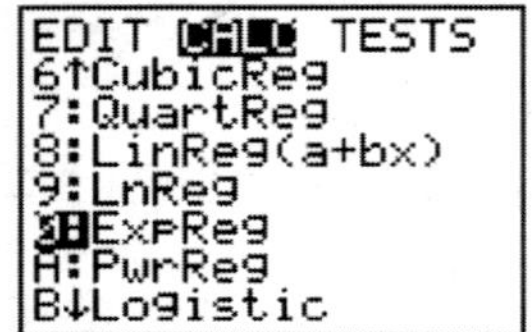

5. Press ENTER to perform the required regression.

Generally, the closer the value of the correlation coefficient (r) is to ±1, the better the equation is at modeling the entered data.

When a sequence of data increases or decreases by a consistent amount for every evenly spaced term, the sequence is linear. When a sequence tends to either increase or decrease to a particular value and then change direction, this indicates a quadratic sequence. On the other hand, if the sequence increases or decreases by an amount that increases or decreases for every term, the sequence is exponential. Finally, a sinusoidal sequence is one in which the values repeatedly increase and decrease through a fixed range.

Example

Consider the following sequence: 150, 133, 116, 99, 82, …

Classify the sequence and identify the next term.

Solution

Step 1

Classify the given sequence.

Determine the difference between successive terms in the sequence.

150 – 133 = 17
133 – 116 = 17
116 – 99 = 17
99 – 82 = 17

Notice that the sequence decreases by a constant amount (17) with each term, which implies that this data represents a linear regression.

Step 2

Perform a linear regression using a TI-83 graphing calculator.

Clear all lists from the calculator and turn on the diagnostic feature. Press STAT and select 1:Edit and enter the term numbers into L1 and the term values of the sequence into L2.

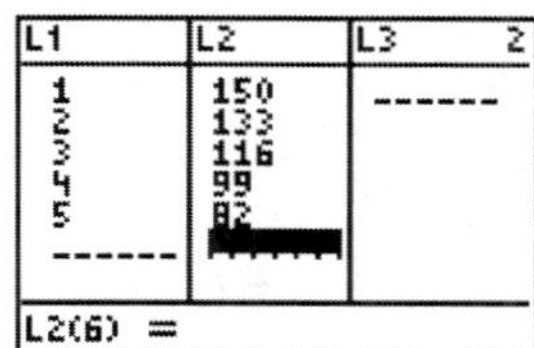

Press STAT, scroll right to highlight "CALC", then scroll down to select 8:LineReg(a+bx). Press ENTER to obtain the following window.

```
LinReg
 y=ax+b
 a=-17
 b=167
 r²=1
 r=-1
```

A linear regression produces the equation, $y = -17x + 167$, with a regression coefficient of $r = -1$. This indicates that the regression equation fits the data perfectly and that there is a downward trend in the data.

Step 3

Identify the sixth term in the sequence.

To find the sixth term in the sequence, evaluate the equation when $x = 6$.

$y = -17x + 167$
$y = -17(6) + 167$
$y = 65$

The sixth term is 65.

There are times when a thorough understanding of the scenario being modeled is necessary to make a decision regarding the appropriate regression equation.

Example

The value of a car decreases as outlined in the chart.

Time since Purchase (years)	Value of the Vehicle ($)
2	14,000
3	10,000
5	5,800
6	4,200
7	2,500

What is the **most appropriate** regression model for the data?

Solution

Step 1

Enter the data into the list feature of a TI-83 graphing calculator.

Clear all lists from the calculator and turn on the diagnostic feature. Press STAT and select 1:Edit and enter the number of years into L1 and the value of the vehicle for each year into L2.

L1	L2	L3 2
2	14000	------
3	10000	
5	5800	
6	4200	
7	2500	

L2(6) =

Step 2
Determine the regression coefficient for a linear regression.

Press STAT, scroll right to highlight "CALC", then scroll down to select 8:LineReg(a+bx). Press ENTER to obtain the following window.

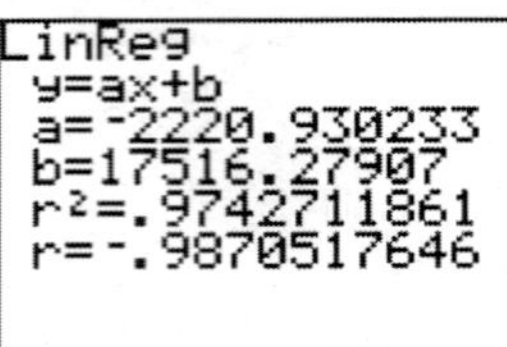

The regression coefficient for a linear regression, to the nearest thousandth, is $r = -0.9871$.

Step 3
Determine the regression coefficient for a quadratic regression.

Press STAT, scroll right to highlight "CALC", then scroll down to select 5:QuadReg. Press ENTER to obtain the following window.

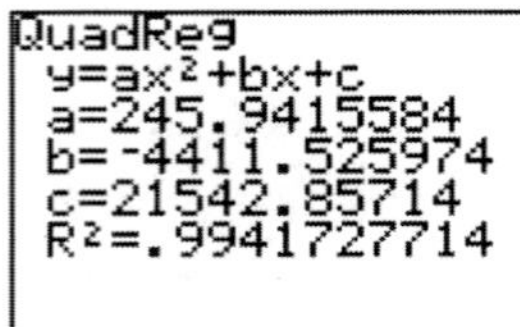

Since $R^2 = 0.9942$, the regression coefficient for a quadratic regression, to the nearest thousandth, is $\sqrt{0.9942} = \pm 0.9971$.

Step 4
Determine the regression coefficient for an exponential regression.

Press STAT, scroll right to highlight "CALC", then scroll down to select 0:ExpReg. Press ENTER to obtain the following window.

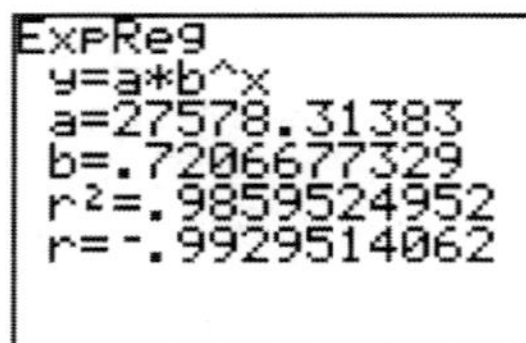

The regression coefficient for an exponential regression, to the nearest thousandth, is $r = -0.9930$.

Step 5
Analyze the regression coefficients.

- Linear: $r = -0.9871$
- Quadratic: $r = \pm 0.9971$
- Exponential: $r = -0.9930$

It seems that the quadratic regression is the most accurate model because the correlation coefficient of regression is closest to 1.
This type of a regression implies that the trend in the data will eventually change from decreasing to increasing once it has reached a minimum value.

Step 6
Consider the reality of the given scenario.
The value of a car decreasing over time is a situation in which the downward trend will continue. Therefore, the data in the chart is more accurately modeled by an exponential function in the form $y = ab^x$. From the exponential regression, the equation is $y = 27{,}578.31(0.7207)^x$, where y is the value of the vehicle and x is the number of years that have passed since purchase.

Solve Problems Involving the Applications of Functions

Different types of functions can be used to represent many types of real-world applications. Many strategies such as reasoning techniques, algebra, and technology can be used to solve problems involving functions.

Example

The distance that a particular car travels after the brakes are applied is measured for several different speeds. The data is given in the following table.

Speed (km/h)	Stopping Distance (m)
5	0.82
10	3.3
15	7.3
20	13.1
25	20.4
30	29.4
35	39.8

Technology can be used to investigate linear, quadratic, and exponential models for the relationship of speed and stopping distance.

Use technology to describe the possible models of the relationship between speed and stopping distance and predict the stopping distance for a speed of 50 km/h, for each.

Solution

Using a TI-83 calculator, graph the data by carrying out the following procedure.

Step 1
Input the data points.

Clear the lists by pressing [2nd] [+] and selecting 4:ClrAllLists. Press [ENTER].

Press [Y =] and clear any functions that were previously graphed. Then press [STAT] [ENTER]. Input the speeds in L1 and the stopping distances in L2.

Step 2
Graph the data.

Set the viewing window to x:[0, 60, 5] y:[0, 100, 10].

Press [2nd] [Y =] [ENTER] and turn Plot 1 on by pressing [ENTER] again.

The type of graph should be a scatter plot, the Xlist is L1, and the Ylist is L2.

Pressing [GRAPH] will show you the following graph.

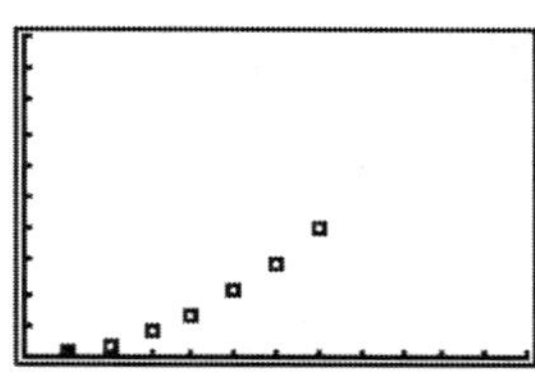

Step 3
Determine the best regression model for the data.

There is no need to do linear regression, since the graph is a curve. However, if you did need to, you would press [STAT], then scroll right to [CALC] and choose 4: LinReg ($ax + b$).

For quadratic regression press [STAT], then scroll right to [CALC] and choose 5:QuadReg. Then press [2nd] [1] [,] [2nd] [2] [,] [VARS], scroll right to [Y-VARS], and press [ENTER] twice. The screen should now display QuadReg L1, L2, Y1.

Pressing [ENTER] will perform the regression and produce the following screen.

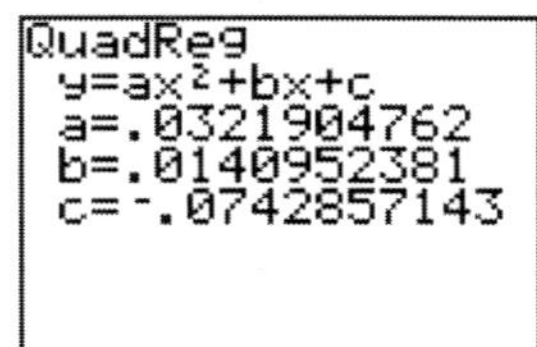

The quadratic function that best fits the data is approximately the equation $y = 0.0321905x^2 + 0.0140952x - 0.0742857$.

If you press GRAPH, the calculator will draw the graph because you have stored the regression equation as Y_1.

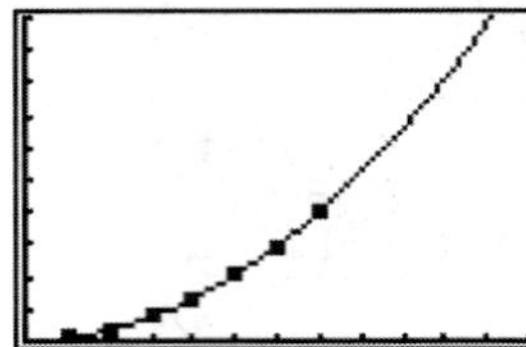

This function appears to be a fairly good fit to the given data.

To determine the predicted stopping distance for a speed of 50 km/h, press 2nd TRACE ENTER and input 50. Press ENTER.

The calculator gives a stopping distance of 81.1 m, to the nearest tenth, for the quadratic model.

To see how well an exponential function fits the data, press STAT, then scroll right to CALC and choose 0:ExpReg. Then press 2nd 1 , 2nd 2 , VARS, scroll right to Y-VARS, and press ENTER twice.

The screen will now display ExpReg L1, L2, Y1.

Press ENTER to perform the regression. The result should be an equation with approximate values of $y = 0.8178(1.1295)^x$

Press GRAPH to see how well this function fits the data.

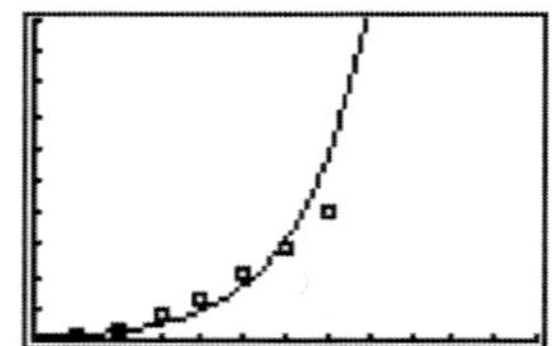

This function does not appear to fit the data as well as the quadratic function did since several points are above the curve and the graph rises rapidly to the right of the final point. To use this model to determine the predicted stopping distance for a speed of 50 km/h, again press 2nd TRACE ENTER and input 50. Press ENTER. The stopping distance for this model is approximately 360.3 m, which is unreasonably large.

The quadratic model is the more realistic relationship for this data.

PC.3.E Solve problems from physical situations using trigonometry, including the use of Law of Sines, Law of Cosines, and area formulas and incorporate radian measure where needed.

Calculating the Area of a Triangle Given One Angle and Two Adjacent Sides

Sometimes, the area of a triangle is required, but the height of the triangle is not given or readily available. Without knowing the height (h) of the triangle, the usual area formulas $A = \frac{bh}{2}$ or $A = \frac{1}{2}bh$ (where b is the base) cannot be used.

With trigonometry, however, it is possible to derive another formula for the area of a triangle.

A New Area Formula

A new formula for the area of the following triangle can be derived.

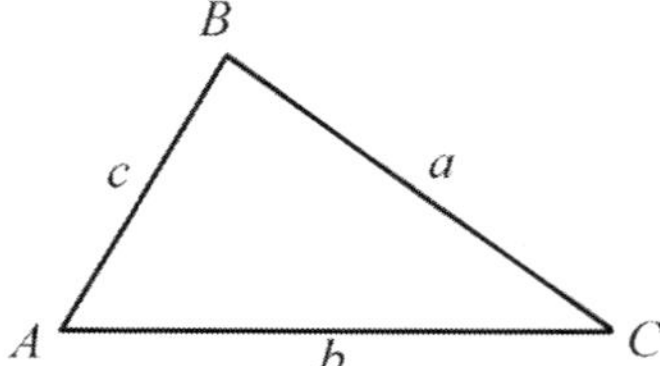

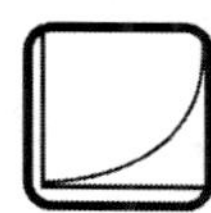

The object is to find an expression for the area of ΔABC in terms of C, a, and b only.

Let h be the height of the triangle from vertex B to side AC.

$\sin C = \frac{h}{a}$

$a\sin C = h$

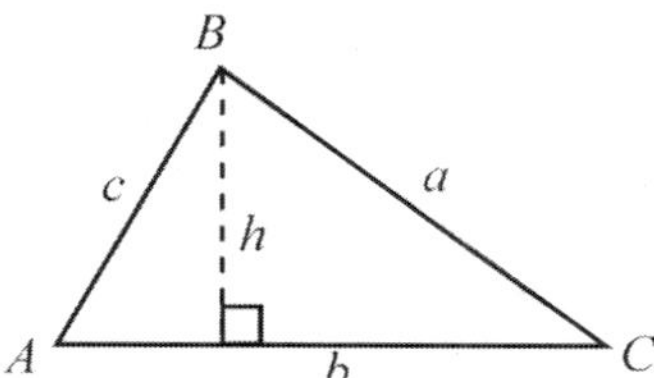

Use the area formula $A = \frac{1}{2}bh$, and substitute $h = a\sin C$ for h to derive a new area formula.

$$A = \frac{1}{2}bh$$
$$= \frac{1}{2}b(a\sin C)$$
$$= \frac{1}{2}ab\sin C$$

The area of a triangle can be found using the formula $A = \frac{1}{2}ab\sin C$, where a and b are side lengths of a triangle, and C is the included angle.

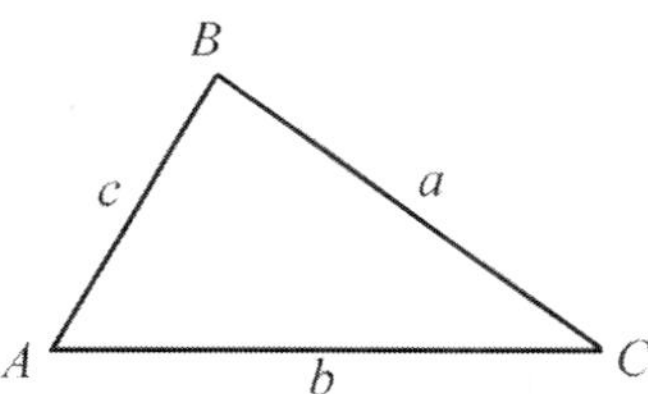

The area formula works using any two known sides and the included angle, as shown in the following formulas:

$$A = \frac{1}{2}ab\sin C$$
$$A = \frac{1}{2}ac\sin B$$
$$A = \frac{1}{2}bc\sin A$$

This particular version of the area formula is not frequently used because of the potential for confusion caused by the use of A to mean area on the left side of formula and to refer to angle A on the right side of the formula.

Example

A seamstress has been commissioned to create 500 mini-pennants for a local sports team. The pennant is designed to have one side measuring 8 cm, another side measuring 10 cm, and the angle between the two sides measuring 50°, as illustrated in the diagram.

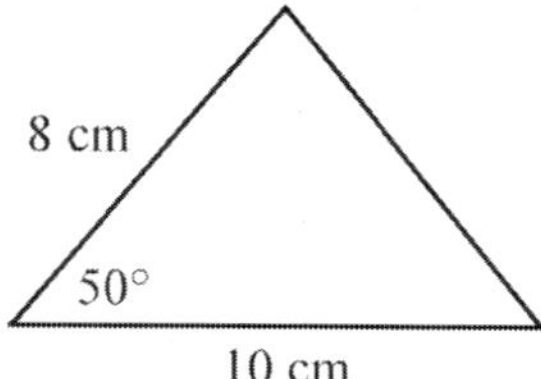

To the nearest square centimeter, what is the minimum amount of fabric required to create the 500 pennants?

Solution

Step 1

Calculate the area of one pennant.

Because the height of the triangle is not given but the lengths of two sides and the included angle are known, use the formula

$A = \frac{1}{2}ac\sin(B)$.

$$A = \frac{1}{2}ac\sin(B)$$
$$= \frac{1}{2}(8 \text{ cm})(10 \text{ cm})\sin(50°)$$
$$\approx 30.6 \text{ cm}^2$$

Step 2

Calculate the amount of material required to create 500 pennants.

Multiply the area of one pennant by 500.

$500 \times 30.6 \text{ cm}^2 = 15{,}320.1 \text{ cm}^2$

Since 15,320 cm^2 will not be enough fabric for the pennants, the amount must be rounded up. To the nearest square centimeter, the minimum amount of fabric required to create 500 mini-pennants is 15,321 cm^2.

Calculating Arc Lengths

One of the advantages of measuring angles in radians becomes evident when calculating arc lengths.

Recall that there is a close relationship between the arc length on a circle and the size of the angle subtended by that arc.

For an angle measuring 2 rad, the corresponding arc length is 2 radii.

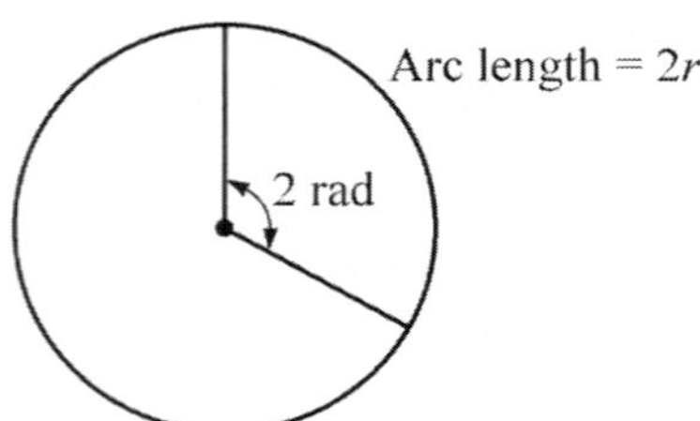

For an angle measuring 3 rad, the corresponding arc length is 3 radii.

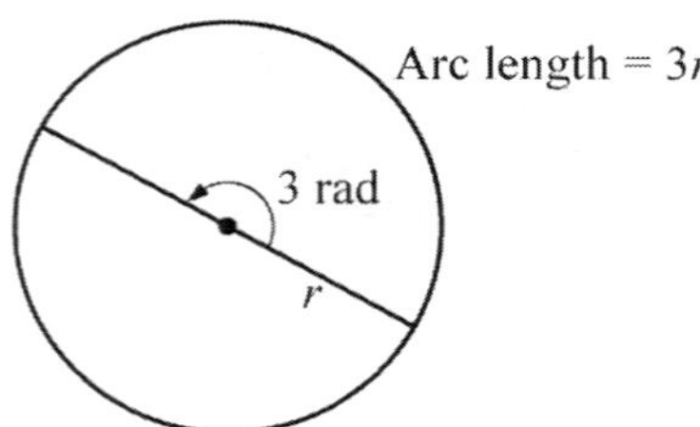

In general, given an angle of θ radians and a radius, r, the arc length, a, can be calculated using the equation $a = r\theta$, where θ is measured in radians, a is the arc length, and r is the radius.

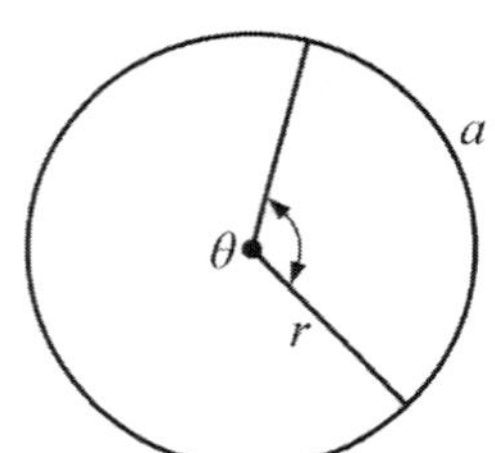

Example

An arc subtends an angle of 1.8 rad. If the radius of the circle is 6 cm, what is the arc length?

Solution

$\theta = 1.8$ rad and $r = 6$ cm

$$\begin{aligned} a &= r\theta \\ &= (6)(1.8) \\ &= 10.8 \end{aligned}$$

The arc length is 10.8 cm.

When the measure of an angle is given in degrees, convert it to radians first, and then apply the formula.

Example

An arc subtends an angle of 150°. The radius of the circle is 11 mm. Find the arc length. Round your answer to the nearest tenth of a millimeter.

Solution

Step 1

Determine the radian measure of the angle.

$$150° = 150 \times \frac{\pi}{180} = \frac{150\pi}{180} = \frac{5\pi}{6} \text{ rad}$$

Step 2

Apply the formula to determine the length of the arc.

$$\begin{aligned} a &= r\theta \\ &= (11)\left(\frac{5\pi}{6}\right) \\ &\doteq 28.8 \end{aligned}$$

The arc length is approximately 28.8 mm.

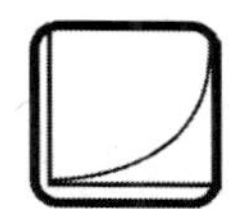

When asked to calculate the unknown measures of the radius or the angle, rearrange the given formula, substitute in the known values, and solve.

Example

An arc subtends the angle θ. If the radius of the circle is 18.5 cm and the arc length is 88.8 cm, what is the measure of angle θ to the nearest tenth of a radian?

Solution

Step 1

Use the formula $a = r\theta$ to solve for θ.

$$\theta = \frac{a}{r}$$

Step 2

Substitute given values and solve for θ.

It is given that $r = 18.5$ and $a = 88.8$.

$$\begin{aligned}\theta &= \frac{a}{r}\\ &= \frac{88.8}{18.5}\\ &\approx 4.8\end{aligned}$$

Therefore, $\theta \approx 4.8$ rad.

Solving Problems Using the Sine Law for Acute Triangles

Problems involving acute triangles can be solved by following these general steps:

1. Read the problem carefully. Determine which measures are given and which measure needs to be calculated.
2. If a diagram is not given, draw a sketch to represent the situation presented in the problem.
3. Make substitutions into the sine law, and use correct algebraic steps to solve for the unknown value. Avoid or minimize rounding until the last step.
4. Check your calculations.
5. Write a concluding statement.

Example

During hockey practice, players performed the following drill: Player *A* passed the puck to player *B*, who was 12 m away. Player *B* redirected the puck at an angle of 40° to player *C*. Player *C* then passed the puck back to player *A*, who was standing 9 m away.

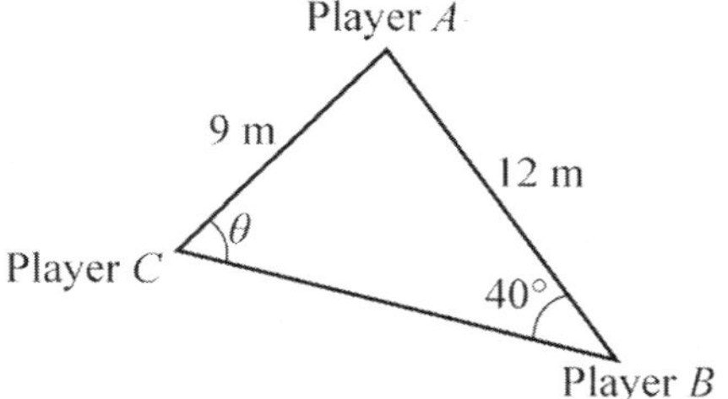

To the nearest degree, determine the measure of angle θ.

Solution

Since it is not a side-side-side situation, apply the sine law. The side measuring 9 m is opposite the 40°angle, and the side measuring 12 m is opposite angle θ. Solve for θ as follows:

$$\begin{aligned}\frac{9}{\sin 40^\circ} &= \frac{12}{\sin \theta}\\ 9\sin \theta &= 12\sin 40^\circ\\ \frac{9\sin \theta}{9} &= \frac{12\sin 40^\circ}{9}\\ \sin \theta &= \frac{12\sin 40^\circ}{9}\\ \theta &\approx 58.99^\circ\end{aligned}$$

The measure of angle θ, to the nearest degree, is 59°.

Example

A surveyor needs to find the length, *b*, of a bridge across a pond in a park.

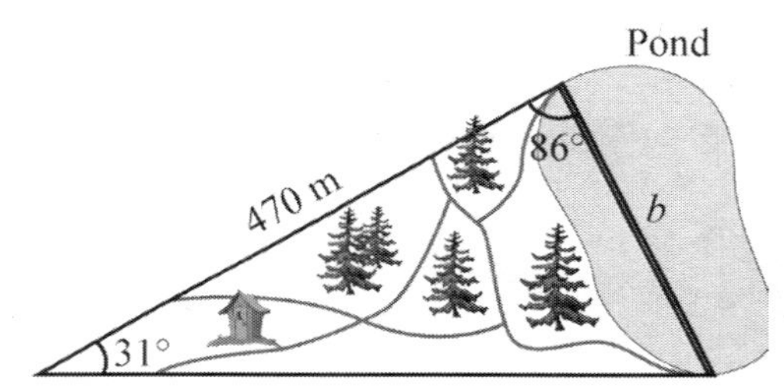

Explain which trigonometric law you would use to find the length of the bridge, *b*. Then, use the trigonometric law to find the length of the bridge, to the nearest whole meter.

Solution

The missing angle in the triangle can be easily determined, since the sum of the measures of the angles must be equal to 180°. This will provide a known pair with the side 470 m. Therefore, the sine law would be the correct formula to use to find the length of the bridge, *b*.

First, find the missing angle, *A*.
$\angle A = 180° - 86° - 31° = 63°$

Next, let side $a = 470$ m and $\angle B = 31°$ in the given triangle. Then, use the sine law to find the value of *b*.

$$\frac{a}{\sin A} = \frac{b}{\sin B}$$
$$\frac{470}{\sin 63°} = \frac{b}{\sin 31°}$$
$$\frac{470(\sin 31°)}{\sin 63°} = b$$
$$b = 271.6791501$$

The length of the bridge, *b*, to the nearest whole meter, is 272 m.

Solving Problems Using the Cosine Law for Acute Triangles

Problems involving acute triangles can be solved by following these general steps:

1. Read the problem carefully. Determine which measures are given and which measure needs to be calculated.
2. If a diagram is not given, draw a sketch to represent the situation presented in the problem.
3. Make substitutions into the cosine law formula, and use correct algebraic steps to solve for the unknown value. Avoid or minimize rounding until the last step.
4. Check your calculations.
5. Write a concluding statement.

Example

A radar tracking station locates two boats: a fishing boat at a distance of 3.4 km from the tracking station, and a passenger ferry at a distance of 5.6 km from the tracking station. From the tracking station, the angle between the line of sight to the two boats is 86°. Determine the distance between the two boats to the nearest tenth of a kilometer.

Solution

Draw a diagram representing the situation. Let *x* represent the distance between the two boats.

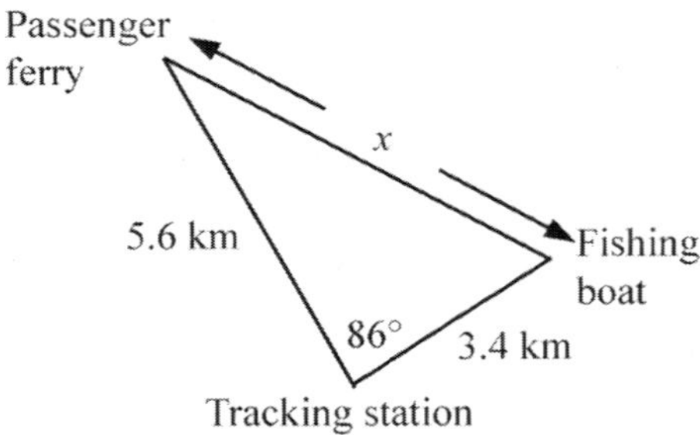

Since the problem is a side-angle-side situation, apply the cosine law. Side *x* is opposite the 86° angle; therefore, solve for *x* as follows:

$$a^2 = b^2 + c^2 - 2bc\cos A$$
$$x^2 = 5.6^2 + 3.4^2 - 2(5.6)(3.4)\cos 86°$$
$$x^2 \approx 31.36 + 11.56 - 2.66$$
$$x^2 \approx 40.26$$
$$x \approx \sqrt{40.26}$$
$$x \approx 6.345 \text{ km}$$

The distance between the fishing boat and the passenger ferry, to the nearest tenth of a kilometer, is 6.3 km.

Example

To display the Stanley Cup, staff at a hockey arena roped off a triangular area and installed a security camera, as illustrated in the given diagram.

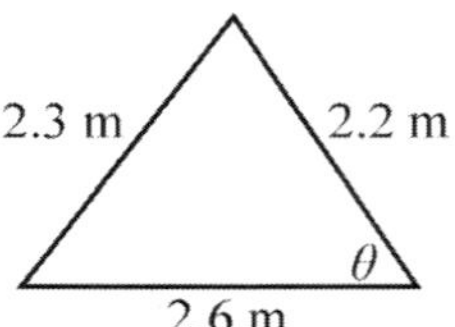

The security camera, located at θ, moves continuously between the two ropes, which measure 2.2 m and 2.6 m, respectively.

To the nearest tenth of a degree, determine the measure of angle θ.

Solution

Since this is a side-side-side situation, apply the cosine law. Angle θ is opposite the side measuring 2.3 m, so solve for θ as follows:

$$\cos A = \frac{b^2 + c^2 - a^2}{2bc}$$
$$\cos \theta = \frac{2.6^2 + 2.2^2 - 2.3^2}{2(2.6)(2.2)}$$
$$\cos \theta = \frac{6.76 + 4.84 - 5.29}{11.44}$$
$$\cos \theta = \frac{6.31}{11.44}$$
$$\theta \approx 56.525^\circ$$

To the nearest tenth of a degree, the measure of angle θ is 56.5°.

Solving Problems Using Sine Laws for Obtuse Triangles

Problems involving obtuse triangles can be solved by following these general steps:

1. Read the problem carefully. Determine what measures are given and what measure needs to be calculated.
2. If a diagram is not given, draw a sketch to represent the situation presented in the problem.
3. Make substitutions into the sine law, and use correct algebraic steps to solve for the unknown value. Avoid or minimize rounding until the last step.
4. Check your calculations for the ambiguous case.
5. Write a concluding statement.

Example

The given image shows where three basketball players were standing as they performed a practice drill. One player stood at point *A* and passed the ball to another player standing at point *B*, which was 6 m away. The player standing at *B* then passed it at an angle of 20° to a player standing at point *C*. The player standing at *C* then passed the ball back to the player standing at point *A*, which was 3 m away.

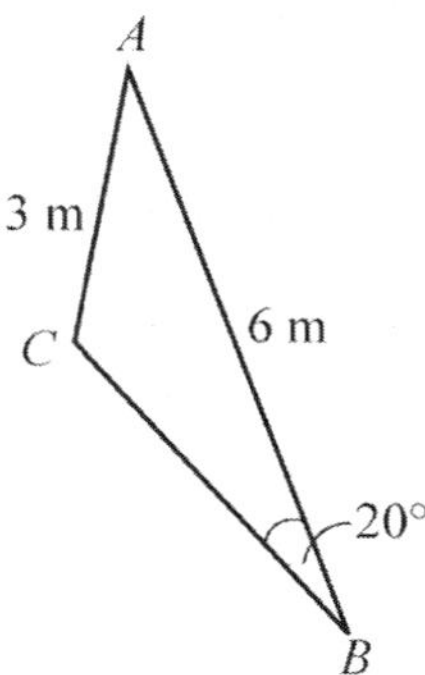

To the nearest degree, determine the measure of $\angle A$.

Solution

Step 1

Apply the sine law to determine the measure of $\angle C$.

The side measuring 3 m is opposite the 20° angle, and the side measuring 6 m is opposite $\angle C$. Solve for $\angle C$.

$$\frac{3}{\sin 20^\circ} = \frac{6}{\sin \angle C}$$
$$3\sin \angle C = 6\sin 20^\circ$$
$$\sin \angle C = 2\sin 20^\circ$$
$$\angle C = \sin^{-1}(2\sin 20^\circ)$$
$$\angle C \approx 43.16^\circ$$

Looking at the given diagram, the value determined for $\angle C$ is too small because an obtuse angle is shown in the diagram. This is a scenario where the ambiguous case is possible.

Step 2

Determine the other possible value of $\angle C$.

Subtract 180° by 43.16° to find the other value of $\angle C$.

$$\angle C \approx 180^\circ - 43.16^\circ$$
$$\angle C \approx 136.84^\circ$$

This is a more reasonable measurement for the given diagram.

Step 3

Determine the measure of $\angle A$.

Apply the property that the sum of the interior angles of a triangle is equal to 180°.

$\angle A = 180° - (\angle B + \angle C)$
$\angle A \approx 180° - (20° + 136.84°)$
$\angle A \approx 180° - (156.84°)$
$\angle A \approx 23.16°$

Rounded to the nearest degree, the measure of $\angle A$ is 23°.

Example

A golfer at point T on the given diagram wishes to sink his golf ball in a hole directly on the other side of a pond at point H. The golfer has two options. He can play two low-risk shots (one from point T to point A and another from point A to point H) or he can play a high-risk shot and attempt to shoot directly from point T to point H. The golfer estimates that the distance from point T to point A is 175 m, the measure of angle ATH is 45°, and the measure of angle TAH is 95°.

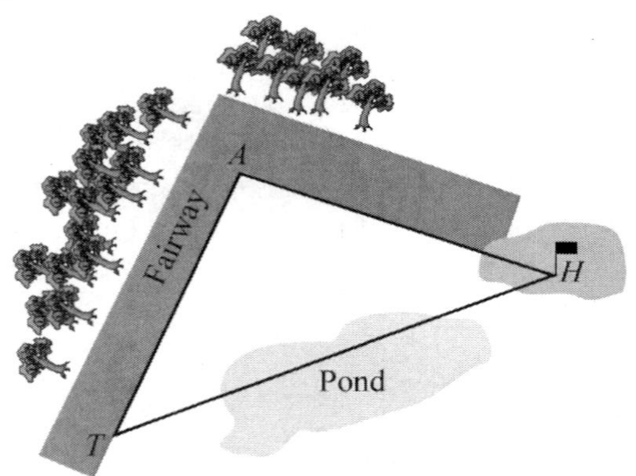

To the nearest meter, what is the distance from point T to point H?

Solution

Step 1

Determine the measure of angle AHT.

$\angle AHT = 180° - (\angle ATH + \angle TAH)$
$\angle AHT = 180° - (45° + 95°)$
$\angle AHT = 40°$

Step 2

Use the sine law to determine the distance from point T to point H.

$$\frac{TH}{\sin TAH} = \frac{TA}{\sin AHT}$$
$$\frac{TH}{\sin 95°} = \frac{175}{\sin 40°}$$
$$TH = \frac{175\sin 95°}{\sin 40°}$$
$$TH = 271.2156699\ldots$$

Step 3

Round the answer to the neatest meter.

The distance from point T to point H is about 271 m.

Solving Problems Using Cosine Laws for Obtuse Triangles

Problems that involve obtuse triangles can be solved by following these general steps:

1. Read the problem carefully. Determine which measures are given and which measure needs to be calculated.
2. If a diagram is not given, draw a sketch to represent the situation presented in the problem.
3. Make substitutions into the cosine law formula, and use correct algebraic steps to solve for the unknown value. Avoid or minimize rounding until the last step.
4. Write a concluding statement.

Example

To navigate his sailboat home at night, a sailor uses a lighthouse as a reference point. He is 1 km away from the lighthouse, and the lighthouse is 2 km away from the harbor, as shown.

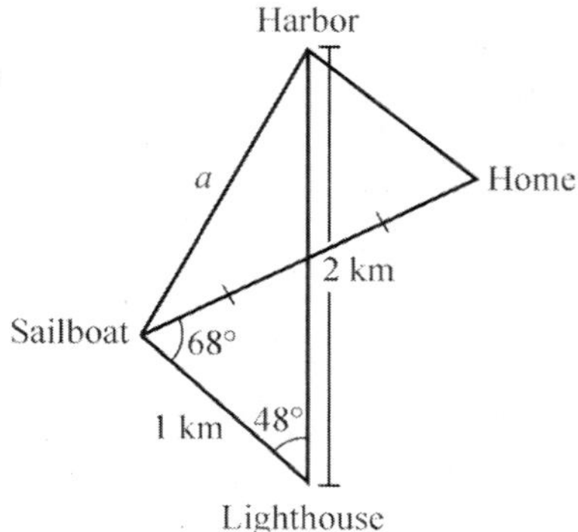

To the nearest tenth of a kilometer, calculate the distance from the sailboat to the harbor.

Solution

Step 1
Draw a diagram.
The sailboat is denoted as B, the lighthouse as A, and the harbor as C.

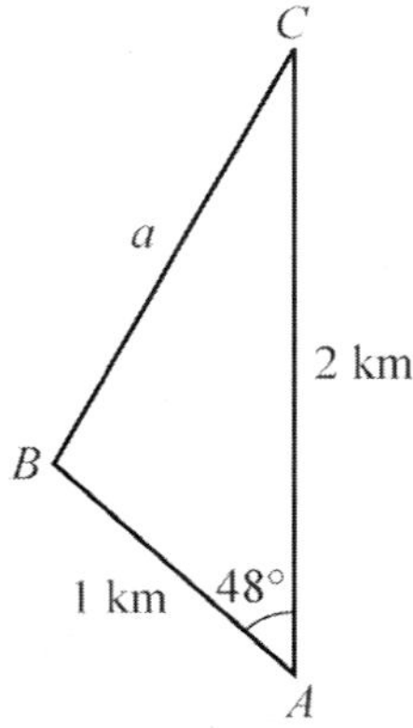

Step 2
Since the triangle is not a right triangle and the measures of two sides and an included angle are known, use the cosine law to solve for a.

$a^2 = b^2 + c^2 - 2bc(\cos A)$
$a^2 = 2^2 + 1^2 - 2(2)(1)\cos 48°$
$a^2 \approx 2.3235$
$a \approx 1.5$ km

The distance from the sailboat to the harbor is approximately 1.5 km.

Example

From the top of a 100 m fire tower, a fire ranger at point R observes smoke coming from two separate fires. The angle of elevation from Fire A is 5° and from Fire B it is 3°. The angle that the two fires make with the base of the tower, T, is 87°.

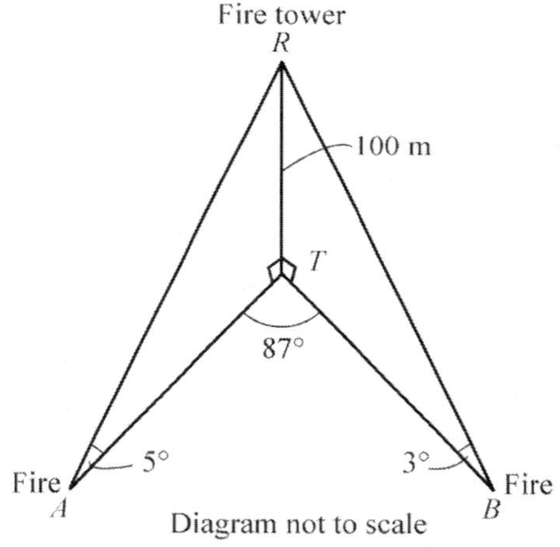

To the nearest meter, what is the distance from Fire A to Fire B?

Solution

Step 1
Draw a diagram, and label it as shown.

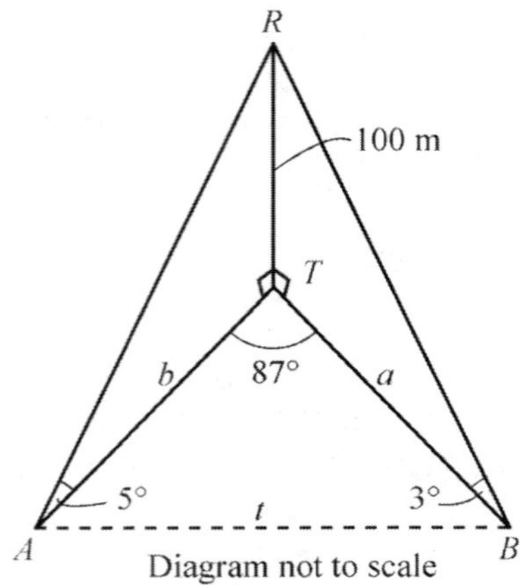

Diagram not to scale

Step 2
Solve for sides a and b.
Since ΔART and ΔBRT are right triangles, use the primary trigonometric ratios to solve for a and b.
Solve for a using the tangent ratio.

$$\tan\theta = \frac{\text{opposite}}{\text{adjacent}}$$
$$\tan 3° = \frac{100}{a}$$
$$a = \frac{100}{\tan 3°}$$
$$a \approx 1{,}908\text{m}$$

Solve for b using the tangent ratio.

$$\tan\theta = \frac{\text{opposite}}{\text{adjacent}}$$
$$\tan 5° = \frac{100}{b}$$
$$b = \frac{100}{\tan 5°}$$
$$b \approx 1{,}143 \text{ m}$$

Step 3
Since two sides and the angle between the two sides are known, solve for t in ΔATB using the cosine law $t^2 = a^2 + b^2 - 2ab(\cos T)$.

$$t^2 = a^2 + b^2 - 2ab(\cos T)$$
$$t^2 \approx 1{,}908^2 + 1{,}143^2 - 2(1{,}908)(1{,}143)\cos 87°$$
$$t^2 \approx 4{,}946{,}913 - 228{,}273.1123$$
$$t^2 \approx 4{,}718{,}639.888$$
$$t \approx 2{,}172 \text{ m}$$

The distance from Fire A to Fire B is 2,172 m.

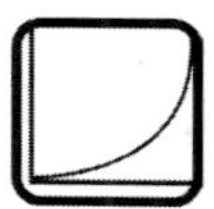

MODELING AND SOLVING FUNCTIONS EXERCISE #1

Use the following information to answer the next question.

While breathing, the volume in your lungs is a periodic function of time. The graph below shows how the volume, V, in liters, changes over time, t, in seconds, for a particular person.

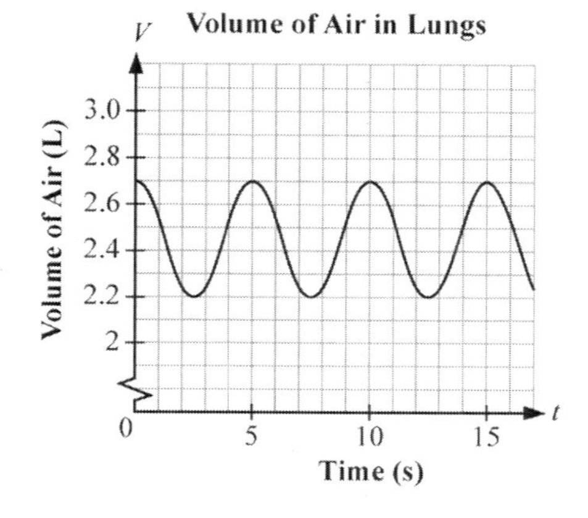

107. If the length of time (period) for the person to inhale and exhale once is P seconds and the total volume exhaled each time a breath is taken is V liters, then the sum of the values $P + V$, to the nearest tenth, is _________.

Use the following information to answer the next question.

The given data represents the change in the sound pitch of a siren over time.

Time (s)	Frequency (Hz)
0	640.0
2	706.6
4	681.1
6	598.9
8	573.4
10	640.0
12	706.6
14	681.1
16	598.8
18	573.4
20	640.0

108. Which of the following graphs and corresponding equations **best** represents the given data?

A.

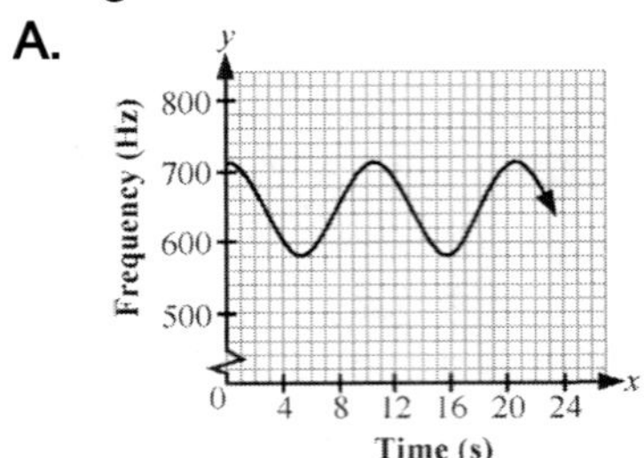

$y = 70\cos(36° x) + 640$

B.

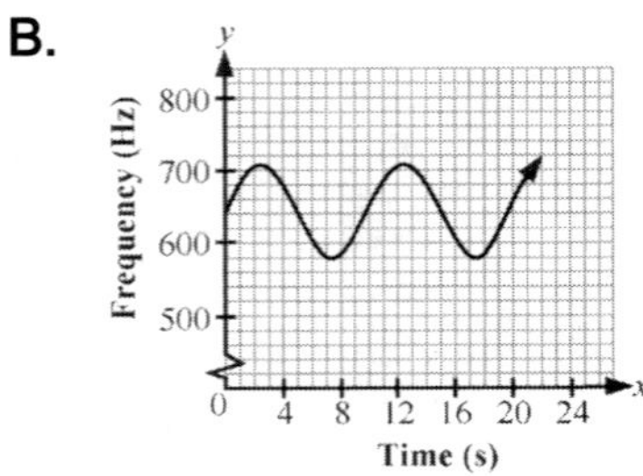

$y = 70\sin(36° x) + 640$

C.

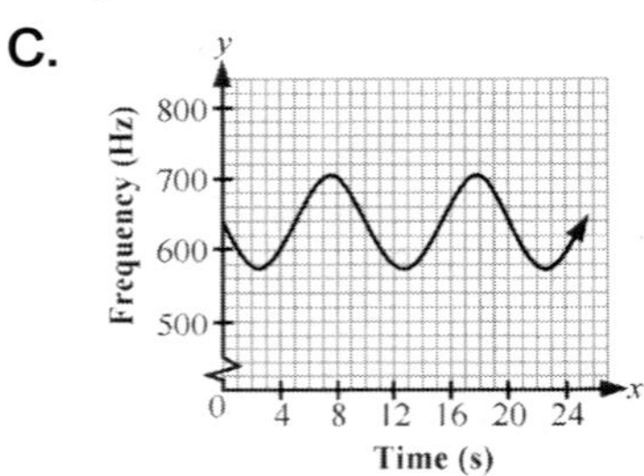

$y = 70\cos(36°(x + 2.57)) + 640$

D.

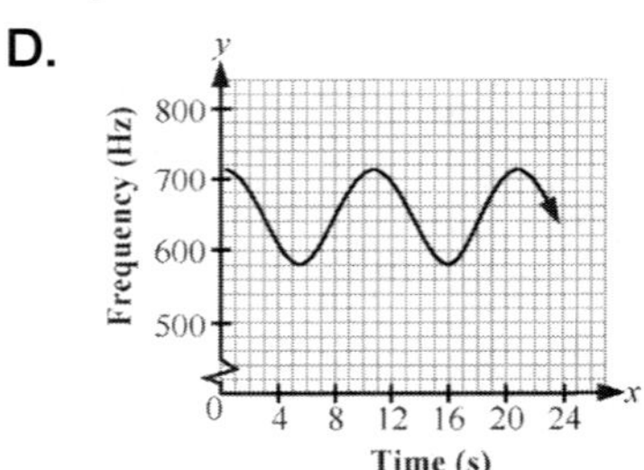

$y = 70\sin(36°(x + 2.57)) + 640$

Use the following information to answer the next question.

The given table of values shows the average amount of daylight in Sudbury, Ontario, for two consecutive years, neither of which were leap years.

Day	Hours of Daylight
1	8.6
60	11.0
121	14.4
182	15.7
213	14.9
274	11.7
305	10.0
366	8.6
397	9.6
456	12.9
486	14.5
547	15.9
609	13.3
639	11.7
700	8.8

109. If the given data represents a periodic function, what is the amplitude of the function?

A. 3.65 h
B. 4.3 h
C. 7.3 h
D. 8.95 h

Use the following information to answer the next question.

The pH scale describes the acidity or basicity of a particular solution. The pH of a solution is the negative logarithm of the concentration of the hydrogen ions, $\left[H^{+}\right]$. In terms of an equation, this can be written as $pH = -\log\left[H^{+}\right]$.

110. If a solution is 7,500 times more acidic than seawater, which has a pH of 8.5, the pH of the solution, to the nearest tenth, is _______.

Use the following information to answer the next question.

The number of hours, h, that milk stays fresh at a given temperature, t, in a particular storage cooler is given by the formula $t = \log \frac{195 - h}{0.28}$.

111. If the temperature of the milk in the cooler is 3.5°C, the milk will stay fresh for _________ days. Record the answer to the nearest tenth.

Use the following information to answer the next question.

The owner of a 300-seat theater sells tickets for $20 each. He believes that for every dollar he increases the price of a ticket, he will lose 10 customers. He has charted his resulting revenue for each $1 increase in ticket price:

Increase in Price ($)	Revenue ($)
0	6,000
1	6,090
2	6,160
3	6,210
4	6,240
5	6,250
6	6,240

112. What is the ticket price at which the owner will earn his maximum revenue?

A. $24.72 **B.** $25.00

C. $25.25 **D.** $25.68

Use the following information to answer the next question.

x	y
10	1,010
20	1,620
30	1,870
40	1,610
50	1,005

113. Perform a quadratic regression to graph the curve of best fit for the function represented by the given table of values.

Use the following information to answer the next question.

The exponential equation $R = 3.7(1.171)^n$, can be used to represent the number of rats, R, in millions, in a certain region, after n number of years since 1997.

114. If the rat population continues to grow at the given rate, then what will be the approximate number of rats in that region in the year 2010?

A. 12.6 million **B.** 14.4 million

C. 28.8 million **D.** 32.3 million

Use the following information to answer the next question.

The population of a small town is 1,400 people, and the population of the town doubles every 20 years.

115. The number of years it will take for the population of the town to reach 50,000 people is between

A. 80 and 90 years

B. 90 and 100 years

C. 100 and 110 years

D. 110 and 120 years

Use the following information to answer the next question.

An equation for determining radioactive decay is $A = A_0\left(\frac{1}{2}\right)^{\frac{t}{h}}$, where

A = the mass present at time t

A_0 = the original mass

t = the time in days

h = the half-life of the material in days

The half-life of iodine-126 is 13 days.

116. To the nearest tenth of a gram, what is the mass of iodine-126 remaining from a 10 g sample after 86 days?

A. 0.1 g **B.** 0.3 g

C. 5.0 g **D.** 9.0 g

Use the following information to answer the next question.

When a large block of ice is put in a tub of water, it melts such that the volume of ice is halved every 12 minutes.

117. Using a graphical approach, determine the amount of time, to the nearest minute, that it takes for the block of ice to melt to one-tenth of its original volume?

A. 3 min **B.** 24 min

C. 33 min **D.** 40 min

Use the following information to answer the next question.

The unit value of a particular stock, in Japanese yen (JPY), followed a quadratic pattern over a period of 20 consecutive days. Part of this trend is portrayed in the bar graph shown below.

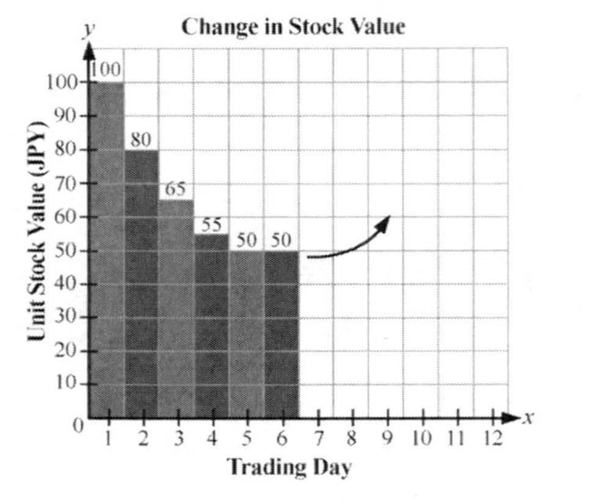

118. Based on the trend, the stock would recover to its original value of 100 JPY on day __________.

Use the following information to answer the next question.

A small model rocket is launched from a second-story balcony deck. The path of the rocket is represented by the given graph.

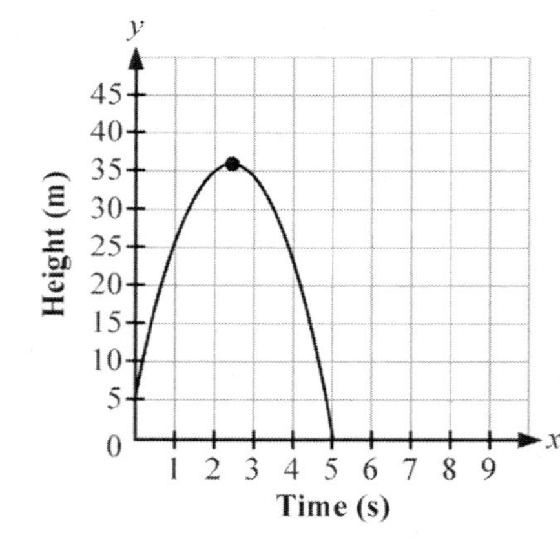

119. Once it is launched, how much time does the rocket take to strike the ground?

A. 3 s **B.** 4 s

C. 5 s **D.** 6 s

Use the following information to answer the next question.

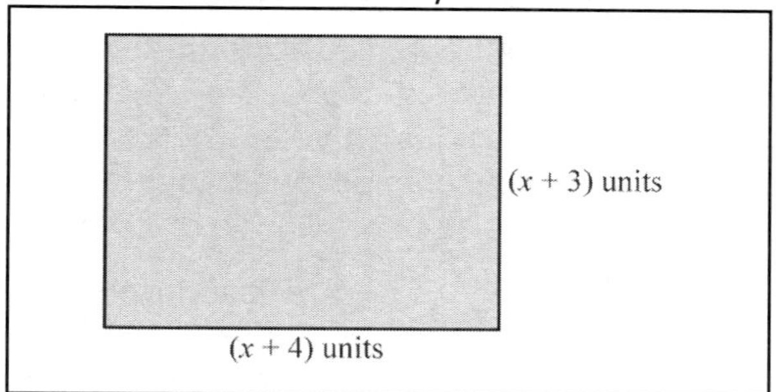

120. The area of the rectangle is

A. $x^2 + 7x + 12$

B. $x^2 + 7x + 7$

C. $x^2 + 12$

D. $x^2 + 7x$

Use the following information to answer the next question.

The design of the side view of a specialized cement staircase is shown, with expressions for all side lengths.

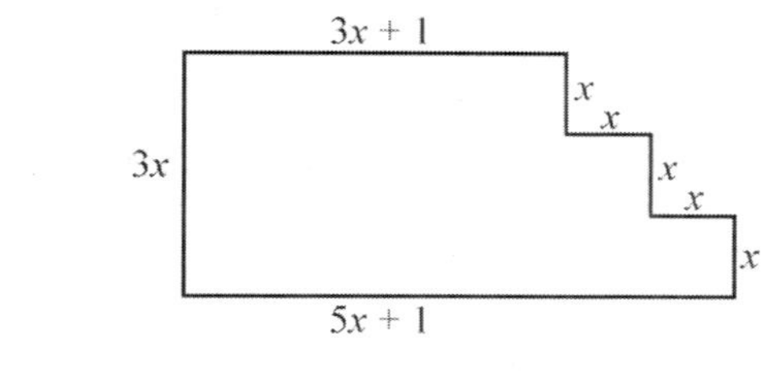

121. Which of the following simplified expressions describes the area of the side view of the staircase?

A. $6x^2$

B. $15x^2$

C. $12x^2 + 3x$

D. $13x^2 + 3x$

Use the following information to answer the next question.

The flight path of a flare fired from the top of a cliff to the ground can be described by the graph of the quadratic function $h(t) = -4.9t^2 + 29.4t + 352.8$, where $h(t)$ is the height, in meters, of the flare above the ground at a time, t, in seconds. Yosef wanted to use his graphing calculator to find the time, in seconds, when the flare hit the ground at $h(t) = 0$, namely the t-intercept.

122. The window Yosef used to display the whole flight of the flare to the ground ($h(t) = 0$) was ____*i*____, and the t-intercept was ____*ii*____.

Which of the following rows correctly completes this statement?

	i	*ii*
A.	x:[−10, 10, 1] y:[−10, 10, 1]	6.0 seconds
B.	x:[−10, 20, 1] y:[−10, 500, 1]	6.0 seconds
C.	x:[−10, 10, 1] y:[−10, 500, 1]	12.0 seconds
D.	x:[−10, 20, 1] y:[−10, 500, 1]	12.0 seconds

Use the following information to answer the next question.

A football kicked during a football game followed a parabolic path. This path can be modeled by graphing the equation $h = -2t^2 + 11t - 3$, $t \geq 1$, where t is the number of seconds that have elapsed since the football was kicked and h is the height of the football above the ground in yards.

123. How long did it take the football to reach a height of 12 yards above the ground after it was kicked?

A. 2.0 seconds

B. 2.5 seconds

C. 3.0 seconds

D. 3.5 seconds

Use the following information to answer the next question.

The mass of a certain radioactive substance is currently 300 g, and its half-life is 7 years.

124. The exponential function of the mass of the given radioactive substance is

A. $N_t = 300(7)^{\frac{t}{2}}$

B. $N_t = 300(2)^{\frac{t}{7}}$

C. $N_t = 300\left(\frac{1}{2}\right)^{\frac{t}{7}}$

D. $N_t = 300\left(\frac{1}{7}\right)^{\frac{t}{2}}$

Use the following information to answer the next question.

A small publishing company initially recorded the number of titles it published every year since it opened in 1999, but it stopped collecting data after six years. The data collected by the company is shown in the given table.

Year	Year Number	Number of Titles Published
1999	0	310
2000	1	327
2001	2	345
2002	3	379
2003	4	402
2004	5	445

Exponential regression can be performed on this data to get a function that gives the number of titles published as a function of the number of years after 1999.

125. According to the regression equation, the number of titles published in 2005 could have been approximately

A. 455 **B.** 463

C. 471 **D.** 495

Use the following information to answer the next question.

The sales staff at a magazine looked at the growth rate in the number of subscribers during the previous 10 years. They found the number of subscriptions had grown exponentially, as shown in the given chart.

Year Recorded	Subscriptions (millions)
1	0.430
2	0.456
3	0.474
4	0.512
5	0.601
6	0.685
7	0.765
8	0.812
9	0.906
10	1.012

An exponential regression was performed on the data to get a function that gives the number of subscriptions, y, in millions, as a function of x, the number of years before the magazine had one million subscribers.

126. Using the exponential regression function, what is the average growth rate percentage for the number of subscribers to the magazine during the past 10 years, to the nearest hundredth?

A. 0.37% **B.** 1.11%

C. 1.63% **D.** 2.27%

Use the following information to answer the next question.

A forestry study was conducted to find the growth rate of the trees in a certain area. The trees in the area had an average starting diameter of 276 cm, and the diameter of each tree increased by an average of 1.3 cm each year over the four-year study.

127. What type of regression would **best** help the researchers predict the future diameter of the trees?

A. Exponential regression
B. Sinusoidal regression
C. Quadratic regression
D. Linear regression

Use the following information to answer the next question.

The given table shows the tidal depths over a 30 hour time span.

Time (h)	0	5	10	15	20	25	30
Change from sea level (m)	−1.8	0.4	2.1	0.2	−2.0	−1.9	0.3

128. If all values are rounded to the nearest hundredth, which of the following regression functions would be **best** to use for the given data?

A. $y = 0.01x^2 + 0.11x + 0.64$

B. $y = -0.01x^2 + 0.11x - 0.64$

C. $y = 2.13\sin(0.25x + 0.86) + 0.25$

D. $y = 2.13\sin(0.25x - 0.86) - 0.25$

Use the following information to answer the next question.

The data in the given table shows the speed, v, in kilometers per hour, of an athlete running a 200 m sprint over a time period, t, in seconds.

Time (t)	**Speed (v)**
1	5.00
2	8.00
3	12.80
4	20.48
5	32.77

129. If this trend continues, after how many seconds will the athlete's speed reach 40 kilometers per hour?

A. 5.36 **B.** 5.42
C. 5.68 **D.** 5.77

Use the following information to answer the next question.

The value of a truck decreases over time, as shown in the given table.

Time Since Purchase (years)	**Value of Truck ($)**
2	28,000
3	20,000
5	11,600
6	8,400
7	5,000

130. If this trend continues, what will the price of the truck be 7 years and 9 months after the time of purchase?

A. $3,965.80 **B.** $3,985.20
C. $4,025.60 **D.** $4,355.57

Use the following information to answer the next question.

Chord BC and line segments AB and AC, which are tangent to the circle, form ΔABC.

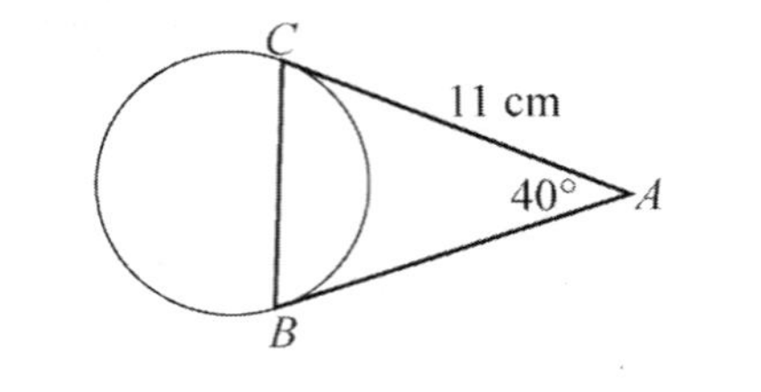

131. Determine the area of ΔABC.

A. 30.25 cm^2

B. 38.89 cm^2

C. 60.50 cm^2

D. 77.78 cm^2

Use the following information to answer the next question.

Along a straight stretch of highway, there are two access roads that lead to a general store. The distance from the highway to the general store along one of the access roads is 3.7 mi. The distance from the highway to the general store along the other access road is 5.4 mi.

132. If the area of the region bordered by the highway and the two access roads is 9.5 mi^2, what is the angle between the two access roads, expressed to the nearest tenth of a degree?

A. 28.4° **B.** 36.0°

C. 68.4° **D.** 72.0°

133. An arc subtends an angle of 320°, and the radius of the circle is 12 mm. Determine the arc length.

Use the following information to answer the next question.

A circle has a radius of 10 cm. A sector within the circle is subtended by an arc with a length of 45 cm.

134. To the nearest degree, what is the measure of the angle subtended by the arc? _______°

Use the following information to answer the next question.

An engineer needs to calculate the distance across a deep canyon. She takes a sighting from a point A and then from a point C, which are both on the same side of the canyon, to a point B on the opposite side of the canyon, as shown in the diagram.

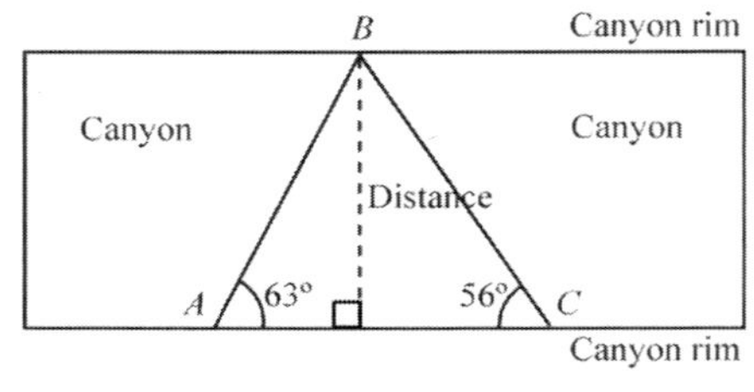

135. If points A and C are 70 m apart, then the distance across the canyon, correct to the nearest tenth of a meter, is

A. 51.9 m **B.** 59.1 m

C. 60.3 m **D.** 68.7 m

Use the following information to answer the next question.

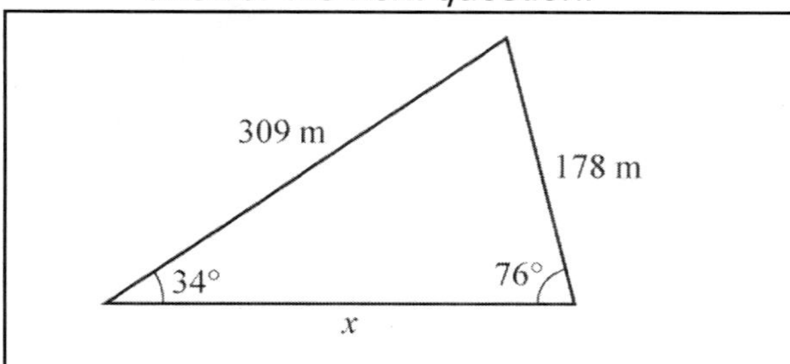

136. An equation that could be used to solve for the length, in meters, of side x in the given diagram is

A. $x = \dfrac{(309)\sin 70°}{\sin 76°}$

B. $x = \dfrac{(178)\sin 70°}{\sin 76°}$

C. $x = \sqrt{309^2 + 178^2 - 2(309)(178)\cos 34°}$

D. $x = \sqrt{309^2 + 178^2 - 2(392)(178)\cos 76°}$

Use the following information to answer the next question.

To display a valuable trophy, the staff at a hockey arena roped off a triangular area and installed a security camera. The security camera was installed so that it rotated continually between the two longest ropes through the angle θ, as shown in the given diagram.

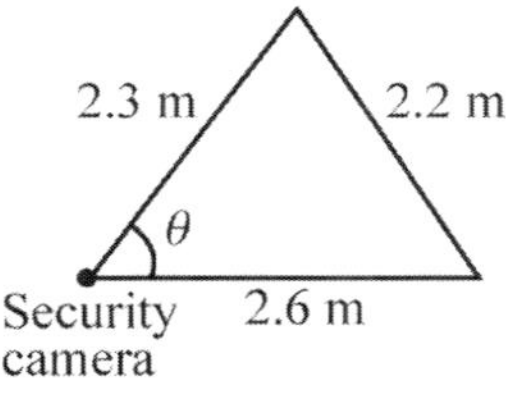

137. The measure of angle θ, rounded to the nearest degree, is

A. 53° **B.** 57°
C. 64° **D.** 70°

Use the following information to answer the next question.

A weather balloon is flying in a field outside of London, Ontario. One end of a lightweight rope is attached to the base of the weather balloon, and the other end of the rope is anchored to the ground at point P. On a windy day, Rachel decides to determine the length of the rope, x, between P and the connection point located at the base of the weather balloon. She locates two points, A and B, that are 200 m apart, and records the measurements shown in the diagram.

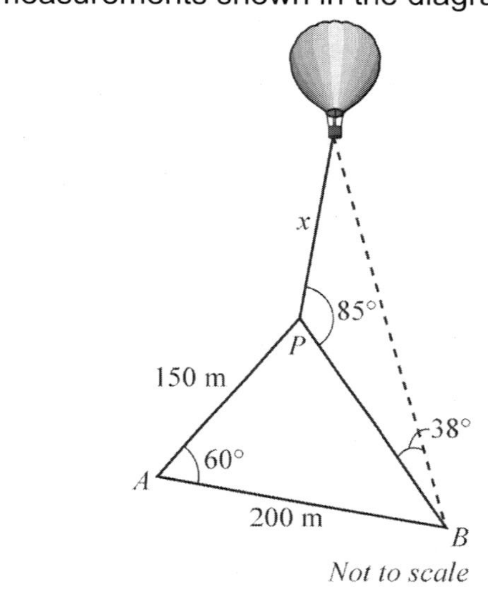

Not to scale

138. The value of x, to the nearest meter, is

A. 128 m **B.** 132 m
C. 136 m **D.** 140 m

Use the following information to answer the next question.

From a particular point, Jennifer determined that the angle of elevation to the top of her school was 18°. When she walked 12.5 m closer to the school, she determined that the angle of elevation to the top of the school was 29°, as illustrated in the diagram.

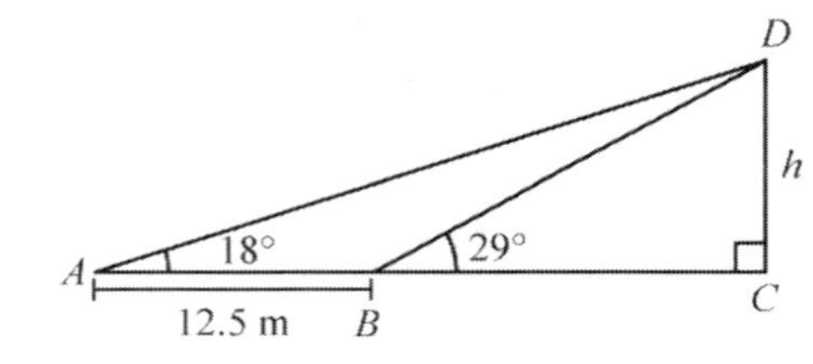

139. Correct to the nearest meter, the height of the school, h, is __________ m.

Use the following information to answer the next question.

At 4:00 P.M., the distance between the tip of the minute hand and the tip of the hour hand on a clock is 20 cm.

140. If the length of the minute hand is 15 cm, then the approximate length of the hour hand is

A. 5.00 cm
B. 7.71 cm
C. 13.23 cm
D. 15.00 cm

Use the following information to answer the next question.

A golf course engineer designs a fairway that curves to the right. In golf terms, this is called a dog-leg right. The designer places four reference points on his sketch of the hole. Reference point T is at the starting location, A and B are at each side of the dog leg, and point G is where the hole is, as shown in the diagram.

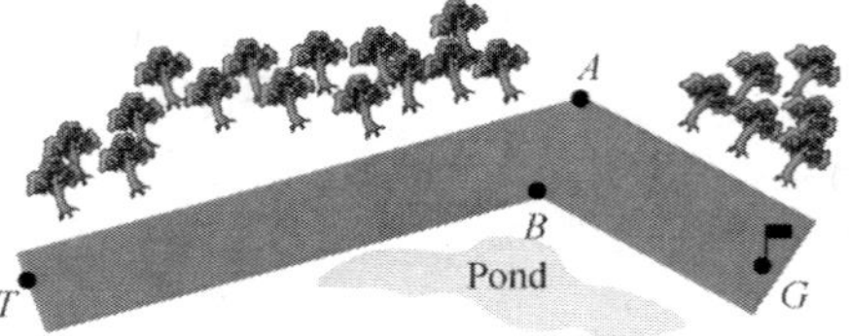

In the sketch, distance TA = 240 m, distance TB = 210 m, $\angle ATB$ = 10°, $\angle GAB$ = 68°, and $\angle GBA$ = 84°.

141. Rounded to the nearest meter, the distance of BG is

A. 46 m
B. 53 m
C. 97 m
D. 104 m

Use the following information to answer the next question.

The given diagram shows a triangle in three dimensions.

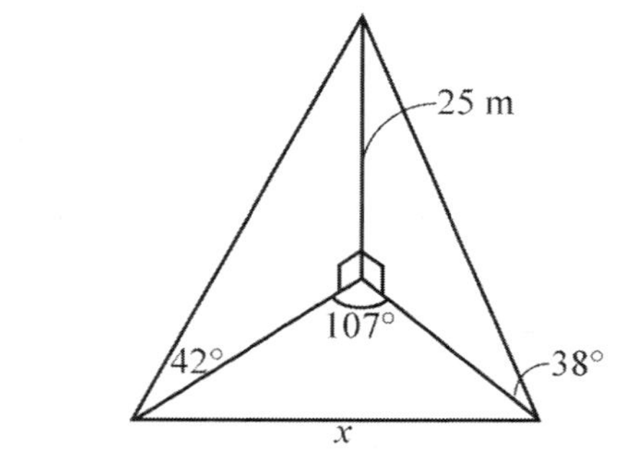

142. To the nearest tenth of a meter, the length of x is __________m.

Use the following information to answer the next question.

Michelle searched a public sector employee database for statistical data that modeled a sine function. She found an example and recorded the data as a graph.

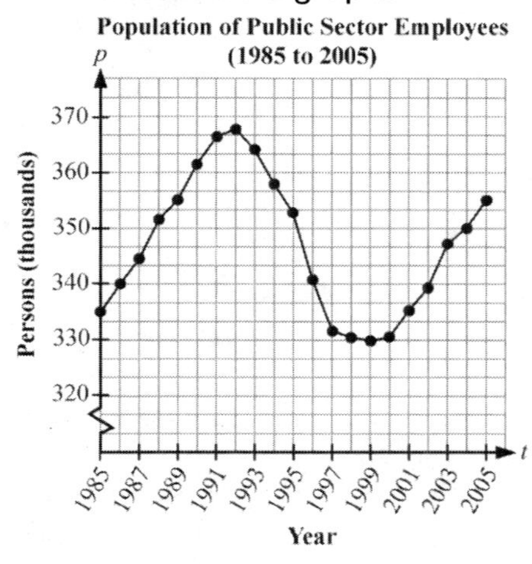

143. According to the approximate sinusoidal graph, the amplitude is about

A. 37,000 people **B.** 27,750 people

C. 18,500 people **D.** 9,250 people

MODELING AND SOLVING FUNCTIONS EXERCISE #1 ANSWERS AND SOLUTIONS

107. 5.5	117. D	127. D	137. A
108. B	118. 10	128. D	138. B
109. A	119. C	129. B	139. 10
110. 4.6	120. A	130. D	140. B
111. 7.7	121. C	131. B	141. C
112. B	122. D	132. D	142. 48.1
113. See solution	123. B	133. See solution	143. C
114. C	124. C	134. 258	
115. C	125. C	135. B	
116. A	126. B	136. A	

107. 5.5

Upon examination of the graph, the length of time between the first two successive maximum values is 5 seconds. This is the time required for the person to inhale and exhale once. Therefore, the value of $P = 5$. To find the total volume exhaled each time you need to find the maximum and minimum volumes of air in the lungs during a breath. According to the graph, the maximum volume is 2.7 liters and the minimum volume is 2.2 liters. Therefore, the total volume exhaled in a breath is 2.7−2.2 = 0.5 liters. Therefore, the sum of the values $P + V$ is 5 + 0.5 = 5.5.

108. B

Step 1

Plot the given points, and draw a curve of best fit.

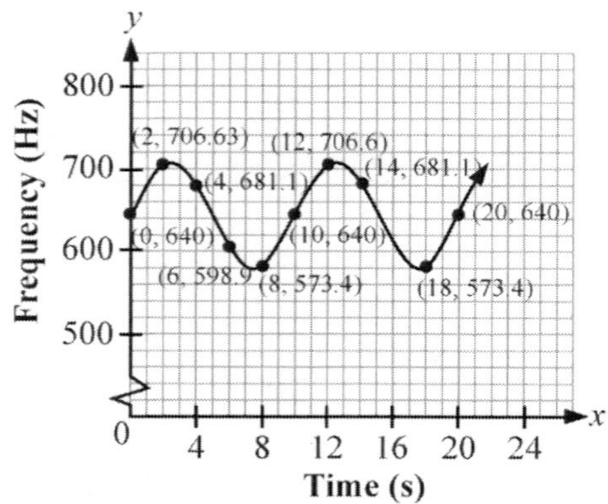

Step 2

Determine the approximate minimum and maximum values.

A sine function has the form $y = a\sin(k(x - c)) + d$.

The minimum value is slightly lower than the given point (8, 573.4), and the maximum value is slightly higher than the given point (2, 706.6).

Therefore, approximate minimum and maximum values can be determined.

Minimum = 570
Maximum = 710

Step 3

Determine the amplitude, a, of the graph using the minimum and maximum values.

$$\begin{aligned} a &= \frac{\max - \min}{2} \\ &= \frac{710 - 570}{2} \\ &= 70 \end{aligned}$$

Step 4

The period of this graph can be determined using the points (0, 640) and (10, 640). Since this shows one cycle, the period is 10. Calculate the value of k.

$$\begin{aligned} k &= \frac{360°}{10} \\ &= 36° \end{aligned}$$

Step 5

Determine the vertical phase shift, d, using the minimum and maximum values.

$$\begin{aligned} d &= \frac{\max + \min}{2} \\ &= \frac{710 + 570}{2} \\ &= 640 \end{aligned}$$

Step 6
From the graph, there is no horizontal translation when compared to the graph of $y = \sin x$, so $c = 0$.

Substituting each value into the equation $y = a\sin(k(x - c)) + d$ gives an approximate sine function of $y = 70\sin(36^\circ x) + 640$.

109. A

The amplitude, a, of a periodic function can be calculated by using the formula $a = \frac{\text{maximum} - \text{minimum}}{2}$.

From the given table of values, the maximum and minimum y-values are 15.9 h and 8.6 h respectively. Substitute these values into the formula, and solve for a.

$$a = \frac{\text{maximum} - \text{minimum}}{2}$$
$$a = \frac{15.9 - 8.6}{2}$$
$$a = 3.65$$

The amplitude of this function is 3.65 h of daylight.

110. 4.6

Step 1
Determine $[H^+]$ for the more acidic solution by applying the formula $pH = -\log[H^+]$.
Let x represent the pH value of the solution more acidic than seawater, and substitute x for pH in the formula.

$$pH = -\log[H^+]$$
$$x = -\log[H^+]$$

Express $\log[H^+]$ as $\log_{10}[H^+]$, and rewrite the resulting equation in exponential form.

$$x = -\log_{10}[H^+]$$
$$-x = \log_{10}[H^+]$$
$$10^{-x} = [H^+]$$

Step 2
Determine $[H^+]$ for seawater by applying the formula $pH = -\log[H^+]$.
Substitute 8.5 for pH.

$$8.5 = -\log[H^+]$$

Express $\log[H^+]$ as $\log_{10}[H^+]$, and rewrite the resulting equation in exponential form.

$$8.5 = -\log_{10}[H^+]$$
$$-8.5 = \log_{10}[H^+]$$
$$10^{-8.5} = [H^+]$$

Step 3
Set up a ratio to determine the pH of the acidic solution, x.
Compare the two acidity levels by dividing their respective $[H^+]$ concentrations.

$$\frac{\text{Acidic solution}[H^+]}{\text{Seawater}[H^+]} = \frac{10^{-x}}{10^{-8.5}}$$

Since it is given that the solution is 7,500 times more acidic than seawater, replace the ratio $\frac{\text{Acidic solution}[H^+]}{\text{Seawater}[H^+]}$ with 7,500.

$$7{,}500 = \frac{10^{-x}}{10^{-8.5}}$$

Step 4
Solve for x in the equation $\frac{10^{-x}}{10^{-8.5}} = 7{,}500$.

Simplify the left side of the equation by applying the quotient law of exponents.

$$\frac{10^{-x}}{10^{-8.5}} = 7{,}500$$
$$10^{-x-(-8.5)} = 7{,}500$$
$$10^{-x+8.5} = 7{,}500$$

Take the common logarithm of each side of the equation.

$$10^{-x+8.5} = 7{,}500$$
$$\log 10^{-x+8.5} = \log 7{,}500$$

Apply the power law of logarithms to the left side of the equation.

$$\log 10^{-x+8.5} = \log 7{,}500$$
$$(-x + 8.5)\log 10 = \log 7{,}500$$

Divide both sides of the equation by log10.

$$(-x + 8.5)\log 10 = \log 7{,}500$$
$$-x + 8.5 = \log \frac{7{,}500}{\log 10}$$

Evaluate $\frac{\log 7{,}500}{\log 10}$, and solve for x.

$$-x + 8.5 = \frac{\log 7{,}500}{\log 10}$$
$$-x + 8.5 \approx 3.9$$
$$8.5 - 3.9 \approx x$$
$$4.6 \approx x$$

The pH value of the solution is 4.6.

111. 7.7

Step 1
Substitute any known values and isolate the logarithm in the formula $t = \frac{\log(195 - h)}{0.28}$.

Substitute 3.5 for t.

$3.5 = \frac{\log(195 - h)}{0.28}$

Simplify the equation by multiplying both sides by 0.28.

$3.5(0.28) = \log(195 - h)$
$0.98 = \log(195 - h)$

Step 2
Convert the equation from logarithmic into exponential form.

Express $\log(195 - h)$ as $\log_{10}(195 - h)$, then rewrite the resulting equation in exponential form.

$0.98 = \log_{10}(195 - h)$
$10^{0.98} = 195 - h$

Step 3
Solve for h, the number of hours that milk will stay fresh at a given temperature.

$10^{0.98} = 195 - h$
$h = 195 - 10^{0.98}$
$h \approx 185.45$

Step 4
Convert 185.45 h into days, to the nearest tenth.

$\frac{185.45}{24} \approx 7.7$

Therefore, the milk in the cooler will stay fresh for 7.7 days.

112. B

Enter the data into a TI-83 Plus calculator and perform a quadratic regression.

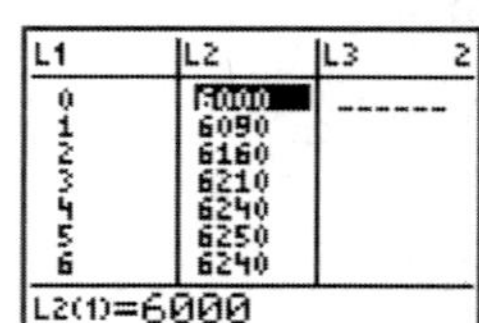

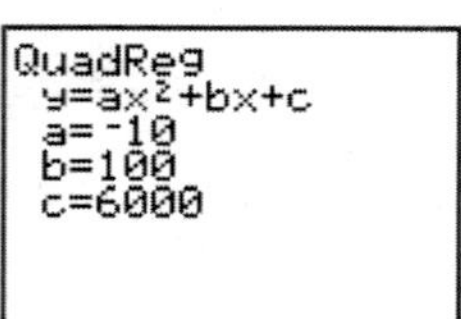

The formula $y = -10x^2 + 100x + 6{,}000$ will result.

Then, use the MAXIMUM feature of a TI-83 Plus graphing calculator and a window setting such as x: $[-1, 30, 2]$ y: $[-1{,}000, 7{,}500, 500]$.

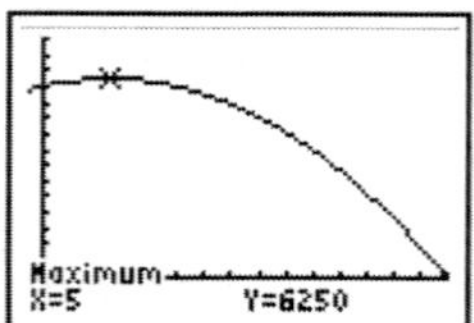

The function's maximum value occurs when $x = 5$.

This means the maximum revenue occurs when the price increases by $5. Therefore, the ticket price that will earn the maximum revenue is $25. (20 + 5 = 25).

113.

Before carrying out the quadratic regression, clear any previous data in the calculator. To clear the data from the calculator, press 2nd + to access the MEMORY menu.

Select 4:ClrAllLists. Press ENTER two times. Any data contained in the lists is cleared.

ClrAllLists
Done
Done

Step 1
Enter the data from the table into the list editor.
Press STAT to view the EDIT menu.

Select 1:Edit.... If there is data in L1, move the cursor up to L1. Press CLEAR ENTER. Move over to L2 and repeat the process.
Using the cursor keys, move the cursor to the first column, as highlighted in the given screen shot.

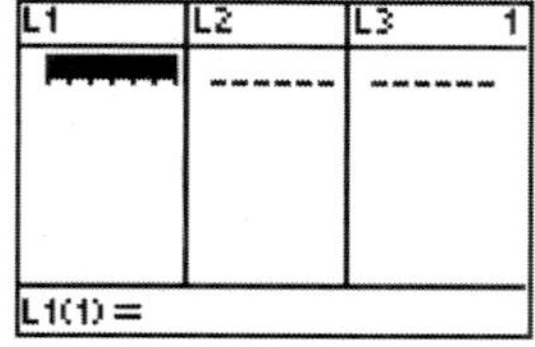

Type in the numbers that represent the *x*-values in L1 (independent variables). Press ENTER after each data entry to move the cursor to the next row. Continue this process until all the *x*-values are entered.

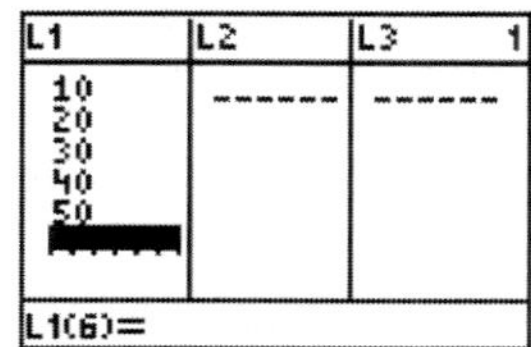

Move to column L2. Enter the numbers representing the *y*-values (dependent variables) in L2.

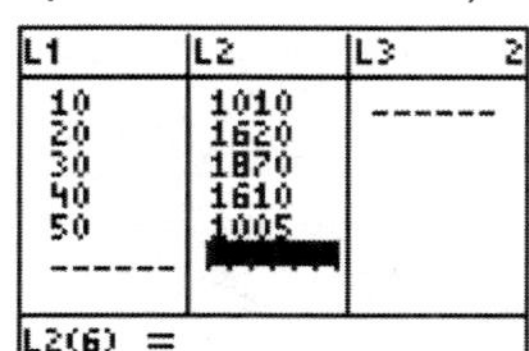

Step 2
Turn on the STAT PLOT.
Press 2nd Y = to view the STAT PLOTS menu.
Select 1:Plot 1...On.

Highlight On with the cursor, and press ENTER. This will turn on the STAT PLOT.

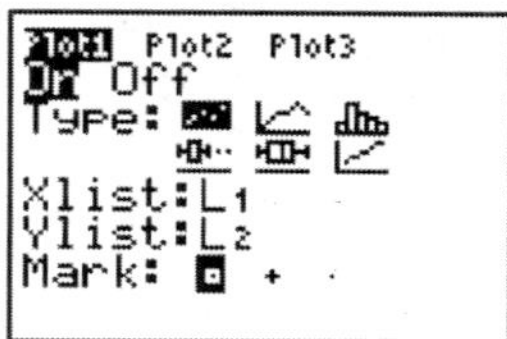

You can change any of the other settings by moving down the rows using the arrow keys. Select the required option by highlighting that option and pressing ENTER.

- On and Off refers to the STAT PLOT function. Select On and the data will be plotted by pressing GRAPH.
- Type shows icons of how the graph will be displayed. Select the first graph.
- Xlist tells the calculator which list should be used for data on the *x*-axis. Select L1.
- Ylist tells the calculator which list should be used for data on the *y*-axis. Select L2.
- Mark shows the icons of how each point will be plotted. Select the first icon.

Step 3
Set an appropriate window setting for the graph to display the data properly.
Setting the window is the graphing calculator's equivalent to choosing and labeling the scale of the graph. Enter the minimum, maximum, and scale for each axis before graphing. Press WINDOW, and type in the appropriate minimum, maximum, and scale values. Press ENTER to navigate from one row to the next row.

```
WINDOW
 Xmin=0
 Xmax=60
 Xscl=10
 Ymin=900
 Ymax=2000
 Yscl=100
 Xres=1
```

- Xmin is the minimum value represented on the *x*-axis. Choose a value one increment less than the least *x*-value in the table of values.
- Xmax is the maximum value represented on the *x*-axis. Choose a value one increment greater than the greatest *x*-value in the table of values.
- Xscl is the scale or spacing between the tick marks on the *x*-axis. Choose an increment that is a factor of most of the values in the table of values.
- Ymin is the minimum value represented on the *y*-axis. Choose a value one increment less than the least *y*-value in the table of values.
- Ymax is the largest value represented on the *y*-axis. Choose a value one increment greater than the greatest *y*-value in the table of values.
- Yscl is the scale or spacing between the tick marks on the *y*-axis.
- Xres defines the distance, in pixels, between consecutive evaluated *x*-values. The default is set at 1.

A shorthand method of communicating the window setting is in the form of $X[X_{min}, X_{max}, X_{scl}]$, $Y[Y_{min}, Y_{max}, Y_{scl}]$.
For most data, a good window setting can be created by pressing the ZOOM button and selecting 9:ZoomStat or 0:ZoomFit.

Step 4
Confirm that the data represents a quadratic function.
Press the GRAPH button to view the graph of the data represented by the table of values.

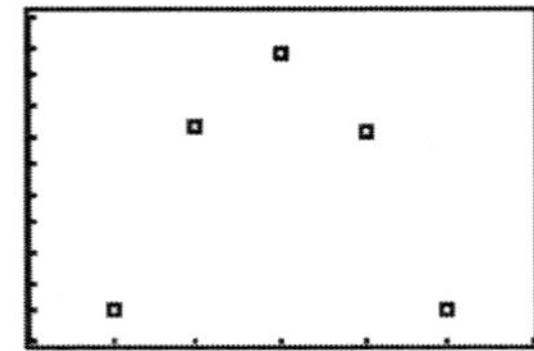

The data points appear to increase and then decrease, forming a parabolic shape. Thus, the data is quadratic.

Step 5
Perform a quadratic regression to determine the defining equation of the curve of best fit.
Press STAT, and then highlight CALC with the cursor. Choose 5:QuadReg.

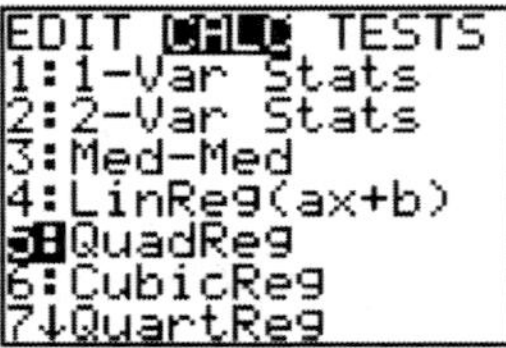

Press 2nd 1 , 2nd 2 to use the values in the lists editor.

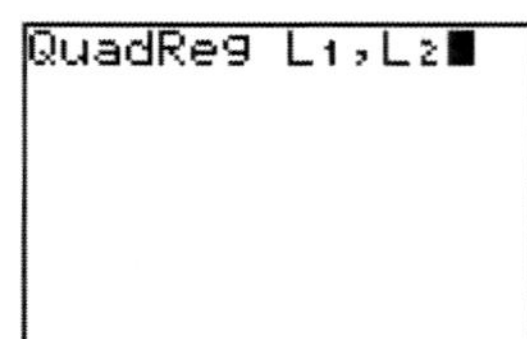

Press ENTER. The screen will appear as shown in the given image.

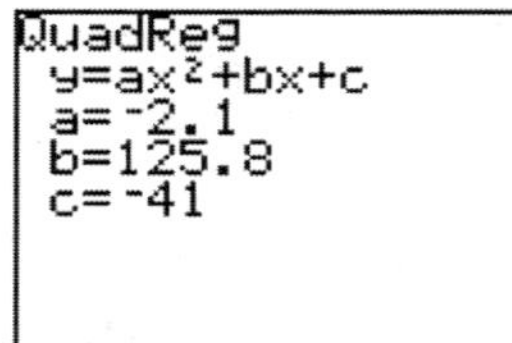

Therefore, the data can be defined by the equation $y = -2.1x^2 + 125.8x - 41$.
In general, to minimize rounding errors, round the values of the coefficients and the constant value in the equation to at least three decimal places.

Step 6
Graph the function.
Press [Y =] and enter the equation $y = -2.1x^2 + 125.8x - 41$ into Y_1. To minimize errors caused by rounding, press [Y=] [VARS], choose 5:Statistics…, highlight the option EQ with the cursor, and press [ENTER] to enter in the equation. Then press [GRAPH]. For the given data, the curve of best fit is shown in the given image.

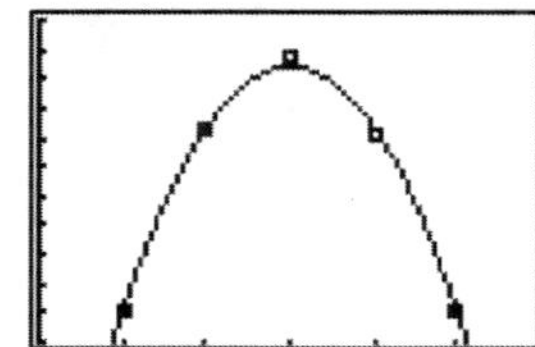

114. C

Step 1
Determine the number of years from 1997 to 2010.
2,010 – 1,997 = 13

Step 2
Substitute 13 for n into the given equation.

$$\begin{aligned} R &= 3.7(1.171)^n \\ &= 3.7(1.171)^{13} \\ &= 3.7(7.784659762) \\ &= 28.8 \end{aligned}$$

In the year 2010, the approximate number of rats in a certain region will be 28.8 million.

115. C

Step 1
Determine what the town's population is every 20 years, and enter the data in a table of values as shown:

Years	Population
0	1,400
20	2,800
40	5,600
60	11,200
80	22,400
100	44,800
120	89,600

Step 2
Graph the ordered pairs as points on a graph, and join the points with a smooth curve. The following is the graph of the relationship between the number of years and the population. From the graph, the population reaches 50,000 between 100 and 110 years.

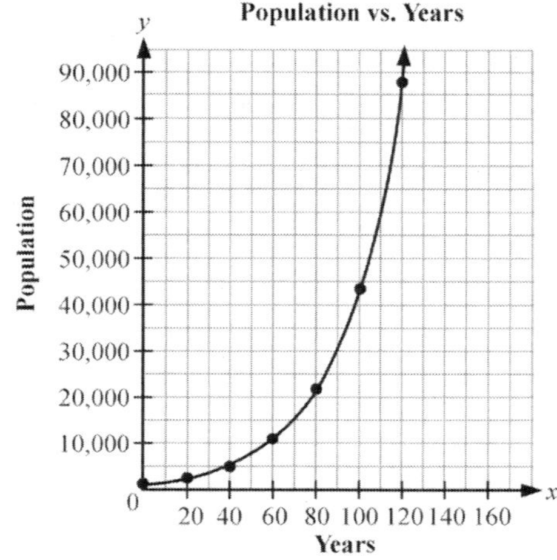

116. A

Step 1
Identify the variables whose values are given.

$$\begin{aligned} A_0 &= 10 \\ t &= 86 \\ h &= 13 \end{aligned}$$

Step 2
Substitute the values into the given equation, and evaluate.

$$\begin{aligned} A &= A_0\left(\frac{1}{2}\right)^{\frac{t}{h}} \\ &= 10\left(\frac{1}{2}\right)^{\frac{86}{13}} \\ &= 10(0.0102) \\ &= 0.1 \text{ g} \end{aligned}$$

117. D

Step 1

Determine the percentage volume of the block of ice after every 12 minutes, and place the data in a table of values.

Time (min)	Volume (%)
0	100.0
12	50.0
24	25.0
36	12.5
48	6.3
60	3.1
72	1.6

Step 2

Plot the ordered pairs as points on a graph, and join the points with a smooth line. The graph generated is shown.

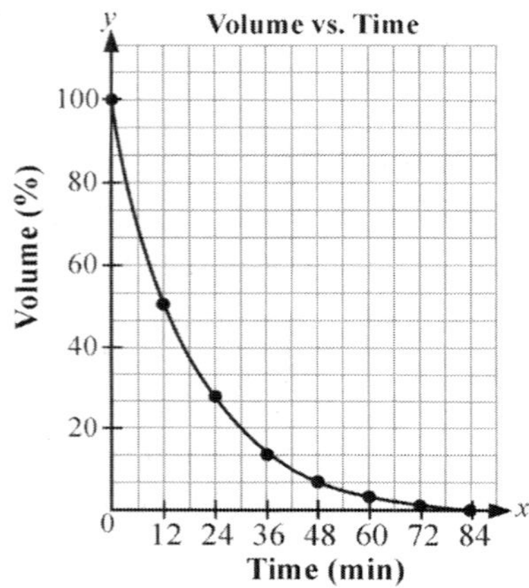

The graph shows that the time it takes for the block of ice to melt to one-tenth, or 10%, of its original volume is about 40 min.

118. 10

A quadratic pattern is symmetrical in that it decreases and increases from its minimum point in equivalent steps. The drops on the left side of the minimum over the first 5 days are

$100 \xrightarrow{-20} 80 \xrightarrow{-15} 65 \xrightarrow{-10} 55 \xrightarrow{-5} 50$. Therefore, the increases on the right side of the graph from day 6 onward will follow the same pattern of

$50 \xrightarrow{+5} 55 \xrightarrow{+10} 65 \xrightarrow{+15} 80 \xrightarrow{+20} 100$.

This increased pattern of the stock can be represented in the completed graph below.

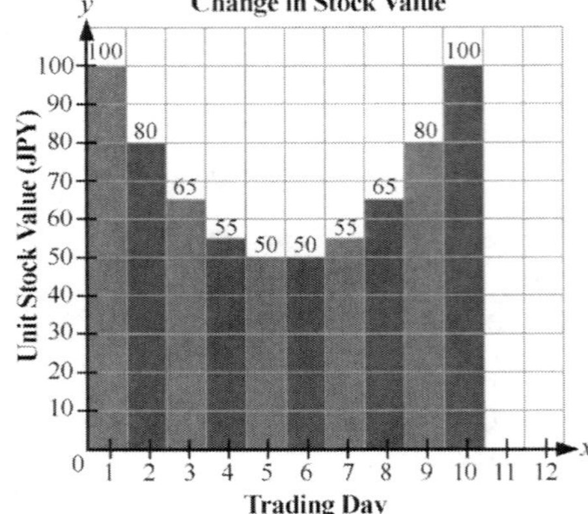

According to the completed pattern shown in the graph, the stock recovers to its original value of 100 JPY on day 10.

119. C

The rocket will strike the ground where the parabola intersects the x-axis after it has reach the vertex. The parabola intersects the x-axis at 5 s, so it takes the rocket 5 s to strike the ground.

Thus, the time it takes the rocket to hit the ground is 5 seconds.

120. A

Step 1

Substitute the given values into the area formula for a rectangle.

$A = l \times w$

$A = (x+3)(x+4)$

Step 2

Multiply each term of the first binomial by each term in the second binomial.

$= (x+3)(x+4)$

$= x(x+4) + 3(x+4)$

$= x^2 + 4x + 3x + 12$

Step 3

Collect like terms and simplify.

$= x^2 + 4x + 3x + 12$

$= x^2 + 7x + 12$

121. C

Method 1

Multiply $3x(5x + 1)$ to find the total rectangular area and then subtract three squares represented by $(x)(x)$.

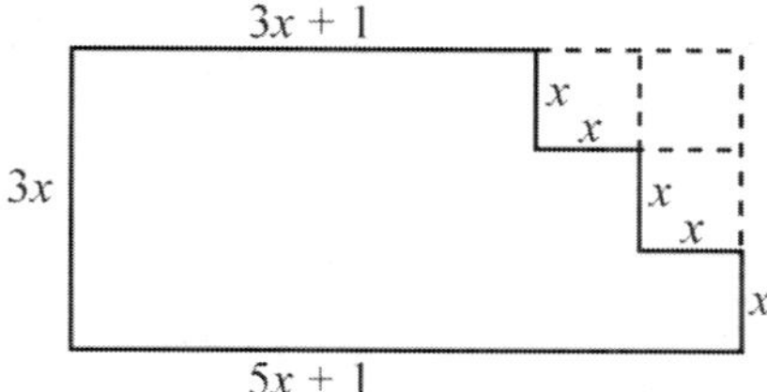

$$A_{rectangle} = 3x(5x + 1)$$
$$= 15x^2 + 3x$$
$$A_{square} = (x)(x) = x^2$$
$$A_{3\ squares} = 3(x^2) = 3x^2$$
$$A_{staircase} = A_{rectangle} - A_{3\ squares}$$
$$= 15x^2 + 3x - 3x^2$$
$$= 12x^2 + 3x$$

Method 2

Multiply three horizontal strips (A, B, and C), making up the stair as shown below.

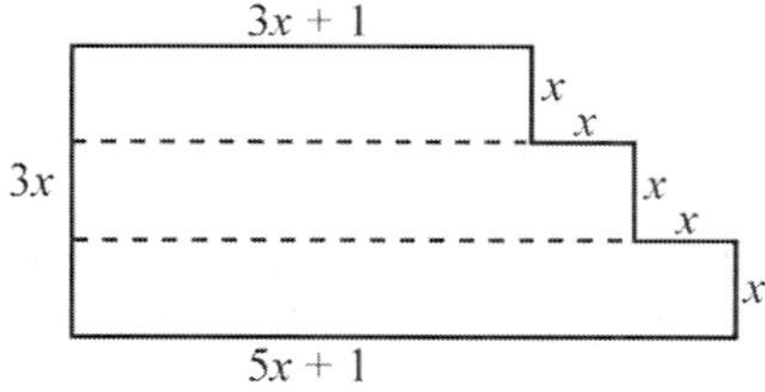

$$\text{Area}_A = (x)(3x + 1)$$
$$\text{Area}_B = (x)(3x + 1 + x)$$
$$\text{Area}_C = (x)(5x + 1)$$
$$\text{Area}_{staircase} = \text{Area}_A + \text{Area}_B + \text{Area}_C$$
$$= (x)(3x + 1)+(x)(4x + 1)+(x)(5x + 1)$$
$$= 3x^2 + x + 4x^2 + x + 5x^2 + x$$
$$= 12x^2 + 3x$$

The simplified expression describing the area of the staircase is $12x^2 + 3x$.

122. D

Enter the function $h(t) = -4.9t^2 + 29.4t + 352.8$ into your $[Y_1 =]$ button on your graphing calculator. Then, press GRAPH and use WINDOW (ZOOM 6).

$Y_1 = -4.9x^2 + 29.4x + 352.8$

The graph only shows the negative x-intercept which does not apply to this question. Also, the top (maximum) of the graph is not visible. Therefore, the WINDOW needs to be made larger to the right (x_{max}) and moved up (y_{max}) a lot. The window that seems appropriate is given in alternatives B or D as:

x:[−10, 20, 1]
y:[−10, 500, 1]

When this WINDOW setting is used, the whole graph is shown with its maximum and the positive x-intercept, namely the point representing when the flare hits the ground. Then, carry out the 2nd TRACE ZERO feature to determine that this x-intercept is 12.0, as shown below:

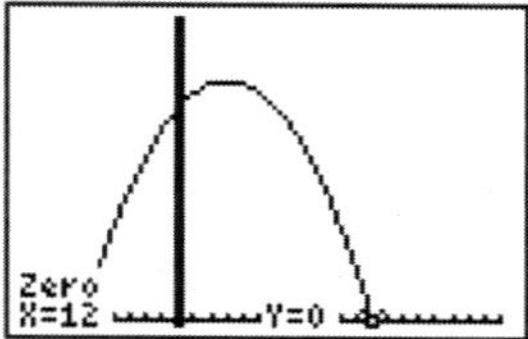

123. B

Use the TI-83 Plus graphing calculator to plot the line $y = 12$ and the parabola $y = -2x^2 + 11x - 3$. Then use the INTERSECTION feature to find the intersection points of the two graphs.

The first intersection point is: (2.5, 12)

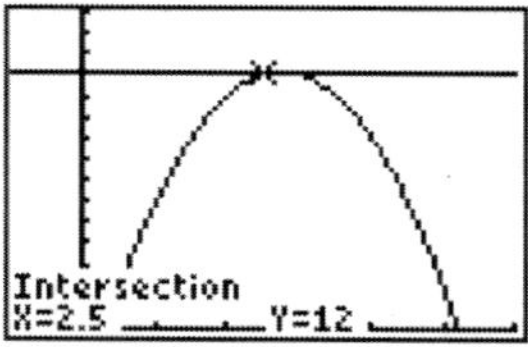

The second intersection point is: (3, 12)

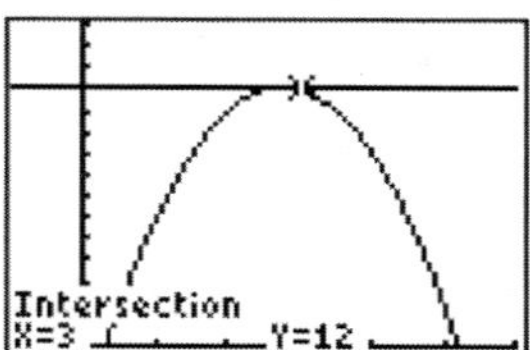

The first value of x is closest to the moment of the kick, so the first value of x is the time taken for the ball to reach a height of 12 m. Therefore, the least number of seconds it took the football to reach a height of 12 yards above the ground is 2.5 seconds.

124. C

Step 1
Define the variables given with respect to the general formula $N_t = N_0 \times R^{\frac{t}{p}}$.

- At time 0, the mass is 300 g.
  $N_0 = 300$
- The substance is reduced to $\frac{1}{2}$ its mass during each period.
  $R = \frac{1}{2}$
- It takes 7 years for the substance to reduce to $\frac{1}{2}$ its mass, so the period is 7.
  $p = 7$

Step 2
Substitute the values $N_0 = 300$, $R = \frac{1}{2}$, and $p = 7$ into the general formula $N_t = N_0 \times R^{\frac{t}{p}}$.

$$N_t = N_0 \times R^{\frac{t}{p}}$$
$$= 300 \times \left(\frac{1}{2}\right)^{\frac{t}{7}}$$
$$= 300\left(\frac{1}{2}\right)^{\frac{t}{7}}$$

125. C

Use a TI-83 or similar graphing calculator to perform the exponential regression and solve the regression equation.

Step 1
Enter the x-values and y-values in lists L_1 and L_2, respectively.
Start by clearing any lists already present. Press [2nd] [+], select 4:ClrAllLists, and press [ENTER].

Press [STAT], and select 1:Edit… to enter the lists.
Enter the year numbers into list L_1 and the number of titles published into list L_2.

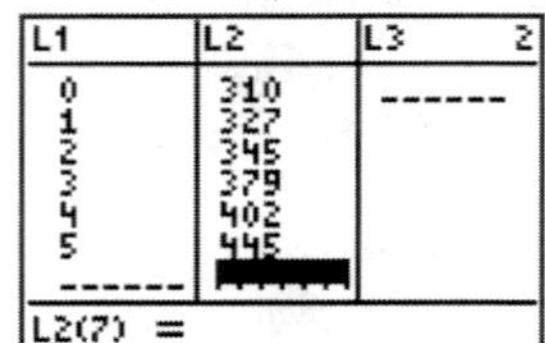

Step 2
Perform the exponential regression.
Press [STAT], and then press the right arrow to access the CALC menu. Select 0:ExpReg.
Specify lists L_1 and L_2 to use with the exponential regression by pressing [2nd] [1] [,] [2nd] [2].

Press [ENTER] to run the exponential regression.

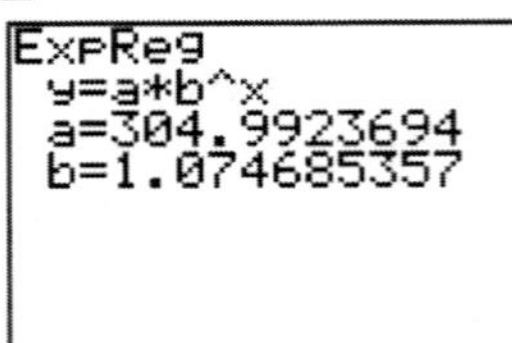

Step 3
Determine the number of books that could have been published in 2005.
Rounded to the nearest thousandth, the regression equation is $y \approx 304.992(1.075)^x$.
Since 2005 is 6 years after 1999, substitute 6 for x in the regression equation.

$y \approx 304.992(1.075)^x$
$y \approx 304.992(1.075)^6$
$y \approx 470.695$
$y \approx 471$

In 2005, the publishing company could have published approximately 471 books.

126. B

Use a TI-83 or similar calculator to perform the exponential regression.

Step 1
Enter the x-values and y-values in lists L_1 and L_2, respectively.
Start by clearing any lists already present. Press [2nd] [+], select 4:ClrAllLists, and press [ENTER].

Press [STAT], and select 1:Edit… to edit the lists.
Enter the years recorded into list L_1 and the number of corresponding subscriptions in millions into list L_2. Press [ENTER] after entering each value.

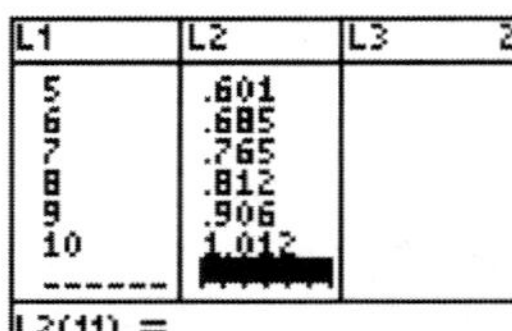

Step 2
Perform the exponential regression.

Press STAT, and then press the right arrow to access the CALC menu. Select 0:ExpReg. Specify lists L_1 and L_2 to use with the exponential regression by pressing 2nd 1 , 2nd 2.

Press ENTER to run the exponential regression.

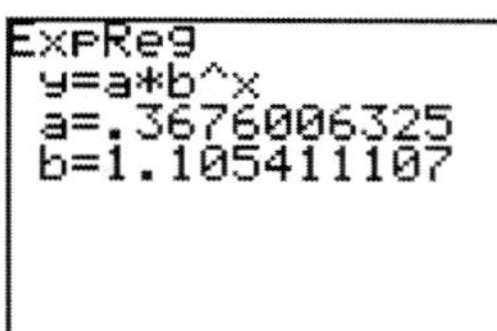

Step 3
Determine the average growth rate for the number of subscriptions.
The regression equation rounded to four decimal places is $y \approx 0.3676(1.1054)^x$. In an exponential function of the form $y = ab^x$, b represents the growth rate. Since $b \approx 1.1054$, this indicates a growth rate of 1.1054%, which rounds to 1.11%.

127. D

It is not necessary to perform each individual regression on the data to determine which is most appropriate because the pattern is evident.

When a sequence of data increases or decreases by a consistent amount for every evenly spaced term, the sequence is linear.

In this case, there is a consistent increase of 1.3 cm each year. Therefore, a linear regression would be the most appropriate regression for the given data.

128. D

Step 1
Enter the data into a TI-83 or similar calculator.

Clear all lists from the calculator. Press 2nd +, select 4:ClrAllLists, and press ENTER. If the diagnostic feature is not on, press 2nd 0, scroll down to DiagnosticOn, and press ENTER twice.

Once the diagnostic feature is on, press STAT, select 1:Edit, and enter the time data into L1 and the sea-level data into L2.

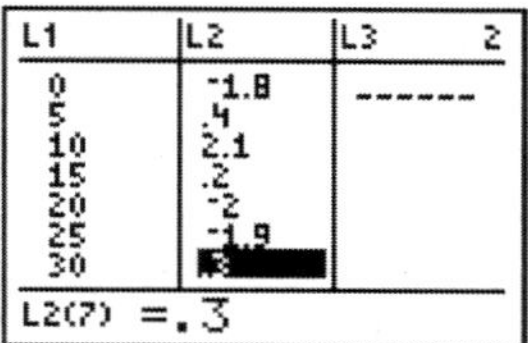

L1	L2	L3
0	-1.8	------
5	.4	
10	2.1	
15	.2	
20	-2	
25	-1.9	
30	.3	

L2(7) =.3

Step 2
Determine the most appropriate regression.
Since the data repeatedly increase and decrease, a sinusoidal function would be most appropriate for the data. Press STAT, scroll to the right to highlight CALC, and then scroll down to C:SinReg. Press ENTER twice to obtain the window shown.

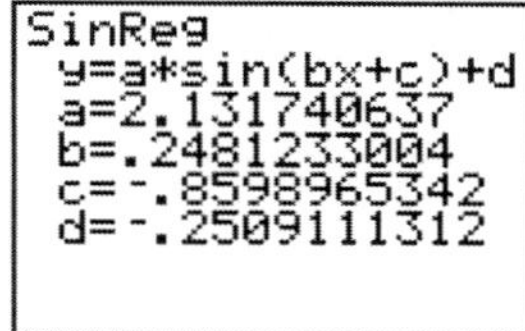

From the sinusoidal regression, the equation is $y = 2.13\sin(0.25x - 0.86) - 0.25$, where y is the change from sea level and x is the time in hours. Note that two of the alternatives are quadratic functions. When a quadratic regression is performed on the data, a correlation coefficient of $R^2 = .75$ is given, which means that the data are a poor fit for a quadratic model.

129. B

Step 1

Plot the data points using a graphing calculator. This can be done by pressing STAT and selecting 1:Edit. Put the values for time in L1 and the values for speed in L2. Press 2nd Y = and select 1:Plot1. Press ENTER to turn on Plot 1. Clear out any equations from Y = and set an appropriate window (in this case X:[0, 8, 1], Y:[0, 50, 5] would be appropriate). Press GRAPH and the points should appear.

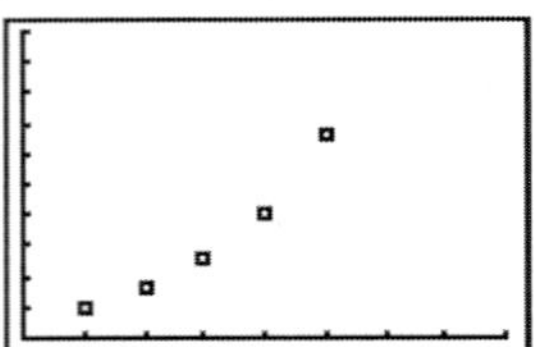

Step 2

Determine the best regression model for the data. Looking at the path of the points, it is clear that the best regression model to begin with is an exponential one. Make sure the Diagnostics are ON so that the value of the correlation coefficient is given before you do the regression. This will indicate the accuracy of the regression model (the closer the value is to 1 or −1, the better the equation fits the data). To do this, press 2nd 0 and then the x^{-1} key. Scroll down to DiagnosticON. Press ENTER twice.

When done correctly, your screen should say Done. Now, perform the exponential regression. Press STAT, scroll right to the CALC menu, and select 0:ExpReg. The screen should show ExpReg. Press the VARS key, scroll right to the Y-VARS menu, select 1:Function, and then 1:Y_1. This will put the exponential regression equation into the Y = feature. Press ENTER and the equation and correlation coefficient should appear.

Note that in this case, $r \approx 1$ which means that the data fits perfectly to an exponential model. Press GRAPH and notice the graph of the equation passes through the center of nearly all 5 points in the data.

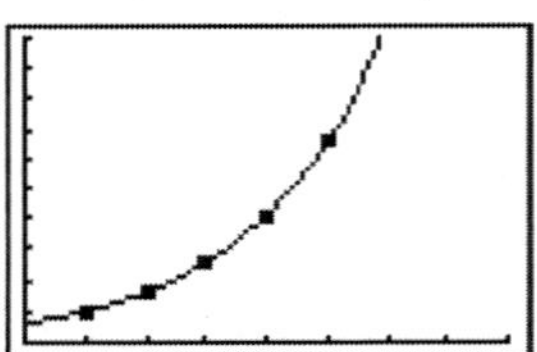

Note: if a quadratic regression is used, then R^2 = .998. This represents a very close fit for the data, but the exponential regression is still slightly better.

Step 3
Determine the time when the athlete's speed will reach 40 kilometers per hour.
To determine when the athlete's speed will reach 40 kilometers per hour, it is necessary to graph $Y_2 = 40$ and find the point of intersection between that line and the curve graphed from the exponential regression.

To find the point of intersection, press [2nd] [TRACE] to access the CALC menu, select 5:intersect and move the cursor until it lies on the point of intersection, then press [ENTER]. Press [ENTER] two more times and the coordinates of the point are given.
The coordinates of the point are (5.42, 40).

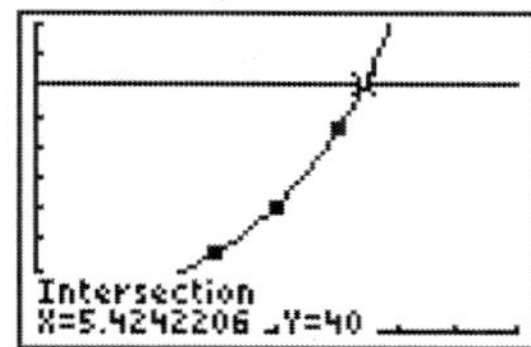

The athlete will reach 40 kilometers per hour, after 5.42 seconds.

130. D

Step 1
Plot the points on a graph.
Press [STAT], and select 1:Edit. Enter the values for the year in *L1* and the values for price in *L2*.
Press [2nd] [Y =], and select 1:Plot1. Press [ENTER] to turn on Plot1.

Clear any equations from [Y =], and set an appropriate window. In this case, X:[0, 8, 1] and Y:[5,000, 29,000, 1] would be appropriate.

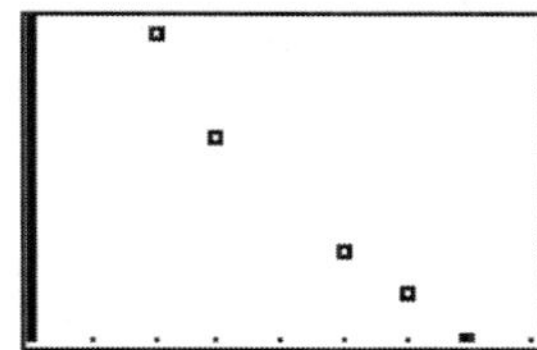

Step 2
Determine the best regression model for the data.
The points in the graph follow a downward trend. The value of the truck decreasing over time is a situation in which the downward trend will continue. Therefore, the exponential regression model would be the best model to use.
Before doing the regression, however, make sure the Diagnostics are on so the value of the correlation coefficient is given. This will indicate the accuracy of the regression model (the closer the value is to 1 or −1, the better the equation fits the data). Press [2nd] [0] and then the [x^{-1}] key. Scroll down to DiagnosticON. Press [ENTER] twice.

Perform the exponential regression. Press [STAT], and scroll to the CALC menu. Select 0:ExpReg. The screen should show ExpReg. Press the [VARS] key, scroll right to the Y-VARS menu, and select 1:Function and then 1:Y_1. This will put the regression equation into the Y = feature. Press [ENTER], and the equation and correlation coefficient should appear.
The regression coefficient for an exponential regression, to the nearest thousandth, is $r \approx -0.993$. Press [GRAPH] to watch as the graph of the equation passes nearly through the center of all points in the data.

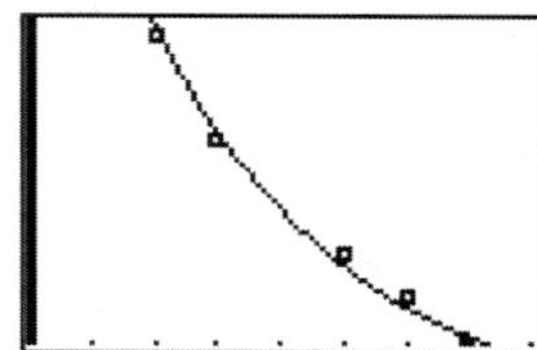

A quadratic model can be used, but because of the reality of the situation it is not the best model because the value of the truck will not increase after decreasing.

Step 3
Determine the price of the truck 7 years and 9 months after the time of purchase.

On the graph screen, press 2nd TRACE to access the CALC menu, and select 1:Value. Enter 7.75 (for 7 and $\frac{9}{12}$ years), and press ENTER.

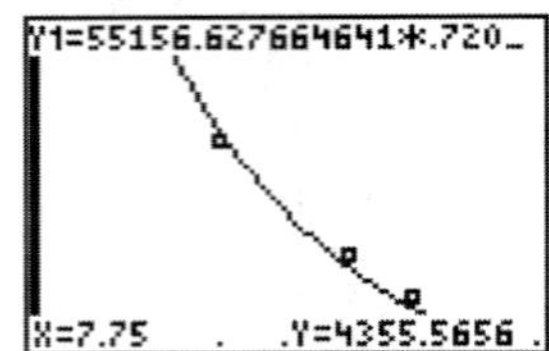

The coordinates of the point are (7.75, 4,355.57). The car will be worth $4,355.577 years and 9 months after the time of purchase.

131. B

Step 1
Apply properties of tangents.
Two tangent segments from one external point are equal in length.
$AB = AC = 11$ cm

Step 2
Find the area of ΔABC.
The height of the triangle is not given. The lengths of two sides and the included angle are known, so use the formula Area = $\frac{1}{2}bc\sin(A)$.

$$\text{Area} = \frac{1}{2}bc\sin(A)$$
$$= \frac{1}{2}(11\text{ cm})(11\text{ cm})\sin(40°)$$
$$\approx 38.89\text{ cm}^2$$

132. D

Draw a sketch to represent the triangle.

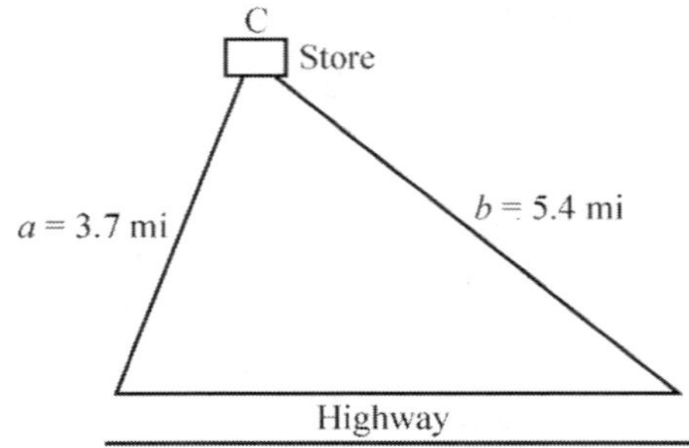

The area and lengths of two sides of a triangle are given. The angle, C, between the two known sides, a and b, can be calculated using the area formula $A = \frac{1}{2}ab\sin C$.

$$A = \frac{1}{2}ab\sin C$$
$$9.5 = \frac{1}{2}(3.7)(5.4)\sin C$$
$$\frac{9.5}{\frac{1}{2}(3.7)(5.4)} = \sin C$$
$$72.0° \approx C$$

The angle between the two access roads is approximately 72.0°.

133.

Step 1
Convert from degrees to radians.

Multiply the angle degree measure by $\frac{\pi}{180}$.

$$320° = 320 \times \frac{\pi}{180}$$
$$320° = \frac{320\pi}{180}$$
$$320° = \frac{16\pi}{9}$$

Step 2
Calculate the arc length using the arc length formula.
$a = r\theta$
$a = (12)\left(\frac{16\pi}{9}\right)$
$a \approx 67.02$
The arc length is about 67.02 mm.

134. 258

The arc length formula, $a = r\theta$, can be used to determine the measure of the central angle θ in radians, where r is the radius of the circle and a is the arc length.

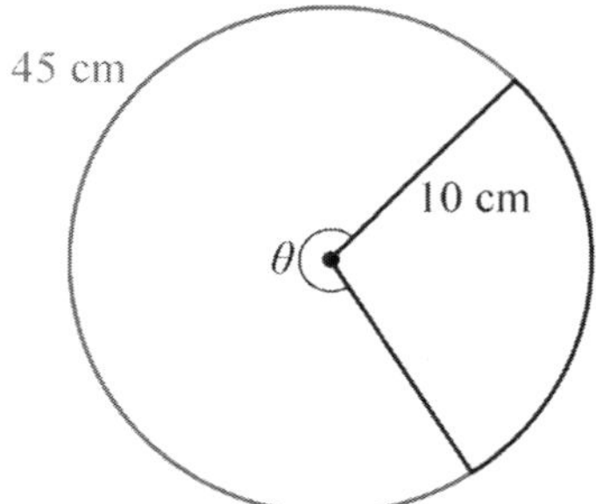

Step 1
Rearrange the formula $a = r\theta$ for θ.

$$\theta = \frac{a}{r}$$

Step 2
Substitute the known values, and solve.
The known values are $a = 45$ and $r = 10$.

$\theta = \frac{a}{r}$

$\theta = \frac{45}{10}$

$\theta = 4.5$

The angle is 4.5 rad.

Step 3
Convert the angle from radians to degrees.
An angle in radians can be converted to degrees by multiplying it by $\frac{180}{\pi}$.

$4.5 \times \frac{180}{\pi} \approx 257.83°$

The central angle to the nearest degree is 258°.

135. B

Step 1
Label the diagram.
The given diagram can be labeled as shown.

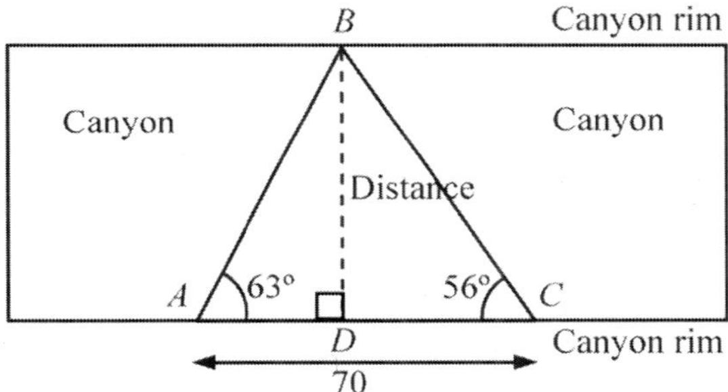

Step 2
Calculate the measure of $\angle B$.
$\angle B = 180° - 63° - 56° = 61°$

Step 3
Determine the length of either side AB or CB by applying the sine law with respect to ΔABC.
The length of AB can be determined as follows:

$\frac{AB}{\sin C} = \frac{AC}{\sin B}$

Substitute 56° for C, 70 for AC, and 61° for B.
Solve for AB.

$\frac{AB}{\sin 56°} = \frac{70}{\sin 61°}$

$AB \times \sin 61° = 70 \times \sin 56°$

$AB = \frac{70 \times \sin 56°}{\sin 61°}$

$AB \approx 66.35$ m

Step 4
Solve for BD by examining ΔADB.

In ΔADB, $\sin A = \frac{BD}{AB}$

Substitute 63° for A and 66.35 for AB.

$\sin 63° = \frac{BD}{66.35}$

$BD = 66.35 \times \sin 63°$

$BD = 59.12$ m

To the nearest tenth, the distance across the canyon BD is 59.1 m.
A similar procedure can be used to determine the length of side BC, and then the sine ratio can be used with respect to ΔBCD.

136. A

Alternative C and D make incorrect use of the Cosine Law because there is no contained angle in between the given sides. To find side x using the Sine Law, the angle opposite of x, plus a side and its opposite angle are used. Therefore, $\frac{309}{\sin 76°} = \frac{x}{\sin 70°}$.

Then. solving for x:

$x = \frac{(309)\sin 70°}{\sin 76°}$

137. A

Substitute the known values into the cosine formula, and solve for θ:

$\cos A = \frac{b^2 + c^2 - a^2}{2bc}$

$\cos \theta = \frac{2.3^2 + 2.6^2 - 2.2^2}{2(2.3)(2.6)}$

$\cos \theta = \frac{7.21}{11.96}$

$\theta = \cos^{-1}\left(\frac{7.21}{11.96}\right)$

$\theta \approx 52.926°$

Rounded to the nearest degree, the measure of θ is 53°.

138. B

Step 1
Label the diagram as shown:

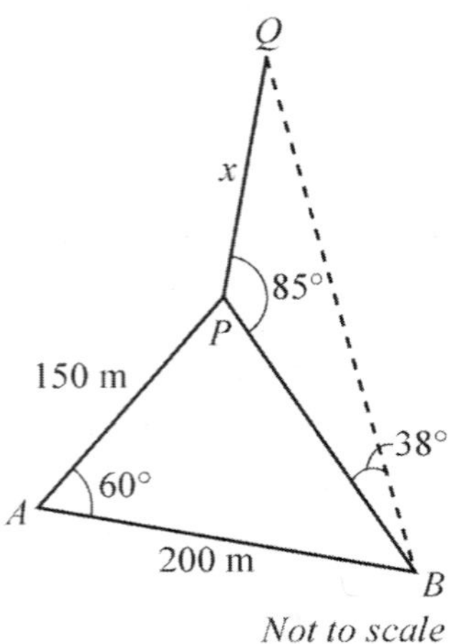

Step 2
Determine the length of BP by applying the cosine law as follows:

$$a^2 = b^2 + c^2 - 2bc\cos A$$
$$(BP)^2 = 150^2 + 200^2 - 2(150)(200)\cos 60$$
$$(BP)^2 = 22{,}500 + 40{,}000 - 30{,}000$$
$$(BP)^2 = 32{,}500$$
$$BP \approx 180.28 \text{ m}$$

Step 3
Calculate the measure of $\angle Q$.
$180° - 85° - 38° = 57°$

Step 4
Calculate the value of x by applying the sine law as follows:

$$\frac{x}{\sin B} = \frac{BP}{\sin Q}$$
$$\frac{x}{\sin 38°} = \frac{180.28}{\sin 57°}$$
$$x = \frac{180.28(\sin 38°)}{\sin 57°}$$
$$x \approx 132.34 \text{ m}$$

The value of x, rounded to the nearest meter, is 132 m.

139. 10

Step 1
Determine the length of side BD by applying the sine law.
In ΔABD, observe that $\angle ABD = 180° - 29° = 151°$.
Thus, the measure of $\angle ADB$ is
$180° - 151° - 18° = 11°$.

$$\frac{BD}{\sin \angle A} = \frac{AB}{\sin \angle ADB}$$

Substitute 18° for $\angle A$, 12.5 for AB, and 11° for $\angle ADB$.

$$\frac{BD}{\sin 18°} = \frac{12.5}{\sin 11°}$$
$$BD \times \sin 11° = 12.5 \times \sin 18°$$
$$BD = \frac{12.5 \times \sin 18°}{\sin 11°}$$
$$BD \approx 20.24 \text{ m}$$

Step 2
Solve for h in right triangle BCD.
Substitute 29° for $\angle DBC$, h for DC, and 20.24 for BD.

$$\sin \angle DBC = \frac{DC}{BD}$$
$$\sin 29° = \frac{h}{20.24}$$
$$h = 20.24 \times \sin 29°$$
$$h \approx 9.81 \text{ m}$$

The height of the school, to the nearest meter, is 10 m.

140. B

Step 1
Draw and label a diagram that represents the situation.

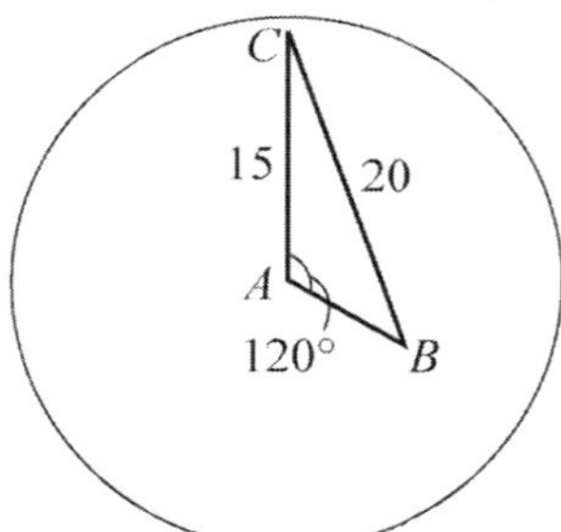

Step 2

Find the measures of angles B and C.

Since two sides and an angle opposite to one of the sides are given, apply the law of sines.

$$\frac{a}{\sin A} = \frac{b}{\sin B}$$
$$\frac{20}{\sin 120°} = \frac{15}{\sin B}$$
$$\frac{\sin 120°}{20} \times 15 = \sin B$$
$$\sin^{-1}\left(\frac{\sin 120°}{20} \times 15\right) = B$$
$$40.5° \approx B$$

The sum of all the interior angles in a triangle is 180°.

$\angle C \approx 180° - (120° + 40.5°)$
$\approx 19.5°$

Step 3

Use the law of sines to determine the side length AB.

$$\frac{a}{\sin A} = \frac{c}{\sin C}$$
$$\frac{20}{\sin 120°} \approx \frac{AB}{\sin 19.5°}$$
$$\frac{20}{\sin 120°} \times \sin 19.5° \approx AB$$
$$7.71 \approx AB$$

The approximate length of the hour hand is 7.71 cm.

141. C

Step 1

Label the diagram.

The given diagram can be labeled as follows:

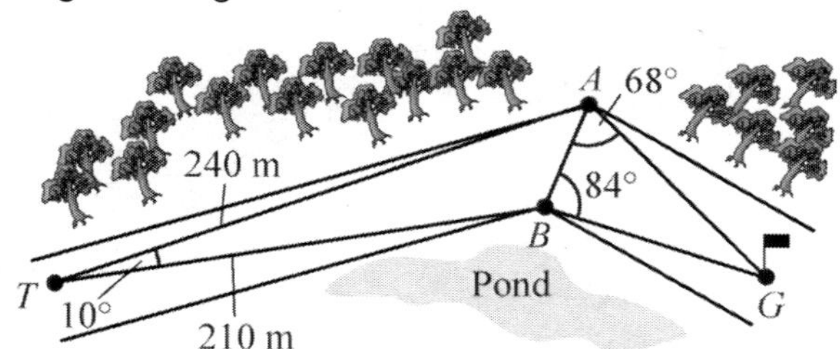

Step 2

Determine the distance from point A to point B.

In ΔATB, it is a side-angle-side situation; therefore, solve for AB by applying the cosine law.

$(AB)^2 = (TA)^2 + (TB)^2 - 2(TA)(TB)\cos \angle T$

Substitute 240 for TA, 210 for TB, and 10° for $\angle T$, and solve for AB.

$(AB)^2 = 240^2 + 210^2 - 2(240)(210)\cos 10°$

$(AB)^2 \approx 57{,}600 + 44{,}100 - 99{,}268.62$

$(AB)^2 \approx 2{,}431.38$

$AB \approx \sqrt{2{,}431.38}$

$AB \approx 49.31$

Step 3

Use ΔGAB, and apply the sine law in order to determine the distance of BG.

$$\frac{BG}{\sin \angle GAB} = \frac{AB}{\sin \angle G}$$

Calculate the measure of $\angle G$ by subtracting the known angle measures of ΔABG from 180°.

$\angle G = 180° - 68° - 84° = 28°$

Substitute 68° for $\angle GAB$, 49.31 for AB, and 28° for $\angle G$, and solve for BG.

$$\frac{BG}{\sin 68°} = \frac{49.31}{\sin 28°}$$
$$BG \times \sin 28° = 49.31 \times \sin 68°$$
$$BG = \frac{49.31 \times \sin 68°}{\sin 28°}$$
$$BG \approx 97.38 \text{ m}$$

To the nearest meter, the distance of BG is 97 m.

142. 48.1

Step 1

Determine the lengths of the bases of the vertical triangles using the tangent ratio.

$\tan 42° = \dfrac{25}{y}$

$y = \dfrac{25}{\tan 42°}$

$y \approx 27.77$

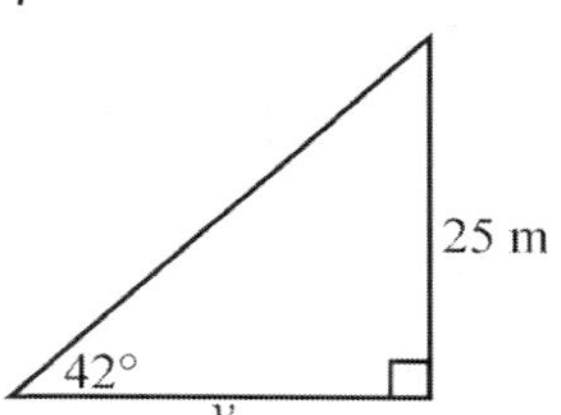

$\tan 38° = \dfrac{25}{z}$

$z = \dfrac{25}{\tan 38°}$

$z \approx 32.00$

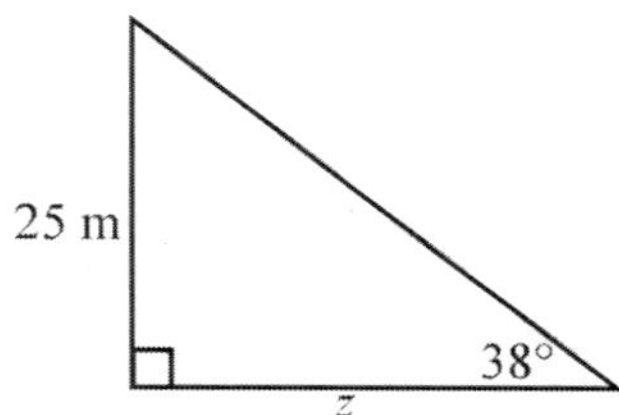

Step 2
Determine x using the cosine law.

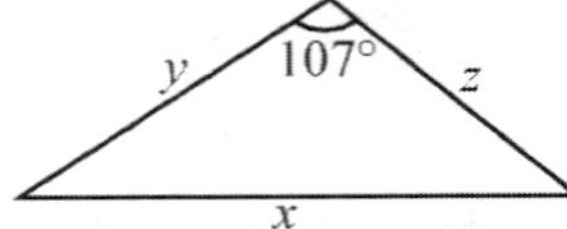

$$a^2 = b^2 + c^2 - 2bc\cos A$$
$$x^2 = y^2 + z^2 - 2(y)(z)\cos 107°$$
$$x \approx \sqrt{(27.77)^2 + (32.00)^2 - 2(27.77)(32.00)\cos 107°}$$
$$x \approx 48.1$$

143. C

Select a maximum point and a minimum point.

In this case, choose the maximum point to be in 1992 and the minimum point to be in 1999. Using the p-coordinate of each of these points, calculate the approximate amplitude. Note that the p-axis values represent thousands.

$$\frac{\text{max} - \text{min}}{2} \approx \frac{367{,}000 - 330{,}000}{2}$$
$$\approx 18{,}500$$

The amplitude of the graph is about 18,500 people.

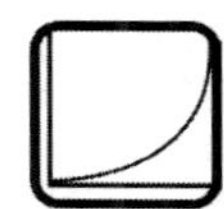

MODELING AND SOLVING FUNCTIONS EXERCISE #2

Use the following information to answer the next question.

September 21 and 22 were two nice sunny days in Laura's city. Starting at 8:00 A.M., when it was sunrise, she measured the length of the shadow of an 80 m tall building at various times until sunset, which occurred at 8:00 P.M. (or 20 hours on Day 1).
Next morning at 8:00 A.M. (or 32 hours after Day 1), she did the same, until the sunset at 8:00 P.M. (or 44 hours after Day 1).
The graph below shows the relationship between the shadow length, l, in meters, and the time, t, in hours from Day 1. This graph portrays a periodic function.

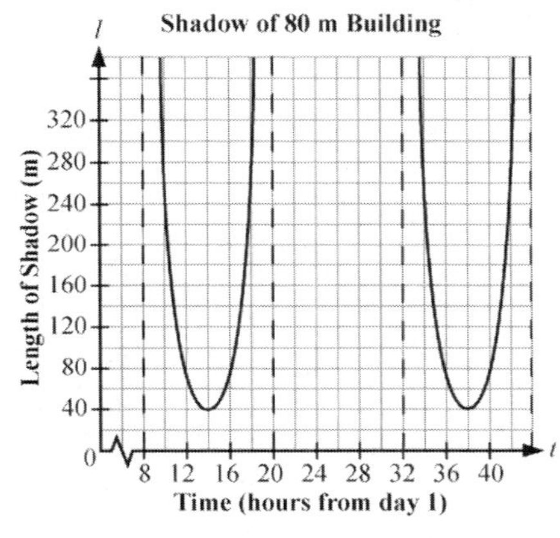

144. What is the period and range of the above graph representing a periodic function?

A. 10 hours, $40 \leq l \leq 360$

B. 10 hours, $l \geq 40$

C. 12 hours, $40 \leq l \leq 360$

D. 12 hours, $l \geq 40$

Use the following information to answer the next question.

At 7 A.M. on a Saturday morning, a person measured the distance between the bottom of his boat dock and the top of the water. He measured this distance again every 10 h over a 60 h period and recorded his data in the given table.

Time (h)	0	10	20	30	40	50	60
Distance (m)	2.7	1.3	2.1	2.1	1.3	2.7	1.3

145. Which of the following graphs **best** models the given sinusoidal data?

A. **B.**

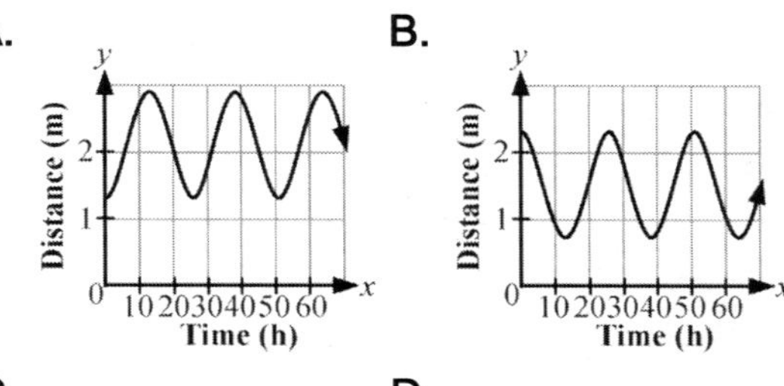

C. **D.**

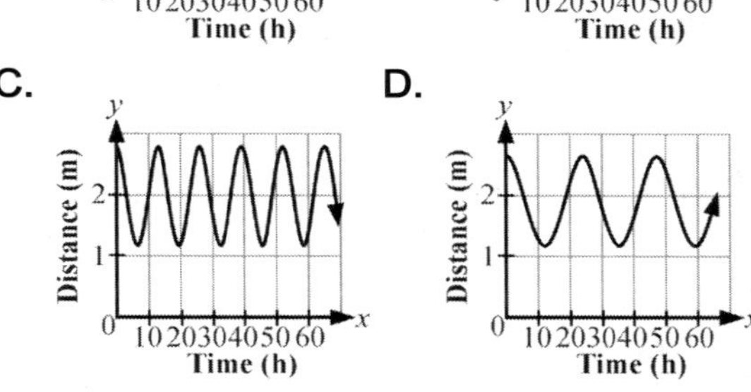

Use the following information to answer the next question.

Sound intensity is measured in decibels, dB. The decibel measurement can be expressed as dB = 10log (L), in which L is the relative intensity of the sound compared to the threshold of hearing.

146. An orchestra with a decibel level of 98 is __________ times louder than a vacuum cleaner with a decibel level of 80. Record answer to the nearest whole number.

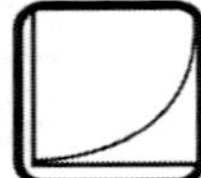

Use the following information to answer the next question.

A model rocket is launched upward from a platform. The height of the rocket *h* meters, with respect to time, *t* seconds, is recorded in the given table.

Time (s)	Height (m)
0	3
1	148
3	410
8	890
14	1,140
20	1,025
25	700

147. Assuming that the flight of the rocket can be modeled by a quadratic relationship, what is the total time that the rocket was in the air?

A. 25.8 s **B.** 30.0 s
C. 31.1 s **D.** 36.2 s

148. A bacteria culture triples every 5 minutes. After 27 minutes, the population grows to 50,000. What was the original population at $t = 0$?

149. Ken's car depreciates at an annual rate of 12 %. If his car is currently worth $5,000, the original amount he paid 8 years ago, to the nearest dollar, was $ _____._____

150. The population of a small city is changing according to the formula $P = 10{,}000(10^{-0.035y})$, where *y* is the time, in years, from the beginning of the year 1998. In which year did the population first fall below 6,000?

A. 2002 **B.** 2003
C. 2004 **D.** 2005

Use the following information to answer the next question.

To host a concert, it costs the owners of an amphitheatre $200,000.00. Currently, ticket prices are $40.00. The owners plan to increase the price of each ticket so as to maximize the profits. The graph below represents the quadratic relation between the gross revenue as the ticket price increases.

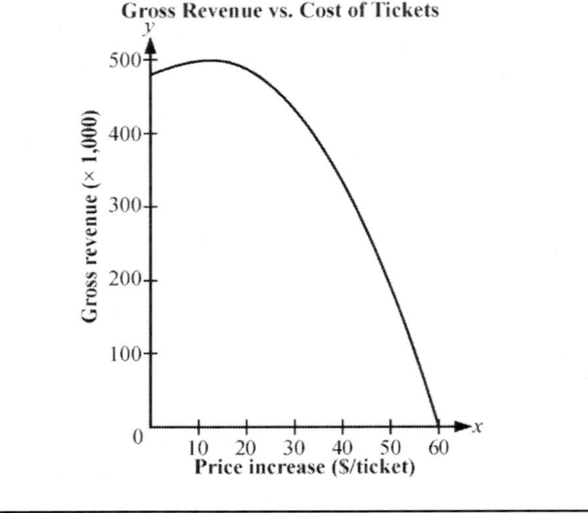

151. What is the maximum profit that can be generated from the concert? $__________

Use the following information to answer the next question.

During the peak season, a men's clothing store can rent 25 tuxedos at $125 each. The latest marketing results indicate that for each $25 increase in price, one less tuxedo will be rented.

152. What is the price, to the nearest dollar, that the store should charge to rent a tuxedo to maximize its revenue? $__________

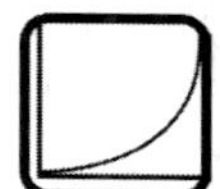

Use the following information to answer the next question.

The half-life of a radioactive substance is 5.2 days.

153. If the original mass of this radioactive substance is 800 g, and it decays exponentially, then the amount left after 15 days is

A. 108.33 g **B.** 100.04 g
C. 33.44 g **D.** 5.69 g

Use the following information to answer the next question.

Iodine-131 is a radioactive isotope used in thyroid uptake tests. Agnes did an experiment for science class in which she measured the number of radioactive decays of a sample of iodine-131 for 1 min each day over a period of 7 days. She recorded her results in a table.

Day	Number of Decays
0	48
1	46
2	41
3	37
4	36
5	31
6	28
7	27

154. How many radioactive decays of iodine-131 would Agnes have observed had she started the experiment two days earlier?

A. 22 **B.** 41
C. 58 **D.** 73

Use the following information to answer the next question.

The internet is huge and it is growing. Grace wanted to know how fast it is growing so she did a little research and found some historical data showing the total number of.com domain names that were registered each year since 1995. She organized the data into a table.

Year	Number of Years Since 1995	Number of.com Domain Names
1995	0	2,573
1996	1	13,555
1997	2	31,657
1998	3	62,898
1999	4	126,591
2000	5	202,484
2001	6	229,339
2002	7	278,903
2003	8	340,589
2004	9	425,698
2005	10	539,248
2006	11	697,763

155. Use exponential regression to find the internet's percentage rate of growth between 1995 and 2006, expressed to the nearest tenth. __________%

Use the following information to answer the next question.

A set of ordered pairs is given.
(0, 15), (9, 18), (25, 20), (42, 19), (62, 14), (89, 10), (104, 12), (118, 15)

156. This data could **most appropriately** be modeled by a

A. linear regression
B. quadratic regression
C. sinusoidal regression
D. exponential regression

Use the following information to answer the next question.

The given table shows the growth of a population of bacteria.

Time (min)	Population
1	6
5	35
8	259
12	4,095
17	131,076

157. To the nearest tenth, how long will it take for the population to reach 237,500?

A. 18.3 min **B.** 19.0 min
C. 21.0 min **D.** 27.5 min

Use the following information to answer the next question.

A boat is towing two water skiers using ropes that have lengths of 36 feet and 40 feet, respectively.

158. If the area of the triangle formed by the two ropes and the distance between the skiers is 410 ft^2, what is the angle to the nearest tenth of a degree between the two ski ropes? __________ °

Use the following information to answer the next question.

A gardener dug a pond in the shape of an equilateral triangle in his backyard to house his exotic fish.

159. If the base of the pond occupies an area of 210 ft^2, determine the perimeter of the pond to the nearest tenth.

A. 46.7 ft **B.** 50.2 ft
C. 66.1 ft **D.** 73.2 ft

160. An arc subtends an angle of 9.5 rad. If the radius of the circle is 7 cm, what is the arc length?

A. 16.5 cm **B.** 56.6 cm
C. 66.5 cm **D.** 67.6 cm

Use the following information to answer the next question.

In the game of pool, a player uses a cue stick to strike the white cue ball so that it, in turn, strikes an object ball (usually the ball that the player wants to sink in a pocket). In the diagram below, the player is attempting to sink two balls, labeled *A* and *B*, with the cue ball, *C*, in one shot.

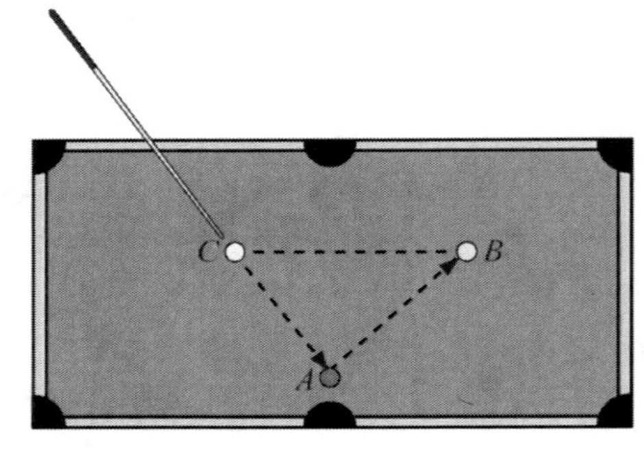

161. The player estimates that balls *C* and *A* are 53 cm apart, balls *A* and *B* are 61 cm apart, and balls *C* and *B* are 77 cm apart. What angle must the cue ball make after it strikes ball A in order for the player to make the shot successfully?

A. 80° **B.** 85°
C. 88° **D.** 90°

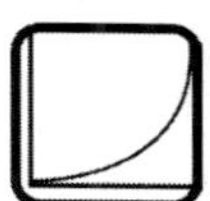

Use the following information to answer the next question.

An engineer needs to calculate the width of a river. He takes a sighting from a point D and then from a point F, both on the same side of the river, to a point E on the opposite side of the river, as illustrated in the following diagram.

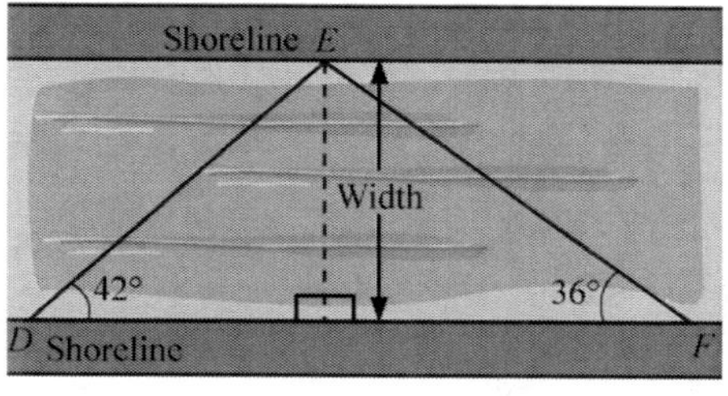

162. If the distance from point D to point F is 250 m, then what is the width of the river correct to the nearest tenth of a meter?

A. 90.8 m **B.** 100.5 m

C. 101.7 m **D.** 112.6 m

Use the following information to answer the next question.

From the top of a 115 m fire tower, Sue observes smoke in two different locations. She dispatches Gaetan and Bryan to investigate. When Gaetan arrives at the scene of the first smoke sighting, he uses his measuring tools to calculate that he is 334 m from the base of the fire tower and that the angle of elevation from where he is standing to the top of the tower is 19°. When Bryan arrives at the scene of the second smoke sighting, he uses his measuring tools to calculate that the angle of elevation from where he is standing to the top of the fire tower is 16°. After Gaetan and Bryan have radioed their information to Sue, she estimates that the angle from Gaetan to the base of the fire tower to Bryan is 110°, as shown in the diagram.

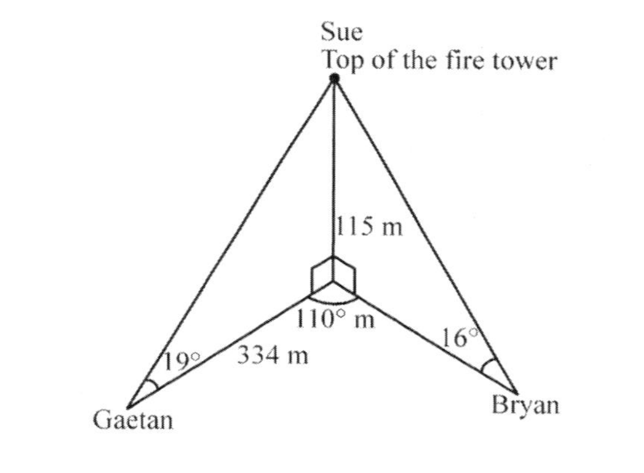

163. What is the distance between Gaetan and Bryan correct to the nearest meter?

A. 346 m **B.** 391 m

C. 584 m **D.** 603 m

To answer the following question, please see: on page ???

Use the following information to answer the next question.

Michelle searched a public sector employee database for statistical data that modeled a sine function. She found an example and recorded the data as a graph.

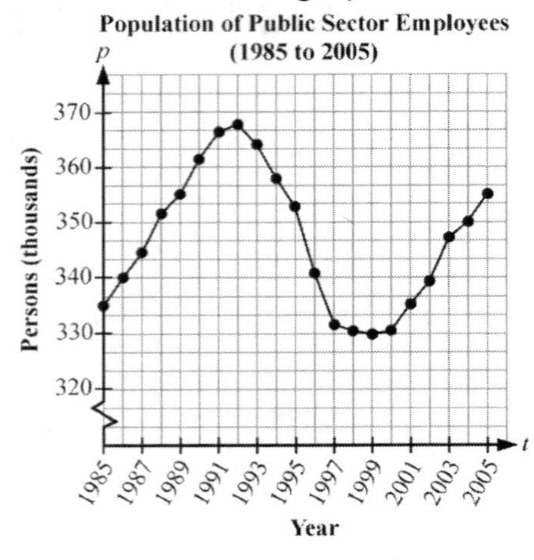

164. According to the approximate sinusoidal graph, the period, or time for one cycle, is about

A. 21 years
B. 16 years
C. 10 years
D. 7 years

Geometric and Arithmetic Sequences and Series

GEOMETRIC AND ARITHMETIC SEQUENCES AND SERIES

Table of Correlations

Standard		Concepts	Exercise #1	Exercise #2
PC.4	The student uses sequences and series as well as tools and technology to represent, analyze, and solve real-life problems.			
PC.4.A	*Represent patterns using arithmetic and geometric sequences and series.*	Deriving the General Term for an Arithmetic Sequence		
		Determine the General Term of an Arithmetic Sequence	165, 166, 167	197, 198
		Finding the Sum of a Finite Geometric Series Using the Summation Formula	168, 169	199
		Deriving the Summation Formula for Finite Arithmetic Series		
		Derive the Summation Formula for Finite Geometric Series		
		Derive the Summation Formula for Infinite Geometric Series		
		Understanding Pascal's Triangle	170, 171	200, 201
		Identify Arithmetic Sequences	177	202, 204
		Find the Sum of an Arithmetic Series Using a Summation Formula	172, 173	203
		Identify Geometric Sequences	174, 175	204, 205
		Determine the General Term of a Geometric Sequence	174, 176	206
		Generating Arithmetic Sequences	177, 178	207
		Generating Geometric Sequences	179, 180	205, 208, 209
		Solving Problems and Applications Involving the Sum of a Geometric Series	169, 181, 182	210
		Solving Problems Using Geometric Sequences	174, 175	208
		Solving Problems Using Basic Arithmetic Sequences	183, 184	211
		Solving Problems Involving the Sums of Arithmetic Series	185, 186	212
		Solving Problems Using the General Term Formula for an Arithmetic Sequence	165, 187	213
		Identifying a Geometric Series	188, 189	214, 215
PC.4.B	*Use arithmetic, geometric, and other sequences and series to solve real-life problems.*	Deriving the General Term for an Arithmetic Sequence		
		Determine the General Term of an Arithmetic Sequence	165, 166, 167	197, 198
		Finding the Sum of a Finite Geometric Series Using the Summation Formula	168, 169	199
		Identify Arithmetic Sequences	177	202, 204
		Find the Sum of an Arithmetic Series Using a Summation Formula	172, 173	203

		Identify Geometric Sequences	174, 175	204, 205
		Determine the General Term of a Geometric Sequence	174, 176	206
		Generating Arithmetic Sequences	177, 178	207
		Generating Geometric Sequences	179, 180	205, 208, 209
		Solving Problems and Applications Involving the Sum of a Geometric Series	169, 181, 182	210
		Solving Problems Using Geometric Sequences	174, 175	208
		Solving Problems Using Basic Arithmetic Sequences	183, 184	211
		Solving Problems Involving the Sums of Arithmetic Series	185, 186	212
		Solving Problems Using the General Term Formula for an Arithmetic Sequence	165, 187	213
		Identifying a Geometric Series	188, 189	214, 215
PC.4.C	*Describe limits of sequences and apply their properties to investigate convergent and divergent series.*	Calculate the Sum of an Infinite Geometric Series	190, 191	216, 217
		Understanding the Difference Between Divergent and Convergent Geometric Series		
PC.4.D	*Apply sequences and series to solve problems including sums and binomial expansion.*	Understanding Pascal's Triangle	170, 171	200, 201
		Understanding the Binomial Theorem	192	
		Applying the Binomial Theorem to Expand Binomial Expressions	193, 194	218, 219
		Determining Terms in the Expansion of a Binomial Power Using the General Term Formula	195, 196	220, 221

PC.4.A Represent patterns using arithmetic and geometric sequences and series.

Deriving the General Term for an Arithmetic Sequence

As problems involving arithmetic sequences become more complex, it is useful to be able to work with them more formally, using formulas and specific variables for the various components of the sequence.

The following list identifies the variables commonly used in the general term formula of an arithmetic sequence:

- a represents the first term in the sequence
- d represents the common difference; this number can be found by choosing any term in the sequence and subtracting the previous term. Most often the value of d is determined by subtracting the first term from the second term.
- n represents the number of terms in the sequence; n is always a whole number
- t_n represents the nth term in the sequence; also referred to as the general term

Example

For the sequence 2, 6, 10, 14, 18, 22, identify a, d, n, and t_4.

Solution

The first term (a) is 2.

The common difference (d) is 4. (For example, $6 - 2 = 4$)

There are 6 terms in the sequence (n).

The fourth term (t_4) in the sequence is 14.

Consider the following general arithmetic sequence:
$t_1, t_2, t_3, t_4, \ldots, t_n$

The sequence can alternatively be written as follows:
$a, a+d, a+d+d, a+d+d+d, \ldots, t_n$

The sequence can then be simplified as follows:
$a, a+d, a+2d, a+3d, \ldots, t_n$

Note that each term can be written as follows:

$t_1 = a$
$t_2 = a+d$
$t_3 = a+2d$
$t_4 = a+3d$
$t_n = a+(n-1)d$

The general term of an arithmetic sequence is defined by $t_n = a+(n-1)d$.

Determine the General Term of an Arithmetic Sequence

The **general term formula** for an arithmetic sequence is as follows: $t_n = a+(n-1)d$

This formula will generate any specified term for which a and d and n are known.

- a represents the first term in the series
- n represents the term number
- d represents the common difference between sequential terms in the sequence
- t_n represents the value of the term in the nth position

To determine the general term for any given sequence, identify the values of a and d, substitute them into the general term formula, and simplify.

Example

For the arithmetic sequence −5, 2, 9, 16, …, find the general term.

Solution

Step 1
In order to apply the general term formula, $t_n = a+(n-1)d$, identify the values of a and d.

$a = -5$
$d = 2-(-5) = 7$

Step 2
Substitute the derived values for a and d into the general term formula and simplify.

$t_n = a + (n - 1)d$
$t_n = -5 + (n - 1)(7)$
$t_n = -5 + 7n - 7$
$t_n = 7n - 12$

Example

For the arithmetic sequence 4, 1, −2, −5,…, determine the value of the 20th term (t_{20}).

Solution

Identify the values of a, d, and n.

$a = 4$
$d = 1 - 4 = -3$
$n = 20$

Substitute the derived values for a, d and n into the general term formula for an arithmetic sequence.

$t_n = a + (n - 1)d$
$t_{20} = 4 + (20 - 1)(-3)$
$= 4 + (19)(-3)$
$= -53$

The value of the 20th term is −53.

In addition to being able to find the value of a desired term, the general term formula can be used to calculate the value of a, d or n, given the other three values.

Example

Which term in the arithmetic sequence −5, 2, 9, 16, …, has a value of 79?

Solution

Identify the values of a, d and t_n.

$a = -5$
$d = 2 - (-5) = 7$
$t_n = 79$

Substitute the derived values for a, d and t_n into the general term formula for an arithmetic sequence and solve for n.

$t_n = a + (n - 1)d$
$79 = -5 + (n - 1)(7)$
$79 = -5 + 7n - 7$
$79 = -12 + 7n$
$91 = 7n$
$13 = n$

The 13th term in the sequence is 79.

Example

A particular arithmetic sequence has a common difference of −2.5. In the same sequence, $t_{41} = -64$.

What is the first term in the given sequence?

Solution

Step 1
Identify the values of t_n, n, and d.

$t_n = -64$
$n = 41$
$d = -2.5$

Step 2
Substitute the derived values into the general term formula, and solve for a.

$t_n = a + (n - 1)d$
$-64 = a + (41 - 1)(-2.5)$
$-64 = a - 100$
$a = 36$

The first term is 36.

Finding the Sum of a Finite Geometric Series Using the Summation Formula

The two formulas for finding the sum of the first n terms of a geometric series are as follows:

$$S_n = \frac{a(r^n - 1)}{r - 1},\ r \neq 1,\ S_n = \frac{rt_n - a}{r - 1},\ r \neq 1$$

- a represents the first term in the series.
- n represents the term number.
- r represents the common ratio between sequential terms in the series.
- t_n represents the value of the term in the nth position.

The first formula is used when the first term, the common ratio, and the number of terms in the series are known.

The second formula is used when the first term, last term, and the common ratio in the series are known.

Example

Find S_{11} of the geometric series $2 + 6 + 18 + 54 + 162 + \ldots$. __________

Solution

Step 1

Identify the given information.

In this series, the first term is 2, so $a = 2$.

To find the common ratio, r, divide $\frac{t_2}{t_1}$.

$$\frac{6}{2} = 3$$

Therefore, $r = 3$.

Step 2

Determine which summation formula to use.

The goal is to find S_{11}, so $n = 11$.

Since the value of n is known, use $S_n = \frac{a(r^n - 1)}{r - 1}$.

Step 3

Substitute the given values into the formula, and evaluate.

Substitute the values $a = 2$, $r = 3$, and $n = 11$ into the formula.

$$\begin{aligned} S_{11} &= \frac{2(3^{11} - 1)}{3 - 1} \\ &= \frac{2(177{,}147 - 1)}{2} \\ &= 177{,}146 \end{aligned}$$

In the geometric series $2 + 6 + 18 + 54 + 162 + \ldots$, $S_{11} = 177{,}146$.

Example

Find the sum of the finite geometric series $64 + 96 + 144 + \ldots + 729$.

Solution

Step 1

Determine the value of a.

The first term is 64. Therefore, $a = 64$.

Step 2

Determine the common ratio, r.

$$\begin{aligned} r &= \frac{t_2}{t_1} \\ &= \frac{96}{64} \\ &= \frac{3}{2} \end{aligned}$$

Step 3

The number of terms, n, is not known. However, the value of the last term in the series, t_n, is known.

The last term in the series is 729. Therefore, $t_n = 729$.

Step 4
Since the values of a, r, and t_n are known, use the formula $S_n = \frac{rt_n - a}{r - 1}$ to determine the sum of the series.

Substitute the values $a = 64$, $r = \frac{3}{2}$, and $t_n = 729$ into the formula $S_n = \frac{rt_n - a}{r - 1}$, and solve for S_n.

$$\begin{aligned} S_n &= \frac{\left(\frac{3}{2}\right)(729) - 64}{\frac{3}{2} - 1} \\ &= \frac{1{,}029.5}{0.5} \\ &= 2{,}059 \end{aligned}$$

The sum of the finite geometric series is 2,059.

Example

If the sum of the first n terms of the geometric series $3 - 6 + 12 - 24 + \ldots$ is equal to $-1{,}023$, determine the value of n.

Solution

Step 1
Determine the value of a.
The first term is 3. Therefore, $a = 3$.

Step 2
Determine the common ratio, r.

$$\begin{aligned} r &= \frac{t_2}{t_1} \\ &= \frac{-6}{3} \\ &= -2 \end{aligned}$$

Step 3
Determine the value of S_n.

The sum of the first n terms is $-1{,}023$. Therefore, $S_n = -1{,}023$.

Step 4
Since the values of a, r, and S_n are known and the problem asks for n, apply the formula $S_n = \frac{a(r^n - 1)}{r - 1}$.

Substitute the values $a = 3$, $r = -2$, and $S_n = -1{,}023$ into the formula and simplify.

$$\begin{aligned} -1{,}023 &= \frac{3((-2)^n - 1)}{(-2) - 1} \\ -1{,}023 &= \frac{3((-2)^n - 1)}{-3} \\ -1{,}023 &= -((-2)^n - 1) \\ 1{,}023 &= (-2)^n - 1 \end{aligned}$$

Step 5
Solve for n.

Add 1 to both sides.

$1{,}024 = (-2)^n$

Rewrite 1,024 as a power with a base of -2, then equate the exponents.

$$\begin{aligned} (-2)^{10} &= (-2)^n \\ 10 &= n \end{aligned}$$

Example

If $t_3 = 128$ and $t_6 = -16$ in a geometric series, what is the value of S_9?

Solution

Step 1
Determine the value of the common ratio, r.
Define the two terms, t_6 and t_3, by applying the formula $t_n = ar^{n-1}$.

$t_6 = a(r)^{6-1} = ar^5 = -16$

$t_3 = a(r)^{3-1} = ar^2 = 128$

Solve the system of equations $ar^5 = -16$ and $ar^2 = 128$ for r by dividing the first equation by the second equation.

$$\begin{aligned} \frac{ar^5}{ar^2} &= \frac{-16}{128} \\ r^3 &= -\frac{1}{8} \\ r &= \sqrt[3]{-\frac{1}{8}} \\ r &= -\frac{1}{2} \end{aligned}$$

Step 2
Determine the value of a by applying the general term formula $t_n = ar^{n-1}$.

The value of a can be determined using the formula with either t_3 or t_6.

Since $t_3 = 128$, substitute 128 for t_n, 3 for n, and $-\frac{1}{2}$ for r, and solve the equation for a.

$$128 = a\left(-\frac{1}{2}\right)^2$$
$$128 = a\left(\frac{1}{4}\right)$$
$$512 = a$$

Step 3
Determine S_9.

Substitute the values $a = 512$, $r = -\frac{1}{2}$, and $n = 9$ into the formula $S_n = \frac{a(r^n - 1)}{r - 1}$ and simplify.

$$S_9 = \frac{512\left(\left(-\frac{1}{2}\right)^9 - 1\right)}{\left(-\frac{1}{2}\right) - 1}$$
$$= \frac{512\left(-\frac{1}{512} - 1\right)}{\left(-\frac{1}{2}\right) - 1}$$
$$= \frac{-513}{\left(-\frac{3}{2}\right)}$$
$$= 342$$

Thus, $S_9 = 342$ for the given geometric series.

Deriving the Summation Formula for Finite Arithmetic Series

When the commas in an arithmetic sequence are replaced with plus signs, the sequence becomes a **series**.

Rewriting the sequence 2, 5, 8, 11, 14 as a series will result in the following:
$2 + 5 + 8 + 11 + 14$

One method of finding the sum of such a series is by adding all the terms. For example, the sum of the series $2 + 5 + 8 + 11 + 14$ is 40.

However, as the number of terms in a series increases, adding the terms becomes less efficient. As such, a formula to find the sum of a series, S_n, is far more helpful.

The general term of an arithmetic sequence is defined by $t_n = a + (n - 1)d$:

- a represents the first term in the series
- n represents the term number
- d represents the common difference between sequential terms in the series
- t_n represents the value of the term in the nth position

Consider the summation of the following general series:
$S_n = a + (a + d) + (a + 2d) + (a + 3d) + \ldots + (a + (n - 2)d) + (a + (n - 1)d)$

Rewrite the sum with the terms on the right side written in reverse order as follows:
$S_n = (a + (n - 1)d) + (a + (n - 2)d) + \ldots + (a + 3d) + (a + 2d) + (a + d) + a$

Now, add the two summation equations together.
$S_n = a + (a + d) + (a + 2d) + (a + 3d) + \ldots + (a + (n - 2)d) + (a + (n - 1)d)$
$S_n = (a + (n - 1)d) + (a + (n - 2)d) + \ldots + (a + 3d) + (a + 2d) + (a + d) + a$

In each summation equation, there are n terms being added together.

In addition, since the equations are written in reverse order, the sum of the first terms of the two equations will be the same as the sum of the second terms, which will be the same as the sum of the third terms, and so on.

As such, the sum of the two equations can be found by multiplying the sum of the first terms by n (n repetitions of the same sum).

The result is as follows:
$2S_n = [a + (a + (n-1)d)]n$
$2S_n = n[2a + (n-1)d]$
$S_n = \frac{n}{2}[2a + (n-1)d]$
$S_n = \frac{n}{2}(a + t_n)$

There are two formulas that can be used to find S_n:

$S_n = \frac{n}{2}(a + t_n)$

$S_n = \frac{n}{2}[2a + (n-1)d]$

The first formula is used when the first term, last term, and the number of terms in the series are known. The second formula is used when the first term, the common difference, and the number of terms in the series are known.

Derive the Summation Formula for Finite Geometric Series

When the commas in a geometric sequence are replaced with plus signs, the sequence becomes a **series**.

Rewriting the sequence 2, 4, 8, 16, 32 as a series will give the following:
2 + 4 + 8 + 16 + 32

One way of finding the sum of such a series is by adding all of the terms. For example, the sum of the series 2 + 4 + 8 + 16 + 32 is 62.

In general, the sum of a series, S_n, is given by $S_n = t_1 + t_2 + \ldots + t_{n-1} + t_n$.

However, as the number of terms in a series increases, adding up the terms becomes less efficient. As such, a formula to find the sum of a geometric series, S_n, is far more helpful.

Recall that the general term of a geometric sequence is defined by:
$t_n = ar^{n-1}$

- a represents the first term in the series
- n represents the term number
- r represents the common ratio between sequential terms in the series
- t_n represents the value of the term in the nth position

Consider the summation of a general series:
$S_n = a + ar + ar^2 + \ldots + ar^{n-1}$

Multiply both sides of the equation by r.
$rS_n = ar + ar^2 + \ldots + ar^{n-1} + ar^n$

Subtract the first equation from the second.
$rS_n = ar + ar^2 + \ldots + ar^{n-1} + ar^n$
$S_n = a + ar + ar^2 + \ldots + ar^{n-1}$

The result is as follows:
$rS_n - S_n = -a + ar^n$
$S_n(r-1) = a(r^n - 1)$
$S_n = \frac{a(r^n - 1)}{r - 1}$

Thus, one formula for finding the sum of a finite geometric series is as follows:

$S_n = \frac{a(r^n - 1)}{r - 1}$

Sometimes, however, different information is given in a problem, making an alternate form of the formula more useful.

Multiply both sides of the general term formula, $t_n = ar^{n-1}$, by r.
$rt_n = ar^n$

Working with the original summation formula $S_n = \frac{a(r^n - 1)}{r - 1}$, expand the numerator and replace ar^n with rt_n as follows:

$$S_n = \frac{ar^n - a}{r - 1} = \frac{rt_n - a}{r - 1}$$

The two formulas for finding the sum of the first n terms of a geometric series are as follows:

$S_n = \frac{a(r^n - 1)}{r - 1}$, $r \neq 1$, $S_n = \frac{rt_n - a}{r - 1}$, $r \neq 1$

The first formula is used when the first term, the common ratio, and the number of terms in the series are known.
The second formula is used when the first term, last term, and the common ratio in the series are known.

Derive the Summation Formula for Infinite Geometric Series

An **infinite series** is a summation of an infinite number of terms (or infinite sequence).
One common way to represent an infinite series is to write the first few terms followed by three dots (...).

For example, the series 2 + 4 + 8 + ... represents an infinite series.

As with a finite series, the symbol t_1 or a is used in an infinite series to refer to the first term, the symbol t_2 refers to the second term, the symbol t_3 refers to the third term, and so on.

$$\underset{t_1}{\overset{\uparrow}{2}} + \underset{t_2}{\overset{\uparrow}{4}} + \underset{t_3}{\overset{\uparrow}{8}} + \ldots$$

When a given infinite geometric series has a common ratio $-1 < r < 1$, the series is **convergent** and its sum has a finite value.

When a given infinite geometric series has a common ratio of $r > 1$ or $r < -1$, the series is **divergent** and its sum cannot be calculated.

As such, to find the sum of an infinite geometric series, the series must be convergent. In other words, the following restriction must be made: $-1 < r < 1$

Consider the summation formula for a finite geometric series.

$$S_n = \frac{a(r^n - 1)}{r - 1}$$

Now consider finding the sum of an infinite geometric series using the above formula. The series must be convergent such that $-1 < r < 1$.

As the number of terms approaches infinity $(n \to \infty)$, the value of r^n (in the numerator of the formula) will approach 0. With $r^n \to 0$, the formula can be rewritten as follows:

$$S_n = \frac{a(-1)}{r - 1}$$

Dividing the numerator and denominator by −1 gives:

$$S_n = \frac{a}{1 - r}$$

The sum of an infinite geometric series can be calculated by the following formula:

$$S_n = \frac{a}{1 - r}, \ -1 < r < 1$$

Understanding Pascal's Triangle

The triangular array of numbers shown here is called Pascal's triangle. It is named after the French mathematician Blaise Pascal who discovered it.

1
1 1
1 2 1
1 3 3 1
1 4 6 4 1
1 5 10 10 5 1

This array is formed by starting with the number 1 in the first row and then two 1s are placed in a second row below and to the left and right of the 1 in the first row. Subsequent rows are formed by again placing 1s diagonally left and right below the 1s in the previous row. The numbers between the 1s are obtained by adding the two numbers that are situated diagonally above them. For example, the numbers 2 and 1 are diagonally above 3 (2 + 1 = 3), and the numbers 4 and 6 are diagonally above 10(4 + 6 = 10).

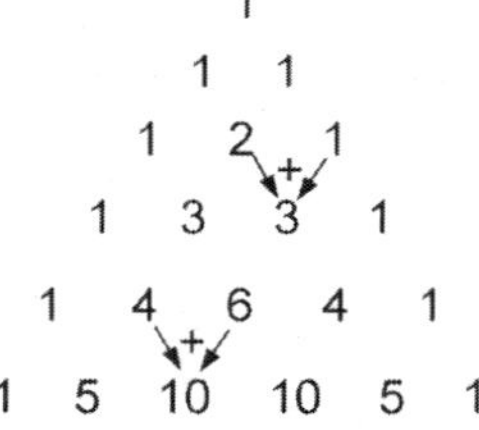

Continuing the pattern of placing 1s at the beginning and end of each row and adding numbers in the sixth row generates the numbers in the seventh row.

1 5 10 10 5 1
1 6 15 20 15 6 1

Every entry in Pascal's triangle is a combination. The 1 in the first row is the combination ${}_0C_0$.

The two 1s in the second row are ${}_1C_0$ and ${}_1C_1$. The entries in the third row are ${}_2C_0$, ${}_2C_1$, and ${}_2C_2$. Similarly, the numbers in row six are ${}_5C_0$, ${}_5C_1$, ${}_5C_2$, ${}_5C_3$, ${}_5C_4$, and ${}_5C_5$. Finally, the entries in the $(n+1)^{\text{th}}$ row are ${}_nC_0$, ${}_nC_1$, ${}_nC_2$, ${}_nC_3$, ..., ${}_nC_n$.

As such, Pascal's triangle can also be written in the following way:

$$
\begin{array}{ccccccccccc}
 & & & & & {}_0C_0 & & & & & \\
 & & & & {}_1C_0 & & {}_1C_1 & & & & \\
 & & & {}_2C_0 & & {}_2C_1 & & {}_2C_2 & & & \\
 & & {}_3C_0 & & {}_3C_1 & & {}_3C_2 & & {}_3C_3 & & \\
 & {}_4C_0 & & {}_4C_1 & & {}_4C_2 & & {}_4C_3 & & {}_4C_4 & \\
{}_5C_0 & & {}_5C_1 & & {}_5C_2 & & {}_5C_3 & & {}_5C_4 & & {}_5C_5
\end{array}
$$

The sum of the numbers in any given row is a power of two—specifically two to the power of one less than the row number.

$$
\begin{aligned}
1 &= 1 = 2^0\\
1+1 &= 2 = 2^1\\
1+2+1 &= 4 = 2^2\\
1+3+3+1 &= 8 = 2^3\\
1+4+6+4+1 &= 16 = 2^4\\
1+5+10+10+5+1 &= 32 = 2^5
\end{aligned}
$$

The seventh row is $1+6+15+20+15+6+1 = 2^6$. The $(n+1)^{\text{th}}$ row is ${}_nC_0 + {}_nC_1 + \ldots + {}_nC_n = 2^n$.

A row in the triangle is generated from the previous row by the formula

${}_nC_r + {}_nC_{r+1} = {}_{n+1}C_{r+1}$, $n, r \in W$, $n \geq 1$.

For example, the sum of the second and third entries in row four gives the third entry in the fifth row, which is ${}_3C_1 + {}_3C_2 = {}_4C_2$. Likewise, the sum of the fifth and sixth entries in row seven yields the sixth entry in row eight $({}_3C_1 + {}_6C_5 = {}_7C_5)$.

The rows of Pascal's triangle are the coefficients of the terms of the expansion of powers of binomials in the form $(x+y)^n$, $n \in W$. The expansion of the first several powers of $(x+y)^n$ shows the pattern.

$$
\begin{aligned}
(x+y)^0 &= 1\\
(x+y)^1 &= 1x+1y\\
(x+y)^2 &= 1x^2+2xy+1y^2\\
(x+y)^3 &= 1x^3+3x^2y+3xy^2+1y^3\\
(x+y)^4 &= 1x^4+4x^3y+6x^2y^2+4xy^3+1y^4\\
(x+y)^5 &= 1x^5+5x^4y+10x^3y^2+10x^2y^3+5xy^4+1y^5
\end{aligned}
$$

Note that the coefficients for the terms of the expansion $(x+y)^n$ come from the $(n+1)^{\text{th}}$ row or the row in which the second number equals the power of the binomial. Thus, the coefficients for the terms of the expansion of $(x+y)^{10}$ come from the eleventh row, which have the first two terms 1 and 10.

Example

Determine the sum of the coefficients of the terms in the expansion of the binomial $(a+b)^7$.

Solution

The coefficients of the terms in the expansion of $(a+b)^7$ come from the eighth row of Pascal's triangle.

The coefficients are ${}_7C_0$, ${}_7C_1$, ${}_7C_2$, ..., ${}_7C_7$.

The sum of these coefficients is $2^7 = 128$.

Identify Arithmetic Sequences

A **number sequence** is a list of numbers that are separated by commas. Some sequences follow rules or patterns. In particular, an **arithmetic sequence** is one in which each term is increasing or decreasing by a constant amount, *d*, called the **common difference**.

Some examples of arithmetic sequences are given in the following list:

- In the sequence 2, 5, 8, 11 … the number 3 is added to each term to get the subsequent term; thus $d = 3$.
- In the sequence 4, 3.5, 3, 2.5, 2 … the number −0.5 is added to each term to get the subsequent term; thus $d = -0.5$.
- In the sequence $\frac{1}{3}, \frac{1}{2}, \frac{2}{3}, \frac{5}{6}, \ldots$, the number $\frac{1}{6}$ is added to each term to get the subsequent term; thus $d = \frac{1}{6}$.

The following sequences are not arithmetic:

- 1, 3, 6, 10, 15 …
- 100, 50, 25, 12.5 …

Although the above sequences follow a pattern, it is not the repeated addition of the same number, so these sequences are not arithmetic.

It is important to distinguish arithmetic sequences from other types of sequences.

Example

Determine whether or not the sequence 4, 9, 14, 19… is an arithmetic sequence. If it is arithmetic, determine the common difference, *d*.

Solution

This sequence is arithmetic because 5 is being added to each term to get the subsequent term. Therefore, $d = 5$.

Example

Determine whether the sequence 3, 6, 12, 24… is an arithmetic sequence. If it is arithmetic, determine the common difference, *d*.

Solution

This sequence is not an arithmetic sequence because the same number is not being added each time to get the subsequent term.

Example

Determine whether the sequence 10, 4, −2, −8 … is an arithmetic sequence. If it is arithmetic, determine the common difference, *d*.

Solution

The sequence is arithmetic because −6 is added to each term to get the subsequent term. Therefore, $d = -6$.

Example

Determine whether the sequence $\frac{1}{3}, \frac{2}{3}, \frac{4}{3}, \frac{8}{3}$ … is an arithmetic sequence. If it is arithmetic, determine the common difference, *d*.

Solution

This is not an arithmetic sequence because the same number is not being added each time to get the subsequent term.

Find the Sum of an Arithmetic Series Using a Summation Formula

There are two formulas that can be used to find the sum of an arithmetic series, S_n:

$$S_n = \frac{n}{2}(a + t_n)$$

$$S_n = \frac{n}{2}[2a + (n-1)d]$$

- *a* represents the first term in the series
- *n* represents the term number
- *d* represents the common difference between sequential terms in the series
- t_n represents the value of the term in the nth position

Example

Find the sum of the arithmetic series 3, …, 95 if $n = 21$.

Solution

Step 1
Identify the given variables.
$a = 3$
$n = 21$
$t_n = 95$

Step 2
Substitute the numbers into the appropriate sum formula and simplify.

Since the first term, last term, and the number of terms in the series are given, apply the formula $S_n = \frac{n}{2}(a + t_n)$.

$$S_n = \frac{n}{2}(a + t_n)$$
$$S_{21} = \frac{21}{2}(3 + 95)$$
$$S_{21} = 1{,}029$$

Example

Find the sum of the arithmetic series 41, 39, 37, … if $n = 12$.

Solution

Step 1
Identify the given variables.
$a = 41$
$n = 12$
$d = 39 - 41 = -2$

Step 2
Substitute the numbers into the appropriate sum formula and simplify.

Since the first term, common difference, and the number of terms in the series are given, apply the formula $S_n = \frac{n}{2}[2a + (n - 1)d]$.

$$S_n = \frac{n}{2}[2a + (n - 1)d]$$
$$S_{12} = \frac{12}{2}[2(41) + (12 - 1)(-2)]$$
$$S_{12} = 360$$

Identify Geometric Sequences

A **sequence** is an ordered list of numbers that are separated by commas.

A common type of number sequence is a geometric sequence.

A sequence is **geometric** if each successive term is obtained by multiplying the previous term by a constant. This constant is called the **common ratio** and is denoted by r.

For example, in the sequence 3, 6, 12, 24, 48, each successive term is obtained by multiplying the previous term by 2. Therefore, the sequence is geometric with a common ratio, r, of 2.
$t_1 = a = 3$
$t_2 = t_1 \times 2 = 3 \times 2 = 6$
$t_3 = t_2 \times 2 = 6 \times 2 = 12$
$t_4 = t_3 \times 2 = 12 \times 2 = 24$
$t_5 = t_4 \times 2 = 24 \times 2 = 48$

The following sequences are examples of geometric sequences:

- 2, 4, 8, 16, 32 … $r = 2$
- −5, −15, −45, −135 … $r = 3$
- 100, 50, 25, 12.5 … $r = 0.5$

Any two successive terms in a sequence can be used to find the common ratio. Terms 1 and 2 are often used, so a possible formula is $r = \frac{t_2}{t_1}$.

When $r > 1$, the terms of a geometric sequence are increasing in value. This is referred to as **geometric growth**.

When $0 \le r < 1$, the terms of a geometric sequence are decreasing in value. This is called **geometric decay**.

When $r < 0$, the terms of a geometric sequence alternate between positive and negative values if the first term is positive or alternate between negative and positive values if the first term is negative.

Example

For the geometric sequence 7, 21, 63, …, determine the value of the common ratio and classify the sequence as growth or decay.

Solution

Find r.
$$r = \frac{21}{7}$$
$$r = 3$$

Since $r > 1$, this sequence is an example of geometric growth.

Example

For the geometric sequence 6, 3, $\frac{3}{2}$, …, determine the value of the common ratio and classify the sequence as growth or decay.

Solution

Find r.

$r = \frac{3}{6}$

$r = \frac{1}{2}$

Since $0 < r < 1$, this sequence is an example of geometric decay.

To determine whether a sequence is geometric, look at the first two ratios. Check whether $\frac{t_2}{t_1} = \frac{t_3}{t_2}$. If the two ratios are equal, then quickly scan the other terms of the sequence to verify that the same common ratio applies to them as well. If it does, then the sequence is geometric.

A sequence, $t_1, t_2, t_3, t_4, \ldots t_{n-1}, t_n$, is geometric if it satisfies this condition:

$$\frac{t_2}{t_1} = \frac{t_3}{t_2} = \frac{t_4}{t_3} = \ldots = \frac{t_n}{t_{n-1}}$$

Example

Given the sequence $\frac{1}{2}, \frac{1}{4}, \frac{1}{8}, \ldots$, explain whether the sequence is geometric.

Solution

Step 1

Determine the common ratio using t_1 and t_2.

$$\frac{t_2}{t_1} = \frac{\left(\frac{1}{4}\right)}{\left(\frac{1}{2}\right)} = \frac{1}{4} \times \frac{2}{1} = \frac{2}{4} = \frac{1}{2}$$

Step 2

Determine the common ratio using t_2 and t_3.

$$\frac{t_3}{t_2} = \frac{\left(\frac{1}{8}\right)}{\left(\frac{1}{4}\right)} = \frac{1}{8} \times \frac{4}{1} = \frac{4}{8} = \frac{1}{2}$$

Step 3

Compare the common ratios.

$$\frac{t_2}{t_1} = \frac{1}{2} = \frac{t_3}{t_2}$$

Since the ratios are the same, the sequence $\frac{1}{2}, \frac{1}{4}, \frac{1}{8}, \ldots$ is a geometric sequence with a common ratio, r, of $\frac{1}{2}$.

Determine the General Term of a Geometric Sequence

The formula for the general term of a geometric sequence is as follows:

$t_n = ar^{n-1}$

This formula will generate any specified term for which a and r and n are known.

To determine the general term for any given geometric sequence, identify the values of a and r, substitute them into the general term formula, and simplify.

Example

What is the general term of the geometric sequence 54, 36, 24, 16, …?

Solution

Step 1

Determine the value of a, the first term.

In this sequence, the first term is 54. Therefore, $a = 54$.

Step 2

Determine the common ratio, r.

$$r = \frac{t_2}{t_1} = \frac{36}{54} = \frac{2}{3}$$

Step 3

Substitute 54 for a and $\frac{2}{3}$ for r in the formula $t_n = ar^{n-1}$.

The general term is $t_n = 54\left(\frac{2}{3}\right)^{n-1}$.

Example

To the nearest hundredth, the 7th term of the geometric sequence 54, 36, 24, 16, … is __________.

Solution

Substitute 7 for n in the formula $t_n = 54\left(\frac{2}{3}\right)^{n-1}$, and then evaluate.

$t_7 = 54\left(\frac{2}{3}\right)^{7-1}$

$t_7 = 54\left(\frac{2}{3}\right)^{6}$

$t_7 \approx 54(0.08779)$

$t_7 \approx 4.74$

The 7th term is 4.74.

In addition to being able to find the value of a desired term, the general term formula can be used to calculate the value of a, r or n, given the other three values.

Example

The number of terms in the geometric sequence 4, 12, 36, 108, …, 78,732 is _______.

Solution

Since this is a finite sequence and the last term is 78,732, then for some value of n, $t_n = 78{,}732$. The number of terms in the sequence can be determined by solving for n.

Step 1

Determine the value of a, the first term.

In this sequence, the first term is 4. Therefore, $a = 4$.

Step 2

Determine the common ratio, r.

$r = \frac{t_2}{t_1}$

$= \frac{12}{4}$

$= 3$

Step 3

Determine the general term.

Substitute 4 for a and 3 for r in the formula $t_n = ar^{n-1}$.

The general term is $t_n = 4(3)^{n-1}$.

Step 4

Substitute 78,732 for t_n in the formula $t_n = 4(3)^{n-1}$.

$78{,}732 = 4(3)^{n-1}$

Step 5

Solve for n.

Divide both sides of the equation by 4.

$(3)^{n-1} = 19{,}683$

Take the common logarithm of both sides of the equation.

$\log (3)^{n-1} = \log 19{,}683$

Apply the power law of logarithms.

$(n-1)\log 3 = \log 19{,}683$

Divide both sides by log 3.

$n - 1 = \frac{\log 19{,}683}{\log 3}$

Add 1 to both sides.

$n = \frac{\log 19{,}683}{\log 3} + 1$

Evaluate.

$n = 10$

The sequence has 10 terms, and 78,732 is the 10th term.

Since n must be a natural number, 19,683 must be a power of 3. The value of n could therefore be determined as follows:

$3^{n-1} = 19{,}683$

$3^{n-1} = 3^9$

$n - 1 = 9$

$n = 10$

Generating Arithmetic Sequences

In order to generate an arithmetic sequence, a starting value and the common difference are required. All terms can then be generated by repeatedly adding the same amount to each term.

Example

Generate the first five terms of the arithmetic sequence that starts with 14 and has a common difference of 7.

Solution

$14 + 7 = 21$
$21 + 7 = 28$
$28 + 7 = 35$
$35 + 7 = 42$

The first five terms of this arithmetic sequence are 14, 21, 28, 35, and 42.

Example

Generate the first five terms of the arithmetic sequence that starts with 1.3 and has a common difference of −2.4.

Solution

$1.3 + (-2.4) = -1.1$
$-1.1 + (-2.4) = -3.5$
$-3.5 + (-2.4) = -5.9$
$-5.9 + (-2.4) = -8.3$

The first five terms in this arithmetic sequence are 1.3, −1.1, −3.5, −5.9, and −8.3.

Example

Generate the first five terms of the arithmetic sequence that starts with $\frac{1}{3}$ and has a common difference of $\frac{2}{3}$.

Solution

$\frac{1}{3} + \frac{2}{3} = 1$
$1 + \frac{2}{3} = 1\frac{2}{3}$
$1\frac{2}{3} + \frac{2}{3} = 2\frac{1}{3}$
$2\frac{1}{3} + \frac{2}{3} = 3$

The first five terms in this arithmetic sequence are $\frac{1}{3}$, 1, $1\frac{2}{3}$, $2\frac{1}{3}$, and 3.

Generating Geometric Sequences

In order to generate a geometric sequence, a starting value and the common ratio, *r*, are required. All terms can then be generated by repeatedly multiplying the common ratio to each term.

Example

Generate the first five terms of the geometric sequence that starts with 11 and has a common ratio of 3.

Solution

$11 \times 3 = 33$
$33 \times 3 = 99$
$99 \times 3 = 297$
$297 \times 3 = 891$

The first five terms of this geometric sequence are 11, 33, 99, 297, and 891.

Example

Generate the first five terms of the geometric sequence that starts with 1.5 and has a common ratio of −3.5.

Solution

$$1.5 \times (-3.5) = -5.25$$
$$-5.25 \times (-3.5) = 18.375$$
$$18.375 \times (-3.5) = -64.3125$$
$$-64.3125 \times (-3.5) = 225.09375$$

The first five terms in this geometric sequence are 1.5, −5.25, 18.375, −64.3125, 225.09375

Alternatively, when at least two consecutive terms of a geometric sequence are given, other terms in the geometric sequence can be determined.

Example

Find the next three terms of the geometric sequence 4, 20, 100, ….

Solution

Find r.

$$r = \frac{20}{4}$$
$$r = 5$$

Calculate the next three terms by multiplying the preceding term by the value of r.

$$t_4 = 100 \times 5 = 500$$
$$t_5 = 500 \times 5 = 2{,}500$$
$$t_6 = 2{,}500 \times 5 = 12{,}500$$

Example

Find the next three terms of the geometric sequence $\sqrt{5}, \sqrt{10}, 2\sqrt{5}, \ldots$.

Solution

Find r.

$$r = \frac{\sqrt{10}}{\sqrt{5}}$$
$$r = \sqrt{2}$$

Calculate the next three terms by multiplying the preceding term by the value of r.

$$t_4 = 2\sqrt{5} \times \sqrt{2} = 2\sqrt{10}$$
$$t_5 = 2\sqrt{10} \times \sqrt{2} = 2\sqrt{20}$$
$$t_6 = 2\sqrt{20} \times \sqrt{2} = 2\sqrt{40}$$

Example

Find the next three terms of the geometric sequence $\frac{3}{2}, \frac{3}{4}, \frac{3}{8}, \ldots$.

Solution

Find r.

$$r = \frac{\frac{3}{4}}{\frac{3}{2}}$$
$$r = \frac{3}{4} \times \frac{2}{3}$$
$$r = \frac{1}{2}$$

Calculate the next three terms by multiplying the preceding term by the value of r.

$$t_4 = \frac{3}{8} \times \frac{1}{2} = \frac{3}{16}$$
$$t_5 = \frac{3}{16} \times \frac{1}{2} = \frac{3}{32}$$
$$t_6 = \frac{3}{32} \times \frac{1}{2} = \frac{3}{64}$$

Solving Problems and Applications Involving the Sum of a Geometric Series

You can solve many real-world problems using the formulae for the sum of a geometric series.

There are two formulae that can be used to find the sum, S_n, of a geometric series:

1. When a, n, and r are known, use
$$S_n = \frac{a(r^n - 1)}{r - 1},\ r \neq 1.$$
2. When a, r, and t_n are known, use
$$S_n = \frac{rt_n - a}{r - 1},\ r \neq 1.$$

The sum of an infinite geometric series is given by the formula $S_\infty = \frac{a}{1-r}$, where $-1 < r < 1$.

Example

Each year, Farmer Brown buys some land to increase the overall size of his farm. In the first year, he bought 4 ha. Each year after, he buys 15% more land than he bought the previous year.

To the nearest hundredth, how much land will he have purchased after 10 years?

Solution

Step 1

Determine the series that represents the given information.

The amounts of land he purchased represent a geometric series. In the first year, he bought 4 ha.

$t_1 = 4$ ha

In the second year, he bought 15% more.

$4 \times 1.15 = 4.6$ ha

In the third year, he bought 15% more.

$4.6 \times 1.15 = 5.29$ ha

Write the first three terms of the geometric series.

$4 + 4.6 + 5.29 + \ldots$

Step 2

Find the total area Farmer Brown purchased over the ten-year period.

Since you are finding the sum of the first 10 terms in the series, $n = 10$. Since the first term is 4, $a = 4$. The common ratio (r) is 1.15 because each term after the first one is obtained by multiplying the previous term by 1.15.

To determine the sum, substitute $a = 4$, $r = 1.15$, and $n = 10$ into the formula $S_n = \frac{a(r^n - 1)}{r-1}$.

$$S_n = \frac{a(r^n - 1)}{r-1}$$

$$S_{10} = \frac{4(1.15^{10} - 1)}{1.15 - 1}$$

$$S_{10} \approx 81.21$$

In 10 years, Farmer Brown will have purchased approximately 81.21 ha of land.

Solving Problems Using Geometric Sequences

You can find many instances of geometric growth in real-life situations. Some of these situations include the following:

- Inflation
- Investments that grow
- Chain letters
- Bacterial growth
- Animal populations

Example

Stephen has a job that pays $25,000 per year in the first year and increases by 5% each year thereafter.

How much will Stephen earn in his fifth year of employment?

Solution

In this instance, the common ratio is 100% + 5% = 105% or 1.05, when 105% is written as a decimal.

First year	$25,000
Second year	$25,000 × 1.05 = $26,250
Third year	$26,250 × 1.05 = $27,562.50
Fourth year	$27,562.50 × 1.05 = $28,940.63
Fifth year	$28,940.63 × 1.05 = $30,387.66

Stephen will earn $30,387.66 in his fifth year of employment.

You can also find geometric decay in situations involving job raises, radioactive isotopes, or the depreciation of vehicles.

Example

A car is originally worth $25,000. Each year it depreciates by 18%.

At the end of which year will the car first be worth less than $10,000?

Solution

If the value of the car decreases 18% each year, then the common ratio is 100% – 18% = 82% or 0.82 when 82% is written as a decimal.

	Value ($)
Initial value	$25,000
End of year 1	$25,000(0.82) = $20,500
End of year 2	$20,500(0.82) = $16,810
End of year 3	$16,810(0.82) = $13,784.20
End of year 4	$13,784.20(0.82) = $11,303.04
End of year 5	$11,303.04(0.82) = $9,268.50

At the end of the fifth year, the car will be worth less than $10,000, for the first time.

Solving Problems Using Basic Arithmetic Sequences

There are many real-world situations that provide examples of arithmetic growth. When a problem arises in which the desired term number of the arithmetic sequence is small, it can be solved by generating the sequence required and then answering the given question.

Example

Each year on his birthday, David's grandparents give him money.

They started on his first birthday by giving him \$10. Each birthday after that, they give him \$5 more than they did the previous year.

How much money will David receive on his 10th birthday?

Solution

First, generate the pattern.

Add 5 to each term to get the subsequent term.
10, 15, 20, 25, 30, 35, 40, 45, 50, 55

On his 10th birthday, David will receive \$55.00.

Solving Problems Involving the Sums of Arithmetic Series

You can solve many real-world problems using one of the formulae for the sum of an arithmetic series.

There are two formulae that can be used to find the sum, S_n, of an arithmetic series:

- When a, n, and d are known, use $S_n = \frac{n}{2}[2a + (n-1)d]$.
- When a, n, and t_n are known, use $S_n = \frac{n}{2}(a + t_n)$.

Example

For eight weeks over the summer, Lexi had a job mowing lawns. She had 5 customers in her first week. Each week after that, she had 2 more lawns to mow than she had during the previous week.

How many lawns did she mow in total during the summer?

Solution

Since the question asks for the total number of lawns mowed over the 8 weeks, determine the sum of the first eight terms of the arithmetic series.

Use the sum formula $S_n = \frac{n}{2}[2a + (n-1)d]$, where $n = 8$, $a = 5$, and $d = 2$.

$$S_n = \frac{n}{2}[2a + (n-1)d]$$

$$S_n = \frac{8}{2}[2(5) + (8-1)2]$$

$$S_n = 96$$

Lexi mowed 96 lawns over the 8 weeks.

Example

For eight weeks over the summer, Lexi had a job mowing lawns.

She started by having 5 customers in her first week. Each week after that she had 2 more lawns to mow than she had during the previous week.

If she charged \$6 per lawn, how much did she make during the first 6 weeks?

Solution

First, calculate the number of lawns mowed in the 6 weeks.

Identify the given variables:
$a = 5$
$d = 2$
$n = 6$

Apply the appropriate sum formula and solve.

$S_n = \frac{n}{2}[2a + (n - 1)d]$

$S_6 = \frac{6}{2}[2(5) + (6 - 1)2]$

$S_6 = 60$

She mowed 60 lawns in the first 6 weeks.

To calculate her revenue, multiply the number of lawns mowed by the price charged per lawn:
Total earned = 60 × 6 = \$360

She earned \$360.00 mowing lawns in the first 6 weeks.

Solving Problems Using the General Term Formula for an Arithmetic Sequence

The general term of an arithmetic sequence is given by $t_n = a + (n - 1)d$, where t_n is the value of the nth term, a is the value of the first term in the sequence, and d is the common difference.

When solving problems using the general term formula, start by identifying all the given information, and decide what information is necessary to generate the general term.
The general term for each situation is different, so it is important to do this step first. Then, substitute the values of the known variables into the general term formula, and solve for the required (unknown) variable.

Example

Amorita starts working for a company at a yearly salary of \$19,000. Each year, she gets a raise of \$1,800.

How much will she be making during her fifth year with the company?

Solution

Step 1
Identify the values of a, d and n from the given information.
$a = 19{,}000$ (her starting salary)
$d = 1{,}800$ (her annual raise)
$n = 5$ (her 5th year)

Step 2
Substitute the derived values for a, d and n into the general term formula for an arithmetic sequence.
$t_n = a + (n - 1)d$
$t_5 = 19{,}000 + (5 - 1)(1{,}800)$

Step 3
Find the value of t_5.
$t_5 = 19{,}000 + (5 - 1)(1{,}800)$
$= 19{,}000 + 4(1{,}800)$
$= 19{,}000 + 7{,}200$
$= 26{,}200$
Amorita will make \$26,200 in her fifth year.

During which year will she make \$40,600?

Solution

Step 1
Identify the values of a, d and t_n from the given information.
$a = 19{,}000$ (her starting salary)
$d = 1{,}800$ (her annual raise)
$t_n = 40{,}600$ (the given salary)

Step 2
Substitute the derived values for a, d and t_n into the general term formula for an arithmetic sequence.
$t_n = a + (n - 1)d$
$40{,}600 = 19{,}000 + (n - 1)(1{,}800)$

Step 3

Solve for n.

$40,600 = 1,900 + (n - 1)(1,800)$
$40,600 = 19,000 + 1,800n - 1,800$
$40,600 = 1,800n + 17,200$
$23,400 = 1,800n$
$13 = n$

Amorita will make $40,600 in her 13th year of work.

IDENTIFYING A GEOMETRIC SERIES

A **series** is a summation of ordered terms of a sequence of numbers. Some examples of series are as follows:

- $1 + 2 + 3 + 4 + \ldots$
- $1 + (-1) + 1 + (-1) + \ldots$
- $1 + \frac{1}{2} + \frac{1}{4} + \frac{1}{8} + \frac{1}{16} + \ldots$

Some series are **finite**, which means they have a fixed number of terms. Other series are **infinite**, which means they have an infinite number of terms. One common way to represent an infinite series is to write the first few terms followed by three dots (...).

For example, the series 2 + 4 + 8 + 16 + 32 + 64 is finite. The series 2 + 4 + 8 + ... is infinite.

Consider the following series:

$$\begin{array}{ccccccccccc} 2 & + & 6 & + & 18 & + & 54 & + & 162 & + & \ldots \\ \uparrow & & \uparrow & & \uparrow & & \uparrow & & \uparrow & & \\ t_1 & & t_2 & & t_3 & & t_4 & & t_5 & & \end{array}$$

The symbol t_1 is used to refer to the first term, t_2 refers to the second term, t_3 refers to the third term, and so on. The symbol t_n refers to the nth term in the series, and t_{n-1} refers to the term just before the nth term.

A series is **geometric** if it is a summation of terms of a geometric sequence. In turn, a sequence is geometric if terms are generated by multiplying previous terms by a constant. This constant is called the **common ratio**, and it is denoted by r. Any two successive terms in the series can be used to find the common ratio, r.

$$r = \frac{t_k}{t_{k-1}}$$

Therefore, a series $t_1 + t_2 + t_3 + \ldots t_{k-1} + t_k + \ldots + t_n$ is geometric if it satisfies the condition

$$\frac{t_2}{t_1} = \frac{t_3}{t_2} = \ldots = \frac{t_k}{t_{k-1}} = \ldots = \frac{t_n}{t_{n-1}}.$$

To determine whether a given series is geometric, compare the ratios $\frac{t_2}{t_1}, \frac{t_3}{t_2}, \frac{t_4}{t_3}$, and so on. If the ratios are all equal, then the series is geometric.

Example

Determine whether the series $4 - 10 + 25 - 62.5 + \ldots$ is a geometric series.

Solution

Step 1

Rewrite the series as an addition of terms.

$4 + (-10) + 25 + (-62.5) + \ldots$

Step 2

Determine the ratio between the first and second terms.

$$r = \frac{t_2}{t_1}$$
$$r = \frac{-10}{4}$$
$$r = -2.5$$

Step 3

Determine the ratio between the second and third terms.

$$r = \frac{t_3}{t_2}$$
$$r = \frac{25}{-10}$$
$$r = -2.5$$

Step 4

Determine the ratio between the third and fourth terms.

$$r = \frac{t_4}{t_3}$$
$$r = \frac{-62.5}{25}$$
$$r = -2.5$$

Step 5
State whether the given series is geometric.
A series is geometric if it is a summation of terms that are generated by multiplying previous terms by a constant. This constant is called the common ratio. Since the ratio between consecutive terms is constant, –2.5 is a common ratio. Therefore, the given series is a geometric series.

PC.4.C Describe limits of sequences and apply their properties to investigate convergent and divergent series.

Calculate the Sum of an Infinite Geometric Series

The formula used to calculate the sum of an infinite geometric series is $S_\infty = \frac{a}{1-r}$, where $-1 < r < 1$.

The sum of an infinite geometric series cannot be calculated when the series has a common ratio $r \geq 1$ or $r \leq -1$.

Example

Determine the sum of the series
$7 + 2.1 + 0.63 + \ldots$.

Solution

Step 1
Determine the first term a and the common ratio r of the given series.
Since 7 is the first term, $a = 7$.

$$\begin{aligned} r &= \frac{t_2}{t_1} \\ &= \frac{2.1}{7} \\ &= 0.3 \end{aligned}$$

Step 2
Since the series is an infinite geometric series where $-1 < r < 1$, apply the formula

$$S_\infty = \frac{a}{1-r}.$$

Substitute 7 for a and 0.3 for r.

$$\begin{aligned} S_\infty &= \frac{7}{1-0.3} \\ &= \frac{7}{0.7} \\ &= 10 \end{aligned}$$

The sum of the given series is 10.

Understanding the Difference Between Divergent and Convergent Geometric Series

An infinite geometric series is said to be **convergent** when the sum of its infinite terms has a finite value.

This occurs when the common ratio of the infinite geometric series is $-1 < r < 1$ because when $-1 < r < 1$, each consecutive term in the series approaches (gets closer to) 0.

As such, it can be concluded that when a given infinite geometric series has a common ratio $-1 < r < 1$, the series is convergent and its sum has a finite value.

Alternatively, an infinite geometric series is said to be **divergent** when the sum of its infinite terms does not have a finite value.

A divergent geometric series exists when the common ratio is either greater than 1 ($r > 1$), in which case each consecutive term in the series becomes infinitely larger, or when the common ratio is less than negative 1 ($r < -1$), in which case each consecutive term in the series becomes infinitely smaller (sometimes this is referred to as infinitely large negative).

As such, it can be concluded that when a given infinite geometric series has a common ratio of $r > 1$ or $r < -1$, its sum cannot be calculated.

When $r = \pm 1$, the sum of an infinite series cannot be calculated. If $r = 1$, every term of the series is identical and the sum approaches infinity (or negative infinity if a is negative). If $r = -1$, the terms of the series oscillate between two values $\pm a$ and thus no sum can be calculated.

PC.4.D Apply sequences and series to solve problems including sums and binomial expansion.

Understanding the Binomial Theorem

The first several expansions of powers of the binomial $x + y$ yield a pattern where the coefficients of the terms form the array known as Pascal's triangle.

$$(x+y)^0 = 1$$
$$(x+y)^1 = 1x + 1y$$
$$(x+y)^2 = 1x^2 + 2xy + 1y^2$$
$$(x+y)^3 = 1x^3 + 3x^2y + 3xy^2 + 1y^3$$
$$(x+y)^4 = 1x^4 + 4x^3y + 6x^2y^2 + 4xy^3 + 1y^4$$
$$(x+y)^5 = 1x^5 + 5x^4y + 10x^3y^2 + 10x^2y^3 + 5xy^4 + 1y^5$$

Since every entry in Pascal's triangle is also a combination, the triangle can be written as follows:

$${}_0C_0$$
$${}_1C_0 \quad {}_1C_1$$
$${}_2C_0 \quad {}_2C_1 \quad {}_2C_2$$
$${}_3C_0 \quad {}_3C_1 \quad {}_3C_2 \quad {}_3C_3$$
$${}_4C_0 \quad {}_4C_1 \quad {}_4C_2 \quad {}_3C_4 \quad {}_4C_4$$
$${}_5C_0 \quad {}_5C_1 \quad {}_5C_2 \quad {}_5C_3 \quad {}_5C_4 \quad {}_5C_5$$

Example

Identify a strategy for determining the coefficients of the terms that result from the expansion of $(x + y)^3$.

Solution

Step 1

Expand the binomial.

$$(x+y)^3$$
$$= (x+y)(x+y)(x+y)$$
$$= (x^2 + xy + xy + y^2)(x+y)$$
$$= x^3 + x^2y + x^2y + xy^2 + x^2y + xy^2 + xy^2 + y^3$$
$$= x^3 + 3x^2y + 3xy^2 + y^3$$

Step 2

Observe patterns in the expansion.

Look at the last line in step 1.

- Each term in the expansion must consist of one factor, either an x or a y, from each of the three binomial $x + y$ factors.
- The first term, x^3, consists of three factors of x and zero factors of y from the product of the three binomials.
- The last term, y^3, consists of zero factors of x and three factors of y from the product of the three binomials.
- For the first term, x^3, there are 0 factors of y. The number of ways to select 0 y factors from the 3 ys in the binomial $x + y$ factors is ${}_3C_0 = 1$.
- For the last term y^3, there are 3 factors of y. The number of ways to select 3 y factors from the 3 ys is ${}_3C_3 = 1$.

  Thus, the coefficients of the first and last terms may be written as ${}_3C_0x^3 + 3x^2y + 3xy + {}_3C_3y^3$.
- The second term contains only 1 y factor from the 3 ys, and the third term contains 2 y factors from the 3 ys.
- The number of ways to select only 1 y from 3 is ${}_3C_1$, and the number of ways to select 2 ys from 3 is ${}_3C_2$.

Therefore, the coefficients of the expansion may be written as follows:

$${}_3C_0 + {}_3C_1x^3y + {}_3C_2xy^2 + {}_3C_3y^3$$
$$= 1x^3 + 3x^2y + 3xy^2 + 1y^3$$

Example

Determine a general approach to expand $(x+y)^n$.

Solution

The first term will contain 0 *y* factors from the *n y*s. The second term will contain 1 *y* factor from the n *y*s, the third term will contain 2 *y* factors from the n *y*s, and so on, until the last term is reached, which will contain all *n* factors of *y*.

Once the factors of *y* are chosen, the factors of *x* must come from the remaining factors of $x+y$ that have not yet been chosen, as each term must contain a factor from each $x+y$ factor.

The expansion of $(x+y)^n$ may then be written as follows:

$$(x+y)^n = {}_nC_0x^n + {}_nC_1x^{n-1}y$$
$$+{}_nC_2x^{n-2}y^2 + \ldots {}_nC_ny^n$$

Note that the first term in the expansion is $t_1 = {}_nC_0x^n$, the second term is $t_2 = {}_nC_1x^{n-1}y^1$, and the third term is $t_3 = {}_nC_2x^{n-2}y^2$.

Continuing this pattern would suggest that $t_4 = {}_nC_3x^{n-3}y^3$ and $t_5 = {}_nC_4x^{n-4}y^4$.

Somewhere in the expansion, the term ${}_nC_kx^{n-k}y^k$ could be identified. This must be t_{k+1}, the $(k+1)^{\text{th}}$ term because the exponent for the variable *y* is always one less than the term number.

This term $t_{k+1} = {}_nC_kx^{n-k}y^k$ is called the general term of the expansion $(x+y)^n$ and can be used to determine individual terms without expanding the entire binomial.

The following are characteristics of the binomial expansion $(x+y)^n$, $n \in W$:

1. $(x+y)^n = {}_nC_0x^n + {}_nC_1x^{n-1}y + {}_nC_2x^{n-2}y^2 + \ldots + {}_nC_ny^n$, $n \in W$
2. The number of terms in the expansion is one more than the power of the binomial.
   For example, $(x+y)^6$ has seven terms, $(x+y)^{10}$ has eleven terms, and $(x+y)^n$ has $n+1$ terms.
3. The degree of every term is equal to the power of the binomial. For example, each term in the expansion of $(x+y)^5$ is of degree 5.
4. In the final expansion, the exponent of *x* in the first term equals *n*, the power of the binomial. Moving from left to right, the exponent of *x* decreases by 1 in each consecutive term. The exponent of *y* is 0 in the first term and increases by 1 for each consecutive term, ending with degree *n* in the final term.
5. The coefficients form the pattern of Pascal's triangle:

```
        1
      1   1
    1   2   1
  1   3   3   1
 1  4   6   4  1
1  5  10  10  5  1
```

6. The general term of the expansion is $t_{k+1} = {}_nC_kx^{n-k}y^k$.

Applying the Binomial Theorem to Expand Binomial Expressions

The binomial theorem for the expansion of $(x+y)^n$, $n \in W$ states:

$$(x+y)^n = {}_nC_0x^n + {}_nC_1x^{n-1}y + {}_nC_2x^{n-2}y^2$$
$$+ \ldots + {}_nC_{n-1}xy^{n-1} + {}_nC_ny^n$$

Although this theorem is stated for the binomial $x+y$, it can be applied to the expansion of any binomial by substitution.

For example, $(x+y)^4 = {}_4C_1x^4 + {}_4C_1x^3y + {}_4C_2x^2y^2 + {}_4C_3xy^3 + {}_4C_4y^4$ shows the expansion of a simple binomial.

However, the binomial $\left(3a+\frac{2}{b}\right)^4$ can also be expanded using the binomial theorem by simply substituting $3a$ for x and $\frac{2}{b}$ for y and then simplifying.

Any binomial to any power can be expanded using this theorem by following these steps:

1. Write the expansion of $(x+y)^n$ using the binomial theorem, substituting x and y with the appropriate terms of the binomial.
2. Simplify the terms of the expansion.

Example

Expand $\left(3a+\frac{2}{b}\right)^4$.

Solution

Step 1

Apply the binomial theorem.

$$\left(3a+\frac{2}{b}\right)^4 = {}_4C_0(3a)^4 + {}_4C_1(3a)^3\left(\frac{2}{b}\right) + {}_4C_2(3a)^2\left(\frac{2}{b}\right)^2 + {}_4C_3(3a)\left(\frac{2}{b}\right)^3 + {}_4C_4\left(\frac{2}{b}\right)^4$$

Step 2

Simplify the preceding equation.

$$= \left(\begin{array}{l} 1(81a^4) + 4(27a^3)\left(\frac{2}{b}\right) + 6(9a^2)\left(\frac{2^2}{b^2}\right) \\ +4(3a)\left(\frac{2^3}{b^3}\right) + 1\left(\frac{2^4}{b^4}\right) \end{array}\right)$$

$$= \left(\begin{array}{l} 81a^4 + 108a^3\left(\frac{2}{b}\right) + 54a^2\left(\frac{4}{b^2}\right) \\ +12a\left(\frac{8}{b^3}\right) + 1\left(\frac{16}{b^4}\right) \end{array}\right)$$

$$= 81a^4 + \frac{216a^3}{b} + \frac{216a^2}{b^2} + \frac{96a}{b^3} + \frac{16}{b^4}$$

Determining Terms in the Expansion of a Binomial Power Using the General Term Formula

The general term of the expansion of the binomial $(x+y)^n$, $n \in W$ is $t_{k+1} = {}_nC_kx^{n-k}y^k$. This term and the pattern contained within it can be used to solve problems related to individual terms of any binomial expansion.

Example

Determine the 8th term in the expansion of $\left(x+\frac{2}{y}\right)^{10}$.

Solution

Step 1

Apply $t_{k+1} = {}_nC_kx^{n-k}y^k$ to determine the 8th term.

The 8th term occurs when $k = 7$. Substitute 7 for k, 10 for n, and $\frac{2}{y}$ for y.

$$t_{7+1} = {}_{10}C_7(x)^{10-7}\left(\frac{2}{y}\right)^7$$

Step 2

Simplify.

$$t_{7+1} = {}_{10}C_7(x)^{10-7}\left(\frac{2}{y}\right)^7$$
$$= 120x^3\left(\frac{2}{y}\right)^7$$
$$= \frac{15{,}360x^3}{y^7}$$

Example

Determine the middle term in the expansion of $\left(2+\frac{x}{2}\right)^{18}$.

Solution

Since the number of terms in a binomial expansion is one more than the power, the expanded form of $\left(2+\frac{x}{2}\right)^{18}$ has 19 terms.

It follows that the middle term is the $\frac{19+1}{2}=$ 10th term.

Step 1
Determine the value of k in the general term formula for a binomial expansion.

Since it is required to determine the 10th term, the value of k is 9.

Step 2
Apply the general term formula for a binomial expansion.

$t_{k+1}={}_nC_k x^{n-k}y^k$

Substitute 9 for k, 18 for n, 2 for x, and $\frac{x}{2}$ for y.

$t_{10}={}_{18}C_9(2)^{18-9}\left(\frac{x}{2}\right)^9$

Step 3
Simplify the equation.

$$\begin{aligned}t_{10}&=48{,}620(2^9)\left(\frac{x^9}{2^9}\right)\\&=48{,}620x^9\end{aligned}$$

Example

Determine the coefficient of y^4 in the expansion of $(y^2-2)^9$.

Solution

Step 1
Apply the general term formula for a binomial expansion.

$t_{k+1}={}_nC_k x^{n-k}y^k$

Substitute 9 for n, y^2 for x, and -2 for y.

$t_{(k+1)}={}_9C_k(y^2)^{9-k}(-2)^k$

Step 2
Simplify the equation by applying the power of a power law for exponents.

$t_{(k+1)}={}_9C_k(y)^{18-2k}(-2)^k$

Step 3
Determine the value of k.

When determining the coefficient of y^4, it follows that y^4 must equal y^{18-2k}.

$$\begin{aligned}4&=18-2k\\2k&=14\\k&=7\end{aligned}$$

Step 4
Substitute 7 for k in the equation $t_{(k+1)}={}_9C_k(y)^{18-2k}(-2)^k$, and then simplify.

$$\begin{aligned}t_{(7+1)}&={}_9C_7(y)^4(-2)^7\\&=36y^4(-128)\\&=-4{,}608y^4\end{aligned}$$

The coefficient of y^4 is $-4{,}608$.

Example

One term in the expansion of the binomial power $(az+4t)^7$ is $336{,}140z^4t^3$.

If $a>0$, determine the value of a to the nearest tenth.

Solution

Step 1
Determine the term number and the values of each parameter in the general term of the expansion of $(az+4t)^7$ given that one term is $336{,}140z^4t^3$.

The general term of the binomial theorem is $t_{k+1}={}_nC_kx^{n-k}y^k$.

For the binomial power $(az+4t)^7$, $n=7$, $x=az$, and $y=4t$.

Since the exponent of t is 3 in the term $336{,}140z^4t^3$, the value of k must also be 3; this is term four.

Step 2
Substitute the values of the parameters into the general term equation, and solve for a.

$$336{,}140z^4t^3 = {}_7C_3(az)^{7-3}(4t)^3$$
$$336{,}140z^4t^3 = (35)(a^4z^4)(64t^3)$$
$$336{,}140z^4t^3 = 2{,}240a^4z^4t^3$$
$$150.0625 = a^4$$
$$\sqrt[4]{150.0625} = a$$
$$3.5 = a$$

GEOMETRIC & ARITHMETIC SEQUENCES & SERIES EXERCISE #1

Use the following information to answer the next question.

A display of baseball cards is arranged in rows in such a way that the number of cards in each row forms an arithmetic sequence. There are 85 cards in row 1, 78 cards in row 2, 71 cards in row 3, and so on.

165. Which row will contain 15 cards?

A. Row 11 **B.** Row 10
C. Row 9 **D.** Row 8

166. The 30th term of the sequence 4, 8, 12, 16, ... is __________.

167. Which of the following equations represents the value of a $500 investment with a simple interest rate of 6%/*a* over several years?

A. $t_n = 30n$

B. $t_n = 3{,}000n$

C. $t_n = 500(1 + 6n)$

D. $t_n = 500(1 + 0.06n)$

168. The sum of the first 10 terms of the series 40 + 20 + 10 + 5 + ... is

A. $79\frac{59}{64}$ **B.** $422\frac{1}{2}$
C. 1,990 **D.** 81,840

Use the following information to answer the next question.

A city plans a monthly lottery where the first prize is $20,000, and the prize money will increase by 10% each month for one year.

169. To the nearest dollar, the amount of prize money that will be awarded is

A. $62,769 **B.** $240,073
C. $427,686 **D.** $627,676

170. What term in Pascal's triangle is formed by the sum ${}_7C_4 + {}_7C_5$?

A. ${}_7C_6$ **B.** ${}_7C_9$
C. ${}_8C_5$ **D.** ${}_8C_6$

171. What is the value of ${}_6C_1 + {}_6C_2 + {}_6C_3 + {}_6C_4 + {}_6C_5 + {}_6C_6$?

A. 31 **B.** 32
C. 63 **D.** 64

172. What is the sum of the first 46 terms in the arithmetic series 10 + 16 + 22 + ...?

A. 280 **B.** 286
C. 6,670 **D.** 6,808

173. The sum of the first 15 terms of the series 40, 35, 30, 25, ... is

A. 75 **B.** 115
C. 825 **D.** 1,125

174. The eighth term of the sequence $\frac{1}{2}$, 2, 8, 32, ... is __________.

Use the following information to answer the next question.

The yearly value for the first four years of an initial investment of $800.00 is given by the sequence $824.00, $848.72, $874.18, and $900.41.

175. Which of the following investments describes the sequence?

A. $800 invested at simple interest of 3%/*a*

B. $800 invested at simple interest of 1.03%/*a*

C. $800 invested at 3%/*a* compounded annually

D. $800 invested at 6%/*a* compounded semi-annually

176. Determine the general term of the sequence $\frac{1}{64}, \frac{1}{32}, \frac{1}{16}, \frac{1}{8}, \ldots$, and then find the 12th term.

177. Classify the sequence $t_n = 13 - 3n$ as arithmetic, geometric, or neither.

178. What are the first five terms of the arithmetic sequence that starts with $-\frac{2}{5}$ and has a common difference of $-\frac{4}{7}$?

A. $-\frac{2}{5}, \frac{34}{35}, -\frac{54}{35}, \frac{74}{35}, -\frac{94}{35}$

B. $-\frac{2}{5}, -\frac{34}{35}, -\frac{54}{35}, -\frac{74}{35}, -\frac{94}{35}$

C. $-\frac{2}{5}, \frac{8}{35}, -\frac{32}{245}, \frac{128}{1{,}715}, -\frac{512}{12{,}005}$

D. $-\frac{2}{5}, -\frac{8}{35}, -\frac{32}{245}, -\frac{128}{1{,}715}, -\frac{512}{12{,}005}$

179. If $\frac{3\sqrt{2}}{4}$ is the first term in a geometric sequence and the common ratio is $\sqrt{2}$, then the sixth term is

A. 6 **B.** 3

C. $6\sqrt{2}$ **D.** $3\sqrt{2}$

180. If the first three terms of a geometric sequence are $\frac{\sqrt{2}}{x}$, a, and $2\sqrt{2}x^3$, what is the fourth term?

A. $\pm 4x^4$ **B.** $\pm 4x^5$

C. $\pm 4\sqrt{2}x^6$ **D.** $\pm 4\sqrt{2}x^7$

Use the following information to answer the next question.

A cellular phone company sold 500,000 cellphones in its first month. Studies show that cellphone purchasing will increase by 8 % every month.

181. To the nearest whole number, what is the number of cellphones that the company will sell in its first 9 months?

A. 3,298,991 **B.** 4,581,364

C. 5,786,942 **D.** 6,243,779

Use the following information to answer the next question.

Andrew won a lottery and decided to donate part of his winnings. Each week, he donated 4% more to charity than he did the previous week. After 26 weeks, he had given away a total of $400,000.

182. To the nearest dollar, the initial amount that Andrew donated was $__________.

Use the following information to answer the next question.

The cost of renting a full-sized car is $38 per day plus 14 ¢ per kilometer for any distance traveled beyond 100 km per day. This chart illustrates the cost of driving a full-sized car up to 350 km per day.

Distance per Day (km)	Cost ($)
100	38.00
150	t_2
200	t_3
250	t_4
300	t_5
350	t_6

183. What is the cost of renting a full-sized car for one day and driving 350 km?

A. $66.00 **B.** $73.00
C. $80.00 **D.** $87.00

Use the following information to answer the next question.

Leroy is learning how to walk on his hands. After 1 week, he can walk for 3 seconds (s) before falling over.

184. If Leroy adds 4 s to the time he can walk on his hands for each additional week of practice, for how many seconds will he be able to walk on his hands after 6 weeks? __________ s

Use the following information to answer the next question.

In order to get in shape for a marathon, Betty decides to run 4,000 m on the first day of a 30-day month. She then increases the distance she runs by 500 m each day.

185. To the nearest meter, what is the total distance Betty runs during that month?

A. 14,500 m **B.** 18,500 m
C. 337,500 m **D.** 675,000 m

Use the following information to answer the next question.

Lauren has a summer job delivering newspapers. In the first week, she delivers newspapers to 40 houses. Each week after that, she delivers to five more houses than the previous week. Each house receives one newspaper.

186. If Lauren gets paid $0.50 per newspaper, how much money does she make in six weeks?

A. $135.45 **B.** $157.50
C. $175.00 **D.** $205.75

Use the following information to answer the next question.

In order to save money to buy a car, Renee decides to start an annuity. She deposits $500 the first month and increases the amount of each monthly deposit by $50 for a period of 15 months.

187. The value of the last deposit Renee makes is

A. $1,200 **B.** $1,900
C. $12,750 **D.** $13,125

188. Which of the following series is **not** geometric?

A. 5 + 15 + 45 + 135 + …
B. 2.4 – 6 + 15 – 37.5 + …
C. –125 – 100 – 80 – 64 – …
D. –75 + 50 – 35.5 + 23.25 – …

189. Which of the following series is geometric?

A. 104 + 52 + 26 + 13 + …

B. 7 + 14 + 21 + 28 + …

C. 3 + 9 + 81 + 729 + …

D. 256 + 16 + 4 + 2 + …

Use the following information to answer the next question.

A ping pong ball is dropped from a height of 20 m. After each bounce, the ping pong ball rises to 50% of its previous height.

190. After the first bounce, the total distance traveled by the ping pong ball before it comes to rest is

A. 20 m **B.** 30 m

C. 40 m **D.** 60 m

191. An infinite geometric series has a sum of 100 and a common ratio of $\frac{1}{5}$. What is the second term of this series?

A. 15 **B.** 16

C. 25 **D.** 26

192. If there are 17 terms in the expansion $(2x+3y)^{3n-5}$, then the value of n is

A. 5 **B.** 7

C. 17 **D.** 18

193. Which of the following expressions is the expanded form of $(5a-3b)^3$?

A. $5a^3-9a^2b+45ab^2-3b^3$

B. $125a^3-45a^2b+45ab^2-27b^3$

C. $125a^3-225a^2b+135ab^2-27b^3$

D. $375a^3-225a^2b+135ab^2-81b^3$

194. The three middle terms in the expansion of $(4x+5)^6$ are

A. $30{,}720x^5+234{,}375x^4+160{,}000x^3$

B. $96{,}000x^4+160{,}000x^3+150{,}000x^2$

C. $160{,}000x^3+150{,}000x^2+75{,}000x$

D. $1{,}500x^4+10{,}000x^3+37{,}500x^2$

195. The sixth term in the expansion of the expression $(3x+1)^7$ has a coefficient of

A. 21 **B.** 42

C. 189 **D.** 378

196. The third term of the expansion of $(x-y)^4$ is

A. $-6x^2y^2$ **B.** $6x^3y$

C. $6x^2y^2$ **D.** $6xy^3$

GEOMETRIC & ARITHMETIC SEQUENCES & SERIES EXERCISE #1 ANSWERS AND SOLUTIONS

165. A	173. A	181. D	189. A
166. 120	174. 8192	182. 9027	190. C
167. D	175. C	183. B	191. B
168. A	176. See solution	184. 23	192. B
169. C	177. See solution	185. C	193. C
170. C	178. B	186. B	194. B
171. C	179. A	187. A	195. C
172. C	180. B	188. D	196. C

165. A

An arithmetic sequence is one that increases or decreases at a constant rate. The difference between two successive terms is called the common difference.

The nth term of an arithmetic sequence is defined by the formula $t_n = a + (n - 1)d$, where n is a positive integer, t_n is the nth term, and d is the common difference.

Step 1
Identify the first term and the common difference of the sequence.
The number of cards in the first row is 85. So, $a = 85$.
Find the common difference, d, by subtracting successive terms.
$78 - 85 = -7$
$71 - 78 = -7$
The value of d is -7.

Step 2
Apply the general term formula.
Since the number of cards in the nth row is 15, the value of t_n is 15.

Substitute the known values into the general term formula, and solve for n.

$$\begin{aligned} t_n &= a + (n - 1)d \\ 15 &= 85 + (n - 1)(-7) \\ 15 &= 85 - 7n + 7 \\ 15 &= -7n + 92 \\ -77 &= -7n \\ 11 &= n \end{aligned}$$

The 11th row will contain 15 cards.

166. 120

The sequence is arithmetic with a first term of $a = 4$ and a common difference of $d = 4$. Substitute these values into the formula $t_n = a + (n - 1)d$.

$$\begin{aligned} t_n &= a + (n - 1)d \\ t_{30} &= 4 + (30 - 1)(4) \\ t_{30} &= 4 + 116 \\ t_{30} &= 120 \end{aligned}$$

167. D

Step 1
Calculate the interest earned each year.

$$\begin{aligned} I &= Prt \\ &= (500)(0.06)(1) \\ &= \$30 \end{aligned}$$

Step 2
Determine the sequence.
The value of the investment at the end of each year would form the arithmetic sequence \$530, \$560, \$590,... with a common difference of \$30.

Step 3
Determine the general term equation using the formula $t_n = a + (n - 1)d$.

Substitute 530 for a and 30 for d.

$$\begin{aligned} t_n &= a + (n - 1)d \\ &= 530 + (n - 1)(30) \\ &= 500 + 30n \\ &= 500(1 + 0.06n) \end{aligned}$$

168. A

The series is geometric with a first term of $a = 40$ and a common ratio of $r = \frac{20}{40} = \frac{1}{2}$. Substitute these values into the formula $S_n = \frac{a(r^n - 1)}{r - 1}$.

$$S_n = \frac{a(r^n - 1)}{r - 1}$$

$$S_{10} = \frac{40\left(\left(\frac{1}{2}\right)^{10} - 1\right)}{\frac{1}{2} - 1}$$

$$= \frac{40\left(\frac{1}{1{,}024} - 1\right)}{-\frac{1}{2}}$$

$$= -80\left(-\frac{1{,}023}{1{,}024}\right)$$

$$= 5\left(\frac{1{,}023}{64}\right)$$

$$= \frac{5{,}115}{64}$$

$$= 79\frac{59}{64}$$

169. C

The 12 prizes will form a geometric series with a first term of $a = \$20{,}000$.

Step 1
Find the common ratio.
$r = 1 + 10\%$
$r = 1 + 0.1$
$r = 1.1$

Step 2
Substitute the variables into the formula $S_n = \frac{a(r^n - 1)}{r - 1}$.

$$S_n = \frac{a(r^n - 1)}{r - 1}$$

$$S_{12} = \frac{20{,}000(1.1^{12} - 1)}{1.1 - 1}$$

$$S_{12} = \$427{,}686$$

170. C

The sum of two consecutive terms in a row of Pascal's triangle gives the value of the term in the row below, located directly between the two given terms. In general, ${}_nC_r + {}_nC_{r+1} = {}_{n+1}C_{r+1}$. Thus, ${}_7C_4 + {}_7C_5 = {}_8C_5$.

171. C

From Pascal's triangle, the sum ${}_6C_0 + {}_6C_1 + {}_6C_2 + {}_6C_3 + {}_6C_4 + {}_6C_5 + {}_6C_6$ equals 2^6, or 64.

The sum ${}_6C_1 + {}_6C_2 + {}_6C_3 + {}_6C_4 + {}_6C_5 + {}_6C_6$ is missing the term ${}_6C_0$, which has a value of 1.

Therefore, the sum is $64 - 1 = 63$.

172. C

Step 1
Identify the values of a, n and d, where a represents the first term, n represents the number of terms and d represents the common difference.
$a = 10$
$n = 46$
$d = 16 - 10 = 6$

Step 2
Substitute into the appropriate sum formula, and simplify.
Determine the sum of the first 46 terms of the given arithmetic sequence by applying the formula

$S_n = \frac{n}{2}(2a + (n - 1)d)$.

Substitute 10 for a, 46 for n, and 6 for d in the given sum formula.

$$S_{46} = \frac{46}{2}[2(10) + (46 - 1)6]$$

$$S_{46} = \frac{46}{2}[2(10) + 45(6)]$$

$$S_{46} = 23(20 + 270)$$

$$S_{46} = 23(290)$$

$$S_{46} = 6{,}670$$

173. A

This is an arithmetic series with a first term of $a = 40$ and a common difference of $d = -5$. Substitute these values into the formula $S_n = \frac{n}{2}(2a + (n - 1)d)$ to find the sum of the first 15 terms of the series.

$$S_n = \frac{n}{2}(2a + (n - 1)d)$$

$$S_{15} = \frac{15}{2}(2(40) + (15 - 1)(-5))$$

$$S_{15} = 7.5(80 - 70)$$

$$S_{15} = 75$$

174. 8192

Step 1
Determine the first differences of the sequence.

$2 - \frac{1}{2} = 1.5$
$8 - 2 = 6$
$32 - 8 = 24$

The differences are not constant, so this sequence is not arithmetic.

Step 2
Determine the ratio of consecutive terms of the sequence.

$\frac{2}{\frac{1}{2}} = 4$
$\frac{8}{2} = 4$
$\frac{32}{8} = 4$

The ratios are constant, a common ratio, so this sequence is geometric.

Step 3
Determine the general term formula for the given sequence using $t_n = ar^{n-1}$.

The sequence is geometric with a first term of $a = \frac{1}{2}$ and a common ratio of $r = 4$. Substitute into the formula $t_n = ar^{n-1}$.

$$t_n = ar^{n-1}$$
$$= \frac{1}{2}(4)^{n-1}$$

Step 4
Substitute 8 for n, and solve.

$$t_n = \frac{1}{2}(4)^{n-1}$$
$$t_8 = \frac{1}{2}(4)^{8-1}$$
$$t_8 = \frac{1}{2}(4)^7$$
$$t_8 = \frac{1}{2}(16{,}384)$$
$$t_8 = 8{,}192$$

175. C

Step 1
Determine the common difference between consecutive terms in the sequence.

$848.72 - 824 = 24.72$
$874.18 - 848.72 = 25.46$
$900.41 - 874.18 = 26.23$

There is no common difference since the differences are not constant (24.72, 25.46, and 26.23).

Step 2
Determine the common ratio between consecutive terms.

$\frac{848.72}{824} = 1.03$
$\frac{874.18}{848.72} = 1.03$
$\frac{900.41}{80{,}074.18} = 1.03$

The common ratio is 1.03.

Step 3
Determine the interest rate.

Because the given sequence is geometric, the function that represents the sequence must represent compound interest.

The function $f(x) = 800(1.03)^x$ will generate the terms of the sequence.
Comparing the function to the compound interest formula $A = P(1 + i)^n$, this function describes a principal amount of \$800 invested at 3%/*a* compounded annually.

176.

Step 1
Determine the general term of the sequence.
The sequence is geometric. The first term (a) is $\frac{1}{64}$, and the common ratio (r) is 2. Substitute the values into the formula for the general term $t_n = ar^{n-1}$, and solve.

$$t_n = \frac{1}{64}(2)^{n-1}$$
$$= (2^{-6})(2)^{n-1}$$
$$= 2^{-6+n-1}$$
$$= 2^{n-7}$$

Therefore, the general term of the sequence is $t_n = 2^{n-7}$.

Step 2
Find the 12th term.

$$t_{12} = 2^{12-7}$$
$$= 2^5$$
$$= 32$$

Therefore, the 12th term is 32.

177.

Step 1
Determine the terms of the sequence.

$t_n = 13 - 3n$
$t_1 = 13 - 3(1)$
$= 10$
$t_2 = 13 - 3(2)$
$= 7$
$t_3 = 13 - 3(3)$
$= 4$
$t_4 = 13 - 3(4)$
$= 1$

Therefore, the sequence is 10, 7, 4, 1, …

Step 2
Determine the first differences of the sequence.

$7 - 10 = -3$
$4 - 7 = -3$
$1 - 4 = -3$

These are constant.

Step 3
Determine the ratio of consecutive terms.

$\frac{7}{10} = 0.7$

$\frac{4}{7} \approx 0.57$

$\frac{1}{4} = 0.25$

These are not constant.
Therefore, this sequence is arithmetic.

178. B

Step 1
Determine the value of the second term.

The first term is $-\frac{2}{5}$, and each subsequent term can be determined by adding $-\frac{4}{7}$ to the previous term.

$t_1 = -\frac{2}{5}$

$t_2 = -\frac{2}{5} + \left(-\frac{4}{7}\right)$
$= -\frac{2}{5}\left(\frac{7}{7}\right) + \left(-\frac{4}{7}\right)\left(\frac{5}{5}\right)$
$= -\frac{14}{35} - \frac{20}{35}$
$= -\frac{34}{35}$

Step 2
Determine the third, fourth, and fifth terms.

$t_2 = -\frac{34}{35}$

$t_3 = -\frac{34}{35} + \left(-\frac{4}{7}\right)$
$= -\frac{54}{35}$

$t_4 = -\frac{54}{35} + \left(-\frac{4}{7}\right)$
$= -\frac{74}{35}$

$t_5 = -\frac{74}{35} + \left(-\frac{4}{7}\right)$
$= -\frac{94}{35}$

The first five terms in this arithmetic sequence are $-\frac{2}{5}, -\frac{34}{35}, -\frac{54}{35}, -\frac{74}{35}$, and $-\frac{94}{35}$.

179. A

Generate the sequence to determine the sixth term. To generate this sequence, multiply each successive term by $\sqrt{2}$, beginning with the first term, $\frac{3\sqrt{2}}{4}$.

$t_2 = t_1 \times r$
$= \frac{3\sqrt{2}}{4} \times \sqrt{2}$
$= \frac{3}{2}$

$t_3 = t_2 \times r$
$= \frac{3}{2} \times \sqrt{2}$
$= \frac{3\sqrt{2}}{2}$

$t_4 = t_3 \times r$
$= \frac{3\sqrt{2}}{2} \times \sqrt{2}$
$= 3$

$t_5 = t_4 \times r$
$= 3 \times \sqrt{2}$
$= 3\sqrt{2}$

$t_6 = t_5 \times r$
$= 3\sqrt{2} \times \sqrt{2}$
$= 6$

180. B

Step 1
Determine the value of a.

Since the given sequence is geometric, there is a common ratio between each pair of successive terms. As such, $\frac{t_2}{t_1} = \frac{t_3}{t_2}$.

$$\frac{\frac{a}{\sqrt{2}}}{x} = \frac{2\sqrt{2}x^3}{a}$$
$$a^2 = \left(2\sqrt{2}x^3\right)\left(\frac{\sqrt{2}}{x}\right)$$
$$a^2 = 2\sqrt{4}x^2$$
$$a^2 = 4x^2$$
$$a = \pm\sqrt{4x^2}$$
$$a = \pm 2x$$

Step 2
Since the second term is $a = \pm 2x$, there are two possible values for the common ratio r.

Find the common ratio when $a = 2x$.

$$\begin{aligned} r &= \frac{t_2}{t_1} \\ &= \frac{2x}{\frac{\sqrt{2}}{x}} \\ &= \frac{2x^2}{\sqrt{2}} \\ &= \sqrt{2}x^2 \end{aligned}$$

Find the common ratio when $a = -2x$.

$$\begin{aligned} r &= \frac{t_2}{t_1} \\ &= \frac{-2x}{\frac{\sqrt{2}}{x}} \\ &= \frac{-2x^2}{\sqrt{2}} \\ &= -\sqrt{2}x^2 \end{aligned}$$

The common ratio is $\pm\sqrt{2}x^2$.

Step 3
Determine the fourth term by multiplying the common ratio by the third term.

$$\begin{aligned} t_4 &= t_3 \times r \\ &= 2\sqrt{2}x^3 \times \sqrt{2}x^2 \\ &= 4x^5 \end{aligned}$$

$$\begin{aligned} t_4 &= t_3 \times r \\ &= 2\sqrt{2}x^3 \times (-\sqrt{2})x^2 \\ &= -4x^5 \end{aligned}$$

The fourth term is $\pm 4x^5$.

181. D

The monthly cellphone sales will form a geometric series with a first term of $a = 500{,}000$ and a common ratio of r.

$r = 1 + 8\%$
$r = 1 + 0.08$
$r = 1.08$

Since the sum of the first 9 terms equals the number of cellphones sold in 9 months, substitute the given values into the formula for the sum of a geometric series, $S_n = \frac{a(r^n - 1)}{r - 1}$.

$$S_n = \frac{a(r^n - 1)}{r - 1}$$
$$S_9 = \frac{500{,}000((1.08)^9 - 1)}{1.08 - 1}$$
$$S_9 \approx 6{,}243{,}778.919$$

The company can expect to sell approximately 6,243,779 cellphones in the first 9 months of business.

182. 9027

The 26 weeks will form a geometric series with a final sum of $S_{26} = \$400{,}000$.

Step 1
Find the common ratio.

$r = 1 + 4\%$
$r = 1 + 0.04$
$r = 1.04$

Step 2
Substitute the values into the formula $S_n = \frac{a(r^n - 1)}{r - 1}$.

$$S_n = \frac{a(r^n - 1)}{r - 1}$$
$$S_{26} = \frac{a(1.04^{26} - 1)}{1.04 - 1}$$
$$(400{,}000)\frac{1.04 - 1}{1.04^{26} - 1} = a$$
$$\$9{,}026.95 \approx a$$

To the nearest dollar, Andrew's initial donation was $9,027.

183. B

Step 1
Determine the common difference.

The amount of money charged for each 50 km over the daily amount of kilometers is the common difference.

$0.14 / km × 50 km = $7.00

Therefore, the common difference is $7.00.

Step 2
Finish the table, and determine the value of t_6.

This process is illustrated in the given table.

Distance per Day (km)	Cost ($)
100	38.00
150	t_2 = 38.00 + 7.00 = 45.00
200	t_3 = 45.00 + 7.00 = 52.00
250	t_4 = 52.00 + 7.00 = 59.00
300	t_5 = 59.00 + 7.00 = 66.00
350	t_6 = 66.00 + 7.00 = 73.00

Therefore, it costs $73.00 to rent a full-sized car for one day and drive 350 km.

184. 23

To calculate the time he can walk on his hands after 6 weeks, add 4 s to his total time for each week until he reaches 6 weeks.

Week of Practice	Time (s)
1	3
2	3 + 4 = 7
3	7 + 4 = 11
4	11 + 4 = 15
5	15 + 4 = 19
6	19 + 4 = 23

After practicing for 6 weeks, Leroy should be able to walk on his hands for 23 s.

185. C

The 30 distances Betty runs form an arithmetic series with a first term of a = 4,000 m and a common difference of d = 500 m. The total distance that Betty runs is the sum of the 30 terms. Substitute the given variables into the formula $S_n = \frac{n}{2}(2a + (n-1)d)$.

$$S_n = \frac{n}{2}(2a + (n-1)d)$$
$$S_{30} = \frac{30}{2}(2(4{,}000) + (30 - 1)(500))$$
$$= 15(8{,}000 + 14{,}500)$$
$$= 337{,}500 \text{ m}$$

186. B

To find the amount of money Lauren earns in six weeks, find the total number of newspapers she delivers.

In order to determine the total number of newspapers Lauren delivers, determine the sum of the first six terms of the arithmetic series.

Step 1
Determine the number of newspapers delivered.

Use the sum formula $S_n = \frac{n}{2}[2a + (n-1)d]$, where n = 6, a = 40, and d = 5.

$$S_n = \frac{n}{2}[2a + (n-1)d]$$
$$S_n = \frac{6}{2}[2(40) + (6 - 1)5]$$
$$S_n = 3[80 + (5)5]$$
$$S_n = 3[105]$$
$$S_n = 315$$

The number of newspapers delivered is 315.

Step 2
Determine the amount of money earned.

Multiply $0.50 by the total number of newspapers delivered.
0.50 × 315 = 157.5

Lauren earned $157.50 in six weeks.

187. A

The 15 deposits form an arithmetic sequence with a first term of a = $500 and a common difference of d = $50.

The last deposit is the 15th term, so substitute n = 15 into the formula $t_n = a + (n-1)d$.

$$t_n = a + (n-1)d$$
$$t_{15} = 500 + (15 - 1)50$$
$$= \$1{,}200$$

188. D

A series is geometric if it is a summation of terms of a geometric sequence. In turn, a sequence is geometric if terms are generated by multiplying previous terms by a constant. This constant is called the common ratio and is denoted by *r*.

Step 1

Determine if the series 5 + 15 + 45 + 135 + ... is geometric by determining if there is a common ratio between the terms.

$$\frac{15}{5} = 3$$
$$\frac{45}{15} = 3$$
$$\frac{135}{45} = 3$$

Since the ratio between each pair of terms is constant, the series is geometric.

Step 2

Determine if the series 2.4 – 6 + 15 – 37.5 + ... is geometric by determining if there is a common ratio between the terms.

$$\frac{-6}{2.4} = -2.5$$
$$\frac{15}{-6} = -2.5$$
$$\frac{-37.5}{15} = -2.5$$

Since the ratio between each pair of terms is constant, the series is geometric.

Step 3

Determine if the series –125 – 100 – 80 – 64 – ... is geometric by determining if there is a common ratio between the terms.

$$\frac{-100}{-125} = 0.8$$
$$\frac{-80}{-100} = 0.8$$
$$\frac{-64}{-80} = 0.8$$

Since the ratio between each pair of terms is constant, the series is geometric.

Step 4

Determine if the series –75 + 50 – 35.5 + 23.25 – ... is geometric by determining if there is a common ratio between the terms.

$$\frac{50}{-75} \approx -0.67$$
$$\frac{-35.5}{50} = -0.71$$
$$\frac{23.25}{-35.5} \approx -0.65$$

Since the ratio between each pair of terms is not constant, the series is not geometric.

189. A

A series is geometric if it is a summation of terms of a geometric sequence. In turn, a sequence is geometric if terms are generated by multiplying previous terms by a constant. This constant is called the common ratio and is denoted by *r*.

Step 1

Determine if the series 104 + 52 + 26 + 13 + ... is geometric.

Determine if there is a common ratio between the terms.

$$\frac{52}{104} = 0.5$$
$$\frac{26}{52} = 0.5$$
$$\frac{13}{26} = 0.5$$

Since the ratio between each pair of terms is constant, the series is geometric.

Step 2

Determine if the series 7 + 14 + 21 + 28 + ... is geometric.

Determine if there is a common ratio between the terms.

$$\frac{14}{7} = 2$$
$$\frac{21}{14} = 1.5$$
$$\frac{28}{21} \approx 1.3$$

Since the ratio between each pair of terms is not constant, the series is not geometric.

Step 3

Determine if the series 3 + 9 + 81 + 729 + … is geometric.

Determine if there is a common ratio between the terms.

$\frac{9}{3} = 3$

$\frac{81}{9} = 9$

$\frac{729}{81} = 9$

Since the ratio between each pair of terms is not constant, the series is not geometric.

Step 4

Determine if the series 256 + 16 + 4 + 2 + … is geometric.

Determine if there is a common ratio between the terms.

$\frac{16}{256} = 0.0625$

$\frac{4}{16} = 0.25$

$\frac{2}{4} = 0.5$

Since the ratio between each pair of terms is not constant, the series is not geometric.

190. C

The ping pong ball was dropped from a height of 20 m. After each bounce, the ping pong ball rose to 50% of its previous height.

The heights reached after each bounce are given as follows:

- After the first bounce: 50% of 20 m = 10 m
- After the second bounce: 50% of 10 m = 5 m
- After the third bounce: 50% of 5 m = 2.5 m

This pattern continues until the ball is at rest.

Adding these values gives an infinite geometric series, 10, 5, 2.5 ..., with common ratio $r = 0.5$ and first term $a = 10$.

The sum of all terms in the series can be determined as follows:

$$S = \frac{a}{1-r}$$

$$= \frac{10}{1-0.5} = \frac{10}{0.5}$$

$$= 20$$

The value of 20 m gives the sum of the heights reached by the ball after each bounce. However, since the ping pong ball travels up and then back down through each calculated height, the total distance traveled by the ball after the first bounce can be determined by doubling this value.

The total distance traveled by the ball after the first bounce before it finally comes to rest is given by the equation $d = 2 \times 20 = 40$ m.

191. B

The common ratio of the series is $\frac{1}{5}$, which is less than 1. Thus, the sum of the series can be calculated using the following formula:

$$S = \frac{a}{1-r}$$

The sum of the series is 100. Thus, the first term of the series can be determined as follows:

$$100 = \frac{a}{1-\left(\frac{1}{5}\right)}$$

$$100 = \frac{a}{\frac{4}{5}}$$

$$100\left(\frac{4}{5}\right) = a$$

$$80 = a$$

The first term of the series is 80.

The second term of the series can be calculated using the following formula:

$$t_n = ar^{n-1}$$

$$t_2 = ar^1$$

$$= ar$$

$$= 80 \times \frac{1}{5}$$

$$= 16$$

192. B

There are $n + 1$ terms in the binomial expansion of $(x + y)^n$. This means that there are $(3n - 5) + 1$ terms in the expansion $(2x + 3y)^{3n-5}$.

If the number of terms in the expansion $(2x+3y)^{3n-5}$ is 17, then let $(3n-5)+1=17$, and solve for n.

$$\begin{aligned}(3n-5)+1&=17\\ 3n-5&=16\\ 3n&=21\\ n&=7\end{aligned}$$

The value of n is 7.

193. C

Step 1

Write the expansion for $(x+y)^3$ by applying the binomial theorem.

$$(x+y)^3={}_3C_0x^3+{}_3C_1x^2y+{}_3C_2xy^2+{}_3C_3y^3$$

Step 2

In the expansion of $(x+y)^3$, replace x by $5a$ and y by $-3b$, and then simplify.

$$\begin{aligned}&(5a-3b)^3\\ &={}_3C_0(5a)^3+{}_3C_1(5a)^2(-3b)\\ &+{}_3C_2(5a)(-3b)^2+{}_3C_3(-3b)^3\\ &=(1)(125a^3)+(3)(25a^2)(-3b)\\ &+3(5a)(9b^2)+(1)(-27b^3)\\ &=125a^3-225a^2b+135ab^2-27b^3\end{aligned}$$

194. B

Step 1

Write the expansion for $(x+y)^6$ using the binomial theorem, and identify the three middle terms.

$$(x+y)^6=\begin{pmatrix}{}_6C_0x^6+{}_6C_1x^5y+{}_6C_2x^4y^2+{}_6C_3x^3y^3\\ +{}_6C_4x^2y^4+{}_6C_5xy^5+{}_6C_6y^6\end{pmatrix}$$

The three middle terms are ${}_6C_2x^4y^2+{}_6C_3x^3y^3$ $+{}_6C_4x^2y^4$.

Step 2

In the three middle terms of the expansion of $(x+y)^6$, replace x by $4x$ and y by 5. Simplify.

$$\begin{aligned}&{}_6C_2(4x)^4(5)^2+{}_6C_3(4x)^3(5)^3+{}_6C_4(4x)^2(5)^4\\ &=\begin{pmatrix}(15)(256x^4)25\\ +\ (20)64x^3(125)\\ +\ (15)(16x^2)(625)\end{pmatrix}\\ &=96{,}000x^4+160{,}000x^3+150{,}000x^2\end{aligned}$$

195. C

Step 1

Interpret all given information and apply the formula for terms of a binomial expansion.

The $(r+1)$th term in the binomial expansion of $(x+y)^n$ is ${}_nC_rx^{n-r}y^r$.

To find the sixth term, let $r=5$.

Substitute $n=7$, $r=5$, $x=3x$, and $y=1$into the expression.

$${}_nC_rx^{n-r}y^r={}_7C_5(3x)^21^5$$

Step 2

Simplify the expression.

$$\begin{aligned}{}_7C_5(3x)^21^5&=\frac{7!}{(7-5)!\,5!}(9x^2)(1)\\ &=\frac{7!}{(2)!\,5!}(9x^2)\\ &=189x^2\end{aligned}$$

The coefficient of the sixth term is 189.

196. C

The $(r+1)^{\text{th}}$ term of the binomial expansion of $(x-y)^n$ is ${}_nC_rx^{n-r}(-y)^r$.

Step 1

Determine an expression for the third term.

To find the third term of the expansion, substitute $n=4$ and $r=2$.

$${}_nC_rx^{n-r}(-y)^r={}_4C_2(x)^2(-y)^2$$

Step 2

Evaluate the coefficient and simplify.

$$\begin{aligned}{}_4C_2(x)^2(-y)^2&=\frac{4!}{(4-2)!\,2!}(x^2)(y^2)\\ &=\left(\frac{4!}{2!\,2!}\right)x^2y^2\\ &=\left(\frac{4\times3\times2\times1}{2\times1\times2\times1}\right)x^2y^2\\ &=6x^2y^2\end{aligned}$$

Therefore, the third term of the expansion of $(x-y)^4$ is $6x^2y^2$.

GEOMETRIC & ARITHMETIC SEQUENCES & SERIES EXERCISE #2

Use the following information to answer the next question.

The general term of a sequence is given by the equation $t_n = 3n + 5$.

197. This sequence is

A. arithmetic with a common difference of 3

B. arithmetic with a common difference of 5

C. geometric with a common ratio of 3

D. geometric with a common ratio of 5

198. In simplified form, determine the equation for the general term of the sequence $-5, -1, 3, 7, \ldots$, and find which term in the sequence has a value of 203.

199. For the geometric series $256 + 192 + 144 + \ldots$, the value of S_{12}, to the nearest hundredth, is

A. 980.75 **B.** 991.56

C. 4,353.98 **D.** 5,869.30

200. The sum of the terms in the sixth row of Pascal's triangle is

A. 16 **B.** 32

C. 64 **D.** 96

201. The value of the sixth term in the tenth row of Pascal's triangle is __________.

202. Which of the following sequences is arithmetic?

A. 5, 25, 125, 625, …

B. 5, 10, 15, 20, …

C. 5, 10, 20, 40, …

D. 5, 7, 11, 17, …

203. The sum of the first 10 terms of the arithmetic series $72 + 69 + 66 + \ldots$ is

A. 1,170 **B.** 615

C. 585 **D.** 570

204. Which of the following sequences is neither arithmetic nor geometric?

A. $\frac{1}{2}, 1, \frac{3}{2}, 2, \ldots$

B. $\frac{1}{2}, 1, \frac{3}{2}, \frac{5}{2}, \ldots$

C. $\frac{1}{2}, -1, 2, -4, \ldots$

D. $\frac{1}{2}, -1, -\frac{5}{2}, -4, \ldots$

205. Which of the following general terms would generate a geometric sequence?

A. $t_n = 4n$

B. $t_n = 4^n$

C. $t_n = 4n^2$

D. $t_1 = 4,\ t_n = 4t_{n-1} + 4,\ n > 1$

Use the following information to answer the next question.

In a geometric sequence, the 4th term is −80, the 8th term is −1,280 and the first term, *a*, is a positive whole number.

206. The value of *a* is

207. Which of the following functions would generate the sequence 4, 8, 12, 16, …?

A. $f(x) = 2^x,\ x \in N,\ x \geq 2$

B. $f(x) = 4(x + 1),\ x \in W$

C. $f(x) = 4x + 8,\ x \in W$

D. $f(x) = 2x^2,\ x \in N$

Use the following information to answer the next question.

A sequence with a first term of 3 is formed by multiplying each preceding number by 2 to obtain the next term.

208. The sixth term in the sequence is ________.

209. If $\frac{y^2}{x}$, a, b, $\frac{x^2}{y}$, and $\frac{x^3}{y^2}$ are five consecutive terms in a geometric sequence, what are the values of a and b?

A. $a = y,\ b = x$

B. $a = x,\ b = xy$

C. $a = \frac{1}{x},\ b = \frac{x}{y}$

D. $a = \frac{1}{x},\ b = \frac{1}{y}$

Use the following information to answer the next question.

Jane deposits $500 at the beginning of each month into an account earning interest at 6%/*a*, compounded monthly.

210. The total value of her investment after one year is

A. $6,016.27 **B.** $6,030.00

C. $6,167.78 **D.** $6,198.62

Use the following information to answer the next question.

Over a period of five years, the price of an ice-cream sundae at an ice-cream shop increased by $0.20 each year. In the fifth year, the price of an ice-cream sundae was $2.20.

211. If the price continues to increase by the same amount each year, in the ninth year, the price of an ice-cream sundae will be $__________.

Use the following information to answer the next question.

Soup cans are arranged in layers such that an arithmetic sequence is formed. There are 46 cans in the bottom layer and 16 cans in the top layer.

212. If there are 6 layers of soup cans, then the number of cans in the display is

A. 168 **B.** 186

C. 292 **D.** 310

Use the following information to answer the next question.

During the summer holidays, Jeremy is collecting pop cans. He collects 12 pop cans on day 1, 16 pop cans on day 2, 20 pop cans on day 3, and so on.

213. If the number of pop cans that Jeremy collects each day forms an arithmetic sequence, then Jeremy will collect 100 pop cans on day

A. 21 **B.** 23

C. 27 **D.** 29

214. Which of the following series is geometric?

A. 1 + 3 + 5 + 7 + …

B. 4 + 16 + 28 + 40 + …

C. 7 + 21 + 63 + 189 + …

D. 25 + 20 + 15 + 10 + …

215. Which of the following series is geometric?

A. $1 - 2 + 4 - 16 + \ldots$

B. $5 - 8 + 18 - 34 + \ldots$

C. $135 - 90 + 60 - 40 + \ldots$

D. $150 - 110 + 70 - 30 + \ldots$

Use the following information to answer the next question.

A ball falls and strikes the floor before rebounding to $\frac{3}{5}$ of the height from which it has fallen. It then continues to fall and rebound each time to $\frac{3}{5}$ of its previous height until it comes to rest.

216. If the ball is dropped from a height of 130 m, the total distance that the ball travels before coming to rest is

A. 325 m **B.** 390 m

C. 520 m **D.** 650 m

217. Steve expresses the recurring decimal $0.\bar{4}$ in the form of an infinite geometric series. From the series, he deduces the value of $(0.444\ldots)^{\frac{1}{2}}$. What is its value in fraction form?

A. $\frac{2}{5}$ **B.** $\frac{2}{3}$

C. $\frac{4}{5}$ **D.** $\frac{1}{2}$

218. What is the sum of the coefficients of the terms in the expansion of the binomial $(2x - 3)^4$?

A. 0 **B.** 1

C. 16 **D.** 625

219. What are the first three terms in the expanded form of the binomial $\left(4x - \frac{2}{x}\right)^6$?

A. $4{,}096x^6 - 12{,}288x^4 + 15{,}360x^2$

B. $4{,}096x^6 - 12{,}288x^5 + 15{,}360x^4$

C. $24x^6 - 120x^4 + 240x^2$

D. $24x^6 - 120x^5 + 240x^4$

220. The fourth term in the expansion of the expression $(2x - 3y)^7$ has a numerical coefficient of

A. $-15{,}120$ **B.** -35

C. 35 **D.** 15,120

221. In the expansion of $\left[x^3 - \frac{3}{x^2}\right]^{10}$, the value of the constant term is

A. $-153{,}090$

B. -210

C. 210

D. 153,090

Conics

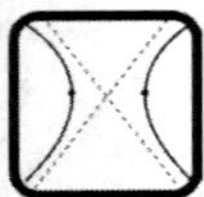

CONICS

Table of Correlations

Standard		Concepts	Exercise #1	Exercise #2
PC.5	The student uses conic sections, their properties, and parametric representations, as well as tools and technology, to model physical situations.			
PC. 5.A	*Use conic sections to model motion, such as the graph of velocity vs. position of a pendulum and motions of planets.*	Solving Problems Using Conic Sections	222, 223	258
		Determining the Key Characteristics of a Circle from the Standard Form Equation	224, 225	259
		Determining the Equation of a Circle when Given Key Characteristics	226, 227	260
		Determining the Equation of a Circle from a Graph	228, 229	261
		Determining the Key Characteristics of an Ellipse Given the Standard Form Equation	230, 231	262
		Determining the Equation of an Ellipse when Given Key Characteristics	232, 233	263
		Determining the Equation of an Ellipse When Given the Graph	234, 235	264
		Determining Key Characteristics of a Hyperbola Given the Standard Form Equation	236, 237	265
		Determining the Equation of a Hyperbola Given Key Characteristics	238, 239	266
		Determining the Equation of a Hyperbola Given the Graph	240, 241	267
		Determining Key Characteristics of a Parabola Given the Standard Form Equation	242, 243	268
		Determining the Equation of a Parabola when Given Key Characteristics	244, 245	269
		Determining the Equation of a Parabola from a Given Graph	246, 247	270
PC. 5.B	*Use properties of conic sections to describe physical phenomena such as the reflective properties of light and sound.*	Solving Problems Using Conic Sections	222, 223	258
		Determining the Key Characteristics of a Circle from the Standard Form Equation	224, 225	259
		Determining the Equation of a Circle when Given Key Characteristics	226, 227	260
		Determining the Equation of a Circle from a Graph	228, 229	261
		Determining the Key Characteristics of an Ellipse Given the Standard Form Equation	230, 231	262
		Determining the Equation of an Ellipse when Given Key Characteristics	232, 233	263
		Determining the Equation of an Ellipse When Given the Graph	234, 235	264
		Determining Key Characteristics of a Hyperbola Given the Standard Form Equation	236, 237	265

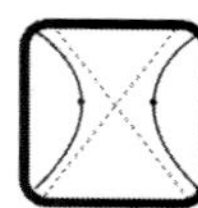

		Determining the Equation of a Hyperbola Given Key Characteristics	238, 239	266
		Determining the Equation of a Hyperbola Given the Graph	240, 241	267
		Determining Key Characteristics of a Parabola Given the Standard Form Equation	242, 243	268
		Determining the Equation of a Parabola when Given Key Characteristics	244, 245	269
		Determining the Equation of a Parabola from a Given Graph	246, 247	270
PC. 5.C	*Convert between parametric and rectangular forms of functions and equations to graph them.*	Sketching Parametric Equations	248, 249	271
		Determining Cartesian Form from Parametric Form	250, 251	272
		Graphing Parametric Equations with Technology	252, 253	273
		Determining the Parametric Form of an Equation from the Cartesian Form	254, 255	274
PC. 5.D	*Use parametric functions to simulate problems involving motion.*	Modeling Projectile Motion Using Parametric Functions	256, 257	275

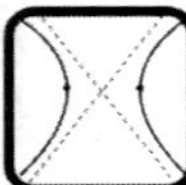

PC.5.A Use conic sections to model motion, such as the graph of velocity vs. position of a pendulum and motions of planets.

Solving Problems Using Conic Sections

For thousands of years, people have been building and experimenting with the principles of conic sections. In the 16th century, Galileo fired projectiles from the top of a tower and discovered that they fell along parabolic paths. Kepler and Newton developed theories describing planetary motion based on elliptical paths. More recently, scientists have launched satellites that travel elliptically around Earth. Bridges and tunnels are designed with conic section shapes because of their load-bearing capacity.

Using conic sections or quadratic relations, practical problems can be modeled and solved.

Example

An overpass above a highway forms a parabolic arch as shown.

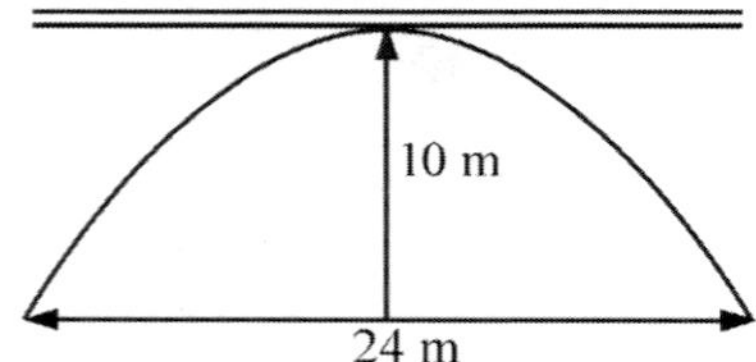

The arch is 24 m wide and 10 m high.

If the top of the arch is considered to be at the origin of a coordinate system, determine an equation in standard form that could be used to describe the arch.

Solution

Step 1
Draw a sketch of the arch on a coordinate grid. Assume that every unit on the grid is equivalent to 1 m (the *x*- and *y*-axis are both measured in meters).

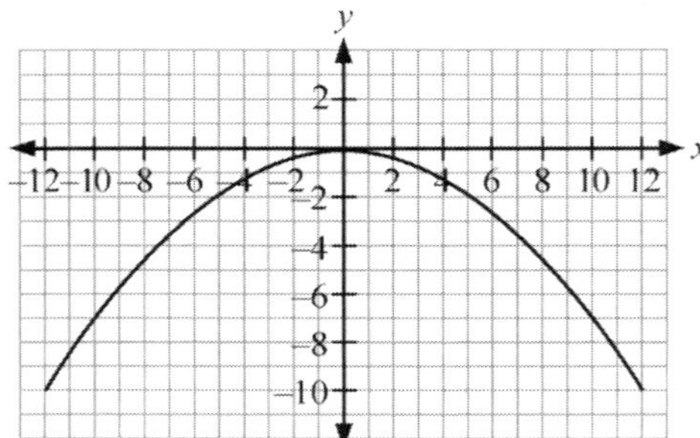

Step 2
Determine the standard form of the parabola represented by the arch.
Since the parabola opens down, the general standard form is $y - k = a(x - h)^2$.

Step 3
Substitute 0 for h and 0 for k in the equation $y - k = a(x - h)^2$ since the vertex of the parabola is at the origin.

$$y - 0 = a(x - 0)^2$$
$$y = ax^2$$

Step 4
Determine a point on the parabola other than the origin.
The endpoints of the arch are 24 m apart and 10 m below the highest point. Therefore, two points on the parabola are located at the ordered pairs (−12, −10) and (12, −10), representing 12 m to the left and to the right and 10 m below the vertex.

Step 5
Using the point (12, −10), substitute 12 for x and −10 for y in the equation $y = ax^2$ in order to solve for a.

$$-10 = a(12)^2$$
$$-10 = 144a$$
$$\frac{-10}{144} = a$$
$$a = \frac{-5}{72}$$

Step 6
Write an equation that describes the arch.
An equation that describes the arch is $y = -\frac{5}{72}x^2$, with the domain $-12 \le x \le 12$.

Determine an equation of the parabola if the base of the arch is considered to be on the x-axis.

Solution

If the base of the arch is now on the x-axis instead of its vertex being located at the origin, the graph that illustrates the newly located arch is translated 10 units up. As such, the equation defining the parabola with vertex at the origin will be transformed from $y = -\frac{5}{72}x^2$ to $y = -\frac{5}{72}x^2 + 10$.

The equation is $y = -\frac{5}{72}x^2 + 10$, $-12 \le x \le 12$.

Once the shape of a structure is successfully modeled with a quadratic relation, some additional practical problems may be investigated.

Would a truck with a load 16 m wide and 6 m high be able to drive on the highway beneath the arch?

Solution

If the truck were to drive under the overpass through the center of the arch, one-half of the truck's 16 m width would be on each side of the center. This means 8 m of the load would be on either side of the center of the parabolic arch. This value of 8 m corresponds to a horizontal coordinate (x-coordinate).

To determine whether a 6 m tall load would pass under the arch, determine the corresponding y-coordinate by substituting 8 for x in the equation $y = -\frac{5}{72}x^2 + 10$.

Recall that the center of the highway, at road level, is located at the origin.

$$y = -\frac{5}{72}(8)^2 + 10$$
$$y = -\frac{5}{72}(64) + 10$$
$$y = 5.6$$

The height of the arch at the points 8 m on either side of the center line of the highway is approximately 5.6 m. Since the load is 6 m high, it would not fit under the arch. It would require at least another 0.4 m of clearance.

Example

A community decides to build an elliptical skating oval that is 80 m long. The design of the rink requires an entry to the ice be placed 10 m from the end and 8 m from the midline.

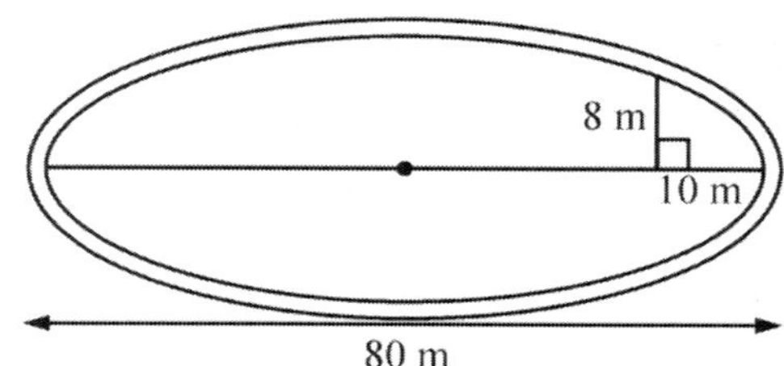

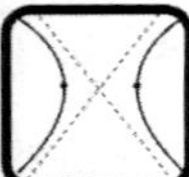

Assuming the center of the oval is located at the origin on a coordinate system, determine the equation in standard form that represents the oval.

Solution

When the ellipse is centered at the origin, the equation will fit the form $\frac{x^2}{a^2} + \frac{y^2}{b^2} = 1$. If it is considered to be oriented horizontally, then $2a = 80$, $a = 40$.

The equation is $\frac{x^2}{40^2} + \frac{y^2}{b^2} = 1$. The position of the entry on the skating oval that is shown is 10 m from the end (or 30 m to the right of the origin) and 8 mabove the midline.
The coordinates of the point can be represented by (30, 8). These coordinates must satisfy the equation and can therefore be substituted into the equation to solve for b^2.

$$\frac{30^2}{40^2} + \frac{8^2}{b^2} = 1$$

Begin by solving the equation for b^2.

Subtract $\frac{30^2}{40^2}$ from both sides of the equation.

$$\frac{64}{b^2} = 1 - \frac{900}{1,600}$$

Simplify.

$$\frac{64}{b^2} = \frac{7}{16}$$

Solve for b^2.

$$b^2 = \frac{64 \times 16}{7} = \frac{1,024}{7}$$

Thus, the equation is $\frac{x^2}{40^2} + \frac{y^2}{\frac{(32)^2}{7}} = 1$, or

$$\frac{x^2}{1,600} + \frac{7y^2}{1,024} = 1.$$

Example

A road passes through a tunnel, whose cross section is in a shape of a parabola, that is 16 m across at the bottom and 5 m high at the highest point. A 4 m wide vehicle enters the tunnel in such a way that the driver's side is exactly in the center of the tunnel.

Assuming that the bottom left corner of the opening of the tunnel is represented by the origin on a coordinate system, what is the maximum height of the vehicle, to the nearest hundredth, in order for it to pass through the tunnel and not cross the center lane?

Solution

Step 1
Draw and label a diagram that represents the information in the given problem.

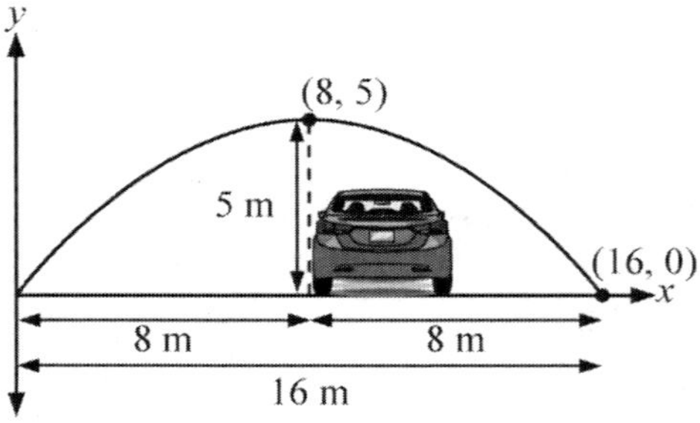

Step 2
Write the standard form of a parabola that opens downward.

$y - k = a(x - h)^2$

Step 3
Substitute 8 for h and 5 for k in the equation $y - k = a(x - h)^2$ since the vertex of the parabola is at the point (8, 5).

$y - 5 = a(x - 8)^2$

Step 4
Determine a point on the parabola other than the vertex.
The endpoints of the parabola are located at the ordered pairs (0, 0) and (16, 0). Thus, one of these points can be selected.

Step 5
Using the point (16, 0), substitute 16 for x and 0 for y in the equation.

$$0-5=a(16-8)^2$$
$$-5=a(8)^2$$
$$-5=64a$$
$$\frac{-5}{64}=a$$

Step 6
Write an equation that describes the parabolic opening of the tunnel.

Substitute $-\frac{5}{64}$ for a.

$$y-5=-\frac{5}{64}(x-8)^2$$
or
$$y=-\frac{5}{64}(x-8)^2+5$$

Step 7
Determine the maximum height of the vehicle.

$$y=-\frac{5}{64}(x-8)^2+5$$

Since the right side of the vehicle is a horizontal distance of 8 m + 4 m = 12 m from the origin, substitute 12 for x, and solve for y.

$$y=-\frac{5}{64}(12-8)^2+5$$
$$y=-\frac{5}{64}(4)^2+5$$
$$y=-\frac{5}{64}(16)+5$$
$$y=-1.25+5$$
$$y=3.75$$

To the nearest hundredth, the maximum allowable height of the vehicle is 3.75 m.

Determining the Key Characteristics of a Circle from the Standard Form Equation

A circle with a center (0, 0) is defined by an equation of the form $x^2+y^2=r^2$, where r represents the radius of the circle. For example, the circle defined by the equation $x^2+y^2=9$ has its center at (0, 0) and a radius of $\sqrt{9}=3$ units.

Generally, the standard form equation for a circle is $(x-h)^2+(y-k)^2=r^2$. The standard form equation is useful for determining the key characteristics of the graph of the circle, such as the center, radius, domain, and range.

The characteristics of the graph of the circle defined by $(x-h)^2+(y-k)^2=r^2$ are as follows:

- The center is at (h, k).
- The radius is r units.
- The domain is $h-r\leq x\leq h+r$.
- The range is $k-r\leq y\leq k+r$.

Example

What is the center and the radius of the circle defined by the equation $(x-1)^2+(y+6)^2=49$?

Solution

The standard form for a circle is $(x-h)^2+(y-k)^2=r^2$, where the center of the circle is at (h, k) and the radius is r units. Therefore, the center is at (1, −6), and the radius, r, is $r=\sqrt{49}=7$ units.

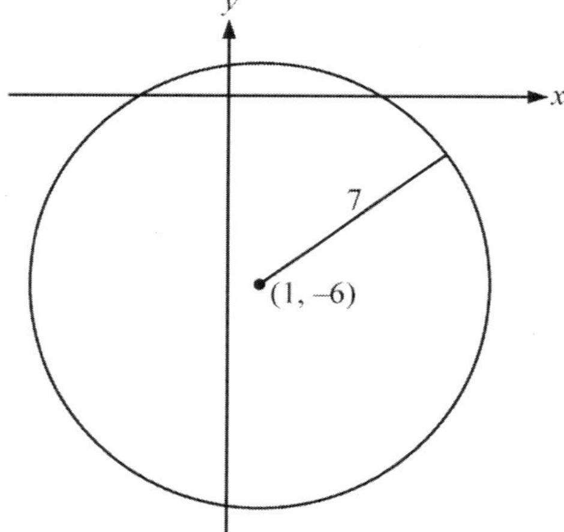

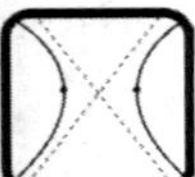

Determine the domain for the graph defined by the equation $(x-1)^2+(y+6)^2=49$.

Solution

The resulting graph of the equation $(x-1)^2+(y+6)^2=49$ is a circle with its center at $(1, -6)$ and a radius of 7 units. To determine the domain, use the center $(1, -6)$ and the radius of 7 units to determine the endpoints of a horizontal diameter.

The endpoints of the horizontal diameter are $(1-7, -6)=(-6, -6)$ and $(1+7, -6)=(8, -6)$.

Therefore, the domain is $-6 \le x \le 8$.

Determine the range for the graph defined by the equation $(x-1)^2+(y+6)^2=49$.

Solution

The resulting graph of the equation $(x-1)^2+(y+6)^2=49$ is a circle with its center at $(1, -6)$ and a radius of 7 units.

To determine the range, use the center $(1, -6)$ and the radius of 7 units to find the endpoints of the vertical diameter.

The endpoints of the vertical diameter are $(1, -6-7)=(1, -13)$ and $(1, -6+7)=(1, 1)$.

Thus, the range is $-13 \le y \le 1$.

Determining the Equation of a Circle when Given Key Characteristics

The equation of a circle in standard or general form can be determined from given characteristics of the circle, such as the center and the radius.

Use the following steps to determine the equation of a circle when given particular characteristics:

1. Determine the center, (h, k), and the radius, r, of the circle. Recall that the center of a circle can be determined by calculating the midpoint of the diameter of the circle, and the radius can be calculated by halving the distance of the diameter or by determining the distance between the center and a point that lies on the circle.
2. Substitute those values into the standard form equation of a circle, $(x-h)^2+(y-k)^2=r^2$, and simplify.
3. If required, convert to general form.

Example

Determine the equation of a circle with its center at $(-5, 2)$ and a radius of 6.

Solution

A circle is defined by the equation $(x-h)^2+(y-k)^2=r^2$, where (h, k) is the center of the circle and r is the radius.

Substitute the given information into the circle equation.

$$\begin{aligned}(x-h)^2+(y-k)^2&=r^2\\(x+5)^2+(y-2)^2&=6^2\\(x+5)^2+(y-2)^2&=36\end{aligned}$$

The equation of a circle with its center at $(-5, 2)$ and a radius of 6 is $(x+5)^2+(y-2)^2=36$.

Example

Given that point $(-3, -5)$ lies on a circle with center $(-7, -8)$, determine the equation of the circle.

Solution

Step 1

Determine the radius of the circle.

The radius of the circle is equal to the distance between the center $(-7, -8)$ and a point on the circumference $(-3, -5)$.

Apply the distance formula.

$$\begin{aligned}r&=\sqrt{(-7-(-3))^2+(-8-(-5))^2}\\&=\sqrt{16+9}\\&=\sqrt{25}\\&=5\end{aligned}$$

Step 2
Determine the equation of the circle.

Substitute the values for the radius and the coordinates of the center into the equation $(x-h)^2+(y-k)^2=r^2$.

$$(x-(-7))^2+(y-(-8))^2=(5)^2$$
$$(x+7)^2+(y+8)^2=25$$

DETERMINING THE EQUATION OF A CIRCLE FROM A GRAPH

Given the graph of a circle, you can determine the equation of the circle in standard or general form by identifying some of the key characteristics of the circle directly from the graph.

To determine the equation of a circle from a graph, follow these general steps:

1. Look at the graph to determine the center, (h, k), and the radius, r.
2. Substitute these values into the standard form of the equation of a circle, $(x-h)^2+(y-k)^2=r^2$.
3. Convert to general form if required.

Example

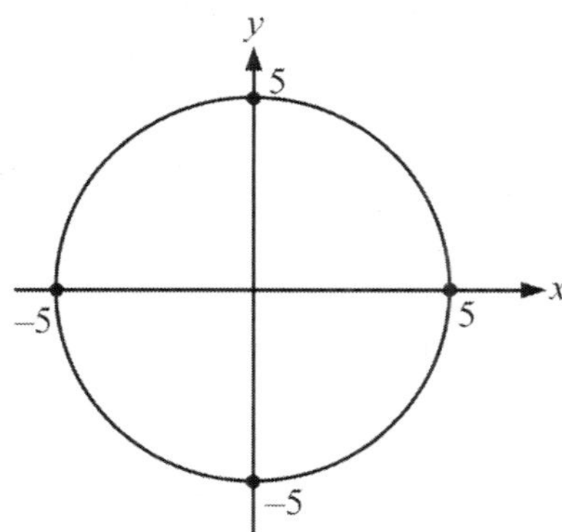

Write an equation in standard form for the given circle.

Solution

The center of the circle is at (0, 0), and the radius is equal to 5.

Thus, the equation is $x^2+y^2=5^2$ or $x^2+y^2=25$.

Example

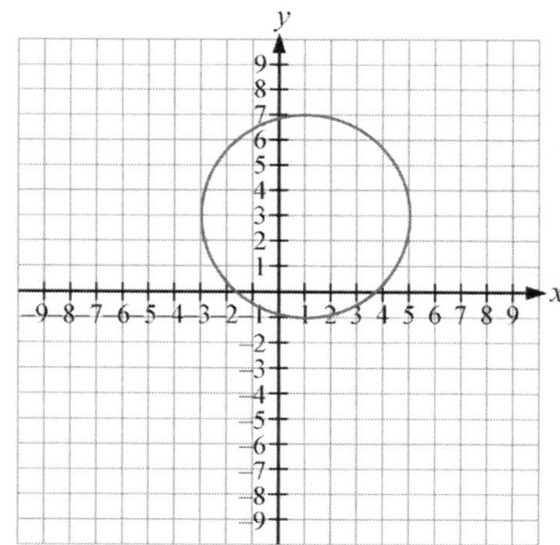

Determine the equation in general form for the given circle.

Solution

Step 1
From the given graph, determine the center, (h, k), and the radius, r, of the circle.

The center of the circle is at (1, 3), and the radius is 4 units.

Step 2
Substitute 1 for h, 3 for k, and 4 for r into the standard form of the equation of a circle, $(x-h)^2+(y-k)^2=r^2$.

$$(x-1)^2+(y-3)^2=4^2$$
$$(x-1)^2+(y-3)^2=16$$

Step 3
Convert to the general form $Ax^2+Cy^2+Dx+Ey+F=0$.

$$(x-1)^2+(y-3)^2=16$$
$$\left(x^2-2x+1\right)+\left(y^2-6y+9\right)=16$$
$$x^2+y^2-2x-6y+1+9-16=0$$
$$x^2+y^2-2x-6y-6=0$$

The general form of the equation of the circle is $x^2+y^2-2x-6y-6=0$.

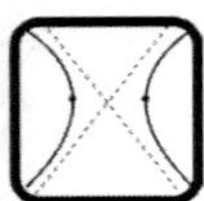

Determining the Key Characteristics of an Ellipse Given the Standard Form Equation

The standard form equation for an ellipse with center (h, k) is $\frac{(x-h)^2}{a^2}+\frac{(y-k)^2}{b^2}=1$. This equation is useful for determining the key characteristics of the graph of an ellipse.

The characteristics of the graph of the ellipse defined by the equation $\frac{(x-h)^2}{a^2}+\frac{(y-k)^2}{b^2}=1$ are as follows:

- The center of the ellipse is at the point (h, k).
- The endpoints of the horizontal axis are a units from the center, and the horizontal length is $2a$.
- The endpoints of the vertical axis are b units from the center, and the vertical length is $2b$.
- The domain of the ellipse is $-a+h \le x \le a+h$.
- The range of the ellipse is $-b+k \le y \le b+k$.

Example

Give the vertices for the equation $\frac{(x-2)^2}{16}+\frac{(y+1)^2}{4}=1$.

Solution

The given equation represents an ellipse with a center at $(2, -1)$. Also from the given equation, $a^2 = 16$ or $a = 4$ and $b^2 = 4$ or $b = 2$.

It can be determined that since $a = 4$, the endpoints of the major axis are 4 units from the center and since $b = 2$, the endpoints of the minor axis are 2 units from the center.

The vertices are at the ordered pairs $(-2, -1)$ and $(6, -1)$, which are 4 units to the left and to the right of the center.

Example

Determine the center, domain, and range of the ellipse defined by the equation $4(x+3)^2+25(y-7)^2=100$.

Solution

Step 1

Write the equation in standard form by dividing both sides of the equation by 100.

$$\frac{4(x+3)^2}{100}+\frac{25(y-7)^2}{100}=\frac{100}{100}$$

$$\frac{(x+3)^2}{25}+\frac{(y-7)^2}{4}=1$$

Step 2

Determine the center of the ellipse.

Since $h = -3$ and $k = 7$, the center of the ellipse is at the point $(-3, 7)$.

Step 3

Determine the values of a and b with respect to the standard form of an ellipse.

$a^2 = 25 \Rightarrow a = 5$

$b^2 = 4 \Rightarrow b = 2$

Step 4

Determine the domain and range of the ellipse.

The domain is $-5-3 \le x \le 5-3$, which is equivalent to $-8 \le x \le 2$. The range is $-2+7 \le y \le 2+7$, which is equivalent to $5 \le y \le 9$.

Determining the Equation of an Ellipse when Given Key Characteristics

The equation of an ellipse in standard or general form can be determined when particular characteristics, such as the center and the horizontal and vertical lengths, are given.

Use the following steps to determine the equation of an ellipse when key characteristics are given:

1. Determine the center, (h, k), and find the values of h and k. The center of an ellipse can be determined by calculating the midpoint of either the horizontal or vertical axis.
2. Determine the values of a and b. Recall that the horizontal length of an ellipse is $2a$, and the vertical length is $2b$. These lengths can be found by calculating the distance between vertices. The values of a and b can also be found by substituting other points that lie on the ellipse into the standard form equation and solving for the required variable.
3. Substitute the values of a, b, h, and k into the standard form equation of an ellipse, $\frac{(x-h)^2}{a^2}+\frac{(y-k)^2}{b^2}=1$, and simplify.
4. If required, convert to general form.

Example

An ellipse has a center at $(2, -1)$, a horizontal length of 8 units, and a vertical length of 6 units.

In standard form, what is the equation of this ellipse?

Solution

The standard form of an ellipse is $\frac{(x-h)^2}{a^2}+\frac{(y-k)^2}{b^2}=1$.

Step 1

Determine the values of h and k.

Given the center $(2, -1)$, it follows that $h = 2$ and $k = -1$.

Step 2

Determine the values of a and b.

The length of the horizontal axis is generalized as $2a$. Since $2a = 8$, then $a = 4$.

The length of the vertical axis is generalized as $2b$. Since $2b = 6$, then $b = 3$.

Step 3

Substitute the values for a, b, h, and k into the standard form equation.

$$\frac{(x-(2))^2}{(4)^2}+\frac{(y-(-1))^2}{(3)^2}=1$$

Therefore, the equation is

$$\frac{(x-2)^2}{16}+\frac{(y+1)^2}{9}=1.$$

Example

What is the equation of an ellipse centered at $(-1, 4)$ that passes through the points $(2, 4)$ and $(-1, -1)$ in both standard and general form?

Solution

Step 1

Determine the center, (h, k), and determine the values for h and k.

The ellipse is centered at $(-1, 4)$; therefore, h is -1, and k is 4.

Substitute the values for h and k into the standard form equation of an ellipse,

$$\frac{(x-h)^2}{a^2}+\frac{(y-k)^2}{b^2}=1.$$

$$\frac{(x+1)^2}{a^2}+\frac{(y-4)^2}{b^2}=1$$

Step 2

Determine the values of a^2 and b^2.

The points (2, 4) and (–1, –1) must satisfy the equation $\frac{(x+1)^2}{a^2}+\frac{(y-4)^2}{b^2}=1$.

Substitute (2, 4) into $\frac{(x+1)^2}{a^2}+\frac{(y-4)^2}{b^2}=1$, and solve for a.

$$\frac{(2+1)^2}{a^2}+\frac{(4-4)^2}{b^2}=1$$
$$\frac{3^2}{a^2}+\frac{0}{b^2}=1$$
$$\frac{9}{a^2}=1$$
$$a^2=9$$

Substitute (–1, –1) into the equation $\frac{(x+1)^2}{a^2}+\frac{(y-4)^2}{b^2}=1$, and solve for b.

$$\frac{(-1+1)^2}{a^2}+\frac{(-1-4)^2}{b^2}=1$$
$$\frac{0}{a^2}+\frac{(-5)^2}{b^2}=1$$
$$\frac{25}{b^2}=1$$
$$b^2=25$$

Step 3

Substitute the values for a^2, b^2, h, and k into the standard form equation of an ellipse, $\frac{(x-h)^2}{a^2}+\frac{(y-k)^2}{b^2}=1$.

Therefore, the equation in standard form is $\frac{(x+1)^2}{9}+\frac{(y-4)^2}{25}=1$.

Step 4

Convert to general form.

$$\frac{(x+1)^2}{9}+\frac{(y-4)^2}{25}=1$$
$$25(x+1)^2+9(y-4)^2=225$$
$$\begin{pmatrix}25(x^2+2x+1)\\+9(y^2-8y+16)\end{pmatrix}=225$$
$$\begin{pmatrix}25x^2+50x+25\\+9y^2-72y+144\end{pmatrix}=225$$
$$25x^2+9y^2+50x-72y-56=0$$

The equation of the ellipse in general form is $25x^2+9y^2+50x-72y-56=0$.

Determining the Equation of an Ellipse When Given the Graph

When you are given the graph of an ellipse, the equation in standard or general form can be determined by identifying some of the key characteristics of the graph.

To determine the equation of an ellipse when given a graph, follow these steps:

1. Locate the center (h, k) on the graph, and determine the values for h and k.
2. Observe the horizontal length ($2a$) and the vertical length ($2b$) of the ellipse. Determine the values of a and b.
3. Substitute the values for a, b, h, and k into the standard form of the equation of an ellipse, $\frac{(x-h)^2}{a^2}+\frac{(y-k)^2}{b^2}=1$, and simplify.
4. Convert to general form, $Ax^2+Cy^2+Dx+Ey+F=0$, if required.

Example

The graph of an ellipse is shown.

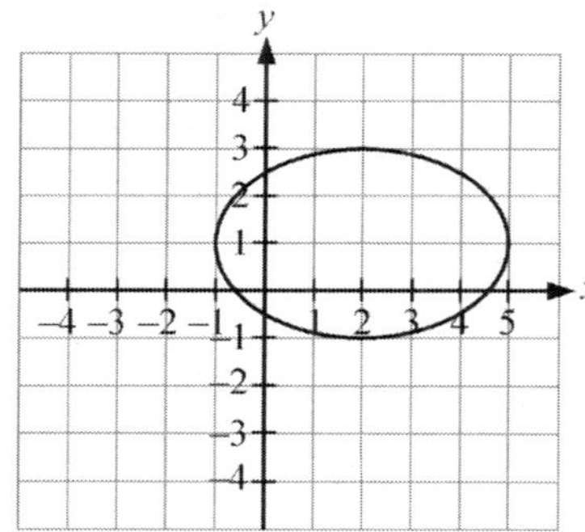

Write the equation of the ellipse in general form.

Solution

The standard form of an ellipse with center (h, k) is $\frac{(x-h)^2}{a^2} + \frac{(y-k)^2}{b^2} = 1$. Determine the standard form of the equation of the given ellipse, and then convert it to general form.

Step 1

Locate the center (h, k) on the graph, and determine the values for h and k.

The center is at (2, 1); therefore, $h = 2$ and $k = 1$.

Step 2

Observe the horizontal length ($2a$) and the vertical length ($2b$) of the ellipse, and determine the values of a and b.

Determine the horizontal length.

$2a = 5 - (-1)$
$2a = 6$
$a = 3$

Determine the vertical length.

$2b = 3 - (-1)$
$2b = 4$
$b = 2$

Step 3

Write the standard form of the equation of the ellipse.

Substituting the values for a, b, h, and k into the standard form of the equation gives $\frac{(x-(2))^2}{(3)^2} + \frac{(y-(1))^2}{(2)^2} = 1$. Therefore, the standard form of the equation of the ellipse is $\frac{(x-2)^2}{9} + \frac{(y-1)^2}{4} = 1$.

Step 4

Convert the standard form of the equation to general form as follows:

$$\begin{aligned} \frac{(x-2)^2}{9} + \frac{(y-1)^2}{4} &= 1 \\ 4(x-2)^2 + 9(y-1)^2 &= 36 \\ 4\left(x^2 - 4x + 4\right) + 9\left(y^2 - 2y + 1\right) &= 36 \\ 4x^2 - 16x + 16 + 9y^2 - 18y + 9 &= 36 \\ 4x^2 + 9y^2 - 16x - 18y + 25 &= 36 \\ 4x^2 + 9y^2 - 16x - 18y - 11 &= 0 \end{aligned}$$

Determining Key Characteristics of a Hyperbola Given the Standard Form Equation

The standard form of a hyperbola can be used to identify the key characteristics of its graph, such as the center, vertices, slopes of asymptotes, domain, and range.

If the graph of a hyperbola has a horizontal orientation, the standard form equation is $\frac{(x-h)^2}{a^2} - \frac{(y-k)^2}{b^2} = 1$. Similarly, if the graph has a vertical orientation, the standard form equation is $\frac{(x-h)^2}{a^2} - \frac{(y-k)^2}{b^2} = -1$.

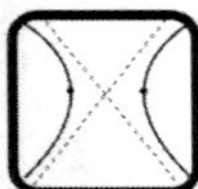

Hyperbolas with a Horizontal Orientation

The characteristics of the graph of the hyperbola defined by $\frac{(x-h)^2}{a^2} - \frac{(y-k)^2}{b^2} = 1$ are as follows:

- Center: (h, k)
- Range: $y \in \mathrm{R}$
- Slopes of the asymptotes: $\pm\frac{b}{a}$
- Domain: $x \leq h - a$ or $x \geq h + a$
- Distance between the vertices: $2a$
- Vertices: $(h - a, k)$ and $(h + a, k)$

Example

A hyperbola is defined by the equation $\frac{x^2}{16} - y^2 = 1$.

Determine the vertices of the given hyperbola.

Solution

Step 1
Relate the values of h, k, b, and a of the standard form, $\frac{(x-h)^2}{a^2} - \frac{(y-k)^2}{b^2} = 1$, to the given equation.
In the given equation, the values of h, k, and b are all 0. Determine the value of a.

$$a^2 = 16$$
$$a = \sqrt{16}$$
$$a = 4$$

Step 2
Determine the vertices.
For a hyperbola of the form $\frac{(x-h)^2}{a^2} - \frac{(y-k)^2}{b^2} = 1$, the vertices are $(h - a, k)$ and $(h + a, k)$.

$$(h - a, k) = (0 - 4, 0) = (-4, 0)$$
$$(h + a, k) = (0 + 4, 0) = (4, 0)$$

Therefore, the vertices are $(-4, 0)$ and $(4, 0)$.

Determine the domain and range of the given hyperbola.

Solution

Step 1
Relate the values of h, k, b, and a of the standard form, $\frac{(x-h)^2}{a^2} - \frac{(y-k)^2}{b^2} = 1$, to the given equation.
In the given equation, the values of h, k, and b are all 0. Determine the value of a.

$$a^2 = 16$$
$$a = \sqrt{16}$$
$$a = 4$$

Step 2
Determine the domain and range of the equation.
For a hyperbola of the form $\frac{(x-h)^2}{a^2} - \frac{(y-k)^2}{b^2} = 1$, the domain is $x \leq h - a$ or $x \geq h + a$, and the range is $y \in \mathbb{R}$.

$$x \leq h - a$$
$$x \leq 0 - 4$$
$$x \leq -4$$
$$x \geq h + a$$
$$x \geq 0 + 4$$
$$x \geq 4$$

Therefore, the range is $y \in \mathbb{R}$, and the domain is $x \leq -4$ or $x \geq 4$.

Hyperbolas with a Vertical Orientation

The characteristics of the graph of the hyperbola defined by $\frac{(x-h)^2}{a^2} - \frac{(y-k)^2}{b^2} = -1$ are as follows:

- Center: (h, k)
- Domain: $x \in \mathrm{R}$
- Slopes of the asymptotes: $\pm\frac{b}{a}$
- Range: $y \leq k - b$ or $y \geq k + b$
- Distance between the vertices: $2b$
- Vertices: $(h, k - b)$ and $(h, k + b)$

Example

A quadratic relation is represented by the equation $9(x+4)^2 - 4(y+3)^2 = -1$.

Determine the coordinates of the center of the given hyperbola.

Solution

Step 1

Put the equation $9(x+4)^2 - 4(y+3)^2 = -1$ into standard form, $\frac{(x-h)^2}{a^2} - \frac{(y-k)^2}{b^2} = -1$.

In standard form, the equation is

$$\frac{(x+4)^2}{\left(\frac{1}{3}\right)^2} - \frac{(y+3)^2}{\left(\frac{1}{2}\right)^2} = -1.$$

Step 2

Determine the center of the hyperbola.

The value of h is –4, and the value of k is –3; therefore, the center (h, k) is $(-4, -3)$.

Determine the slopes of the asymptotes for the given hyperbola.

Solution

Step 1

Put the equation $9(x+4)^2 - 4(y+3)^2 = -1$ into standard form, $\frac{(x-h)^2}{a^2} - \frac{(y-k)^2}{b^2} = -1$.

In standard form, the equation is

$$\frac{(x+4)^2}{\frac{1}{9}} - \frac{(y+3)^2}{\frac{1}{4}} = -1.$$

Step 2

Determine the slopes of the asymptotes.

Since $a^2 = \frac{1}{9}$ and $b^2 = \frac{1}{4}$, it follows that

$a = \frac{1}{3}$ and $b = \frac{1}{2}$. Substitute these values to determine the slopes of the asymptotes.

$$\pm\frac{b}{a} = \pm\frac{\frac{1}{2}}{\frac{1}{3}}$$

$$\pm\frac{b}{a} = \pm\frac{3}{2}$$

Determining the Equation of a Hyperbola Given Key Characteristics

The equation of a hyperbola in standard or general form can be determined by considering certain key characteristics of the hyperbola.

To determine the equation of a hyperbola when key characteristics are given, follow these steps:

1. Determine the orientation of the hyperbola.
   - For a vertical orientation, use the standard form $\frac{(x-h)^2}{a^2} - \frac{(y-k)^2}{b^2} = -1$.
   - For a horizontal orientation, use the standard form $\frac{(x-h)^2}{a^2} - \frac{(y-k)^2}{b^2} = 1$.
2. Determine the coordinates of the center (h, k) of the hyperbola, and determine the values of h and k.
   The center of a hyperbola can be determined by calculating the midpoint of either the horizontal or vertical vertices.
3. Determine the values of a and b. The values of a and b can be determined by calculating the distance between vertices —$2a$ for horizontal length and $2b$ for vertical length. These values can also be found by using the slopes of the asymptotes $\pm\frac{b}{a}$. If particular points that lie on the hyperbola are given, the values of a and b can also be determined by substituting these points into the standard form equation and solving for the required variable.
4. Substitute the values of a, b, h, and k into the standard form equation for the hyperbola, and simplify.
5. Convert to general form if required.

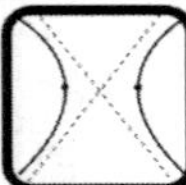

Example

Where $y \le -7$ or $y \ge 3$, determine the value of b^2 in the equation $\frac{(x-1)^2}{16} - \frac{(y+2)^2}{b^2} = -1$.

Solution

Step 1

Identify the type of conic from the given standard form equation.

The equation $\frac{(x-1)^2}{16} - \frac{(y+2)^2}{b^2} = -1$ is of the form $\frac{(x-h)^2}{a^2} - \frac{(y-k)^2}{b^2} = -1$. Therefore, the given equation defines a hyperbola with a vertical orientation.

Step 2

Determine the center of the hyperbola.

The center of the hyperbola is the point $(1, -2)$ since $h = 1$ and $k = -2$.

Step 3

Determine the value of b.

The vertical distance from $y = -2$ to $y = -7$, as well as from $y = -2$ to $y = 3$, is 5 units. Thus, $b = 5$.

The value of b can also be determined in another way. Since the vertices of the hyperbola are at $(1, -7)$ and $(1, 3)$, the distance between the vertices is 10 units.

$2b = 10$

$b = 5$

Therefore, $b = 5$.

Step 4

Determine the value of b^2.

Since $b = 5$, it follows that $b^2 = 25$.

Example

A hyperbola has vertices at points $(-2, 4)$ and $(6, 4)$. One of the asymptotes has a slope of $-\frac{4}{3}$.

Determine the equation of the given hyperbola in standard form.

Solution

Step 1

Determine the orientation and model form of the hyperbola.

Since the y-values of the vertices are equal, the hyperbola has a horizontal orientation and the standard form equation

$$\frac{(x-h)^2}{a^2} - \frac{(y-k)^2}{b^2} = 1.$$

Step 2

Determine the coordinates of the center (h, k) of the hyperbola.

Use the midpoint of the horizontal vertices $(-2, 4)$ and $(6, 4)$ to determine the center.

$$\begin{aligned}(x, y) &= \left(\frac{x_1 + x_2}{2}, \frac{y_1 + y_2}{2}\right) \\ &= \left(\frac{-2+6}{2}, \frac{4+4}{2}\right) \\ &= (2, 4)\end{aligned}$$

Step 3

Determine the values of a and b.

Since the vertices of the hyperbola are at $(-2, 4)$ and $(6, 4)$, the horizontal distance between the vertices is 8 units.

$2a = 8$

$a = 4$

Therefore, $a = 4$.

Since the slope of an asymptote is $-\frac{4}{3}$, it follows that $\frac{b}{4} = \frac{4}{3}$; thus, $b = \frac{16}{3}$.

Step 4
Substitute the values of a, b, h, and k into the standard form equation for the hyperbola, and simplify.

$$\frac{(x-2)^2}{4^2} - \frac{(y-4)^2}{\left(\frac{16}{3}\right)^2} = 1$$

$$\frac{(x-2)^2}{16} - \frac{(y-4)^2}{\frac{256}{9}} = 1$$

$$\frac{(x-2)^2}{16} - \frac{9(y-4)^2}{256} = 1$$

The equation of the hyperbola in standard form is $\frac{(x-2)^2}{16} - \frac{9(y-4)^2}{256} = 1$.

Determining the Equation of a Hyperbola Given the Graph

When given the graph of a hyperbola, you can determine the equation in standard or general form by identifying some of the key characteristics directly from the graph.

To determine the equation of a hyperbola when given a graph, follow these steps:

1. Observe the orientation of the hyperbola to determine the proper standard form equation. For a vertical orientation, use the standard form $\frac{(x-h)^2}{a^2} - \frac{(y-k)^2}{b^2} = -1$.
   For a horizontal orientation, use the standard form $\frac{(x-h)^2}{a^2} - \frac{(y-k)^2}{b^2} = 1$.
2. Locate the center (h, k) of the hyperbola to determine the values of h and k.
3. Locate the vertices and the value of the slope of an asymptote, and determine the values of a and b.
4. Substitute the values of a, b, h, and k into the standard form equation for the hyperbola, and simplify.
5. Convert to general form if required.

Example

A conic where the straight dotted lines are asymptotes is shown here.

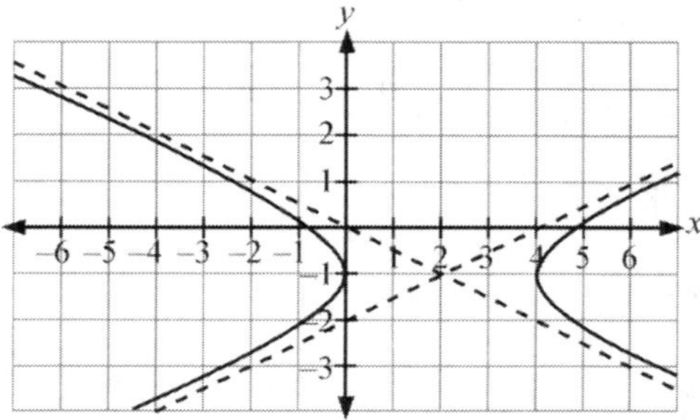

Determine the equation for the given conic in the form $\frac{(x-h)^2}{a^2} \pm \frac{(y-k)^2}{b^2} = 1$.

Solution

Step 1
Use the graph, and classify the conic section. The quadratic relation shown in the graph is a hyperbola with a horizontal orientation.
It models an equation of the form
$\frac{(x-h)^2}{a^2} - \frac{(y-k)^2}{b^2} = 1$.

Step 2
Analyze the key features of the graph.

- The center is at $(2, -1)$; therefore, $h = 2$ and $k = -1$.
- The distance between the vertices is 4 units, which is equivalent to $2a$; therefore, $a = 2$.
- The slopes of the asymptotes are $\pm\frac{1}{2}$.

  A slope of an asymptote is $\pm\frac{b}{a}$; therefore,

  $\frac{1}{2} = \frac{b}{2}$ and $b = 1$.

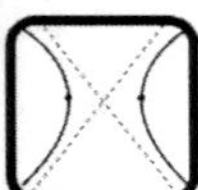

Step 3
Determine the equation of the hyperbola.
Substitute the values of a, b, h, and k into the equation $\frac{(x-h)^2}{a^2} - \frac{(y-k)^2}{b^2} = 1$.

$$\frac{(x-2)^2}{2^2} - \frac{(y+1)^2}{1^2} = 1$$

Simplify.

$$\frac{(x-2)^2}{4} - (y+1)^2 = 1$$

Example

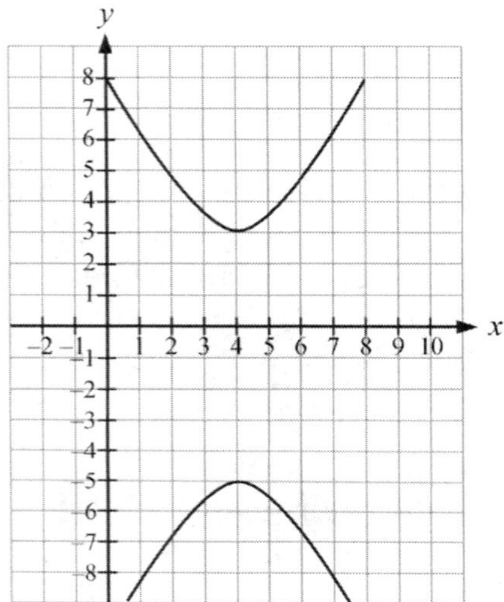

Determine the equation, in general form, of the given hyperbola if $\frac{b}{a} = 2$.

Solution

This is a vertically oriented hyperbola that models the standard form equation $\frac{(x-h)^2}{a^2} - \frac{(y-k)^2}{b^2} = -1$.

Step 1
From the graph, locate the vertices and center. The vertices are (4, 3) and (4, −5). The center is located in the middle between the two vertices: (4, −1). Therefore, $h = 4$ and $k = -1$.

Step 2
Determine the distance from the center to the vertex to find the value of b.
The distance from the center to a vertex is 4 units. This is a vertical hyperbola, and thus, $b = 4$.

Step 3
Determine the value of a.
It is given that $\frac{b}{a} = 2$, since $b = 4$ and $a = 2$.

Step 4
Substitute the values for a, b, h, and k into the standard form hyperbola equation.
The equation in standard form is $\frac{(x-4)^2}{4} - \frac{(y+1)^2}{16} = -1$.

Step 5
Multiply both sides of the equation by the lowest common multiple of 4 and 16. $4(x-4)^2 - (y+1)^2 = -16$
Expand the binomials.
$4(x^2 - 8x + 16) - (y^2 + 2y + 1) = -16$
Multiply to remove the brackets.
$4x^2 - 32x + 64 - y^2 - 2y - 1 = -16$
Add 16 to both sides, collect like terms, and rearrange.
$4x^2 - y^2 - 32x - 2y + 79 = 0$

Determining Key Characteristics of a Parabola Given the Standard Form Equation

The standard form of a parabola is convenient for identifying key characteristics such as the vertex, axis of symmetry, domain, and range.

In general, the standard form for the equation of a parabola opening up or down is $y - k = a(x-h)^2$. The parabola opens upward if $a > 0$, and it opens downward if $a < 0$. Similarly, the standard form for the equation of a parabola opening right or left is $x - h = a(y-k)^2$. The parabola opens to the right if $a > 0$, and it opens to the left if $a < 0$.

Characteristics of a Parabola

	Vertical Orientation $y-k=a(x-h)^2$	Horizontal Orientation $x-h=a(y-k)^2$
Vertex	(h, k)	(h, k)
Axis of Symmetry	$x=h$	$x=h$
Domain	$x \in \mathbb{R}$	$x \geq h$ if $a>0$ $x \leq h$ if $a<0$
Range	$y \geq h$ if $a>0$ $y \leq h$ if $a<0$	$y \in \mathbb{R}$

Example

Consider the graph of $x-3=-\frac{1}{9}(y+5)^2$.

Determine the coordinates of the vertex.

Solution

Since $h=3$ and $k=-5$, the vertex is at $(3, -5)$.

Determine the domain and the range.

Solution

Because $a<0$, the parabola opens to the left. The vertex of the parabola is point $(3, -5)$. The domain is $x \leq 3$, and the range is $y \in \mathbb{R}$.

Example

Consider the graph of $y+3=2(x+7)^2$.

Determine the equation of the axis of symmetry.

Solution

The axis of symmetry is a vertical line that passes through the vertex. For an equation of the form $y-k=a(x-h)^2$, the equation of the axis of symmetry is $x=h$. Since $h=-7$, the equation of the axis of symmetry is $x=-7$.

Determining the Equation of a Parabola when Given Key Characteristics

The equation of a parabola in standard or general form can be determined by using particular characteristics of the parabola.

To determine the equation of a parabola when given key characteristics, follow these steps:

1. Determine the orientation of the parabola to establish the proper standard form equation. For a vertical orientation, use the standard form $y-k=a(x-h)^2$, and for a horizontal orientation, use the standard form $x-h=a(y-k)^2$.
2. Determine the vertex (h, k) of the parabola, substitute the values of h and k into the standard form equation for the parabola, and simplify.
3. Determine the value of a by using a given point (x, y) that lies on the parabola. Substitute the values of x, y, h, and k into the standard form equation for the parabola, and then solve for a.
4. Write the equation in standard form by using the values for a, h, and k.
5. Convert to general form if required.

Example

The graph of a vertically orientated parabola has its vertex at $(-4, 5)$ and a y-intercept at -27.

Determine the equation, in standard form, of the given parabola.

Solution

Step 1

Determine the orientation and vertex of the parabola.

Since the parabola has a vertical orientation, it will have $y-k=a(x-h)^2$ as its standard form equation. Since the vertex (h, k) is $(-4, 5)$, substitute the values for h and k into the equation $y-k=a(x-h)^2$.

The equation becomes $y-5=a(x+4)^2$.

Step 2

Determine the value of a.

Since -27 is the y-intercept, substitute $(0, -27)$, into the equation, and solve for a.

$$\begin{aligned} y-5 &= a(x+4)^2 \\ (-27)-5 &= a(0+4)^2 \\ -32 &= 16a \\ -\frac{32}{16} &= a \\ -2 &= a \end{aligned}$$

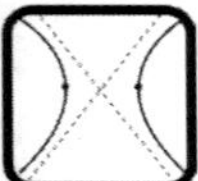

Step 3
Write the equation in standard form by using the values for a, h, and k.
$y - 5 = -2(x + 4)^2$

Example

The graph of a parabola has a horizontal orientation, its vertex is at (2, −1), and it passes through the point (−4, 2). Determine its equation, and write it in general form.

Solution

Since the parabola has horizontal orientation, in standard form, the equation fits the form of $x - h = a(y - k)^2$. The vertex is (2, −1). Therefore, $h = 2$ and $k = -1$ and the equation is $x - 2 = a(y + 1)^2$. Since the graph passes through (−4, 2), this ordered pair satisfies the equation.

$$-4 - 2 = a(2 + 1)^2$$
$$-6 = 9a$$
$$-\frac{2}{3} = a$$

In standard form, the equation is
$x - 2 = -\frac{2}{3}(y + 1)^2.$

Convert the equation to general form. Multiply both sides of the equation by 3.
$3x - 6 = -2(y + 1)^2$

Expand $(y + 1)^2$.
$3x - 6 = -2(y^2 + 2y + 1)$

Multiply to remove brackets.
$3x - 6 = -2y^2 - 4y - 2$

Add and subtract terms to make the RHS = 0.
$2y^2 + 3x + 4y - 4 = 0$

Determining the Equation of a Parabola from a Given Graph

If the graph of a parabola is given, the equation of the parabola in standard or general form can be determined by identifying some of the key characteristics of the graph.

To determine the equation of a parabola when given a graph, use the following general guidelines:

- Observe the orientation of the parabola to determine the proper standard form of the equation. If the parabola has a vertical orientation, use the standard form $y - k = a(x - h)^2$. For a horizontal orientation, use the standard form $x - h = a(y - k)^2$.
- Locate the vertex (h, k) of the parabola. Substitute the values of h and k into the standard form of the equation, and simplify.
- Locate one other point (x, y) on the graph, such as the y-intercept, x-intercept, etc. Substitute the values of x, y, h, and k into the standard form of the equation, and solve for a.
- Write the equation in standard form using the values for a, h, and k.
- Convert to general form, $Ax^2 + Cy^2 + Dx + Ey + F = 0$, if required.

Example

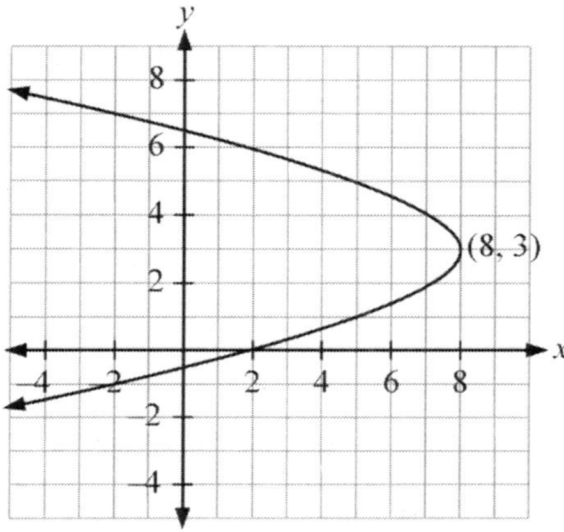

The graph of a parabola is given.

Write the equation of the parabola shown in standard form.

Solution

The standard form of the equation of a parabola opening right or left (horizontal orientation) is $x - h = a(y - k)^2$, where (h, k) is the vertex of the parabola.

Step 1

Locate the vertex, and substitute the values of h and k into the equation $x - h = a(y - k)^2$.

The vertex of the given parabola is (8, 3).

Substitute 8 for h and 3 for k.

$x - 8 = a(y - 3)^2$

Step 2

Determine the value of a.

Locate one other point (x, y) on the graph, such as the x-intercept (2, 0).

Substitute (2, 0) in $x - 8 = a(y - 3)^2$, and solve for a.

$$\begin{aligned} 2 - 8 &= a(0 - 3)^2 \\ -6 &= a(-3)^2 \\ -6 &= 9a \\ -\frac{6}{9} &= a \\ -\frac{2}{3} &= a \end{aligned}$$

Step 3

Write the equation in standard form using the values for a, h, and k.

$x - 8 = -\frac{2}{3}(y - 3)^2$

PC.5.C Convert between parametric and rectangular forms of functions and equations to graph them.

Sketching Parametric Equations

A parametric equation is formed by separating the Cartesian equation into two parts, one for each variable, x and y. The two parts have a common variable, t.

When sketching parametric equations, substitute values of t into both of the equations to build a table of values consisting of x and y.

In some problems involving graphing parametric equations, restrictions on the t-variable may be given. This will result in a segment of a graph with defined endpoints. If the problems asks for the general shape of the graph, a good starting point is to use values of t that are close to 0 and then go higher and lower from there until the general shape of the graph is determined.

To graph a parametric equation, follow these steps:

1. Determine the x-values.
2. Determine the y-values.
3. Build a table of values.
4. Plot the ordered pairs on the Cartesian plane.
5. Join the points with a straight or curved line.

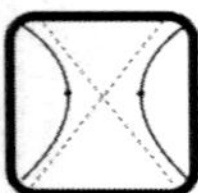

Example

A set of parametric equations is given.

$x = 1 + 2t$
$y = 5 - 3t$

Sketch the graph of the given set of parametric equations if $-1 \le t \le 3$.

Solution

Step 1

Determine the values of x.

Given the restriction on the t-variable, substitute the values –1, 0, 1, 2, and 3 into the equation $x = 1 + 2t$.

t	x
–1	$x = 1 + 2(-1)$ $x = 1 - 2$ $x = -1$
0	$x = 1 + 2(0)$ $x = 1$
1	$x = 1 + 2(1)$ $x = 1 + 2$ $x = 3$
2	$x = 1 + 2(2)$ $x = 1 + 4$ $x = 5$
3	$x = 1 + 2(3)$ $x = 1 + 6$ $x = 7$

Step 2

Determine the values of y.

Given the restriction on the t-variable, substitute the values –1, 0, 1, 2, and 3 into the equation $y = 5 - 3t$.

t	y
–1	$y = 5 - 3(-1)$ $y = 5 + 3$ $y = 8$
0	$y = 5 - 3(0)$ $y = 5$
1	$y = 5 - 3(1)$ $y = 5 - 3$ $y = 2$
2	$y = 5 - 3(2)$ $y = 5 - 6$ $y = -1$
3	$y = 5 - 3(3)$ $y = 5 - 9$ $y = -4$

Step 3

Build a table of values.

x	y
–1	8
1	5
3	2
5	–1
7	–4

Step 4

Plot the ordered pairs on the Cartesian plane.

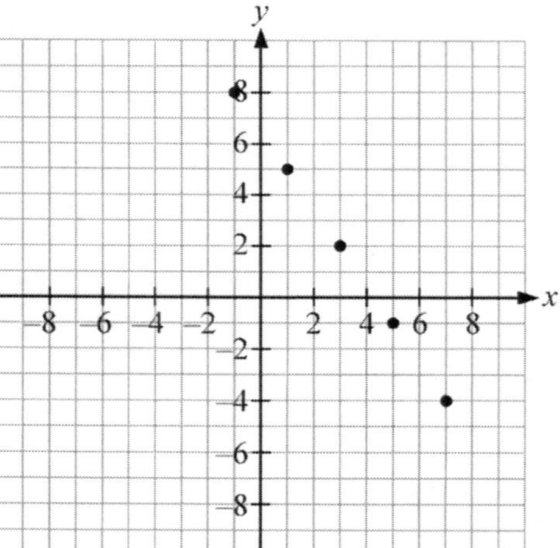

Step 5
Join the points with a straight or curved line.

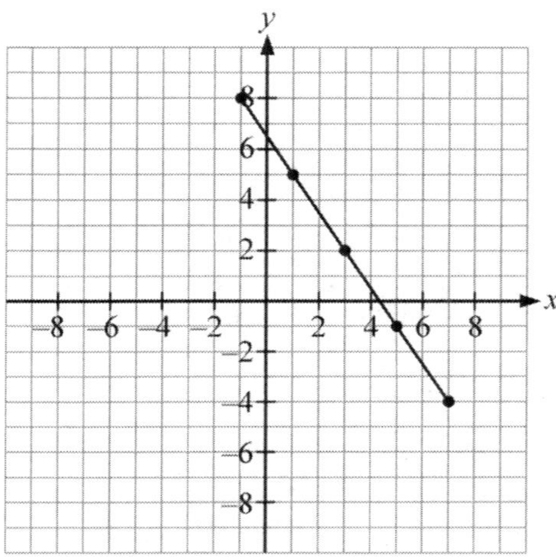

Determining Cartesian Form from Parametric Form

Lines and curves on the Cartesian plane can be represented in different forms. The most common form used in school is the Cartesian form.
The Cartesian form describes all points (x, y) of the line or curve that satisfy the equation. This form may also be referred to as rectangular form or scalar form.

Another form is called parametric form. It is formed by separating the Cartesian equation into two parts, one for each of the variables (x and y) that have a common variable (t).

Converting Linear Parametric Equations to Cartesian Form

The equation of a line in two dimensions can be written in the following two forms:

1. Cartesian: $Ax + By + C = 0$
2. Parametric: $x = x_0 + at$, $y = y_0 + bt$

To convert an equation from parametric form to Cartesian form, follow these steps:

1. Solve each part of the parametric equation for t.
2. Equate the equations.
3. Rearrange the new equation into the form $Ax + By + C = 0$.

Example

A group of parametric equations is given.
$x = 2 - 3t$
$y = 5 + 6t$

What is the Cartesian form of the given parametric equations?

Solution

Step 1
Solve each equation for t.

$$x = 2 - 3t$$
$$x - 2 = -3t$$
$$\frac{x-2}{-3} = t$$
$$\frac{2-x}{3} = t$$

$$y = 5 + 6t$$
$$y - 5 = 6t$$
$$\frac{y-5}{6} = t$$

Step 2
Equate the two equations.

$$\frac{2-x}{3} = \frac{y-5}{6}$$

Step 3
Rearrange the equation into the form $Ax + By + C = 0$.

$$\frac{2-x}{3} = \frac{y-5}{6}$$
$$6\left(\frac{2-x}{3}\right) = y - 5$$
$$2(2 - x) = y - 5$$
$$4 - 2x = y - 5$$
$$-2x - y + 4 + 5 = 0$$
$$-2x - y + 9 = 0$$
$$2x + y - 9 = 0$$

Converting Quadratic Parametric Equations to Cartesian Form

The equation of a parabola in two dimensions can be written in the following two forms:

1. Cartesian: $Ax^2 + Dx + Ey + F = 0$
2. Parametric: $x = x_0 + at$, $y = y_0 + bt + ct^2$

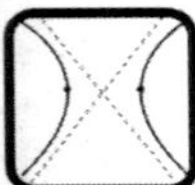

For parabolas represented in parametric equations, if the t^2 is in the x-variable equation, the parabola will be rotated 90°. The resulting Cartesian form, $Cy^2 + Dx + Ey + F = 0$, is not a function.

To convert an equation from parametric form to Cartesian form, follow these steps:

1. Solve each part of the parametric equation for t.
2. Equate the equations.
3. Rearrange the new equation into the form $Ax^2 + Dx + Ey + F = 0$ or $Cy^2 + Dx + Ey + F = 0$.

Example

A group of parametric equations is given.

$x = 1 - 3t$

$y = 7 + 2t^2$

What is the Cartesian form of the given parametric equations?

Solution

Step 1

Solve each equation for t.

$$\begin{aligned} x &= 1 - 3t \\ x - 1 &= -3t \\ 1 - x &= 3t \\ \frac{1-x}{3} &= t \end{aligned}$$

$$\begin{aligned} y &= 7 + 2t^2 \\ y - 7 &= 2t^2 \\ \frac{y-7}{2} &= t^2 \\ \sqrt{\frac{y-7}{2}} &= t \end{aligned}$$

Step 2

Equate the two equations.

$$\frac{1-x}{3} = \sqrt{\frac{y-7}{2}}$$

Step 3

Rearrange the equation into the form $Ax^2 + Dx + Ey + F = 0$.

$$\begin{aligned} \frac{1-x}{3} &= \sqrt{\frac{y-7}{2}} \\ \left(\frac{1-x}{3}\right)^2 &= \left(\sqrt{\frac{y-7}{2}}\right)^2 \\ \frac{(1-x)^2}{9} &= \frac{y-7}{2} \\ 2(1 - 2x + x^2) &= 9(y-7) \\ 2(x^2 - 2x + 1) &= 9(y-7) \\ 2x^2 - 4x + 2 &= 9y - 63 \\ 2x^2 - 4x - 9y + 65 &= 0 \end{aligned}$$

Graphing Parametric Equations with Technology

Using technology such as a TI-83 Plus calculator to graph a parametric equation requires the use of proper window settings, the appropriate selection of calculator buttons, and the proper calculator mode.

To graph a parametric equation on a graphing calculator, follow these steps:

1. Put the calculator into parametric mode by pressing MODE, scroll down to the fourth line, highlight Par, and then press ENTER.
2. Press the Y = button on your graphing calculator. Type in the function for the x-variable into the line labeled X_{1T} = and the function for the y-variable into the line labeled Y_{1T} = . Use the X,T,θ,n button to input the variable t from the parametric equation.
3. Set an appropriate window setting so that the graph will be adequately portrayed on the screen. To access this setting, press the WINDOW button.
4. Press the GRAPH button to view the graph representing the parametric equation.

To make appropriate window settings for parametric equations, you must set the parameters X_{min}, X_{max}, X_{scl}, Y_{min}, Y_{max}, and Y_{scl}. There will also be a third variable, t. This variable will also have parameters that will need to be set as T_{min}, T_{max}, and T_{step}.

Sometimes, problems involving graphing parametric equations will give the restrictions on the t-variable. In these cases, enter the given restrictions on the t-variable for the window settings. Then, either manually input the parameters of the x- and y-variables, or press ZOOM and select 0:ZoomFit. The calculator will adjust the x and y window settings to fit the entered restrictions on the t-variable.

Example

A set of parametric equations is given.

$$\begin{matrix} x = 2t^2 - 9 \\ y = 3 + 2t \end{matrix}, \text{ where } -3 \le t \le 2.$$

Graph the parametric equations.

Solution

Step 1

Put the calculator into parametric mode.

Press MODE, scroll down to the fourth line, highlight Par, and press ENTER.

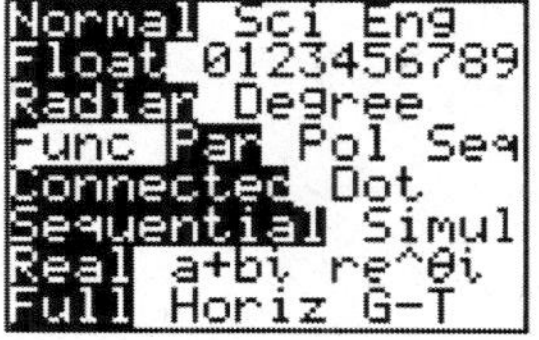

Step 2

Enter the parametric equations into the calculator.

Press the Y = button on your graphing calculator. Type the equation for the x-variable into the line labeled X_{1T} = and the equation for the y-variable into the line Y_{1T} = . Use the X,T,θ,n button to input the variable t from the parametric equation.

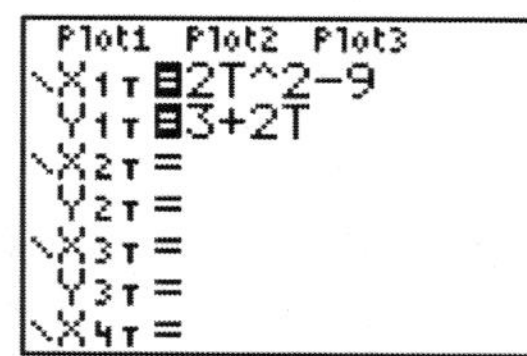

Step 3

Set an appropriate window setting.

Since there are restrictions on the t-variable given, press the WINDOW button, and enter the restrictions.

$T_{min} = -3$

$T_{max} = 2$

$T_{step} = 0.1$

Press ZOOM, and select 0:ZoomFit.

The calculator will adjust the x and y window settings to fit the entered restrictions on the t-variable.

Step 4

Graph the parametric equation.

Press the GRAPH button.

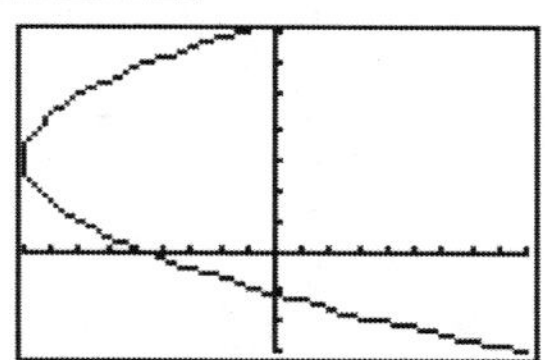

If the problem asks you to give the general shape of the graph, a good starting point for the parameters of the t-variable is $T_{min} = -5$, $T_{max} = 5$, and $T_{step} = 0.1$. If the graph does not show up, the values may need to be adjusted.

Example

A set of parametric equations is given.
$x = t + 1$
$y = t^2 - 2$

Use technology to graph the general shape formed from the parametric equations.

Solution

Step 1
Put the calculator into parametric mode.

Press MODE, scroll down to the fourth line, highlight Par, and press ENTER.

Step 2
Enter the parametric equations into the calculator.

Press the Y = button on your graphing calculator. Type the equation for the x-variable into the line labeled X_{1T} = and the equation for the y-variable into the line labeled Y_{1T} = .

Use the X,T,θ,n button to input the variable t from the parametric equation.

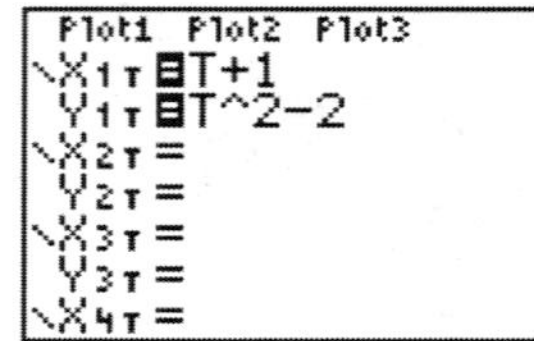

Step 3
Set an appropriate window setting.
Since the question asks for the general shape of the graph, the window settings T:[−5, 5, 0.1], X:[−10, 10, 1], and Y:[−10, 10, 1] can be used.

Step 4
Graph the parametric equation.

Press the GRAPH button.

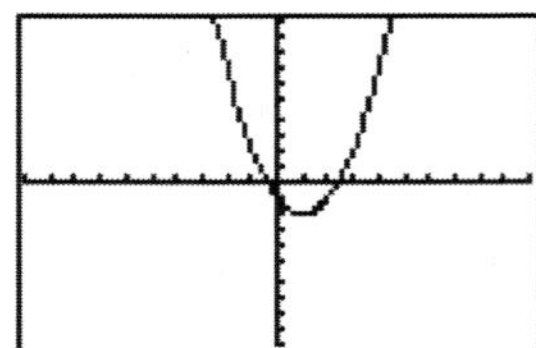

Determining the Parametric Form of an Equation from the Cartesian Form

The equations of lines and curves on the Cartesian plane can be represented in different forms. The most common form used in schools is the Cartesian form. The Cartesian form describes all points (x, y) of the line or curve that satisfy the equation. This form may also be referred to as rectangular form or scalar form.

Another form of an equation is called the parametric form. It is formed by separating the Cartesian equation into two parts, one for each variable (x and y) that have a common variable (t).

Converting Linear Cartesian Equations to Parametric Form

The equation of a line in two dimensions can be written in one of the following two forms:

1. Parametric: $x = x_0 + at$, $y = y_0 + bt$
2. Cartesian: $Ax + By + C = 0$

To convert a linear equation from Cartesian form to parametric form, use the following steps:

1. Introduce a parameter, such as t, to define the x- or y-variable from the Cartesian form.
2. Determine the x-variable of the parametric equation in the form $x = x_0 + at$.
3. Determine the y-variable of the parametric equation in the form $y = y_0 + bt$.

Depending on which variable t equals, the other variable can be found by substituting t into the equation and solving for x or y.

Note that linear Cartesian equations can have many different parametric equations, depending on what the parameter, t, is set to equal.

Example

Determine a parametric form of the Cartesian equation $4x + 3y - 6 = 0$.

Solution

Step 1

Introduce a parameter, such as t, to define the x- or y-variable from the Cartesian form.

Let $t = x$.

Step 2

Determine the x-variable of the parametric equation in the form $x = x_0 + at$.

In this case, $x = t$

Step 3

Determine the y-variable of the parametric equation in the form $y = y_0 + bt$.

Substitute t for x in the equation $4x + 3y - 6 = 0$, and solve for y.

$$
\begin{aligned}
4t + 3y - 6 &= 0 \\
3y &= 6 - 4t \\
y &= 2 - \frac{4t}{3}
\end{aligned}
$$

A possible parametric form of the Cartesian equation $4x + 3y - 6 = 0$ is as follows:

$x = t$

$y = 2 - \frac{4t}{3}$

Converting Quadratic Cartesian Equations to Parametric Form

The equation of a parabola in two dimensions can be written in one of the following two forms:

1. Cartesian: $Ax^2 + Dx + Ey + F = 0$
2. Parametric: $x = x_0 + at$, $y = y_0 + bt + ct^2$

For parabolas represented in parametric equations, if the t^2 is in the x-variable equation, the parabola will be rotated 90°. The resulting Cartesian form will not be a function: $Cy^2 + Dx + Ey + F = 0$.

To convert a quadratic equation from Cartesian form to parametric form, use the following steps:

1. Introduce a parameter, such as t, to define the x- or y-variable from the Cartesian form.
2. Determine the x-variable of the parametric equation in the form $x = x_0 + at$.
3. Determine the y-variable of the parametric equation in the form $y = y_0 + bt + ct^2$.

Note that quadratic Cartesian equations can have many different parametric equations, depending on what the parameter, t, is set to equal.

Example

Determine a parametric form of the Cartesian equation $x^2 - 6x - y + 9 = 0$.

Solution

Step 1

Introduce a parameter, such as t, to define the x- or y-variable from the Cartesian form.

Convert the Cartesian equation into factored form, and then set a parameter by using the variable t.

$$
\begin{aligned}
x^2 - 6x - y + 9 &= 0 \\
-y &= -x^2 + 6x - 9 \\
y &= x^2 - 6x + 9 \\
y &= (x - 3)^2
\end{aligned}
$$

Let $t = x - 3$.

Step 2

Determine the x-variable of the parametric equation in the form $x = x_0 + at$.

Rearrange the parameter $t = x - 3$ to solve for x.

$$
\begin{aligned}
t &= x - 3 \\
-x &= -3 - t \\
x &= t + 3
\end{aligned}
$$

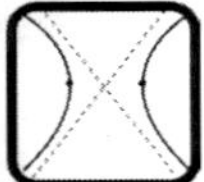

Step 3

Determine the y-variable of the parametric equation in the form $y = y_0 + bt + ct^2$.

Substitute $t = x - 3$ into the equation $y = (x - 3)^2$.

$y = t^2$

A parametric form of the Cartesian equation $x^2 - 6x - y + 9 = 0$ is as follows:

$x = t + 3$
$y = t^2$

PC.5.D Use parametric functions to simulate problems involving motion.

Modeling Projectile Motion Using Parametric Functions

Parametric functions can be used to represent projectile motion. It is easiest to parametrize the time variable, t, which is used to determine relevant information such as displacement and velocity.

Projectile motion is best described as two individual, separate motions: uniform motion in the horizontal plane and uniformly accelerated motion in the vertical plane. A projectile launched at an angle to the horizontal will have both horizontal and vertical components to its initial launch velocity. The horizontal component is given by $v\cos\theta$, and the vertical component is given by $v\sin\theta$.

Horizontally, the projectile continues to travel with the same velocity. The formula that expresses this motion is $d = vt$. In a parametric equation, the x-variable equation represents the horizontal distance traveled, with x_0 representing the initial horizontal distance. The equation that represents the horizontal distance traveled is determined by substituting x for d and $v\cos\theta$ for v into the equation $d = vt$.

$d = vt$
$x = (v\cos\theta)t$
$x = vt\cos\theta$

Next, the value x_0 is added to the equation to incorporate its initial horizontal distance.

$x = vt\cos\theta + x_0$

The vertical consideration of the projectile's motion is more involved. The projectile begins with an initial vertical velocity, as described, but also experiences a uniform acceleration in the opposite direction (toward Earth) of 9.81 m/s^2. This causes the projectile to slow its ascent over time, eventually reaching a peak where its velocity is zero. At this peak, however, there is still the constant acceleration acting on the projectile in the negative direction. After the momentary lapse in vertical motion, the projectile begins to accelerate toward the ground. The formula that expresses this motion is $d = vt - \frac{1}{2}gt^2$, where g is the acceleration due to gravity. For a parametric equation, the y-variable equation represents the vertical distance traveled, with y_0 representing the initial vertical distance. The equation that represents the vertical distance traveled is determined by substituting y for d and $v\sin\theta$ for v into the equation $d = vt - \frac{1}{2}gt^2$.

$d = vt - \frac{1}{2}gt^2$

$y = (v\sin\theta)t - \frac{1}{2}gt^2$

$y = -\frac{1}{2}gt^2 + vt\sin\theta$

Next, the value y_0 is added to the equation to incorporate its initial vertical distance.

$y = -\frac{1}{2}gt^2 + vt\sin\theta + y_0$

Example

A ball leaves a ramp 2 m above the ground with an angle of elevation of 14° and a speed of 5 m/s.

Determine the parametric equations that represent the ball's path.

Solution

Let v represent velocity, t represent time, g represent acceleration due to gravity (9.81 m/s^2), x represent the horizontal component of motion, x_0 represent the initial horizontal distance, y represent the vertical component of motion, and y_0 represent the initial vertical distance.

Step 1
Sketch a diagram.

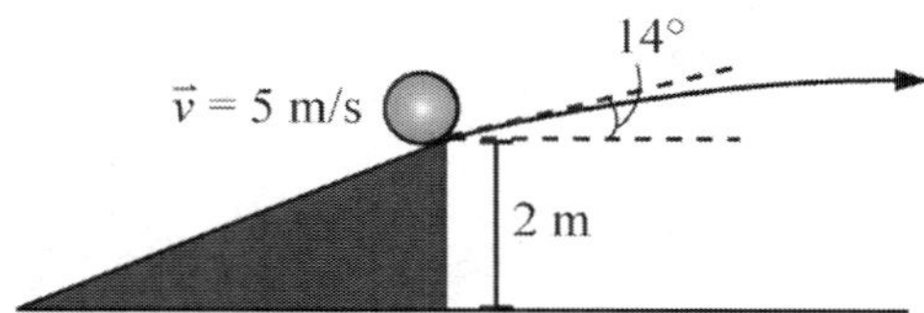

Step 2
Write the parametric equation for the horizontal component of motion.
$x = vt\cos\theta + x_0$

Step 3
Substitute the known values into the parametric equation for the horizontal component of the ball's motion, x.
$x = vt\cos\theta + x_0$
$x = 5t\cos 14° + 0$
$x = 5t\cos 14°$
$x \approx 4.8515t$

Step 4
Write the parametric equation for the vertical component of motion.

$y = -\frac{1}{2}gt^2 + vt\sin\theta + y_0$

Step 5
Substitute the known values into the parametric equation for the vertical component of the ball's motion, y.

$y = -\frac{1}{2}gt^2 + vt\sin\theta + y_0$

$y = -\frac{1}{2}9.81t^2 + 5t\sin 14° + 2$

$y = -4.905t^2 + 5t\sin 14° + 2$
$y \approx -4.905t^2 + 1.2096t + 2$

The parametric equations that describe the ball's path are given as follows:
$x \approx 4.8515t$
$y \approx -4.905t^2 + 1.2096t + 2$

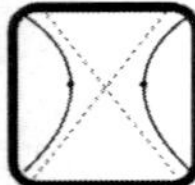

CONICS EXERCISE #1

Use the following information to answer the next question.

The roadway of a bridge is supported by a parabolic arch that is 12 m high and 50 m long. A horizontal girder is located 8 m below the vertex of the parabola to provide support for the arch. This information is shown on a coordinate system.

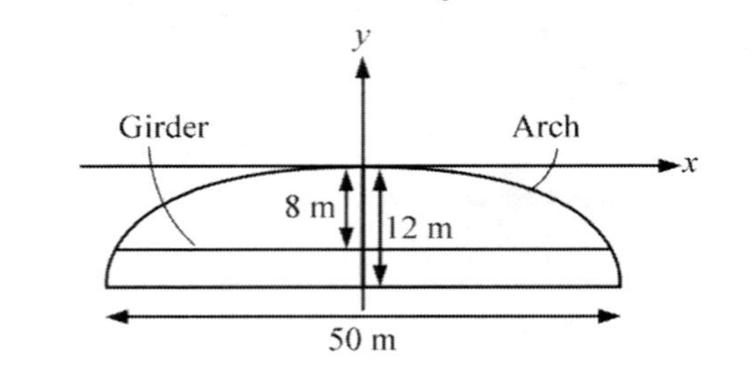

222. Rounded to the nearest tenth of a meter, the length of the horizontal girder is

A. 20.4 m **B.** 33.3 m

C. 40.8 m **D.** 46.1 m

Use the following information to answer the next question.

Ted is playing golf. From the distance of 147 m from the hole, Ted hits the golf ball directly at the flag stick. The golf ball lands a short distance from the hole. The flight of the golf ball may be modeled with a parabolic curve given by the formula

$y - 36 = \frac{-1}{144}x^2$

The diagram shows this information on a coordinate system.

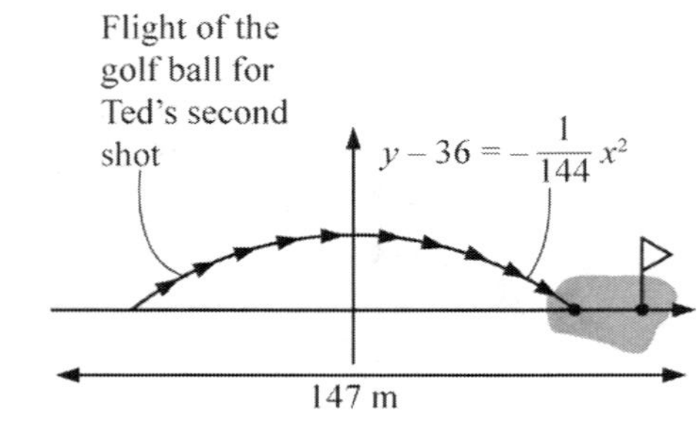

223. If the golf ball stops exactly where it lands (the ball does not roll), then the distance from the ball to the hole is

A. 2.0 m **B.** 2.5 m

C. 3.0 m **D.** 3.5 m

224. The range of the graph of the quadratic relation defined by the equation $(x+3)^2 + (y-1)^2 = 4$ is

A. $-1 \leq y \leq 3$ **B.** $-3 \leq y \leq 1$

C. $-5 \leq y \leq -1$ **D.** $-7 \leq y \leq 1$

225. Which of the following equations represents a circle with a radius of 3 units?

A. $2x^2 + 2(y+1)^2 = 6$

B. $3(x-2)^2 + 3(y+1)^2 = 9$

C. $\frac{(x+1)^2}{3} + \frac{(y-2)^2}{3} = 1$

D. $\frac{(x+4)^2}{9} + \frac{(y-7)^2}{9} = 1$

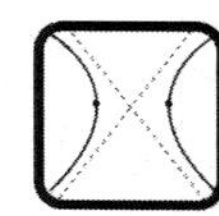

226. The general form equation that defines a circle that is centered at point (–3, 5) and has a diameter of 10 units is

A. $x^2 + y^2 + 6x - 10y + 59 = 0$

B. $x^2 + y^2 - 6x + 10y + 41 = 0$

C. $x^2 + y^2 + 6x - 10y + 9 = 0$

D. $x^2 + y^2 - 6x + 10y - 9 = 0$

227. Which equation defines a circle centered at point (2, –5) with a diameter of 12 units?

A. $x^2 + y^2 - 4x + 10y - 115 = 0$

B. $x^2 + y^2 + 4x - 10y - 115 = 0$

C. $x^2 + y^2 + 4x - 10y - 7 = 0$

D. $x^2 + y^2 - 4x + 10y - 7 = 0$

Use the following information to answer the next question.

The graph of a circle is shown.

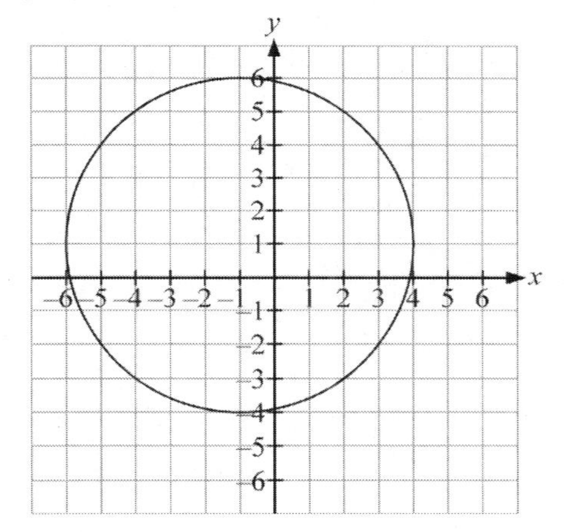

228. If an equation for the given circle is written in the general form $Ax^2 + Cy^2 + Dx + Ey + F = 0$, the value of $|A + C + D + E + F|$ is ________.

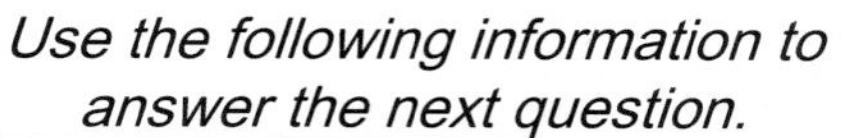

Use the following information to answer the next question.

The graph of a circle is shown.

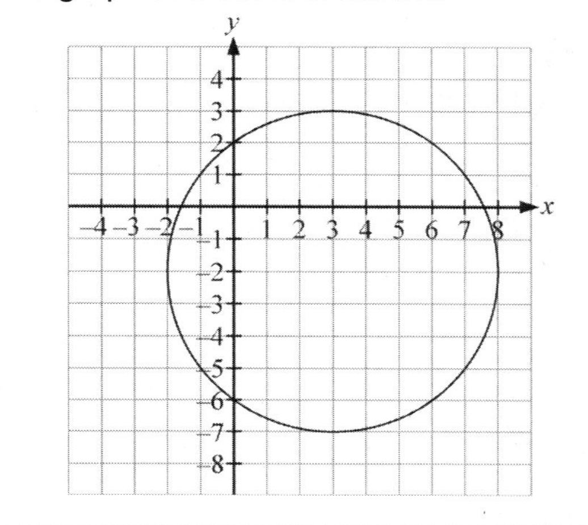

229. What is the equation of the given circle in standard form?

A. $(x - 3)^2 + (y + 2)^2 = 5^2$

B. $(x + 3)^2 + (y - 2)^2 = 5^2$

C. $(x - 2)^2 + (y + 3)^2 = 5^2$

D. $(x + 2)^2 + (y - 3)^2 = 5^2$

230. What is the domain of the graph of the conic defined by the equation $\frac{(x-2)^2}{4} + \frac{(y+3)^2}{9} = 1$?

A. $0 \le x \le 4$ **B.** $-2 \le x \le 6$

C. $-4 \le x \le 0$ **D.** $-6 \le x \le -2$

231. The range of the ellipse $\frac{x^2}{81} + \frac{y^2}{25} = 1$ is

A. $-9 \le y \le 9$ **B.** $-5 \le y \le 9$

C. $-9 \le y \le 5$ **D.** $-5 \le y \le 5$

232. An ellipse is centered at (–3, 2) and passes through the points (2, 2) and (–3, 5). What is the equation of the ellipse in general form?

A. $25x^2 - 9y^2 - 100x + 54y - 100 = 0$

B. $9x^2 + 25y^2 + 54x - 100y - 44 = 0$

C. $25x^2 + 9y^2 + 54x - 44y - 100 = 0$

D. $9x^2 - 25y^2 - 54x + 100y + 44 = 0$

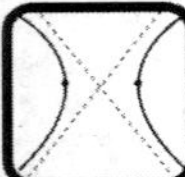

Use the following information to answer the next question.

A conic has the domain $-2 \le x \le 10$ and the range $-8 \le y \le 2$.

233. The standard form equation of this conic is

A. $\frac{(x-6)^2}{16} + \frac{(y+5)^2}{9} = 1$

B. $\frac{(x+6)^2}{16} + \frac{(y-5)^2}{9} = 1$

C. $\frac{(x-4)^2}{36} + \frac{(y+3)^2}{25} = 1$

D. $\frac{(x+4)^2}{36} + \frac{(y-3)^2}{25} = 1$

Use the following information to answer the next question.

A graph of an ellipse is shown.

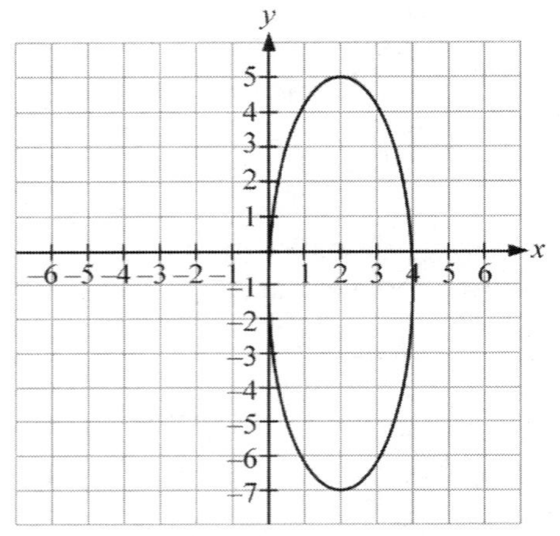

234. What is the equation of the given graph in general form?

A. $x^2 - y^2 + 36x - 2y - 1 = 0$

B. $9x^2 + y^2 - 36x + 2y + 1 = 0$

C. $9x^2 - y^2 + 36x - 2y - 1 = 0$

D. $x^2 + 9y^2 - 2x + 36y + 1 = 0$

Use the following information to answer the next question.

The graph of a conic is illustrated in the given diagram.

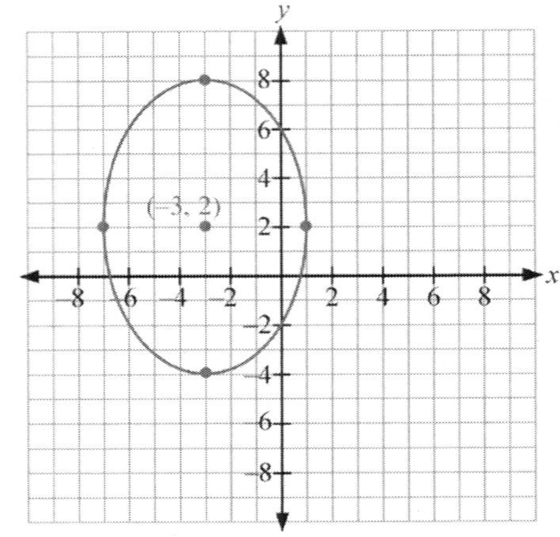

235. Which of the following equations could represent the given conic?

A. $\frac{(x+3)^2}{36} + \frac{(y-2)^2}{16} = 1$

B. $\frac{(x-3)^2}{36} + \frac{(y+2)^2}{16} = 1$

C. $\frac{(x+3)^2}{16} + \frac{(y-2)^2}{36} = 1$

D. $\frac{(x-3)^2}{16} + \frac{(y+2)^2}{36} = 1$

236. The vertices of the graph of the relation defined by the equation $\frac{(x+2)^2}{4} - \frac{(y-1)^2}{9} = -1$ are

A. (−2, −2) and (−2, 4)

B. (0, 1) and (−4, 1)

C. (0, −1) and (4, −1)

D. (2, 2) and (2, 4)

237. The equation of the conic $\frac{(x-3)^2}{25} - \frac{(y+2)^2}{9} = 1$ represents a hyperbola with one vertex at point

A. (3, 1) **B.** (2, 2)

C. (−8, 2) **D.** (−2, −2)

Use the following information to answer the next question.

A hyperbola in standard form is expressed by the equation $\frac{(x-h)^2}{16} - \frac{(y-k)^2}{b^2} = -1$.
The center of the hyperbola is at point (−4, 3), and the hyperbola passes through point (−4, 5).

238. What is the value of b^2?

A. 4 **B.** 8
C. 16 **D.** 64

Use the following information to answer the next question.

A hyperbola in standard form is expressed by the equation $\frac{(x-h)^2}{a^2} - \frac{(y-k)^2}{12} = 1$.
The center of the hyperbola is at point (−3, −4), and the hyperbola passes through point (5, −4).

239. What is the value of a^2?

A. 6 **B.** 8
C. 36 **D.** 64

Use the following information to answer the next question.

A hyperbola is given.

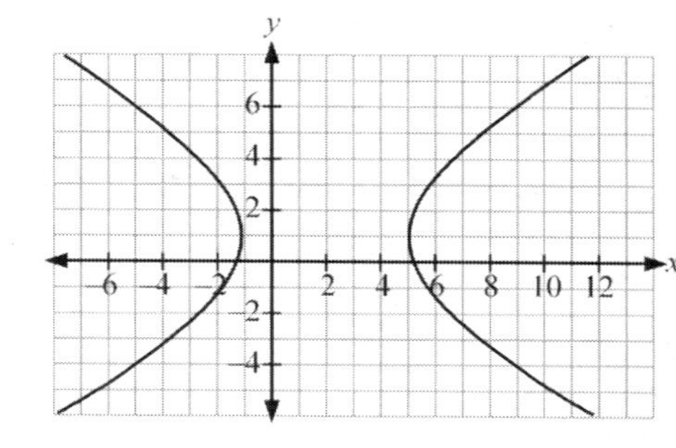

240. If $\frac{b}{a} = 1$, what is the equation, in general form, of the given hyperbola?

A. $x^2 - y^2 - 4x - 2y - 4 = 0$
B. $x^2 - y^2 - 4x + 2y - 6 = 0$
C. $2x^2 - y^2 + 2x + y - 9 = 0$
D. $2x^2 - 2y^2 + 8x - 4y - 8 = 0$

Use the following information to answer the next question.

The graph of a conic is illustrated in the given diagram.

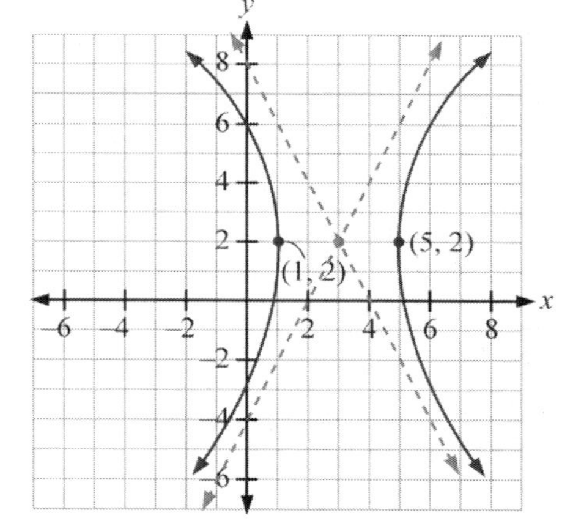

241. The equation of the conic shown could be

A. $16(x-3)^2 - 4(y-2)^2 = 64$
B. $16(x-3)^2 - 4(y-2)^2 = -64$
C. $4(x-3)^2 - 16(y-2)^2 = 64$
D. $4(x-3)^2 - 16(y-2)^2 = -64$

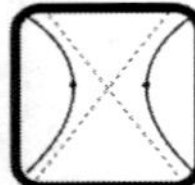

Use the following information to answer the next question.

A student is asked to determine the range of each of four different conics. The table shows the four conics and the student's solution for each.

	Conic	Student's Solution
I	$x^2 - 4y^2 = 36$	$y \in \mathrm{R}$
II	$x^2 + 4y^2 = 36$	$-3 \le y \le 3$
III	$y^2 - 4x = 8$	$y \in \mathrm{R}$
IV	$x^2 - 4y = 8$	$y \le 2$

242. Which conic has an incorrect range?

A. Conic I
B. Conic II
C. Conic III
D. Conic IV

Use the following information to answer the next question.

A student is asked to determine the domain of each of four different conics. The table shows the four conics and the student's solutions.

	Conic	Student's Solution
I	$x^2 - 9y^2 = -36$	$x \le -6$or $x \ge 6$
II	$9x^2 + y^2 = 36$	$-4 \le x \le 4$
III	$y^2 - 2x = 8$	$x \ge -4$
IV	$x^2 + 3y = -12$	$x \le -4$

243. Which conic shows the correct solution for the domain?

A. Conic I
B. Conic II
C. Conic III
D. Conic IV

Use the following information to answer the next question.

The vertex of a parabola is at (–3, 2).

244. If the parabola opens to the right and has a *y*-intercept of 5, then the equation of the parabola is

A. $y - 2 = \frac{1}{3}(x + 3)^2$

B. $x + 3 = \frac{1}{3}(y - 2)^2$

C. $y - 2 = -\frac{1}{3}(x + 3)^2$

D. $x + 3 = -\frac{1}{3}(y - 2)^2$

Use the following information to answer the next question.

The vertex of a parabola is at (4, –2).

245. If the parabola opens to the left and has an *x*-intercept of (2, 0), then the equation of the parabola can be written as

A. $y + 2 = \frac{1}{2}(x - 4)^2$

B. $y + 2 = -\frac{1}{2}(x - 4)^2$

C. $x - 4 = \frac{1}{2}(y + 2)^2$

D. $x - 4 = -\frac{1}{2}(y + 2)^2$

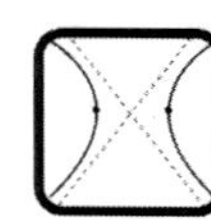

Use the following information to answer the next question.

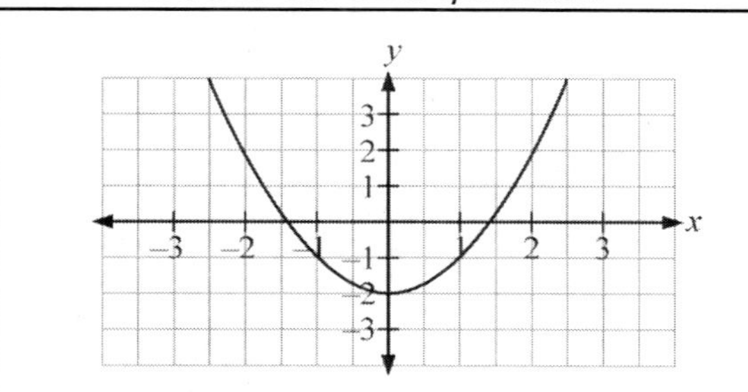

246. The graph shown can be represented by the equation

A. $y = 2x^2$

B. $y = (x + 2)^2$

C. $y = (x - 2)^2$

D. $y = x^2 - 2$

Use the following information to answer the next question.

The graph shown can be represented by the equation $x - h = a(y - k)^2$.

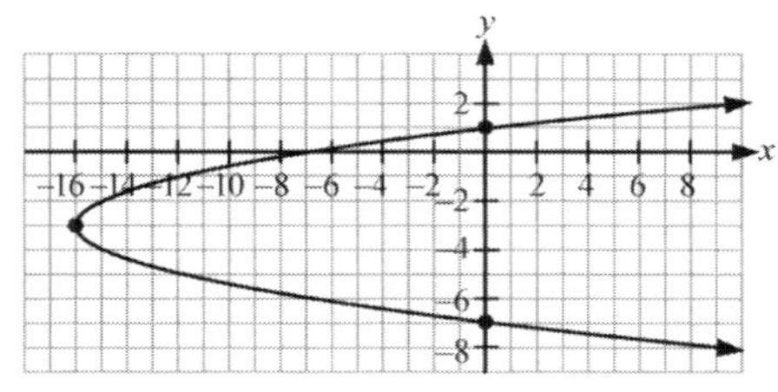

247. The value of a in the equation is _________.

Use the following information to answer the next question.

A set of parametric equations is given.

$x = \frac{t}{2} + 3$

$y = 10 + 2t$

248. Which of the following graphs represents the set of parametric equations if $-8 \le t \le -3$?

A.

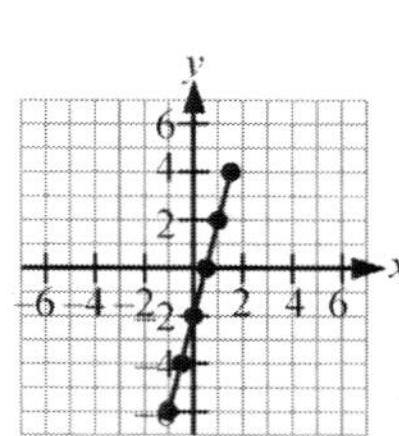

B.

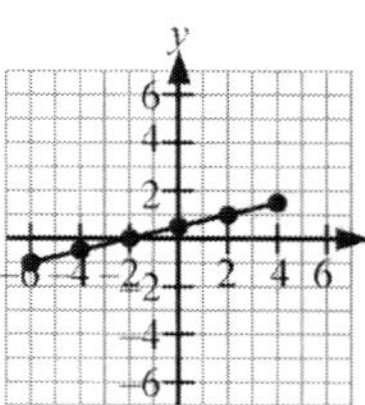

C.

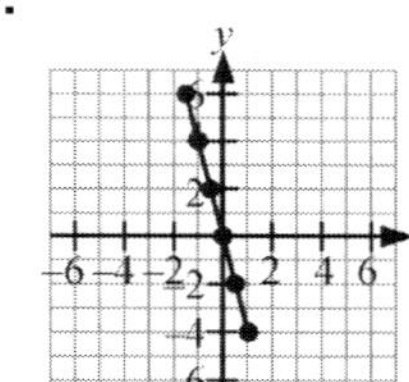

D.

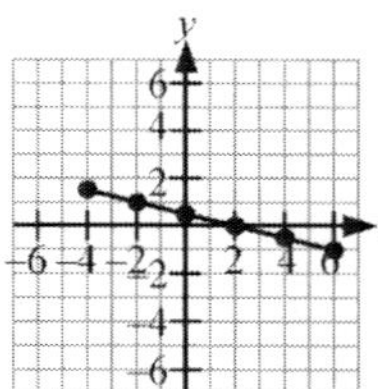

Use the following information to answer the next question.

A parametric equation is given.

$x = -\frac{t^3}{2} - 3$

$y = 5 - \frac{3t}{2}$

249. Given that $-2 \le t \le 2$, which of the following graphs represents this parametric equation?

A.

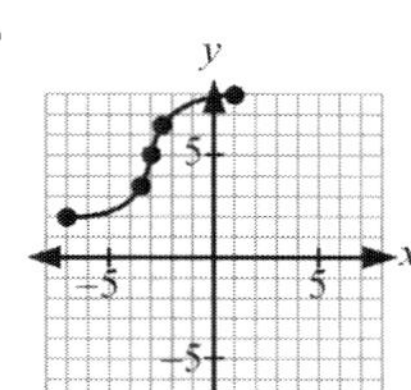

B.

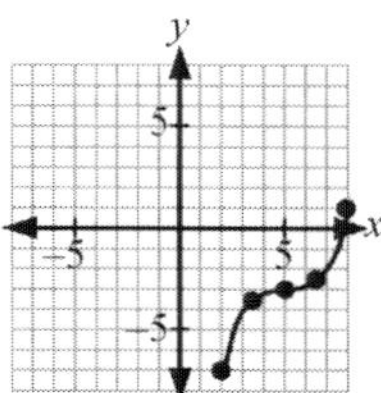

C.

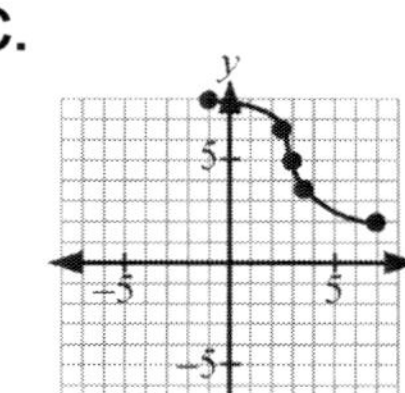

D.

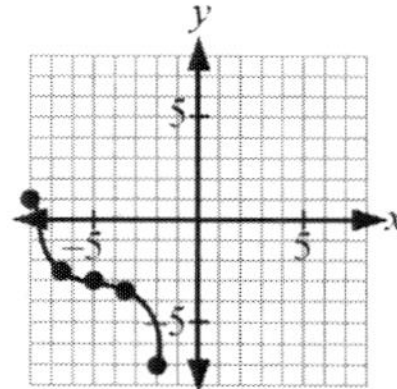

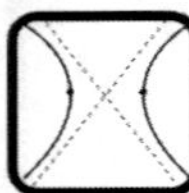

Use the following information to answer the next question.

A parametric equation is given.
$x = \sqrt{3} + \sqrt{4.5}t$
$y = \sqrt{2} + \sqrt{3}t$

250. What is the Cartesian form of the given parametric equation?

A. $\sqrt{4.5}x - \sqrt{3}y = 0$

B. $\sqrt{3}x - \sqrt{4.5}y = 0$

C. $\sqrt{4.5}x - \sqrt{3}y + 2\sqrt{9} = 0$

D. $\sqrt{3}x - \sqrt{4.5}y - 2\sqrt{9} = 0$

Use the following information to answer the next question.

A parametric equation is given.
$x = \sqrt{2} + \frac{5}{6}t$
$y = 3t$

251. What is the Cartesian form of the given parametric equation?

A. $x - 5y - \sqrt{2} = 0$

B. $5x - 18y - 5\sqrt{2} = 0$

C. $18x - 5y - 18\sqrt{2} = 0$

D. $5\sqrt{2}x - 18y - \sqrt{2} = 0$

Use the following information to answer the next question.

A pair of parametric equations are shown.
$x = -t^2$
$y = 3t - 2$

252. Given that $-2 \le t \le 2$, which of the following graphs is formed from these parametric equations?

A. **B.**

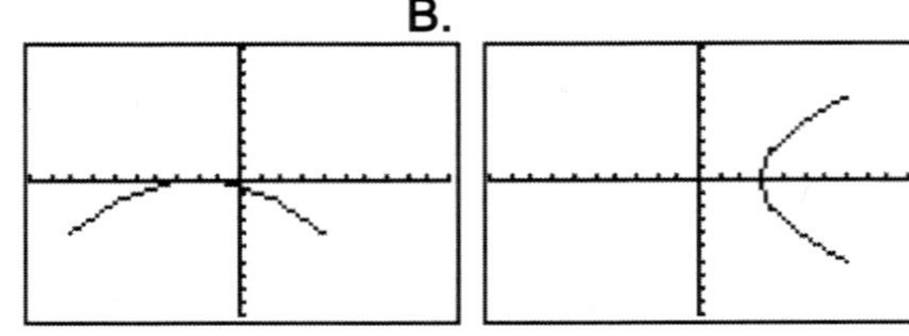

C. **D.**

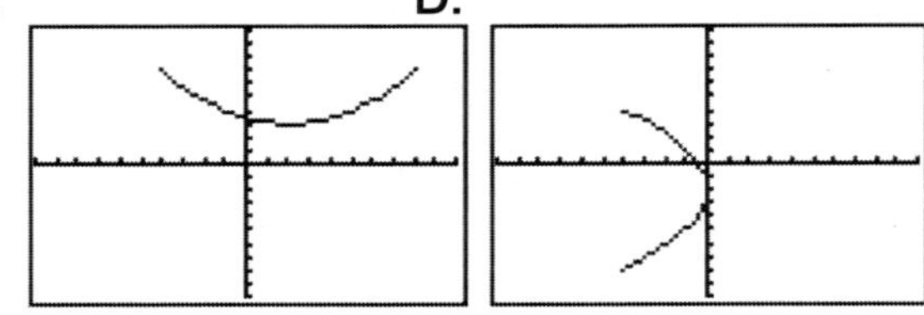

Use the following information to answer the next question.

A parametric equation is given.
$x = 1 - 3t$
$y = 7 - 5t$

253. Which of the following graphs is formed from the given parametric equation?

A. **B.**

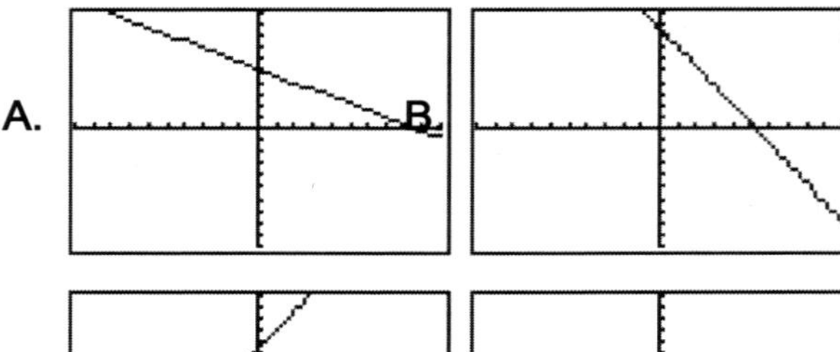

C. **D.**

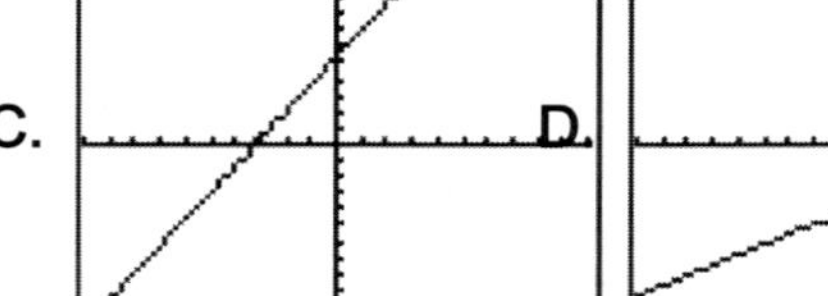

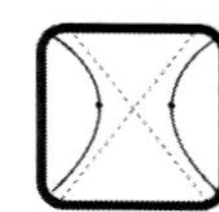

254. Which of the following equations are a possible parametric form of the Cartesian equation $2y^2 + 2x + 4y + 18 = 0$?

A. $x = t$
$y = -t^2 - 2t - 9$

B. $x = -t^2 - 2t - 9$
$y = t$

C. $x = t + 9$
$y = t^2 - 1$

D. $x = t^2 + 9$
$y = t - 1$

255. Which of the following pairs of parametric equations could represent the Cartesian equation $x^2 + 8x - y + 18 = 0$?

A. $x = t - 4$
$y = t^2 + 2$

B. $x = 4 - t^2$
$y = t + 2$

C. $x = t + 2$
$y = 4 - t^2$

D. $x = t^2 + 2$
$y = t - 4$

Use the following information to answer the next question.

A baseball is 1 m above the ground when it is hit. It travels at 22 m/s at an angle of elevation of 35°.

256. The distance the baseball will travel horizontally before it hits the ground is

A. 15.1 m **B.** 22.4 m

C. 31.9 m **D.** 47.8 m

Use the following information to answer the next question.

A motocross rider goes off a ramp that is 15 m above the ground. His initial trajectory is at an angle of elevation of 55°, traveling at 40 m/s.

257. Which of the following parametric equations represent the path of the motocross rider?

A. $x \approx -4.905t^2 + 22.943t$
$y \approx 32.766t + 15$

B. $x \approx -4.905t^2 + 32.766t$
$y \approx 22.943t + 15$

C. $x \approx 32.766t$
$y \approx -4.905t^2 + 22.943t + 15$

D. $x \approx 22.943t$
$y \approx -4.905t^2 + 32.766t + 15$

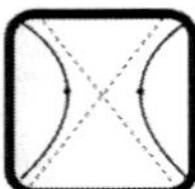

CONICS EXERCISE #1 ANSWERS AND SOLUTIONS

222. C	231. D	240. B	249. A
223. C	232. B	241. A	250. B
224. A	233. C	242. D	251. C
225. D	234. B	243. C	252. D
226. C	235. C	244. B	253. C
227. D	236. A	245. D	254. B
228. 21	237. D	246. D	255. A
229. A	238. A	247. 1	256. D
230. A	239. D	248. A	257. D

222. C

Step 1

Determine the equation of the parabola.

If the parabola has its vertex at (0, 0) and opens downward, then the form of the equation is $y = ax^2$ where $a < 0$.

From the diagram, point (25, −12) is on the parabola.

Substitute this value into the equation for a parabola, and solve for a.

$$y = ax^2$$
$$-12 = a(25^2)$$
$$a = -\frac{12}{625}$$
$$a = -0.0192$$

Therefore, the equation is $y = -0.0192x^2$.

Step 2

Determine half the length of the horizontal girder x by substituting $y = -8$ in the equation.

$$y = -0.0192x^2$$
$$-8 = -0.0192x^2$$
$$x^2 = \frac{8}{0.0192}$$
$$x^2 \approx 416.7$$
$$x \approx 20.4$$

Step 3

Determine the length of the horizontal girder.

The length of the horizontal girder is double the length of half the girder.

$2 \times 20.4 = 40.8$

Rounded to the nearest tenth of a meter, the length of the horizontal girder is 40.8 m.

223. C

In order to determine the distance between the ball and the hole, the total length of Ted's shot must be determined and then subtracted from Ted's distance from the hole.

Step 1

Determine the x-intercepts of the given equation.

Substitute 0 for y in the equation $y - 36 = -\frac{1}{144}x^2$, and simplify.

$$(0) - 36 = -\frac{1}{144}x^2$$
$$-36(-144) = x^2$$
$$5,184 = x^2$$
$$\pm\sqrt{5,184} = \sqrt{x}$$
$$\pm 72 = x$$

Step 2

Determine the horizontal distance that the golf ball travels.

The horizontal distance is the distance between the two x-intercepts and is equal to the difference:

$72 - (-72) = 144$

Step 3

Determine the difference between Ted's distance from the hole and Ted's drive.

Ted is 147 m from the hole.

The difference is 147 − 144 = 3 m.

Thus, the distance from the ball to the hole is 3 m.

224. A

Step 1

Determine the center and the radius of the circle defined by the equation $(x + 3)^2 + (y - 1)^2 = 4$.

Rewrite the equation $(x + 3)^2 + (y - 1)^2 = 4$ so that 4 is a power of 2.

$(x + 3)^2 + (y - 1)^2 = 2^2$

The equation represents a circle with a radius of 2 units and a center at (−3, 1).

Step 2
Determine the endpoints of the vertical diameter of the circle using the center and the radius of 2 units.
The endpoints of the vertical diameter are
$(-3, 1-2) = (-3, -1)$ and $(-3, 1+2) = (-3, 3)$.
The range is $-1 \le y \le 3$.

225. D

Step 1
Identify the standard form of the equation of a circle.
The standard form of the equation of a circle is $(x-h)^2 + (y-k)^2 = r^2$, where (h, k) is the center and r is the radius.

Step 2
Write the equation $2x^2 + 2(y+1)^2 = 6$ in standard form to determine the radius of the circle defined by the equation.
Divide both sides of the equation by 2.
$x^2 + (y+1)^2 = 3$
$x^2 + (y+1)^2 = (\sqrt{3})^2$
The radius of the circle defined by the equation $2x^2 + 2(y+1)^2 = 6$ is $\sqrt{3}$ units.

Step 3
Write the equation $3(x-2)^2 + 3(y+1)^2 = 9$ in standard form to determine the radius of the circle defined by the equation.
Divide both sides of the equation by 3.
$(x-2)^2 + (y+1)^2 = 3$
$(x-2)^2 + (y+1)^2 = (\sqrt{3})^2$
The radius of the circle defined by the equation $3(x-2)^2 + 3(y+1)^2 = 9$ is $\sqrt{3}$ units.

Step 4
Write the equation $\dfrac{(x+1)^2}{3} + \dfrac{(y-2)^2}{3} = 1$ in standard form to determine the radius of the circle defined by the equation.
Multiply both sides of the equation by 3.
$(x+1)^2 + (y-2)^2 = 3$
$(x+1)^2 + (y-2)^2 = (\sqrt{3})^2$
The radius of the circle defined by the equation $\dfrac{(x+1)^2}{3} + \dfrac{(y-2)^2}{3} = 1$ is $\sqrt{3}$ units.

Step 5
Write the equation $\dfrac{(x+4)^2}{9} + \dfrac{(y-7)^2}{9} = 1$ in standard form to determine the radius of the circle defined by the equation.
Multiply both sides of the equation by 9.
$(x+4)^2 + (y-7)^2 = 9$
$(x+4)^2 + (y-7)^2 = 3^2$
The radius of the circle defined by the equation $\dfrac{(x+4)^2}{9} + \dfrac{(y-7)^2}{9} = 1$ is 3 units.

226. C

Step 1
Identify the standard form of the equation of a circle.
The standard form of the equation of a circle is $(x-h)^2 + (y-k)^2 = r^2$, where (h, k) is the center of the circle and r is the radius.
Given that the center of the circle is at $(-3, 5)$ and the diameter is 10 units, the radius is $\dfrac{10}{2}$, or 5 units.
Substitute -3 for h, 5 for k, and 5 for r in the equation $(x-h)^2 + (y-k)^2 = r^2$.
The standard form of the equation of the circle is $(x+3)^2 + (y-5)^2 = 5^2$.

Step 2
Expand the binomials.
$(x^2 + 6x + 9) + (y^2 - 10y + 25) = 25$

Step 3
Collect the like terms, and set the right side of the equation equal to 0.
$x^2 + y^2 + 6x - 10y + 9 = 0$

227. D

Step 1
Determine the standard form of the equation of the circle, $(x-h)^2 + (y-k)^2 = r^2$, where (h, k) is the center of the circle and r is the radius.
The center of the circle is at $(2, -5)$ and the diameter is 12 units, so the radius is $\dfrac{12}{2}$, or 6 units. Substitute 2 for h, -5 for k, and 6 for r in the equation $(x-h)^2 + (y-k)^2 = r^2$.
Therefore, the standard form of the equation of the circle is $(x-2)^2 + (y+5)^2 = 6^2$.

Step 2
Expand the binomials.
$(x^2 - 4x + 4) + (y^2 + 10y + 25) = 36$

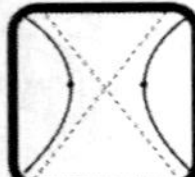

Step 3
Collect the like terms, and set the right-hand side of the equation equal to 0.
$x^2 + y^2 - 4x + 10y - 7 = 0$

228. 21

Step 1
From the given graph, determine the center, (h, k), and the radius, r, of the circle.
The center of the circle is at $(-1, 1)$, and the radius is 5 units.

Step 2
Substitute -1 for h, 1 for k, and 5 for r into the standard form of the equation of a circle,
$(x - h)^2 + (y - k)^2 = r^2$.
$(x - (-1))^2 + (y - 1)^2 = 5^2$
$(x + 1)^2 + (y - 1)^2 = 25$

Step 3
Convert to the general form,
$Ax^2 + Cy^2 + Dx + Ey + F = 0$.

$$(x + 1)^2 + (y - 1)^2 = 25$$
$$\left(x^2 + 2x + 1\right) + \left(y^2 - 2y + 1\right) = 25$$
$$x^2 + y^2 + 2x - 2y + 1 + 1 - 25 = 0$$
$$x^2 + y^2 + 2x - 2y - 23 = 0$$

The general form of the equation of the circle is
$x^2 + y^2 + 2x - 2y - 23 = 0$.

Step 4
Determine the value of $|A + C + D + E + F|$.
$|A + C + D + E + F|$
$= |1 + 1 + 2 + (-2) + (-23)|$
$= |1 + 1 + 2 - 2 - 23|$
$= |-21|$
$= 21$

229. A

Step 1
Determine the center, (h, k), and the radius, r, of the circle from the given graph.
The center of the circle is at $(3, -2)$, and the radius is 5 units.

Step 2
Substitute 3 for h, -2 for k, and 5 for r into the standard form of the equation of a circle,
$(x - h)^2 + (y - k)^2 = r^2$.
$(x - 3)^2 + (y - (-2))^2 = 5^2$
$(x - 3)^2 + (y + 2)^2 = 5^2$

230. A

Step 1
Write the denominators as perfect squares.

$$\frac{(x-2)^2}{2^2} + \frac{(y+3)^2}{3^2} = 1$$

Step 2
Compare with the standard equation for an ellipse.

$$\frac{(x-h)^2}{a^2} + \frac{(y-k)^2}{b^2} = 1$$

The ellipse has its center at (h, k), or $(2, -3)$.
The values of a and b are 2 and 3, respectively.
Since $a < b$, the major axis is vertical. The vertices will be 3 units above and below the center, and the covertices, or minor axis endpoints, will be 2 units to the right and left of the center.
The vertices are $(2, 0)$ and $(2, -6)$, and the covertices are $(0, -3)$ and $(4, -3)$.

Step 3
Since $a < b$, the domain of the equation is between the covertices.
Therefore, the domain of the equation is $0 \le x \le 4$.

231. D

Step 1
Graph the ellipse.
The equation in this question is in standard form.

$$\frac{x^2}{a^2} + \frac{y^2}{b^2} = 1$$

$$\frac{x^2}{9^2} + \frac{y^2}{5^2} = 1$$

The center of the ellipse is $(0, 0)$, the y-intercepts are $(0, -5)$, $(0, 5)$, and the x-intercepts are $(0, -9)$, $(0, 9)$.

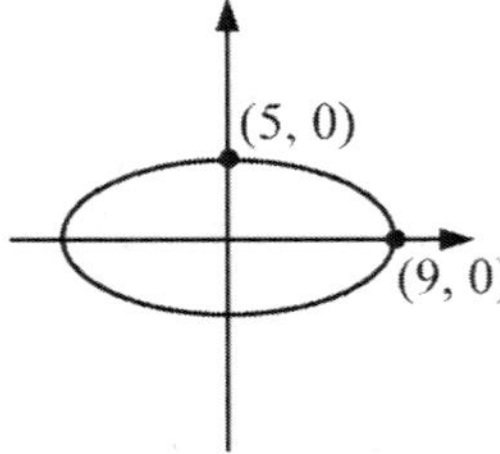

Step 2
State the range.
The range of the ellipse is $-5 \le y \le 5$.

232. B

Step 1
Determine the values of h and k.
The ellipse is centered at $(-3, 2)$, so $h = -3$ and $k = 2$.
Substitute the values for h and k into the standard form equation of an ellipse, $\frac{(x-h)^2}{a^2}+\frac{(y-k)^2}{b^2}=1$.

$$\frac{(x+3)^2}{a^2}+\frac{(y-2)^2}{b^2}=1$$

Step 2
Determine the values of a^2 and b^2.
The points $(2, 2)$ and $(-3, 5)$ must satisfy the equation $\frac{(x+3)^2}{a^2}+\frac{(y-2)^2}{b^2}=1$.

Substitute $(2, 2)$ into $\frac{(x+3)^2}{a^2}+\frac{(y-2)^2}{b^2}=1$, and solve for a^2.

$$\frac{(2+3)^2}{a^2}+\frac{(2-2)^2}{b^2}=1$$
$$\frac{(5)^2}{a^2}+\frac{0}{b^2}=1$$
$$\frac{25}{a^2}=1$$
$$25=a^2$$

Substitute $(-3, 5)$ into $\frac{(x+3)^2}{a^2}+\frac{(y-2)^2}{b^2}=1$, and solve for b^2.

$$\frac{(-3+3)^2}{a^2}+\frac{(5-2)^2}{b^2}=1$$
$$\frac{0}{a^2}+\frac{(3)^2}{b^2}=1$$
$$\frac{9}{b^2}=1$$
$$9=b^2$$

Step 3
Substitute the values for a^2, b^2, h, and k into the standard form equation of an ellipse,
$\frac{(x-h)^2}{a^2}+\frac{(y-k)^2}{b^2}=1$.
Therefore, the equation in standard form is
$\frac{(x+3)^2}{25}+\frac{(y-2)^2}{9}=1$.

Step 4
Convert to general form.

$$\frac{(x+3)^2}{25}+\frac{(y-2)^2}{9}=1$$

Multiply both sides by 25 and 9.

$$9(x+3)^2+25(y-2)^2=225$$

Simplify.

$$\begin{pmatrix} 9(x^2+6x+9) \\ +25(y^2-4y+4) \end{pmatrix}=225$$
$$\begin{pmatrix} 9x^2+54x+81 \\ +25y^2-100y+100 \end{pmatrix}=225$$
$$9x^2+25y^2+54x-100y-44=0$$

The equation of the ellipse in general form is
$9x^2+25y^2+54x-100y-44=0$.

233. C

Since the domain and range indicate a contained conic, the conic is either a circle or an ellipse.

Step 1
Determine the major axis length and minor axis length.
The horizontal distance between the end points of the domain is $10-(-2)=12$. The vertical distance between the end points of the range is
$2-(-8)=10$.
$2a=12$ and $2b=10$
Therefore, $a=6$ and $b=5$. The conic is an ellipse.

Step 2
Find the coordinates of the center.
The x-coordinate of the center will be halfway between the minimum and maximum values of the domain, and the y-coordinate of the center will be halfway between the minimum and maximum values of the range.
The coordinates of the center are
$\left(\frac{-2+10}{2}, \frac{-8+2}{2}\right)$ or $(4, -3)$.

Step 3
Substitute the values for h, k, a, and b in the standard form of an ellipse with center (h, k) and axes of length $2a$ and $2b$, $\frac{(x-h)^2}{a^2}+\frac{(y-k)^2}{b^2}=1$.

$$\frac{(x-4)^2}{6^2}+\frac{(y+3)^2}{5^2}=1$$

Simplify.

$$\frac{(x-4)^2}{36}+\frac{(y+3)^2}{25}=1$$

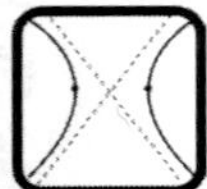

234. B

Step 1
Locate the center (h, k) on the graph, and determine the values of h and k.

The center is $(2, -1)$; therefore, $h = 2$ and $k = -1$.

Step 2
Observe the horizontal length ($2a$) and the vertical length ($2b$) of the ellipse. Determine the values of a and b.

Determine the horizontal length.

$$2a = 4 - 0$$
$$2a = 4$$
$$a = 2$$

Determine the vertical length.

$$2b = 5 - (-7)$$
$$2b = 5 + 7$$
$$2b = 12$$
$$b = 6$$

Step 3
Write the standard form of the equation of the ellipse.

Substitute the values of a, b, h, and k into the standard form of the equation of an ellipse,

$$\frac{(x-h)^2}{a^2} + \frac{(y-k)^2}{b^2} = 1.$$

$$\frac{(x-2)^2}{2^2} + \frac{(y-(-1))^2}{6^2} = 1$$

Simplify.

$$\frac{(x-2)^2}{4} + \frac{(y+1)^2}{36} = 1$$

Step 4
Convert the standard form of the equation to general form.

Multiply both sides by 36.

$$9(x-2)^2 + (y+1)^2 = 36$$
$$9\left(x^2 - 4x + 4\right) + y^2 + 2y + 1 = 36$$
$$9x^2 - 36x + 36 + y^2 + 2y + 1 = 36$$
$$9x^2 + y^2 - 36x + 2y + 1 = 0$$

235. C

The standard form for the equation of an ellipse is $\frac{(x-h)^2}{a^2} + \frac{(y-k)^2}{b^2} = 1.$

Step 1
Identify the coordinates of the vertices for the major and minor axes.

The conic is an ellipse with center $(-3, 2)$. Thus, $h = -3$ and $k = 2$.

The coordinates of the major-axis vertices are $(-3, 8)$ and $(-3, -4)$. The coordinates of the minor-axis vertices are $(-7, 2)$ and $(1, 2)$.

Step 2
Determine the length of the major and minor axes.
The length of the major axis is $8 - (-4) = 12$.
The length of the minor axis is $1 - (-7) = 8$.
From the figure, the ellipse has a vertical major axis and a horizontal minor axis.
Since the length of the major axis is 12, $b = 6$.
Similarly, since the length of the minor axis is 8, $a = 4$.

Step 3
Substitute the values of a, b, h, and k into the equation $\frac{(x-h)^2}{a^2} + \frac{(y-k)^2}{b^2} = 1.$

The equation becomes

$\frac{(x-(-3))^2}{4^2} + \frac{(y-(2))^2}{6^2} = 1$, which simplifies to

$\frac{(x+3)^2}{16} + \frac{(y-2)^2}{36} = 1.$

236. A

The vertices of the hyperbola

$\frac{(x-h)^2}{a^2} - \frac{(y-k)^2}{b^2} = -1$ are $(h, k \pm b)$.

The equation $\frac{(x+2)^2}{4} - \frac{(y-1)^2}{9} = -1$ can be rewritten as $\frac{(x+2)^2}{2^2} - \frac{(y-1)^2}{3^2} = -1.$

The value of b is 3, the value of k is 1, and the value of h is -2.

The vertices are $(-2, 1 \pm 3)$, or $(-2, -2)$ and $(-2, 4)$.

237. D

Step 1
Determine the values of a, h, and k.
The given hyperbola is in the form

$\frac{(x-h)^2}{a^2} - \frac{(y-k)^2}{b^2} = 1.$

The equation $\frac{(x-3)^2}{25} - \frac{(y+2)^2}{9} = 1$ can be rewritten as $\frac{(x-3)^2}{5^2} - \frac{(y+2)^2}{3^2} = 1.$

The value of a is 5, the value of h is 3, and the value of k is -2.

Step 2
Determine the vertices of the given hyperbola.

The vertices of a hyperbola in the form $\frac{(x-h)^2}{a^2} - \frac{(y-k)^2}{b^2} = 1$ are located at $(h \pm a, k)$.

The vertices for the given hyperbola are then located at $(3 \pm 5, -2)$; that is, $(8, -2)$ and $(-2, -2)$.

238. A

The standard form of the equation of a hyperbola with a vertical orientation and with center (h, k) is $\frac{(x-h)^2}{a^2} - \frac{(y-k)^2}{b^2} = -1$. The center of the given hyperbola is $(-4, 3)$, and the point $(-4, 5)$ lies on the hyperbola.

Step 1
Substitute $h = -4$, $k = 3$, $x = -4$, and $y = 5$ into the given equation.

$$\frac{(-4+4)^2}{16} - \frac{(5-3)^2}{b^2} = -1$$

Step 2
Simplify.

$$\frac{0^2}{16} - \frac{2^2}{b^2} = -1$$
$$-\left(\frac{4}{b^2}\right) = -1$$
$$\frac{4}{b^2} = 1$$

Multiply each side by b^2.

$$b^2\left(\frac{4}{b^2}\right) = 1\left(b^2\right)$$
$$4 = b^2$$

Therefore, $b^2 = 4$.

239. D

The standard form of the equation of a hyperbola with center (h, k) is $\frac{(x-h)^2}{a^2} - \frac{(y-k)^2}{b^2} = 1$.

The center of the given hyperbola is $(-3, -4)$, and the point $(5, -4)$ is on the hyperbola.

Step 1
Substitute $h = -3$, $k = -4$, $x = 5$, and $y = -4$ in $\frac{(x-h)^2}{a^2} - \frac{(y-k)^2}{12} = 1$.

$$\frac{(5+3)^2}{a^2} - \frac{(-4+4)^2}{12} = 1$$

Step 2
Simplify.

$$\frac{8^2}{a^2} - \frac{0^2}{12} = 1$$
$$\frac{64}{a^2} = 1$$

Multiply each side by a^2.

$$a^2\left(\frac{64}{a^2}\right) = 1\left(a^2\right)$$
$$a^2 = 64$$

240. B

Step 1
Classify the conic section by using the graph.

The quadratic relation shown in the graph is a hyperbola with a horizontal orientation. It models an equation of the form $\frac{(x-h)^2}{a^2} - \frac{(y-k)^2}{b^2} = 1$.

Step 2
Locate the vertices and center on the graph.

The vertices are $(-1, 1)$ and $(5, 1)$. The center is located in the middle between the two vertices, $(2, 1)$; therefore, $h = 2$ and $k = 1$.

Step 3
Determine the distance from the center to a vertex to find the value of a.

The distance from the center to a vertex is 3 units. This is a horizontal hyperbola, thus $a = 3$.

Step 4
Determine the value of b.

It is given that $\frac{b}{a} = 1$.

$$\frac{b}{3} = 1$$
$$b = 3$$

Step 5
Substitute the values for a, b, h, and k into the standard form hyperbola equation, and simplify.

$$\frac{(x-2)^2}{3^2} - \frac{(y-1)^2}{3^2} = 1$$
$$\frac{(x-2)^2}{9} - \frac{(y-1)^2}{9} = 1$$

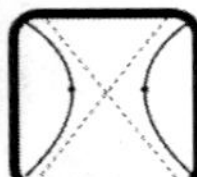

Step 6
Convert the standard form of the equation to general form. Multiply both sides by 9.

$$\frac{(x-2)^2}{9}-\frac{(y-1)^2}{9}=1$$
$$(x-2)^2-(y-1)^2=9$$
$$x^2-4x+4-\left(y^2-2y+1\right)=9$$
$$x^2-4x+4-y^2+2y-1=9$$
$$x^2-y^2-4x+2y-6=0$$

241. A

Step 1
Analyze the graph.
The center of the hyperbola (h, k) is (3, 2).
The distance between the vertices is 4 units, so $a=2$. Observe that the slopes of the asymptotes are ±2. Recall that the general form for the slopes of the asymptotes of a hyperbola are $\pm\frac{b}{a}$.
Substitute known values to determine the value of b.
$\pm\frac{b}{(2)}=\pm2$, so $b=4$.

Step 2
Write in standard form.
The standard form of the equation of the hyperbola is $\frac{(x-h)^2}{a^2}-\frac{(y-k)^2}{b^2}=1$.
Substitute 3 for h, 2 for k, 2 for a, and 4 for b.
$$\frac{(x-3)^2}{4}-\frac{(y-2)^2}{16}=1$$

Step 3
Simplify.
$$16(x-3)^2-4(y-2)^2=64$$

242. D

Step 1
Rewrite the equation of conic I, and find its range.
$$4y^2=x^2-36$$
$$y^2=\frac{x^2-36}{4}$$
$$y=\pm\frac{\sqrt{x^2-36}}{2}$$
The expression under the radicand should not be negative. The right side of the expression can take any real value, so the range is all real numbers.

Step 2
Rewrite the equation of conic II, and find its range.
$$4y^2=-x^2+36$$
$$y^2=\frac{-x^2+36}{4}$$
$$y=\pm\frac{\sqrt{-x^2+36}}{2}$$
The expression under the radicand should not be negative, so x must be greater than -6 and less than 6.
The maximum and minimum values of y are obtained when $x=0$.
Therefore, the range is $-\frac{\sqrt{36}}{2}\le y\le\frac{\sqrt{36}}{2}$ or $-3\le y\le3$.

Step 3
Rewrite the equation of conic III, and find its range.
$$y^2=4x+8$$
$$y=\pm\sqrt{4x+8}$$
$$y=\pm2\sqrt{x+2}$$
The expression under the radicand should not be negative. The right side of the expression can take any real value, so the range is all real numbers.

Step 4
Rewrite the equation of conic IV, and find its range.
$$4y=x^2-8$$
$$y=\frac{x^2-8}{4}$$
The value of x^2 is always greater than or equal to 0.
Therefore, the range is $y\ge-\frac{8}{4}$ or $y\ge-2$.
The student has reversed the inequality in the range for conic IV.

243. C

Step 1
Rewrite the equation of conic I.
$$x^2=-36+9y^2$$
$$x=\pm\sqrt{-36+9y^2}$$
The equation shows that for all possible values of y ($y\le-2$ and $y\ge2$), the domain is all real numbers.

Step 2
Rewrite the equation of conic II.
$9x^2 = 36 - y^2$
$x = \pm\frac{\sqrt{36 - y^2}}{9}$

The value of y^2 is always greater than or equal to 0, so the maximum and minimum values for x are $\frac{\sqrt{36}}{9} = \frac{2}{3}$ and $-\frac{\sqrt{36}}{9} = -\frac{2}{3}$, respectively.

Therefore, the domain is $-\frac{2}{3} \le x \le \frac{2}{3}$.

Step 3
Rewrite the equation of conic III.
$2x = y^2 - 8$
$x = \frac{y^2 - 8}{2}$

The value of y^2 is always greater than or equal to 0, so the minimum value for x is $-\frac{8}{2} = -4$.

Therefore, the domain is $x \ge -4$.

Step 4
Rewrite the equation of conic IV.
$x^2 = -12 - 3y$
$x = \pm\sqrt{-12 - 3y}$
The expression under the radicand must be positive, but the right side of the equation can still take any real value. Therefore, the domain is all real numbers.

When you compare these domains with those listed in the given table, only conic III is shown with the correct solution for the domain.

244. B

The standard form of a parabola that opens to the right with vertex (h, k) is $x - h = a(y - k)^2$, where $a > 0$.

Since the y-intercept is 5, the point (0, 5) lies on the parabola.

The vertex of the parabola is (–3, 2).

Step 1
Substitute $h = -3$, $k = 2$, $x = 0$, and $y = 5$ in the standard form of the equation.
$0 - (-3) = a(5 - 2)^2$

Step 2
Simplify.
$3 = 9a$
Divide each side by 9.
$a = \frac{1}{3}$

Step 3
Substitute $h = -3$, $k = 2$, and $a = \frac{1}{3}$ in
$x - h = a(y - k)^2$.
$x + 3 = \frac{1}{3}(y - 2)^2$

245. D

The standard form of equation of a parabola with a vertex (h, k) and that opens left is
$x - h = a(y - k)^2$, where $a < 0$.

Here, the vertex (h, k) is (4, –2), and the point (2, 0) is on the parabola.

Step 1
Substitute $h = 4$, $k = -2$, $x = 2$, and $y = 0$.
$2 - 4 = a(0 + 2)^2$
Simplify.
$-2 = 4a$

Step 2
Divide both sides by 4, and simplify.
$a = -\frac{1}{2}$

Step 3
Use the value of a and the coordinates of the vertex to write the equation.

Substitute $h = 4$, $k = -2$, and $a = -\frac{1}{2}$ in
$x - h = a(y - k)^2$.
$x - 4 = -\frac{1}{2}(y + 2)^2$

246. D

The graph shown is that of a parabola. The standard form of the equation of a parabola is
$y - k = a(x - h)^2$, where (h, k) is the vertex of the parabola.

The vertex of the given parabola is at (0, –2), so the values of h and k are 0 and –2, respectively.

Step 1
Substitute the values of h and k in the standard form.
$y - (-2) = a(x - 0)^2$

The equation simplifies to $y = ax^2 - 2$.

Step 2
Since the parabola contains the point (2, 2), this point must satisfy the equation of the parabola.

Substitute (2, 2) in $y = ax^2 - 2$.
$2 = a(2)^2 - 2$
$2 = 4a - 2$

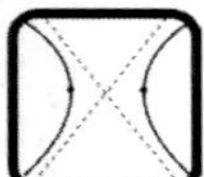

Step 3
Solve for a.

$$4a - 2 = 2$$
$$4a = 4$$
$$a = 1$$

Step 4
Use the value of a in the equation of the graph.
Substitute the value of a in the equation $y = ax^2 - 2$.
Therefore, the equation of the quadratic function is $y = x^2 - 2$.

247. 1

The graph shown is a parabola. The standard form of the equation of a parabola that opens right or left is $x - h = a(y - k)^2$, where (h, k) is the vertex of the parabola.

The vertex of the given parabola is at (–16, –3), so the values of h and k are –16 and –3, respectively.

Step 1
Substitute the values of h and k in the equation $x - h = a(y - k)^2$, and simplify.

$$x - (-16) = a(y - (-3))^2$$
$$x + 16 = a(y + 3)^2$$
$$x = a(y + 3)^2 - 16$$

Step 2
Since the parabola contains the point (0, 1), this point must satisfy the equation of the parabola.

Substitute (0, 1) in $x = a(y + 3)^2 - 16$, and solve for a.

$$0 = a(1 + 3)^2 - 16$$
$$0 = a(4)^2 - 16$$
$$16 = 16a$$
$$a = 1$$

Therefore, the equation of the parabola is $x = (y + 3)^2 - 16$ and the value of a is 1.

248. A

Step 1
Determine the values of x.
Taking into account the restriction on the t-variable, substitute the values –8, –7, –6, –5, –4, and –3 into the equation $x = \frac{t}{2} + 3$.

t	x
–8	$x = \frac{-8}{2} + 3$ $x = -4 + 3$ $x = -1$
–7	$x = \frac{-7}{2} + 3$ $x = -3.5 + 3$ $x = -0.5$
–6	$x = \frac{-6}{2} + 3$ $x = -3 + 3$ $x = 0$
–5	$x = \frac{-5}{2} + 3$ $x = -2.5 + 3$ $x = 0.5$
–4	$x = \frac{-4}{2} + 3$ $x = -2 + 3$ $x = 1$
–3	$x = \frac{-3}{2} + 3$ $x = -1.5 + 3$ $x = 1.5$

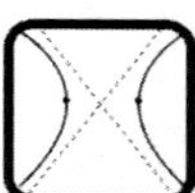

Step 2
Determine the values of y.
Taking into account the restriction on the t-variable, substitute the values –8, –7, –6, –5, –4, and –3 into the equation $y = 10 + 2t$.

t	y
–8	$y = 10 + 2(-8)$ $y = 10 - 16$ $y = -6$
–7	$y = 10 + 2(-7)$ $y = 10 - 14$ $y = -4$
–6	$y = 10 + 2(-6)$ $y = 10 - 12$ $y = -2$
–5	$y = 10 + 2(-5)$ $y = 10 - 10$ $y = 0$
–4	$y = 10 + 2(-4)$ $y = 10 - 8$ $y = 2$
–3	$y = 10 + 2(-3)$ $y = 10 - 6$ $y = 4$

Step 3
Build a table of values.

x	y
–1	–6
–0.5	–4
0	–2
0.5	0
1	2
1.5	4

Step 4
Plot the points, and sketch the graph.

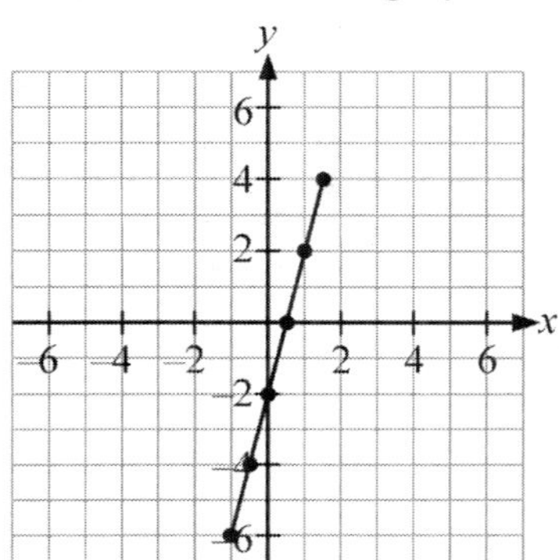

249. A

Step 1
Determine the values of x.
Looking at the restriction given to the t-variable, substitute the values –2, –1, 0, 1, and 2 into the equation $x = -\frac{t^3}{2} - 3$.

t	x
–2	$x = -\frac{(-2)^3}{2} - 3$ $x = -\frac{-8}{2} - 3$ $x = 1$
–1	$x = -\frac{(-1)^3}{2} - 3$ $x = -\frac{-1}{2} - 3$ $x = -2.5$
0	$x = -\frac{(0)^3}{2} - 3$ $x = -3$
1	$x = -\frac{(1)^3}{2} - 3$ $x = -\frac{1}{2} - 3$ $x = -3.5$
2	$x = -\frac{(2)^3}{2} - 3$ $x = -\frac{8}{2} - 3$ $x = -7$

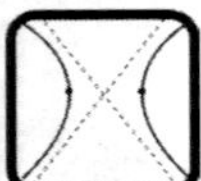

Step 2
Determine the values of y.
Looking at the restriction given to the t-variable, substitute the values –2, –1, 0, 1, and 2 into the equation $y = 5 - \frac{3t}{2}$.

t	y
–2	$y = 5 - \frac{3(-2)}{2}$ $y = 5 + 3$ $y = 8$
–1	$y = 5 - \frac{3(-1)}{2}$ $y = 5 + 1.5$ $y = 6.5$
0	$y = 5 - \frac{3(0)}{2}$ $y = 5$
1	$y = 5 - \frac{3(1)}{2}$ $y = 5 - 1.5$ $y = 3.5$
2	$y = 5 - \frac{3(2)}{2}$ $y = 5 - 3$ $y = 2$

Step 3
Build a table of values.

x	y
1	8
–2.5	6.5
–3	5
–3.5	3.5
–7	2

Step 4
Plot the points, and sketch the graph.

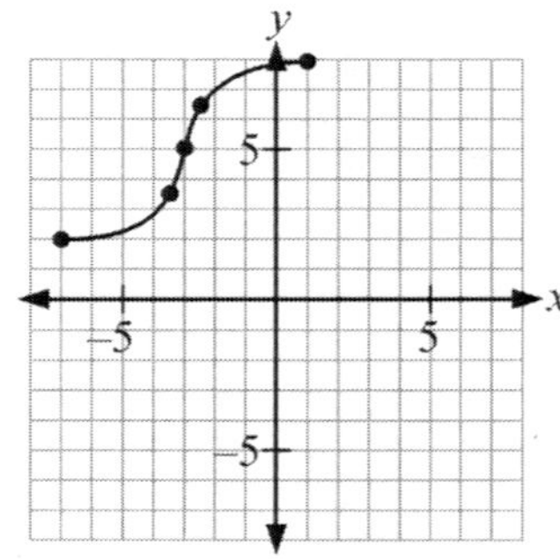

250. B

Step 1
Solve each equation for t.

$$x = \sqrt{3} + \sqrt{4.5}t$$
$$x - \sqrt{3} = \sqrt{4.5}t$$
$$\frac{x - \sqrt{3}}{\sqrt{4.5}} = t$$

$$y = \sqrt{2} + \sqrt{3}t$$
$$y - \sqrt{2} = \sqrt{3}t$$
$$\frac{y - \sqrt{2}}{\sqrt{3}} = t$$

Step 2
Equate the two equations.

$$\frac{x - \sqrt{3}}{\sqrt{4.5}} = \frac{y - \sqrt{2}}{\sqrt{3}}$$

Step 3
Rearrange the equation into the form $Ax + By + C = 0$.

$$\frac{x - \sqrt{3}}{\sqrt{4.5}} = \frac{y - \sqrt{2}}{\sqrt{3}}$$
$$\sqrt{3}(x - \sqrt{3}) = \sqrt{4.5}(y - \sqrt{2})$$
$$\sqrt{3}x - \sqrt{3 \times 3} = \sqrt{4.5}y - \sqrt{4.5 \times 2}$$
$$\sqrt{3}x - \sqrt{9} = \sqrt{4.5}y - \sqrt{9}$$
$$\sqrt{3}x - \sqrt{4.5}y = 0$$

251. C

Step 1
Solve each equation for t.

$$x = \sqrt{2} + \frac{5}{6}t$$
$$x - \sqrt{2} = \frac{5}{6}t$$
$$\frac{x - \sqrt{2}}{\frac{5}{6}} = t$$
$$\frac{6(x - \sqrt{2})}{5} = t$$

$$y = 3t$$
$$\frac{y}{3} = t$$

Step 2
Equate the two equations.

$$\frac{6(x - \sqrt{2})}{5} = \frac{y}{3}$$

Step 3
Rearrange the new equation into the form $Ax + By + C = 0$.

$$\frac{6(x-\sqrt{2})}{5} = \frac{y}{3}$$
$$18(x-\sqrt{2}) = 5y$$
$$18x - 18\sqrt{2} = 5y$$
$$18x - 5y - 18\sqrt{2} = 0$$

Expressed in Cartesian form, the equation is $18x - 5y - 18\sqrt{2} = 0$.

252. D

Use a TI-83 or similar calculator to generate the graph of the parametric equations.

Step 1
Put the calculator into parametric mode.

Press MODE, scroll down to the fourth line, highlight Par, and press ENTER.

Step 2
Enter the parametric equations into the calculator.

Press the Y = button, and type in the equation for the x-variable into the line labeled X_{1T} = and the equation for the y-variable into the line labeled Y_{1T} = . Use the X,T,θ,n button to input the variable t from the parametric equations.

```
Plot1 Plot2 Plot3
\X1T = -T^(2)
 Y1T = 3T-2
\X2T =
 Y2T =
\X3T =
 Y3T =
\X4T =
```

Step 3
Set an appropriate window setting.
There are restrictions on the t-variable given, so enter the window settings t:[−2, 2, 0.1], x:[−10, 10, 1], and y:[−10, 10, 1].

Step 4
Graph the parametric equations.

Press the GRAPH button.

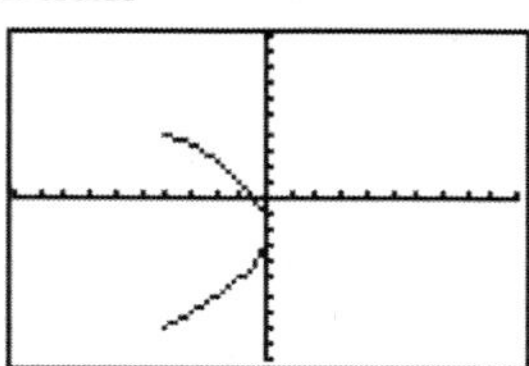

253. C

Step 1
Put the calculator into parametric mode.

Press MODE, scroll down to the fourth line, highlight Par, and press ENTER.

Step 2
Enter the parametric equations into the calculator.

Press the Y = button on the calculator. Type the equation for the x-variable into the line labeled X_{1T} = and the equation for the y-variable into the line labeled Y_{1T} = . Use the X,T,θ,n button to input the variable t from the parametric equation.

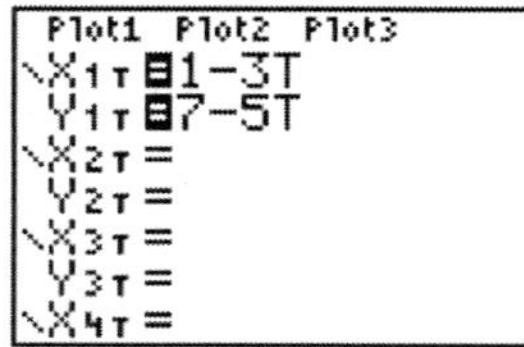

Step 3
Set an appropriate window setting.
Since there are no restrictions given, the window settings T:[−5, 5, 0.1], X:[−10, 10, 1] and Y:[−10, 10, 1] can be used.

Press WINDOW, and enter the values for the window settings.

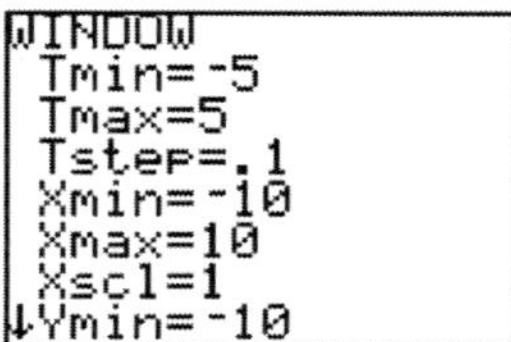

Note that Y_{max} and Y_{scl} do not show up on the given screenshot, but they can be found by scrolling farther down the screen.

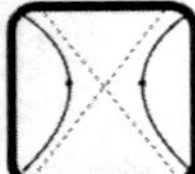

Step 4
Graph the parametric equation.

Press the GRAPH button.

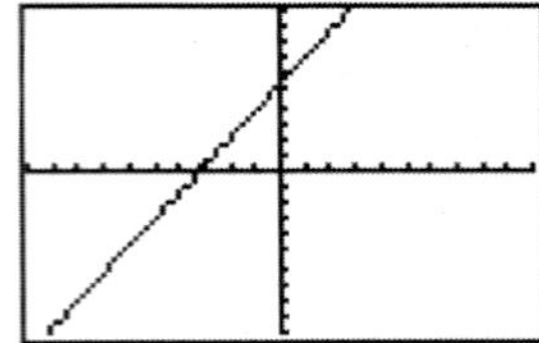

254. B

Step 1
Introduce a parameter, such as t, to define the variables x or y from the Cartesian form.
Let $t = y$.

Step 2
Determine the x-variable of the parametric equation in the form $x = x_0 + at + ct^2$.

Substitute t for y in the equation, and solve for x.

$$2t^2 + 2x + 4t + 18 = 0$$
$$2x = -2t^2 - 4t - 18$$
$$x = -t^2 - 2t - 9$$

Step 3
Determine the y-variable of the parametric equation in the form $y = y_0 + bt$.

Since $t = y$, then $y = t$.

A possible parametric form of the Cartesian equation $2y^2 + 2x + 4y + 18 = 0$ is therefore as follows:

$x = -t^2 - 2t - 9$
$y = t$

Note that quadratic Cartesian equations can have many different parametric equations depending on what the parameter t is set to equal.

255. A

Step 1
Introduce a parameter, such as t, to define the x- or y-variable from the Cartesian form.
You can convert the equation into vertex form by completing the square and then setting a parameter.

$$x^2 + 8x - y + 18 = 0$$
$$y = x^2 + 8x + 18$$
$$y + 16 = \left(x^2 + 8x + 16\right) + 18$$
$$y = (x + 4)^2 + 2$$

Let $t = x + 4$.

Step 2
Determine the x-variable of the parametric equation in the form $x = x_0 + at$.

Rearrange the parameter $t = x + 4$ to solve for x.

$$t = x + 4$$
$$-x = 4 - t$$
$$x = t - 4$$

Step 3
Determine the y-variable of the parametric equation in the form $y = y_0 + bt + ct^2$.

Substitute $t = x + 4$ into the equation $y = (x + 4)^2 + 2$.

$y = t^2 + 2$

A parametric form of the Cartesian equation $x^2 + 8x - y + 18 = 0$ is therefore as follows:

$x = t - 4$
$y = t^2 + 2$

Note that quadratic Cartesian equations can have many different parametric equations depending on what the parameter t is set to equal.

256. D

Let v represent velocity, t represent time, x represent the horizontal component of motion, and y represent the vertical component of motion. The acceleration due to gravity is g (9.81 m/s^2), and θ represents the angle of elevation.

Step 1
Write the parametric equation for the horizontal component of motion.

$x = vt(\cos\theta) + x_o$, where x_o is the horizontal distance relative to the initial point of measurement

Step 2
Substitute the known values into the parametric equation for the horizontal component of the ball's motion, x.

$$x = vt(\cos\theta) + x_o$$
$$x = 22t(\cos 35°) + 0$$
$$x \approx 18.0213t$$

Step 3
Write the parametric equation for the vertical component of motion.

$y = -\frac{1}{2}g\left(t^2\right) + vt(\sin\theta) + y_o$, where y_o is the vertical distance relative to the ground

Step 4
Substitute the known values into the parametric equation for the vertical component of the ball's motion, y.

$y = -\frac{1}{2}g(t^2) + vt(\sin\theta) + y_o$

$y = -\frac{1}{2}(9.81)t^2 + 22t(\sin 35°) + 1$

$y \approx -4.905t^2 + 12.6187t + 1$

The following parametric equations describe this problem:
$x \approx 18.0213t$
$y \approx -4.905t^2 + 12.6187t + 1$

Step 5
Determine how much time goes by before the baseball hits the ground.

The baseball will hit the ground when y is equal to 0. Substitute 0 for y into the equation
$y = -4.905t^2 + 12.6187t + 1$.
$0 = -4.905t^2 + 12.6187t + 1$

Use the quadratic formula to solve for t.

$t = \frac{-b \pm \sqrt{b^2 - 4ac}}{2a}$

$t \approx \frac{-(12.6187) \pm \sqrt{(12.6187)^2 - 4(-4.905)(1)}}{2(-4.905)}$

$t \approx \frac{-12.6187 \pm \sqrt{159.2316 + 19.62}}{-9.81}$

$t \approx \frac{12.6187 \pm 13.3734}{9.81}$

Solve for the two possible solutions for t.

$t \approx \frac{12.6187 + 13.3734}{9.81}$

$t \approx \frac{25.9921}{9.81}$

$t \approx 2.65$ s

$t \approx \frac{12.6187 - 13.3734}{9.81}$

$t \approx \frac{-0.7547}{9.81}$

$t \approx -0.08$ s

Since there cannot be a negative time, $t \approx -0.08$ s is not a possible solution. Therefore, the time before the baseball hits the ground is approximately 2.65 s.

Step 6
Determine the horizontal distance traveled.

Substitute 2.65 s for t into the equation
$x \approx 18.0213t$.
$x \approx 18.0213t$
$x \approx 18.0213(2.65)$
$x \approx 47.76$ m

Therefore, the baseball will travel approximately 47.8 m before hitting the ground.

257. D

Let v represent velocity, t represent time, x represent the horizontal component of motion, and y represent the vertical component of motion. The acceleration due to gravity is g (9.81 m/s^2).

Step 1
Write the parametric equation for the horizontal component of motion.
The equation is $x = vt(\cos\theta) + x_0$, where x_0 is the horizontal distance relative to the initial point of measurement.

Step 2
Substitute the known values into the parametric equation for the horizontal component of the motocross rider's motion, x.
$x = vt(\cos\theta) + x_0$
$x = 40t(\cos 55°) + 0$
$x = 40t\cos 55°$
$x \approx 22.943t$

Step 3
Write the parametric equation for the vertical component of motion.

The equation is $y = -\frac{1}{2}g(t^2) + vt(\sin\theta) + y_0$, where y_0 is the vertical distance relative to the ground.

Step 4
Substitute the known values into the parametric equation for the vertical component of the motocross rider's motion, y.

$y = -\frac{1}{2}g(t^2) + vt(\sin\theta) + y_0$

$y = -\frac{1}{2}(9.81)t^2 + 40t(\sin 55°) + 15$

$y \approx -4.905t^2 + 32.766t + 15$

The parametric equations that describe this problem are $x \approx 22.943t$ and $y \approx -4.905t^2 + 32.766t + 15$.

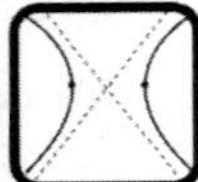

CONICS EXERCISE #2

Use the following information to answer the next question.

A large tornado is spotted on a radar screen. The tornado has a shape of a cone with a vertical axis of symmetry. It is determined that the eye (or the center) of the tornado is at the point $(-1, 7)$ on the radar screen; and the point $(4, 7)$ is on the outer edge of the boundary affected by the tornado.
Each point on the radar is equivalent to 0.5 km.

258. Rounded to the nearest square km, what is the area affected by the tornado? _________

259. The diameter of the circle defined by the equation $16x^2 + 16y^2 - 17 = 0$ is

A. $\frac{\sqrt{17}}{4}$ units

B. $\frac{\sqrt{17}}{2}$ units

C. $\sqrt{17}$ units

D. $2\sqrt{17}$ units

260. The graph of which of the following equations would produce a circle?

A. $(x-1)^2 + y = 25$

B. $x^2 - (y+3)^2 = 16$

C. $\frac{(x-3)^2}{9} + \frac{(y+2)^2}{9} = 1$

D. $2(x+8)^2 + 3(y-2)^2 = 36$

Use the following information to answer the next question.

The graph of a circle is shown.

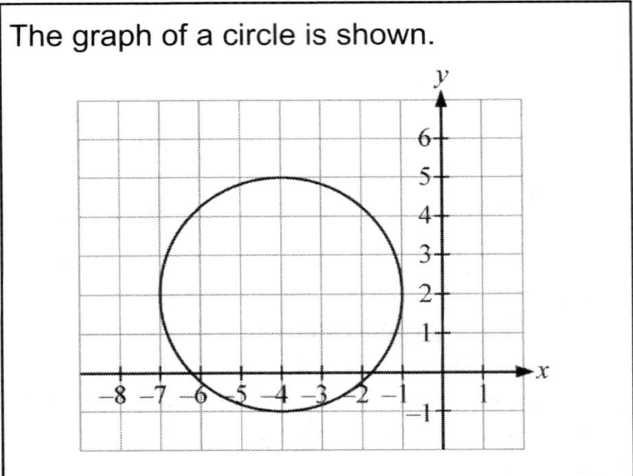

261. If an equation for the given circle is written in general form,
$Ax^2 + Cy^2 + Dx + Ey + F = 0$, the value of $A + C + D + E + F$ is _________.

262. What is the range of the graph of the quadratic relation defined by the equation $4x^2 + 25y^2 = 100$?

A. $-2 \leq y \leq 2$

B. $-5 \leq y \leq 5$

C. $y \geq 2$ or $y \leq -2$

D. $y \geq 5$ or $y \leq -5$

263. A conic has domain $-2 \leq x \leq 4$ and range $-5 \leq y \leq 7$. The standard form equation that defines the conic is

A. $\frac{(x-1)^2}{144} + \frac{(y-1)^2}{36} = 1$

B. $\frac{(x-1)^2}{36} + \frac{(y-1)^2}{144} = 1$

C. $\frac{(x-1)^2}{36} + \frac{(y-1)^2}{9} = 1$

D. $\frac{(x-1)^2}{9} + \frac{(y-1)^2}{36} = 1$

Use the following information to answer the next question.

The graph of an ellipse is shown.

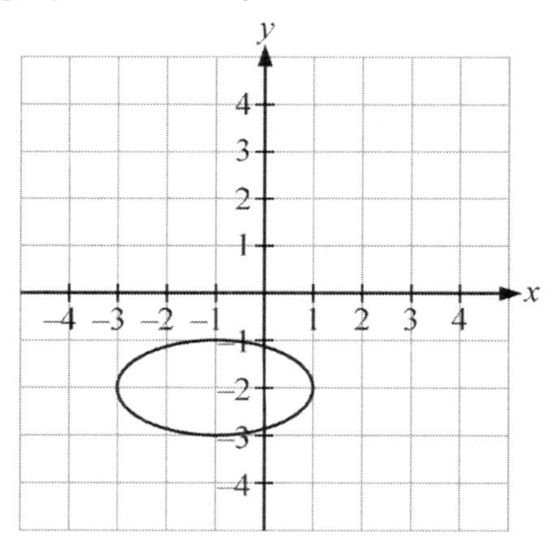

264. What is the equation in standard form of the given graph?

A. $\frac{(x-1)^2}{4} + \frac{(y-2)^2}{1} = -1$

B. $\frac{(x+1)^2}{4} + \frac{(y+2)^2}{1} = 1$

C. $\frac{x^2}{4} + \frac{y^2}{1} = -1$

D. $\frac{x^2}{4} + \frac{y^2}{1} = 1$

265. The range of the graph of the conic defined by the equation $y^2 - 9(x-1)^2 = 9$ is

A. $y \geq 1$

B. $y \geq 0$ or $y \leq -4$

C. $y \geq 3$ or $y \leq -3$

D. $y \geq 9$ or $y \leq -9$

266. The domain of a conic is $x \leq -4$ and $x \geq 6$, and its range is $y \in \mathbb{R}$. What is the standard form equation of this conic?

A. $\frac{(x+1)^2}{25} - \frac{(y+3)^2}{4} = 1$

B. $\frac{(x-1)^2}{25} - \frac{(y+3)^2}{4} = 1$

C. $\frac{(x+1)^2}{100} - \frac{(y+3)^2}{49} = 1$

D. $\frac{(x-1)^2}{100} - \frac{(y+3)^2}{49} = 1$

Use the following information to answer the next question.

A hyperbola of the form $\frac{(x-h)^2}{a^2} - \frac{(y-k)^2}{b^2} = -1$, where $a = 4$, is shown.

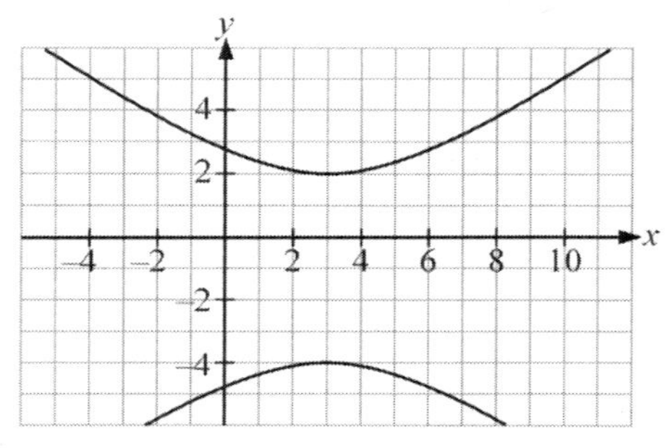

267. What is the equation of the given graph in standard form?

A. $\frac{(x-3)^2}{16} - \frac{(y+1)^2}{9} = -1$

B. $\frac{(x+3)^2}{16} - \frac{(y+1)^2}{9} = 1$

C. $\frac{x^2}{9} - \frac{(y+1)^2}{16} = 1$

D. $\frac{x^2}{16} - \frac{y^2}{9} = -1$

268. The domain of the graph of the parabola defined by the equation $x - 7 = -5(y-3)^2$ is

A. $x \geq 7$ B. $x \leq 7$

C. $x \geq 3$ D. $x \leq 3$

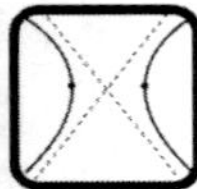

Use the following information to answer the next question.

This diagram illustrates a parabola of the form $y - k = a(x - h)^2$.

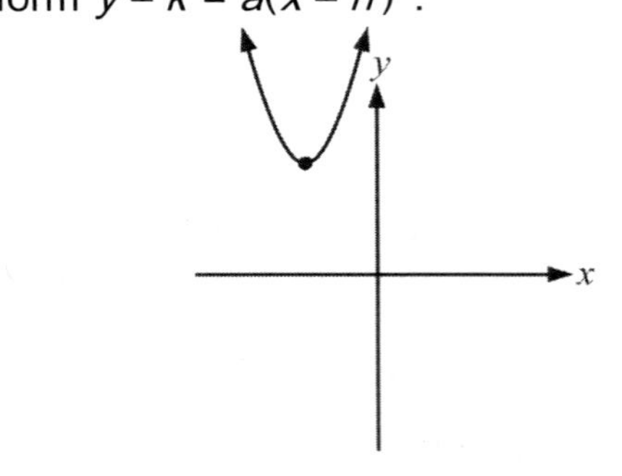

269. If the vertex of the parabola is at the point (–3, 4) and the graph passes through the point (–1, 14), then what is the value of a to the nearest tenth? ___________

Use the following information to answer the next question.

The graph shown can be represented by the equation $y - k = a(x - h)^2$.

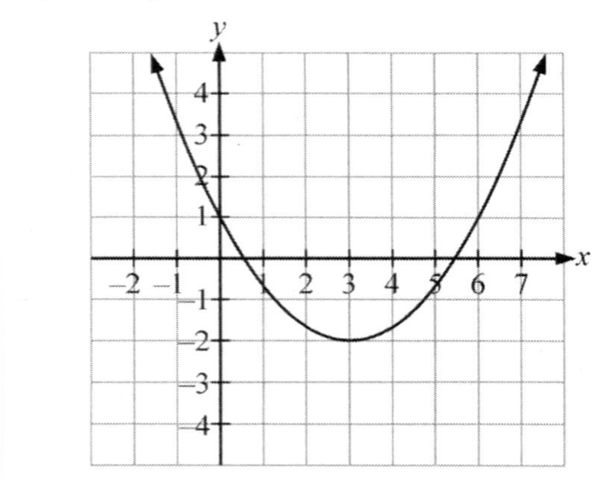

270. What is the value of a in the equation?

A. 3

B. $\frac{1}{3}$

C. $\frac{1}{9}$

D. –2

Use the following information to answer the next question.

A parametric equation is shown.
$x = 2t^2 - 7$
$y = 3t + 1$

271. If this parametric equation was to be graphed, given that $0 \le t \le 4$, which of the following tables of values could be used?

A.

x	y
–1	–25
–4	–11
–7	–1
–10	5
–13	7

B.

x	y
–25	–1
–11	–4
–1	–7
5	–10
7	–13

C.

x	y
1	–7
4	–5
7	1
10	11
13	25

D.

x	y
–7	1
–5	4
1	7
11	10
25	13

Use the following information to answer the next question.

A parametric equation is given.
$x = 5 - \frac{4}{3}t$
$y = 3 - \frac{1}{6}t$

272. What is the Cartesian form of this parametric equation?

A. $x - 8y + 57 = 0$

B. $24x - 3y - 57 = 0$

C. $3x - 24y + 57 = 0$

D. $12x - 24y - 72 = 0$

Use the following information to answer the next question.

A parametric equation is given.
$x = 3t + 5$
$y = 4 - t$
It is also known that $-4 \leq t \leq 0$.

273. Which of the following graphs is formed from this parametric equation?

A. **B.**

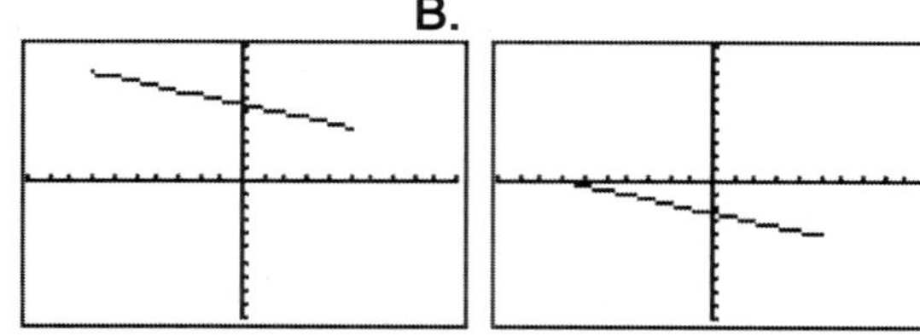

C. **D.**

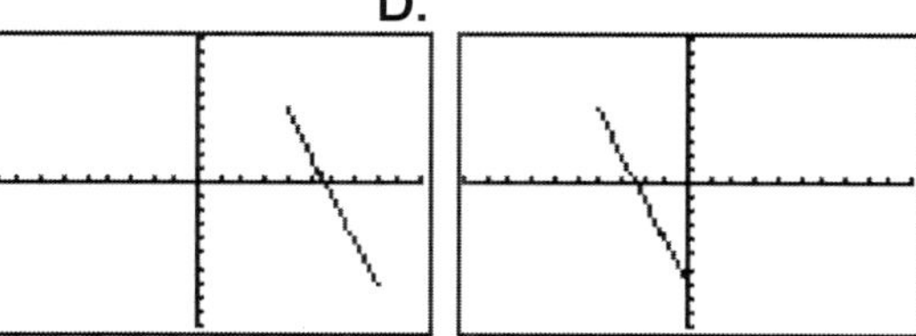

274. Which of the following pairs of parametric equations could represent the Cartesian equation $2y - 4x - 14 = 0$?

A. $x = t - 7$
$y = t$

B. $x = t$
$y = 2t + 7$

C. $x = t$
$y = t - 7$

D. $x = 2t + 7$
$y = t$

Use the following information to answer the next question.

Carlos tosses a pebble over the edge of a canyon. The pebble is tossed at an angle of elevation of 70° and is traveling at a speed of 12 m/s.
The distance traveled is written as (x, y), where x is the horizontal distance and y is the vertical distance traveled from its starting point.

275. Five seconds after the pebble was tossed, what is the value of $x - y$ rounded to the nearest tenth? __________

NOTES

Vectors

VECTORS

Table of Correlations

Standard		Concepts	Exercise #1	Exercise #2
PC.6	The student uses vectors to model physical situations.			
PC.6.A	*Use the concept of vectors to model situations defined by magnitude and direction.*	How Vectors Relate to Scalars	276, 277	285, 286
		Vector Components		
		Modeling Situations by Using Vectors	278, 279	
PC.6.B	*Analyze and solve vector problems generated by real-life situations.*	Modeling Situations by Using Vectors	278, 279	
		Adding Vectors Using the Parallelogram Method	280, 281	287, 288
		Drawing and Measuring a Resultant Vector in a Plane	282	
		Representing Vectors Geometrically in a Plane	283, 284	289, 290
		Negative Vectors		
		Vector Diagrams in One Dimension		

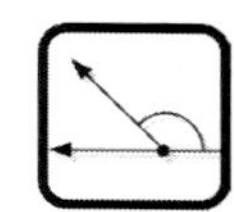

PC.6.A Use the concept of vectors to model situations defined by magnitude and direction.

How Vectors Relate to Scalars

Similar to scalars, vectors are used to describe physical quantities occurring in nature. A vector quantity is described by both a magnitude and a direction. Some vector quantities in physics include displacement, velocity, acceleration, and force.

Vectors differ from scalars because scalars are fully defined by a magnitude but have no direction. Examples of scalars include time, mass, distance, and speed.

To clearly differentiate between vectors and scalars, vectors are written with vector notation above them. For example, displacement is written as $\vec{d}$, while the scalar quantity speed is written as d. Although not used here, writing variables in boldface is another common notation to show that a variable is a vector and not a scalar quantity.

Although vectors are described by a magnitude and a direction, it is often necessary to use only the magnitude in calculations. The magnitude of a vector is represented as follows:

$|\vec{v}| = v$

This is also sometimes known as the absolute value of the vector.

Example

Distance (d) is a scalar quantity. Displacement, a vector quantity ($\Delta\vec{d}$), is a measure of the space between the starting point of an object and its current point of reference. Although often used interchangeably, displacement and distance are different. The difference is illustrated in the following diagram:

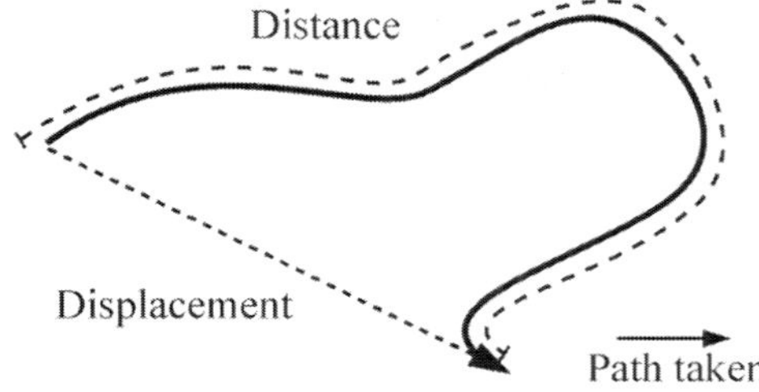

Although the start and end points are the same, the values for distance and displacement are vastly different in this example. Distance is the total distance traveled, whereas displacement is the change in position $(\vec{d}_f - \vec{d}_i)$. Distance and displacement are describing two entirely different things.

Example

Speed (v) is an example of a scalar quantity. If a car is described as traveling at 50 km/h, it tells nothing about the direction the car is moving in. Velocity ($\vec{v}$) is different from speed. A car's velocity might be described as 50 km/h east. Since velocity gives information about the direction of travel, velocity is a vector quantity.

Vector Components

Only two directions are possible in one-dimensional motion. Two-dimensional motion is far more complex. An object in two-dimensional space can travel in any compass direction. A two-dimensional space in which an object is moving is often called a plane or grid. Vectors are necessary to describe and quantify the direction and magnitude of an object's motion in a plane.

Vectors in a plane have both horizontal (x), and vertical (y) components, similar to how a sloped line on a graph has both rise and run. The addition of these components gives the resultant vector ($\vec{R}$).

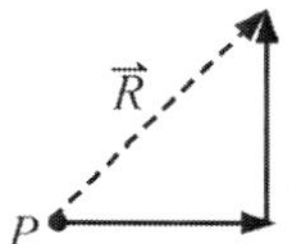

The resultant vector has both horizontal and vertical components

Modeling Situations by Using Vectors

Vectors have both length and direction. When they are used to model real-life situations, vectors convey information regarding magnitude and direction. For example, vectors can be used to describe natural phenomena such as force, displacement, and acceleration.

Example

A blue jay is flying north at 32 km/h and encounters a 27 km/h wind blowing from west to east. What is the velocity of the blue jay relative to Earth?

Solution

Step 1

Make a sketch of the problem. Sketch a vector to represent the blue jay's velocity of 32 km/h north. Sketch another vector to represent the wind's velocity of 27 km/h from west to east. Join the two vectors to form a right triangle. In the given diagram, the joining line (hypotenuse) labeled c represents the vector of the blue jay's resultant velocity relative to Earth.

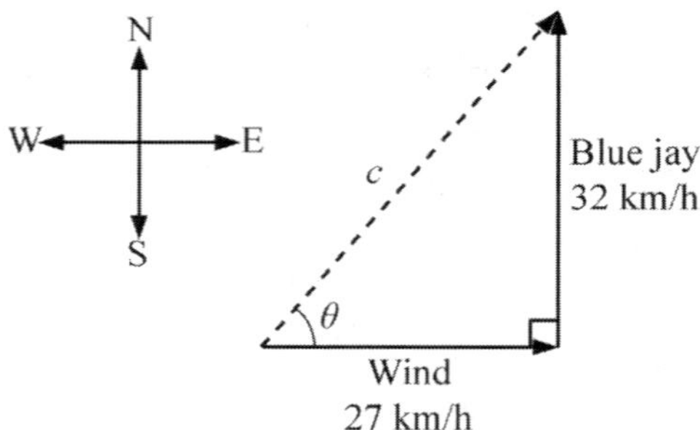

Step 2

Determine the resultant speed of the blue jay by using the Pythagorean theorem.

The Pythagorean theorem is defined as $c^2 = a^2 + b^2$, where c is the hypotenuse of the triangle and a and b are the sides that join at a right angle.

Vectors a and b are given as 32 km/h north and 27 km/h east respectively.

$$c^2 = a^2 + b^2$$
$$c^2 = 32^2 + 27^2$$
$$c^2 = 1,753$$
$$c = \sqrt{1,753}$$
$$c \approx 41.8688$$

The blue jay's speed relative to Earth is approximately 41.8688 km/h.

Step 3

Determine the direction of the blue jay's velocity relative to Earth.

Remember that vectors have both magnitude and direction. The magnitude of the resultant velocity of the blue jay is 41.8688 km/h. Trigonometric functions can be used to determine the direction in which the blue jay is traveling.

Since sides a and b are given, use the trigonometric function $\tan\theta = \frac{a}{b}$ and solve for θ to determine the direction of travel.

$$\tan\theta = \frac{a}{b}$$
$$\tan\theta = \frac{32}{27}$$
$$\theta = \tan^{-1}\left(\frac{32}{27}\right)$$
$$\theta \approx 49.8440°$$

The velocity of the blue jay relative to Earth is approximately 41.8688 km/h E 49.8440° N. This can also be written as 41.8688 km/h N 40.1560° E.

Example

In a 30 m wide river, a sailboat leaves shore from point A, traveling 2 m/s east. It encounters a current traveling north at 5 m/s.

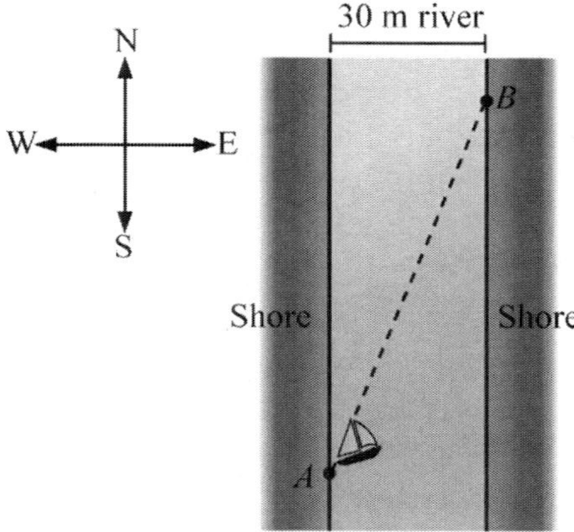

To the nearest whole second, how long does it take the sailboat to travel to point B on the opposite shore?

Solution

Step 1

Make a sketch of the problem. Sketch a vector to represent the sailboat's velocity of 2 m/s east and the current's velocity of 5 m/s north.

Join the two vectors to form a right triangle.

In the given diagram, the joining line (hypotenuse) labeled c represents the vector of the sailboat's resultant velocity on the river.

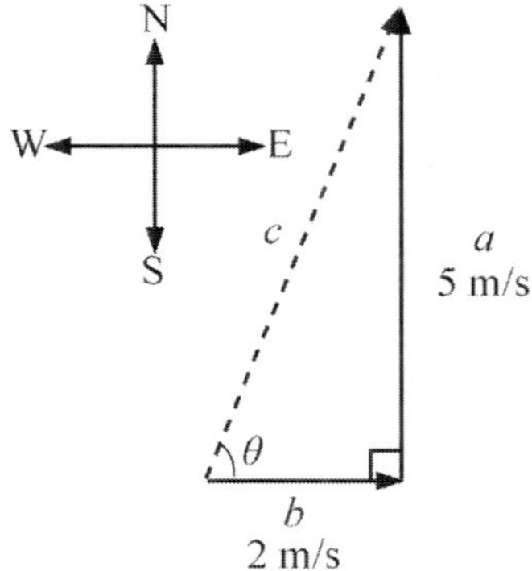

Step 2

Determine the resultant speed of the sailboat by using the Pythagorean theorem.

The Pythagorean theorem is defined as $c^2 = a^2 + b^2$, where c is the hypotenuse of the triangle and a and b are the sides that join at a right angle.

In this example, vectors a and b are given as 5 m/s north and 2 m/s east respectively. This is enough information to solve for the unknown c, which represents the sailboat's resultant speed.

$$c^2 = a^2 + b^2$$
$$c^2 = 5^2 + 2^2$$
$$c^2 = 25 + 4$$
$$c^2 = 29$$
$$c = \sqrt{29}$$
$$c \approx 5.3852$$

The resultant speed of the sailboat is approximately 5.3852 m/s.

Step 3

Determine the direction of the sailboat's resultant velocity.

Remember that vectors have both magnitude and direction. The magnitude of the resultant velocity of the sailboat is approximately 5.3852 m/s. Trigonometric functions can be used to determine the direction in which the sailboat is traveling.

Since sides a and b are given, use the trigonometric function $\tan\theta = \frac{a}{b}$ and solve for θ to determine the direction of travel.

$$\tan\theta = \frac{a}{b}$$
$$\tan\theta = \frac{5}{2}$$
$$\theta = \tan^{-1}\left(\frac{5}{2}\right)$$
$$\theta \approx 68.1986^\circ$$

The resultant velocity of the sailboat is approximately 5.3852 m/s E 68.1986° N. This can also be written as 5.3852 m/s N 21.8014° E.

Step 4

Make a sketch of the river to help determine the distance to point B.

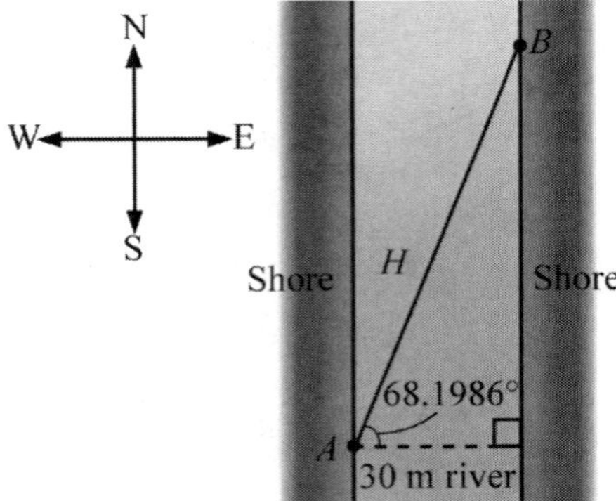

Step 5

The sailboat's resultant velocity travels along the hypotenuse (labeled H) of the triangle to point B. To solve for the distance to point B (the length of the hypotenuse), use the cosine trigonometric function $\cos\theta = \frac{\text{adjacent}}{\text{hypotenuse}}$ and solve for H.

$$\begin{aligned} \cos\theta &= \frac{\text{adjacent}}{\text{hypotenuse}} \\ \cos\theta &= \frac{30}{H} \\ \cos 68.1986° &= \frac{30}{H} \\ H &= \frac{30}{\cos 68.1986°} \\ H &\approx 80.7775 \end{aligned}$$

The distance the sailboat travels from point A to point B is approximately 80.7775 m.

Step 6

Determine the time in seconds that it will take the sailboat to travel from point A to point B. Velocity (v) is equal to distance (d) divided by time (t), or $v = \frac{d}{t}$. The resultant velocity of the sailboat is 5.3852 m/s E 68.1986° N.

The sailboat is traveling over a distance of approximately 80.7775 m. Substitute these values into the velocity formula, and solve for the variable t.

$$\begin{aligned} v &= \frac{d}{t} \\ 5.3852 &\approx \frac{80.7775}{t} \\ t &\approx \frac{80.7775}{5.3852} \\ t &\approx 15 \end{aligned}$$

It will take the sailboat approximately 15 s to get across the river from point A to point B.

PC.6.B Analyze and solve vector problems generated by real-life situations.

Adding Vectors Using the Parallelogram Method

The **parallelogram method** (or tail-to-tail method) is used to add geometric vectors with the same initial point. Consider the vectors $\vec{x}$ and $\vec{y}$. They can be added using this method by following these steps:

1. Rearrange $\vec{x}$ and $\vec{y}$ so the tail of $\vec{x}$ is touching the tail of $\vec{y}$.
2. Complete the parallelogram by using $\vec{x}$ and $\vec{y}$ as its sides. Denote the side opposite $\vec{x}$ as $\vec{z}$.
3. Sketch the vector $\vec{z} + \vec{y}$ by using the triangle method.

According to the properties of parallelograms, $\vec{x}$ is equivalent to $\vec{z}$. Therefore, $\vec{x} + \vec{y} = \vec{z} + \vec{y}$.

Example

Vectors $\vec{u}$ and $\vec{v}$ are shown.

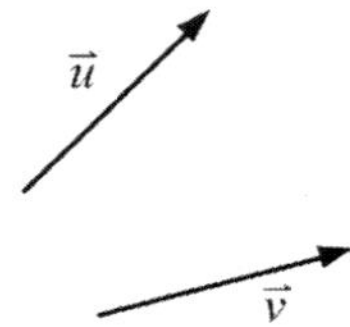

Sketch the resultant vector of $\vec{u}$ and $\vec{v}$ by using the parallelogram method.

Solution

Step 1
Rearrange $\vec{u}$ and $\vec{v}$ so the tail of $\vec{u}$ is touching the tail of $\vec{v}$.

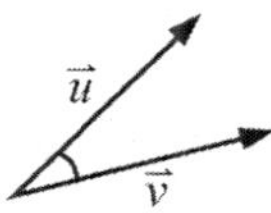

Step 2
Complete the parallelogram by using $\vec{u}$ and $\vec{v}$ as its sides. Denote the side opposite $\vec{u}$ as $\vec{w}$.

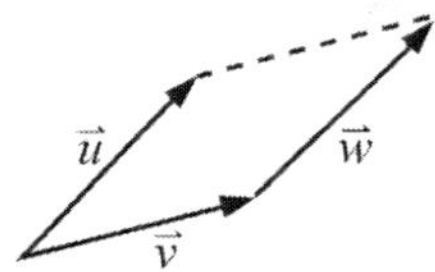

Step 3
Sketch the resultant vector of $\vec{u}$ and $\vec{v}$.

According to the properties of parallelograms, $\vec{u}$ is equivalent to $\vec{w}$.

$\vec{u}+\vec{v}$
$=\vec{v}+\vec{u}$
$=\vec{v}+\vec{w}$

Sketch the vector $\vec{v}+\vec{w}$ by using the triangle method.

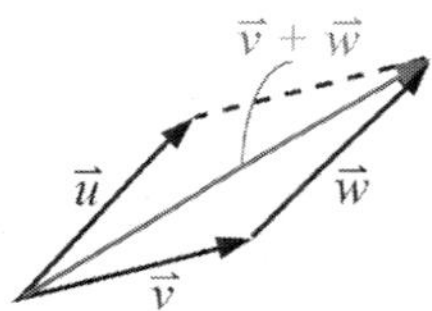

The resultant vector $\vec{v}+\vec{w}=\vec{u}+\vec{v}$ is the diagonal of the parallelogram.

Drawing and Measuring a Resultant Vector in a Plane

Vectors have both length and direction. A resultant vector is formed when two or more vectors are added together. You can add two vectors by using a scale drawing and applying the triangle (head-to-tail) method. The length of the resultant vector can be measured with a ruler, and the direction can be measured with a protractor.

Consider the two vectors $\vec{x}$ = 4 E and $\vec{y}$ = 5 S 30° W. If they are added together using the triangle method, the resultant vector $\vec{r}=\vec{x}+\vec{y}$ can be determined by following these general steps:

1. Select a suitable scale.
2. Draw $\vec{x}$ using the selected scale.
3. Using the same scale, draw $\vec{y}$ so that its tail touches the head of $\vec{x}$.
4. Draw the resultant vector. Draw a line from the tail of $\vec{x}$ to the head of $\vec{y}$.
5. Determine the resultant vector. Measure its length and angle, and convert the length to its original units by applying the selected scale.

Example

Two vectors are given.
$\vec{a}$ = 3 E 36° N
$\vec{b}$ = 2 N

If the two vectors are added together, what is the resultant vector?

Solution

Step 1
Select a suitable scale.

Only the length needs to be scaled.
Let 1 unit = 1 cm.

Step 2
Draw $\vec{a}$ by applying the selected scale.

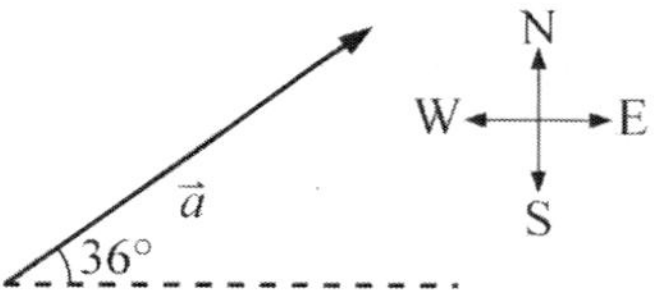

Step 3
Draw $\vec{b}$ so that its tail touches the head of $\vec{a}$.

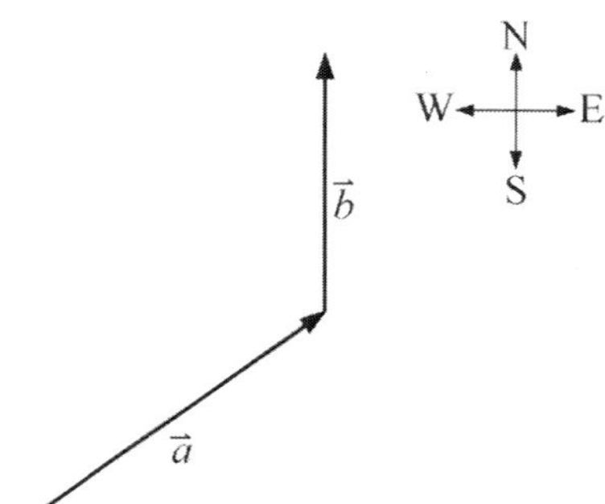

Step 4
Draw the resultant vector, $\vec{r}$.
Draw a line from the tail of $\vec{a}$ to the head of $\vec{b}$.

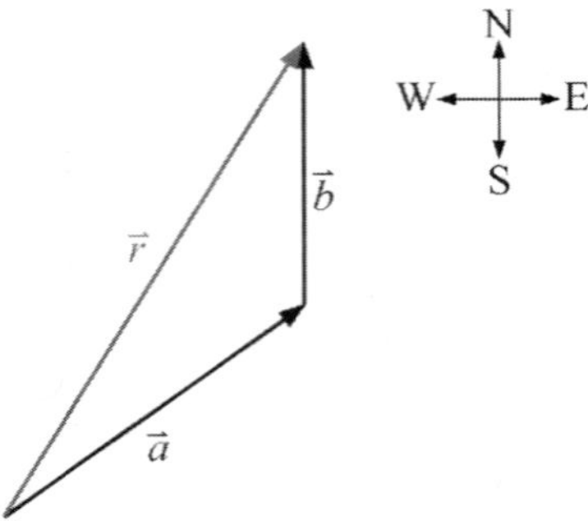

Step 5
Determine the resultant vector.
Measure the length and angle of the resultant. Use a ruler to determine its length and a protractor to determine its angle.

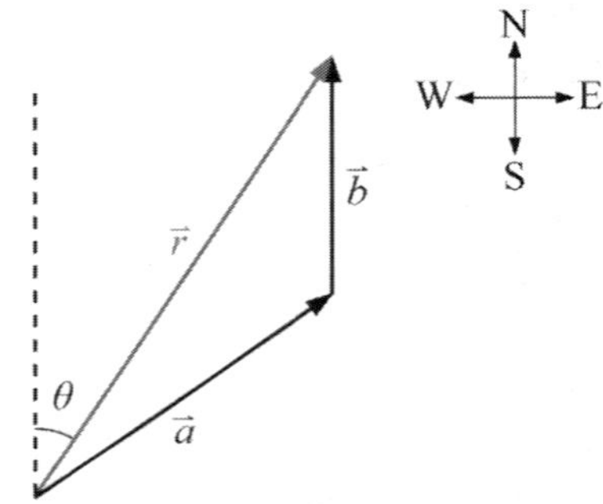

The length of the resultant is 4.5 cm, and the angle, θ, from its tail is 33°.
Convert the length to its original units by applying the selected scale.
Since 1 unit = 1 cm, the length of the resultant is 4.5 units. Therefore, the resultant vector is 4.5 N 33° E. This can also be written as 4.5 E 33° E.

The order in which two or more vectors are added does not matter as long as each vector is placed head to tail.

Example

Three vectors are given.
$\vec{t}$ = 1.5N
$\vec{u}$ = 2W26°N
$\vec{v}$ = 3W

If the three vectors are added together, what is the resultant vector?

Solution

Step 1
Select a suitable scale.
Only the length needs to be scaled.
Let 1 unit = 1 cm.

Step 2
Draw $\vec{t}$ by applying the selected scale.

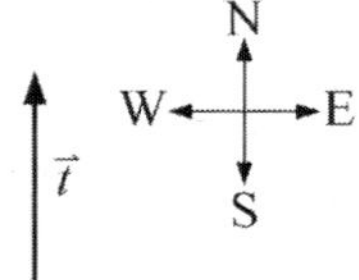

Step 3
Using the same scale, draw $\vec{u}$ so that its tail touches the head of $\vec{t}$.

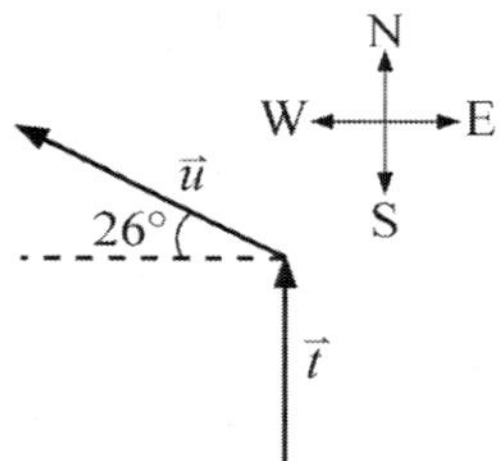

Step 4
Draw $\vec{v}$ so that its tail touches the head of $\vec{u}$.

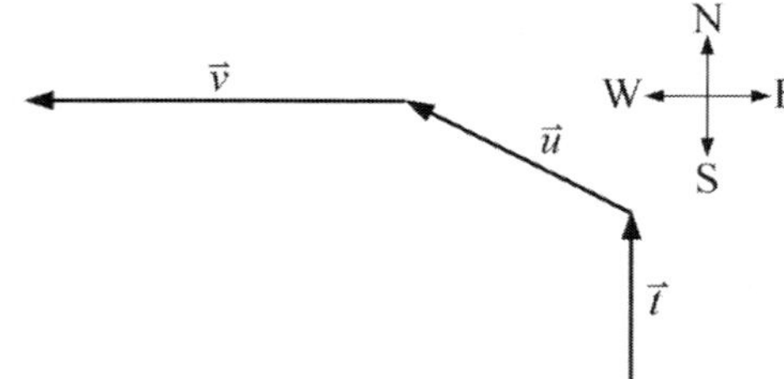

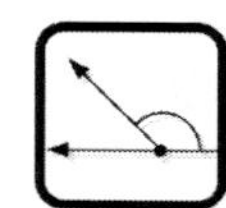

Step 5
Draw a line from the tail of $\vec{t}$ to the head of $\vec{v}$.

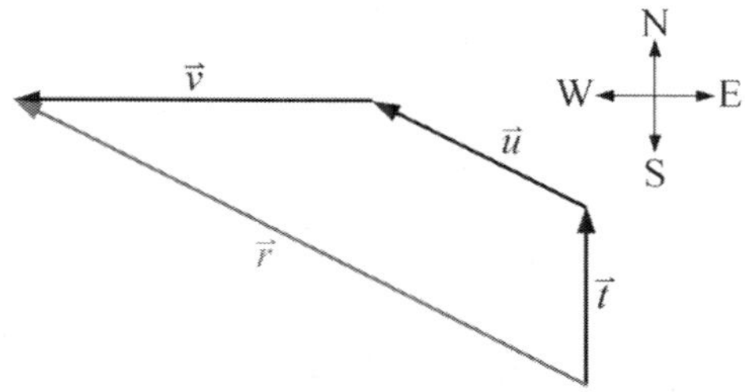

Step 6
Determine the resultant vector.
Measure the length and angle of the resultant. Use a ruler to determine its length and a protractor to determine its angle.

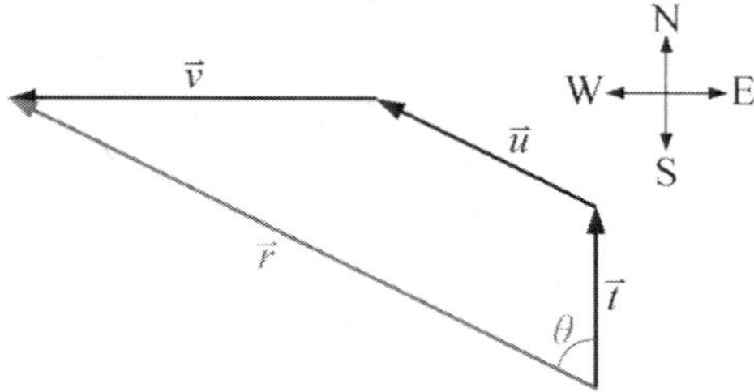

The length of the resultant is 5.4 cm, and the angle, θ, from its tail is 63°.
Convert the length to its original units by applying the selected scale.
Since 1 unit = 1 cm, the length of the resultant is 5.4 units. Therefore, the resultant vector is 5.4 N 63° W. This can also be written as 5.4 W 63° W.

Representing Vectors Geometrically in a Plane

A **geometric vector** is represented in a plane (also called two space) by a directed line segment that is drawn as an arrow. The length of the line segment represents the **magnitude**, and the arrowhead points in the direction of the vector.

A geometric vector can be shown using two letters such as $\overrightarrow{AB}$, with an arrow above the letters to indicate that the direction is from A to B. A vector can also be shown by a single letter such as $\vec{v}$.

Vectors $\overrightarrow{AB}$, $\overrightarrow{CD}$, $\overrightarrow{EF}$, $\overrightarrow{JK}$, and $\vec{v}$ are as shown.

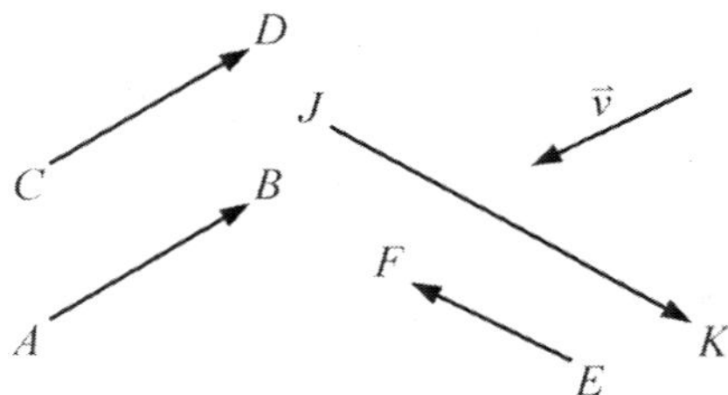

The magnitude of a vector is written using absolute value signs. Thus, the magnitude of $\overrightarrow{AB}$ can be written as $|\overrightarrow{AB}|$. Vectors that have the same length have the same magnitude. Therefore, in the given diagram, $|\overrightarrow{AB}| = |\overrightarrow{CD}|$ and $|\overrightarrow{EF}| = |\vec{v}|$.

Vectors that have the same magnitude and are in the same direction are equal. For example, in the given diagram, $\overrightarrow{AB} = \overrightarrow{CD}$. The magnitudes of $\overrightarrow{EF}$ and $\vec{v}$ are the same, but they are in different directions. Therefore, $\overrightarrow{EF}$ and $\vec{v}$ are not equal.

Example

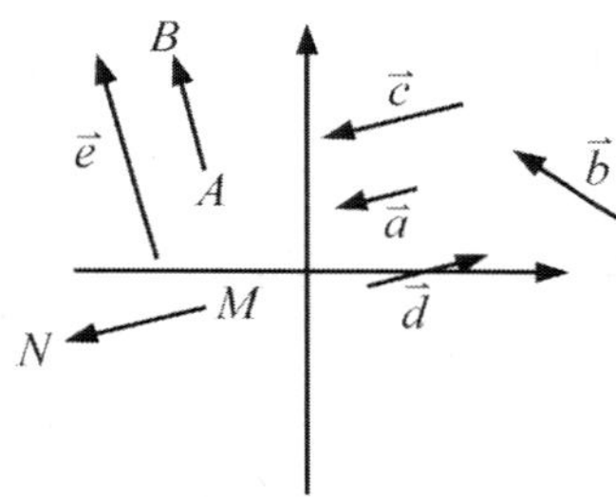

Some vectors are shown.

Which of the given vectors has a greater magnitude than $\overrightarrow{NM}$?

Solution

Vectors that have a greater magnitude are vectors that have a longer length. In the given diagram, $\vec{e}$ has a greater magnitude than $\overrightarrow{NM}$.

Which of the given vectors appear to be equal?

Solution

Equal vectors have the same magnitude (length) and direction. In the given diagram, vectors $\vec{c}$ and $\overrightarrow{MN}$ are equal in length and point in the same direction. Therefore, $\vec{c} = \overrightarrow{MN}$.

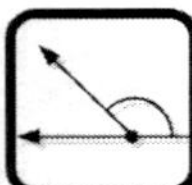

A geometric vector can be shown on a Cartesian plane. A vector on the Cartesian plane is shown with its tail at the origin. The direction can be expressed as an angle measure relative to the positive horizontal axis.

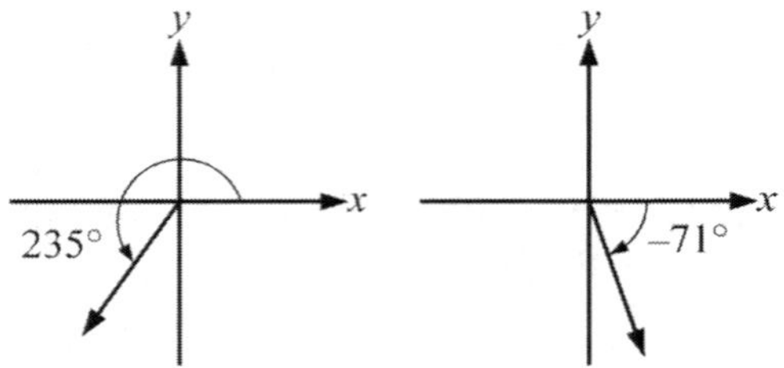

Negative Vectors

Vectors always have direction. When dealing with motion occurring in only one dimension, such as water flowing through a straight pipe or an object falling straight down from a given height, there are only two directions of motion possible. These directions could be upward or downward, left or right, or forward or backward. In the case of one-dimensional motion, direction can be shown as either positive or negative. This notation works as long as you specify which direction is positive and which is negative.

Example

A ball is rolling down a ramp at 2 m/s. You can express this as a vector quantity in two ways.

You can simply indicate the direction after the magnitude. The ball has a velocity of 2 m/s down the ramp.

You can also precede your answer by stating which direction is positive and which is negative. If the positive direction is up the ramp, the ball has a velocity of –2 m/s.

Vector Diagrams in One Dimension

When dealing with vectors that have different directions, it can be difficult to keep all the values organized. A useful tool to organize and understand what vectors mean is a vector diagram. A vector diagram is a simple drawing that uses arrows to represent the vectors on a number line or grid. The direction each arrow points represents the direction of the vector, and the length of the arrow represents its magnitude. The vectors are arranged so that the tail of a vector touches the head of another vector on the diagram. All the arrows can then be added together to find the resultant. These diagrams work for any vector quantity, including displacement, velocity, acceleration, and force.

Example

Sam walks 2.0 m east, 3.0 m east, and 6.0 m west. Find Sam's total displacement.

Solution

Step 1

Draw a vector diagram showing Sam's movement. Mark starting point with a dot. Each line segment of Sam's movement is given a vector. Place the vectors tip-to-tail on a vector diagram. The direction of each vector is important.

R
–1.0 2.0 3.0
–6.0

Vector R is the resultant vector. It represents Sam's total displacement.

Step 2

Use vector addition to determine the value of the vector *R*.

$\vec{d}$ = 2.0 m + 3.0 m – 6.0 m
= –1.0 m

The total displacement is –1.0 m east, or 1.0 m west.

VECTORS EXERCISE #1

276. Which of the following pairs of fields are examples of vector fields?

A. Electric and air pressure
B. Gravitational and electric
C. Temperature and electric
D. Air pressure and gravitational

277. The difference between vectors and scalars is that vectors

A. are negative while scalars are positive
B. point in the opposite direction to scalars
C. are used for forces and scalars for motion
D. have direction while scalars have no direction

278. A plane takes 45 min to fly 300 km due north from one city to another when there is no wind. If the plane were to experience a 70 km/h wind blowing directly from the west, what would be the magnitude of the resultant velocity to the nearest whole number?

A. 413 km/h **B.** 406 km/h
C. 394 km/h **D.** 387 km/h

Use the following information to answer the next question.

Jack is attempting to canoe across a river. The river flows at a speed of 4 km/h directly east. In still water, he paddles north at a rate of 6 km/h.

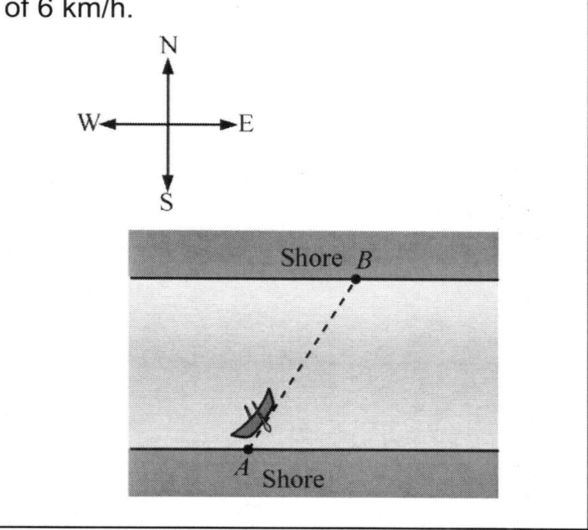

279. What is Jack's resultant velocity?

A. 7.2 km/hN 56° E
B. 7.2 km/hN 34° E
C. 4.5 km/hN 56° E
D. 4.5 km/hN 34° E

Use the following information to answer the next question.

The diagram shows two vectors, $\vec{o}$ and $\vec{s}$.

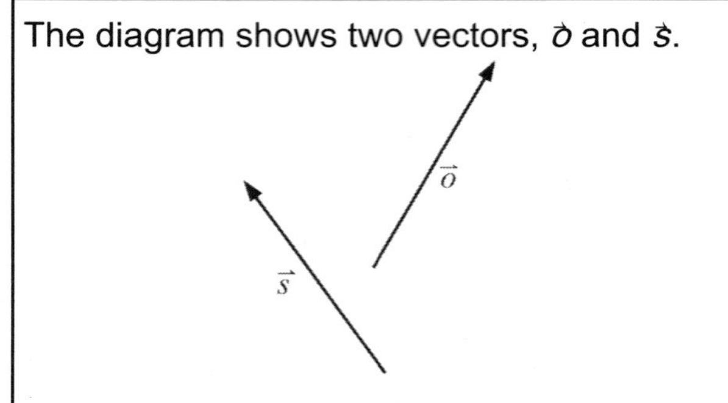

280. If the two vectors are added together by using the parallelogram method, which of the following diagrams shows the resultant vector?

A.

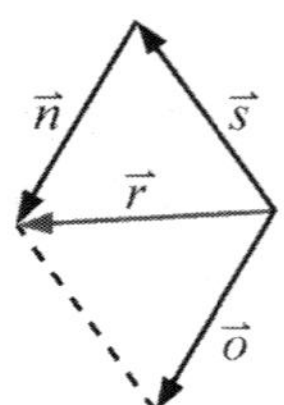

B.

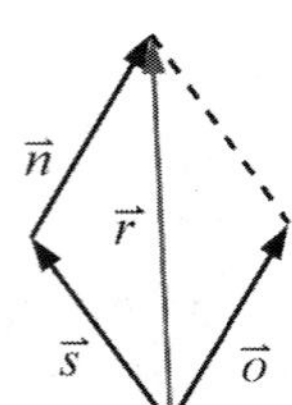

C.

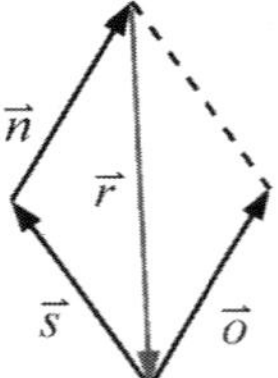

D.

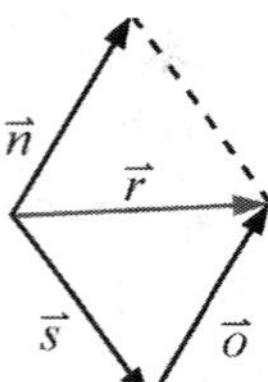

Use the following information to answer the next question.

Four vectors are given.

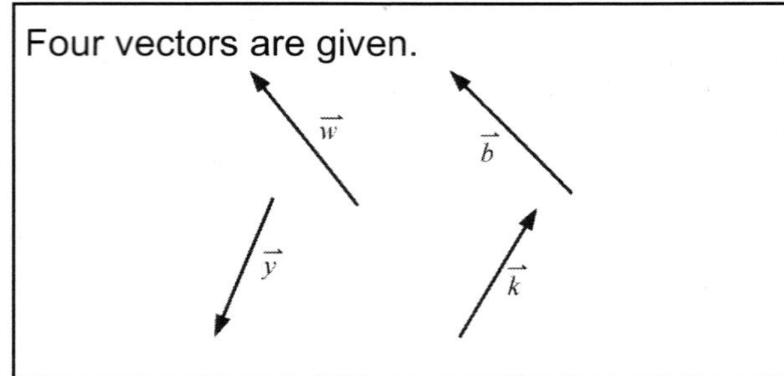

281. If $\vec{w}$ and $\vec{y}$ are added together and $\vec{b}$ and $\vec{k}$ are added together, what are the directions of the resultant vectors?

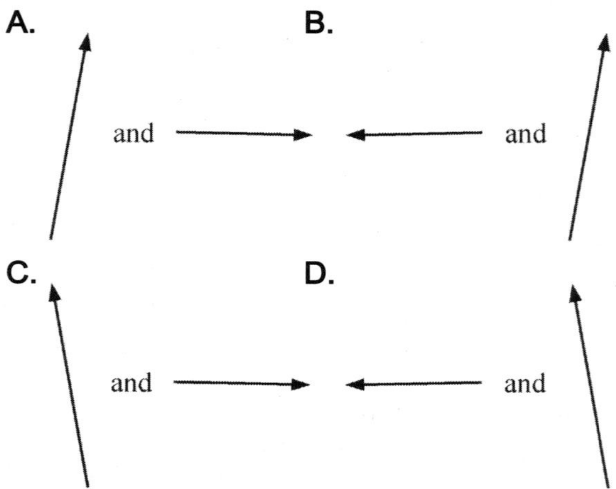

Use the following information to answer the next question.

Two vectors are given.
$\vec{m} = 4.5$ E
$\vec{n} = 2$ S

282. If the vectors are added together using the triangle method, the magnitude of the resultant vector to the nearest whole number is __________.

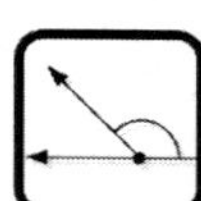

Use the following information to answer the next question.

A diagram of vectors is shown.

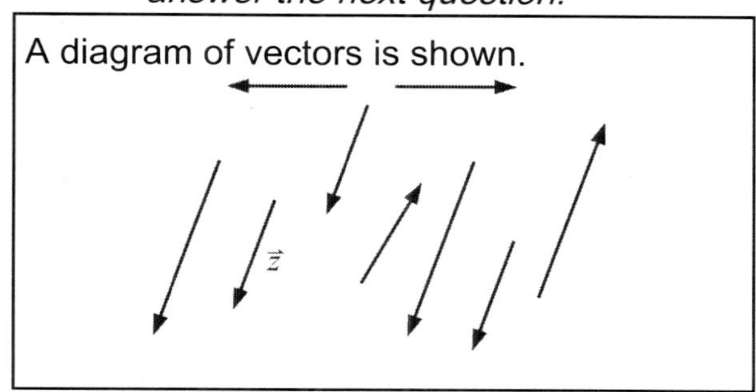

283. How many of the given vectors appear to be equal to $\vec{z}$?

A. 1 **B.** 2

C. 4 **D.** 5

Use the following information to answer the next question.

Vector $\vec{h}$ is given.

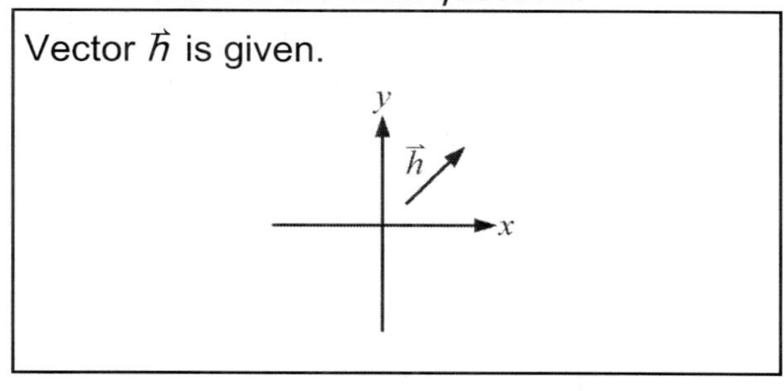

284. Which of the following diagrams shows a vector equal to $\vec{h}$?

A.

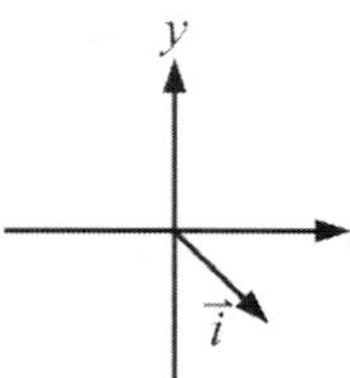

B.

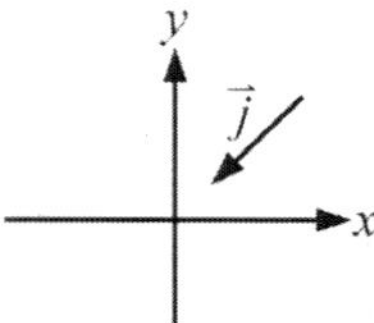

C.

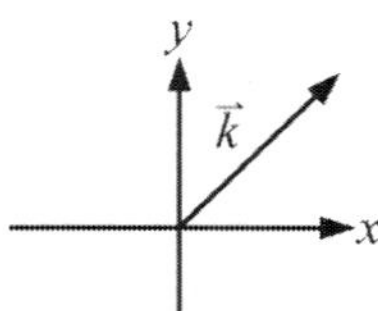

D.

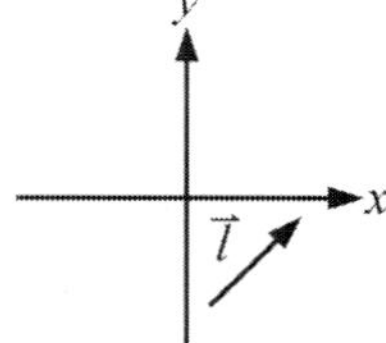

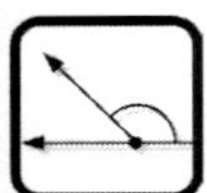

VECTORS EXERCISE #1 ANSWERS AND SOLUTIONS

276. B	279. B	282. 5
277. D	280. B	283. B
278. B	281. D	284. D

276. B

Vector fields have both a magnitude and a direction. Scalar fields only have a magnitude. Both electric and gravitational fields have direction. Temperature and air pressure do not.

277. D

Scalars have no direction. Examples of scalars are time, mass, speed, and distance.

Vectors have direction. Examples are weight, velocity, and displacement.

278. B

Step 1
Determine the velocity of the plane when there is no wind.
Convert 45 min to hours.

$h = \frac{45}{60}$

$h = 0.75$ h

Substitute 300 for d and 0.75 for t in the equation $v = \frac{d}{t}$, where d equals distance and t equals time.

$v = \frac{300}{0.75}$

$v = 400$

The velocity of the plane is 400 km/h N.

Step 2
Make a sketch of the problem.

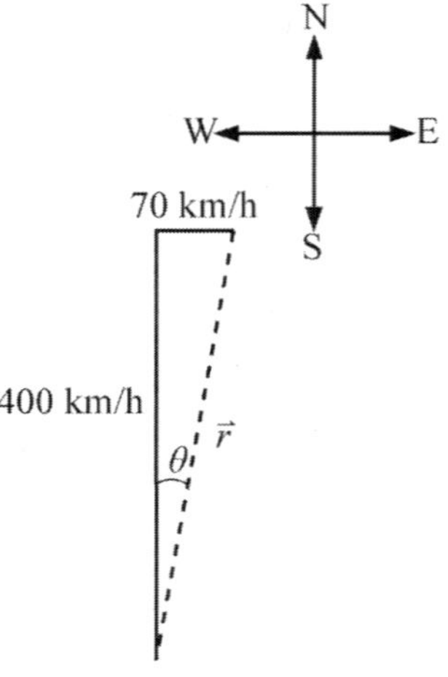

Step 3
Determine the resultant speed of the plane by using the Pythagorean theorem.

$$c^2 = a^2 + b^2$$
$$|\vec{r}|^2 = 400^2 + 70^2$$
$$|\vec{r}| = \sqrt{164{,}900}$$
$$|\vec{r}| \approx 406.08$$

The magnitude of the resultant velocity is equal to the resultant speed of the plane. Therefore, to the nearest whole number, the magnitude of the resultant velocity is 406 km/h.

279. B

Step 1
Make a sketch of the problem.

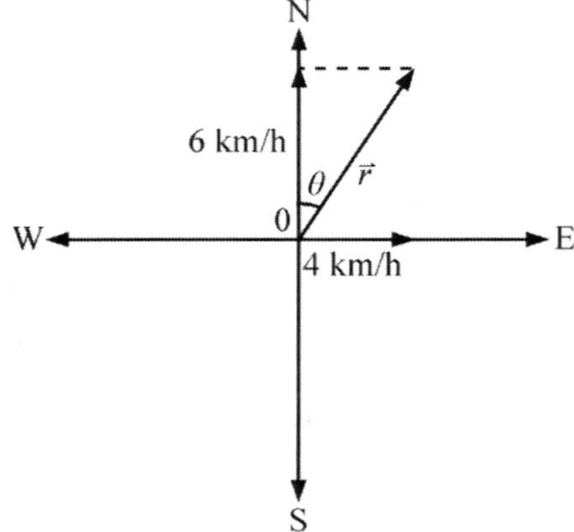

Step 2
Determine Jack's resultant speed by using the Pythagorean theorem, $c^2 = a^2 + b^2$.

$$c^2 = a^2 + b^2$$
$$|\vec{r}|^2 = 6^2 + 4^2$$
$$|\vec{r}| = \sqrt{36 + 16}$$
$$|\vec{r}| = \sqrt{52}$$
$$|\vec{r}| \approx 7.2\text{km/h}$$

Step 3
Determine the direction of the resultant.

Use the trigonometric function $\tan\theta = \frac{a}{b}$ to solve for θ.

$$\tan\theta = \frac{4}{6}$$
$$\theta = \tan^{-1}\left(\frac{4}{6}\right)$$
$$\theta \approx 33.69^\circ$$

Jack's resultant velocity is approximately 7.2 km/hN 34° E, which can also be written as 7.2 km/hE 56° N.

280. B

The parallelogram method is used to add geometric vectors with the same initial point.

Step 1
Rearrange $\vec{o}$ and $\vec{s}$ so that the tail of $\vec{o}$ is touching the tail of $\vec{s}$.

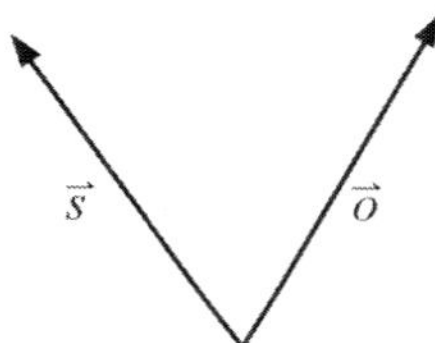

Step 2
Complete the parallelogram by using $\vec{o}$ and $\vec{s}$ as its sides. Denote one of the new sides as $\vec{n}$.

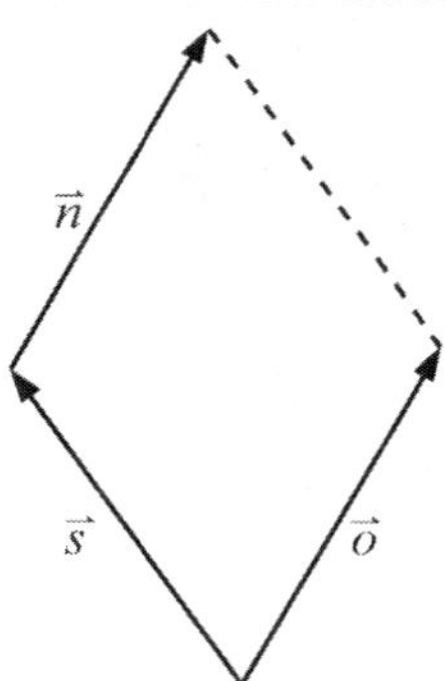

Step 3
Sketch the vector $\vec{r}$ by using the triangle method.

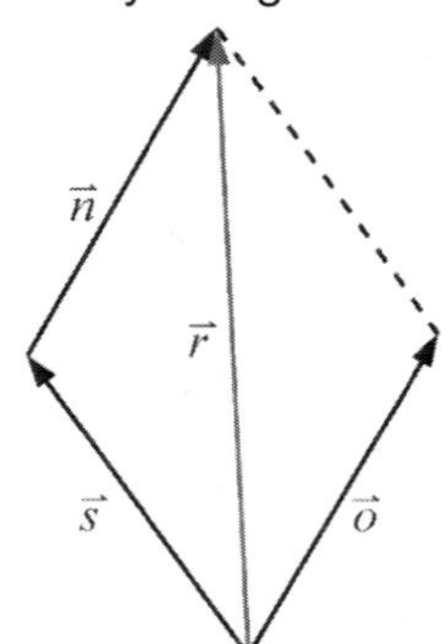

281. D

To determine the direction of the resultant vector, add each set of vectors using the parallelogram method.

Step 1
Determine the direction of the resultant vector for $\vec{w}$ and $\vec{y}$.

Rearrange $\vec{w}$ and $\vec{y}$ so that the tail of $\vec{w}$ is touching the tail of $\vec{y}$.

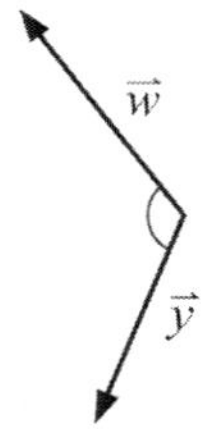

Complete the parallelogram by using $\vec{w}$ and $\vec{y}$ as its sides. Denote one of the sides as $\vec{x}$.

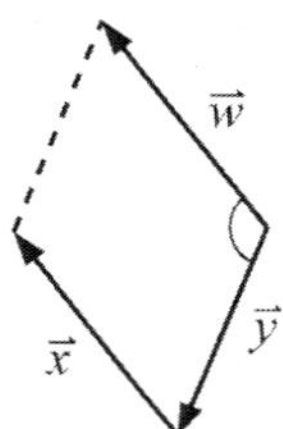

Step 2
Sketch the vector $\vec{x} + \vec{y}$ using the triangle method.

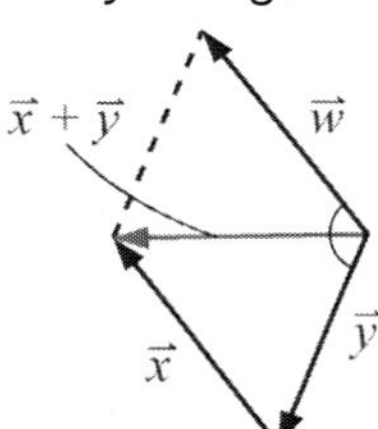

Step 3
Determine the direction of the resultant vector for $\vec{b}$ and $\vec{k}$.

Rearrange $\vec{b}$ and $\vec{k}$ so that the tail of $\vec{b}$ is touching the tail of $\vec{k}$.

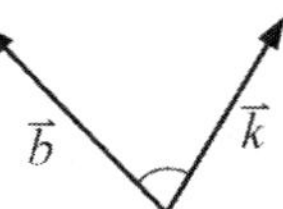

Complete the parallelogram by using $\vec{b}$ and $\vec{k}$ as its sides. Denote one of the sides as $\vec{j}$.

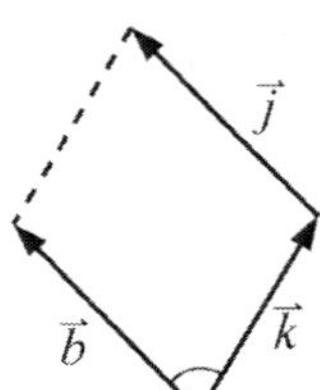

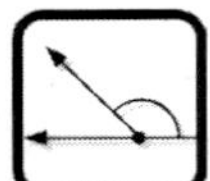

Step 4
Sketch the vector $\vec{k} + \vec{j}$ using the triangle method.

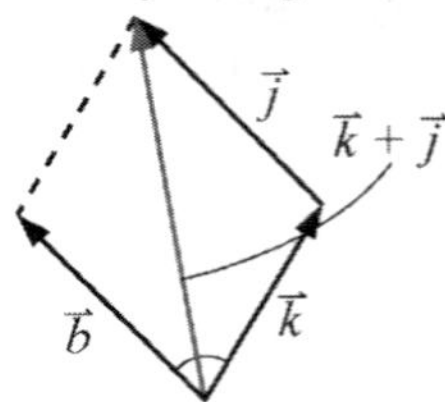

282. 5

The magnitude of the resultant vector is equal to the length of the resultant vector. Add the two vectors together, and measure the resultant vector to determine its magnitude.

Step 1
Select a suitable scale.

Let 1 unit = 1 cm.

Step 2
Draw $\vec{m}$ by applying the selected scale.

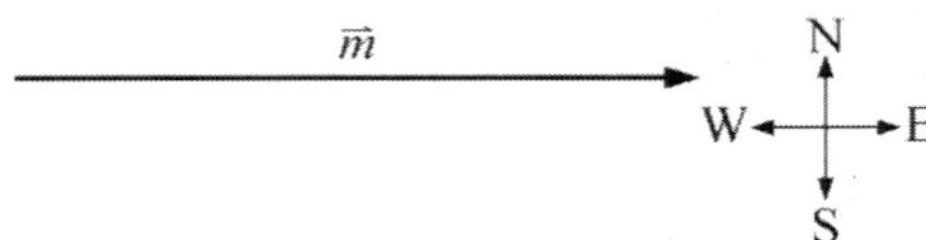

Step 3
Draw $\vec{n}$ by applying the selected scale.

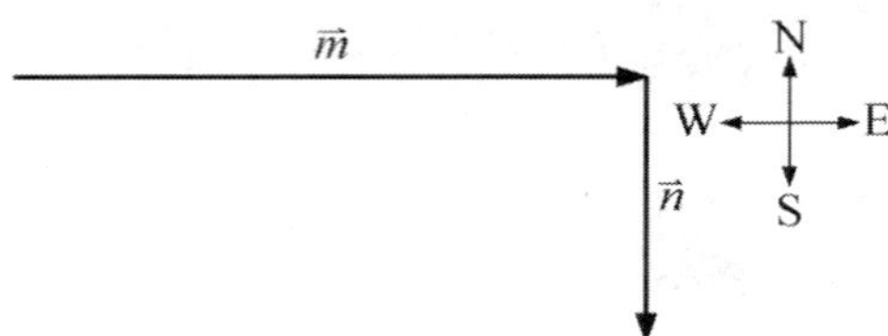

Step 4
Draw the resultant vector.

Draw a line from the tail of $\vec{m}$ to the head of $\vec{n}$.

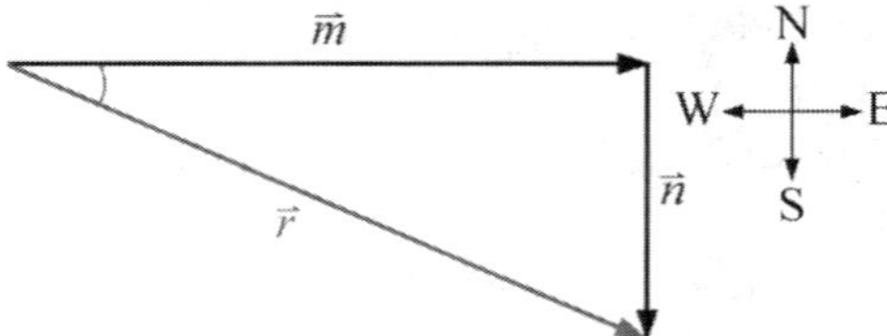

Step 5
Determine the magnitude of the resultant vector.

Use a ruler to measure the line, and convert the length back to the original units.

The length of the resultant is approximately 4.92 cm. Since 1 unit = 1 cm, the magnitude of the resultant vector to the nearest whole number is 5.

283. B

For vectors to be equal, they must have the same magnitude and direction. Only two of the given vectors have both the same magnitude and direction as $\vec{z}$.

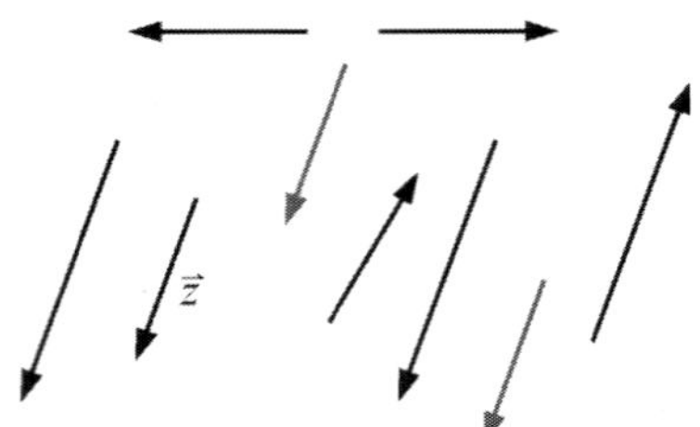

284. D

For vectors to be equal, they must have the same magnitude and direction. The only vector with the same magnitude and direction as $\vec{h}$ is $\vec{l}$.

VECTORS EXERCISE #2

285. Force, mass, and acceleration are correctly identified as vector or scalar quantities in which of the following tables?

A.

Force	Mass	Acceleration
Scalar	Scalar	Scalar

B.

Force	Mass	Acceleration
Scalar	Vector	Scalar

C.

Force	Mass	Acceleration
Vector	Scalar	Vector

D.

Force	Mass	Acceleration
Vector	Vector	Vector

286. Which of the following quantities is a vector quantity?

A. Velocity **B.** Length
C. Mass **D.** Time

Use the following information to answer the next question.

Vectors $\vec{m}$ and $\vec{n}$ are shown.

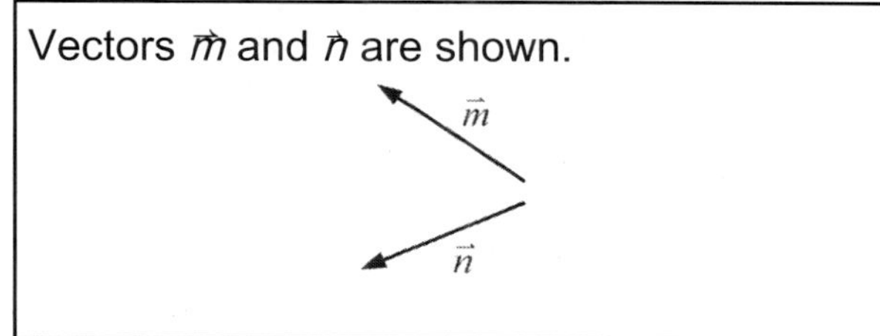

287. If the parallelogram method is used to add these vectors, which direction will the resultant vector point?

A.

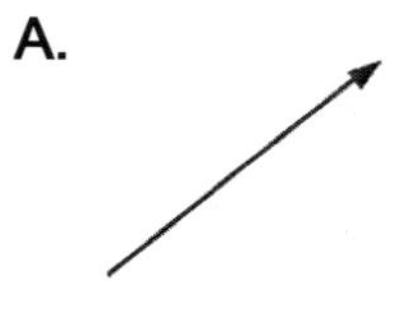

B.

C.

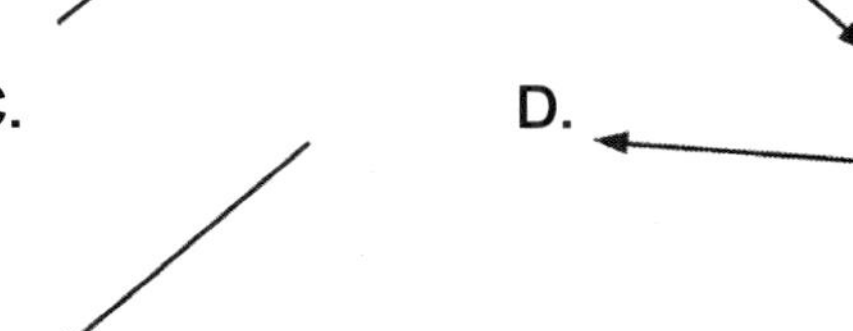

D.

Use the following information to answer the next question.

Two vectors, $\vec{w}$ and $\vec{x}$, are added together by using the parallelogram method.

288. The resultant vector, $\vec{r}$, is equivalent to

A. $\vec{w} + \vec{w}$ **B.** $\vec{x} + \vec{x}$
C. $\vec{y} + \vec{x}$ **D.** $\vec{y} + \vec{w}$

Use the following information to answer the next question.

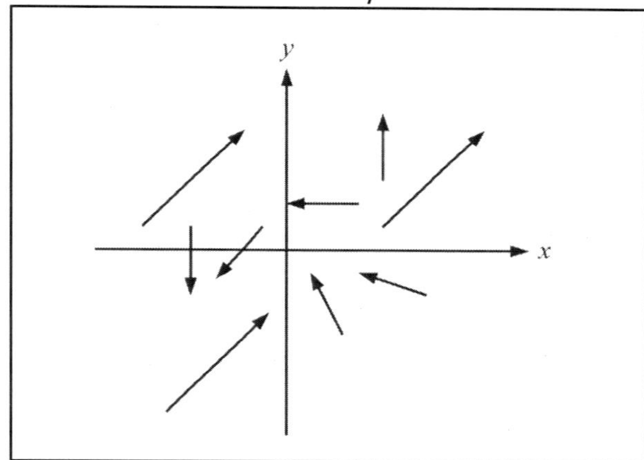

289. How many of the vectors shown in the given diagram appear to be equal?

A. 0 **B.** 2
C. 3 **D.** 4

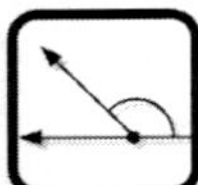

Use the following information to answer the next question.

A diagram of vectors is given.

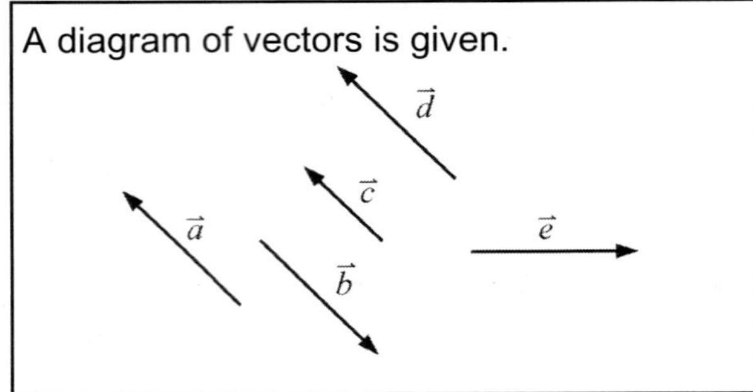

290. Which of the given vectors has a magnitude that is different than $\vec{a}$?

A. $\vec{b}$ **B.** $\vec{c}$

C. $\vec{d}$ **D.** $\vec{e}$

NOTES

SOLARO Study Guides
Ordering Information

Every SOLARO Study Guide unpacks the curriculum standards and provides an overview of all curriculum concepts, practice questions with full solutions, and assignment questions for students to fully test their knowledge.

Visit www.solaro.com/orders to buy books and learn how SOLARO can offer you an even more complete studying solution.

SOLARO Study Guide—$29.95 each plus applicable sales tax

SOLARO
Study Guides

SOLARO Texas State Standard Titles

Science Grade 3	**English Language Arts Grade 3**
Science Grade 4	**English Language Arts Grade 4**
Science Grade 5	**English Language Arts Grade 5**
Science Grade 6	**English Language Arts Grade 6**
Science Grade 7	**English Language Arts Grade 7**
Science Grade 8	**English Language Arts Grade 8**
High School Biology	**High School English Language Arts I**
High School Chemistry	**High School English Language Arts II**
High School Physics	**High School English Language Arts III**
High School Algebra I	**High School English Language Arts IV**
High School Algebra II	
High School Geometry	
High School Precalculus	

To order books, please visit
http://www.store.solaro.com/

Volume pricing is available. Contact us at orderbooks@solaro.com